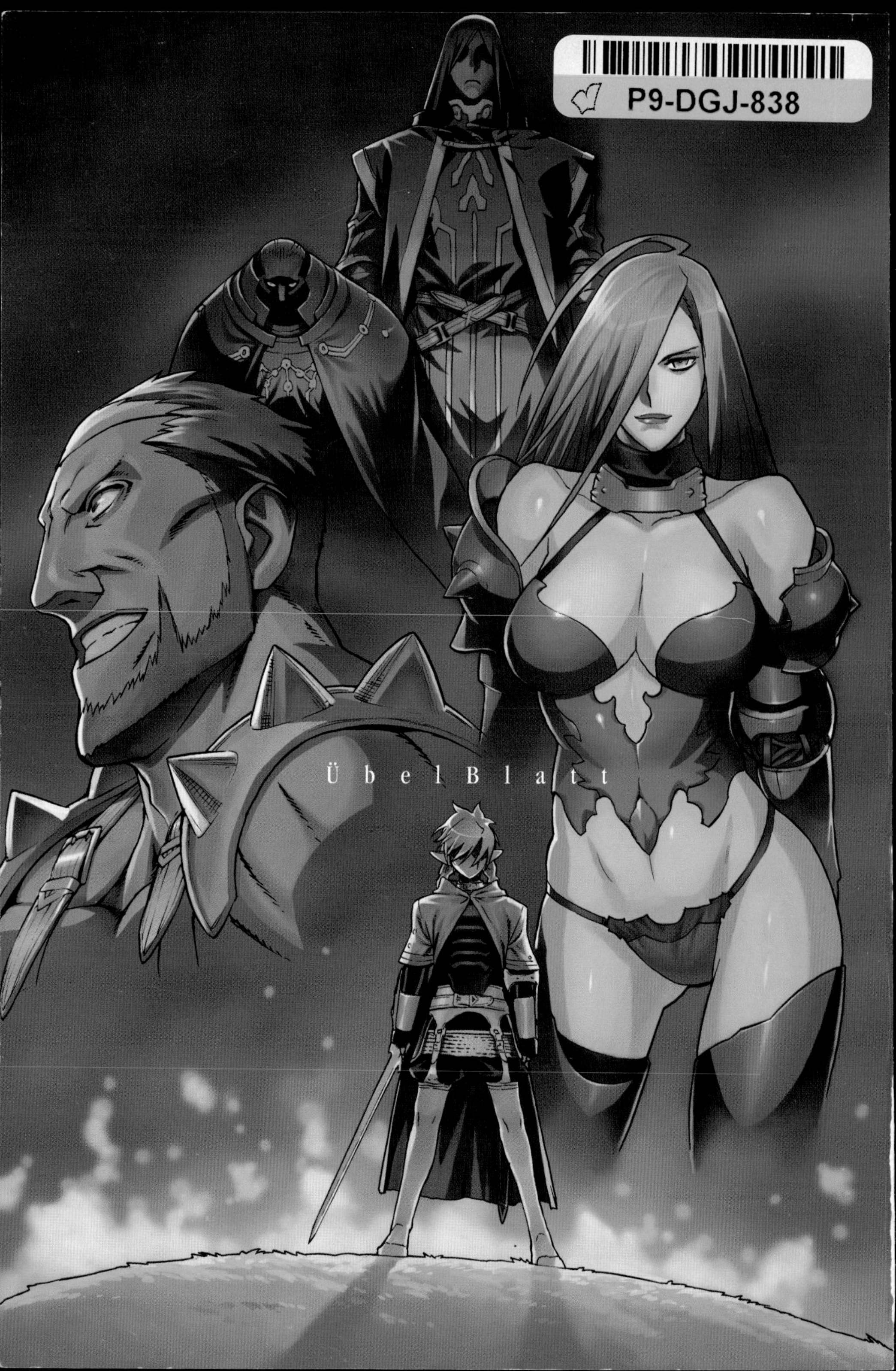
Übel Blatt

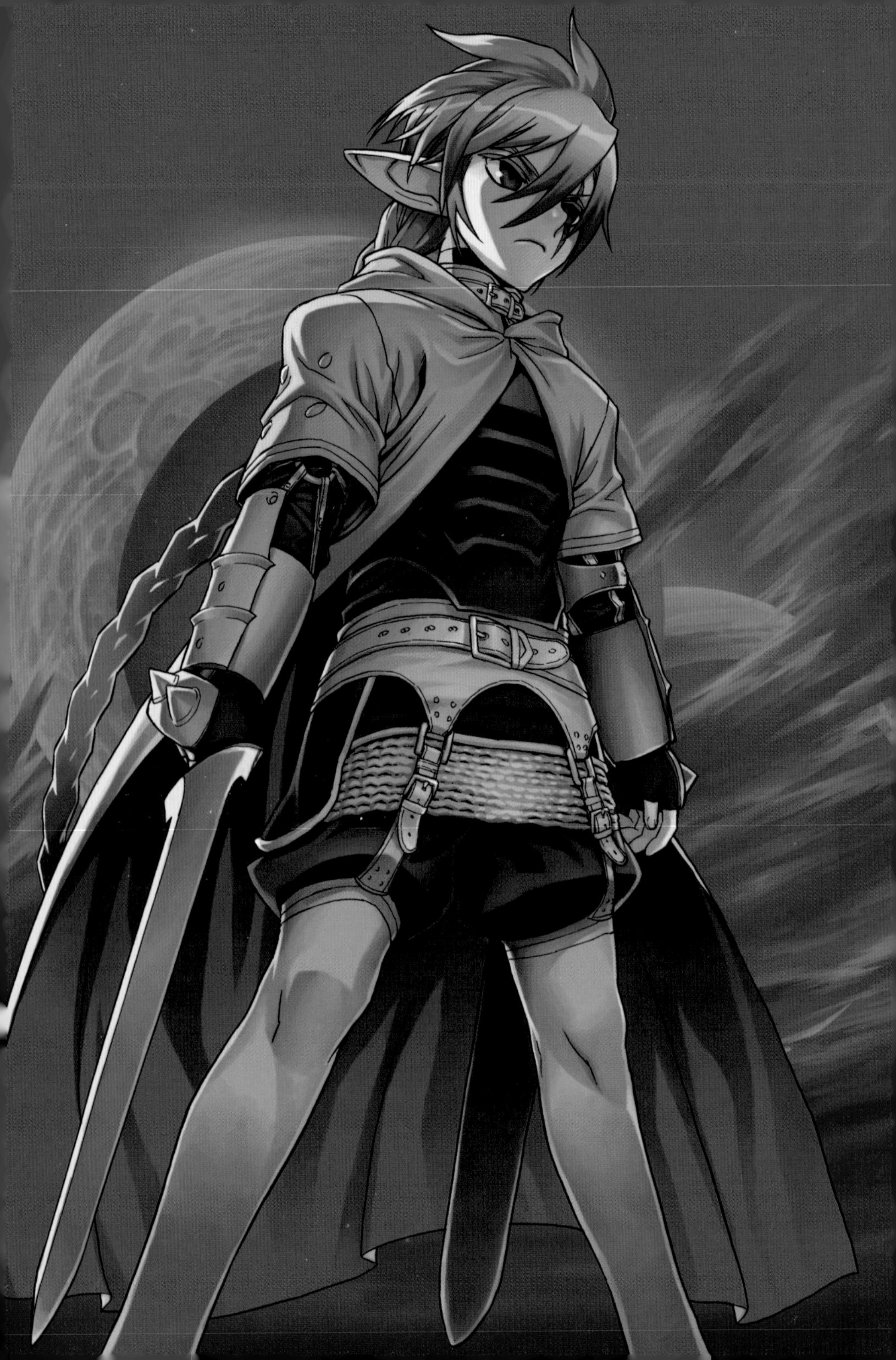

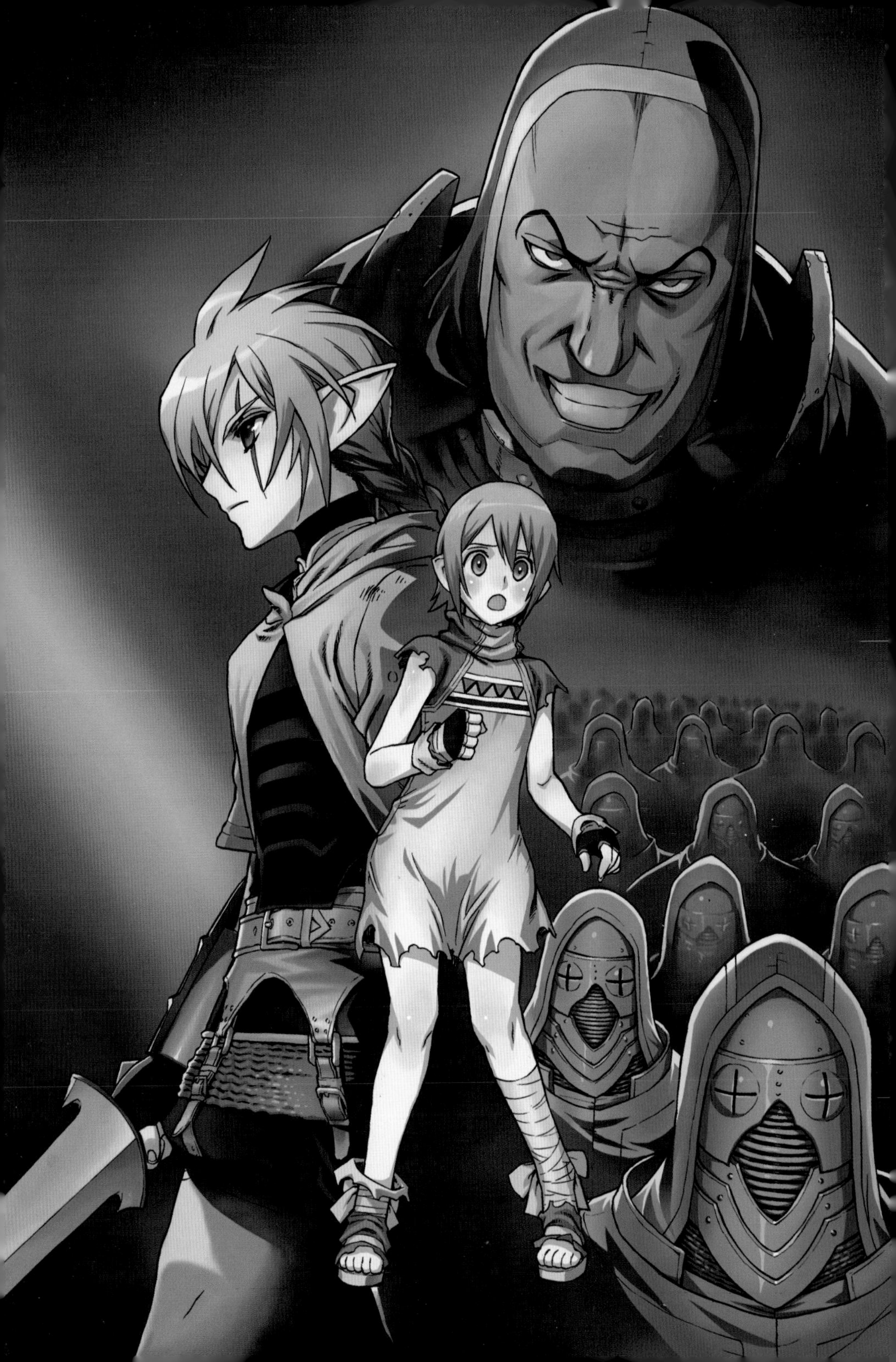

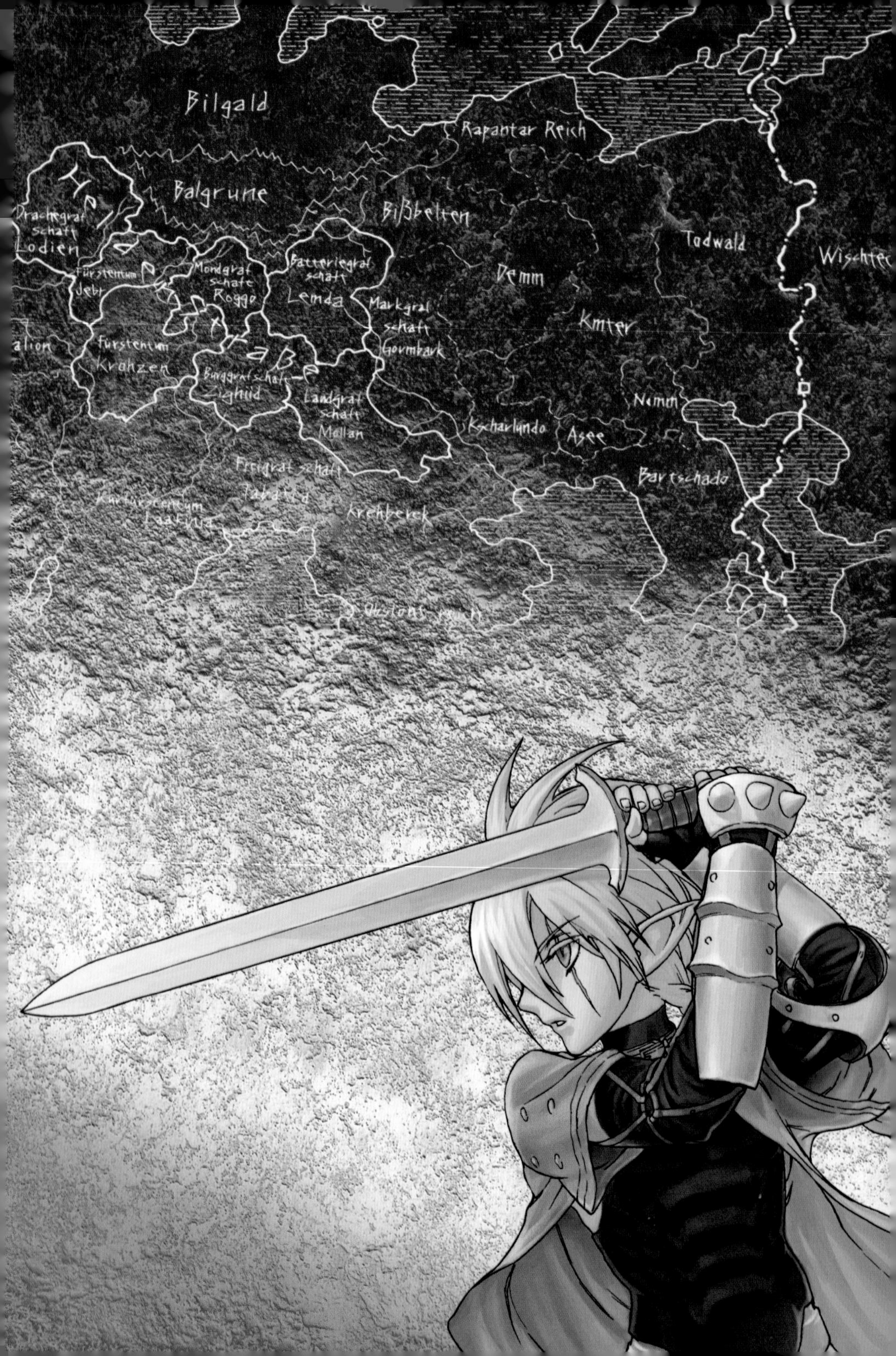

Bilgald
Rapantar Reich
Balgrune
Bißbelten
Todwald
Wischtec
Drachegrafschaft Lodien
Fürstentum Jebr
Mondgrafschaft Roggo
Batteriegrafschaft Lemda
Demm
Markgrafschaft Gourmbark
Kmter
Fürstentum Krahzen
Burggrafschaft Zighiid
Landgrafschaft Mellan
Nemm
Kscharlundo
Asee
Bartschado
Freigrafschaft
Krehberek

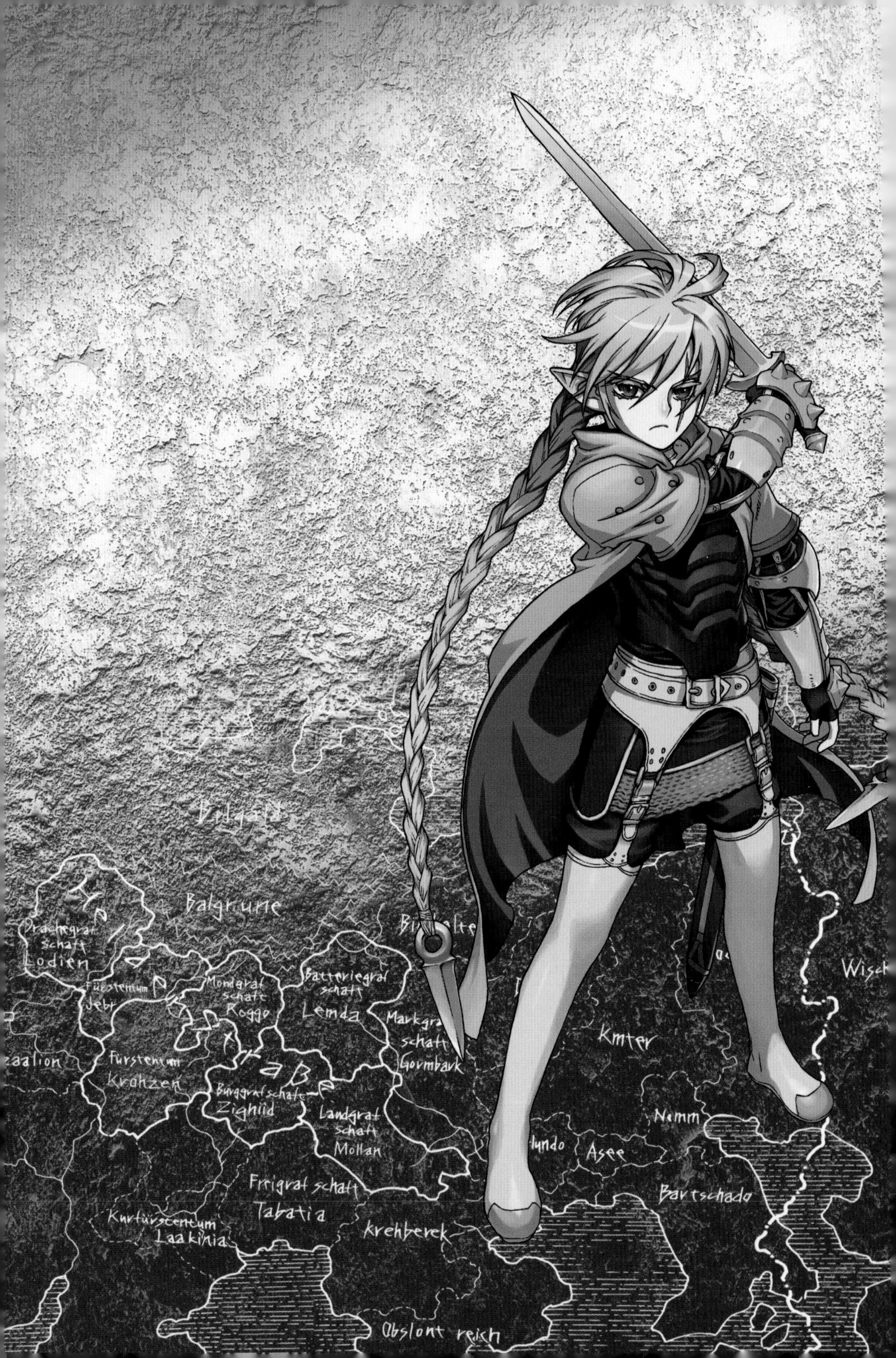
Balgrurie
Drachegraf schaft Lodien
Fürstentum Jebr
Mondgraf schaft Roggo
Batteriegraf schaft Lemda
Markgraf schaft Gormbark
Kmter
Fürstentum Krohzen
Burggrafschaft Zighiid
Landgraf schaft Mollan
Nemm
Asee
Freigraf schaft Tabatia
Bartschado
Kurfürstentum Laakinia
Krehberek
Obslont reich

contents

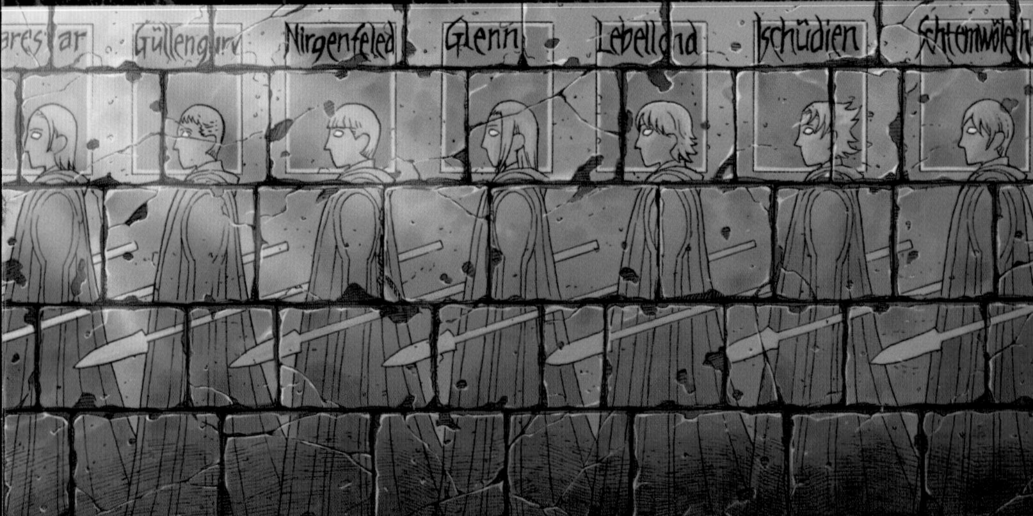

Güllengurv
Nirgenfeled
Glenn
Lebelland
Ischüdien

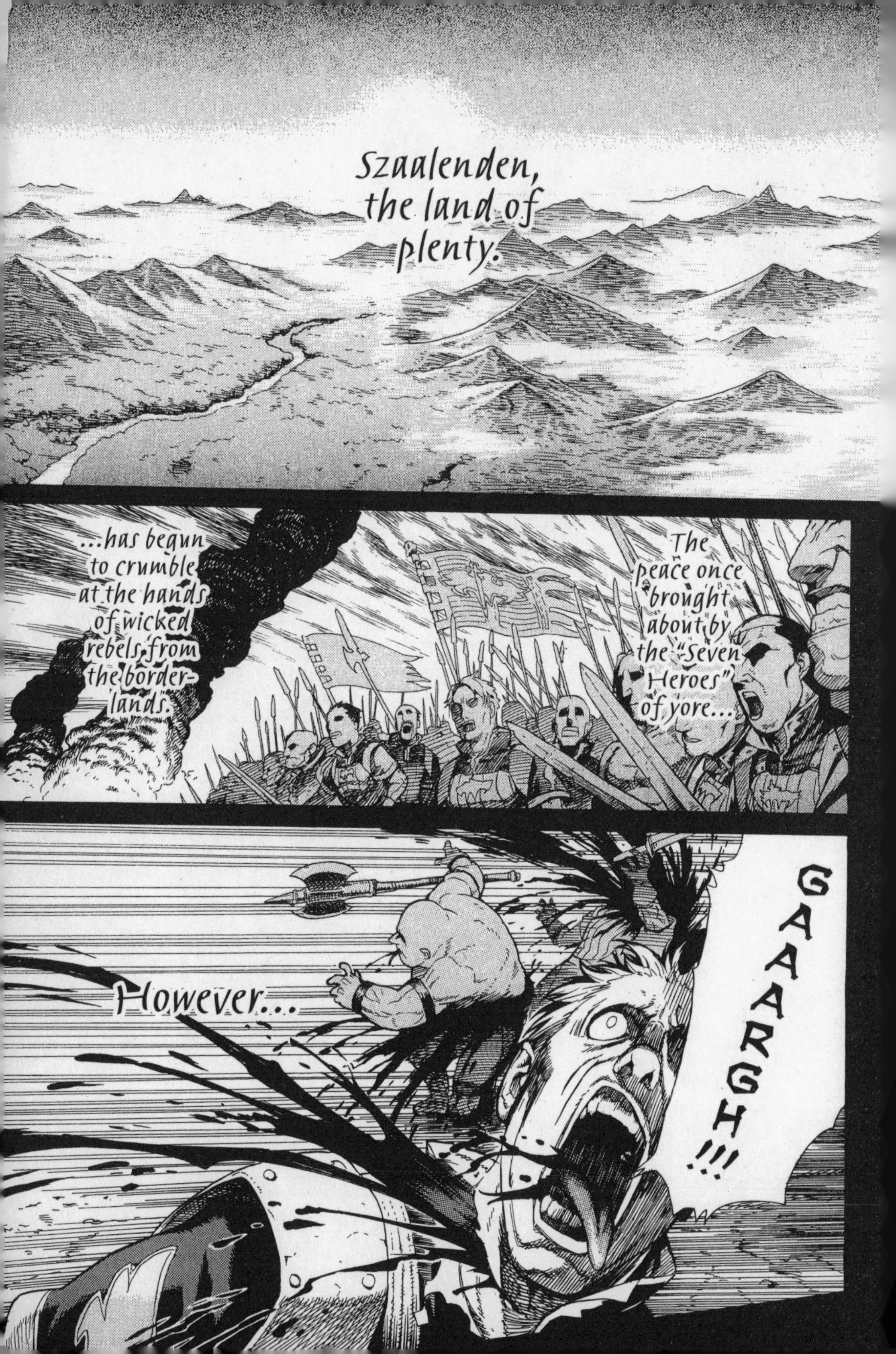

Szaalenden, the land of plenty.
The peace once brought about by the "Seven Heroes" of yore...
...has begun to crumble at the hands of wicked rebels from the borderlands.
GAAARGH!!!
However...

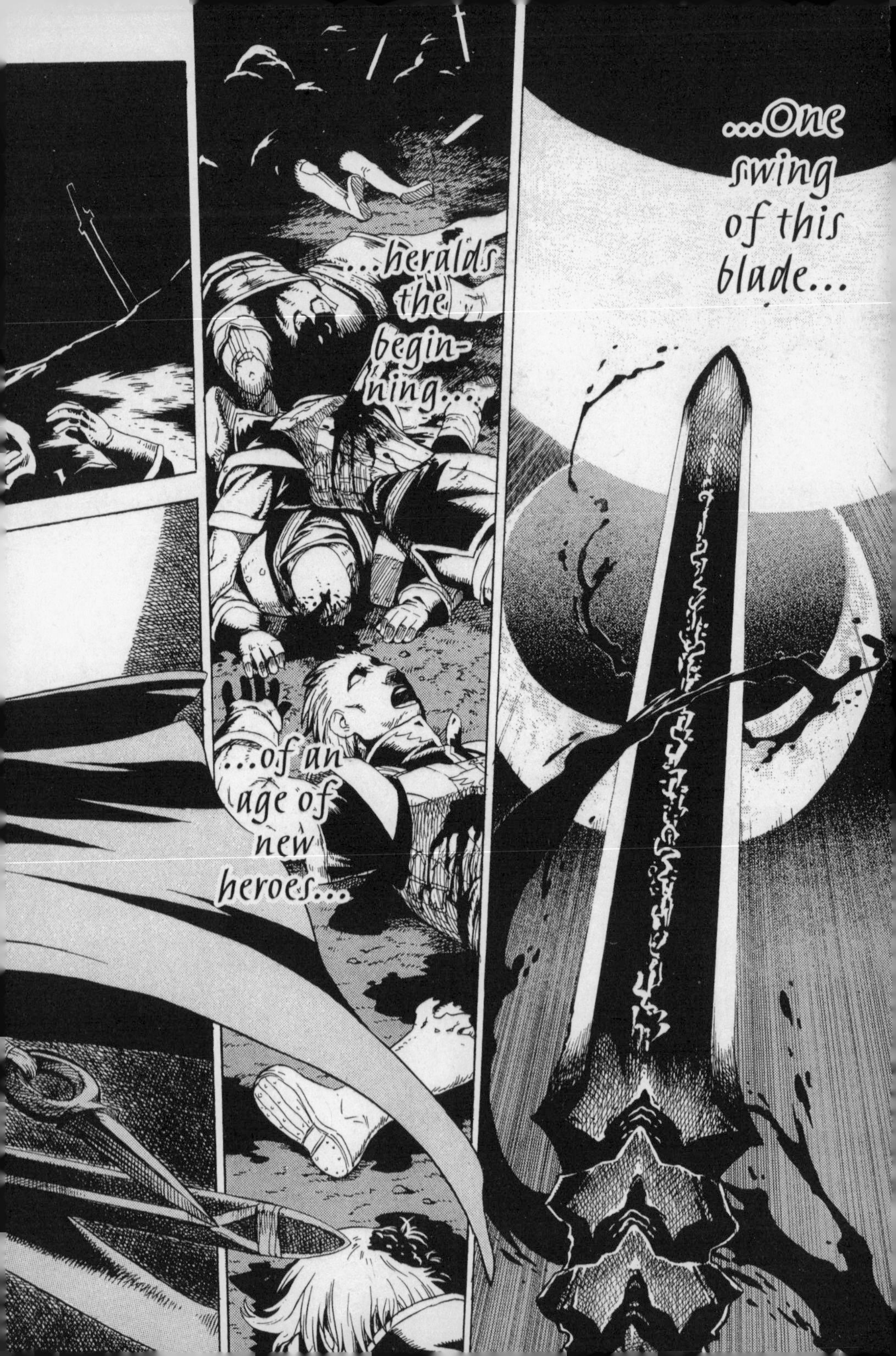
...One swing of this blade...
...heralds the begin-ning...
...of an age of new heroes...

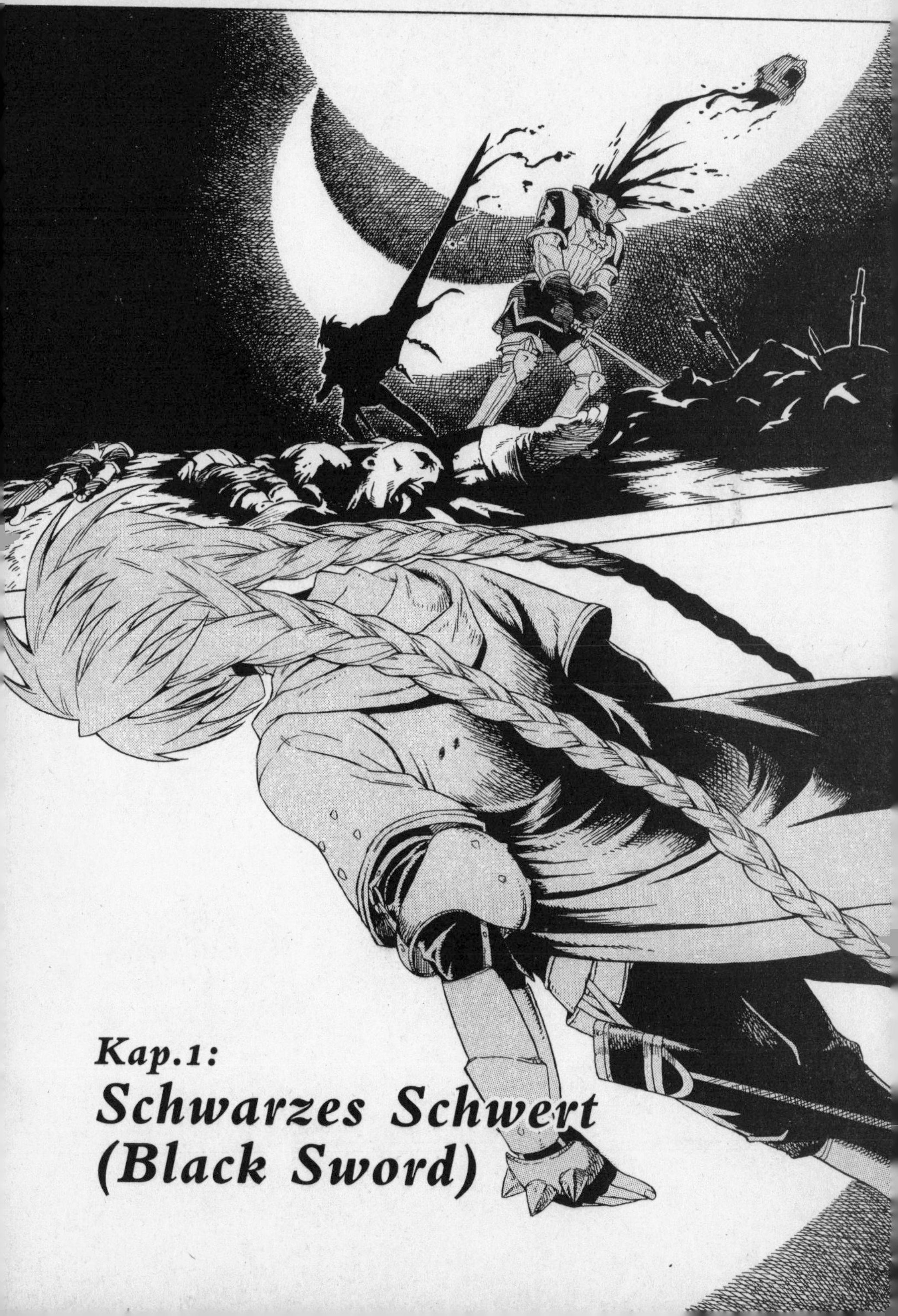

Kap.1: Schwarzes Schwert (Black Sword)

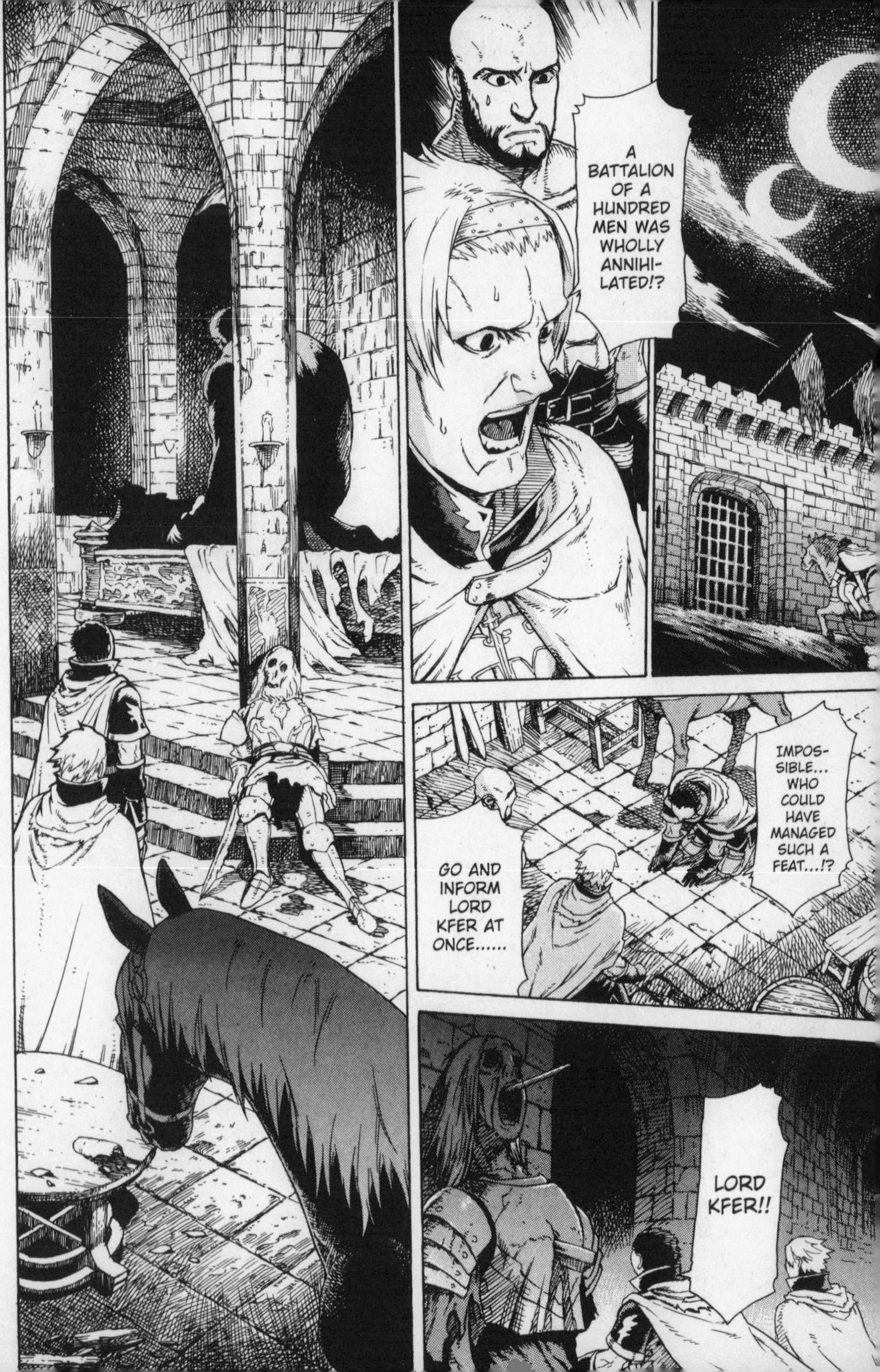
A BATTALION OF A HUNDRED MEN WAS WHOLLY ANNIHI-LATED!?
IMPOS-SIBLE... WHO COULD HAVE MANAGED SUCH A FEAT...!?
GO AND INFORM LORD KFER AT ONCE......
LORD KFER!!

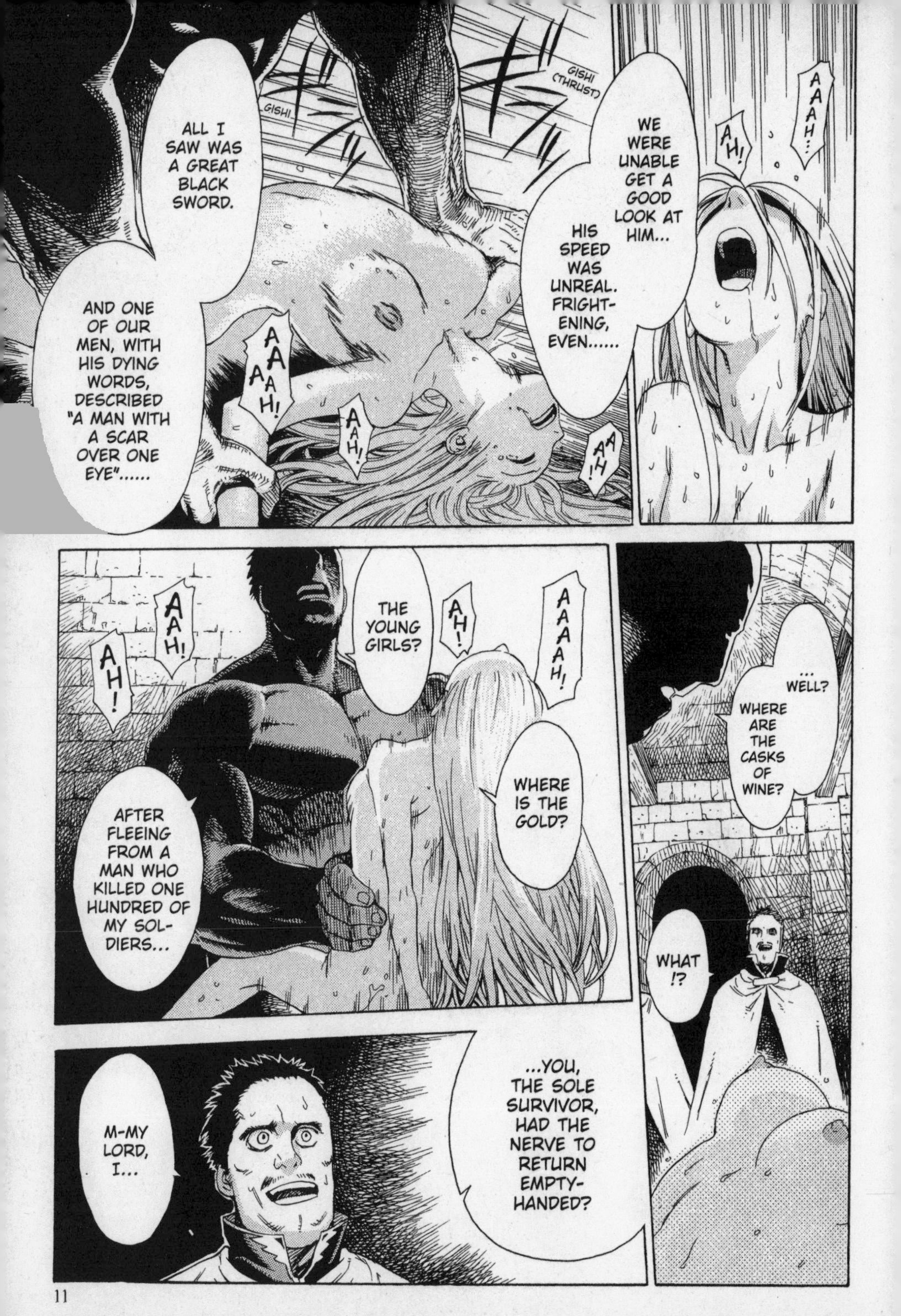
AAAH...
AH!
WE WERE UNABLE GET A GOOD LOOK AT HIM...
HIS SPEED WAS UNREAL. FRIGHT-ENING, EVEN......
GISHI (THRUST)
GISHI
AH AH!
AAH!
AAAH!
ALL I SAW WAS A GREAT BLACK SWORD.
AND ONE OF OUR MEN, WITH HIS DYING WORDS, DESCRIBED "A MAN WITH A SCAR OVER ONE EYE"......
... WELL?
WHERE ARE THE CASKS OF WINE?
WHAT !?
AAAAAH!
AH!
THE YOUNG GIRLS?
WHERE IS THE GOLD?
AAH!
AH!
AFTER FLEEING FROM A MAN WHO KILLED ONE HUNDRED OF MY SOL-DIERS...
...YOU, THE SOLE SURVIVOR, HAD THE NERVE TO RETURN EMPTY-HANDED?
M-MY LORD, I...

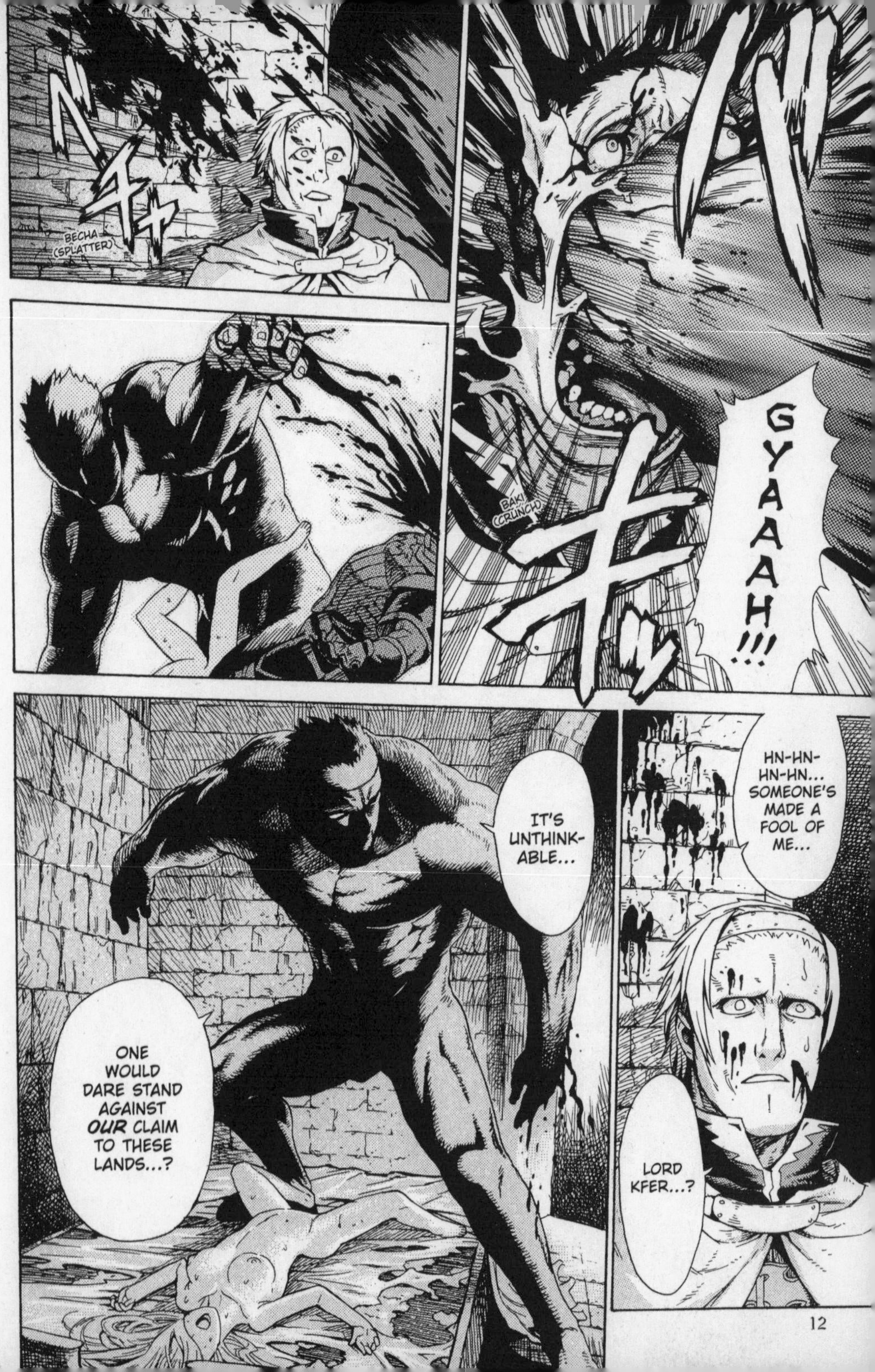
BAKI (CRUNCH)
GYAAAH!!!
BECHA (SPLATTER)
HN-HN-HN-HN... SOMEONE'S MADE A FOOL OF ME...
LORD KFER...?
IT'S UNTHINKABLE...
ONE WOULD DARE STAND AGAINST ***OUR*** CLAIM TO THESE LANDS...?

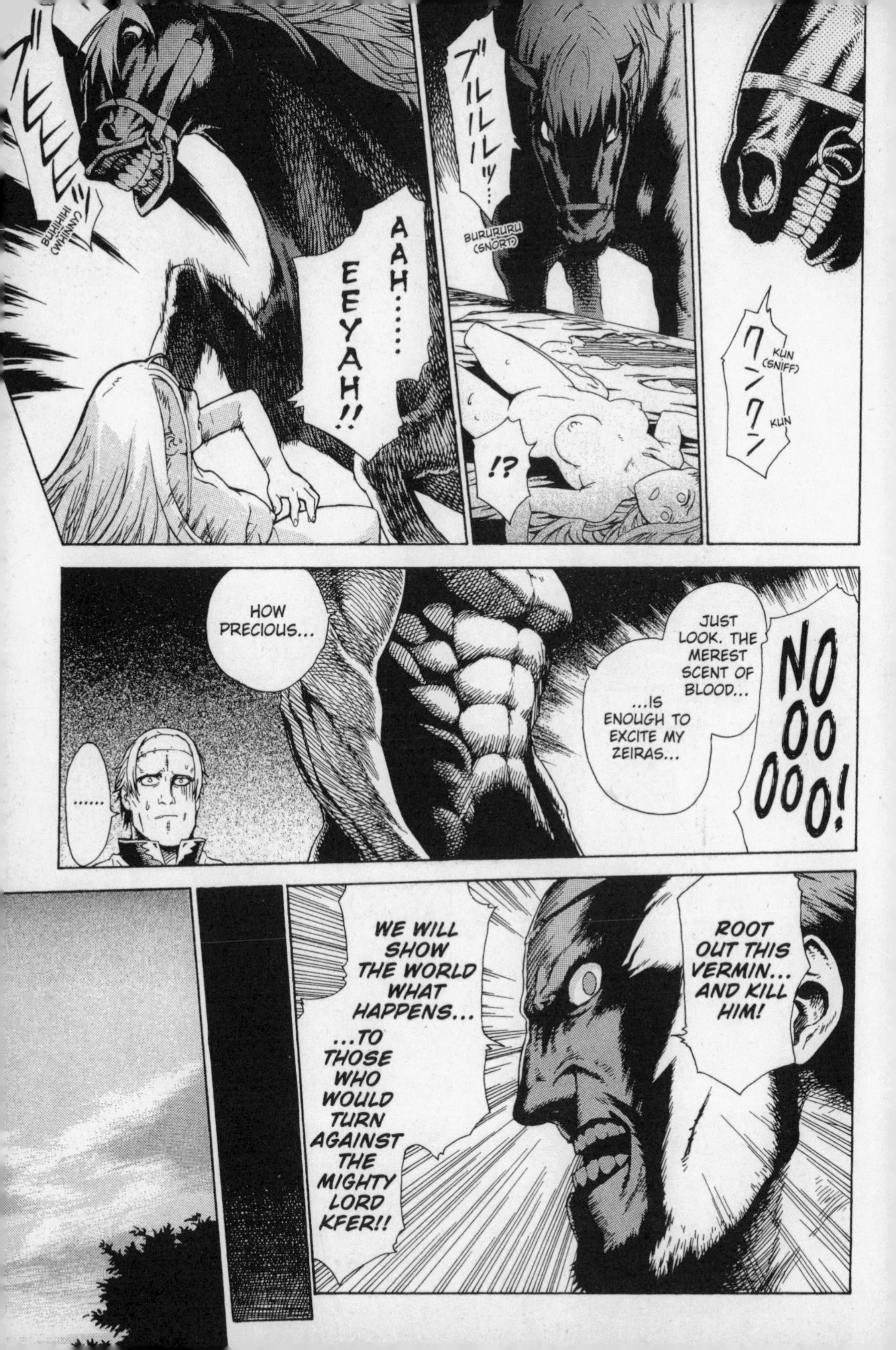

クンクン
KUN (SNIFF)
KUN
ブルルルルッ…
BURURURU (SNORT)
!?
ブヒヒヒーンッ
BUHIHIHI (WHINNY)
AAH.....
EEYAH!!
NOOOOOO!
JUST LOOK. THE MEREST SCENT OF BLOOD...
...IS ENOUGH TO EXCITE MY ZEIRAS...
HOW PRECIOUS...
......
ROOT OUT THIS VERMIN... AND KILL HIM!
WE WILL SHOW THE WORLD WHAT HAPPENS...
...TO THOSE WHO WOULD TURN AGAINST THE MIGHTY LORD KFER!!

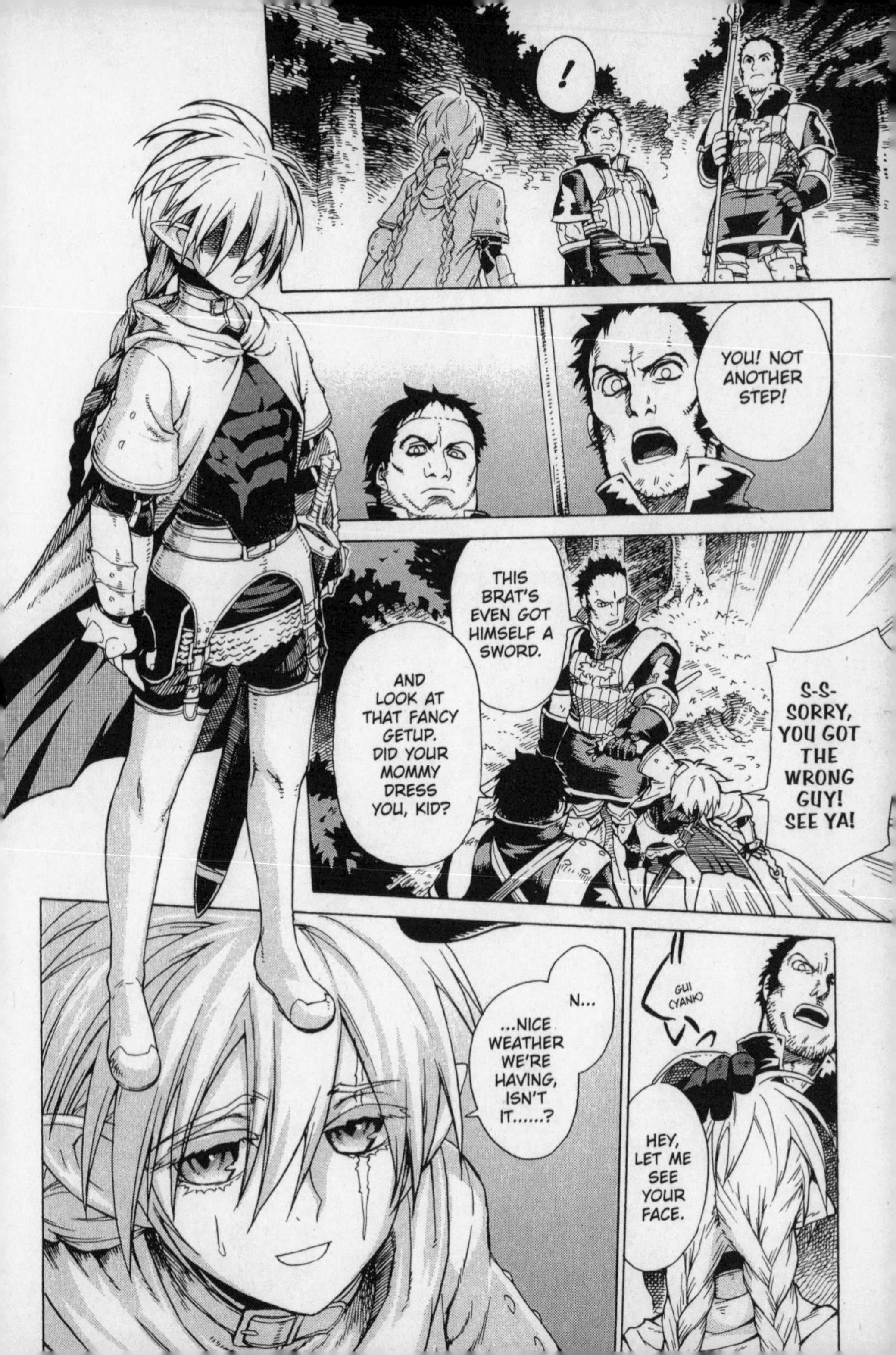
!
YOU! NOT ANOTHER STEP!
THIS BRAT'S EVEN GOT HIMSELF A SWORD.
AND LOOK AT THAT FANCY GETUP. DID YOUR MOMMY DRESS YOU, KID?
S-S-SORRY, YOU GOT THE WRONG GUY! SEE YA!
GUI (YANK)
HEY, LET ME SEE YOUR FACE.
N...
...NICE WEATHER WE'RE HAVING, ISN'T IT......?

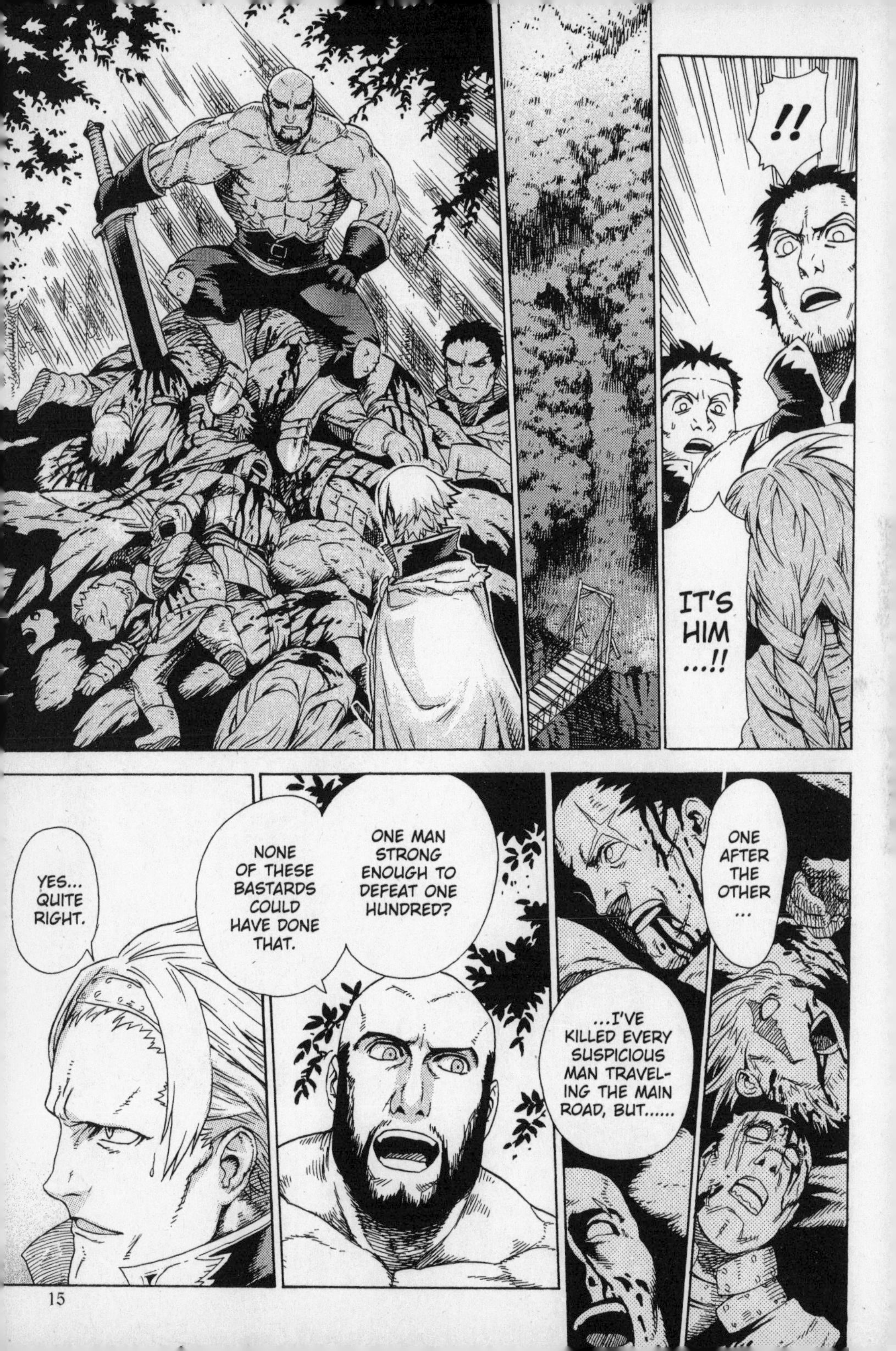
!!
IT'S HIM ...!!
ONE AFTER THE OTHER ...
...I'VE KILLED EVERY SUSPICIOUS MAN TRAVELING THE MAIN ROAD, BUT......
ONE MAN STRONG ENOUGH TO DEFEAT ONE HUNDRED?
NONE OF THESE BASTARDS COULD HAVE DONE THAT.
YES... QUITE RIGHT.

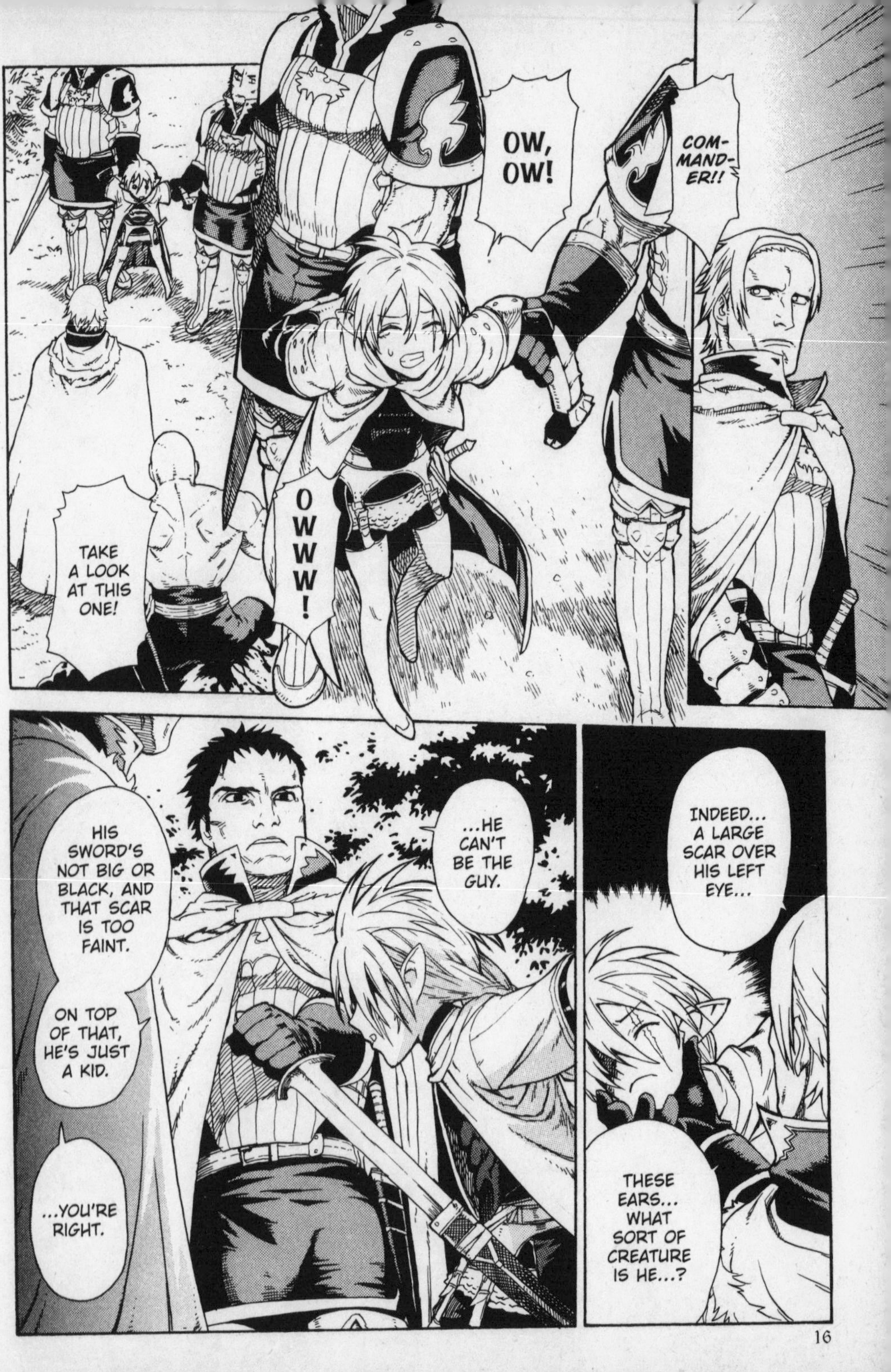
COM-MAND-ER!!
OW, OW!
OWWW!
TAKE A LOOK AT THIS ONE!
INDEED... A LARGE SCAR OVER HIS LEFT EYE...
THESE EARS... WHAT SORT OF CREATURE IS HE...?
...HE CAN'T BE THE GUY.
HIS SWORD'S NOT BIG OR BLACK, AND THAT SCAR IS TOO FAINT.
ON TOP OF THAT, HE'S JUST A KID.
...YOU'RE RIGHT.

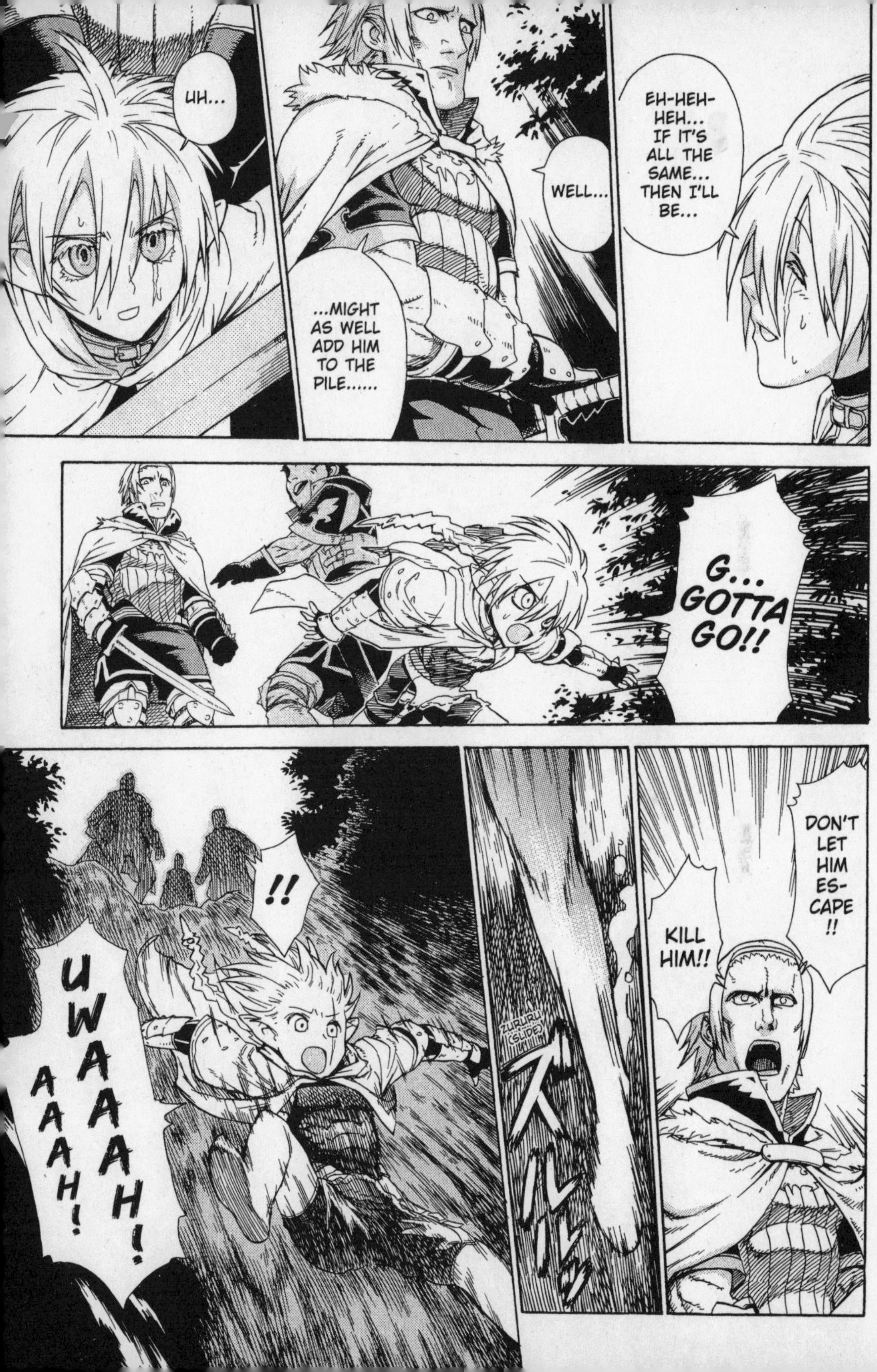
EH-HEH-HEH... IF IT'S ALL THE SAME... THEN I'LL BE...
WELL...
...MIGHT AS WELL ADD HIM TO THE PILE......
UH...
G... GOTTA GO!!
DON'T LET HIM ES-CAPE!!
KILL HIM!!
ZURURU (SLIDE)
!!
UWAAAAAH! AAAAH!

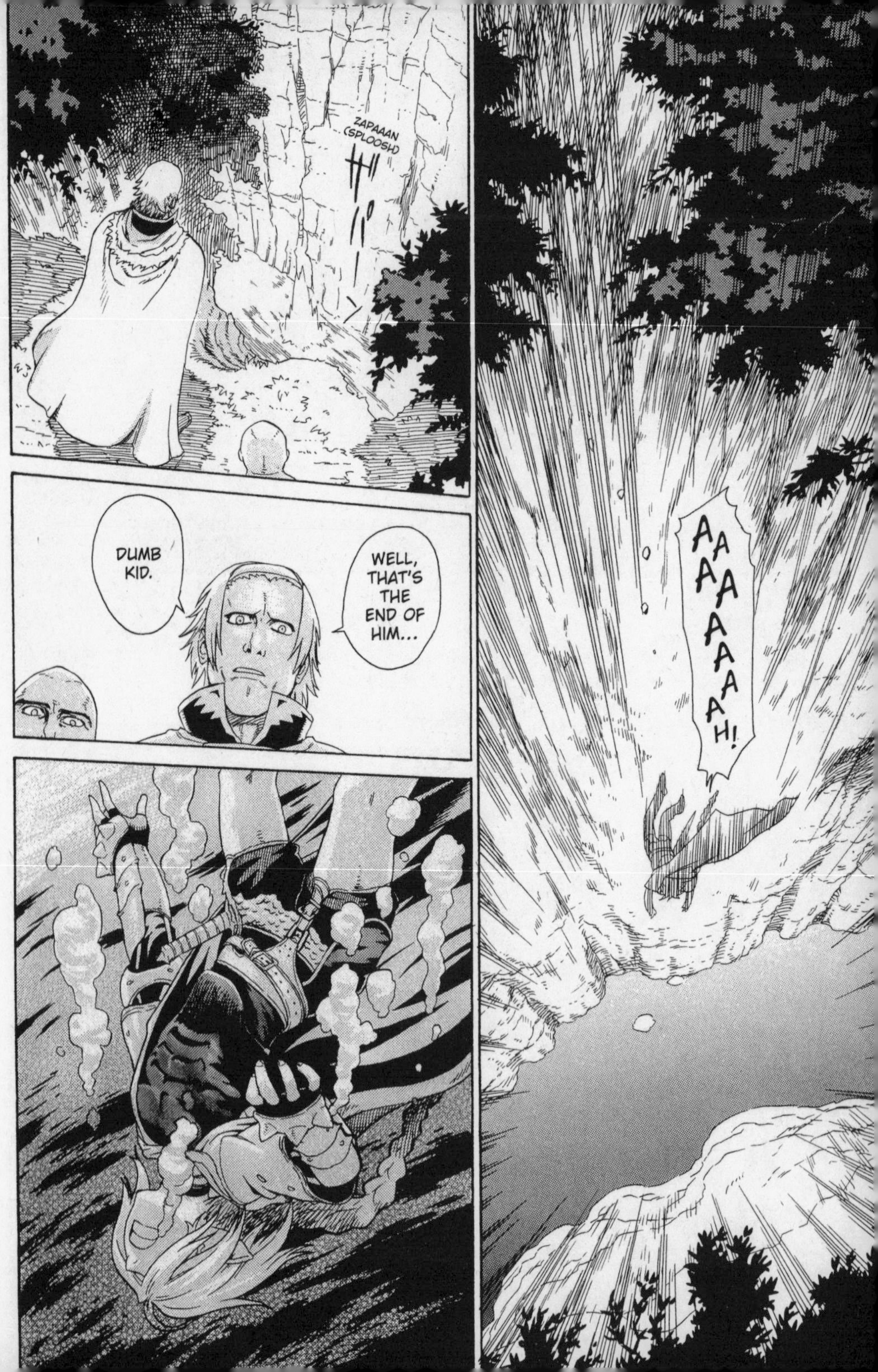
AAAAAAAAH!
ZAPAAAN (SPLOOSH)
WELL, THAT'S THE END OF HIM...
DUMB KID.

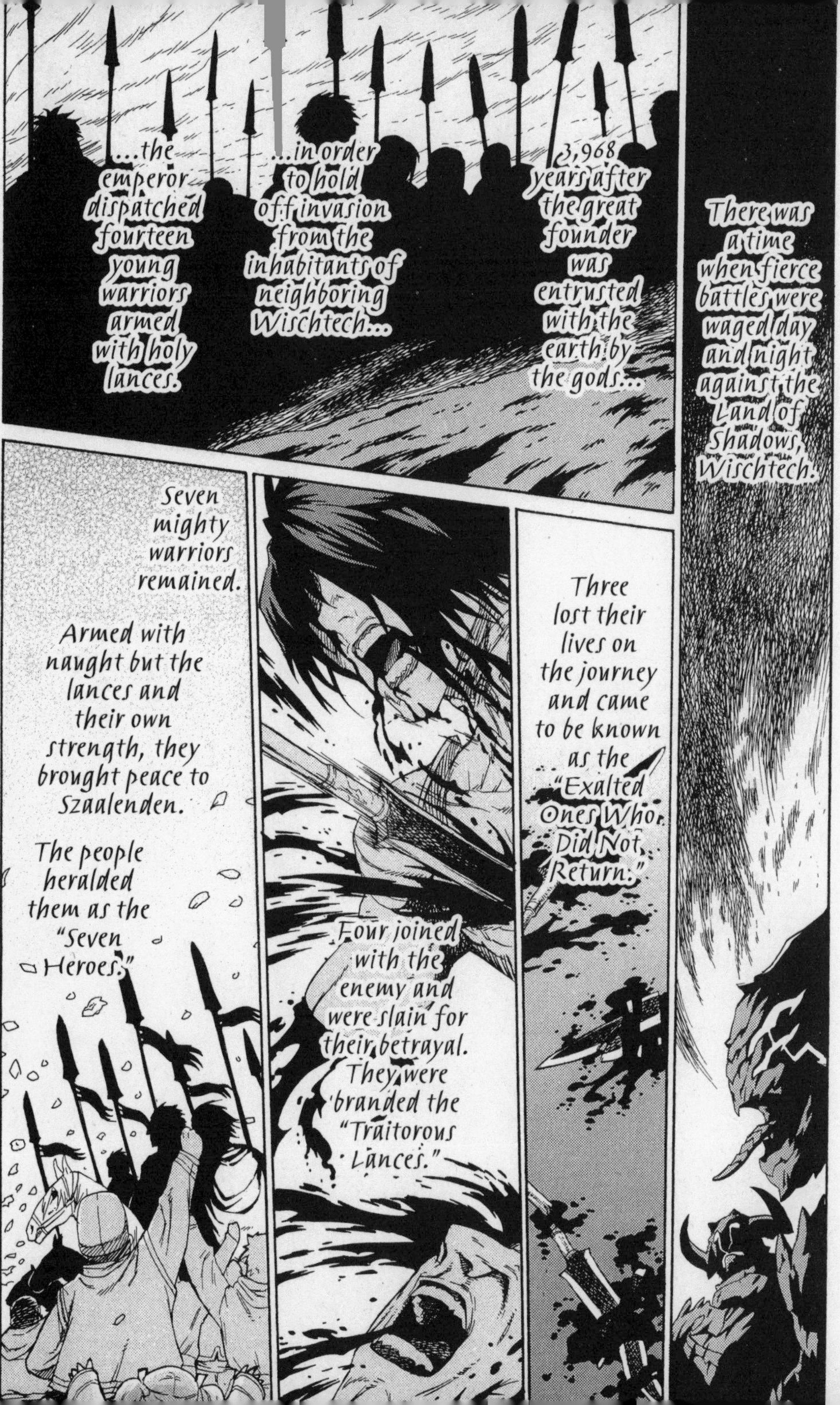
There was a time when fierce battles were waged day and night against the Land of Shadows, Wischtech.
3,968 years after the great founder was entrusted with the earth by the gods...
...in order to hold off invasion from the inhabitants of neighboring Wischtech...
...the emperor dispatched fourteen young warriors armed with holy lances.
Three lost their lives on the journey and came to be known as the "Exalted Ones Who Did Not Return."
Four joined with the enemy and were slain for their betrayal. They were branded the "Traitorous Lances."
Seven mighty warriors remained.
Armed with naught but the lances and their own strength, they brought peace to Szaalenden.
The people heralded them as the "Seven Heroes."

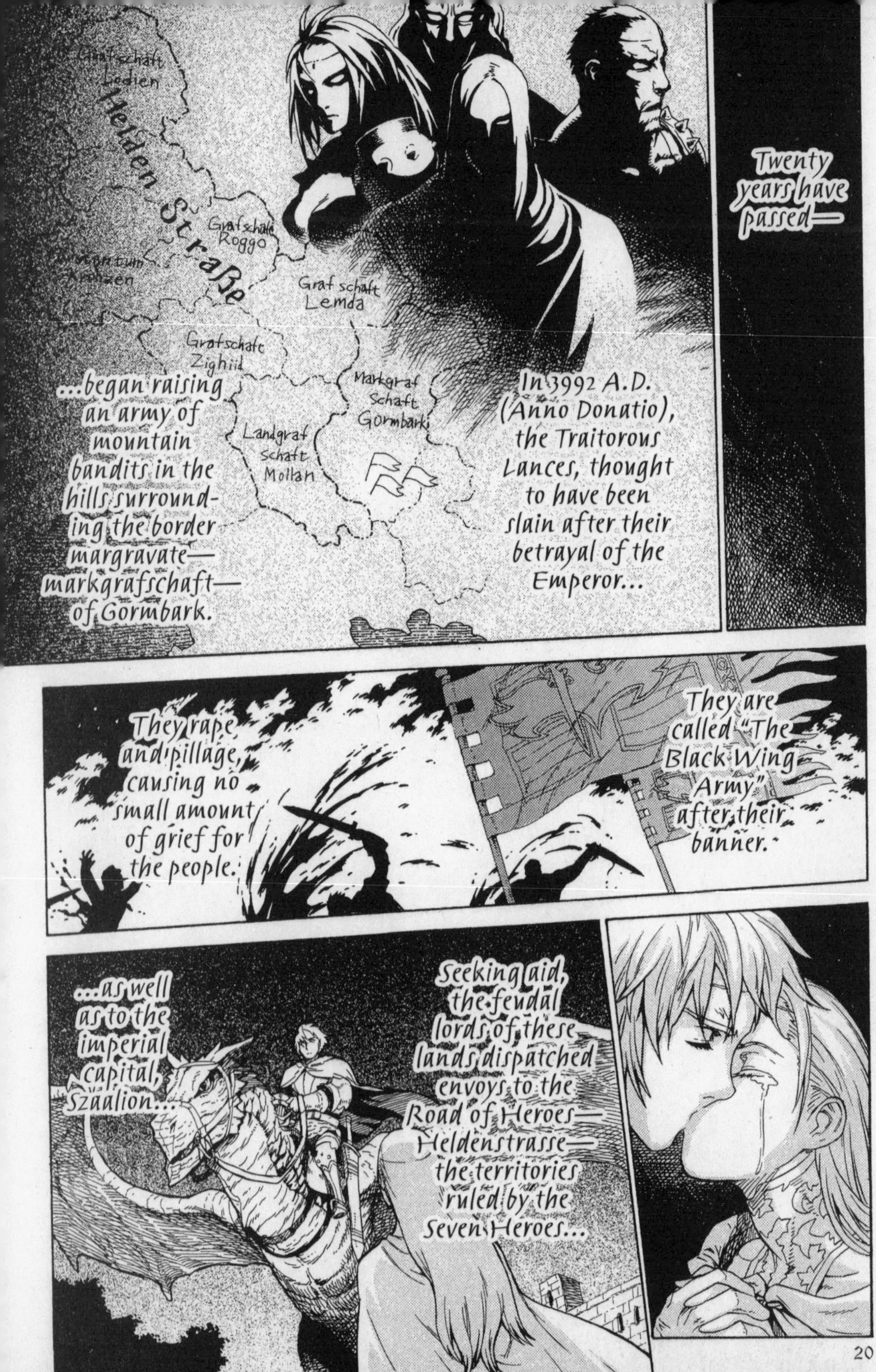
Twenty years have passed—
In 3992 A.D. (Anno Donatio), the Traitorous Lances, thought to have been slain after their betrayal of the Emperor...
...began raising an army of mountain bandits in the hills surrounding the border margravate—markgrafschaft—of Gormbark.
Helden Straße
Grafschaft Roggo
Grafschaft Lemda
Grafschaft Zighiid
Markgraf Schaft Gormbarki
Landgraf Schaft Mollan
They are called "The Black Wing Army" after their banner.
They rape and pillage, causing no small amount of grief for the people.
Seeking aid, the feudal lords of these lands dispatched envoys to the Road of Heroes—Heldenstrasse—the territories ruled by the Seven Heroes...
...as well as to the imperial capital, Szaalion...

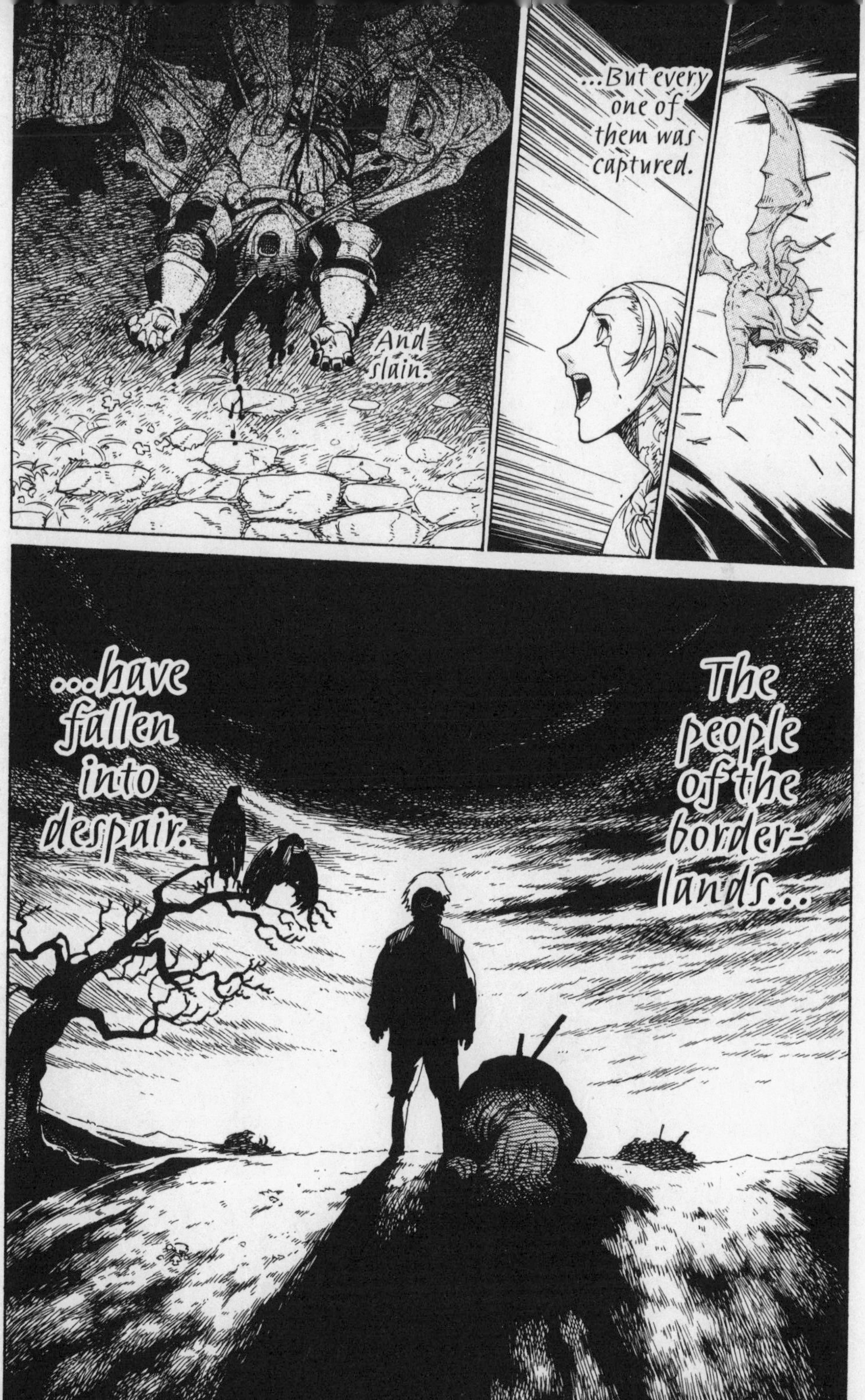
...But every one of them was captured.
And slain.
The people of the borderlands...
...have fallen into despair.

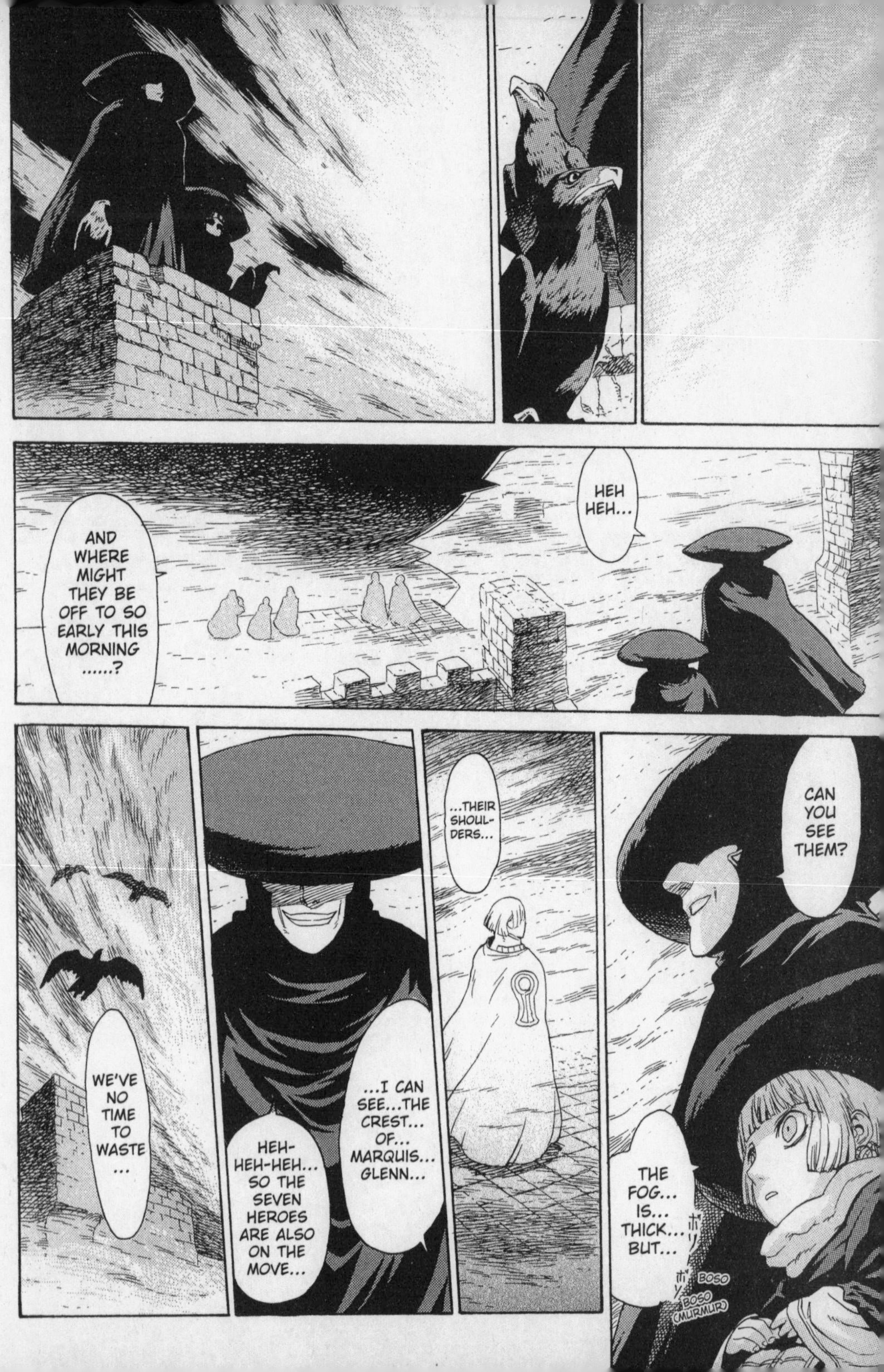
HEH HEH...
AND WHERE MIGHT THEY BE OFF TO SO EARLY THIS MORNING ......?
CAN YOU SEE THEM?
THE FOG... IS... THICK... BUT...
BOSO BOSO (MURMUR)
...THEIR SHOULDERS...
...I CAN SEE...THE CREST... OF... MARQUIS... GLENN...
HEH-HEH-HEH... SO THE SEVEN HEROES ARE ALSO ON THE MOVE...
WE'VE NO TIME TO WASTE...

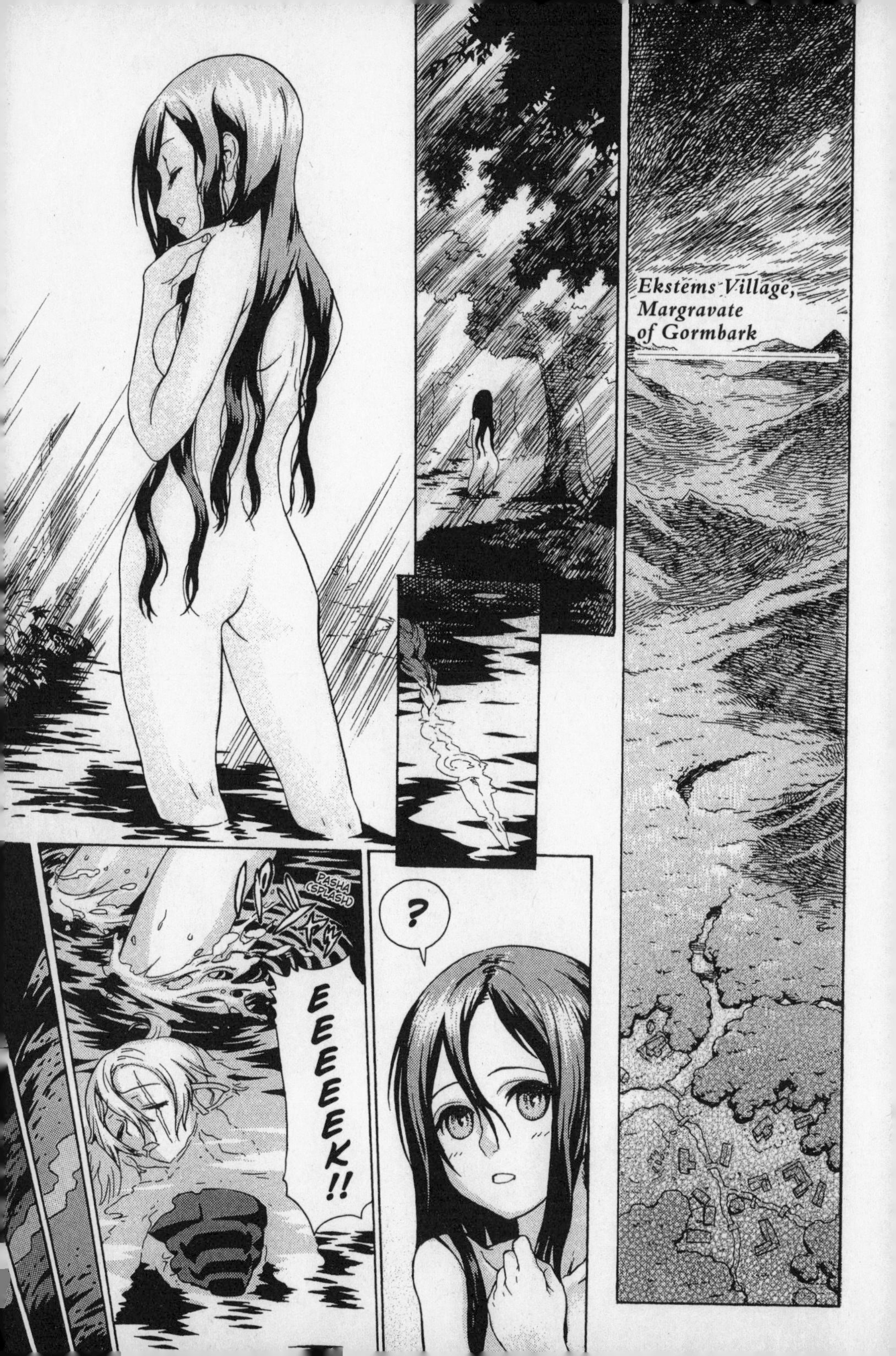

Ekstems Village,
Margravate
of Gormbark
?
PASHA
(SPLASH)
EEEEEEK!!

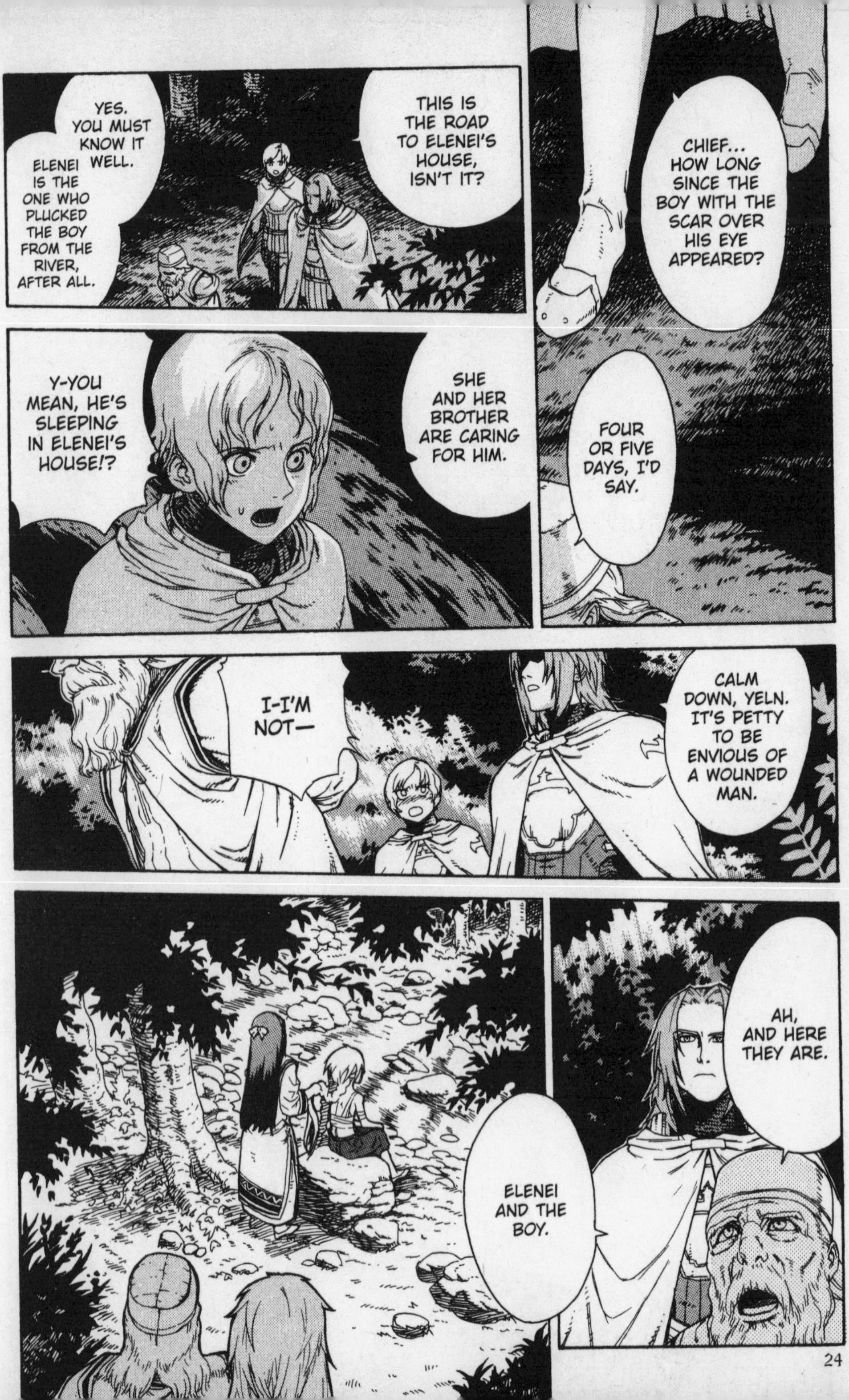
CHIEF... HOW LONG SINCE THE BOY WITH THE SCAR OVER HIS EYE APPEARED?
FOUR OR FIVE DAYS, I'D SAY.
THIS IS THE ROAD TO ELENEI'S HOUSE, ISN'T IT?
YES. YOU MUST KNOW IT WELL.
ELENEI IS THE ONE WHO PLUCKED THE BOY FROM THE RIVER, AFTER ALL.
SHE AND HER BROTHER ARE CARING FOR HIM.
Y-YOU MEAN, HE'S SLEEPING IN ELENEI'S HOUSE!?
CALM DOWN, YELN. IT'S PETTY TO BE ENVIOUS OF A WOUNDED MAN.
I-I'M NOT—
AH, AND HERE THEY ARE.
ELENEI AND THE BOY.

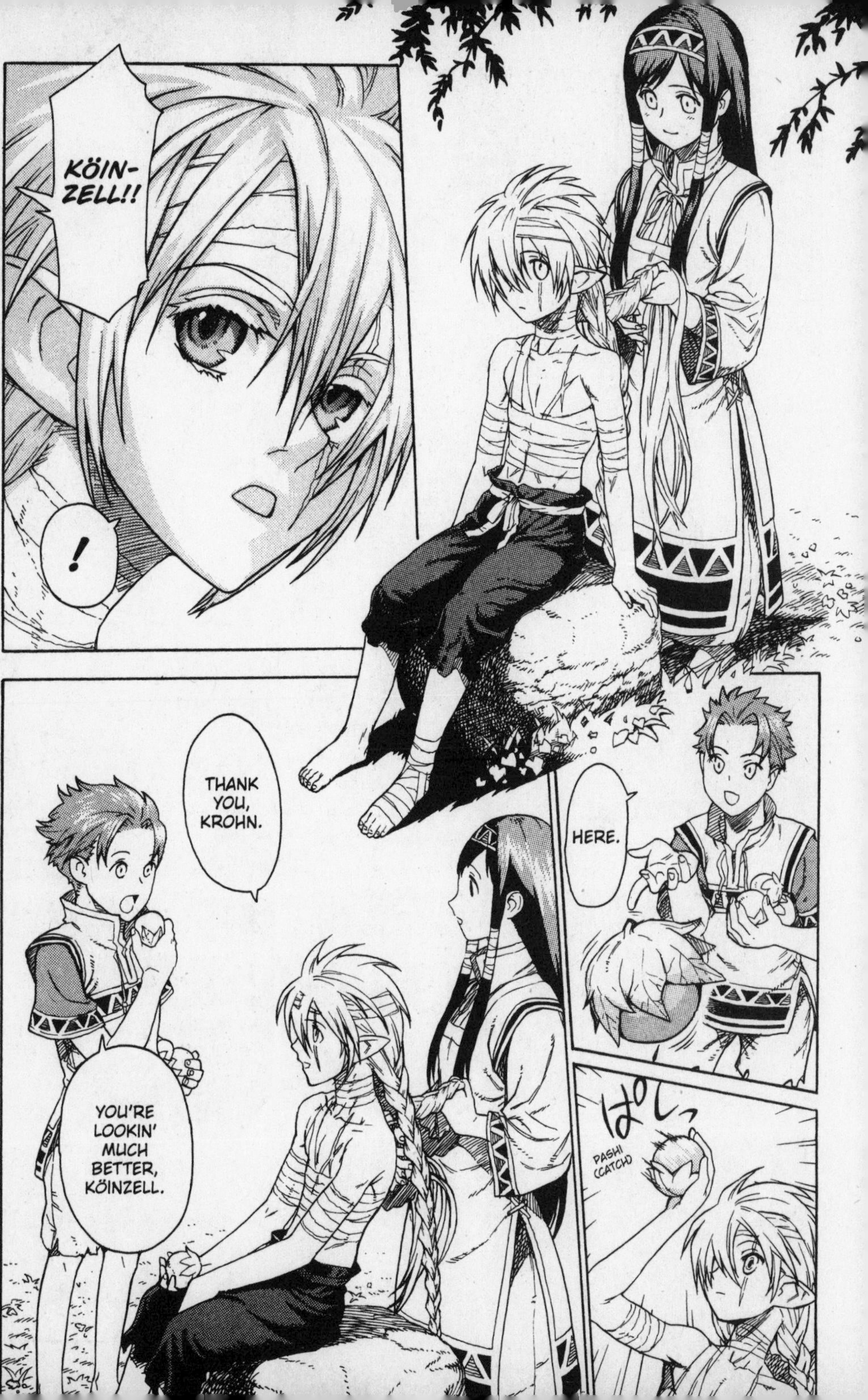
KÖIN-ZELL!!
!
HERE.
ぱしっ
PASHI (CATCH)
THANK YOU, KROHN.
YOU'RE LOOKIN' MUCH BETTER, KÖINZELL.

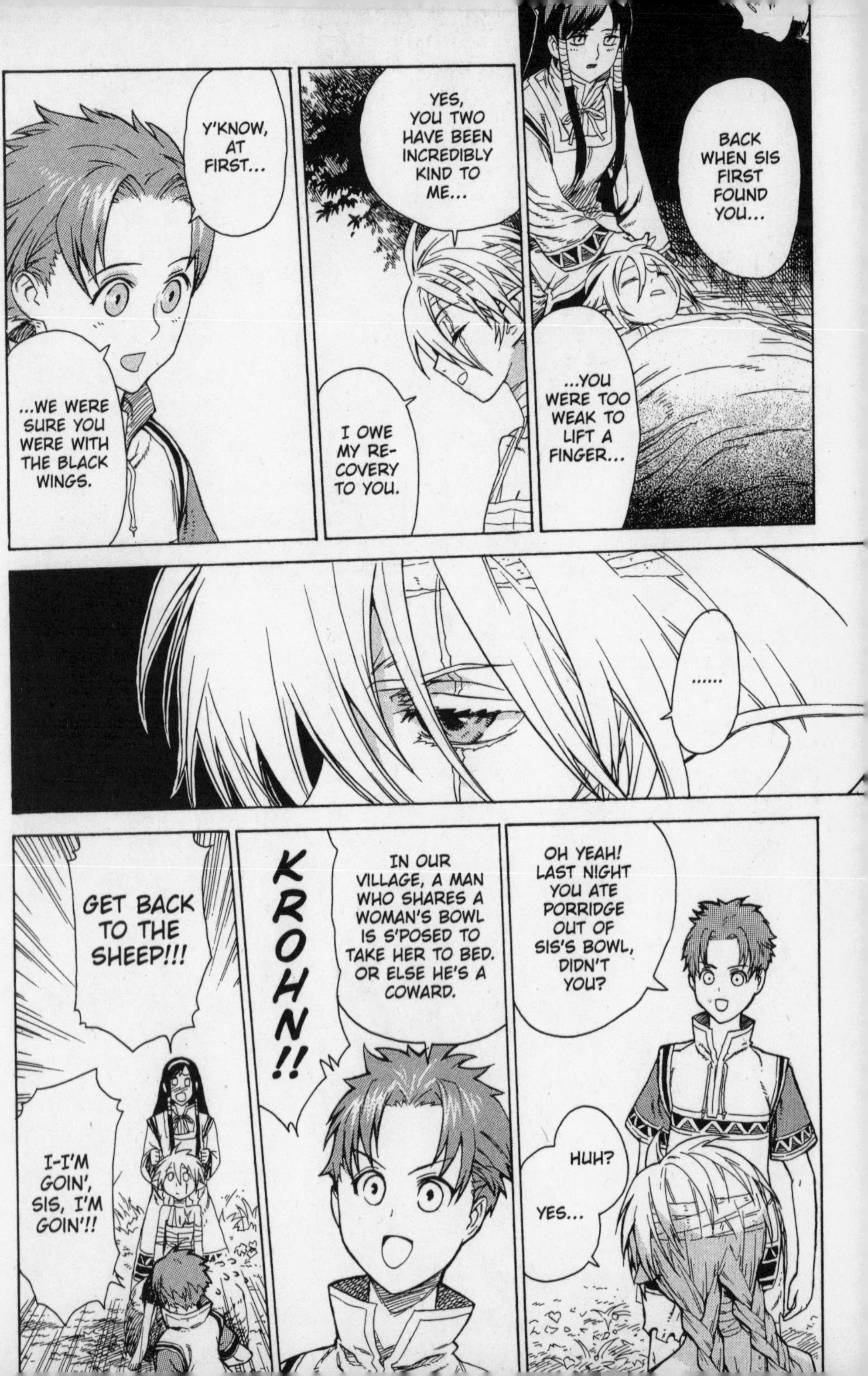
BACK WHEN SIS FIRST FOUND YOU...
...YOU WERE TOO WEAK TO LIFT A FINGER...
YES, YOU TWO HAVE BEEN INCREDIBLY KIND TO ME...
I OWE MY RECOVERY TO YOU.
Y'KNOW, AT FIRST...
...WE WERE SURE YOU WERE WITH THE BLACK WINGS.
......
OH YEAH! LAST NIGHT YOU ATE PORRIDGE OUT OF SIS'S BOWL, DIDN'T YOU?
HUH?
YES...
IN OUR VILLAGE, A MAN WHO SHARES A WOMAN'S BOWL IS S'POSED TO TAKE HER TO BED. OR ELSE HE'S A COWARD.
KROHN!!
GET BACK TO THE SHEEP!!!
I-I'M GOIN', SIS, I'M GOIN'!!

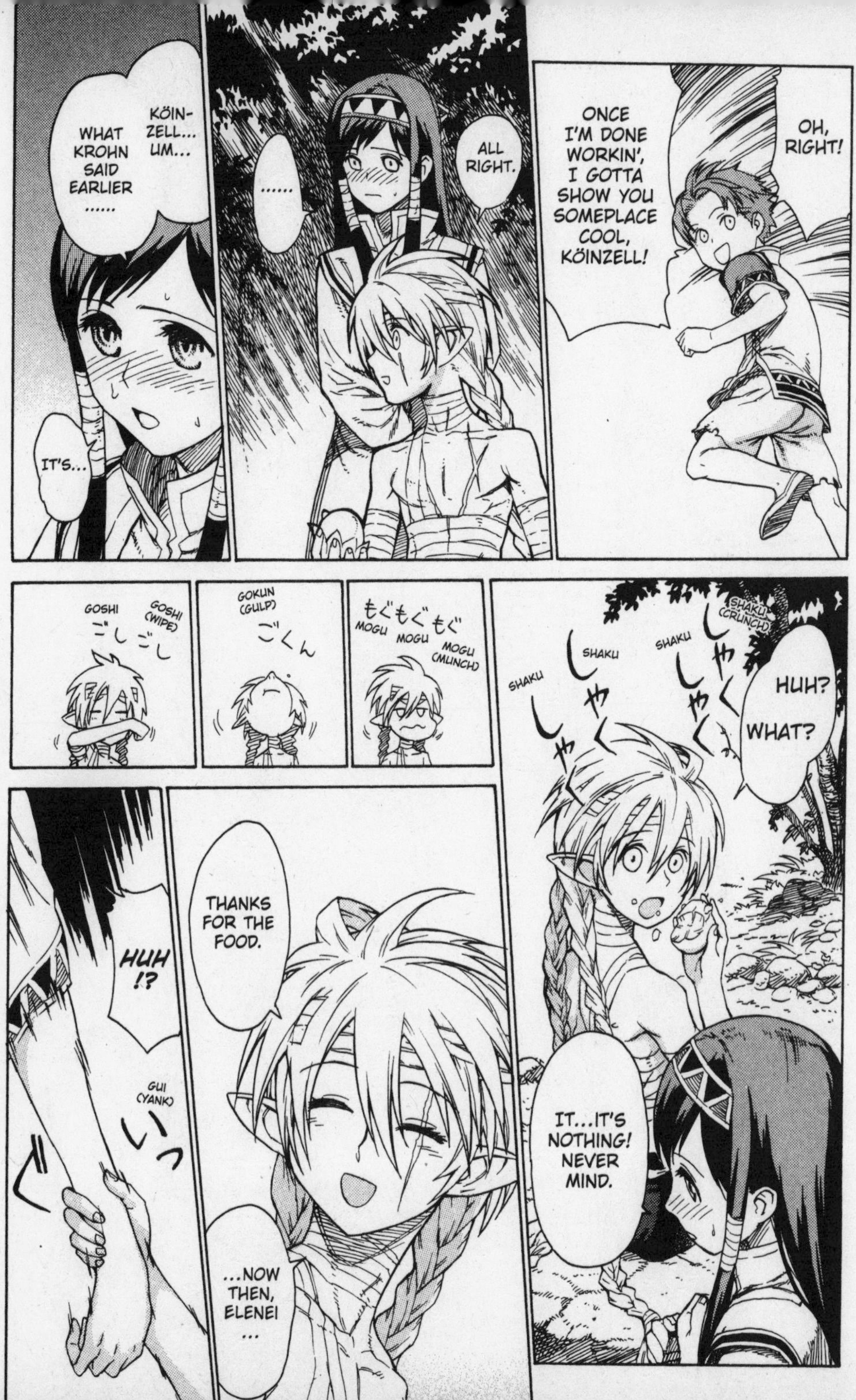

OH, RIGHT!
ONCE I'M DONE WORKIN', I GOTTA SHOW YOU SOMEPLACE COOL, KÖINZELL!
ALL RIGHT.
......
KÖIN-ZELL... UM...
WHAT KROHN SAID EARLIER ......
IT'S...
SHAKU (CRUNCH) SHAKU SHAKU SHAKU
しゃくしゃくしゃくしゃく
HUH? WHAT?
IT...IT'S NOTHING! NEVER MIND.
もぐもぐもぐ
MOGU MOGU MOGU (MUNCH)
GOKUN (GULP)
ごくん
GOSHI GOSHI (WIPE)
ごしごし
THANKS FOR THE FOOD.
...NOW THEN, ELENEI ...
HUH !?
GUI (YANK)
ぐいっ

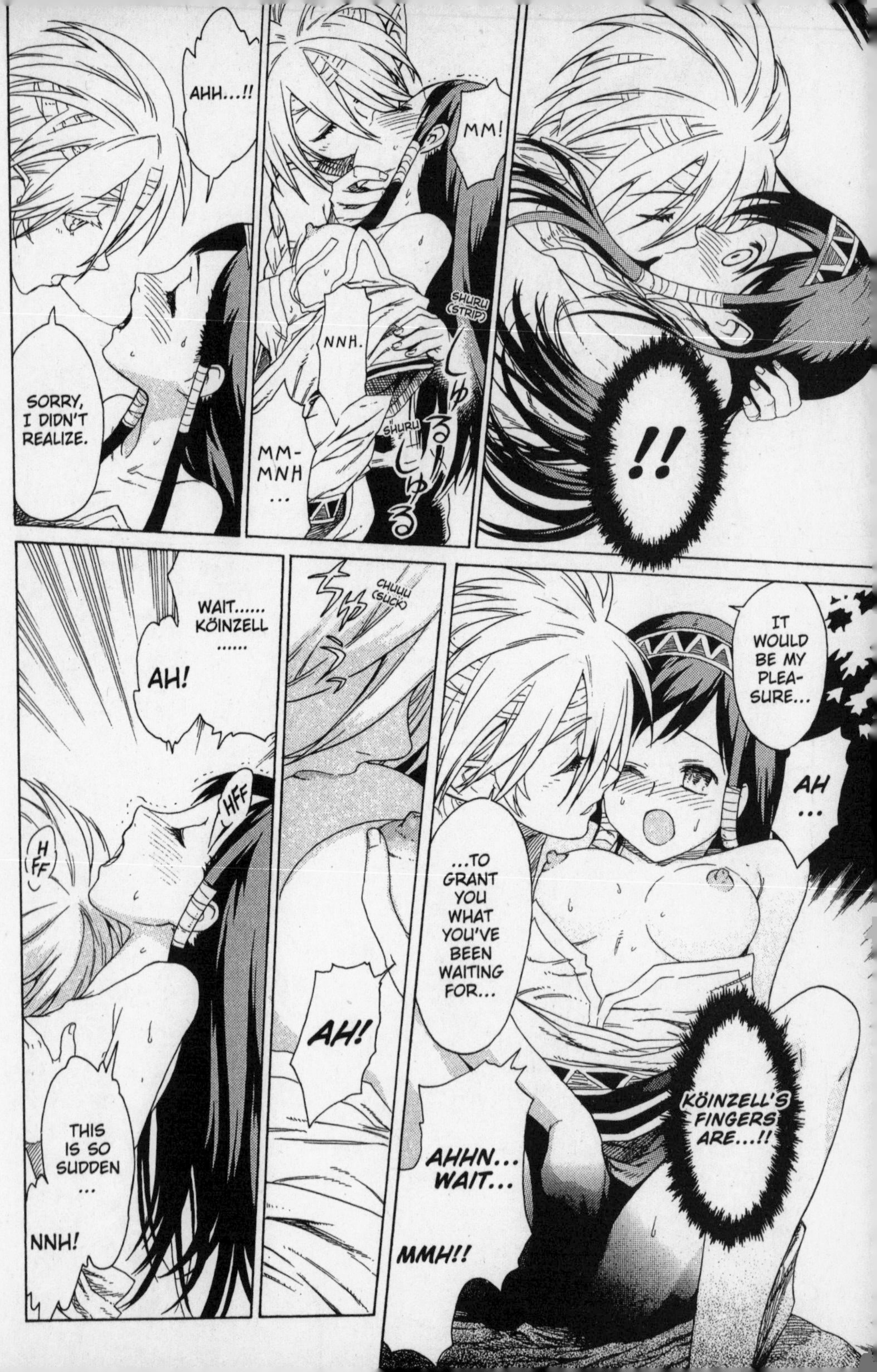
!!
MM!
SHURU (STRIP)
NNH.
SHURU
MM-MNH ...
AHH...!!
SORRY, I DIDN'T REALIZE.
IT WOULD BE MY PLEA-SURE...
AH ...
...TO GRANT YOU WHAT YOU'VE BEEN WAITING FOR...
KÖINZELL'S FINGERS ARE...!!
AHHN... WAIT...
MMH!!
CHUUU (SUCK)
AH!
WAIT...... KÖINZELL ......
AH!
HFF
HFF
THIS IS SO SUDDEN ...
NNH!

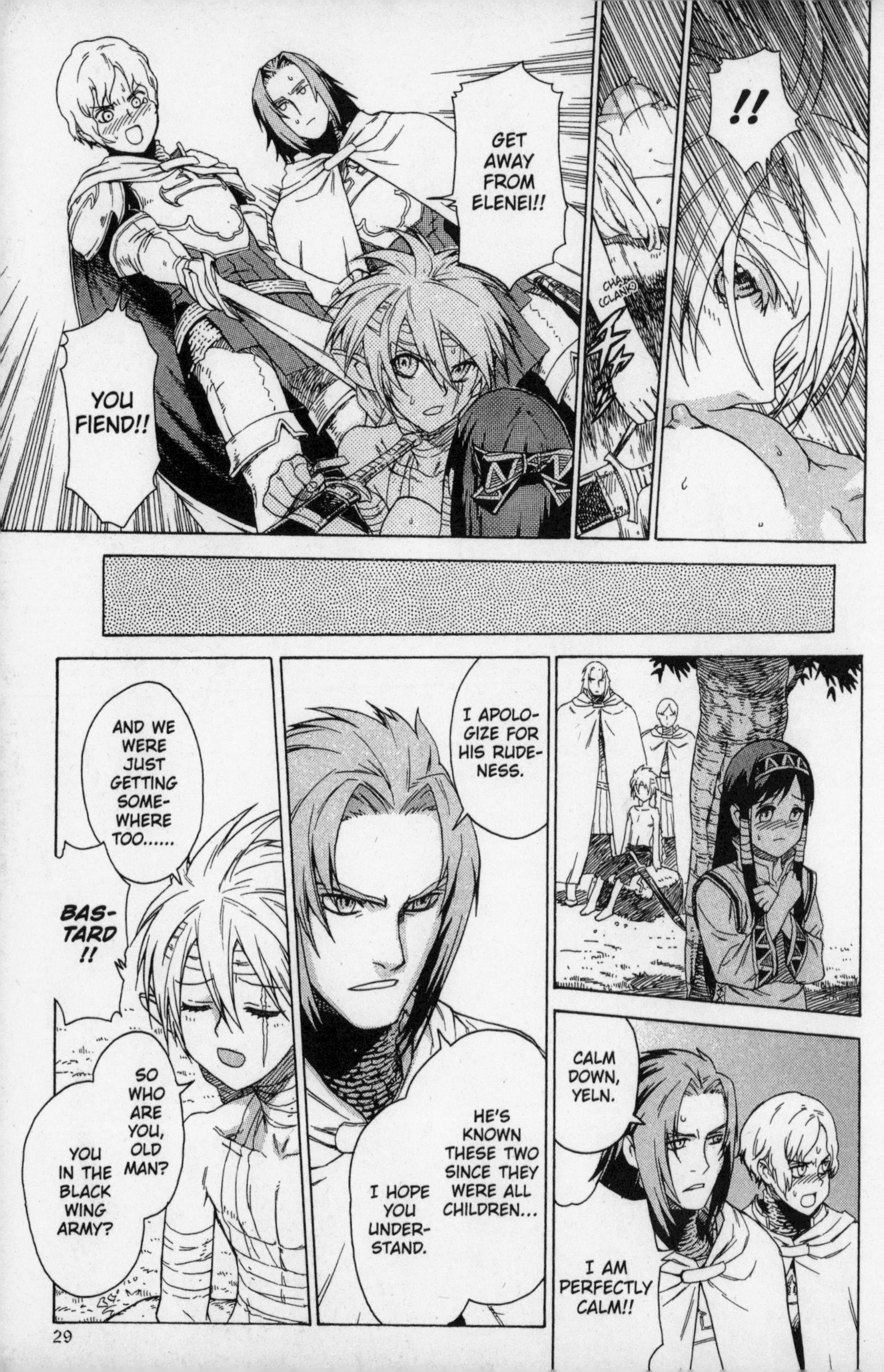
!!
CHA (CLANK)
GET AWAY FROM ELENEI!!
YOU FIEND!!
CALM DOWN, YELN.
I AM PERFECTLY CALM!!
I APOLOGIZE FOR HIS RUDENESS.
HE'S KNOWN THESE TWO SINCE THEY WERE ALL CHILDREN...
I HOPE YOU UNDERSTAND.
AND WE WERE JUST GETTING SOMEWHERE TOO......
BASTARD!!
SO WHO ARE YOU, OLD MAN?
YOU IN THE BLACK WING ARMY?

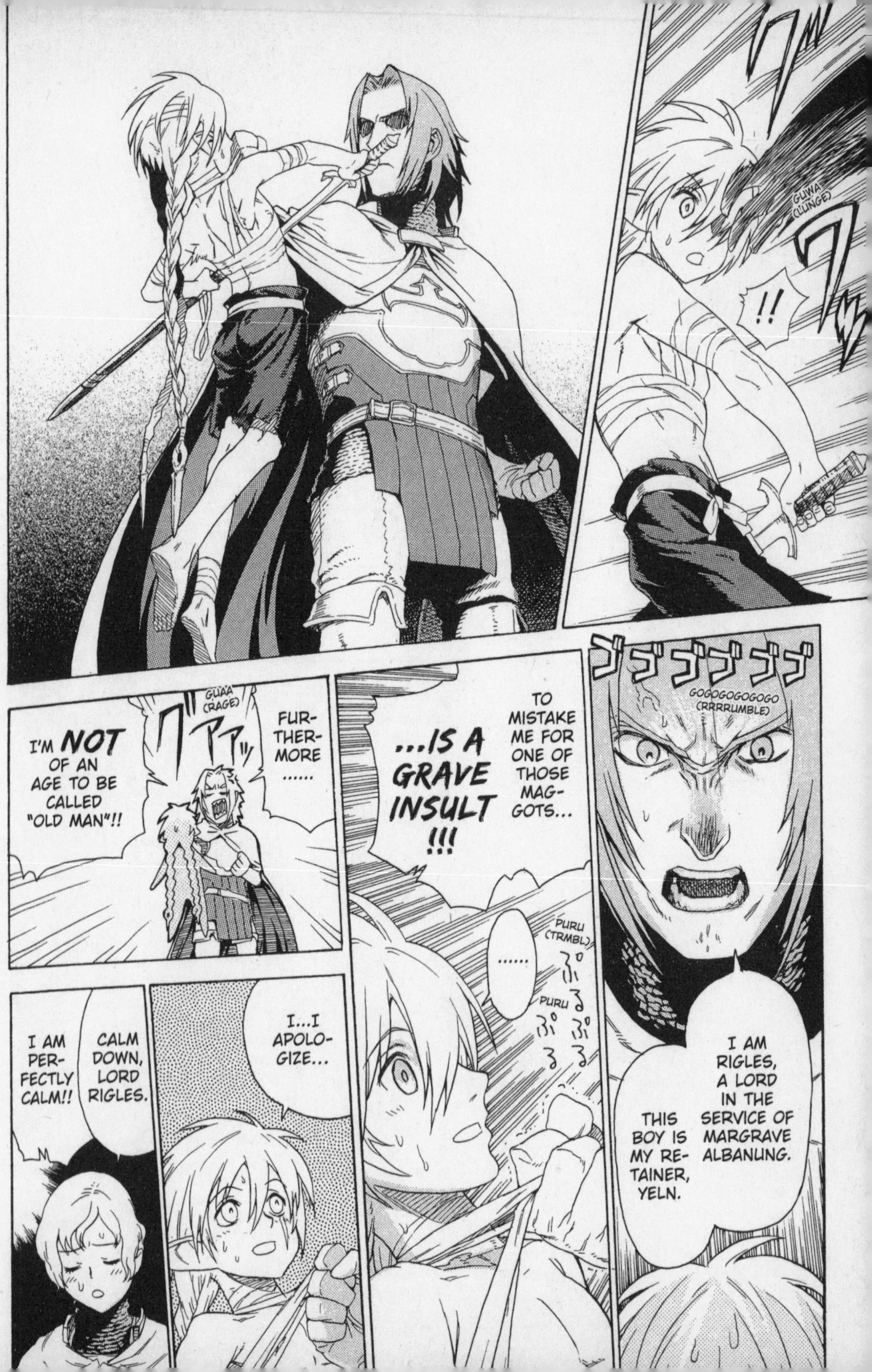

グワッ
GUWA (CLUNGE)
!!
ゴゴゴゴゴゴ
GOGOGOGOGOGO (RRRRUMBLE)
TO MISTAKE ME FOR ONE OF THOSE MAG-GOTS...
...IS A GRAVE INSULT!!!
FUR-THER-MORE......
グアアッ
GUAA (RAGE)
I'M NOT OF AN AGE TO BE CALLED "OLD MAN"!!
I AM RIGLES, A LORD IN THE SERVICE OF MARGRAVE ALBANUNG.
THIS BOY IS MY RE-TAINER, YELN.
......
PURU (TRMBL)
PURU
ぷるぷる
ぷるぷる
I...I APOLO-GIZE...
CALM DOWN, LORD RIGLES.
I AM PER-FECTLY CALM!!

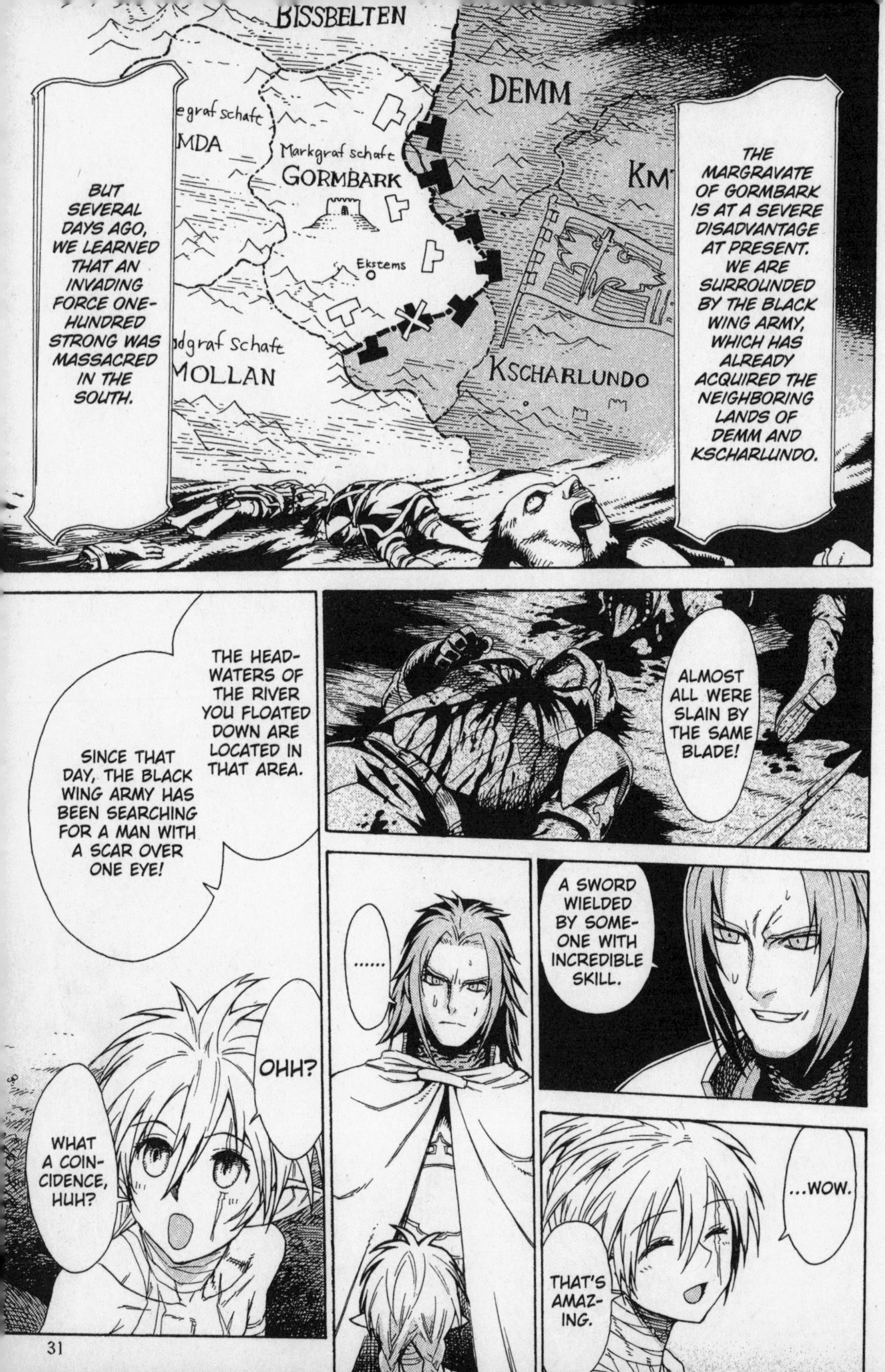
BISSBELTEN
DEMM
egraf schaft
MDA
Markgraf schaft
GORMBARK
Ekstems
KM
dgraf schaft
MOLLAN
KSCHARLUNDO
THE MARGRAVATE OF GORMBARK IS AT A SEVERE DISADVANTAGE AT PRESENT. WE ARE SURROUNDED BY THE BLACK WING ARMY, WHICH HAS ALREADY ACQUIRED THE NEIGHBORING LANDS OF DEMM AND KSCHARLUNDO.
BUT SEVERAL DAYS AGO, WE LEARNED THAT AN INVADING FORCE ONE-HUNDRED STRONG WAS MASSACRED IN THE SOUTH.
ALMOST ALL WERE SLAIN BY THE SAME BLADE!
A SWORD WIELDED BY SOME-ONE WITH INCREDIBLE SKILL.
......
THE HEAD-WATERS OF THE RIVER YOU FLOATED DOWN ARE LOCATED IN THAT AREA.
SINCE THAT DAY, THE BLACK WING ARMY HAS BEEN SEARCHING FOR A MAN WITH A SCAR OVER ONE EYE!
OHH?
WHAT A COIN-CIDENCE, HUH?
...WOW.
THAT'S AMAZ-ING.

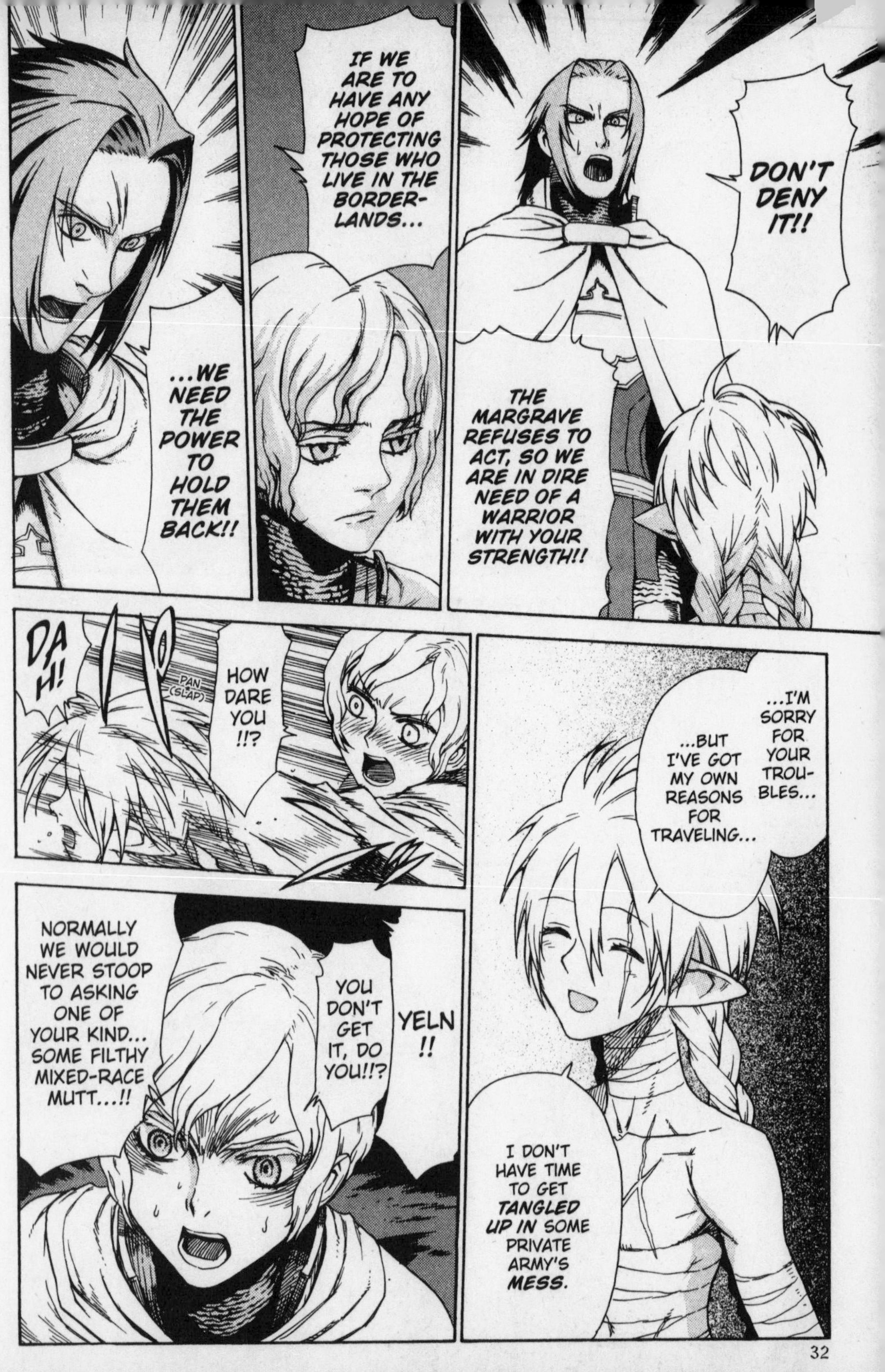
DON'T DENY IT!!
THE MARGRAVE REFUSES TO ACT, SO WE ARE IN DIRE NEED OF A WARRIOR WITH YOUR STRENGTH!!
IF WE ARE TO HAVE ANY HOPE OF PROTECTING THOSE WHO LIVE IN THE BORDER-LANDS...
...WE NEED THE POWER TO HOLD THEM BACK!!
...I'M SORRY FOR YOUR TROU-BLES...
...BUT I'VE GOT MY OWN REASONS FOR TRAVELING...
I DON'T HAVE TIME TO GET TANGLED UP IN SOME PRIVATE ARMY'S MESS.
HOW DARE YOU!!?
PAN (SLAP)
DAH!
YELN!!
YOU DON'T GET IT, DO YOU!!?
NORMALLY WE WOULD NEVER STOOP TO ASKING ONE OF YOUR KIND... SOME FILTHY MIXED-RACE MUTT...!!

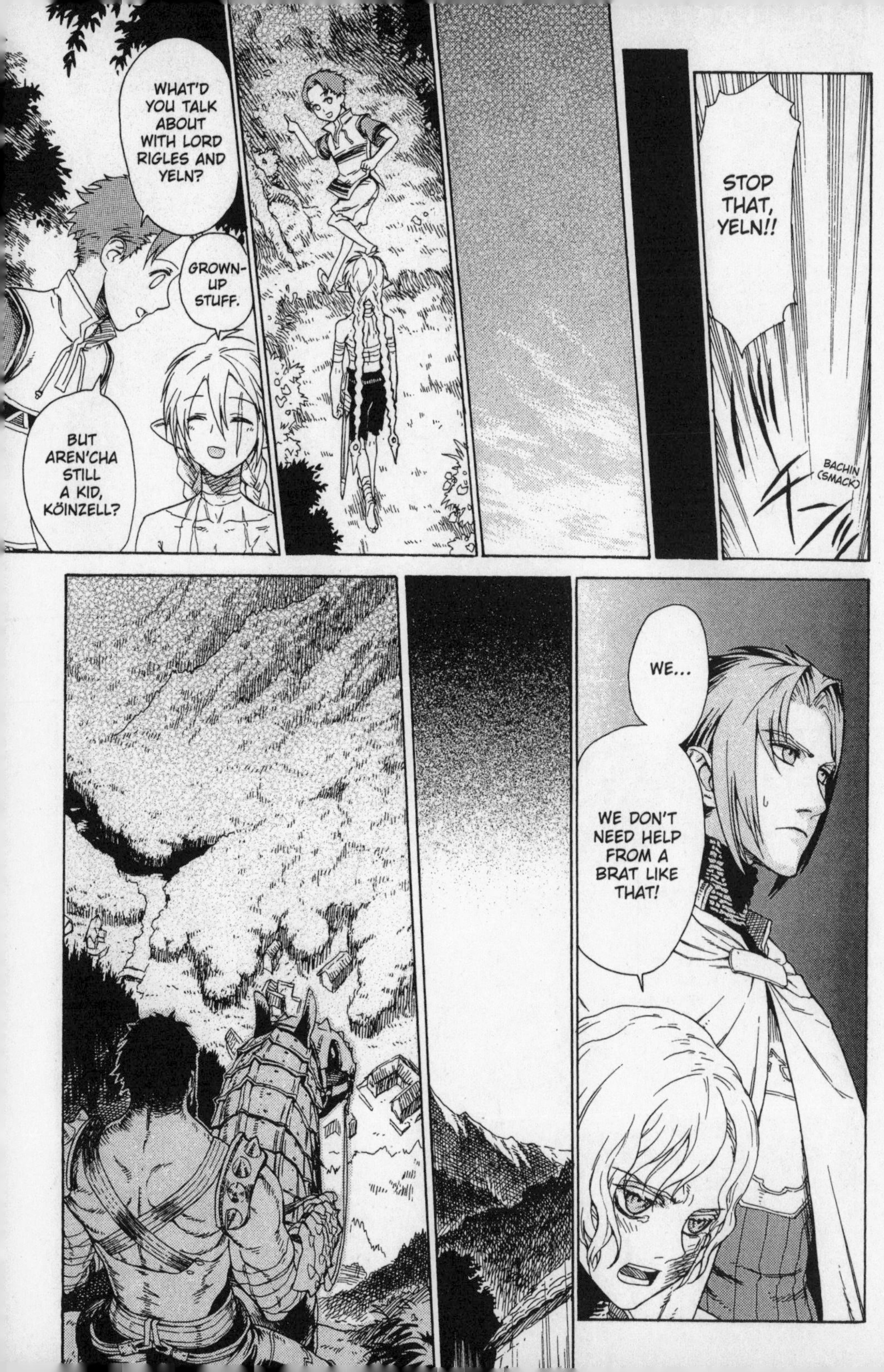
STOP THAT, YELN!!
BACHIN (SMACK)
WHAT'D YOU TALK ABOUT WITH LORD RIGLES AND YELN?
GROWN-UP STUFF.
BUT AREN'CHA STILL A KID, KÖINZELL?
WE...
WE DON'T NEED HELP FROM A BRAT LIKE THAT!

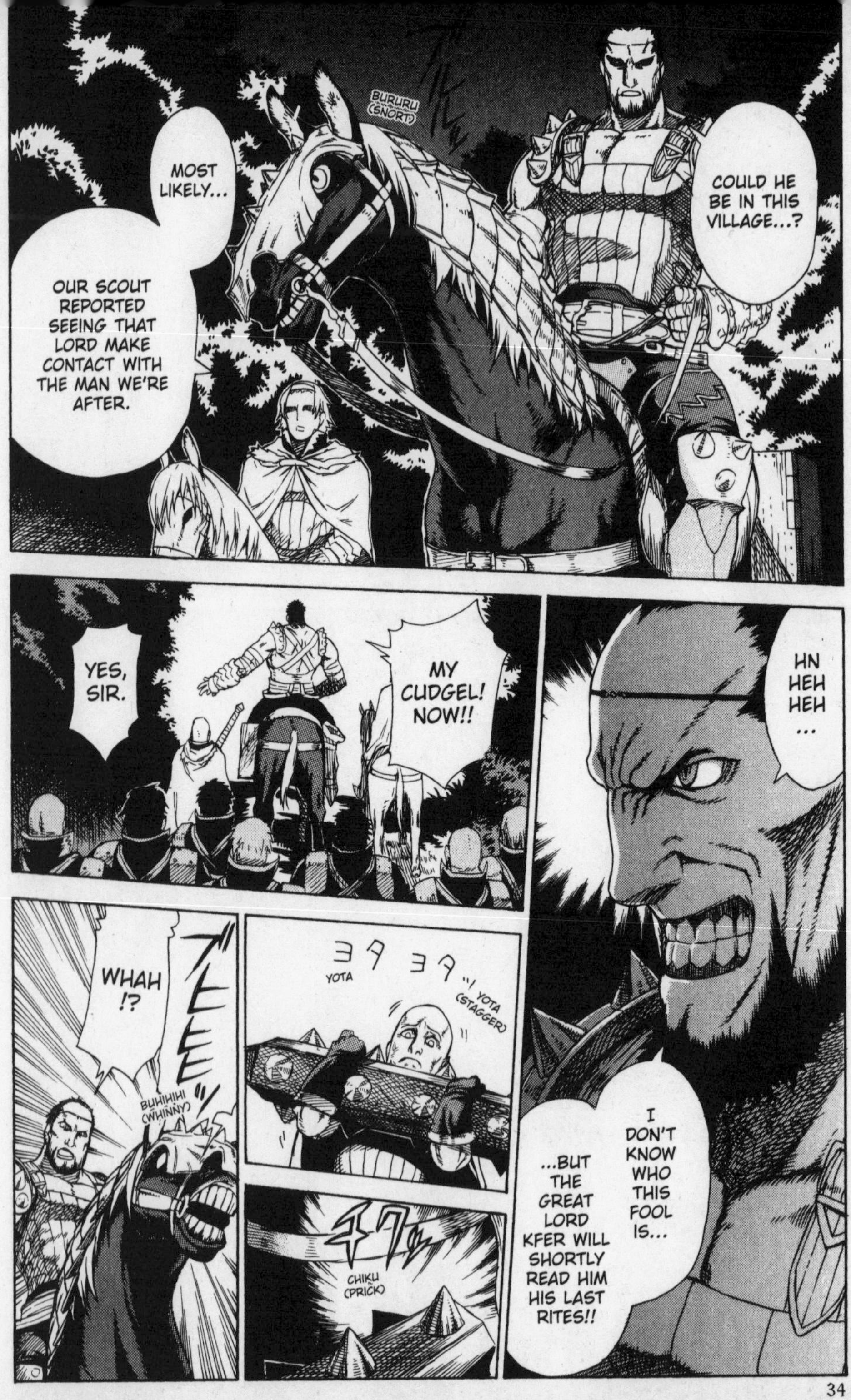
COULD HE BE IN THIS VILLAGE...?
BURURU (SNORT)
MOST LIKELY...
OUR SCOUT REPORTED SEEING THAT LORD MAKE CONTACT WITH THE MAN WE'RE AFTER.
HN HEH HEH...
I DON'T KNOW WHO THIS FOOL IS...
...BUT THE GREAT LORD KFER WILL SHORTLY READ HIM HIS LAST RITES!!
MY CUDGEL! NOW!!
YES, SIR.
ヨタ ヨタ
YOTA YOTA (STAGGER)
チクッ
CHIKU (PRICK)
WHAH !?
BUHIHIHI (WHINNY)

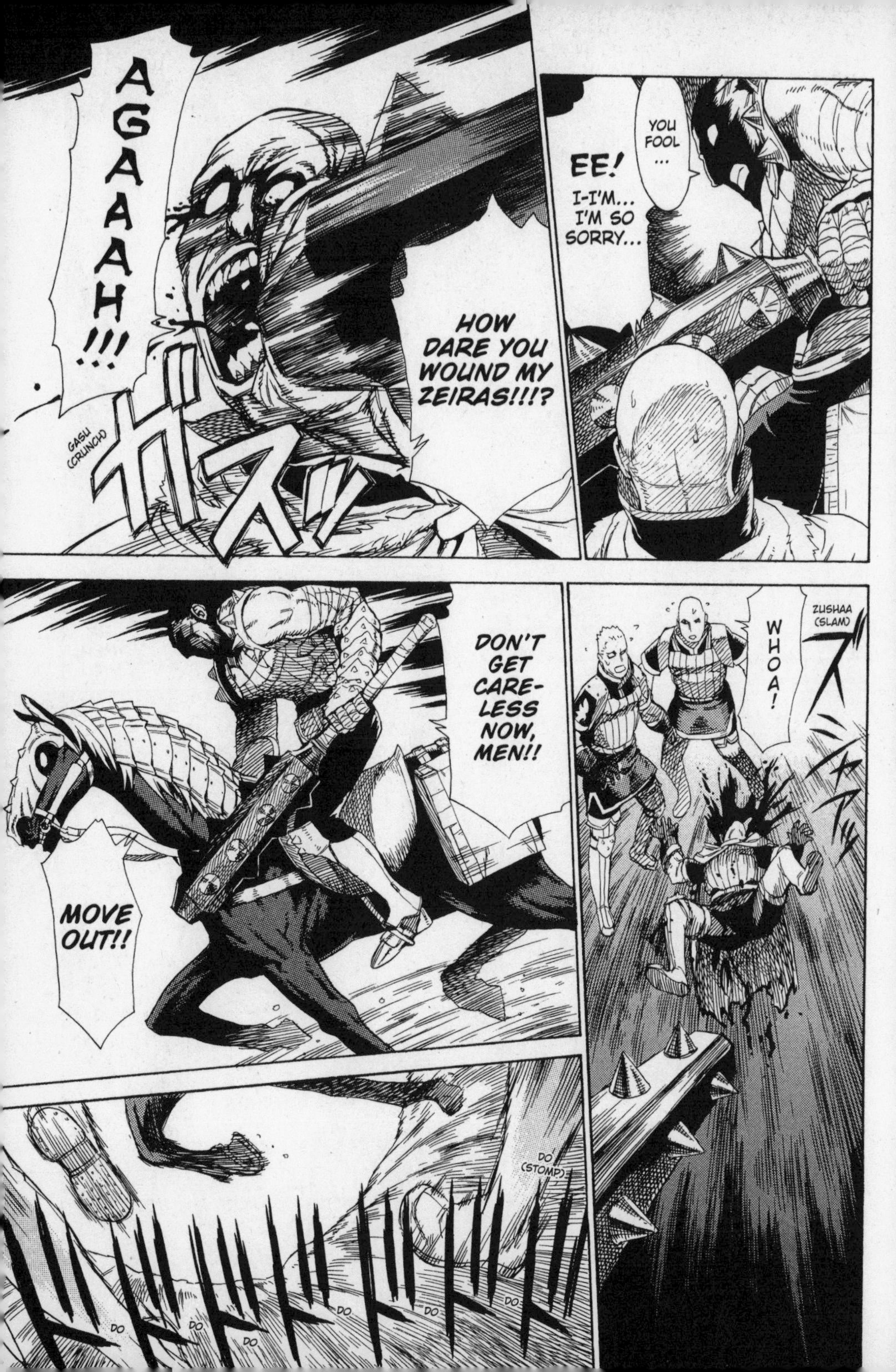
YOU FOOL ...
EE!
I-I'M... I'M SO SORRY...
HOW DARE YOU WOUND MY ZEIRAS!!!?
AGAAAAH!!!
GASU (CRUNCH)
ZUSHAA (SLAM)
WHOA!
DON'T GET CARE-LESS NOW, MEN!!
MOVE OUT!!
DO (STOMP)
DO
DO
DO
DO
DO

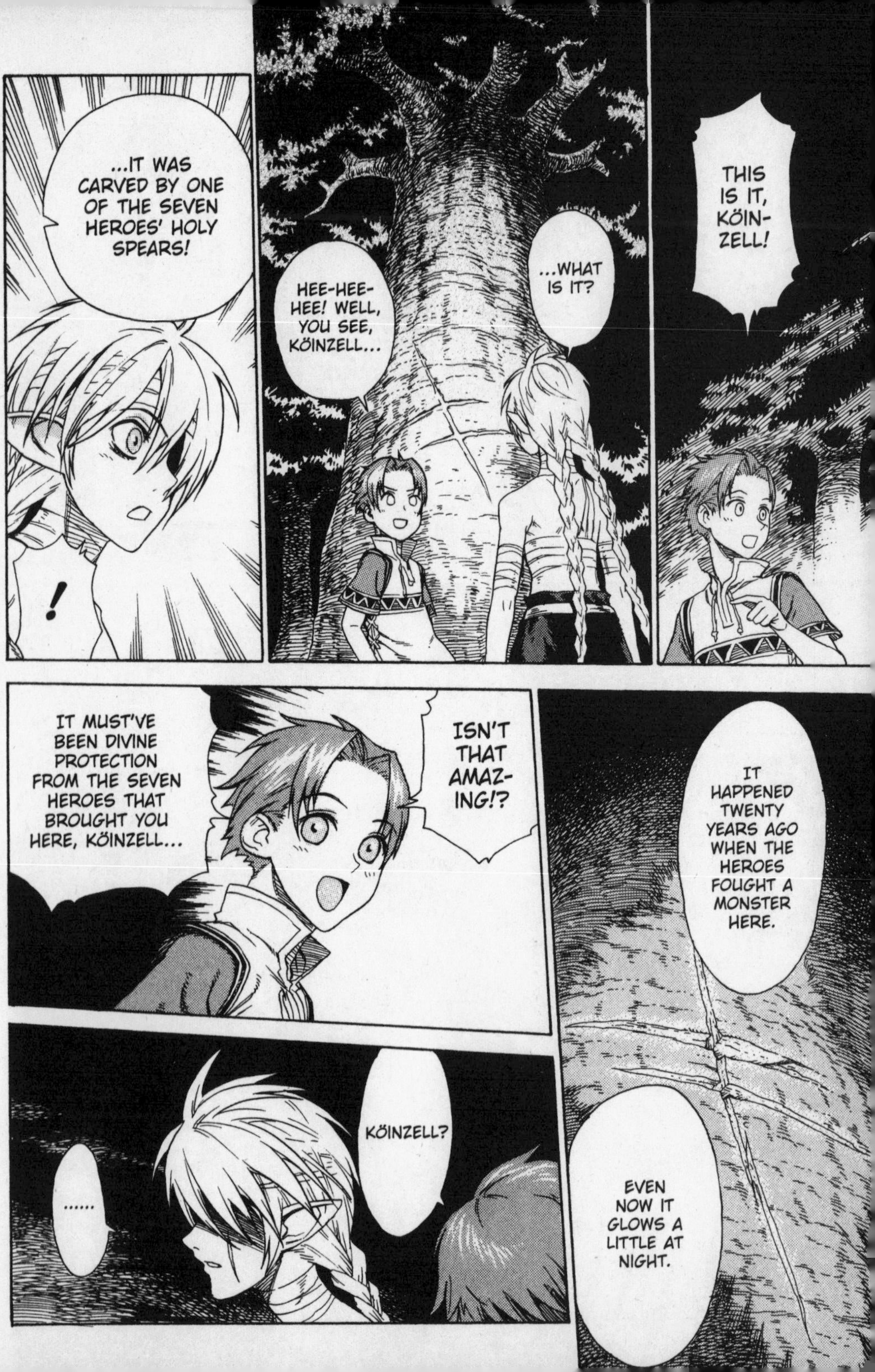
THIS IS IT, KÖIN-ZELL!
...WHAT IS IT?
HEE-HEE-HEE! WELL, YOU SEE, KÖINZELL...
...IT WAS CARVED BY ONE OF THE SEVEN HEROES' HOLY SPEARS!
!
IT HAPPENED TWENTY YEARS AGO WHEN THE HEROES FOUGHT A MONSTER HERE.
EVEN NOW IT GLOWS A LITTLE AT NIGHT.
ISN'T THAT AMAZ-ING!?
IT MUST'VE BEEN DIVINE PROTECTION FROM THE SEVEN HEROES THAT BROUGHT YOU HERE, KÖINZELL...
KÖINZELL?
......

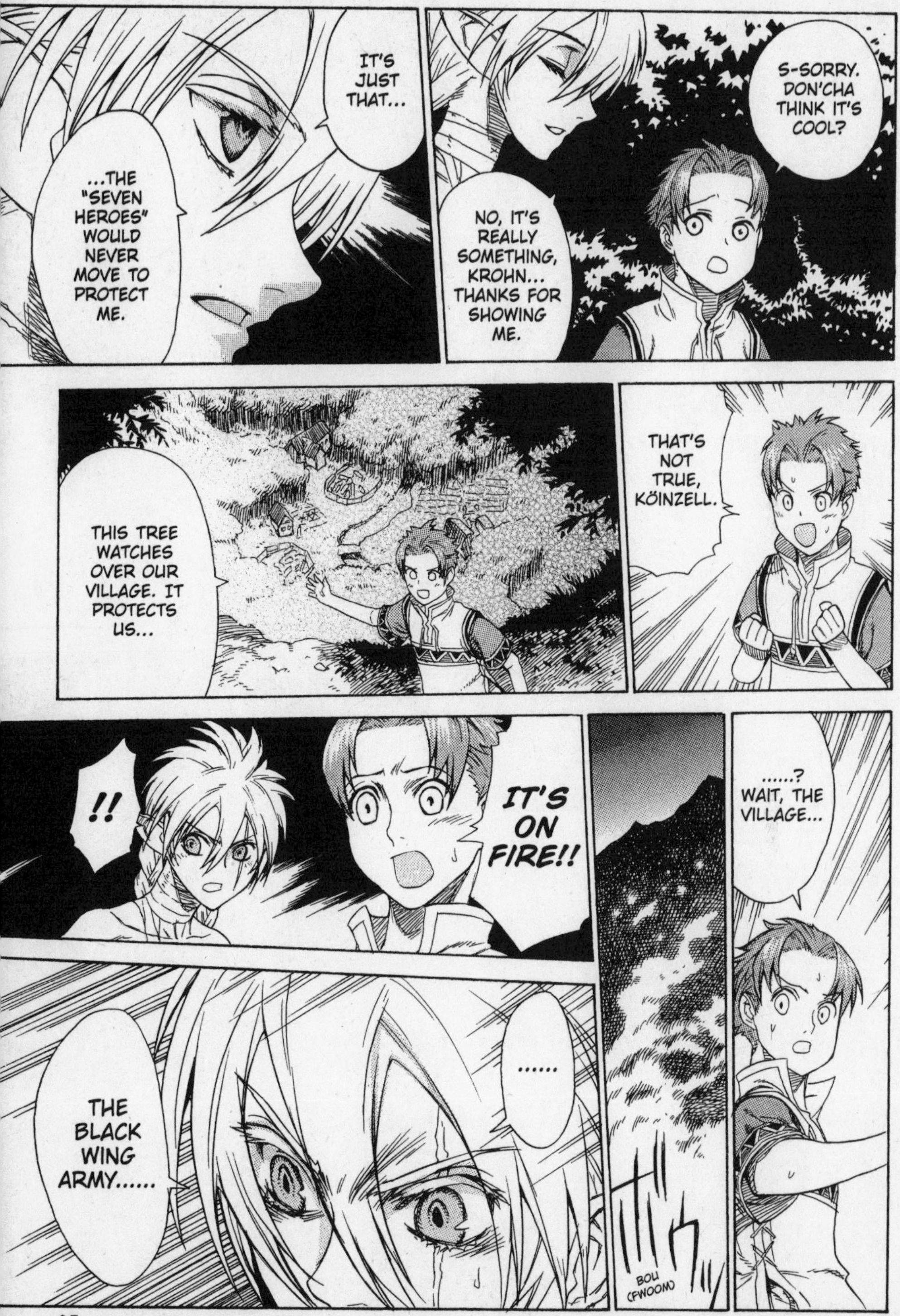
S-SORRY. DON'CHA THINK IT'S COOL?
NO, IT'S REALLY SOMETHING, KROHN... THANKS FOR SHOWING ME.
IT'S JUST THAT...
...THE "SEVEN HEROES" WOULD NEVER MOVE TO PROTECT ME.
THAT'S NOT TRUE, KÖINZELL.
THIS TREE WATCHES OVER OUR VILLAGE. IT PROTECTS US...
......? WAIT, THE VILLAGE...
BOU (FWOOM)
IT'S ON FIRE!!
!!
......
THE BLACK WING ARMY......

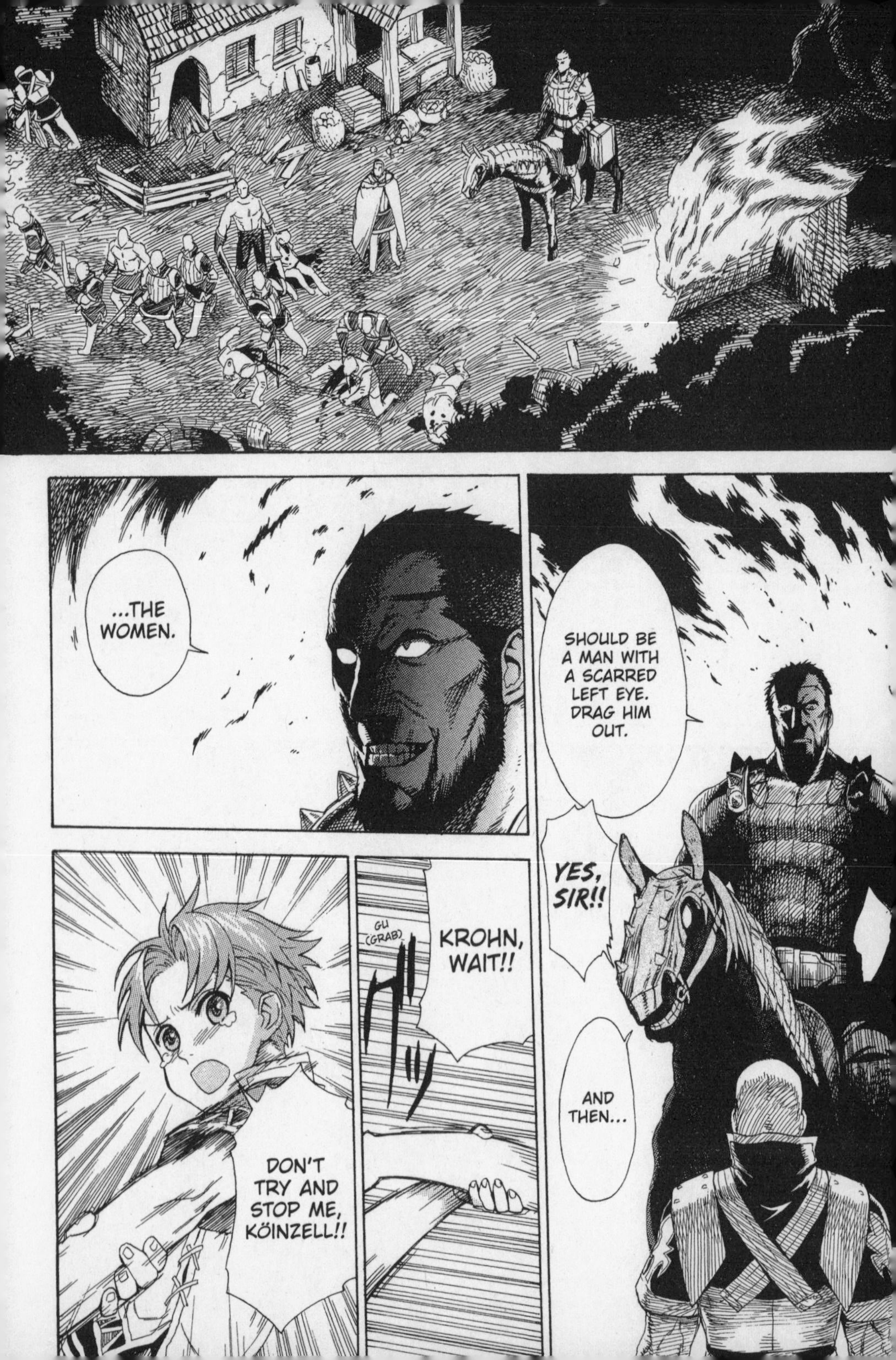
SHOULD BE A MAN WITH A SCARRED LEFT EYE. DRAG HIM OUT.
YES, SIR!!
AND THEN...
...THE WOMEN.
GU (GRAB)
KROHN, WAIT!!
DON'T TRY AND STOP ME, KÖINZELL!!

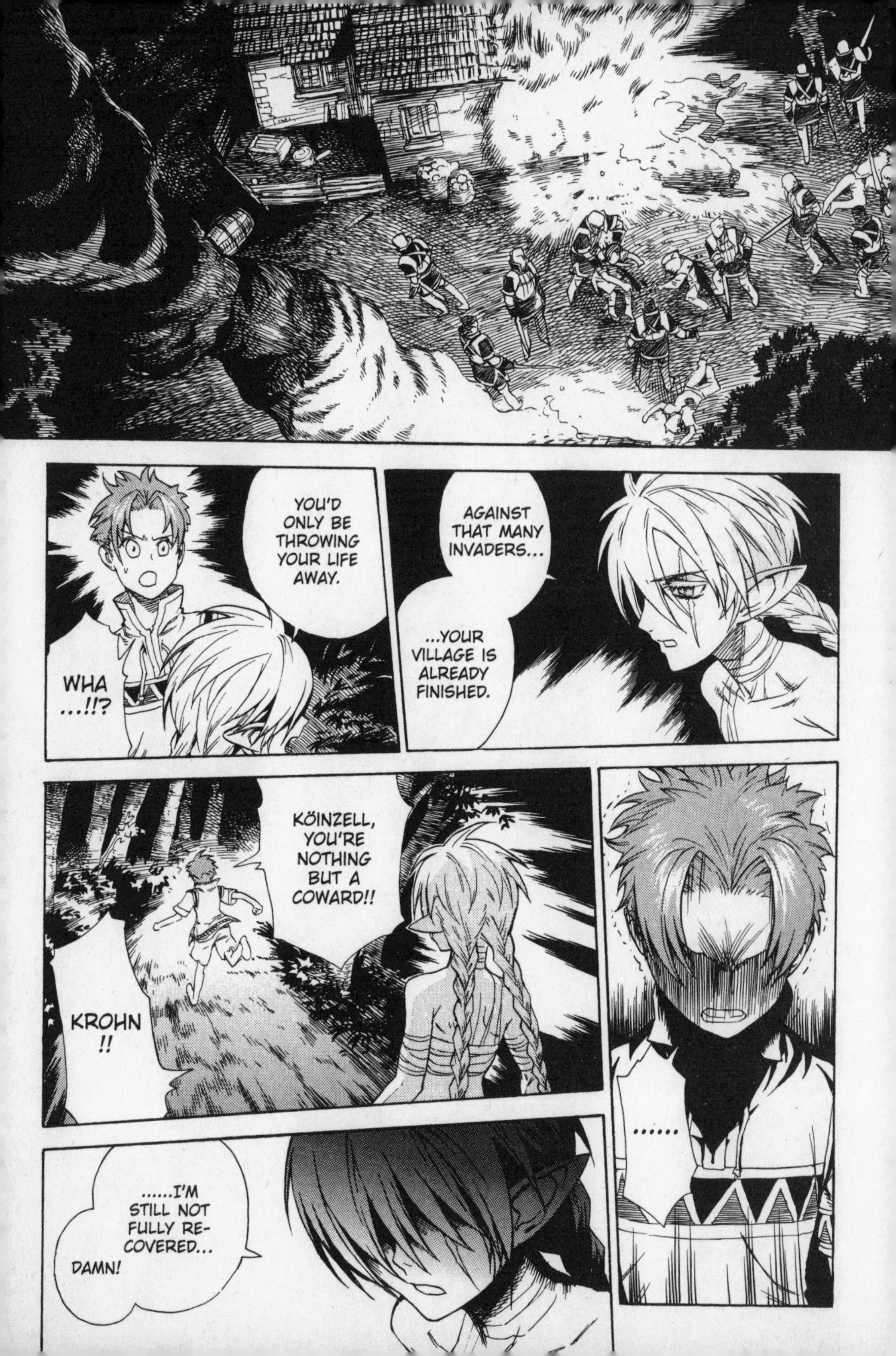
AGAINST THAT MANY INVADERS...
...YOUR VILLAGE IS ALREADY FINISHED.
YOU'D ONLY BE THROWING YOUR LIFE AWAY.
WHA ...!!?
......
KÖINZELL, YOU'RE NOTHING BUT A COWARD!!
KROHN !!
......I'M STILL NOT FULLY RE-COVERED...
DAMN!

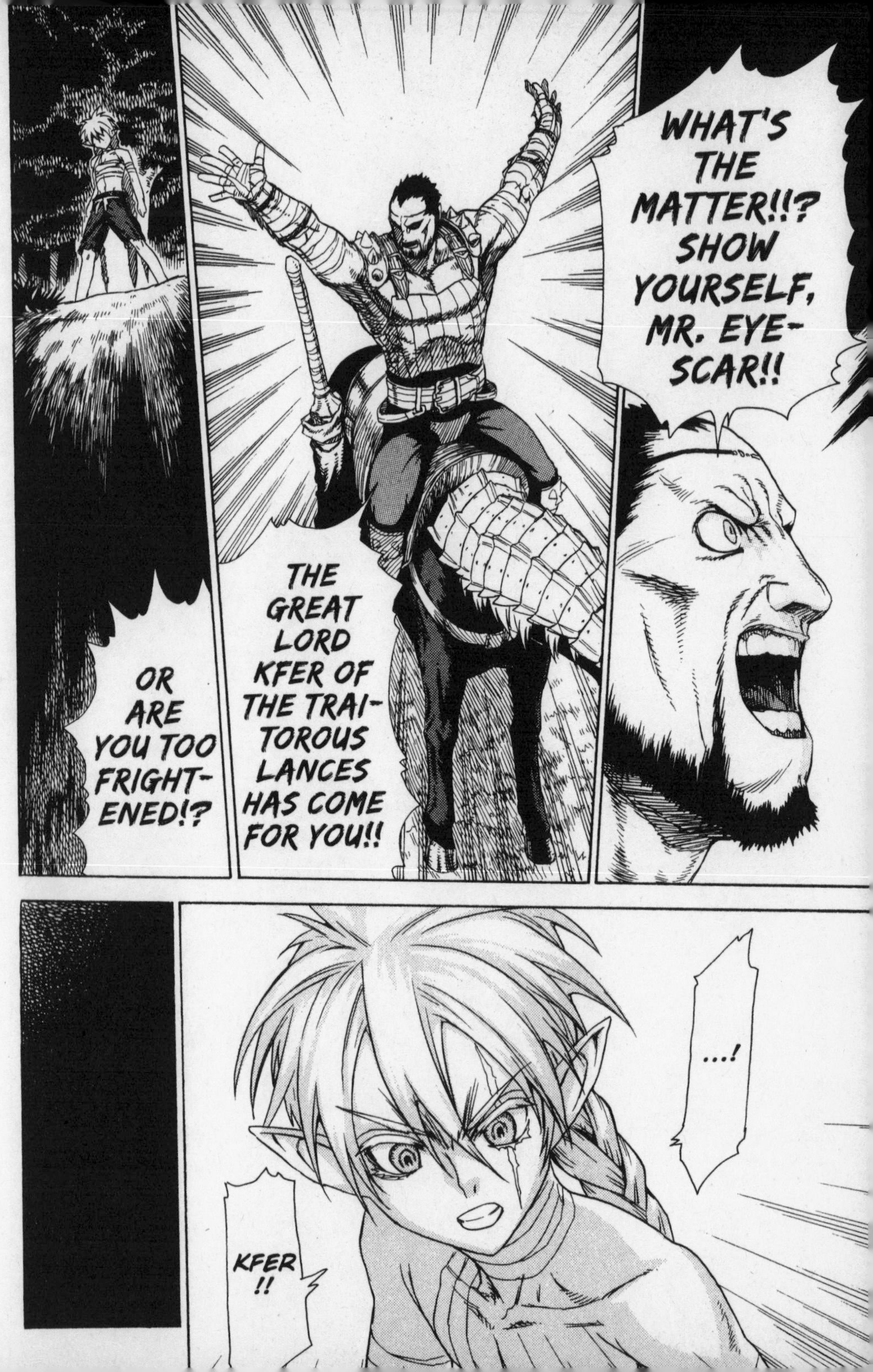
WHAT'S THE MATTER!!? SHOW YOURSELF, MR. EYE-SCAR!!
THE GREAT LORD KFER OF THE TRAITOROUS LANCES HAS COME FOR YOU!!
OR ARE YOU TOO FRIGHTENED!?
...!
KFER!!

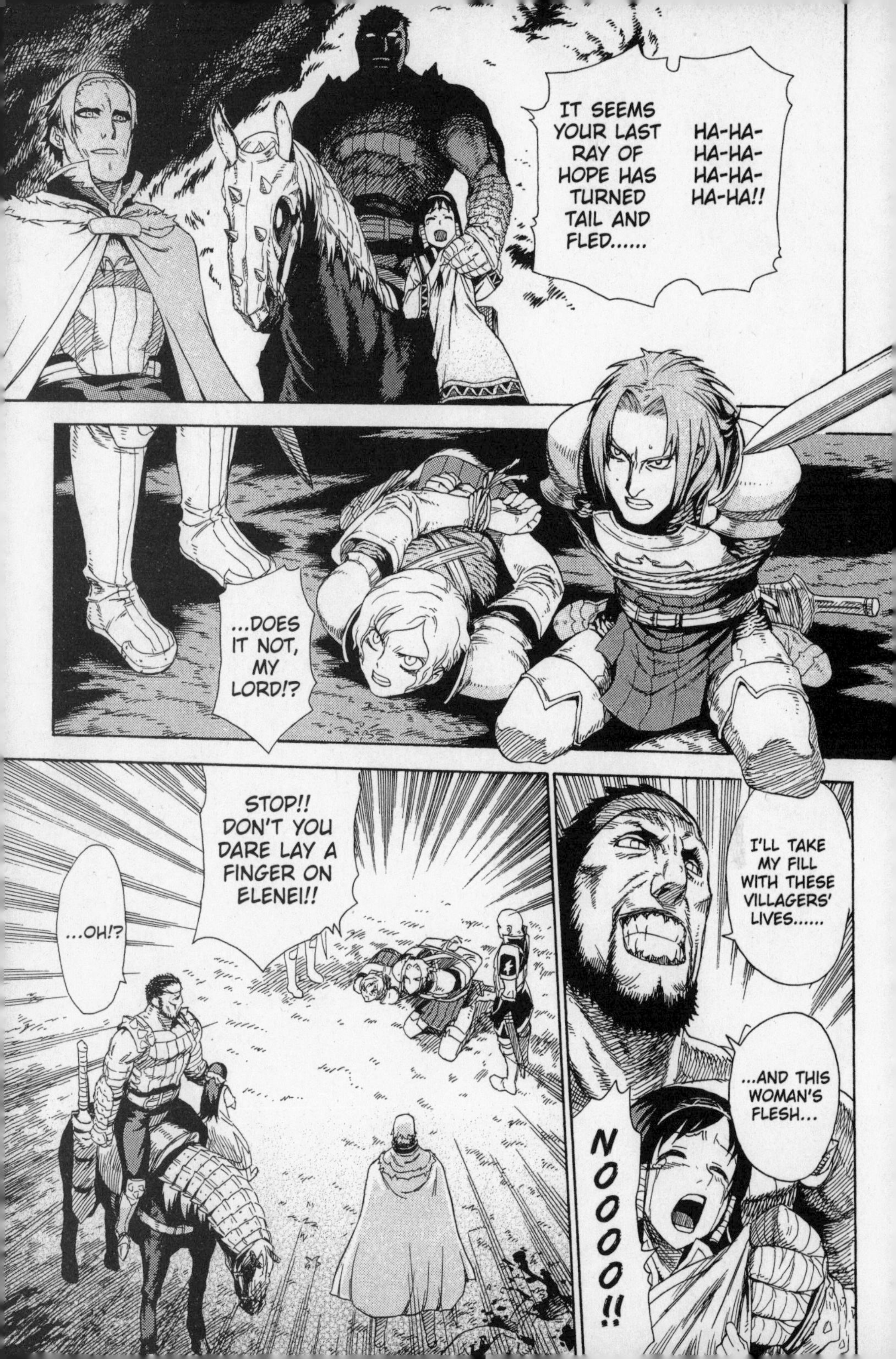
IT SEEMS YOUR LAST RAY OF HOPE HAS TURNED TAIL AND FLED......
HA-HA-HA-HA-HA-HA-HA-HA!!
...DOES IT NOT, MY LORD!?
I'LL TAKE MY FILL WITH THESE VILLAGERS' LIVES......
...AND THIS WOMAN'S FLESH...
NOOOOO!!
STOP!! DON'T YOU DARE LAY A FINGER ON ELENEI!!
...OH!?

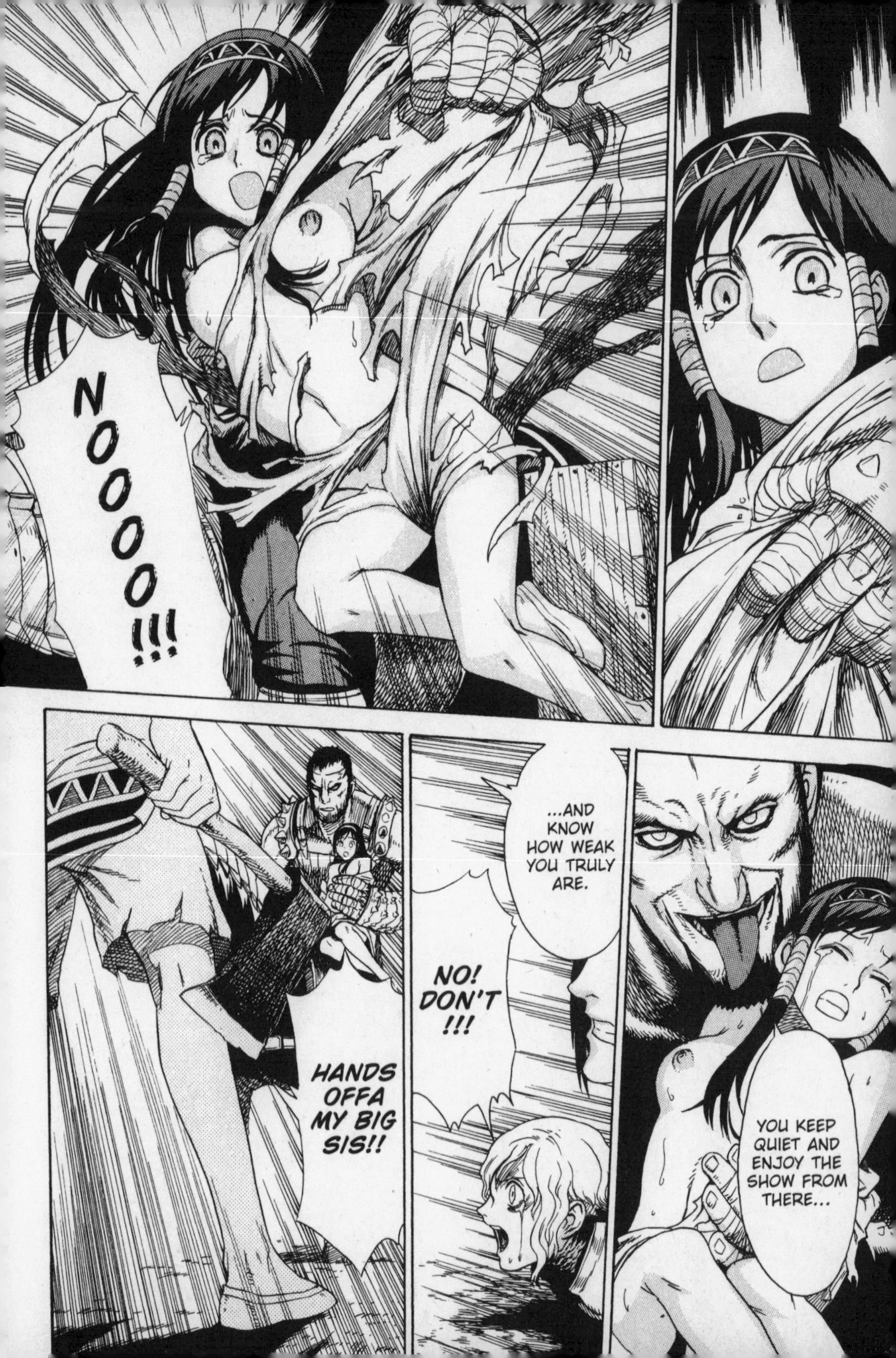
NOOOO!!!
YOU KEEP QUIET AND ENJOY THE SHOW FROM THERE...
...AND KNOW HOW WEAK YOU TRULY ARE.
NO! DON'T!!!
HANDS OFFA MY BIG SIS!!

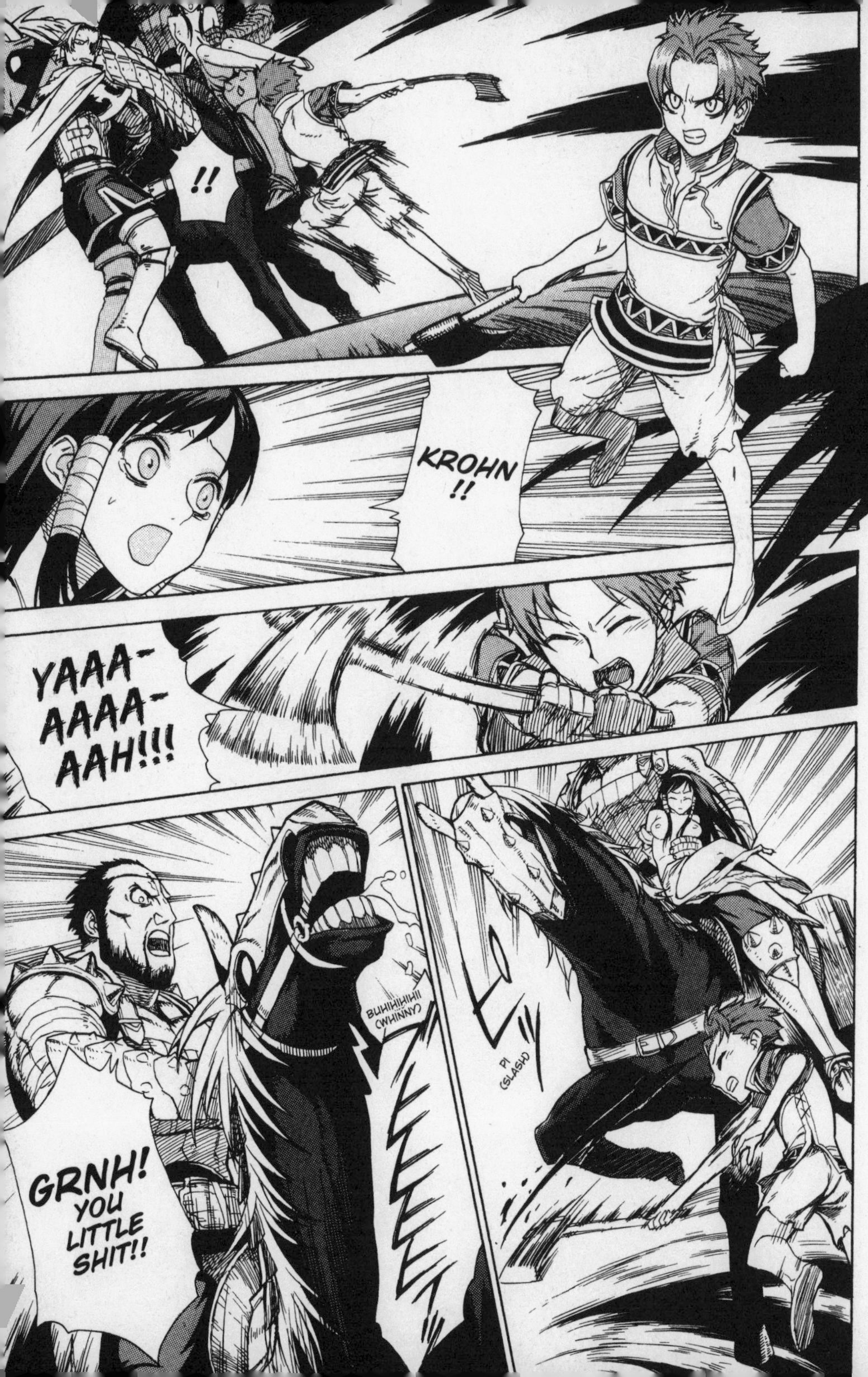
!!
KROHN !!
YAAA-AAAA-AAH!!!
PI (SLASH)
BUHIHIHIHIII (WHINNY)
GRNH! YOU LITTLE SHIT!!

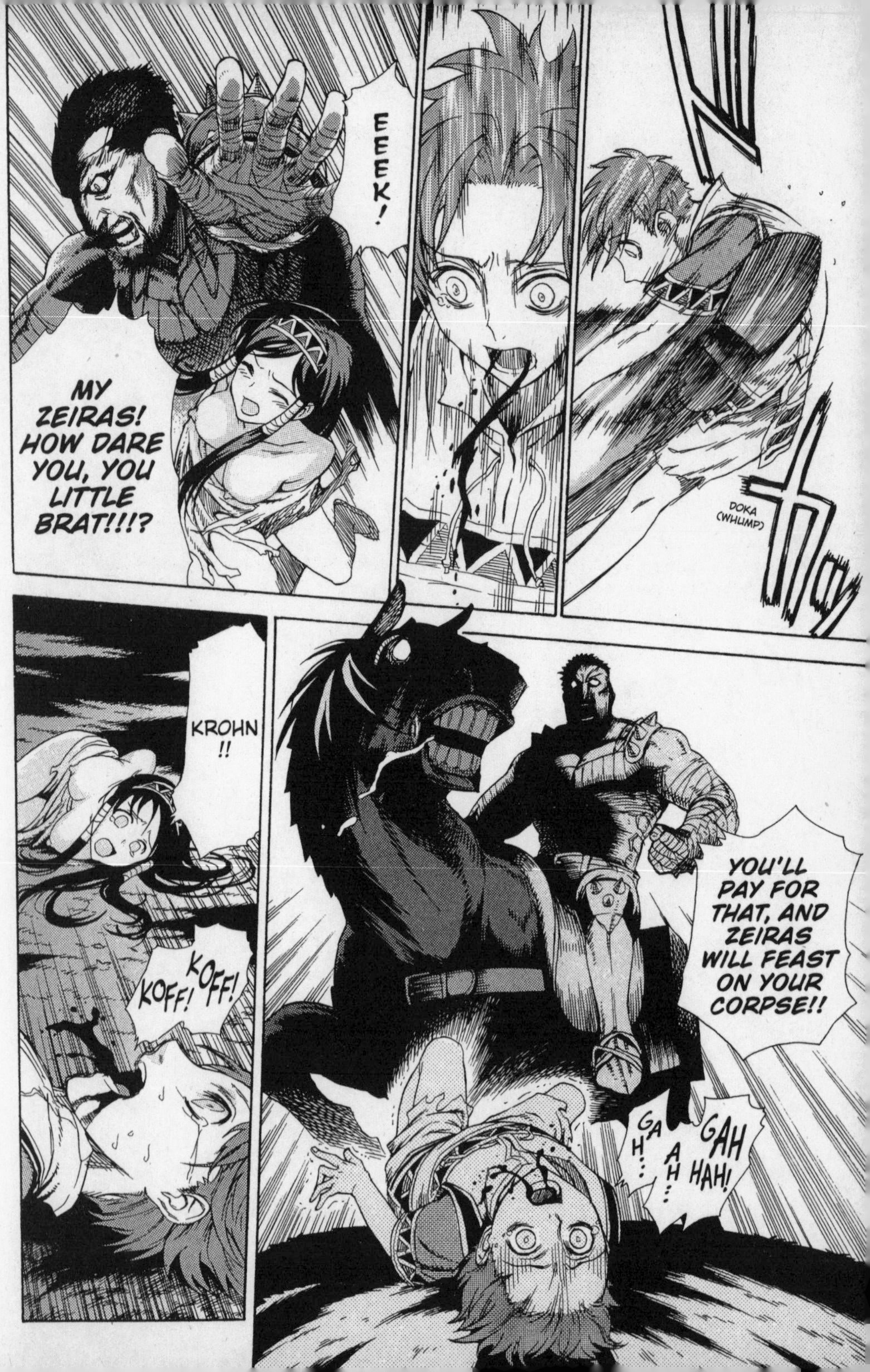
DOKA (WHUMP)
EEEK!
MY ZEIRAS! HOW DARE YOU, YOU LITTLE BRAT!!!?
YOU'LL PAY FOR THAT, AND ZEIRAS WILL FEAST ON YOUR CORPSE!!
GAH HAH!
GAH... AH...
KROHN!!
KOFF! KOFF!

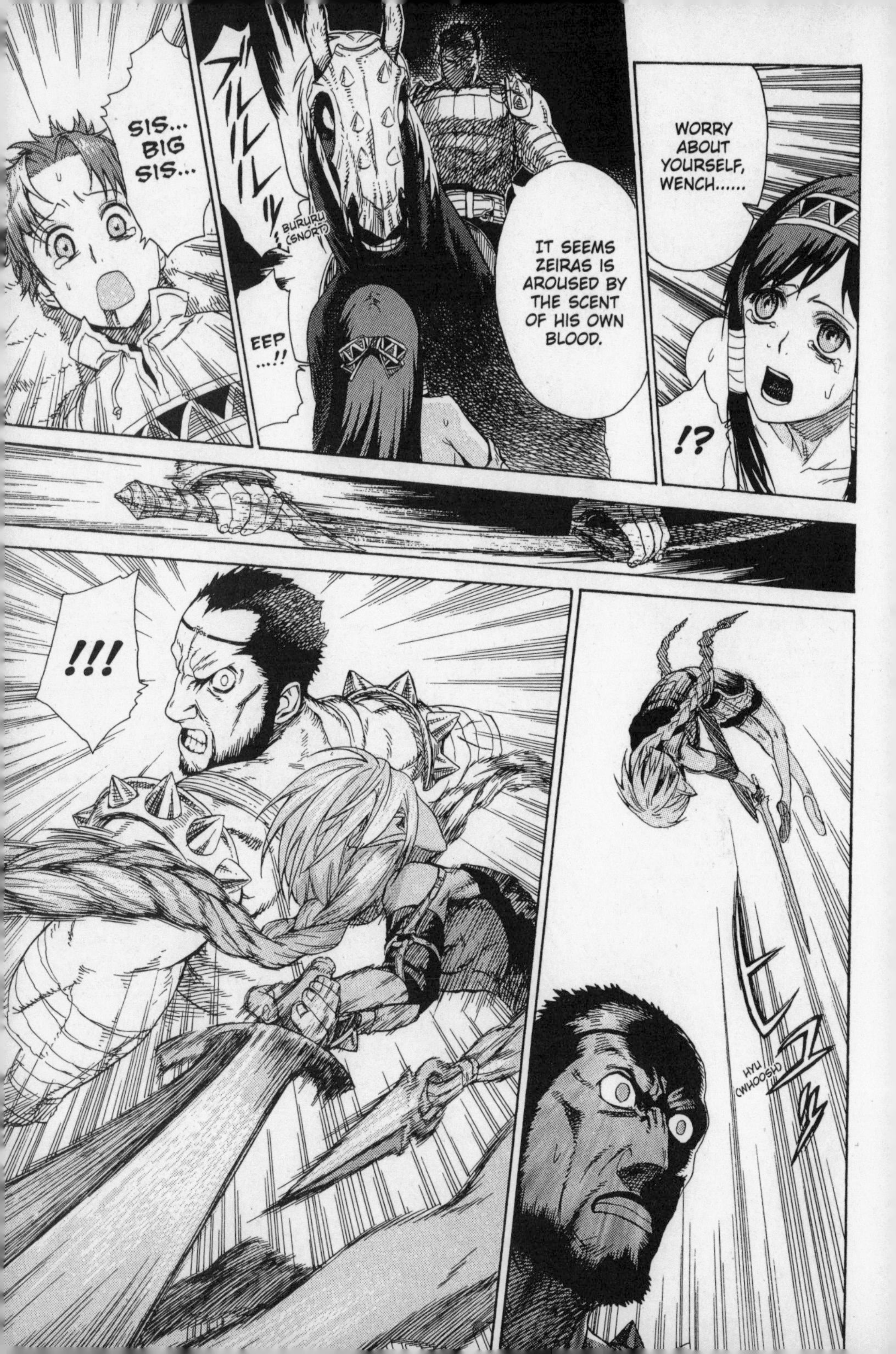
WORRY ABOUT YOURSELF, WENCH......
!?
IT SEEMS ZEIRAS IS AROUSED BY THE SCENT OF HIS OWN BLOOD.
BURURU (SNORT)
EEP ...!!
SIS... BIG SIS...
HYU (WHOOSH)
!!!

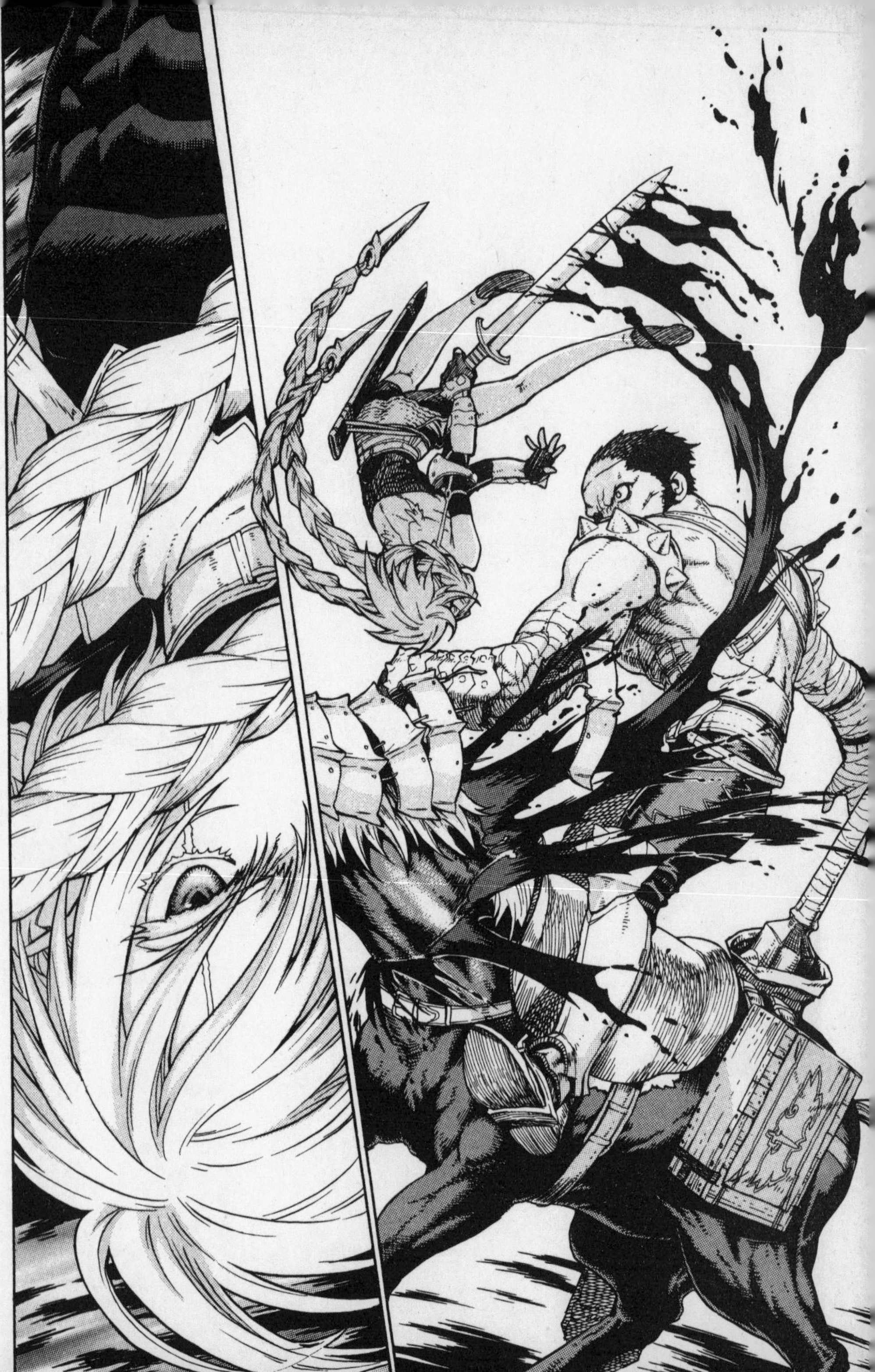

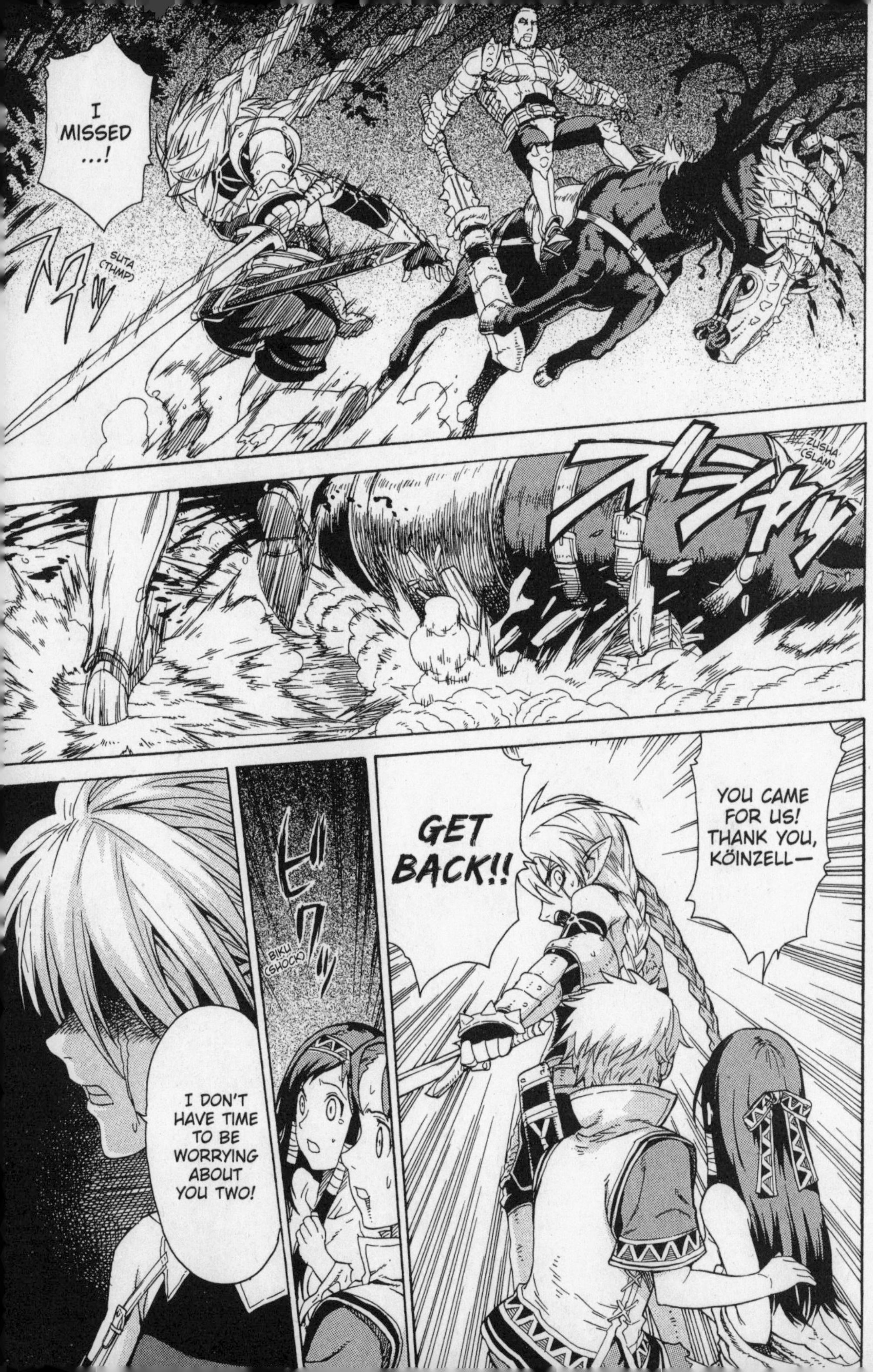
I MISSED ...!
SUTA (THMP)
ZUSHA (SLAM)
YOU CAME FOR US! THANK YOU, KÖINZELL—
GET BACK!!
BIKU (SHOCK)
I DON'T HAVE TIME TO BE WORRYING ABOUT YOU TWO!

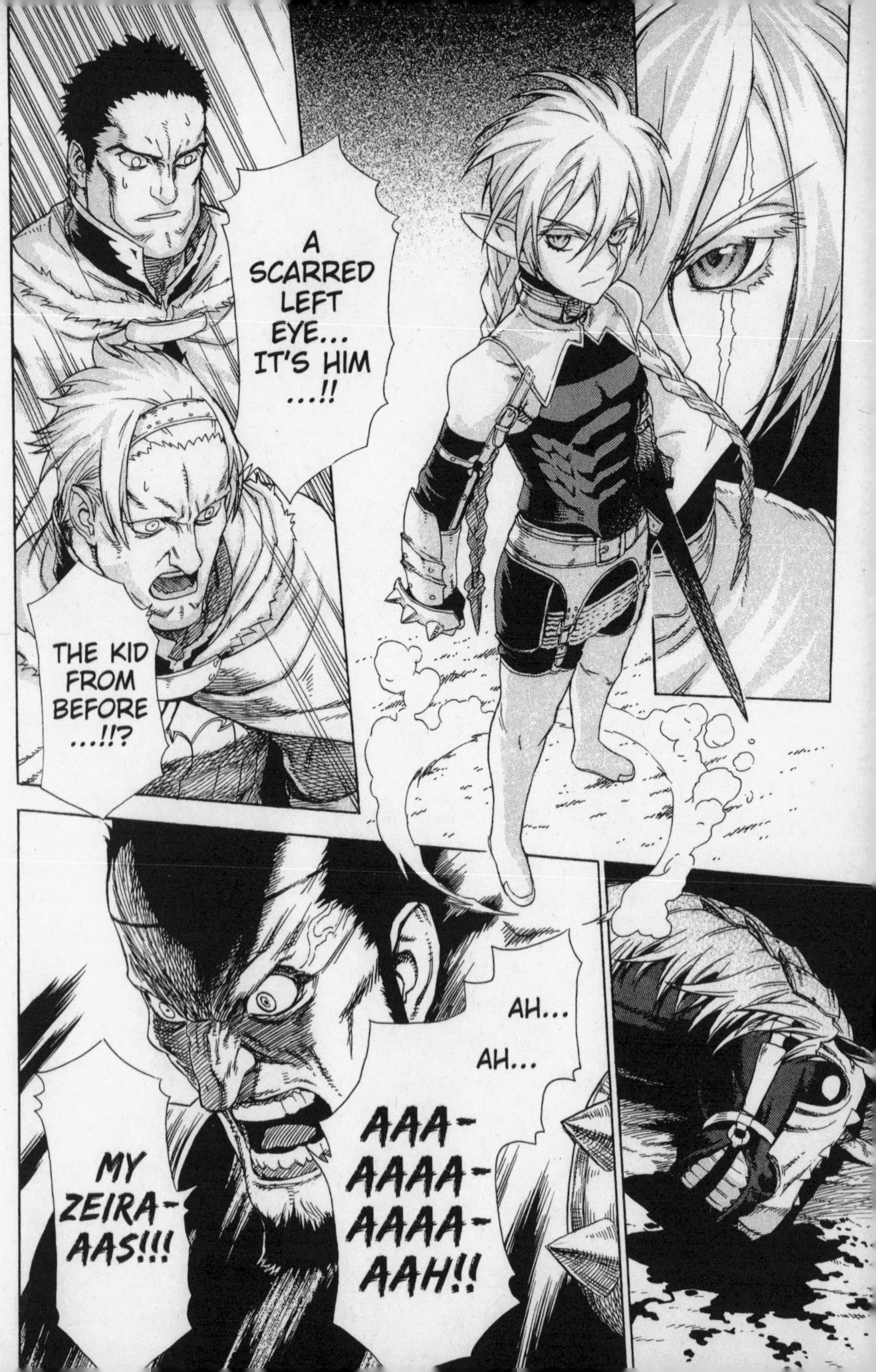
A SCARRED LEFT EYE... IT'S HIM ...!!
THE KID FROM BEFORE ...!!?
AH...
AH...
AAA-AAAA-AAAA-AAH!!
MY ZEIRA-AAS!!!

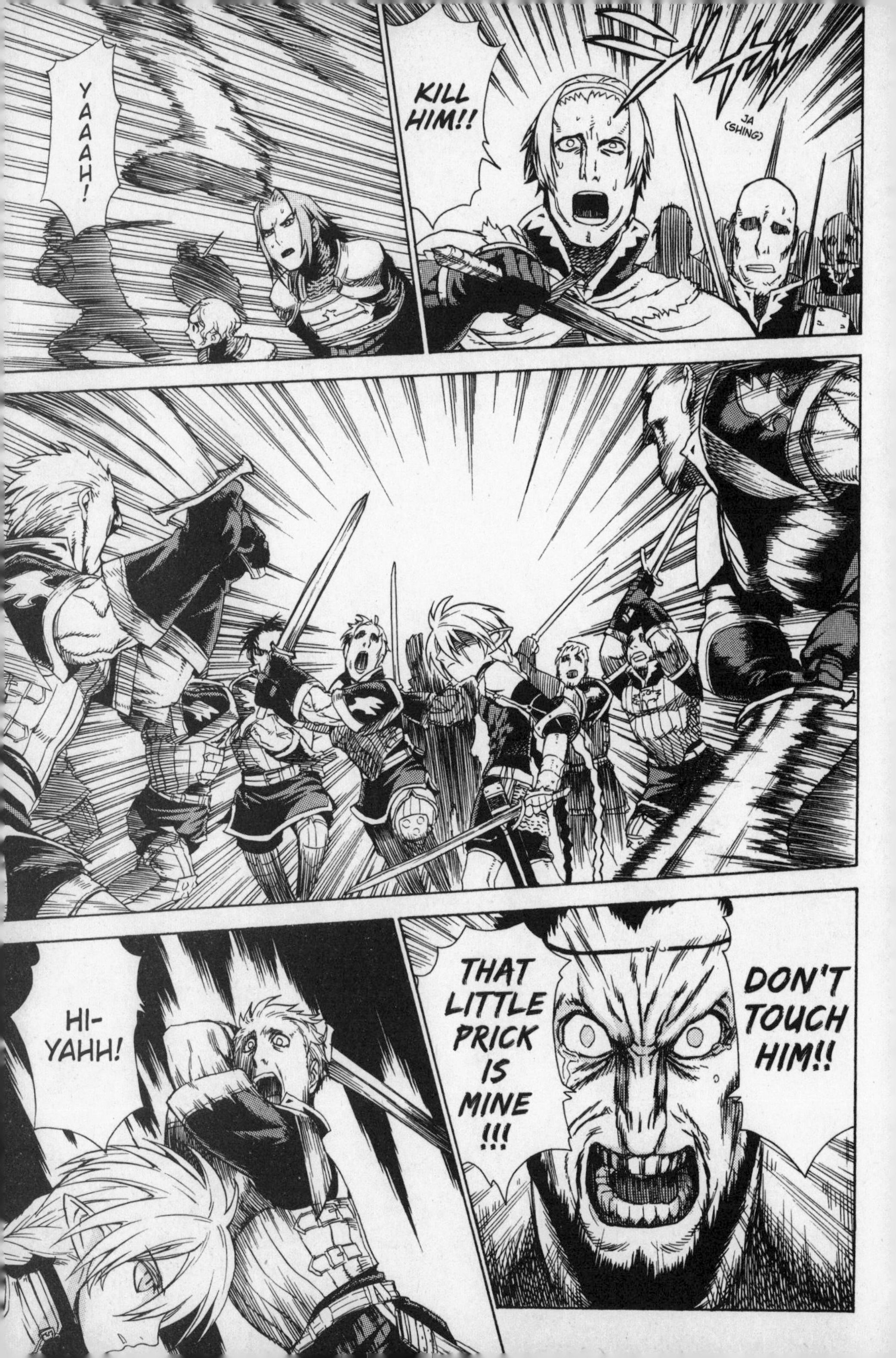
JA (SHING)
KILL HIM!!
YAAAAH!
DON'T TOUCH HIM!!
THAT LITTLE PRICK IS MINE!!!
HI-YAHH!

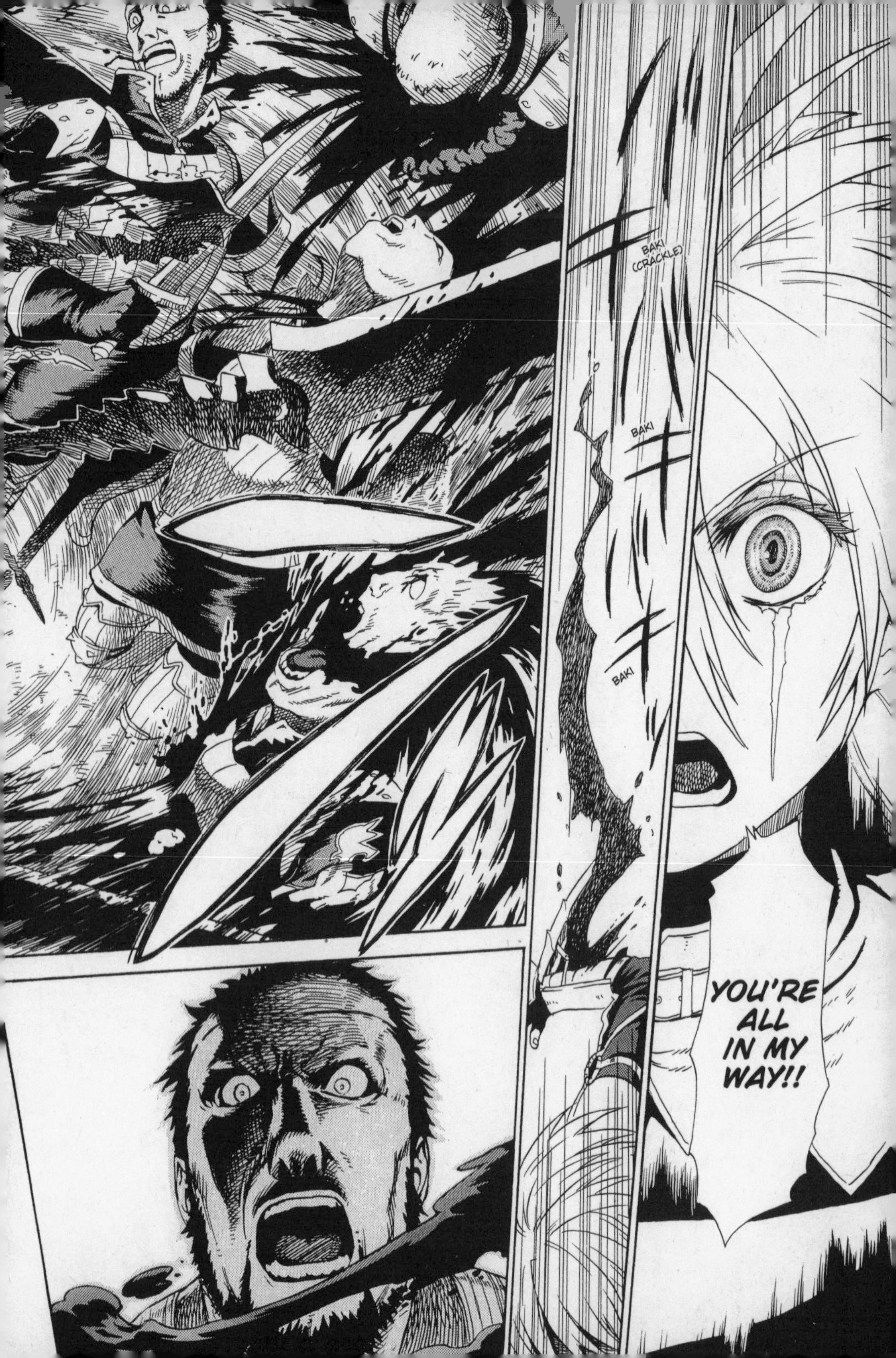
BAKI (CRACKLE)
BAKI
BAKI
YOU'RE ALL IN MY WAY!!

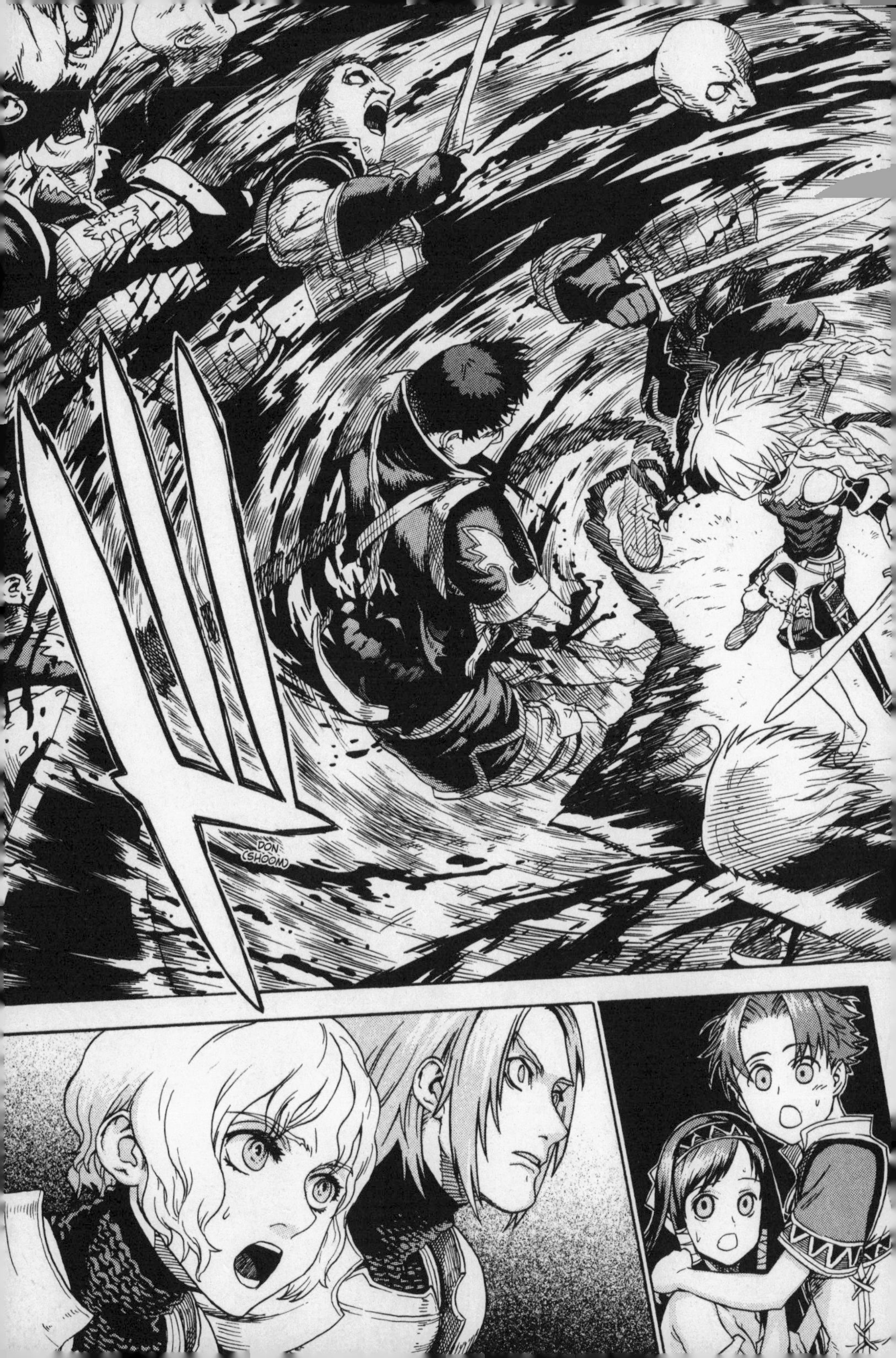
DON
(SHOOM)

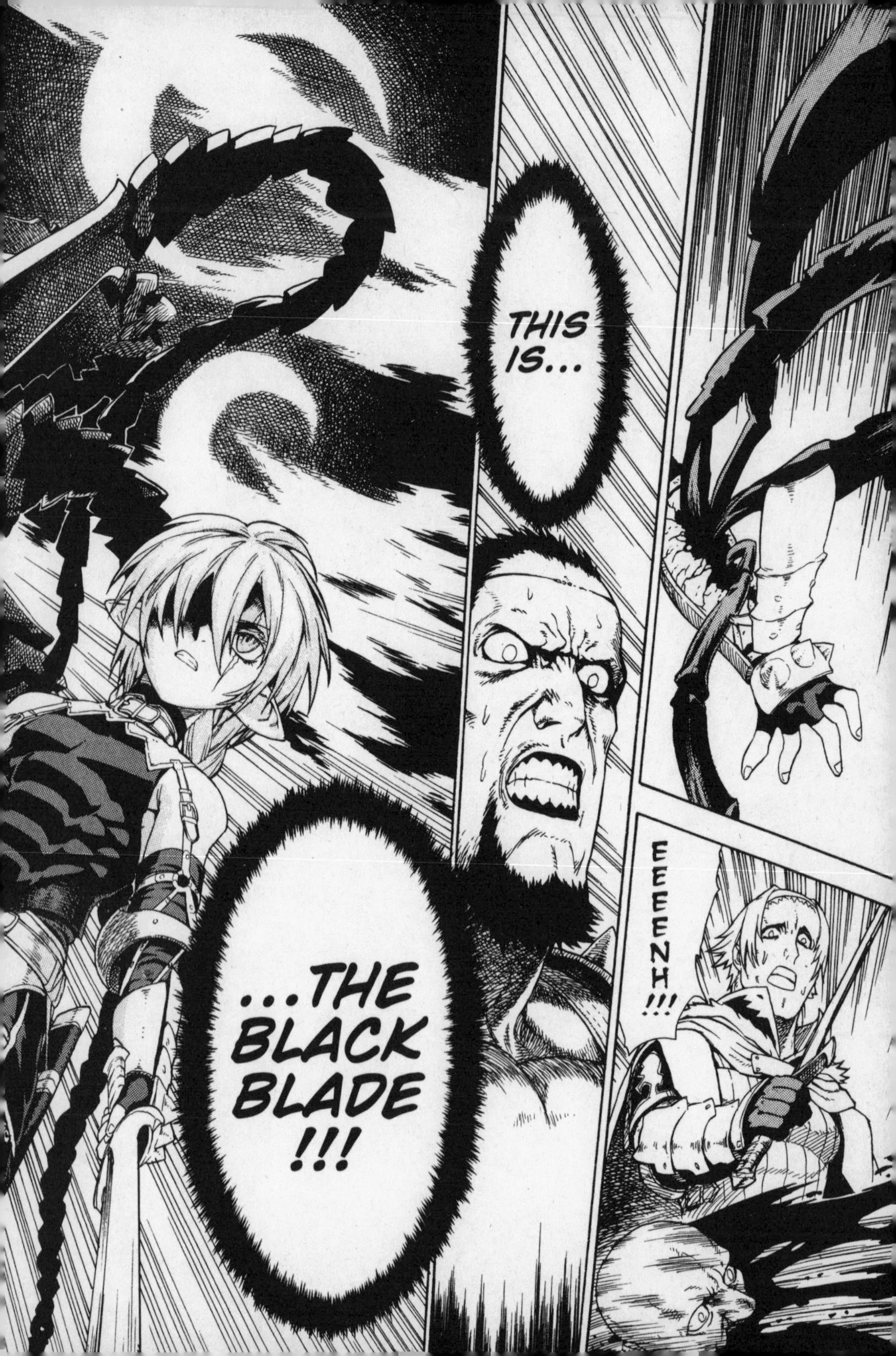
EEEEENH!!!
THIS IS...
...THE BLACK BLADE!!!

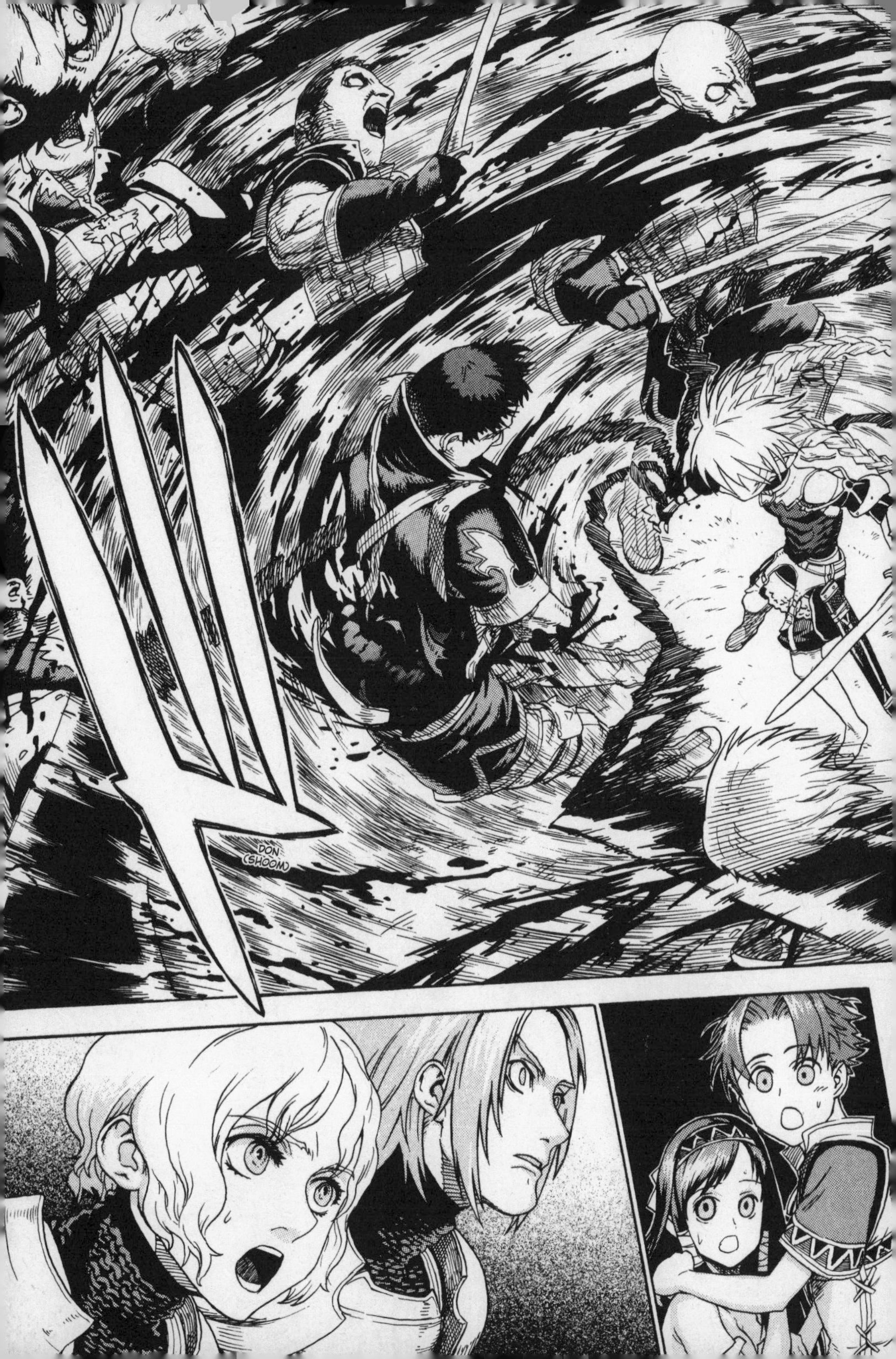
DON
(SHOOM)

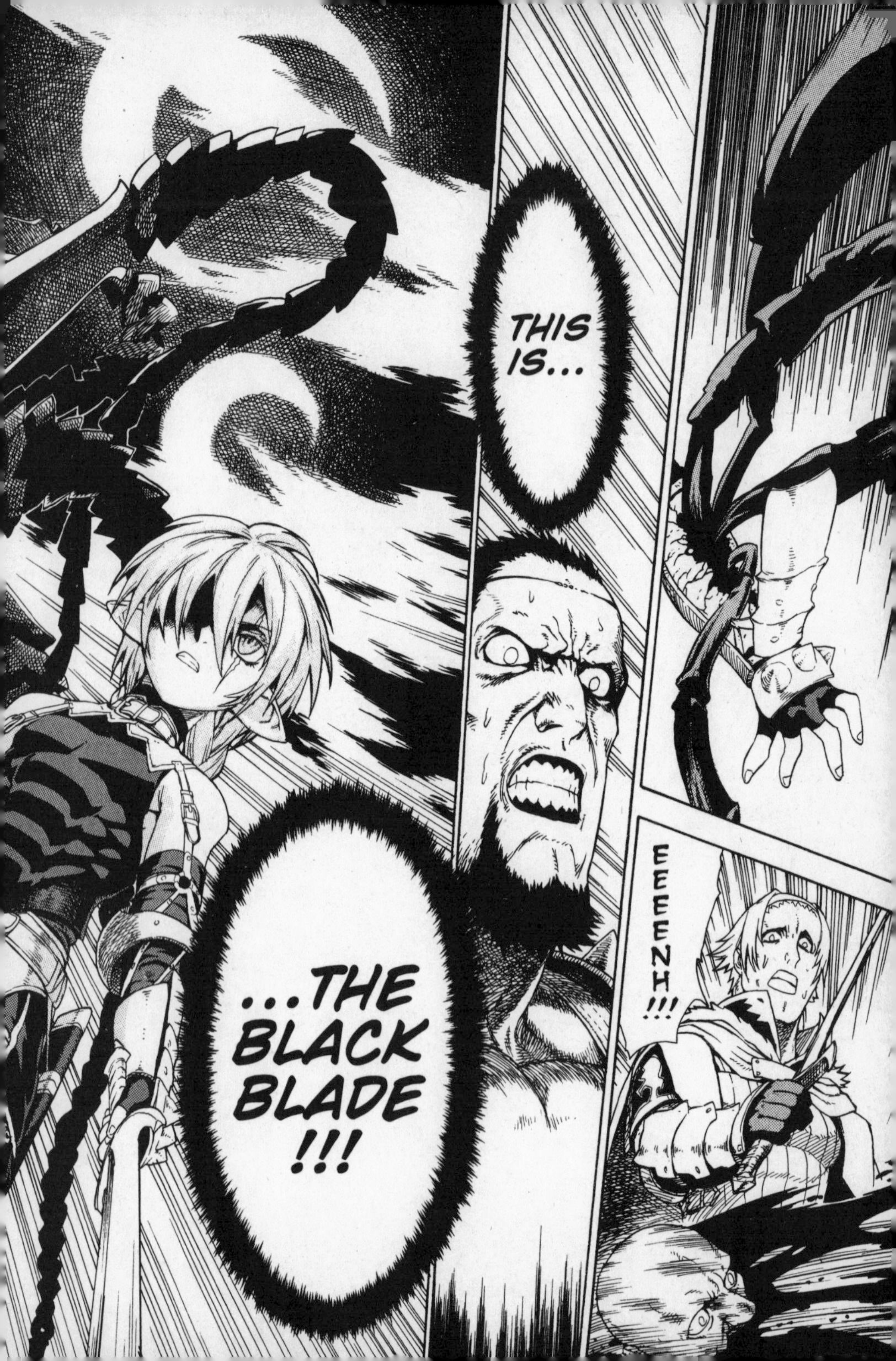
EEEEENH!!!
THIS IS...
...THE BLACK BLADE!!!

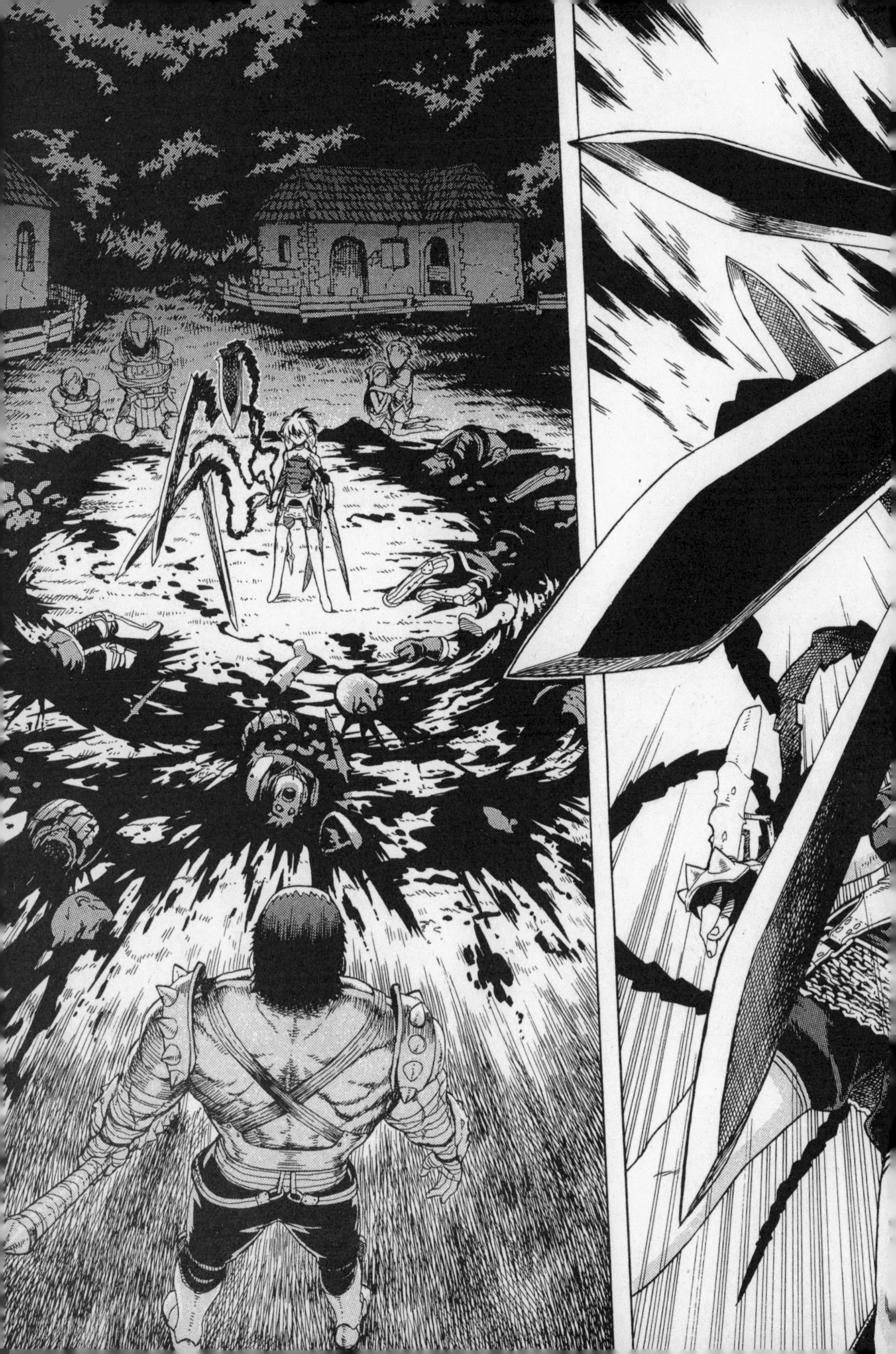

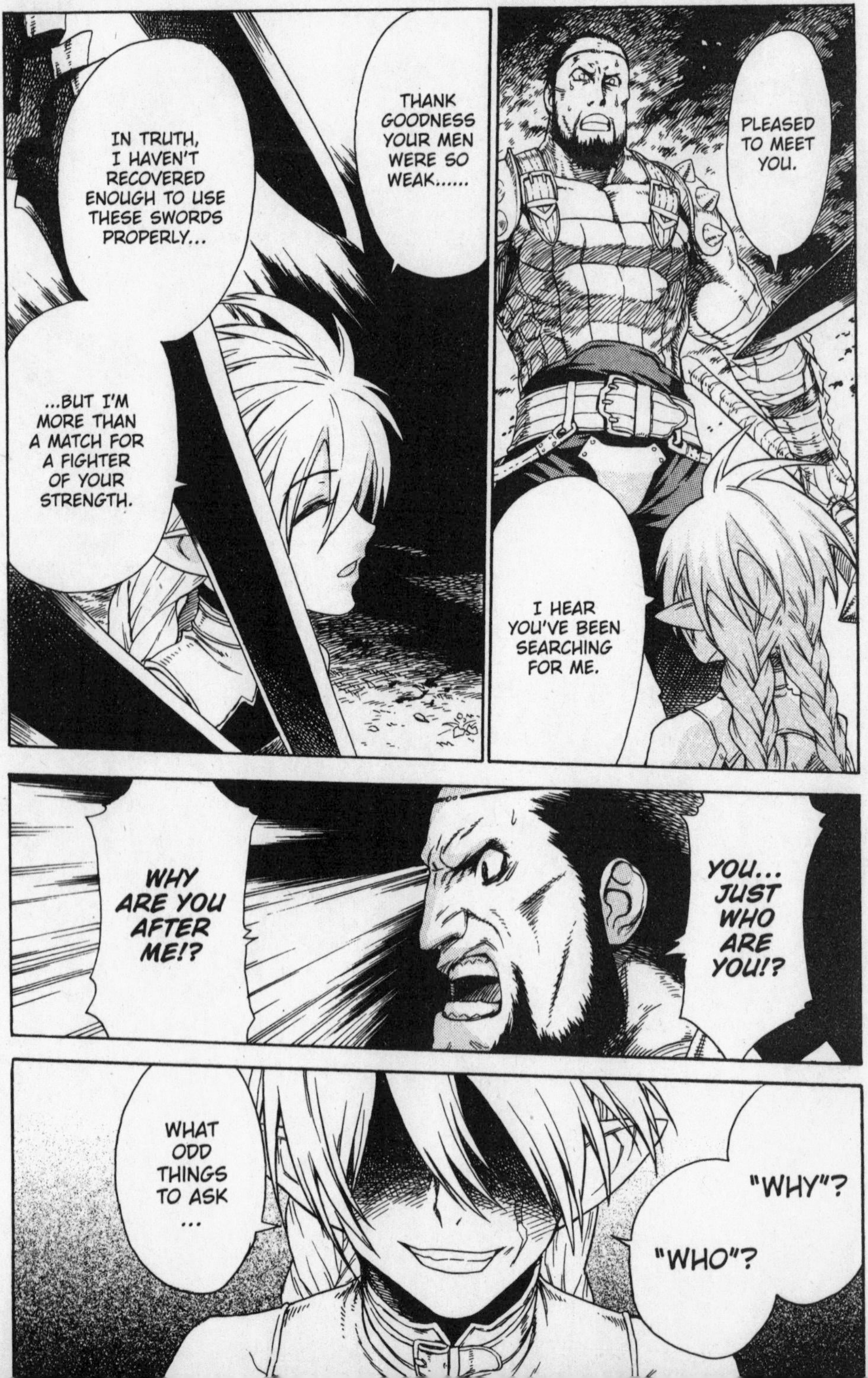
PLEASED TO MEET YOU.
I HEAR YOU'VE BEEN SEARCHING FOR ME.
THANK GOODNESS YOUR MEN WERE SO WEAK......
IN TRUTH, I HAVEN'T RECOVERED ENOUGH TO USE THESE SWORDS PROPERLY...
...BUT I'M MORE THAN A MATCH FOR A FIGHTER OF YOUR STRENGTH.
YOU... JUST WHO ARE YOU!?
WHY ARE YOU AFTER ME!?
"WHY"?
"WHO"?
WHAT ODD THINGS TO ASK ...

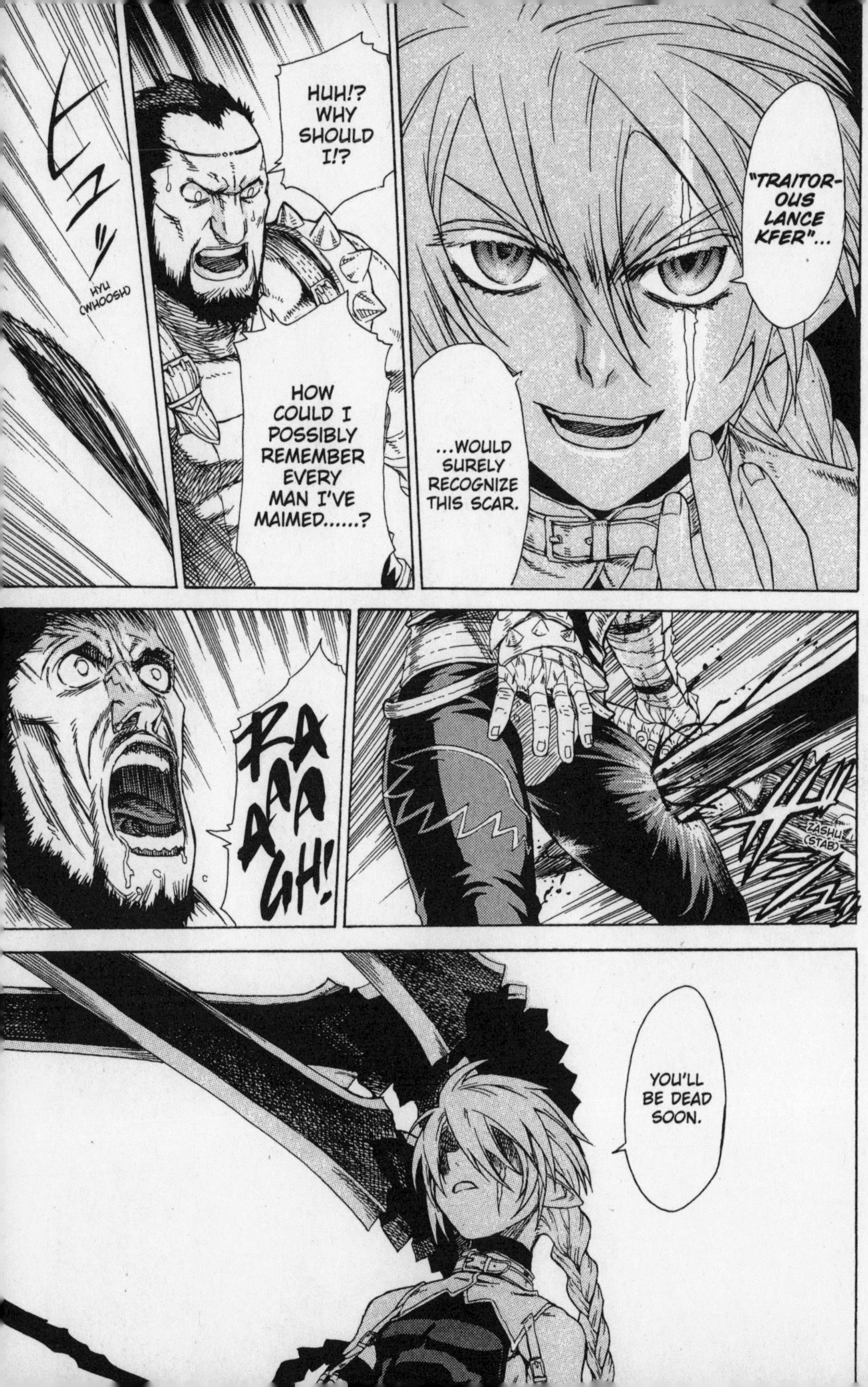
"TRAITOROUS LANCE KFER"...
...WOULD SURELY RECOGNIZE THIS SCAR.
HUH!? WHY SHOULD I!?
HOW COULD I POSSIBLY REMEMBER EVERY MAN I'VE MAIMED......?
HYU (WHOOSH)
ZASHU (STAB)
RAAAAAGH!
YOU'LL BE DEAD SOON.

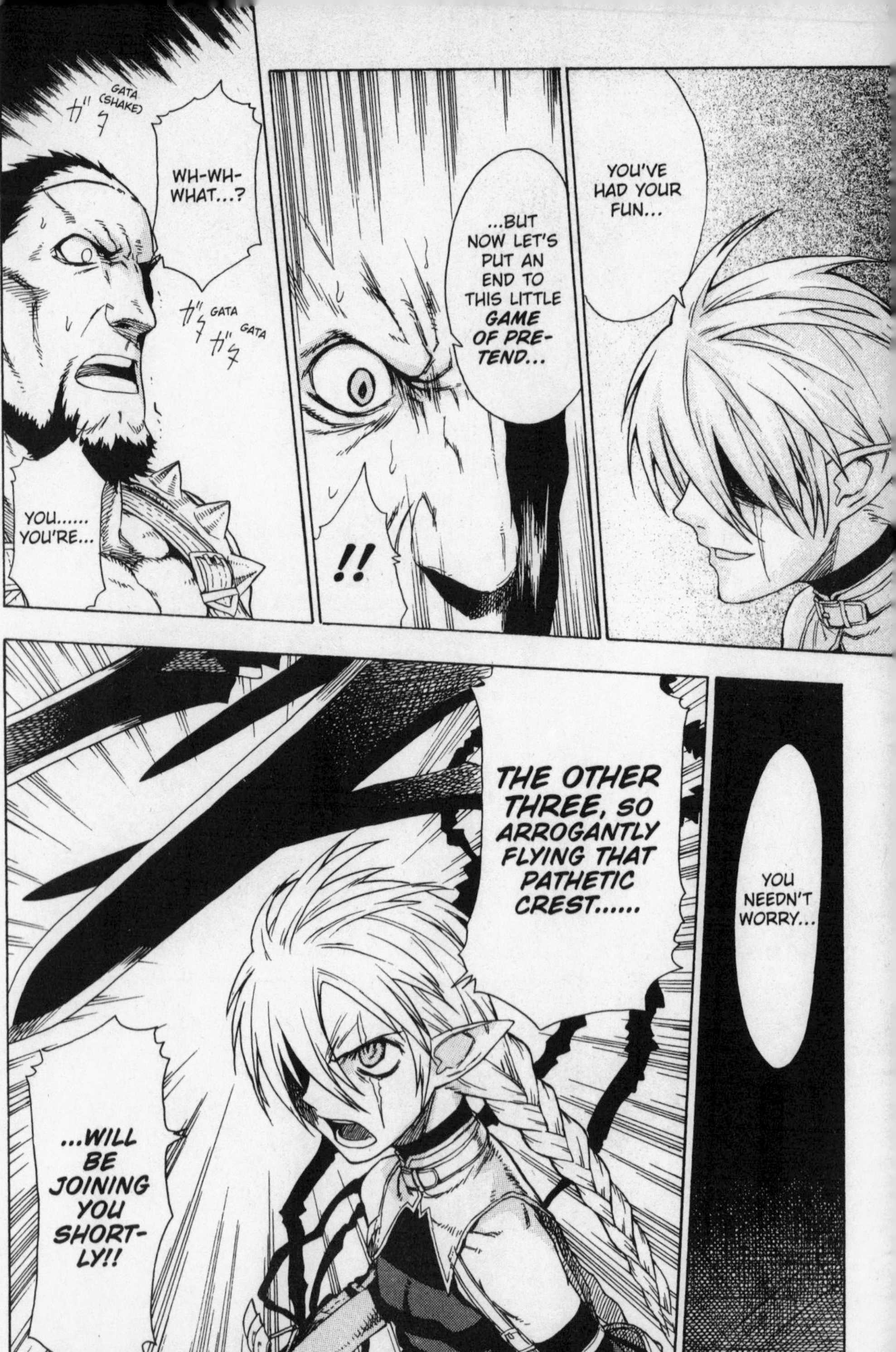
YOU'VE HAD YOUR FUN...
...BUT NOW LET'S PUT AN END TO THIS LITTLE *GAME OF PRE-TEND...*
!!
ガタ
GATA (SHAKE)
WH-WH-WHAT...?
ガタ GATA
ガタ GATA
YOU...... YOU'RE...
YOU NEEDN'T WORRY...
THE OTHER THREE, SO *ARROGANTLY FLYING THAT PATHETIC CREST......*
...WILL BE JOINING YOU SHORT-LY!!

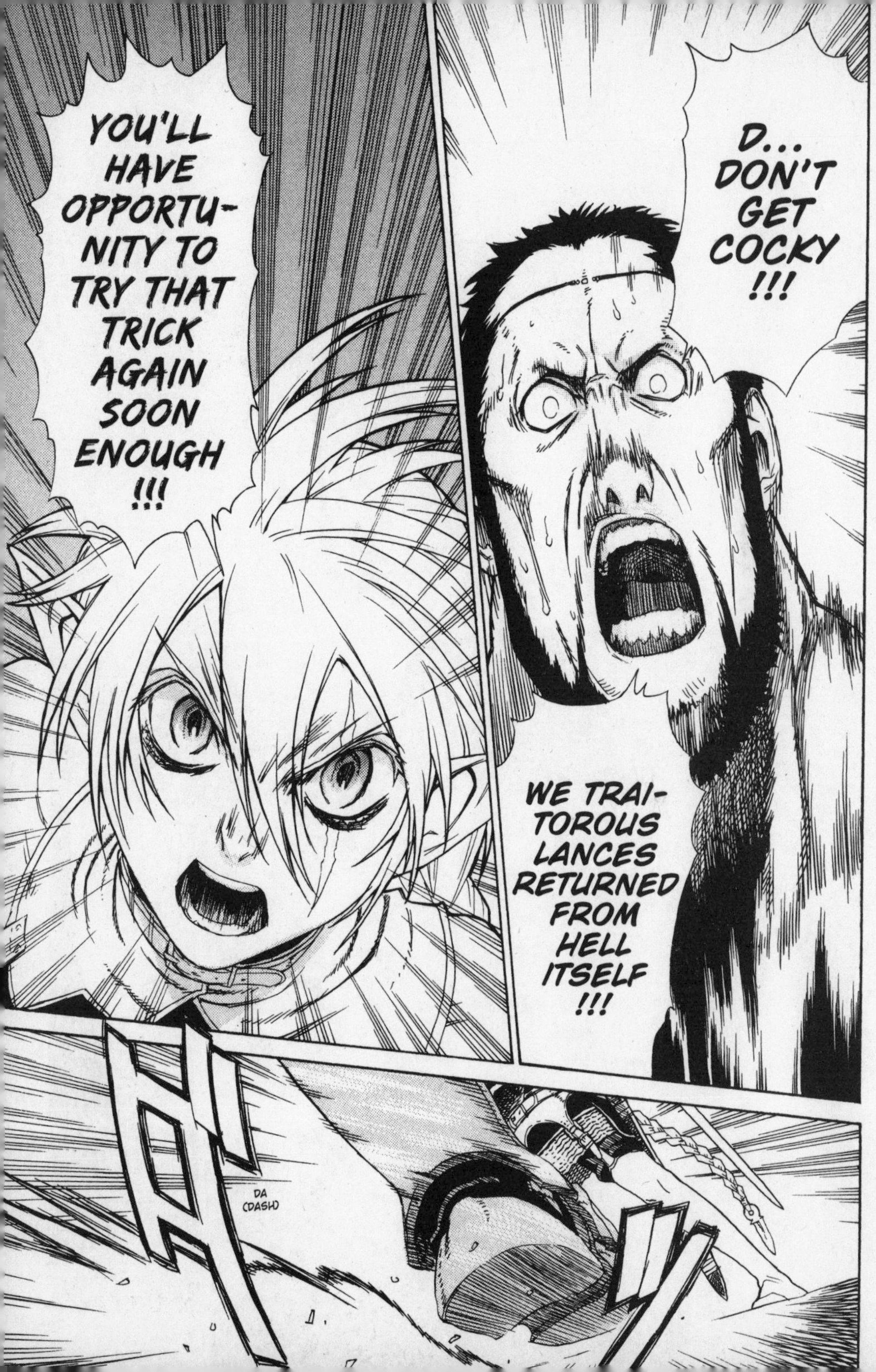
D... DON'T GET COCKY!!!
WE TRAITOROUS LANCES RETURNED FROM HELL ITSELF!!!
YOU'LL HAVE OPPORTUNITY TO TRY THAT TRICK AGAIN SOON ENOUGH!!!
DA (DASH)

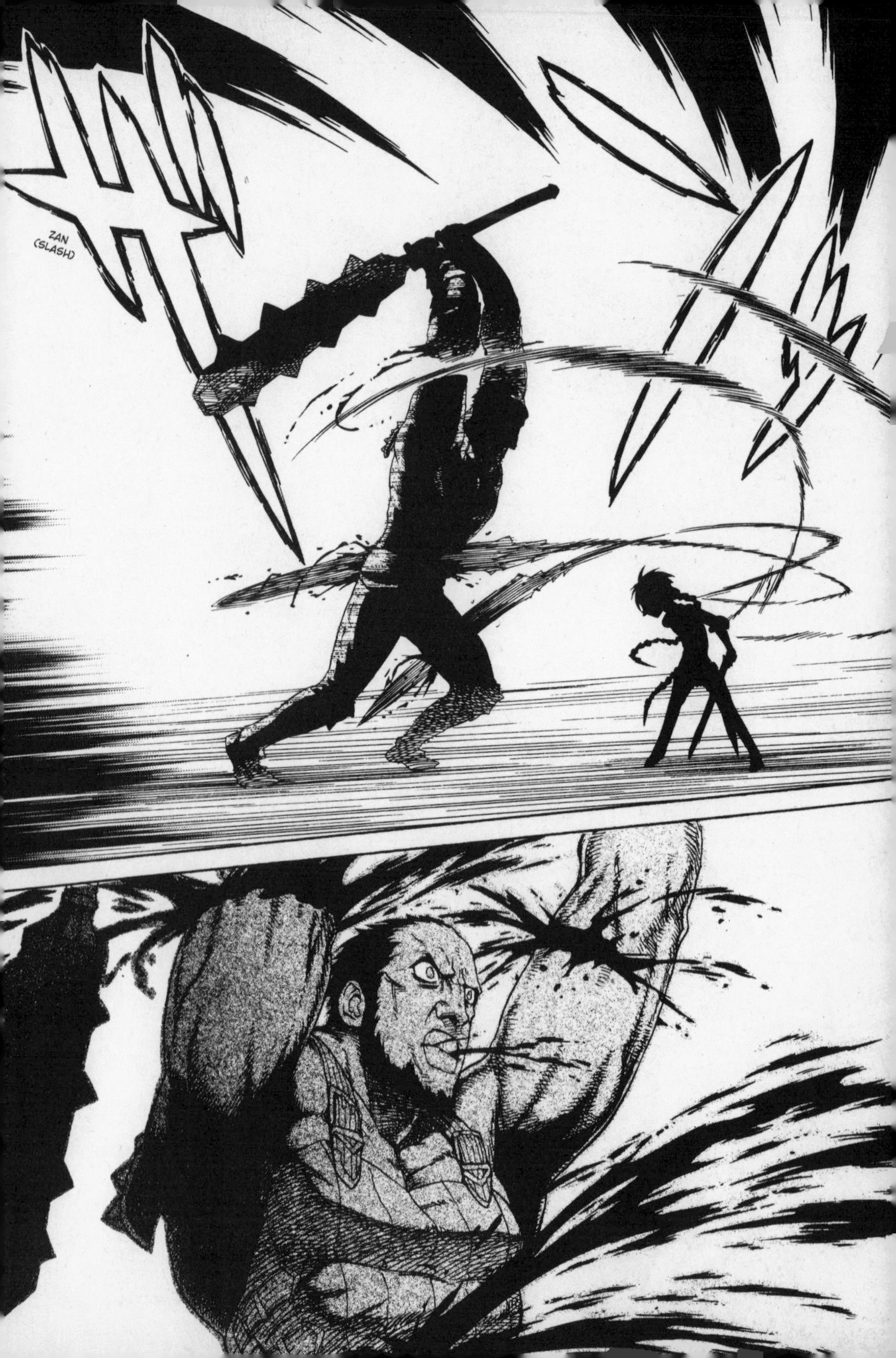
ZAN
(SLASH)

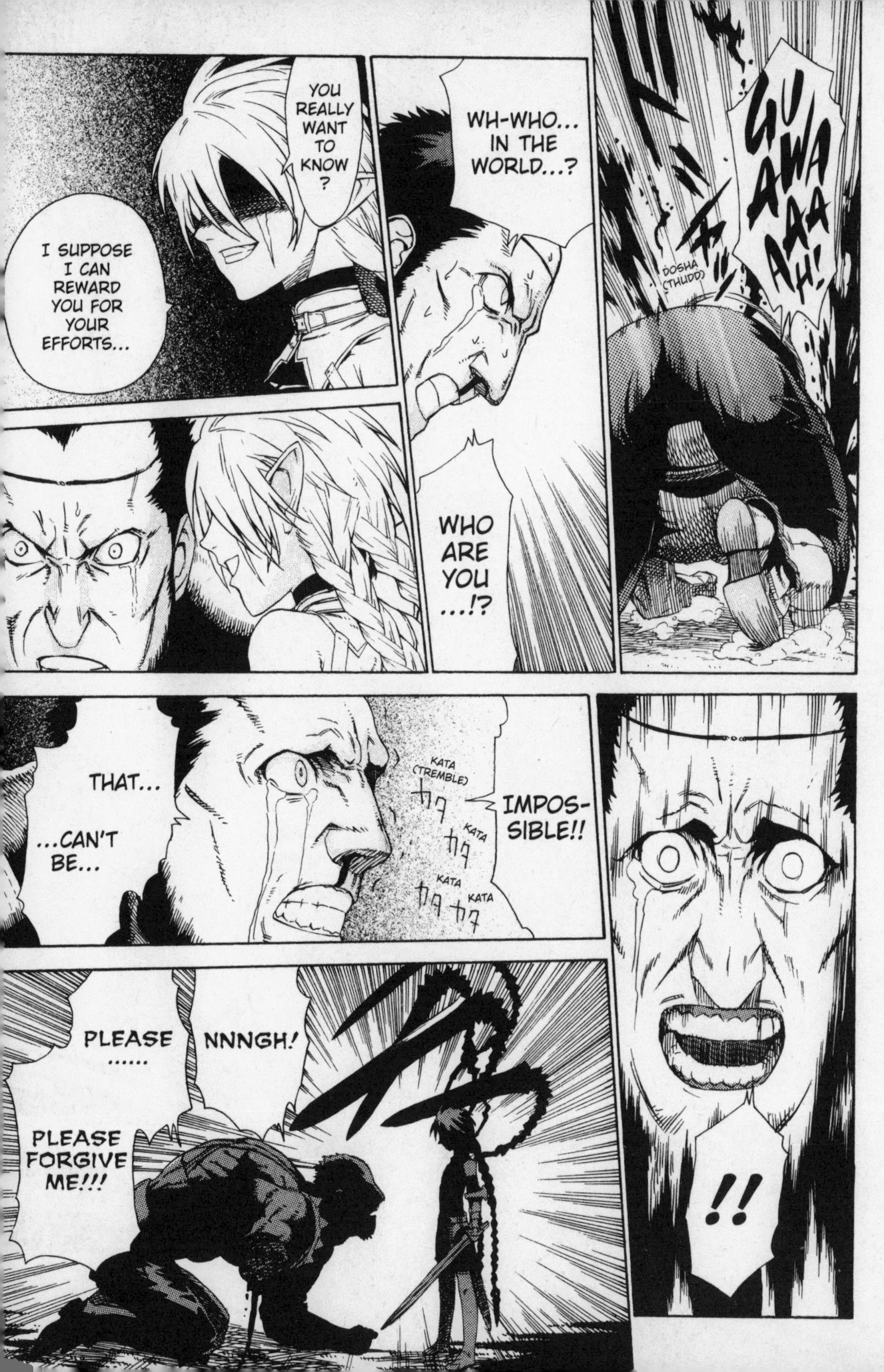
GUWAAAAAH!
DOSHA (THUDD)
WH-WHO... IN THE WORLD...?
WHO ARE YOU...!?
YOU REALLY WANT TO KNOW?
I SUPPOSE I CAN REWARD YOU FOR YOUR EFFORTS...
!!
IMPOSSIBLE!!
KATA (TREMBLE) KATA KATA KATA
THAT...
...CAN'T BE...
NNNGH!
PLEASE......
PLEASE FORGIVE ME!!!

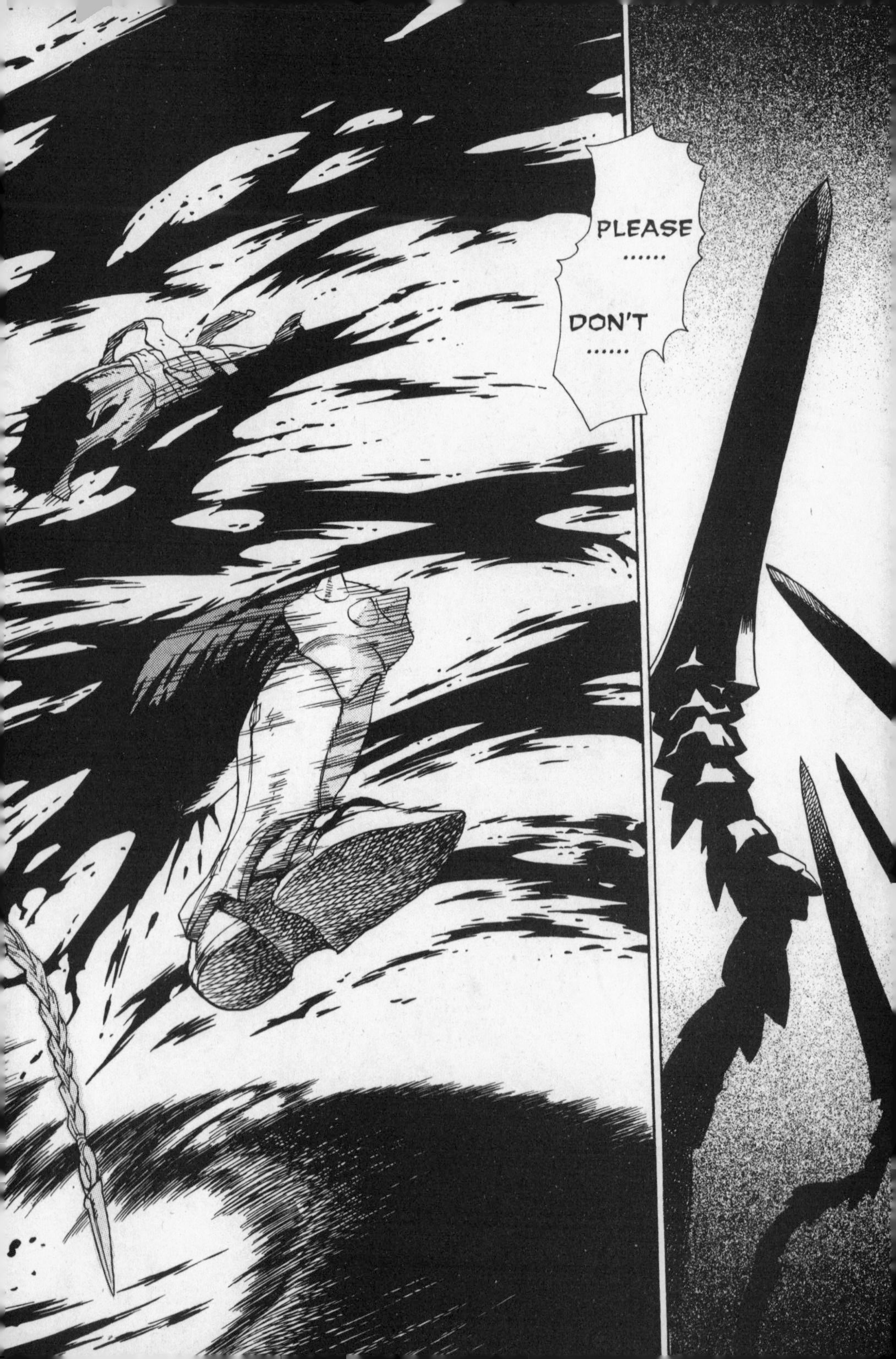
PLEASE …… DON'T ……

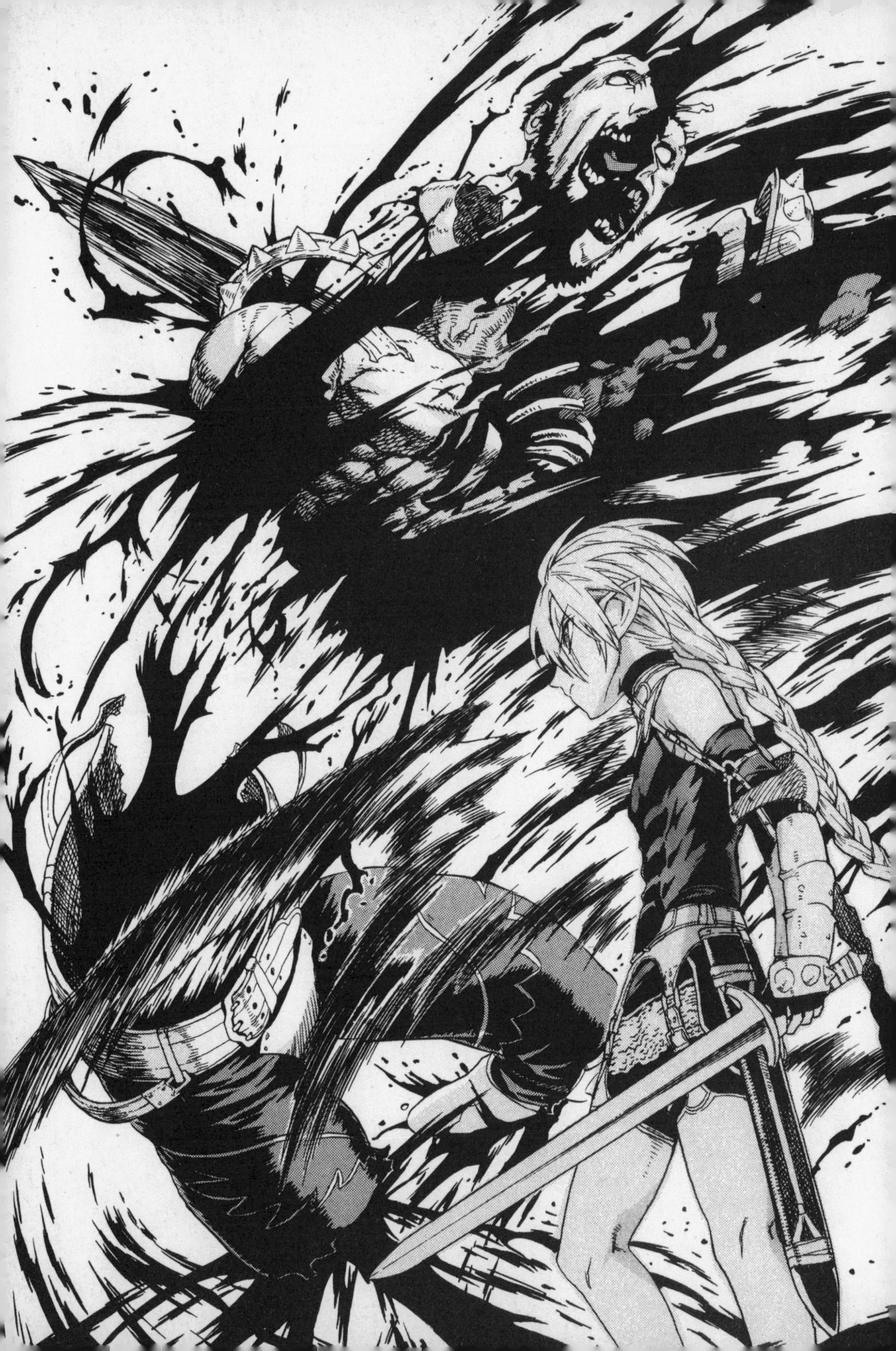

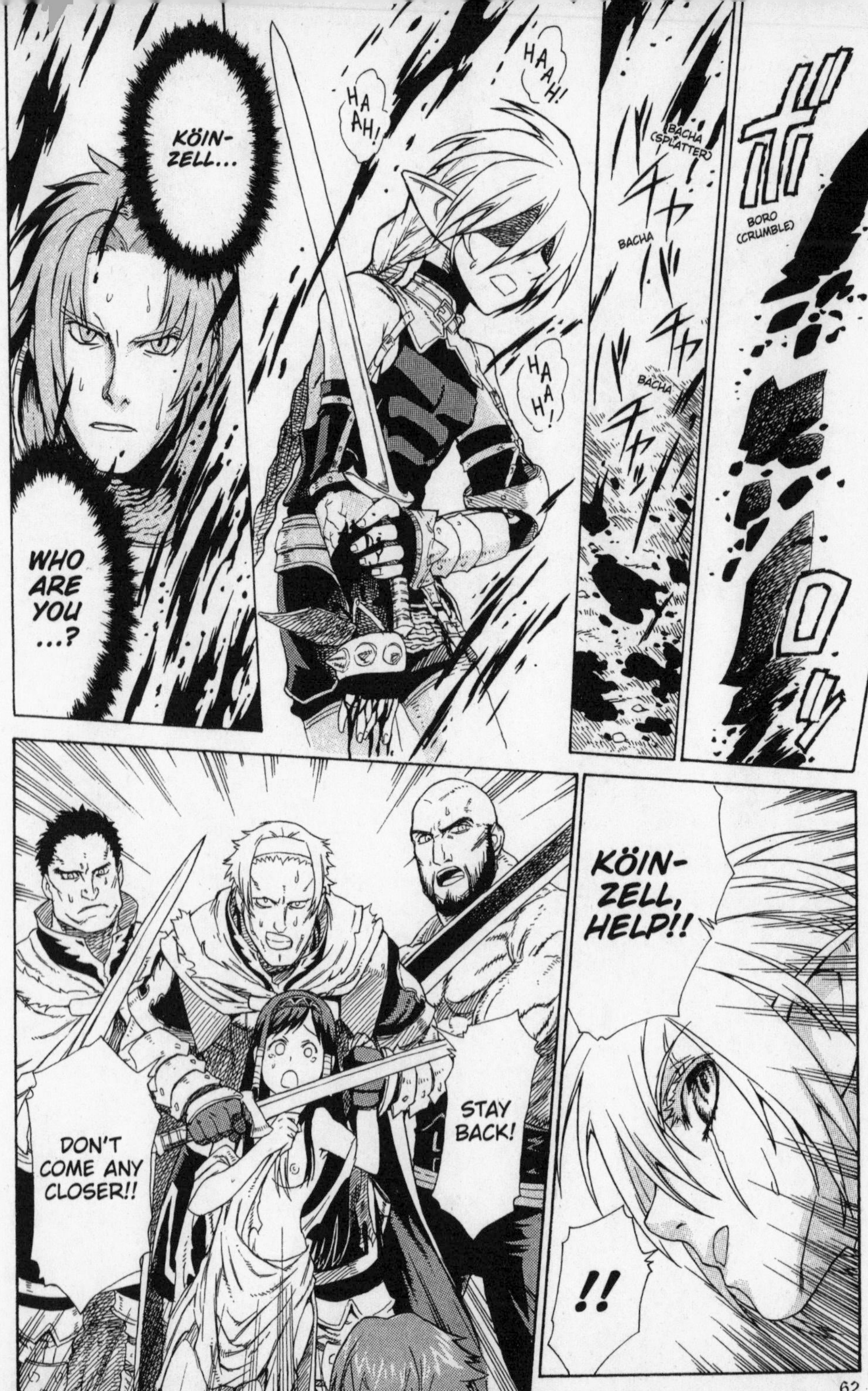
BORO (CRUMBLE)
BACHA (SPLATTER)
BACHA
BACHA
HAAAH!
HA AH!
HAAAH!
KÖIN-ZELL...
WHO ARE YOU...?
KÖIN-ZELL, HELP!!
!!
STAY BACK!
DON'T COME ANY CLOSER!!

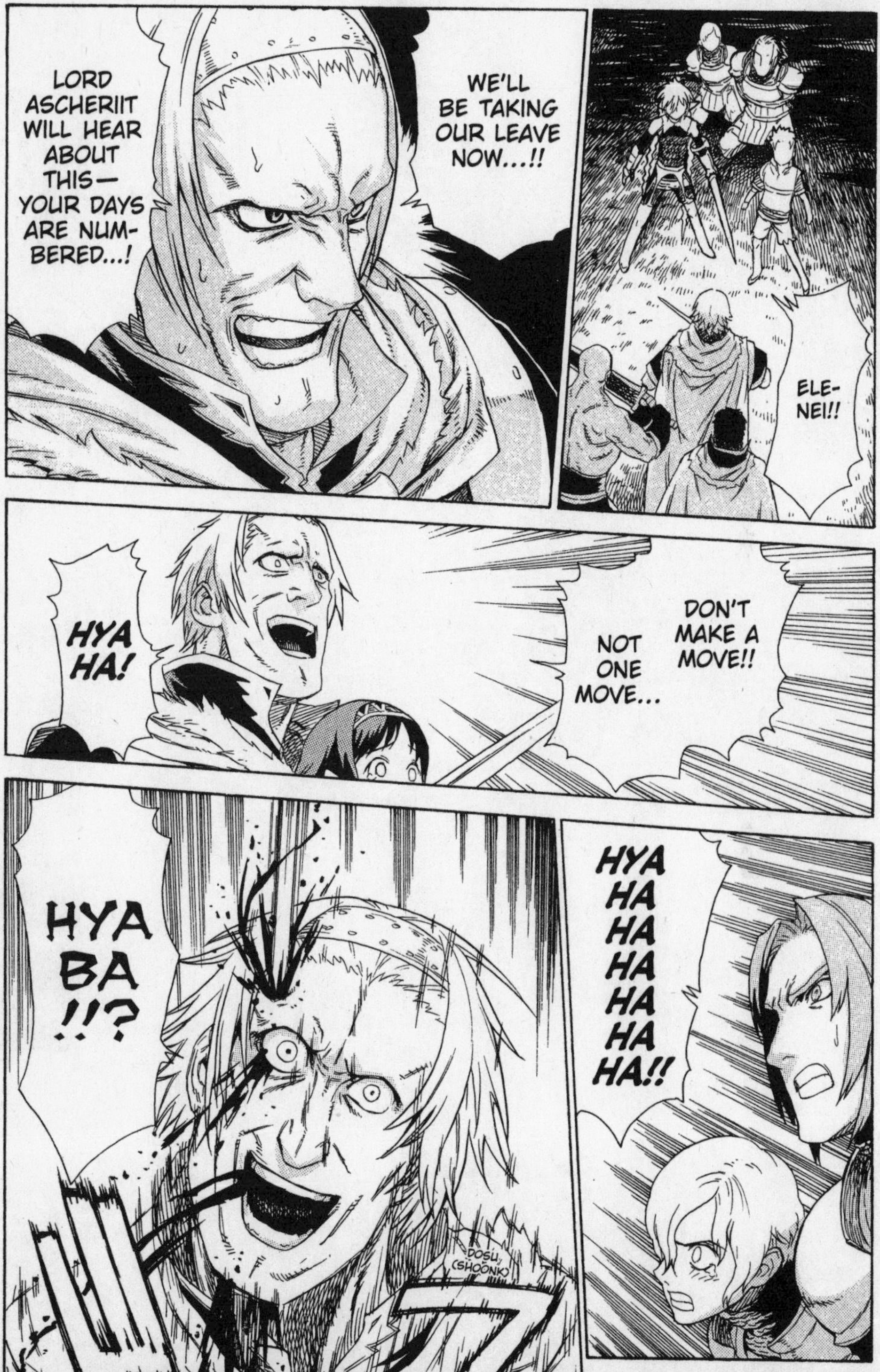
ELE-NEI!!
WE'LL BE TAKING OUR LEAVE NOW...!!
LORD ASCHERIIT WILL HEAR ABOUT THIS— YOUR DAYS ARE NUM-BERED...!
DON'T MAKE A MOVE!!
NOT ONE MOVE...
HYA HA!
HYA HA HA HA HA HA HA HA!!
HYA BA!!?
DOSU (SHOONK)

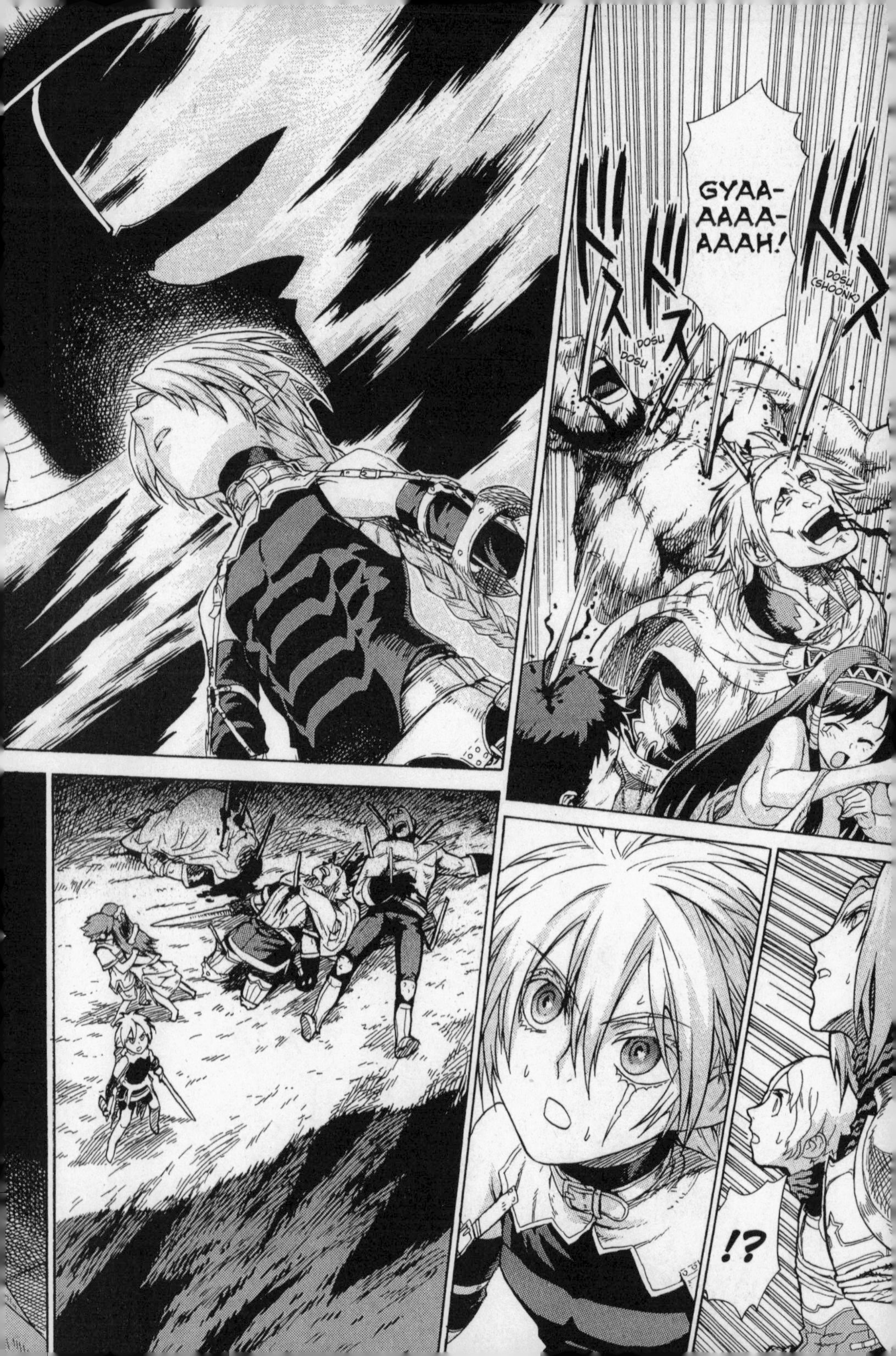
ドス
DOSU (SHOONK)
GYAA-AAAA-AAAH!
ドス
DOSU
ドス
DOSU
!?

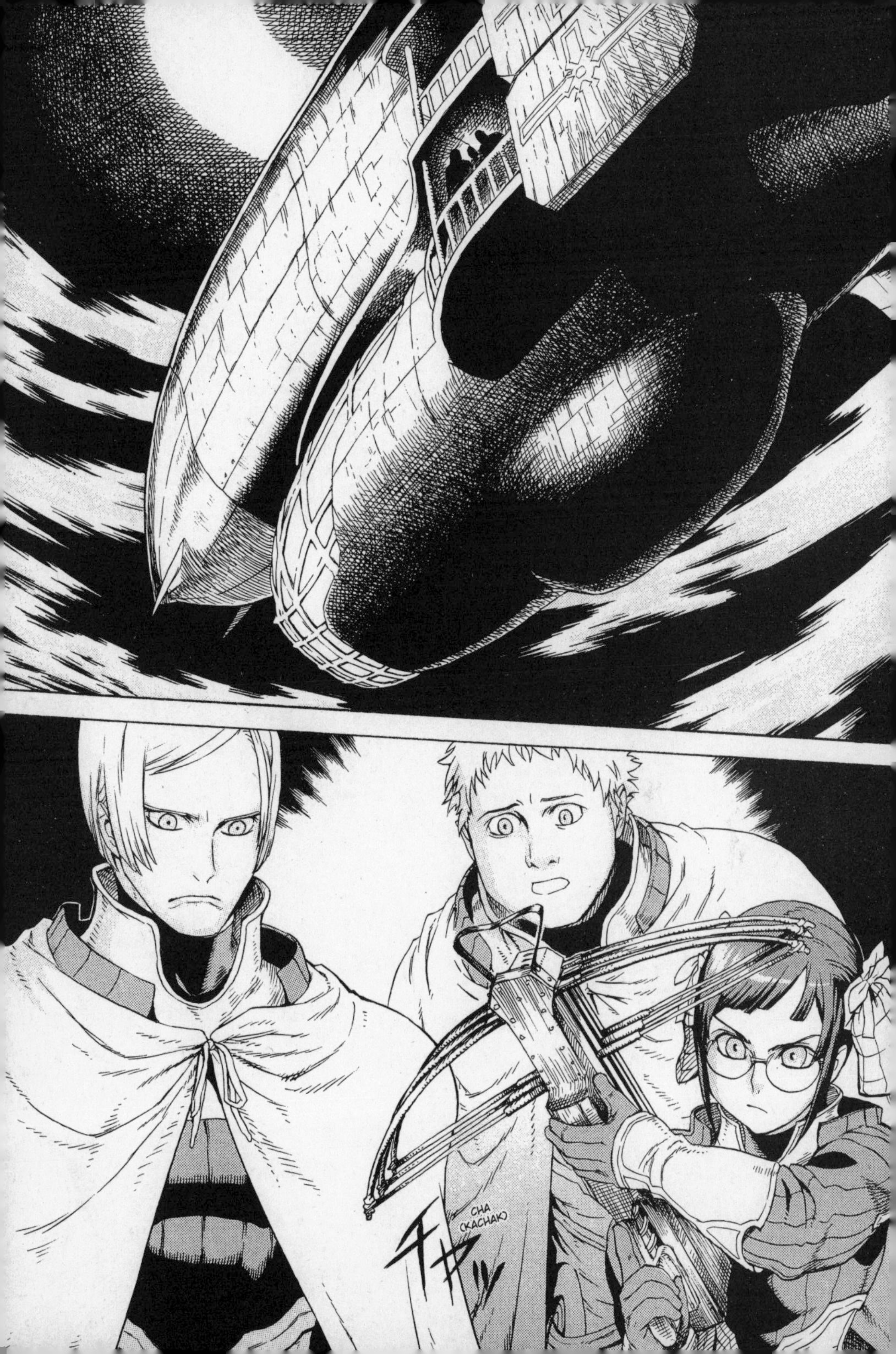
CHA
(KACHAK)

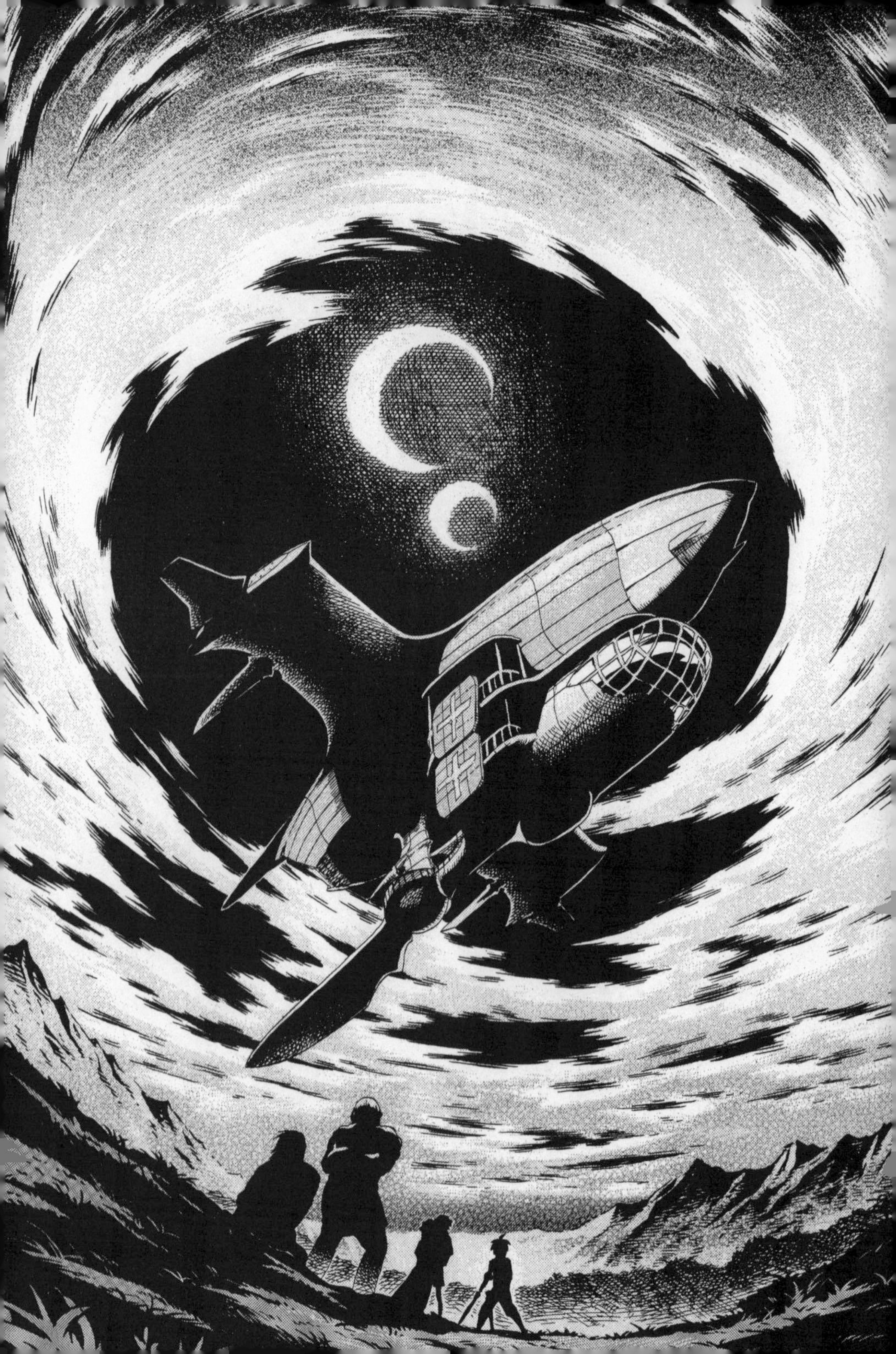

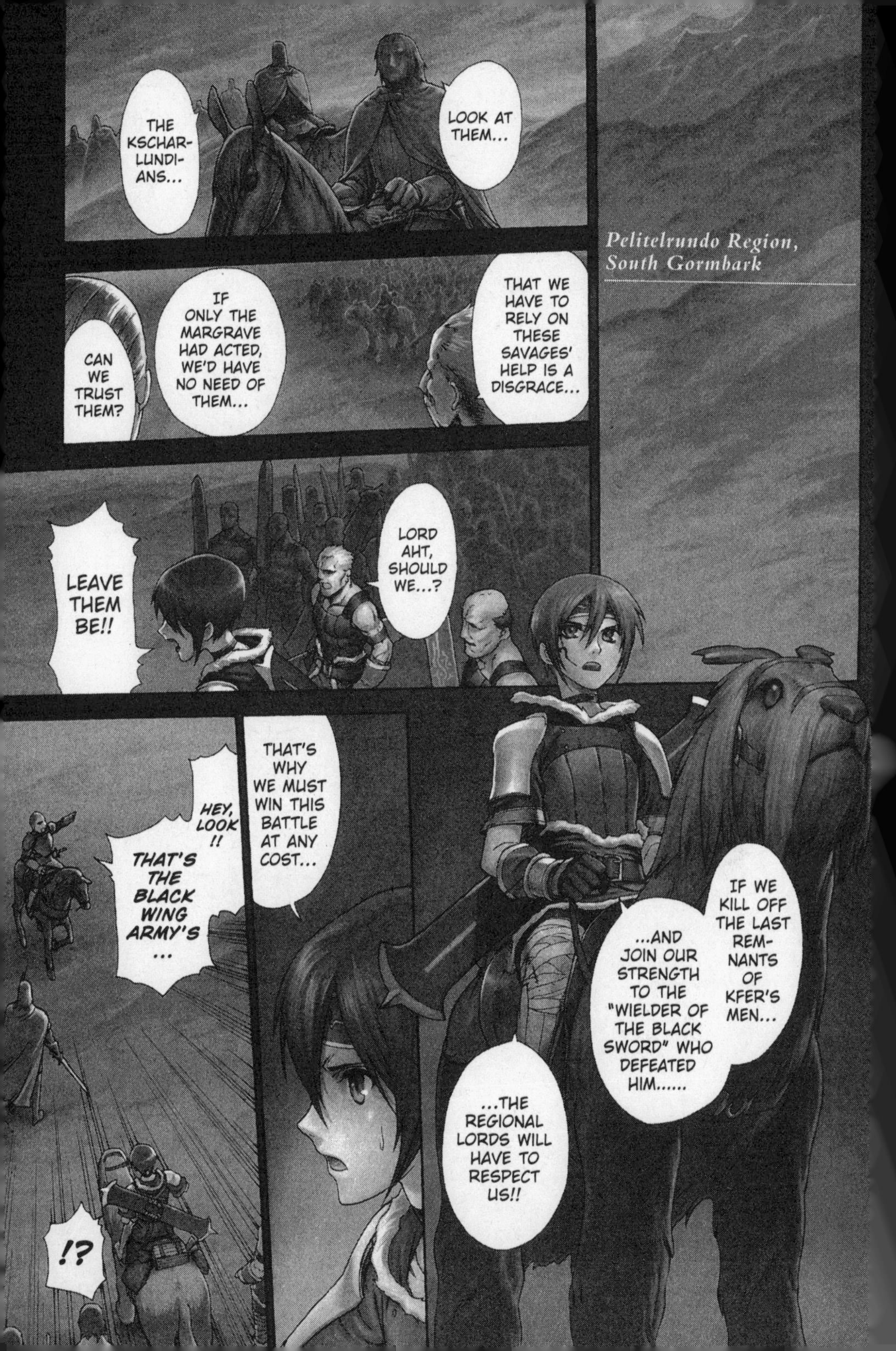
Pelitelrundo Region, South Gormbark
LOOK AT THEM...
THE KSCHAR-LUNDI-ANS...
THAT WE HAVE TO RELY ON THESE SAVAGES' HELP IS A DISGRACE...
IF ONLY THE MARGRAVE HAD ACTED, WE'D HAVE NO NEED OF THEM...
CAN WE TRUST THEM?
LORD AHT, SHOULD WE...?
LEAVE THEM BE!!
IF WE KILL OFF THE LAST REM-NANTS OF KFER'S MEN...
...AND JOIN OUR STRENGTH TO THE "WIELDER OF THE BLACK SWORD" WHO DEFEATED HIM......
...THE REGIONAL LORDS WILL HAVE TO RESPECT US!!
THAT'S WHY WE MUST WIN THIS BATTLE AT ANY COST...
HEY, LOOK!!
THAT'S THE BLACK WING ARMY'S ...
!?

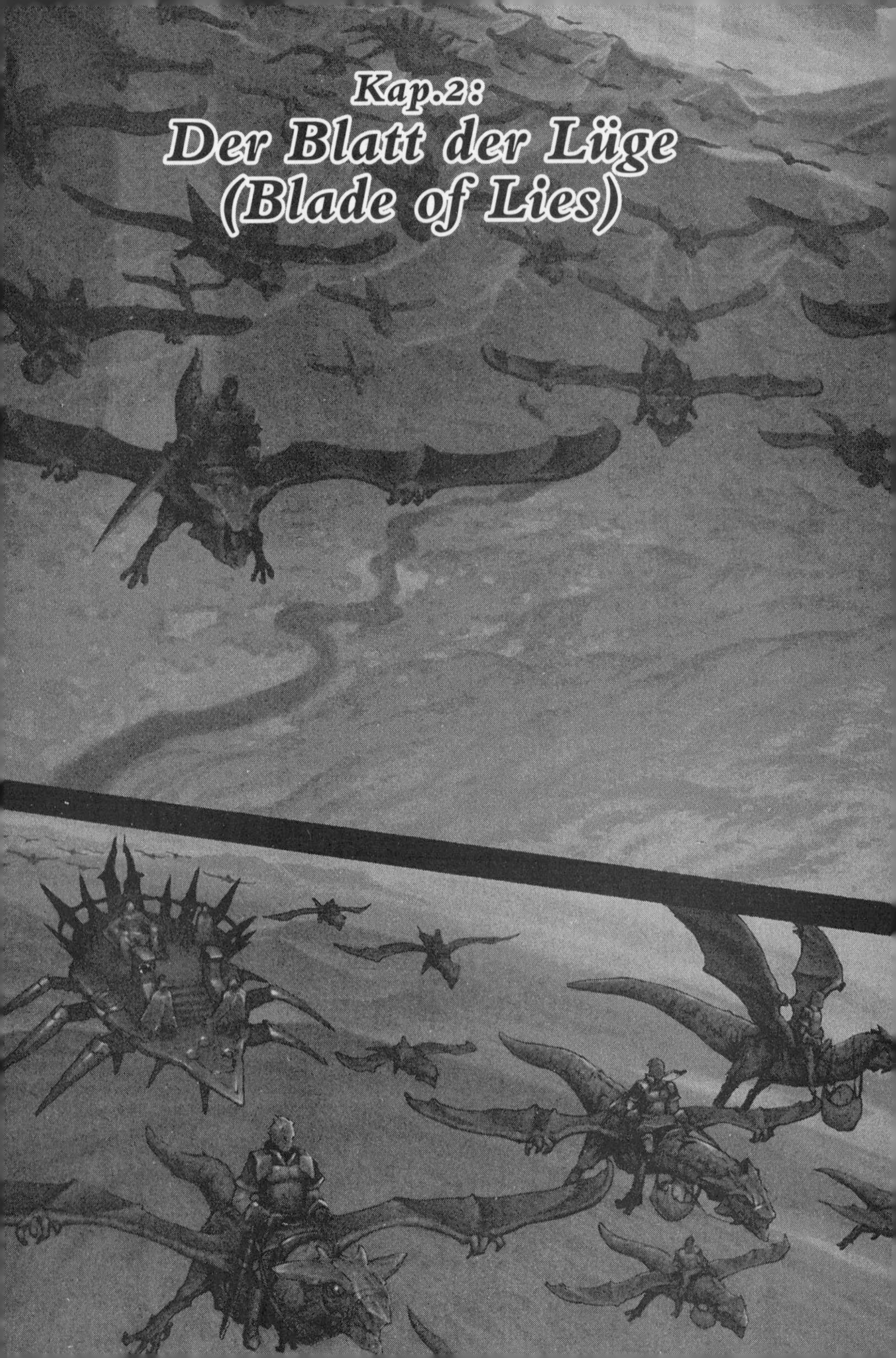
Kap.2:
Der Blatt der Lüge
(Blade of Lies)

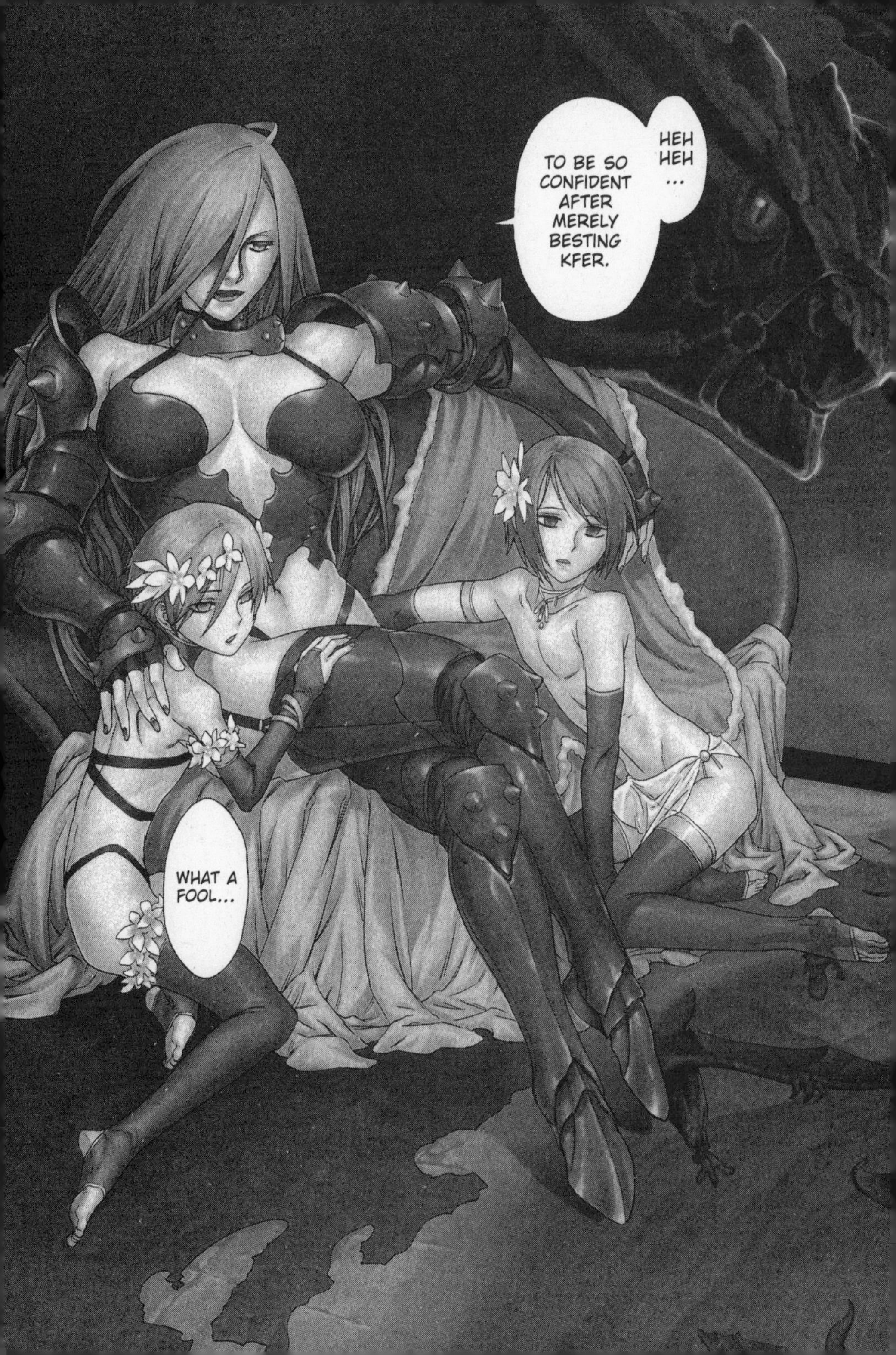
HEH HEH...
TO BE SO CONFIDENT AFTER MERELY BESTING KFER.
WHAT A FOOL...

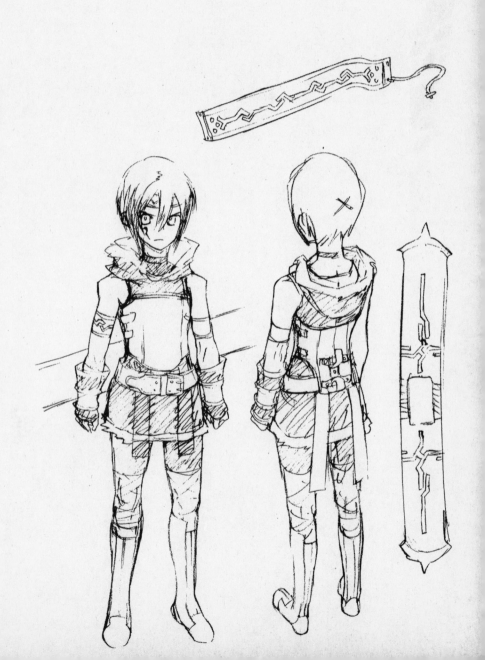

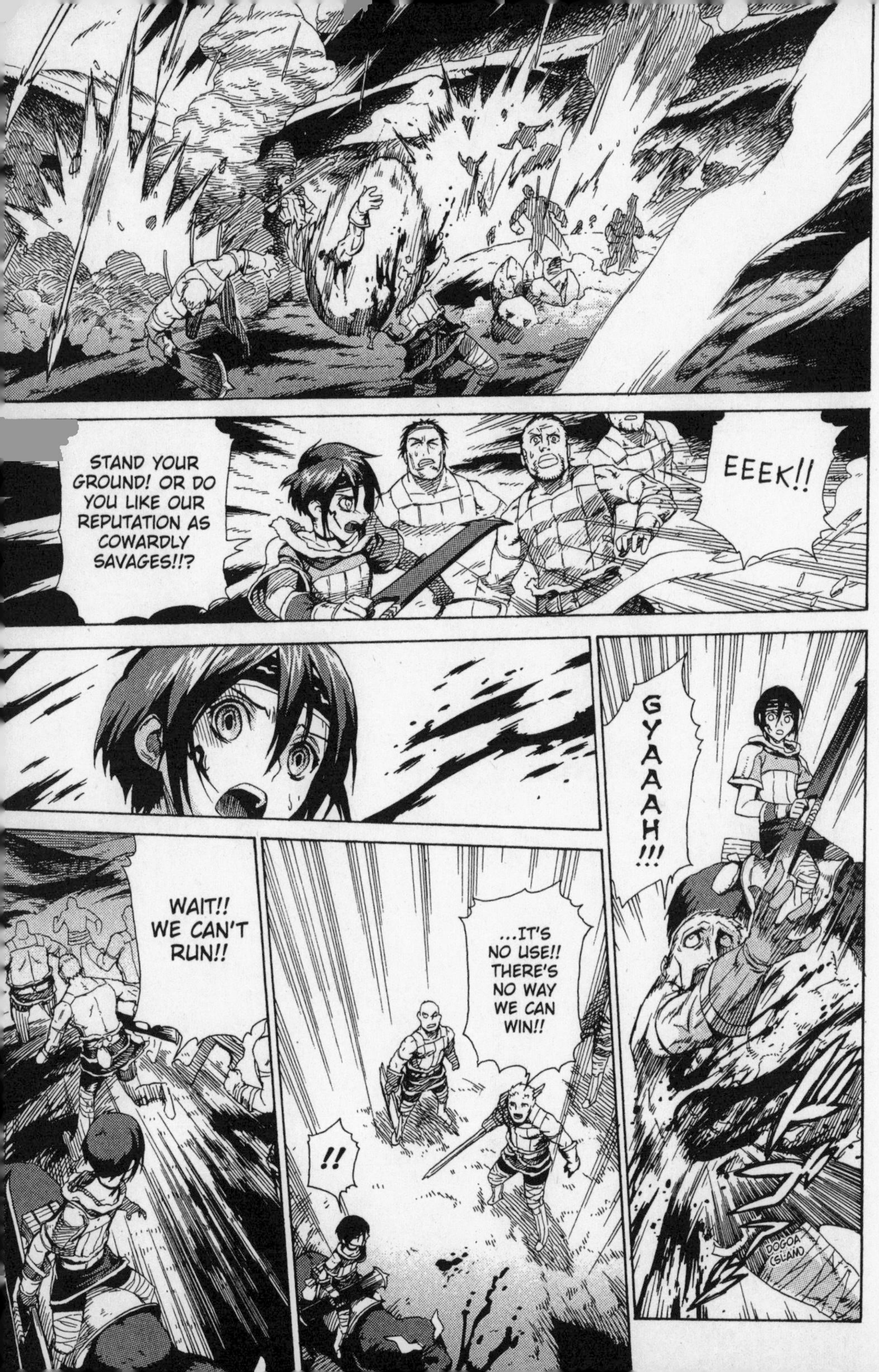
EEEK!!
STAND YOUR GROUND! OR DO YOU LIKE OUR REPUTATION AS COWARDLY SAVAGES!!?
GYAAAH!!!
DOGOA (SLAM)
...IT'S NO USE!! THERE'S NO WAY WE CAN WIN!!
!!
WAIT!! WE CAN'T RUN!!

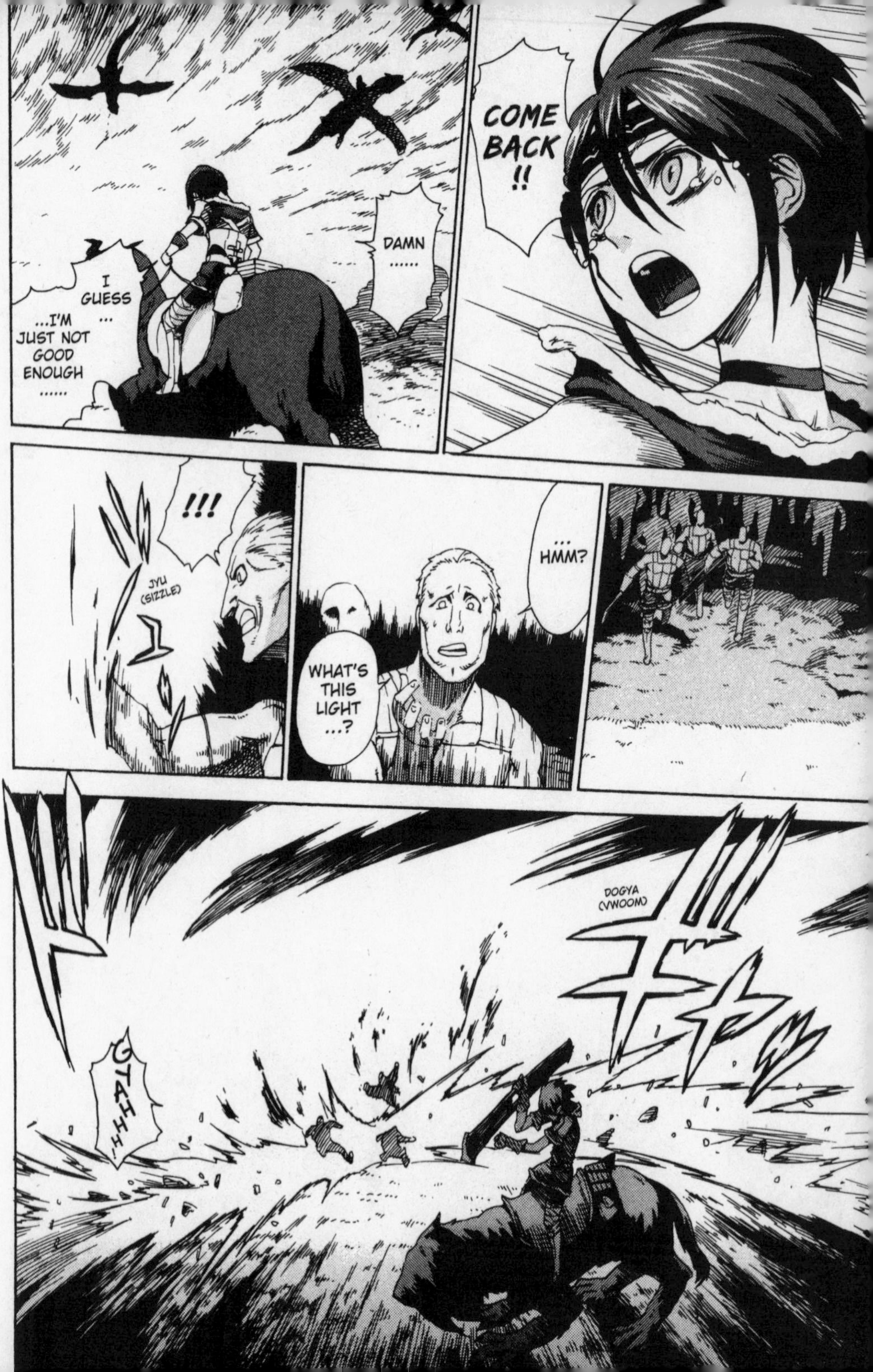
COME BACK !!
DAMN ......
I GUESS ... ...I'M JUST NOT GOOD ENOUGH ......
...HMM?
WHAT'S THIS LIGHT ...?
!!!
JYU (SIZZLE)
DOGYA (VWOOM)
GTAHHH!

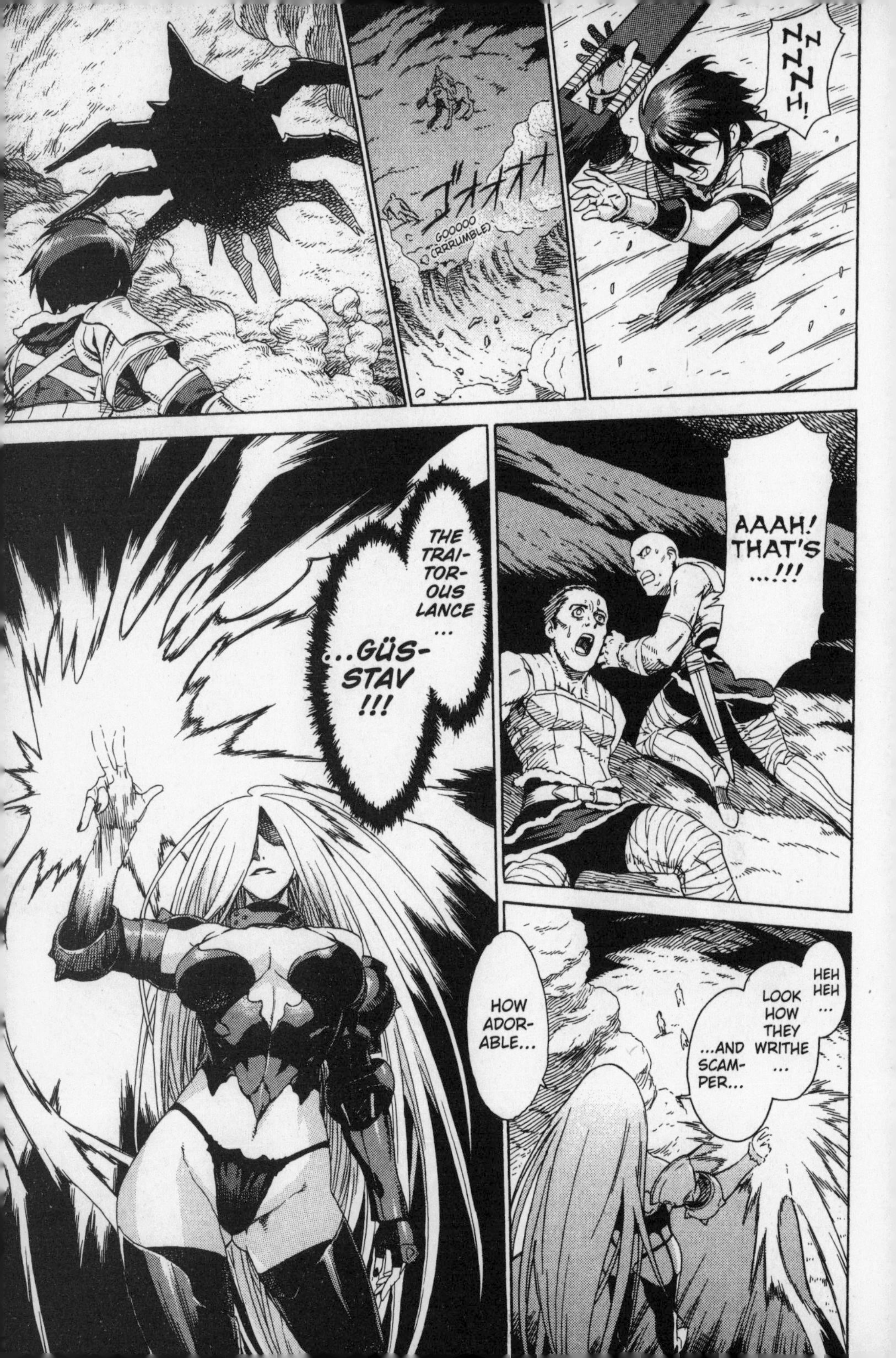
NNNH!
ゴオオオ
GOOOOO (RRRUMBLE)
AAAH! THAT'S ...!!!
HEH HEH... LOOK HOW THEY WRITHE...
...AND SCAMPER...
HOW ADORABLE...
THE TRAITOROUS LANCE...
...GÜSTAV!!!

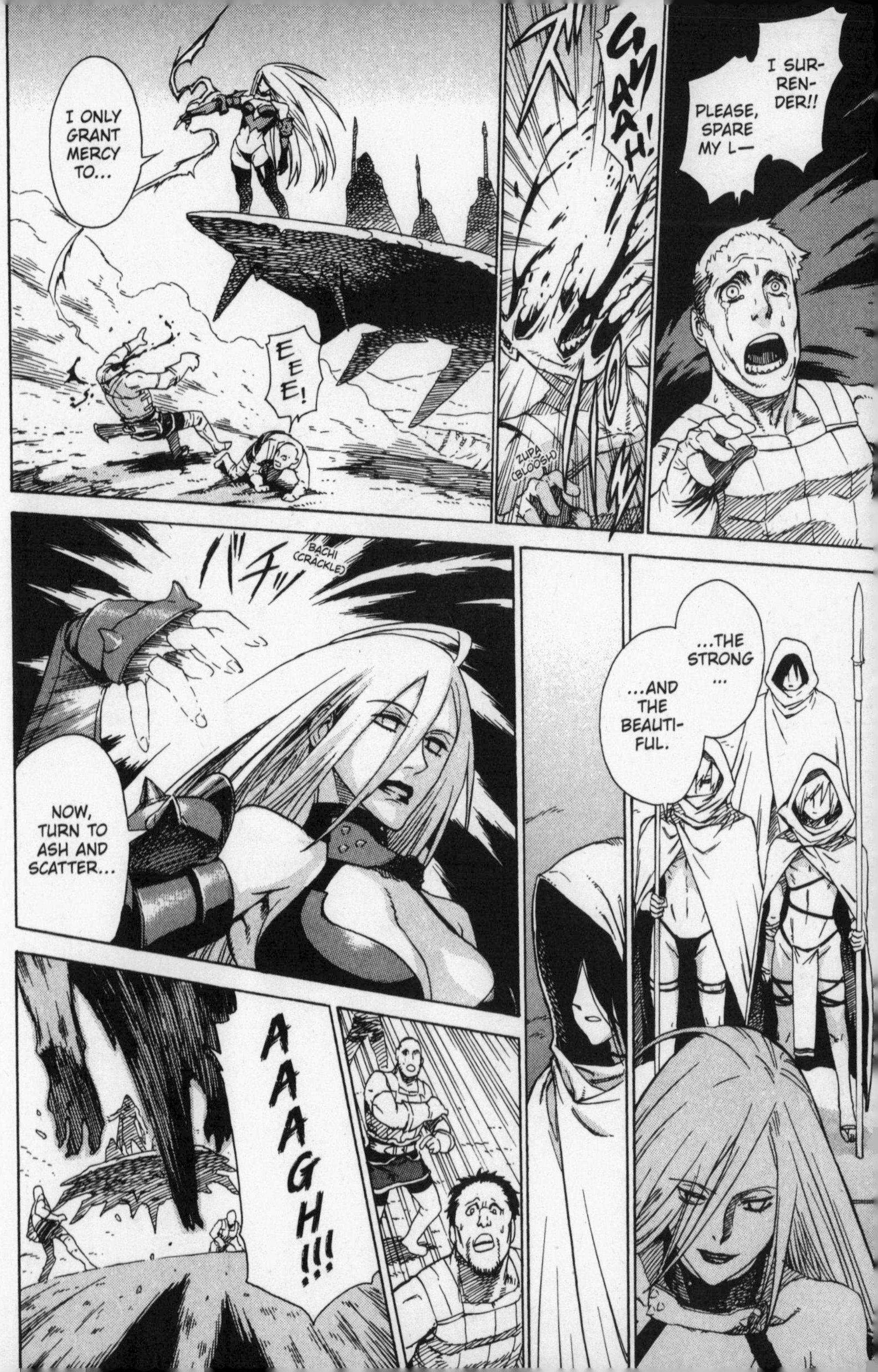
I SURREN-DER!!
PLEASE, SPARE MY L—
GWAAH!
ZUPA (BLOOSH)
I ONLY GRANT MERCY TO...
EEE!
...THE STRONG...
...AND THE BEAUTI-FUL.
バチッ
BACHI (CRACKLE)
NOW, TURN TO ASH AND SCATTER...
AAAGH!!!

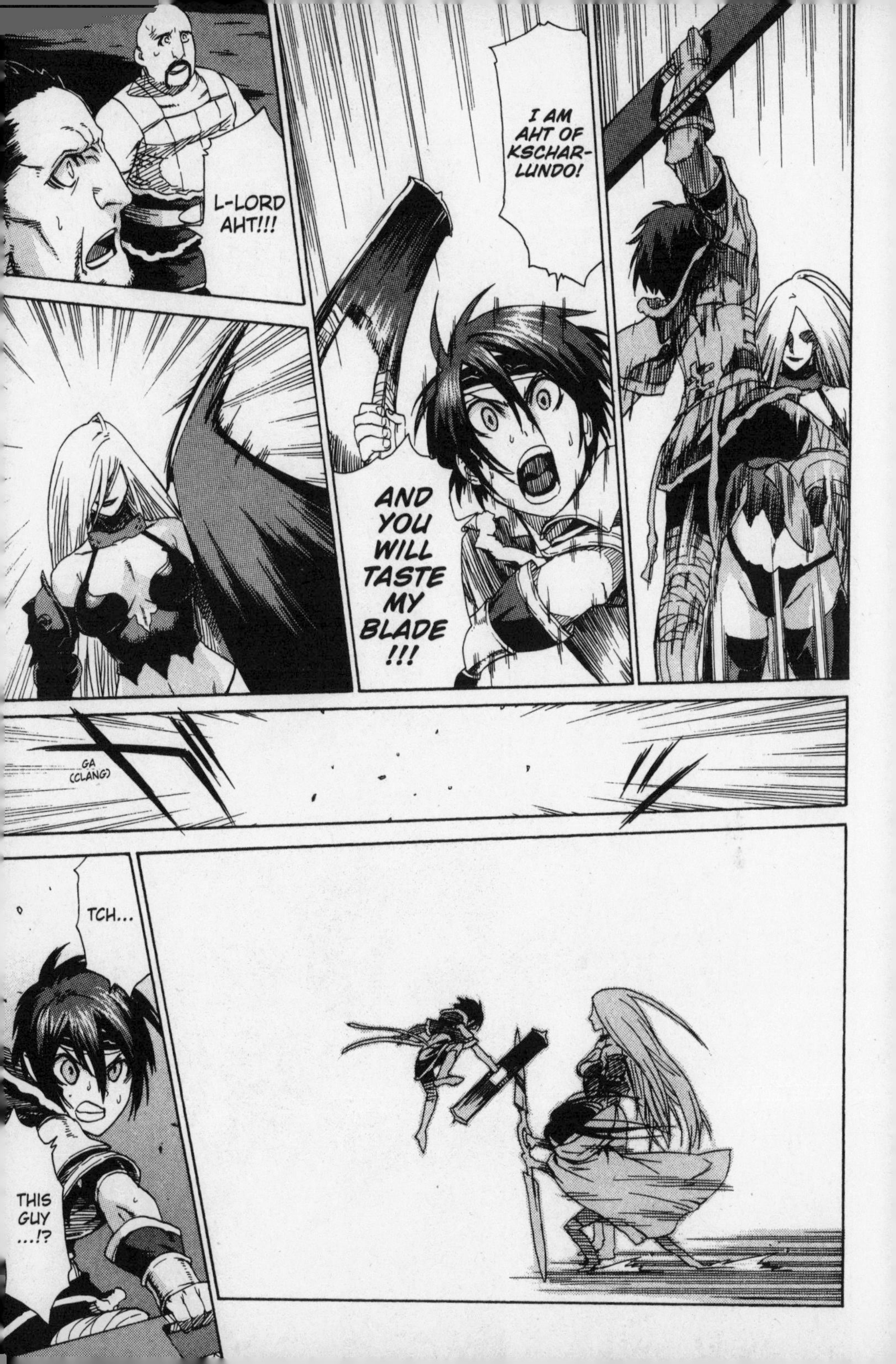

I AM AHT OF KSCHAR-LUNDO!
AND YOU WILL TASTE MY BLADE!!!
L-LORD AHT!!!
GA (CLANG)
TCH...
THIS GUY ...!?

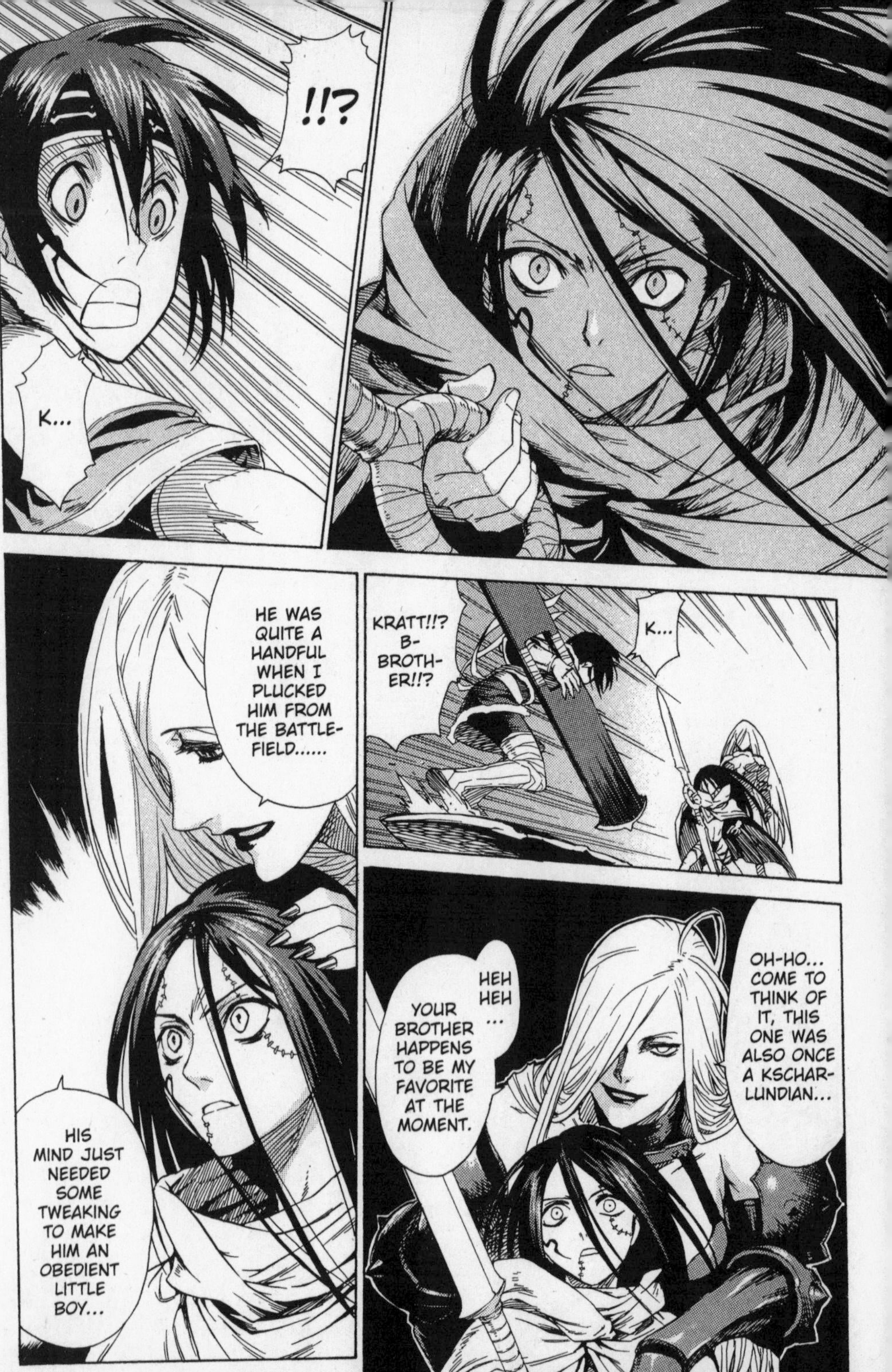
!!?
K...
K...
KRATT!!? B-BROTHER!!?
OH-HO... COME TO THINK OF IT, THIS ONE WAS ALSO ONCE A KSCHAR-LUNDIAN...
HEH HEH ...
YOUR BROTHER HAPPENS TO BE MY FAVORITE AT THE MOMENT.
HE WAS QUITE A HANDFUL WHEN I PLUCKED HIM FROM THE BATTLE-FIELD......
HIS MIND JUST NEEDED SOME TWEAKING TO MAKE HIM AN OBEDIENT LITTLE BOY...

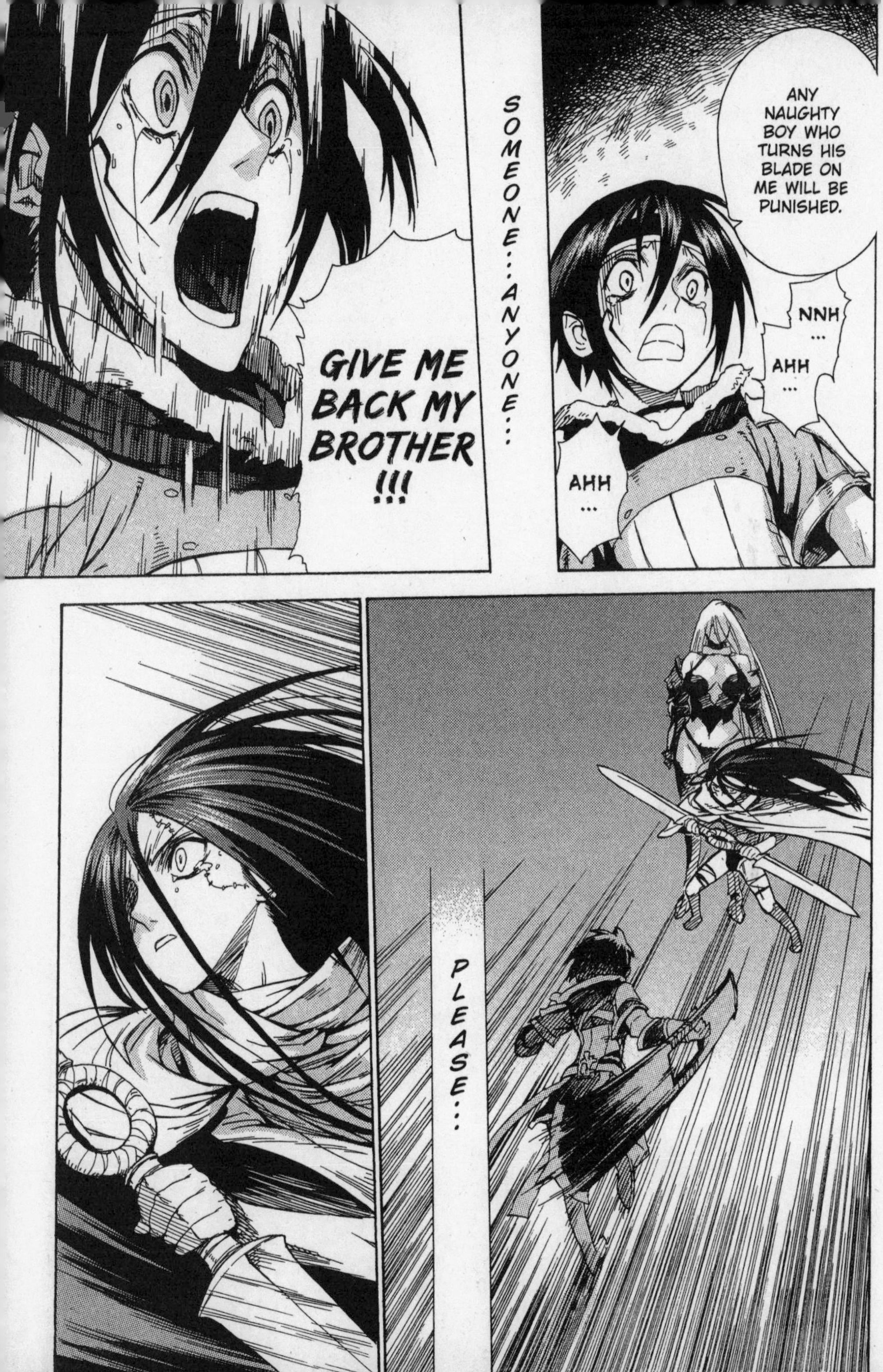
ANY NAUGHTY BOY WHO TURNS HIS BLADE ON ME WILL BE PUNISHED.
NNH ...
AHH ...
AHH ...
SOMEONE... ANYONE...
GIVE ME BACK MY BROTHER !!!
PLEASE...

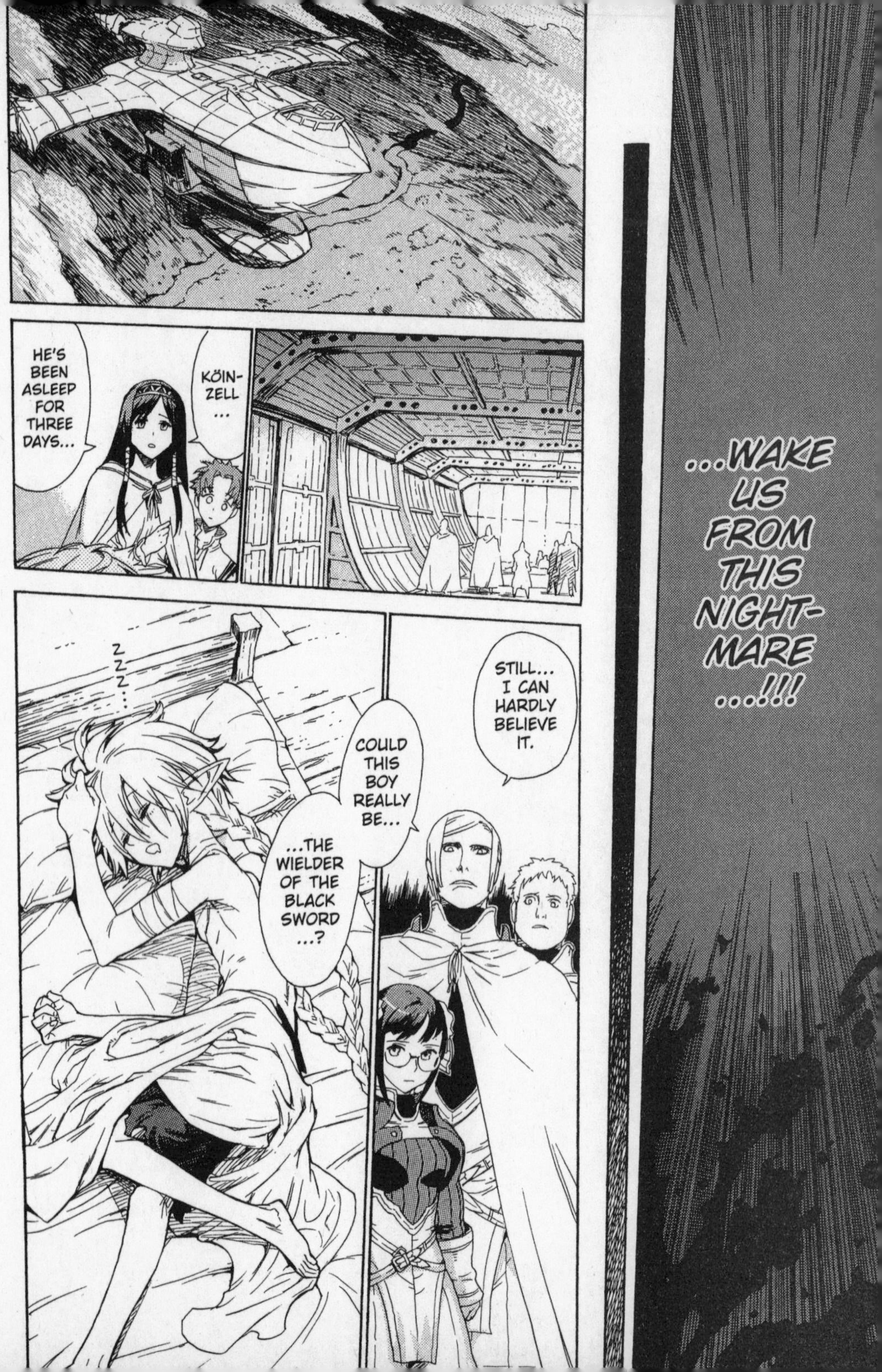
...WAKE US FROM THIS NIGHT-MARE...!!!
KÖIN-ZELL...
HE'S BEEN ASLEEP FOR THREE DAYS...
STILL... I CAN HARDLY BELIEVE IT.
COULD THIS BOY REALLY BE...
...THE WIELDER OF THE BLACK SWORD...?
ZZZ...

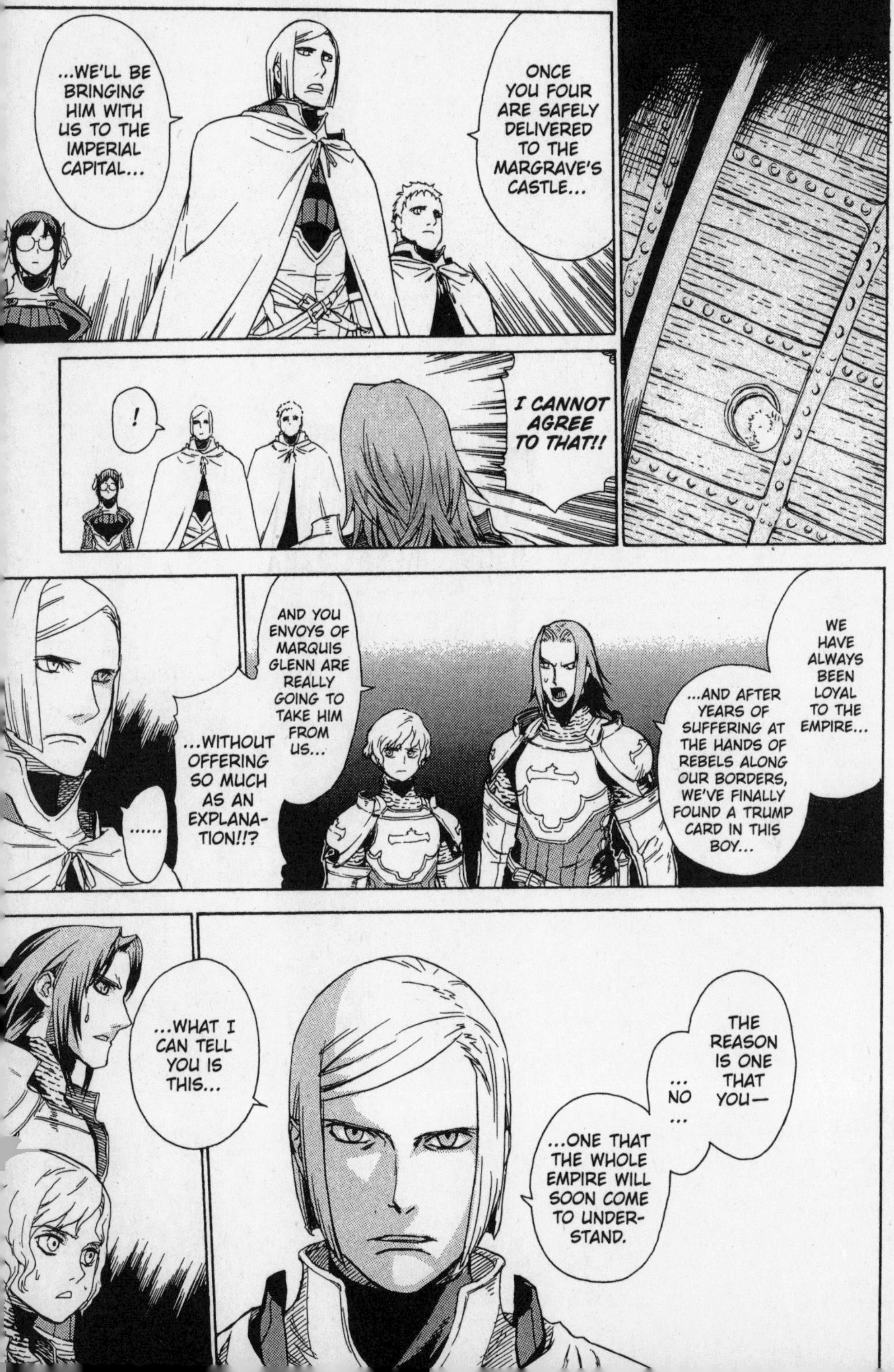
ONCE YOU FOUR ARE SAFELY DELIVERED TO THE MARGRAVE'S CASTLE...
...WE'LL BE BRINGING HIM WITH US TO THE IMPERIAL CAPITAL...
I CANNOT AGREE TO THAT!!
!
WE HAVE ALWAYS BEEN LOYAL TO THE EMPIRE...
...AND AFTER YEARS OF SUFFERING AT THE HANDS OF REBELS ALONG OUR BORDERS, WE'VE FINALLY FOUND A TRUMP CARD IN THIS BOY...
AND YOU ENVOYS OF MARQUIS GLENN ARE REALLY GOING TO TAKE HIM FROM US...
...WITHOUT OFFERING SO MUCH AS AN EXPLANATION!!?
......
...WHAT I CAN TELL YOU IS THIS...
THE REASON IS ONE THAT YOU—
...NO...
...ONE THAT THE WHOLE EMPIRE WILL SOON COME TO UNDERSTAND.

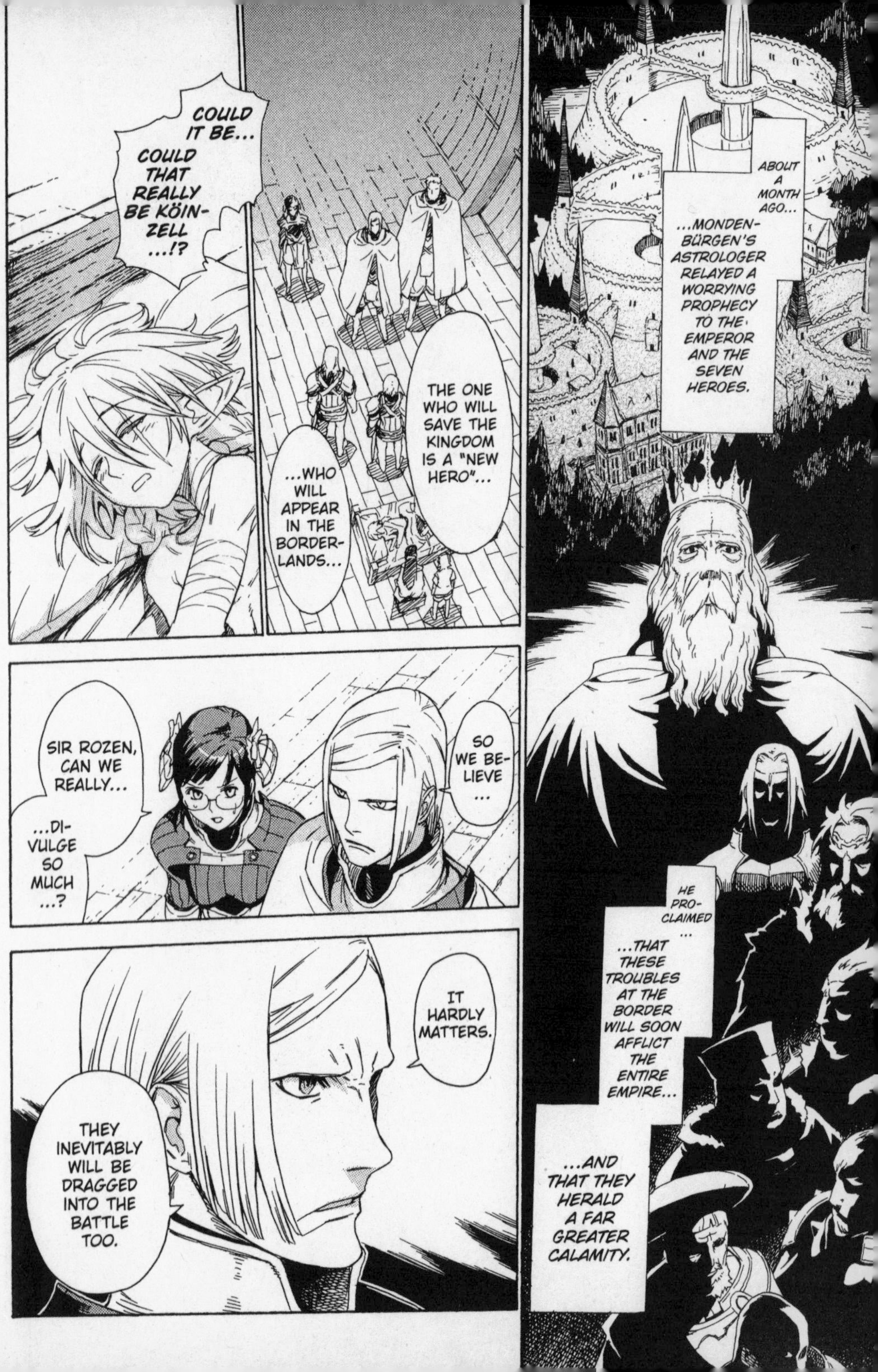
ABOUT A MONTH AGO...
...MONDEN-BÜRGEN'S ASTROLOGER RELAYED A WORRYING PROPHECY TO THE EMPEROR AND THE SEVEN HEROES.
HE PROCLAIMED...
...THAT THESE TROUBLES AT THE BORDER WILL SOON AFFLICT THE ENTIRE EMPIRE...
...AND THAT THEY HERALD A FAR GREATER CALAMITY.
THE ONE WHO WILL SAVE THE KINGDOM IS A "NEW HERO"...
...WHO WILL APPEAR IN THE BORDERLANDS...
COULD IT BE...
COULD THAT REALLY BE KÖINZELL...!?
SO WE BELIEVE...
SIR ROZEN, CAN WE REALLY...
...DIVULGE SO MUCH...?
IT HARDLY MATTERS.
THEY INEVITABLY WILL BE DRAGGED INTO THE BATTLE TOO.

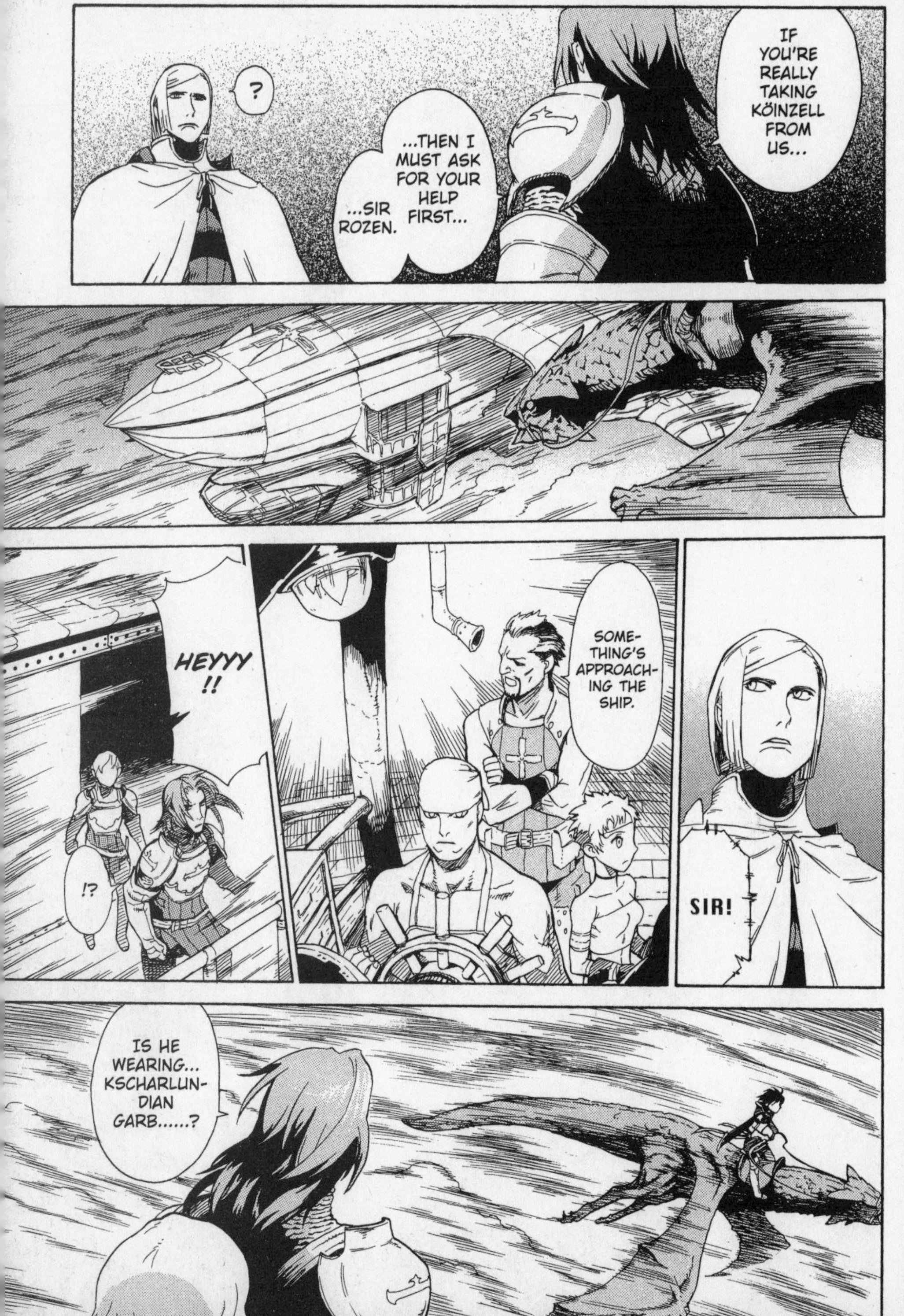
IF YOU'RE REALLY TAKING KÖINZELL FROM US...
...THEN I MUST ASK FOR YOUR HELP FIRST...
...SIR ROZEN.
?
SIR!
SOME-THING'S APPROACH-ING THE SHIP.
HEYYY !!
!?
IS HE WEARING... KSCHARLUN-DIAN GARB......?

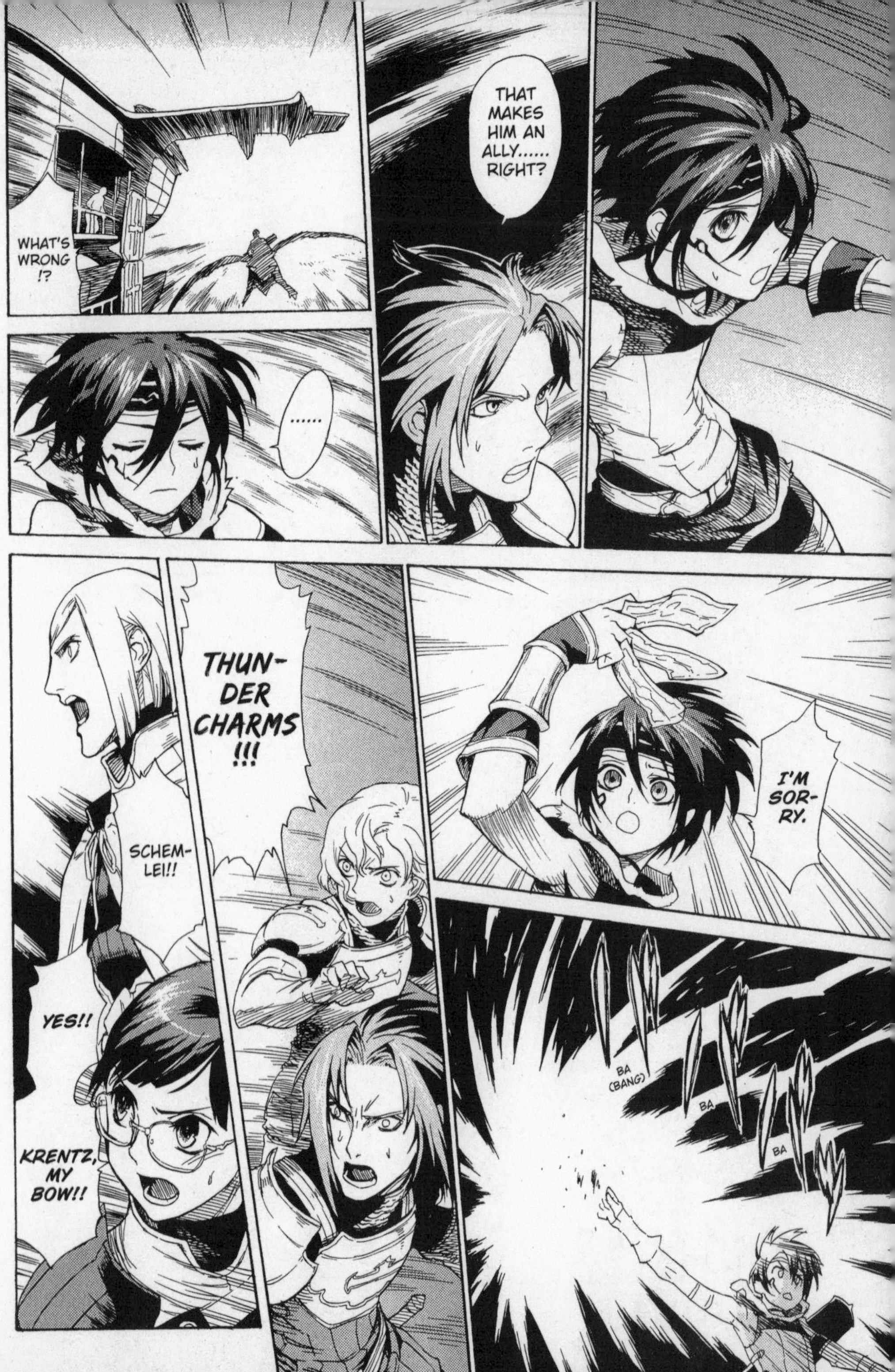
THAT MAKES HIM AN ALLY...... RIGHT?
WHAT'S WRONG !?
......
I'M SOR-RY.
BA (BANG)
BA
BA
THUN-DER CHARMS !!!
SCHEM-LEI!!
YES!!
KRENTZ, MY BOW!!

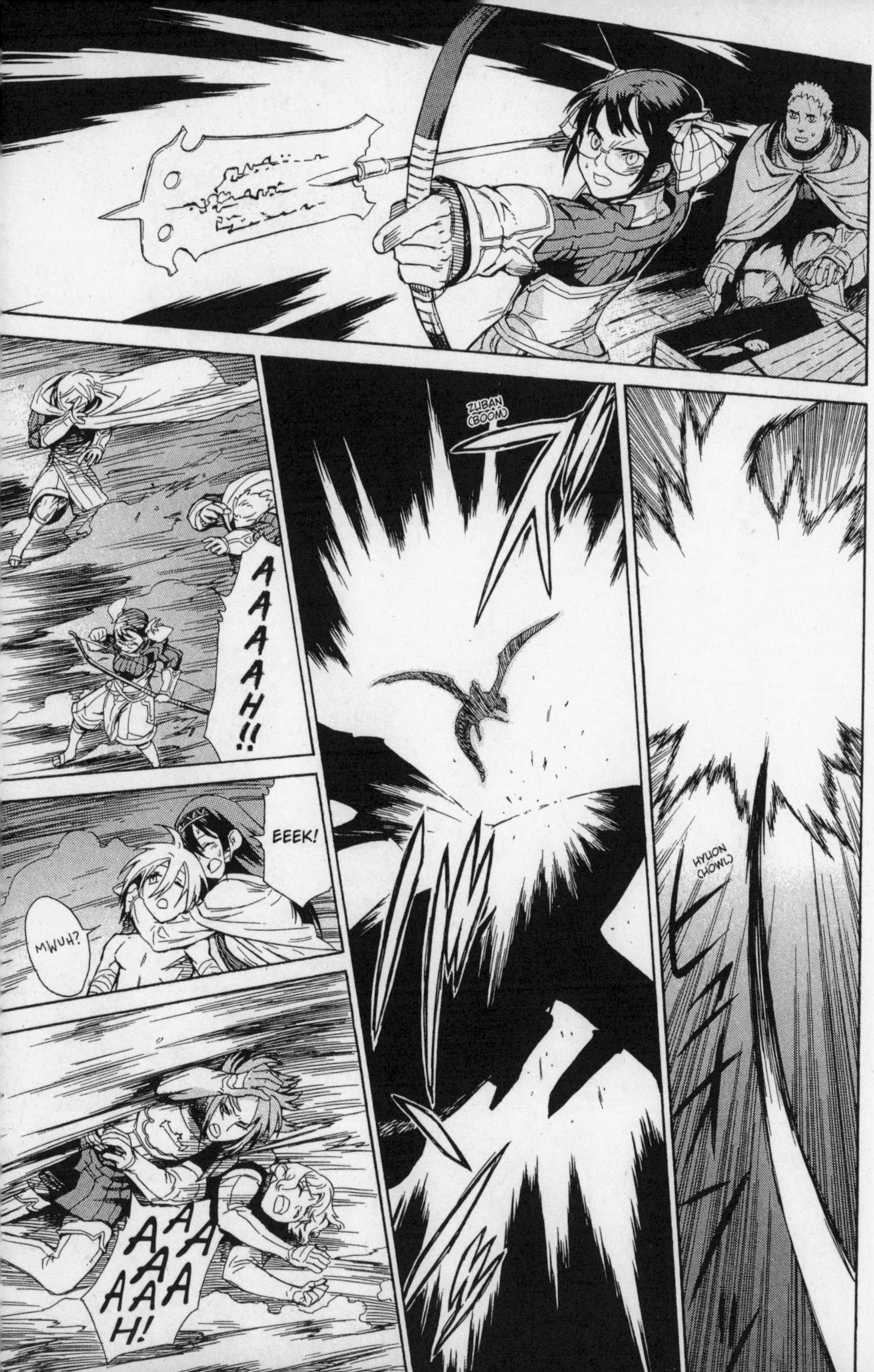
HYUON (HOWL)
ZUBAN (BOOM)
AAAAAAH!!
EEEK!
MWUH?
AAAAAAAAH!

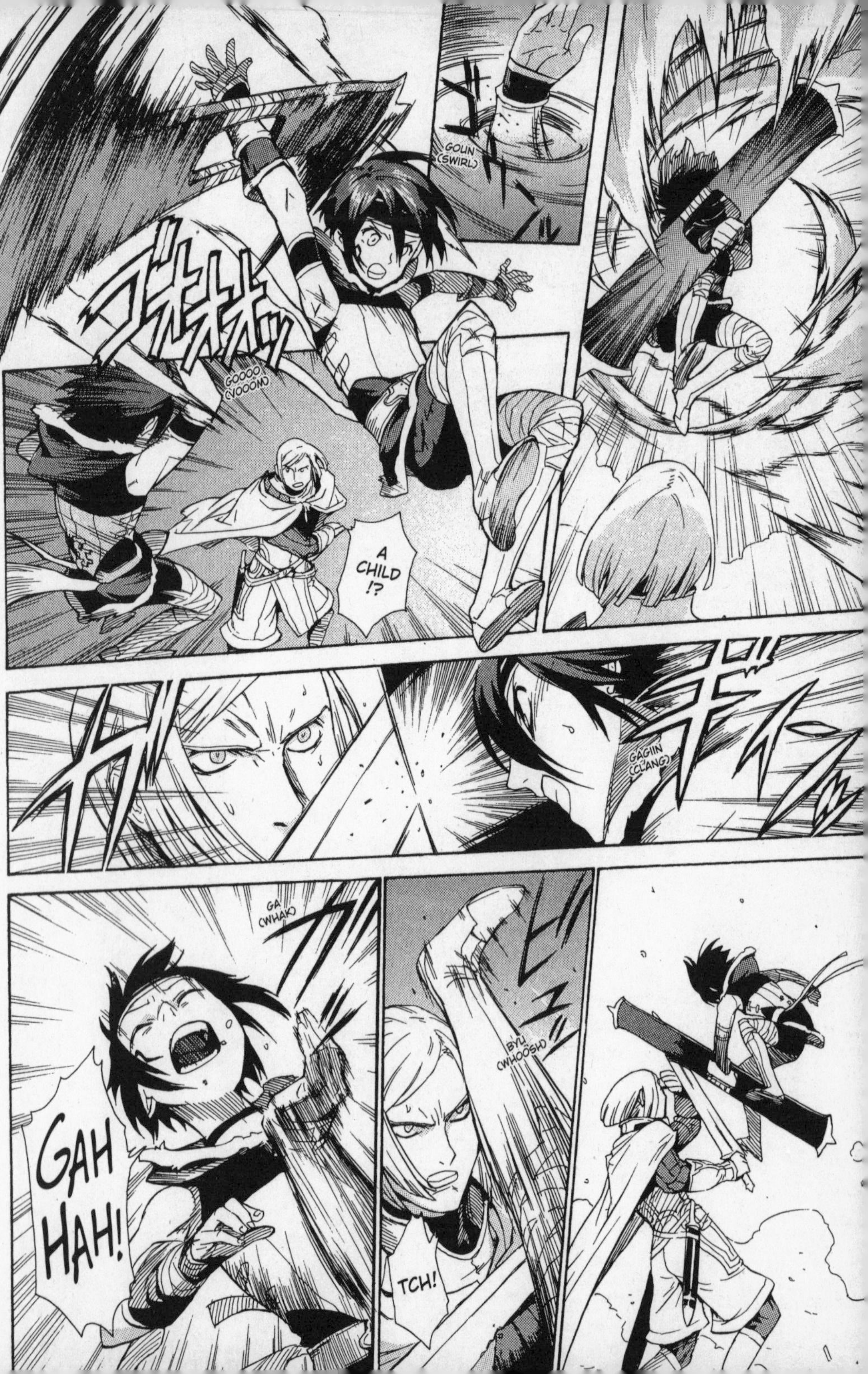
GOUN (SWIRL)
GOOOO (VOOOM)
A CHILD !?
GAGIIN (CLANG)
BYU (WHOOSH)
TCH!
GA (WHAK)
GAH HAH!

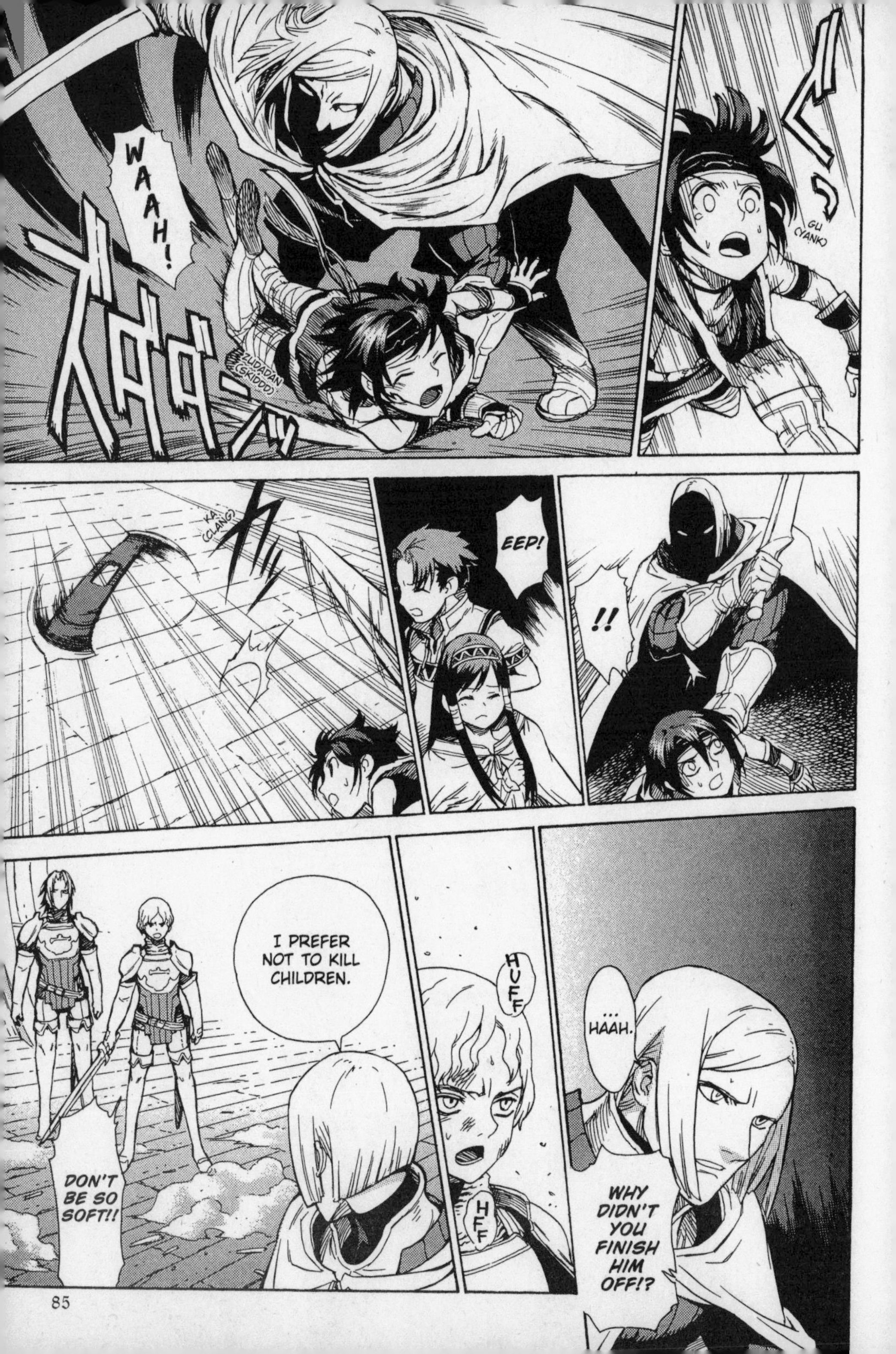
GU (YANK)
WAAAH!
ZUDADAN (SKIDDD)
!!
EEP!
KA (CLANG)
... HÄÄH.
WHY DIDN'T YOU FINISH HIM OFF!?
HUFF
HFF
I PREFER NOT TO KILL CHILDREN.
DON'T BE SO SOFT!!

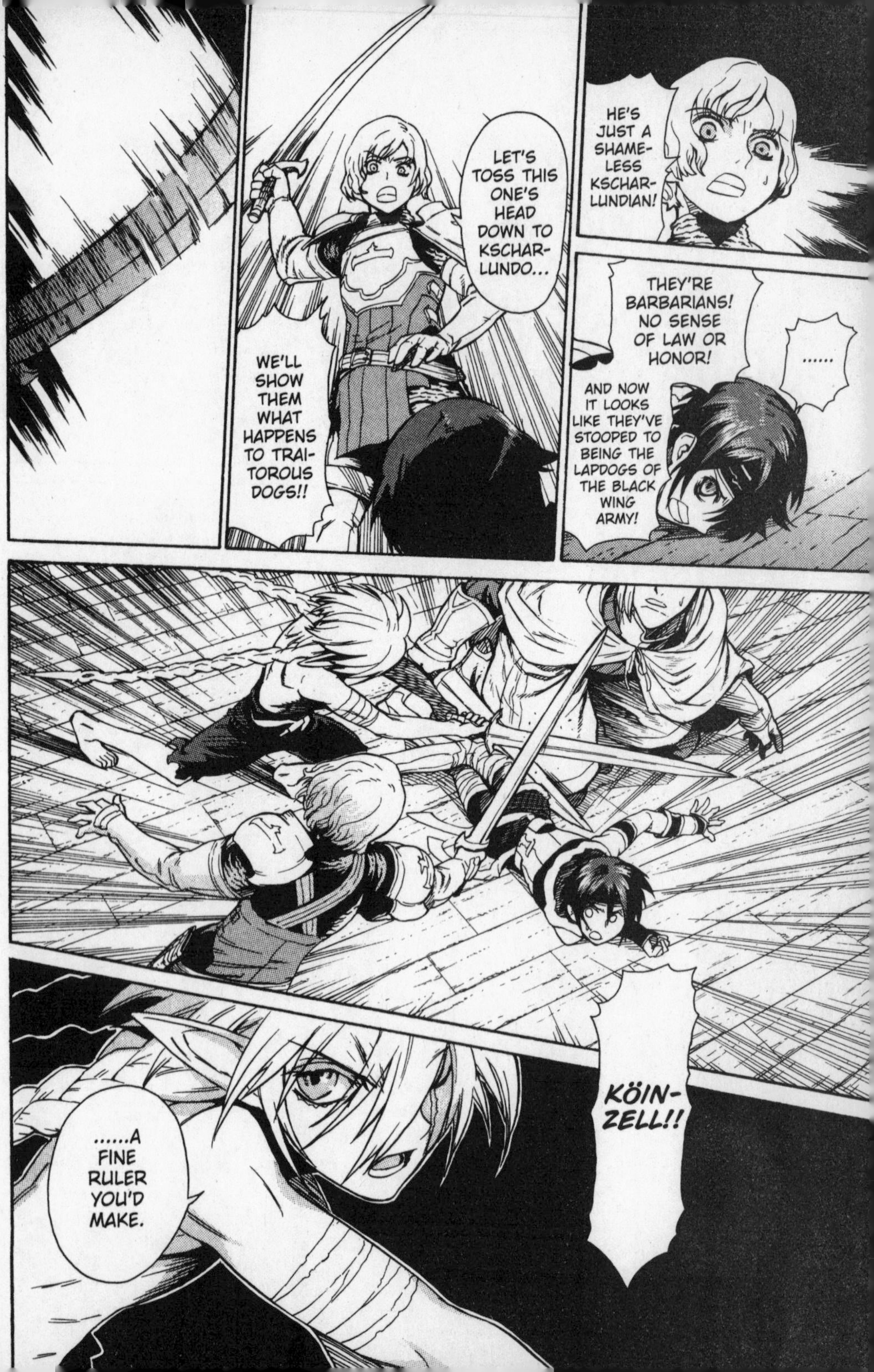
HE'S JUST A SHAMELESS KSCHARLUNDIAN!
THEY'RE BARBARIANS! NO SENSE OF LAW OR HONOR!
AND NOW IT LOOKS LIKE THEY'VE STOOPED TO BEING THE LAPDOGS OF THE BLACK WING ARMY!
......
LET'S TOSS THIS ONE'S HEAD DOWN TO KSCHARLUNDO...
WE'LL SHOW THEM WHAT HAPPENS TO TRAITOROUS DOGS!!
KÖIN-ZELL!!
......A FINE RULER YOU'D MAKE.

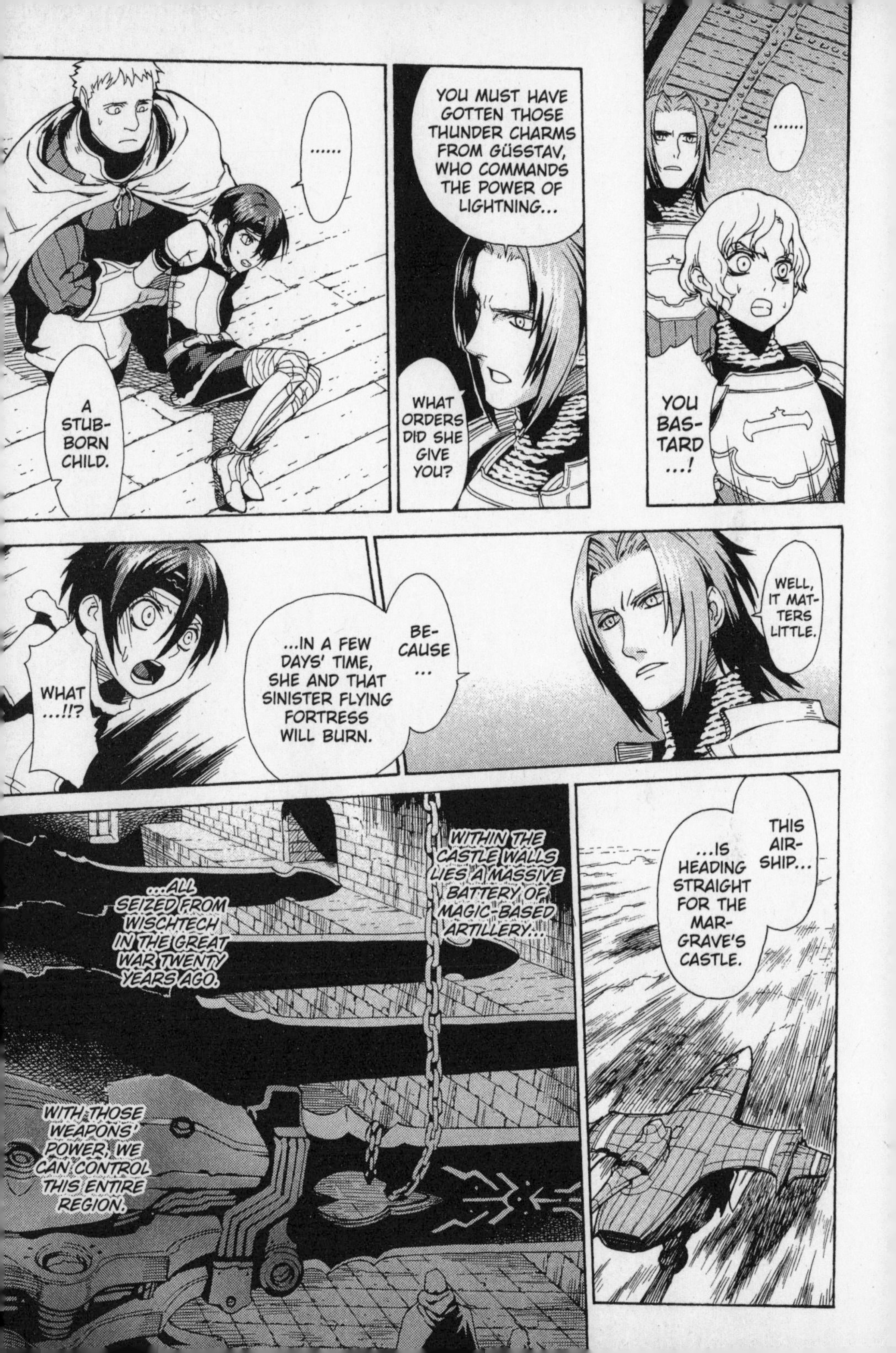
......
YOU BAS-TARD ...!
YOU MUST HAVE GOTTEN THOSE THUNDER CHARMS FROM GÜSSTAV, WHO COMMANDS THE POWER OF LIGHTNING...
WHAT ORDERS DID SHE GIVE YOU?
......
A STUB-BORN CHILD.
WELL, IT MAT-TERS LITTLE.
BE-CAUSE ...
...IN A FEW DAYS' TIME, SHE AND THAT SINISTER FLYING FORTRESS WILL BURN.
WHAT ...!!?
THIS AIR-SHIP...
...IS HEADING STRAIGHT FOR THE MAR-GRAVE'S CASTLE.
WITHIN THE CASTLE WALLS LIES A MASSIVE BATTERY OF MAGIC-BASED ARTILLERY...
...ALL SEIZED FROM WISCHTECH IN THE GREAT WAR TWENTY YEARS AGO.
WITH THOSE WEAPONS' POWER, WE CAN CONTROL THIS ENTIRE REGION.

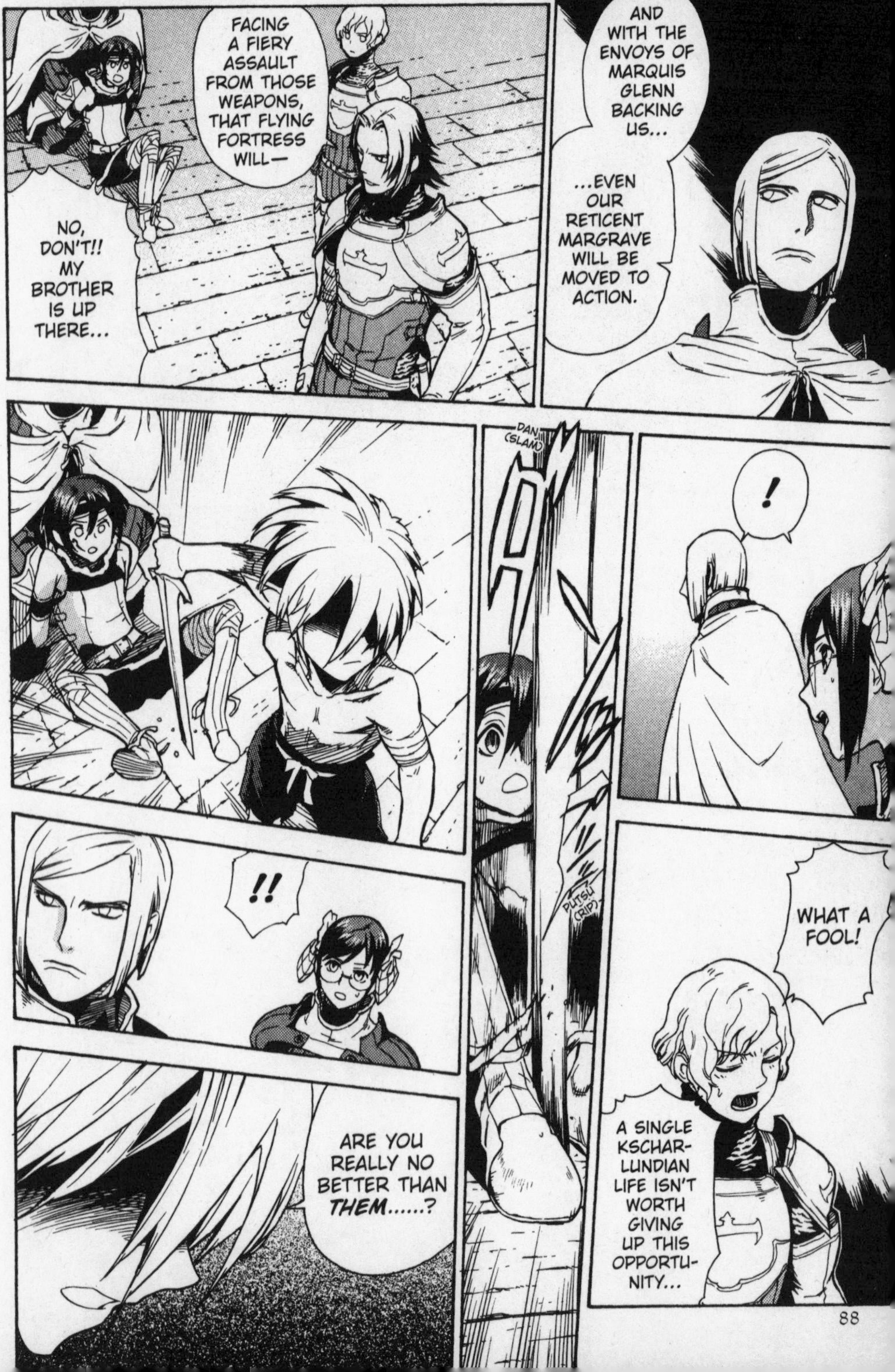
AND WITH THE ENVOYS OF MARQUIS GLENN BACKING US...
...EVEN OUR RETICENT MARGRAVE WILL BE MOVED TO ACTION.
FACING A FIERY ASSAULT FROM THOSE WEAPONS, THAT FLYING FORTRESS WILL—
NO, DON'T!! MY BROTHER IS UP THERE...
!
WHAT A FOOL!
A SINGLE KSCHARLUNDIAN LIFE ISN'T WORTH GIVING UP THIS OPPORTUNITY...
DAN (SLAM)
PUTSU (RIP)
!!
ARE YOU REALLY NO BETTER THAN *THEM*......?

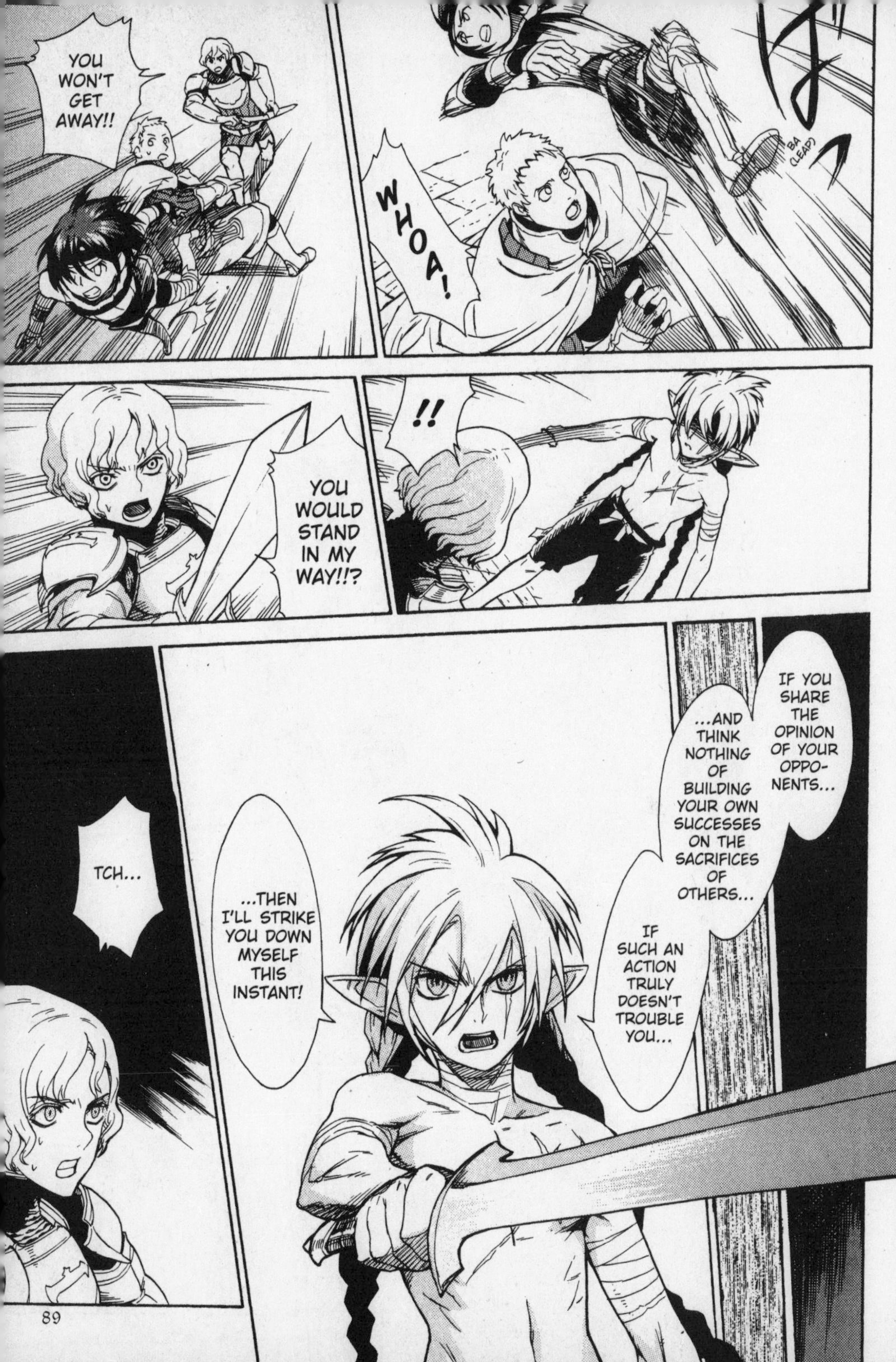
ばっ
BA (LEAP)
WHOA!
YOU WON'T GET AWAY!!
!!
YOU WOULD STAND IN MY WAY!!?
IF YOU SHARE THE OPINION OF YOUR OPPO-NENTS...
...AND THINK NOTHING OF BUILDING YOUR OWN SUCCESSES ON THE SACRIFICES OF OTHERS...
IF SUCH AN ACTION TRULY DOESN'T TROUBLE YOU...
...THEN I'LL STRIKE YOU DOWN MYSELF THIS INSTANT!
TCH...

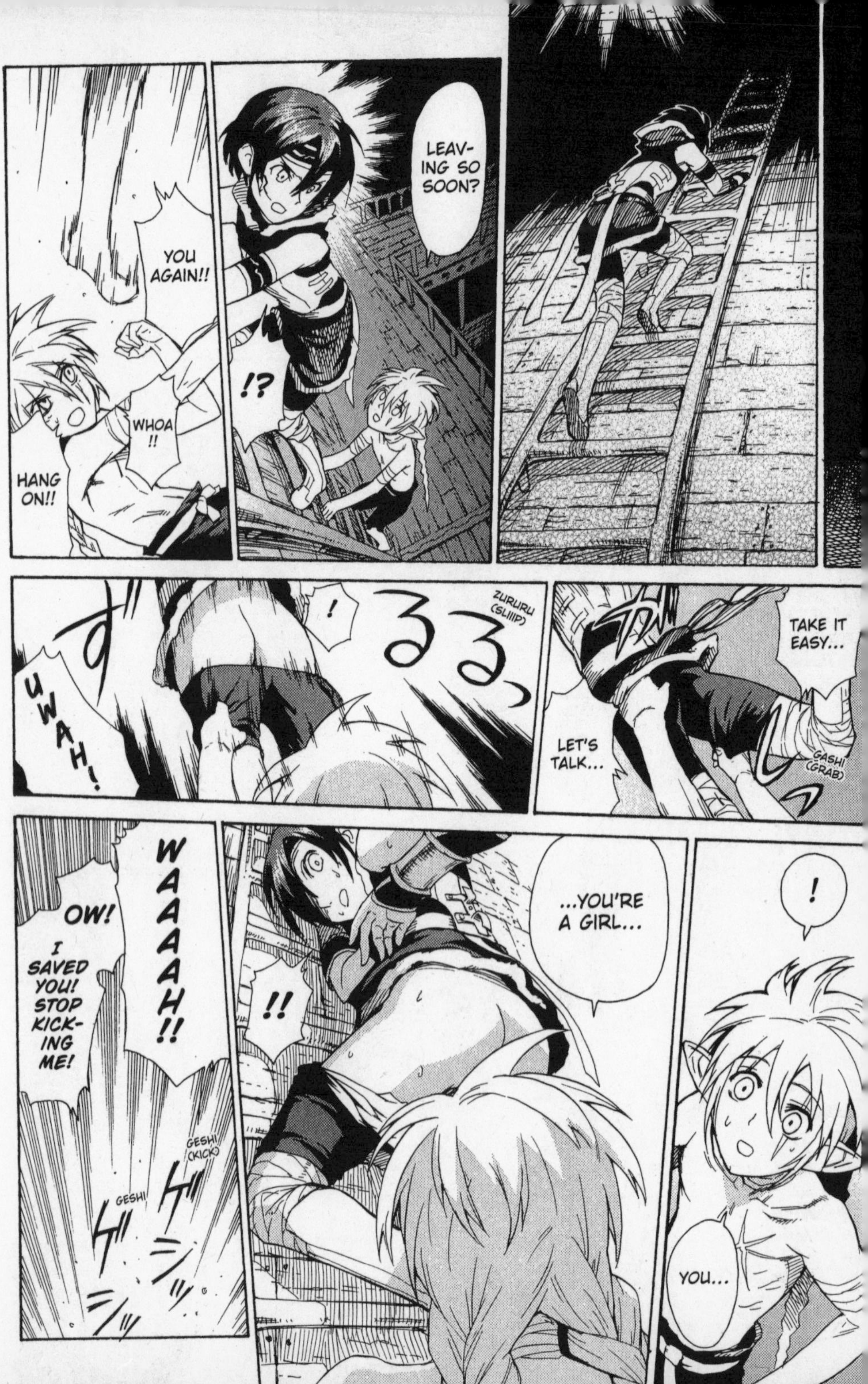
LEAVING SO SOON?
!?
YOU AGAIN!!
WHOA !!
HANG ON!!
TAKE IT EASY...
LET'S TALK...
GASHI (GRAB)
ZURURU (SLIIIP)
!
ずるるっ
UWAH!
!
YOU...
...YOU'RE A GIRL...
!!
WAAAAAH!!
OW! I SAVED YOU! STOP KICKING ME!
GESHI (KICK)
GESHI

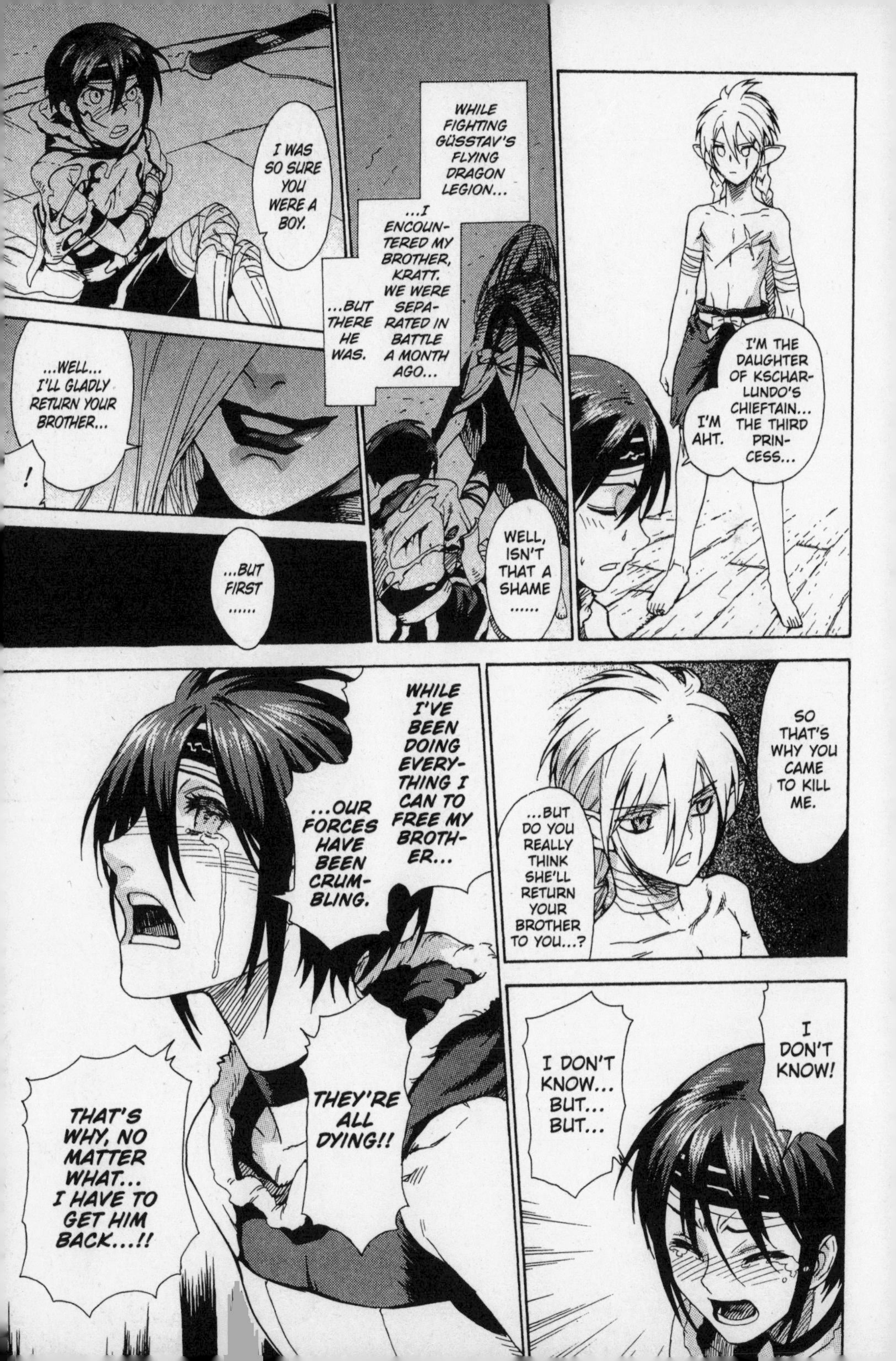
I'M THE DAUGHTER OF KSCHARLUNDO'S CHIEFTAIN... THE THIRD PRINCESS...
I'M AHT.
WELL, ISN'T THAT A SHAME ......
I WAS SO SURE YOU WERE A BOY.
WHILE FIGHTING GÜSSTAV'S FLYING DRAGON LEGION...
...I ENCOUNTERED MY BROTHER, KRATT. WE WERE SEPARATED IN BATTLE A MONTH AGO...
...BUT THERE HE WAS.
...WELL... I'LL GLADLY RETURN YOUR BROTHER...
!
...BUT FIRST ......
SO THAT'S WHY YOU CAME TO KILL ME.
...BUT DO YOU REALLY THINK SHE'LL RETURN YOUR BROTHER TO YOU...?
I DON'T KNOW!
I DON'T KNOW... BUT... BUT...
WHILE I'VE BEEN DOING EVERYTHING I CAN TO FREE MY BROTHER...
...OUR FORCES HAVE BEEN CRUMBLING.
THEY'RE ALL DYING!!
THAT'S WHY, NO MATTER WHAT... I HAVE TO GET HIM BACK...!!

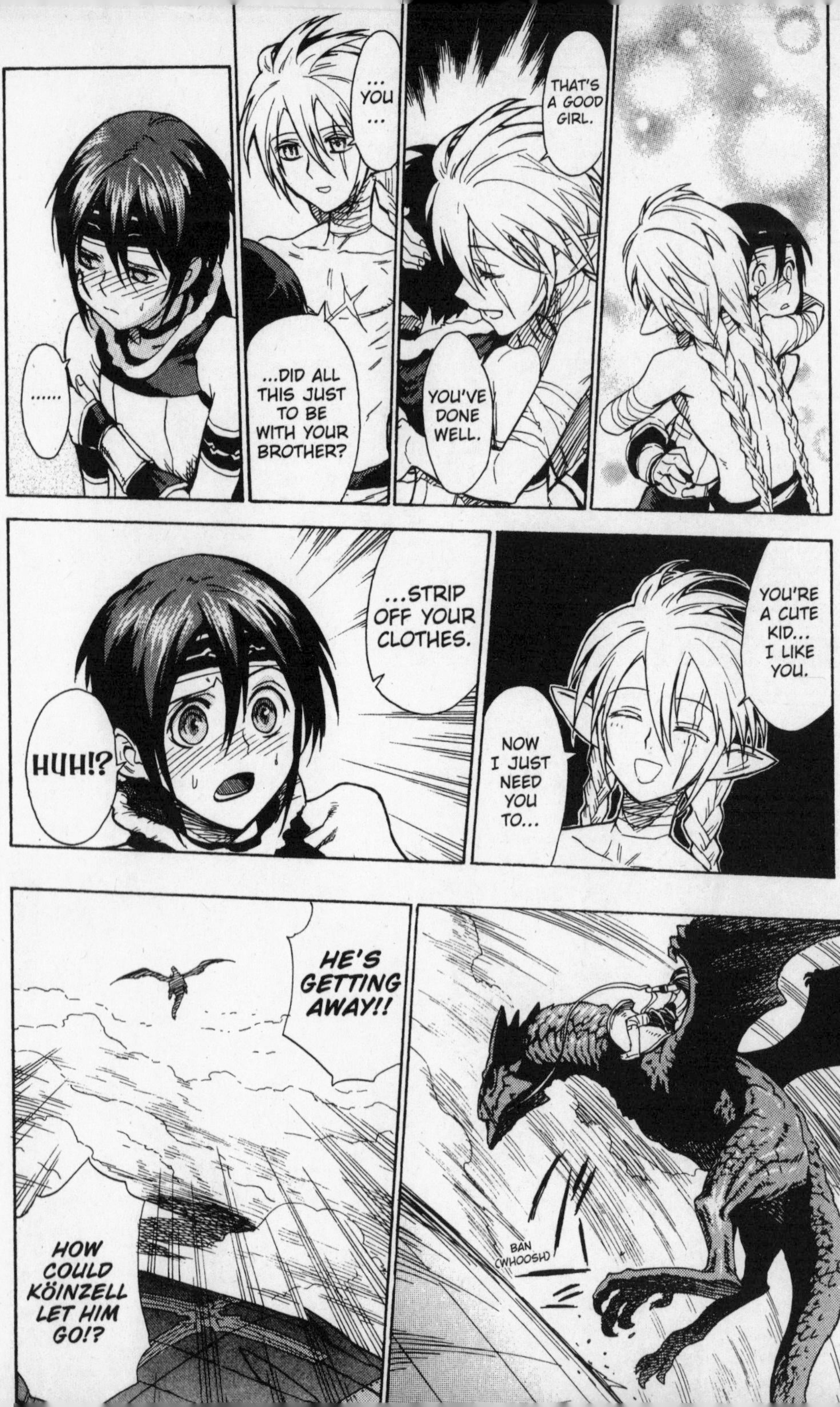

THAT'S A GOOD GIRL.
YOU'VE DONE WELL.
... YOU ...
...DID ALL THIS JUST TO BE WITH YOUR BROTHER?
......
YOU'RE A CUTE KID... I LIKE YOU.
NOW I JUST NEED YOU TO...
...STRIP OFF YOUR CLOTHES.
HUH!?
BAN (WHOOSH)
HE'S GETTING AWAY!!
HOW COULD KÖINZELL LET HIM GO!?

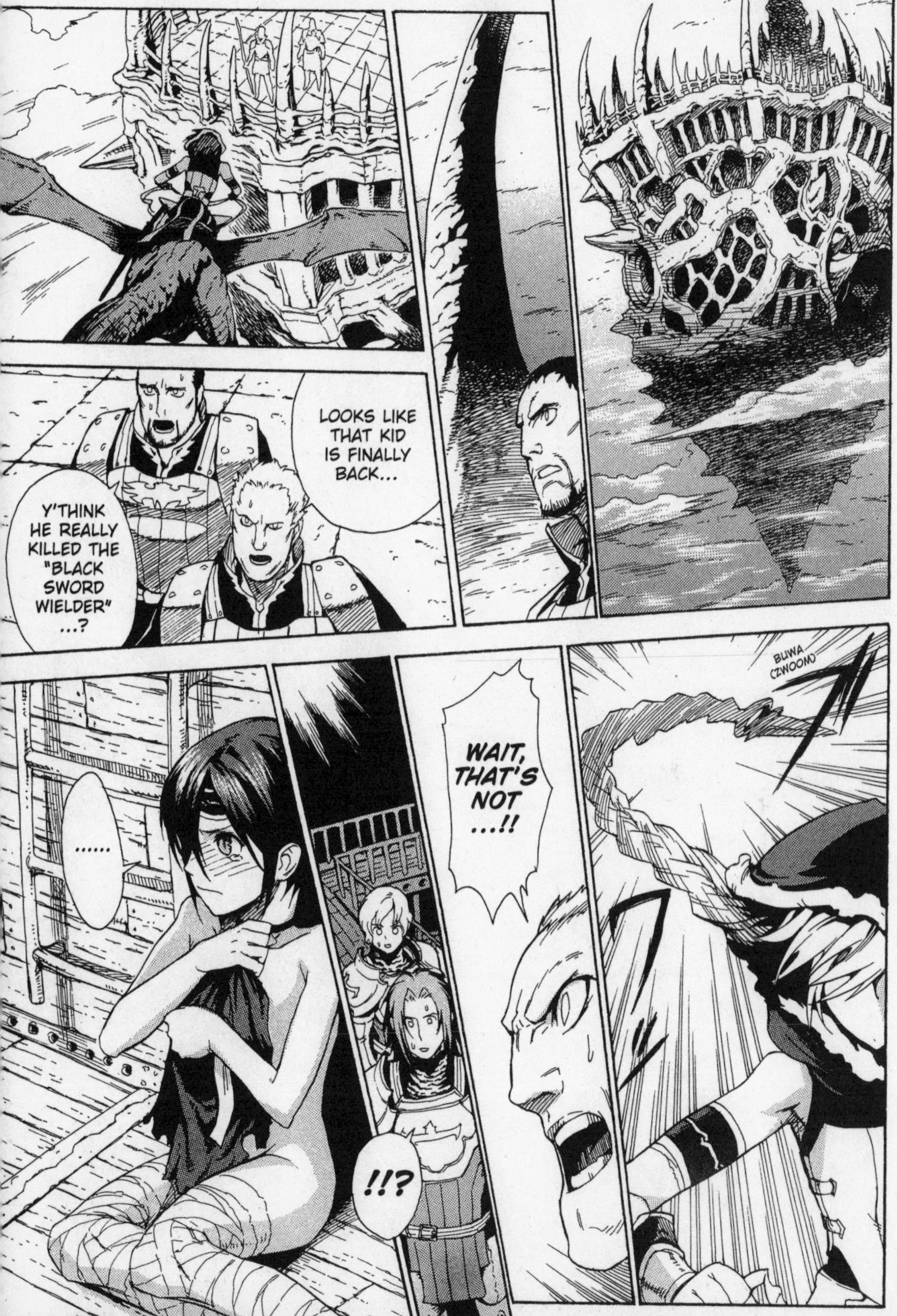
LOOKS LIKE THAT KID IS FINALLY BACK...
Y'THINK HE REALLY KILLED THE "BLACK SWORD WIELDER" ...?
BUWA (ZWOOM)
WAIT, THAT'S NOT ...!!
!!?
......

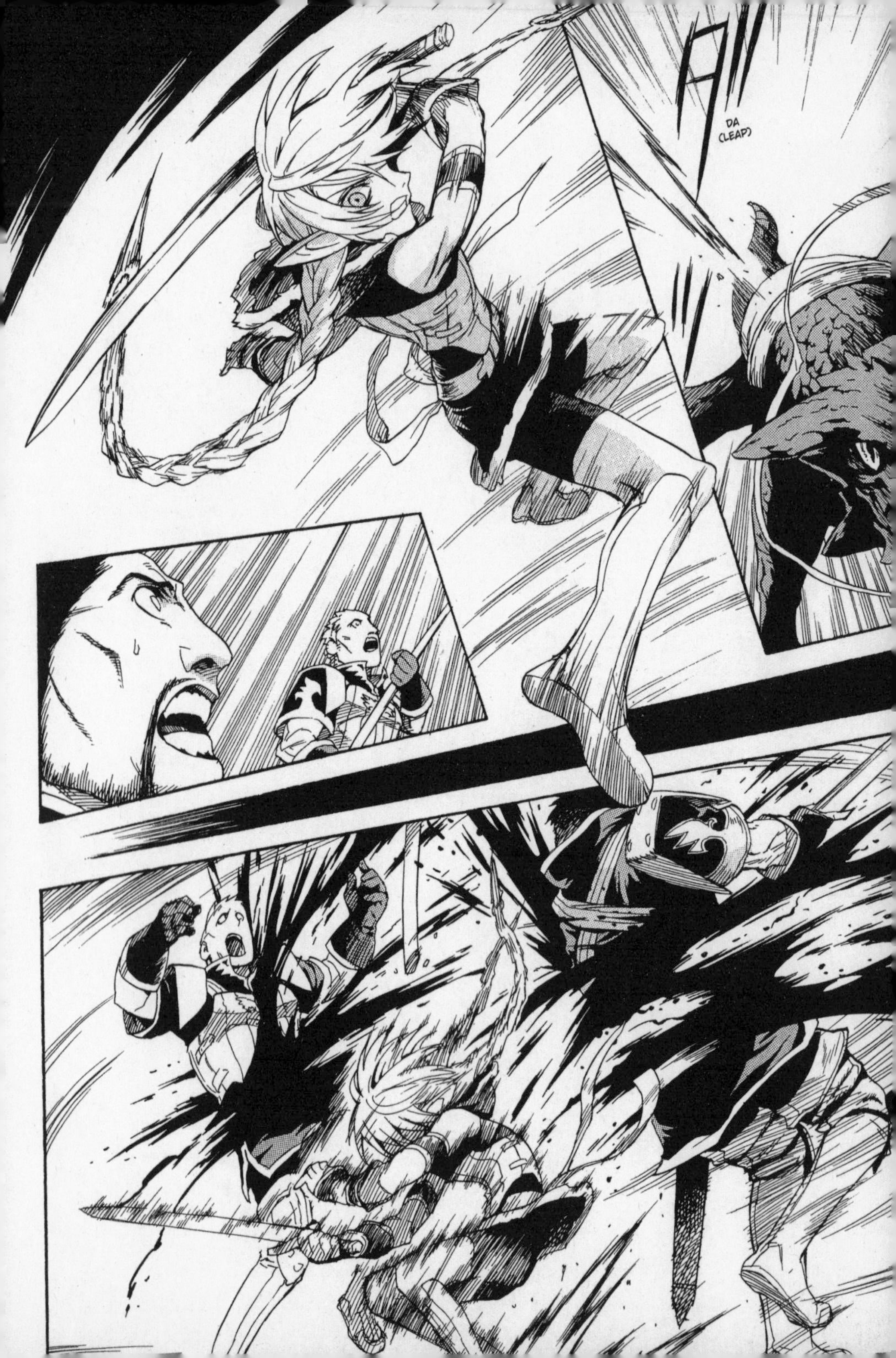
DA
(LEAP)

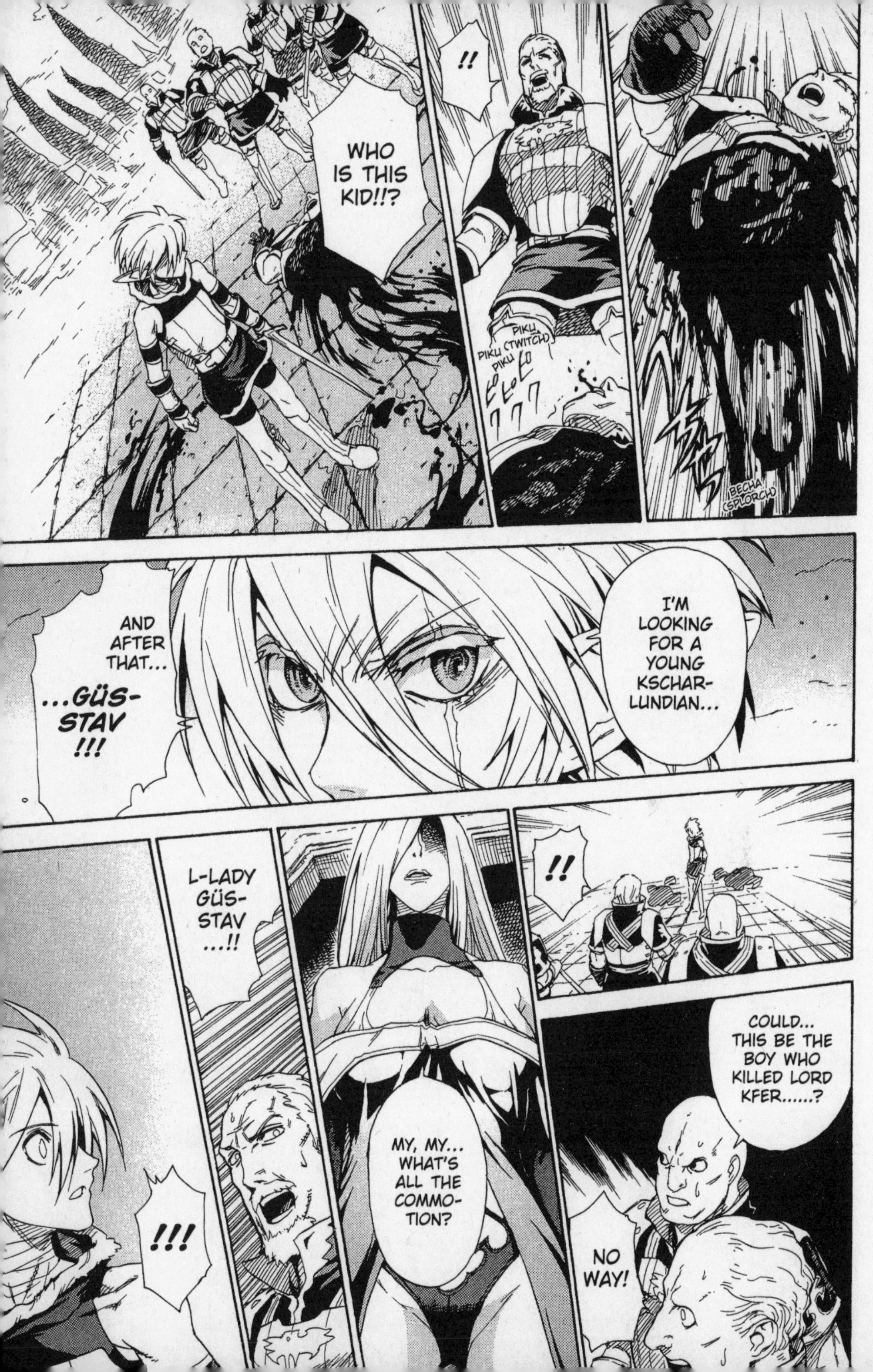
BECHA (SPLORCH)
!!
PIKU PIKU PIKU (TWITCH)
ピクピクピク
WHO IS THIS KID!!?
I'M LOOKING FOR A YOUNG KSCHARLUNDIAN...
AND AFTER THAT...
...GÜS-STAV!!!
!!
COULD... THIS BE THE BOY WHO KILLED LORD KFER......?
NO WAY!
MY, MY... WHAT'S ALL THE COMMOTION?
L-LADY GÜS-STAV...!!
!!!

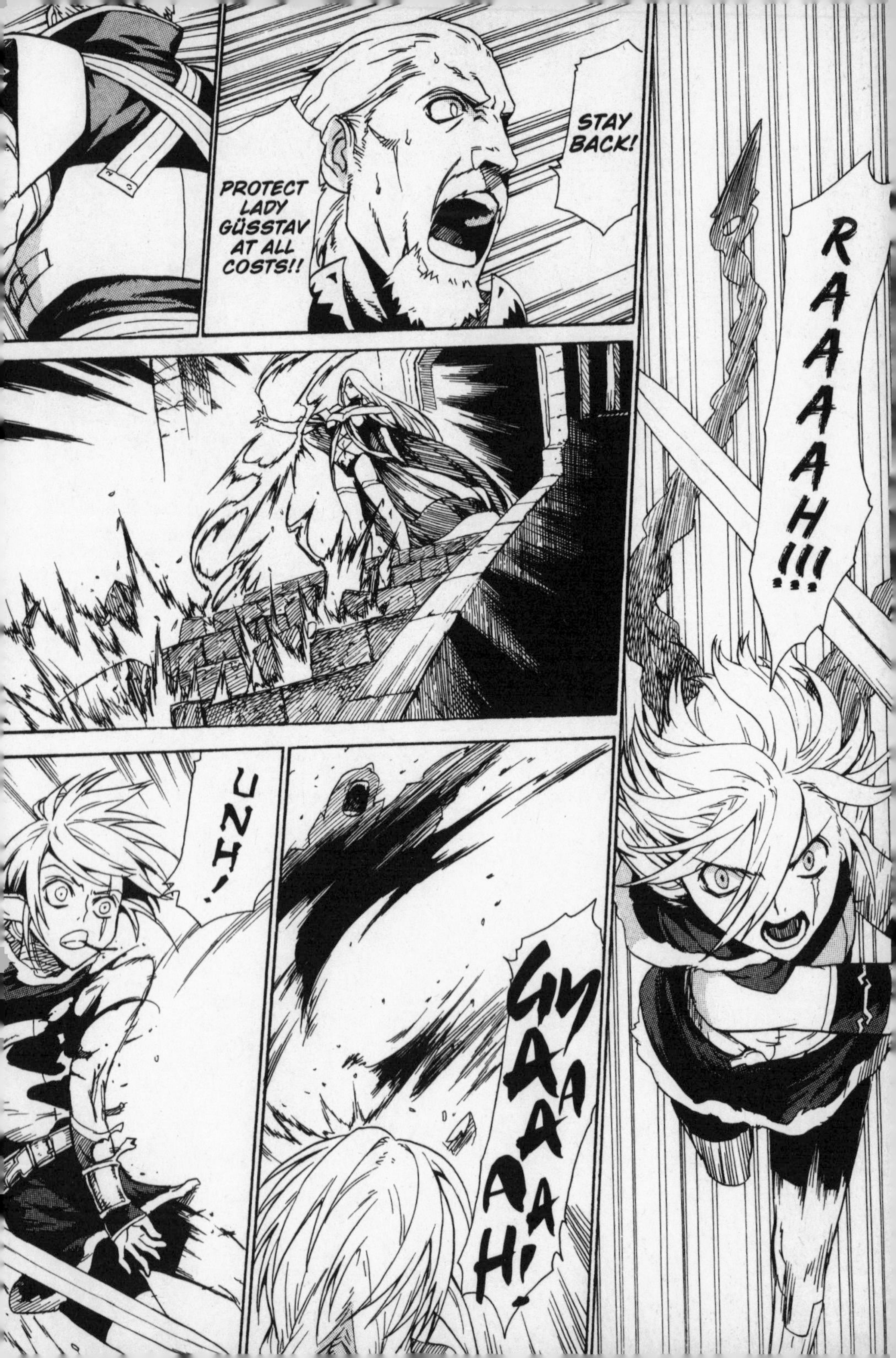
RAAAAH!!!
STAY BACK!
PROTECT LADY GÜSSTAV AT ALL COSTS!!
GYAAAAAH!
UNH!

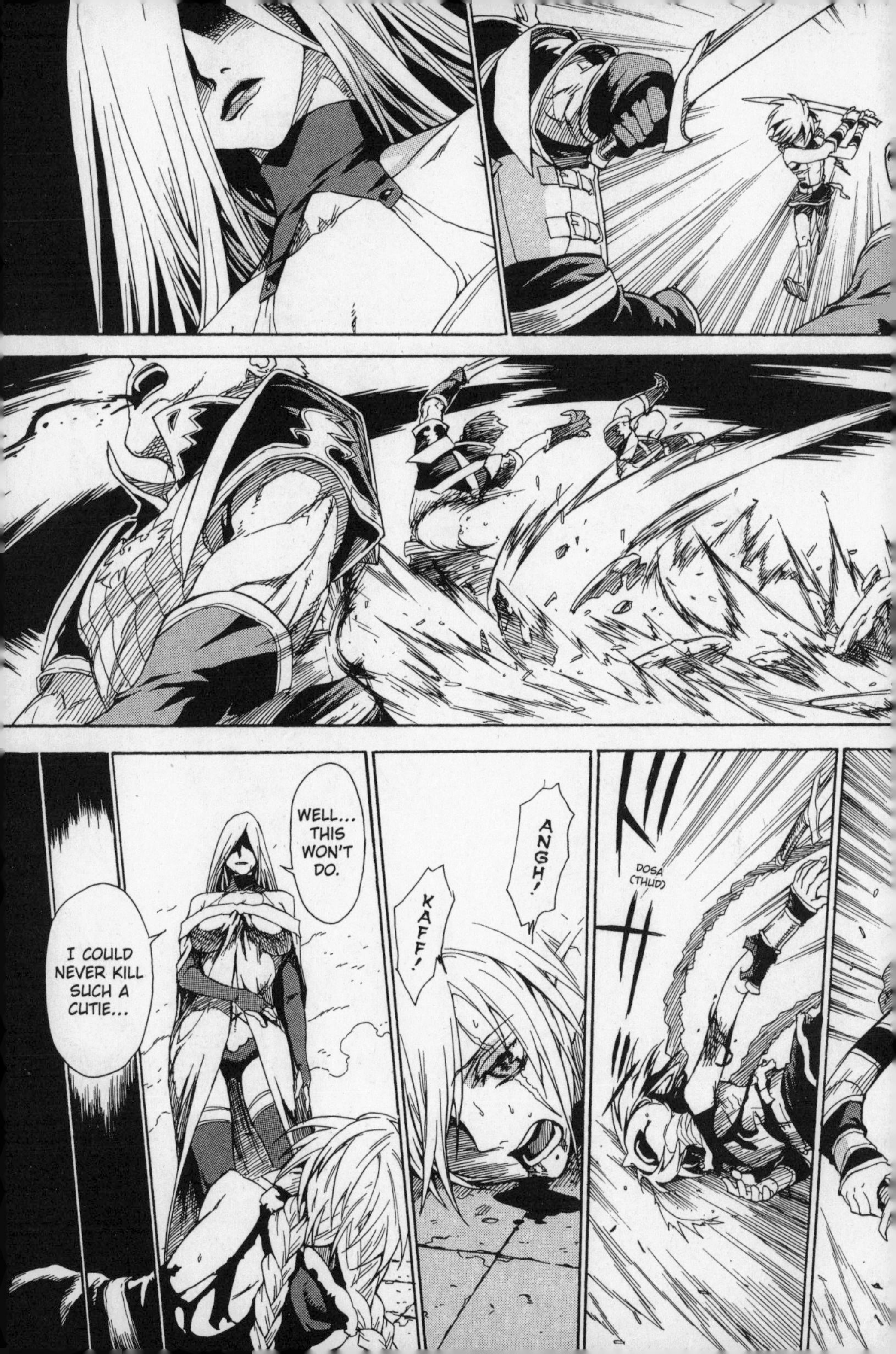
DOSA (THUD)
ANGH!
KAFF!
WELL... THIS WON'T DO.
I COULD NEVER KILL SUCH A CUTIE...

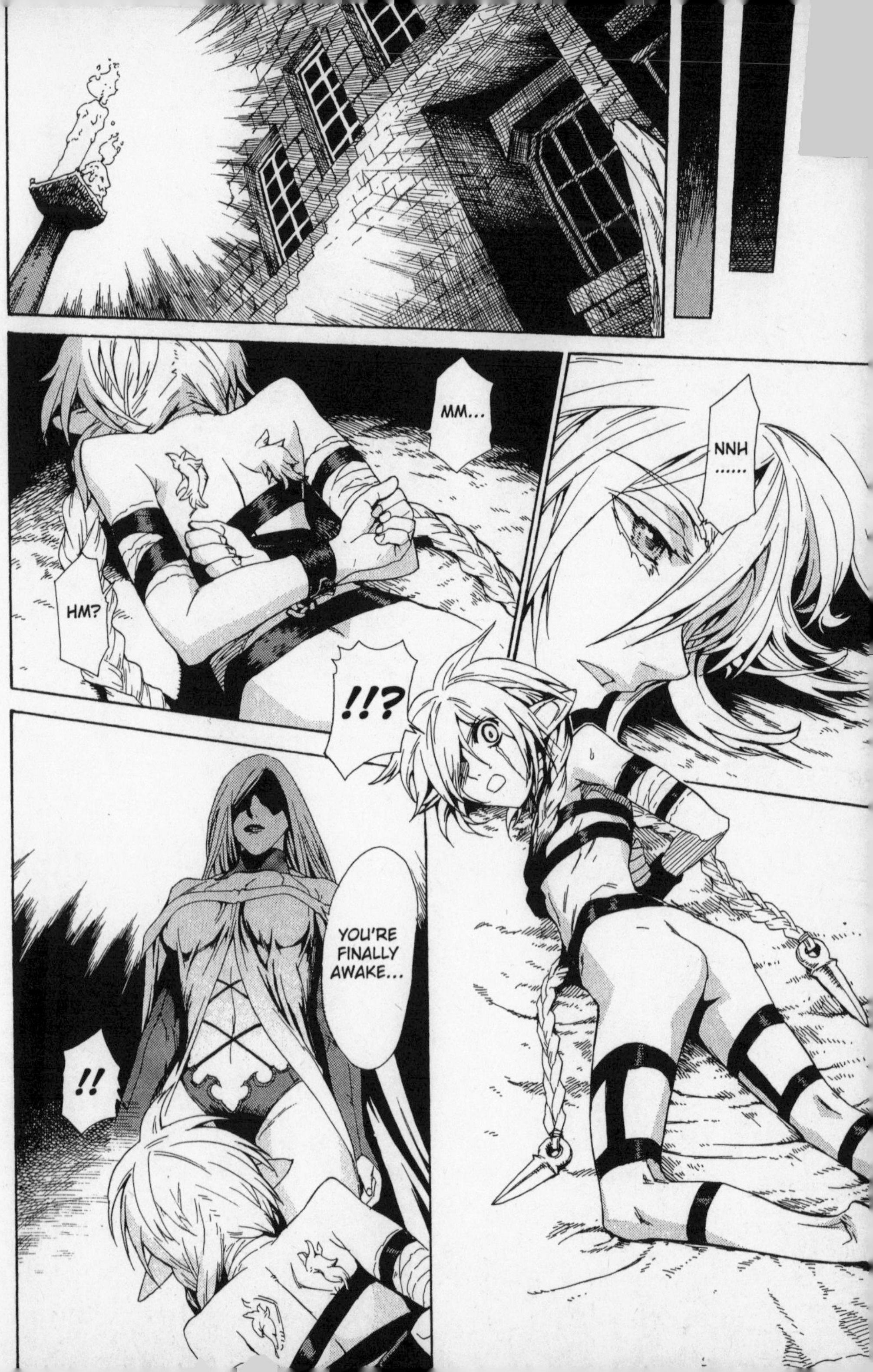
NNH ......
MM...
HM?
!!?
YOU'RE FINALLY AWAKE...
!!

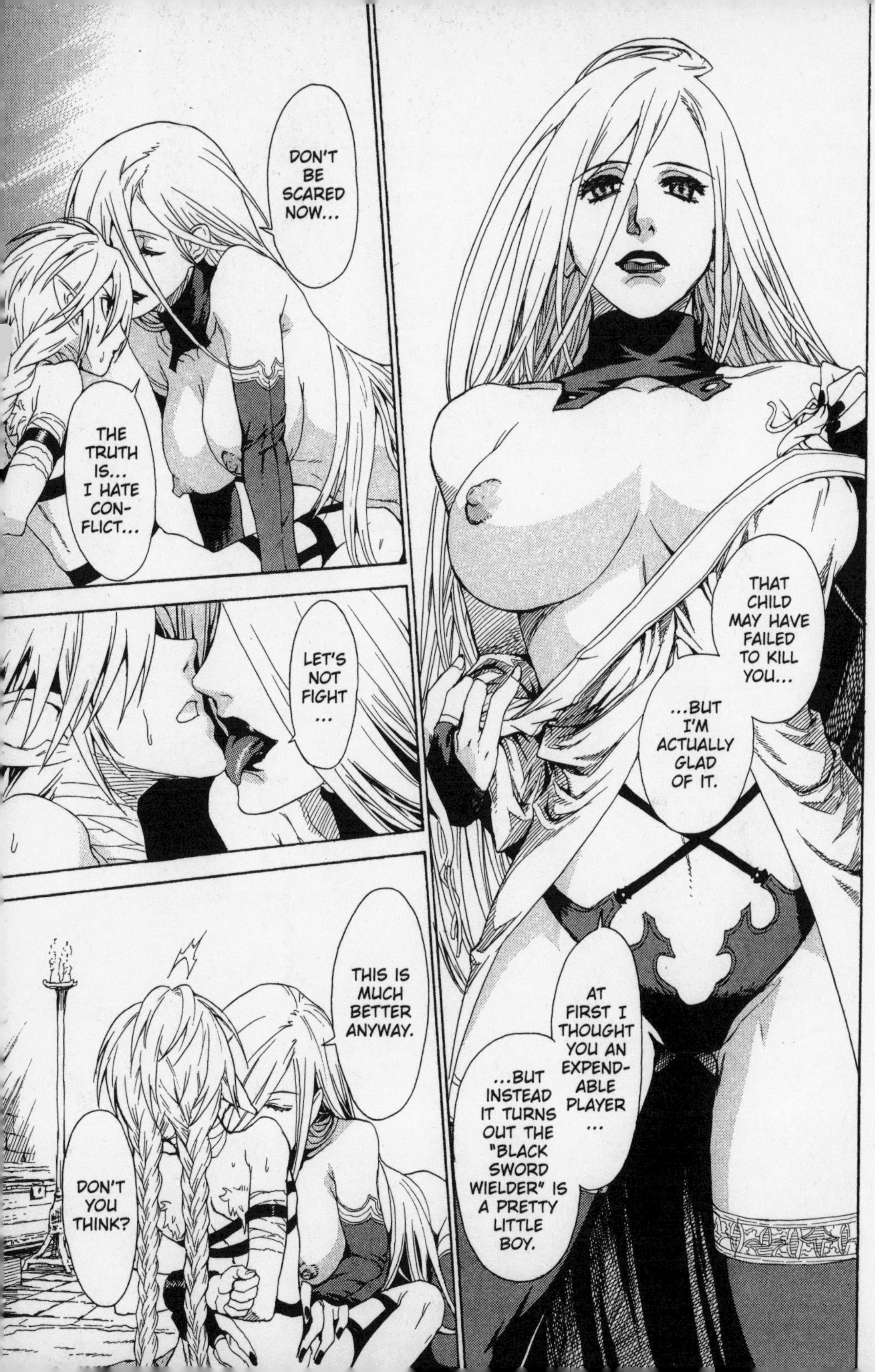
THAT CHILD MAY HAVE FAILED TO KILL YOU...
...BUT I'M ACTUALLY GLAD OF IT.
AT FIRST I THOUGHT YOU AN EXPEND-ABLE PLAYER...
...BUT INSTEAD IT TURNS OUT THE "BLACK SWORD WIELDER" IS A PRETTY LITTLE BOY.
DON'T BE SCARED NOW...
THE TRUTH IS... I HATE CON-FLICT...
LET'S NOT FIGHT...
THIS IS MUCH BETTER ANYWAY.
DON'T YOU THINK?

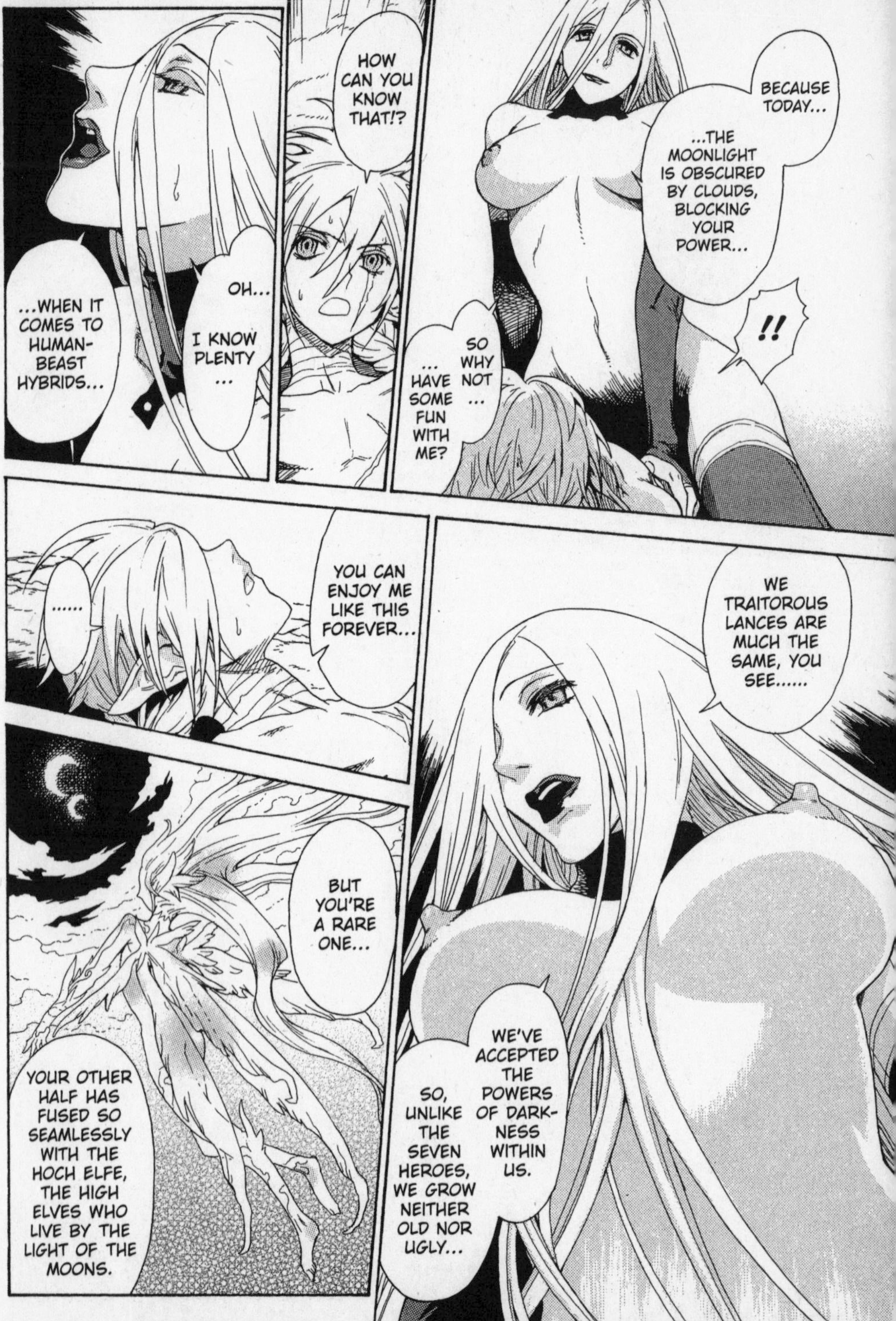
BECAUSE TODAY...
...THE MOONLIGHT IS OBSCURED BY CLOUDS, BLOCKING YOUR POWER...
!!
SO WHY NOT ...
... HAVE SOME FUN WITH ME?
HOW CAN YOU KNOW THAT!?
OH...
I KNOW PLENTY ...
...WHEN IT COMES TO HUMAN-BEAST HYBRIDS...
WE TRAITOROUS LANCES ARE MUCH THE SAME, YOU SEE......
WE'VE ACCEPTED THE POWERS OF DARKNESS WITHIN US.
SO, UNLIKE THE SEVEN HEROES, WE GROW NEITHER OLD NOR UGLY...
YOU CAN ENJOY ME LIKE THIS FOREVER...
......
BUT YOU'RE A RARE ONE...
YOUR OTHER HALF HAS FUSED SO SEAMLESSLY WITH THE HOCH ELFE, THE HIGH ELVES WHO LIVE BY THE LIGHT OF THE MOONS.

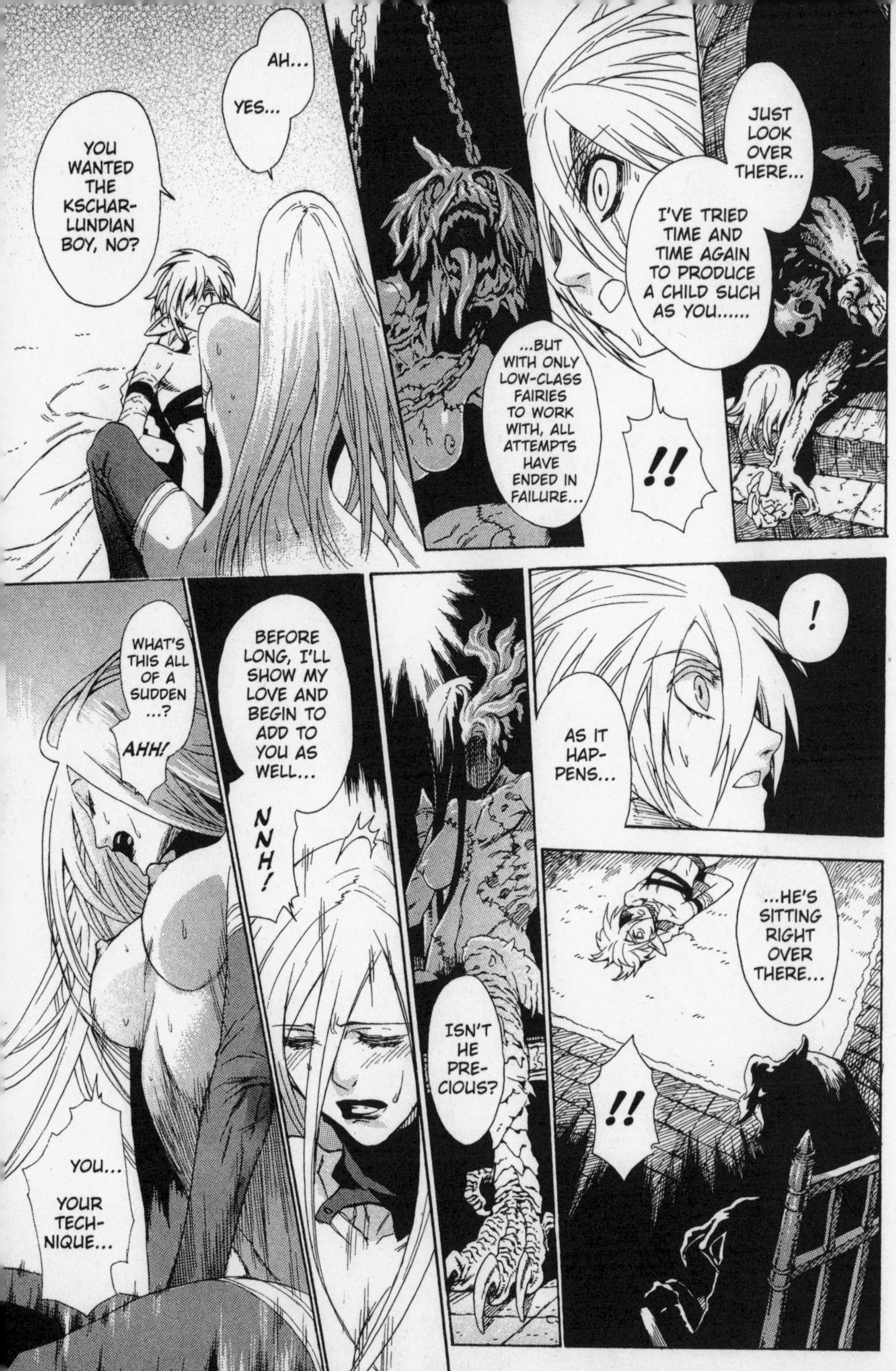
JUST LOOK OVER THERE...
I'VE TRIED TIME AND TIME AGAIN TO PRODUCE A CHILD SUCH AS YOU......
!!
...BUT WITH ONLY LOW-CLASS FAIRIES TO WORK WITH, ALL ATTEMPTS HAVE ENDED IN FAILURE...
AH... YES...
YOU WANTED THE KSCHAR-LUNDIAN BOY, NO?
!
AS IT HAP-PENS...
...HE'S SITTING RIGHT OVER THERE...
!!
ISN'T HE PRE-CIOUS?
BEFORE LONG, I'LL SHOW MY LOVE AND BEGIN TO ADD TO YOU AS WELL...
NNH!
WHAT'S THIS ALL OF A SUDDEN ...?
AHH!
YOU... YOUR TECH-NIQUE...

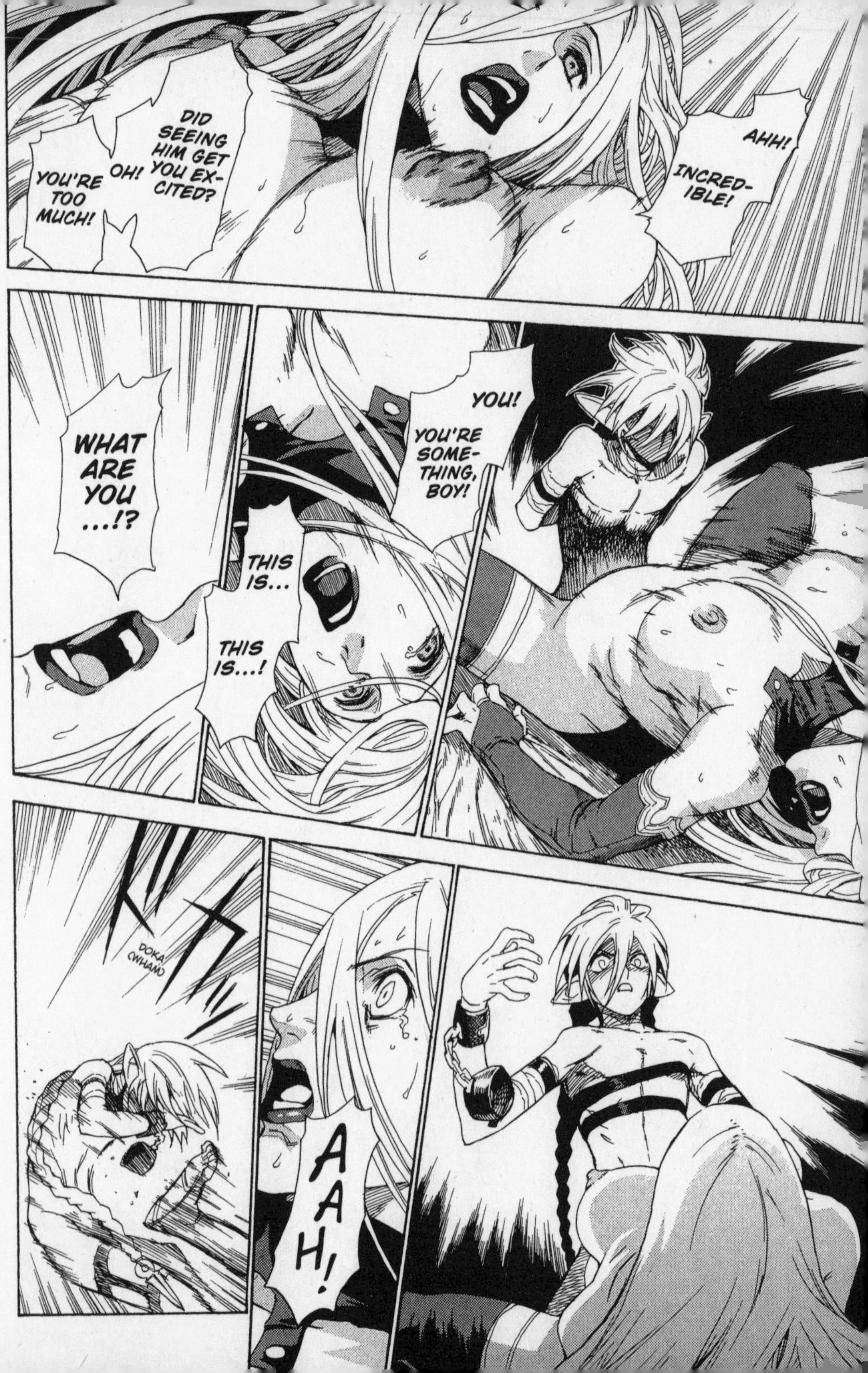
AHH! INCREDIBLE!
DID SEEING HIM GET YOU EXCITED?
OH! YOU'RE TOO MUCH!
YOU! YOU'RE SOMETHING, BOY!
THIS IS... THIS IS...!
WHAT ARE YOU ...!?
AAH!
DOKA (WHAM)

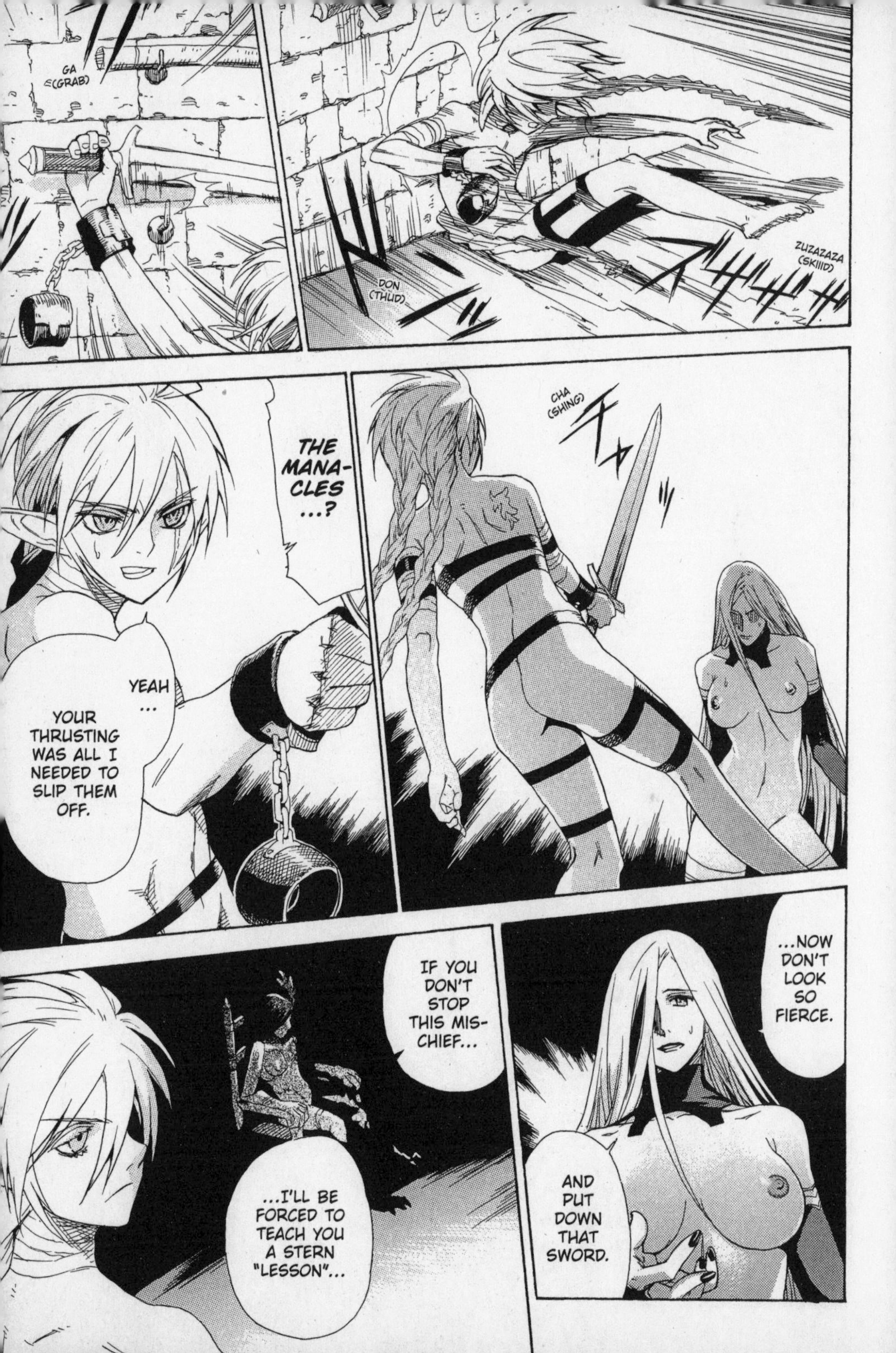
ZUZAZAZA (SKIIID)
DON (THUD)
GA (GRAB)
CHA (SHING)
THE MANA-CLES ...?
YEAH ...
YOUR THRUSTING WAS ALL I NEEDED TO SLIP THEM OFF.
...NOW DON'T LOOK SO FIERCE.
AND PUT DOWN THAT SWORD.
IF YOU DON'T STOP THIS MIS-CHIEF...
...I'LL BE FORCED TO TEACH YOU A STERN "LESSON"...

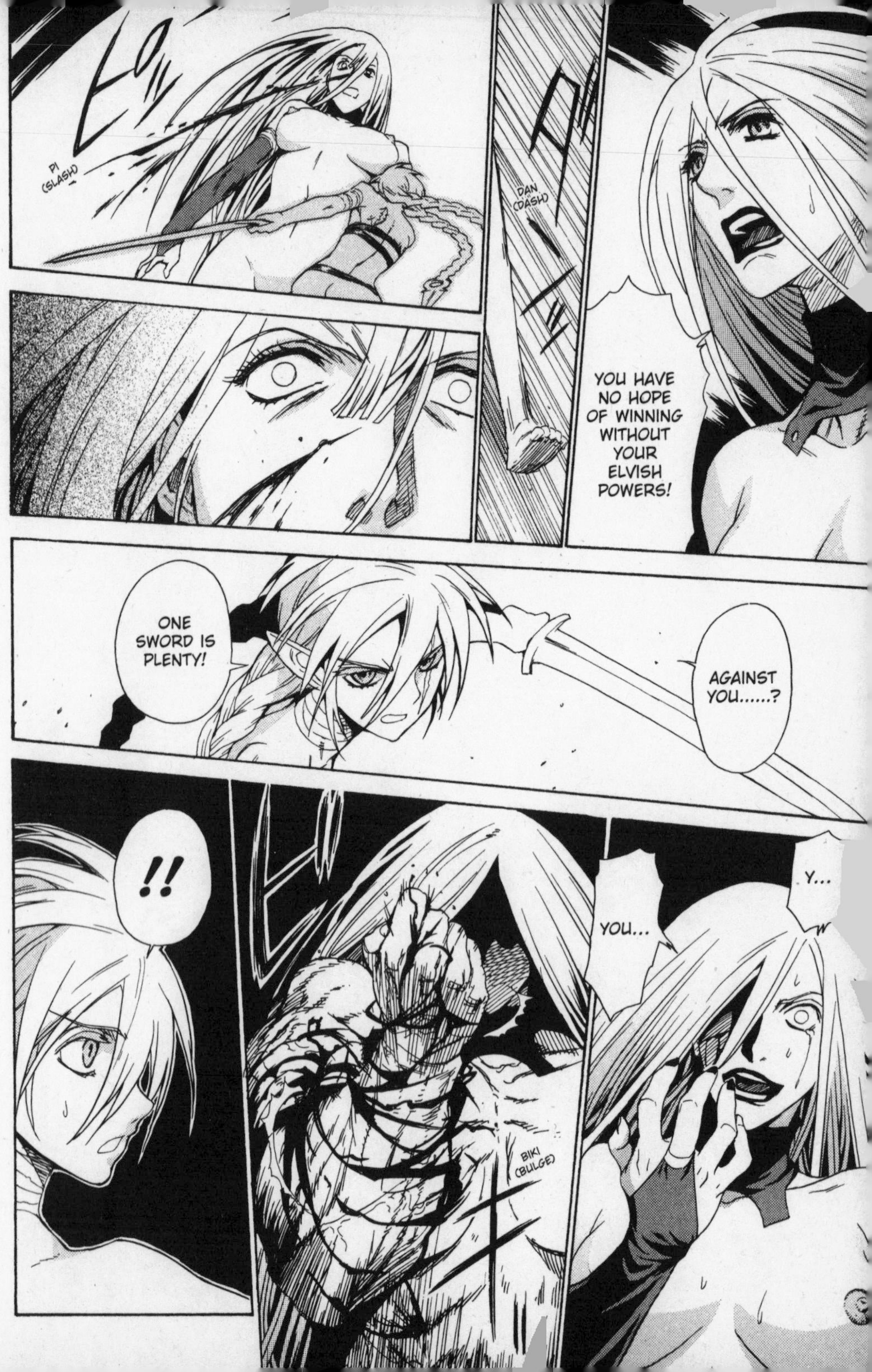
YOU HAVE NO HOPE OF WINNING WITHOUT YOUR ELVISH POWERS!
DAN (DASH)
PI (SLASH)
AGAINST YOU......?
ONE SWORD IS PLENTY!
Y...
YOU...
BIKI (BULGE)
!!

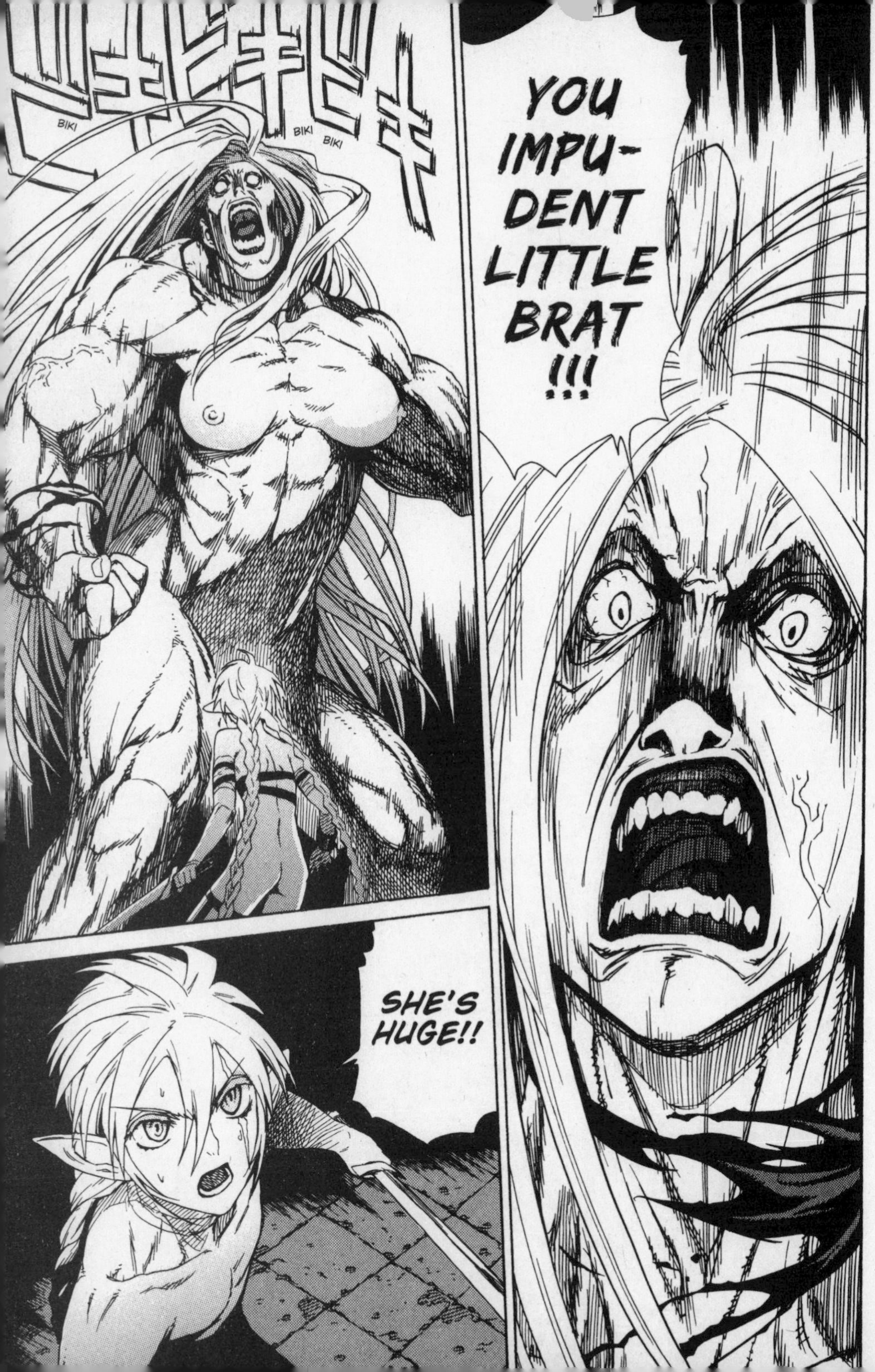
YOU IMPU-DENT LITTLE BRAT!!!
BIKI
BIKI
BIKI
SHE'S HUGE!!

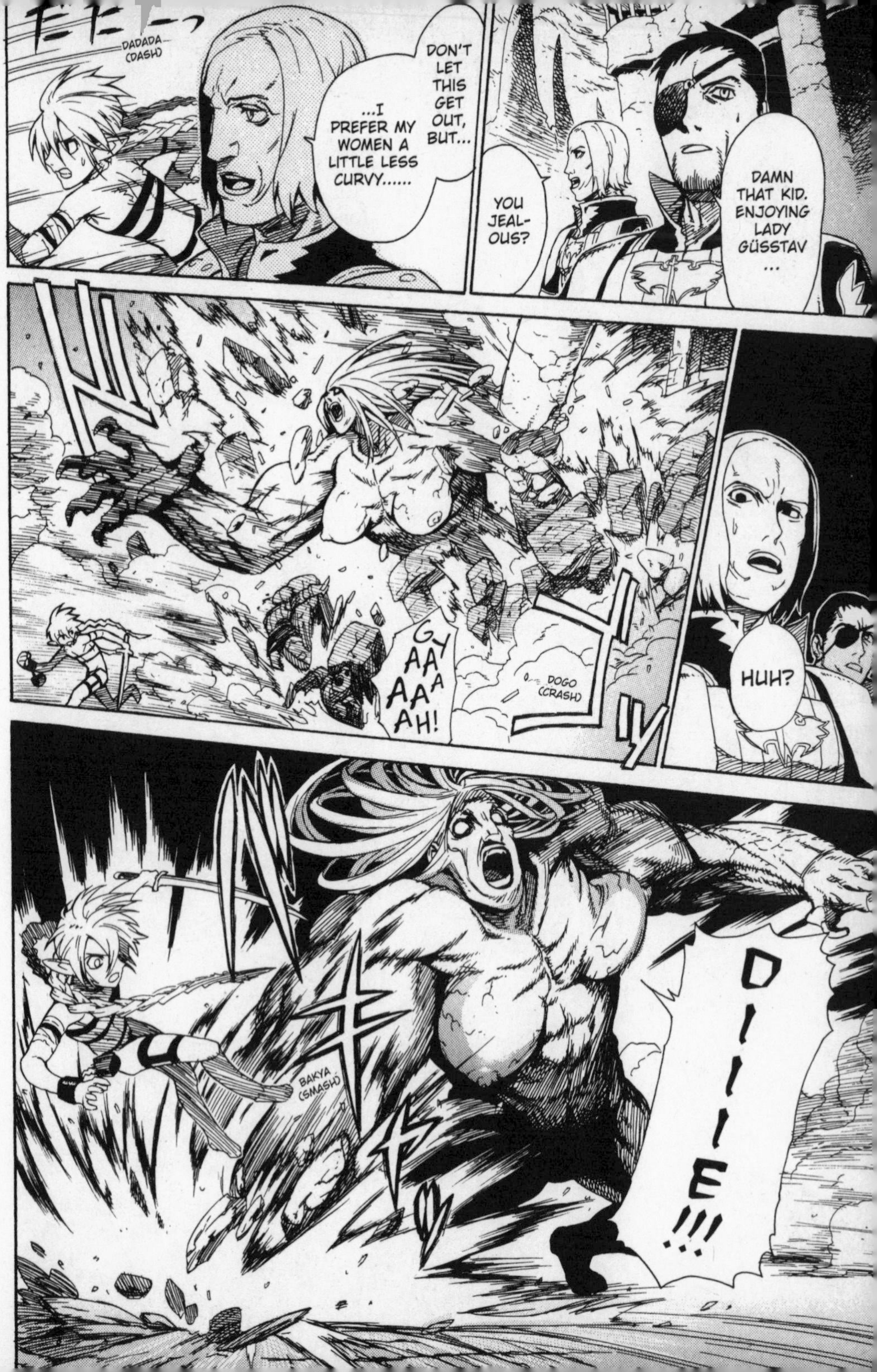
DAMN THAT KID. ENJOYING LADY GÜSSTAV ...
YOU JEAL-OUS?
DON'T LET THIS GET OUT, BUT...
...I PREFER MY WOMEN A LITTLE LESS CURVY......
DADADA (DASH)
HUH?
DOGO (CRASH)
GYAAAAAAH!
DIIIE!!!
BAKYA (SMASH)

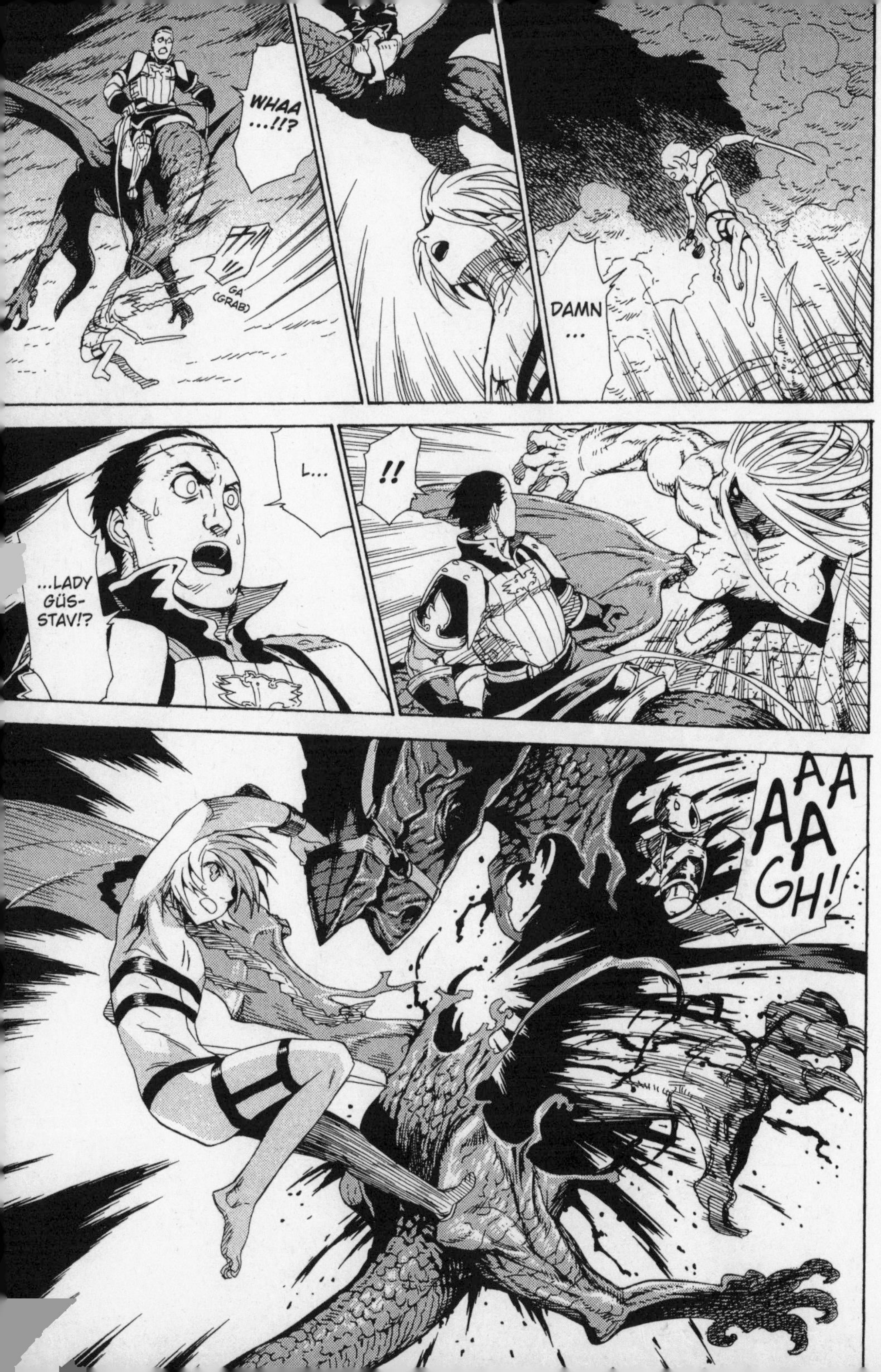
DAMN
...
WHAA
...!!?
GA
(GRAB)
!!
L...
...LADY GÜS-STAV!?
AAAAAGH!

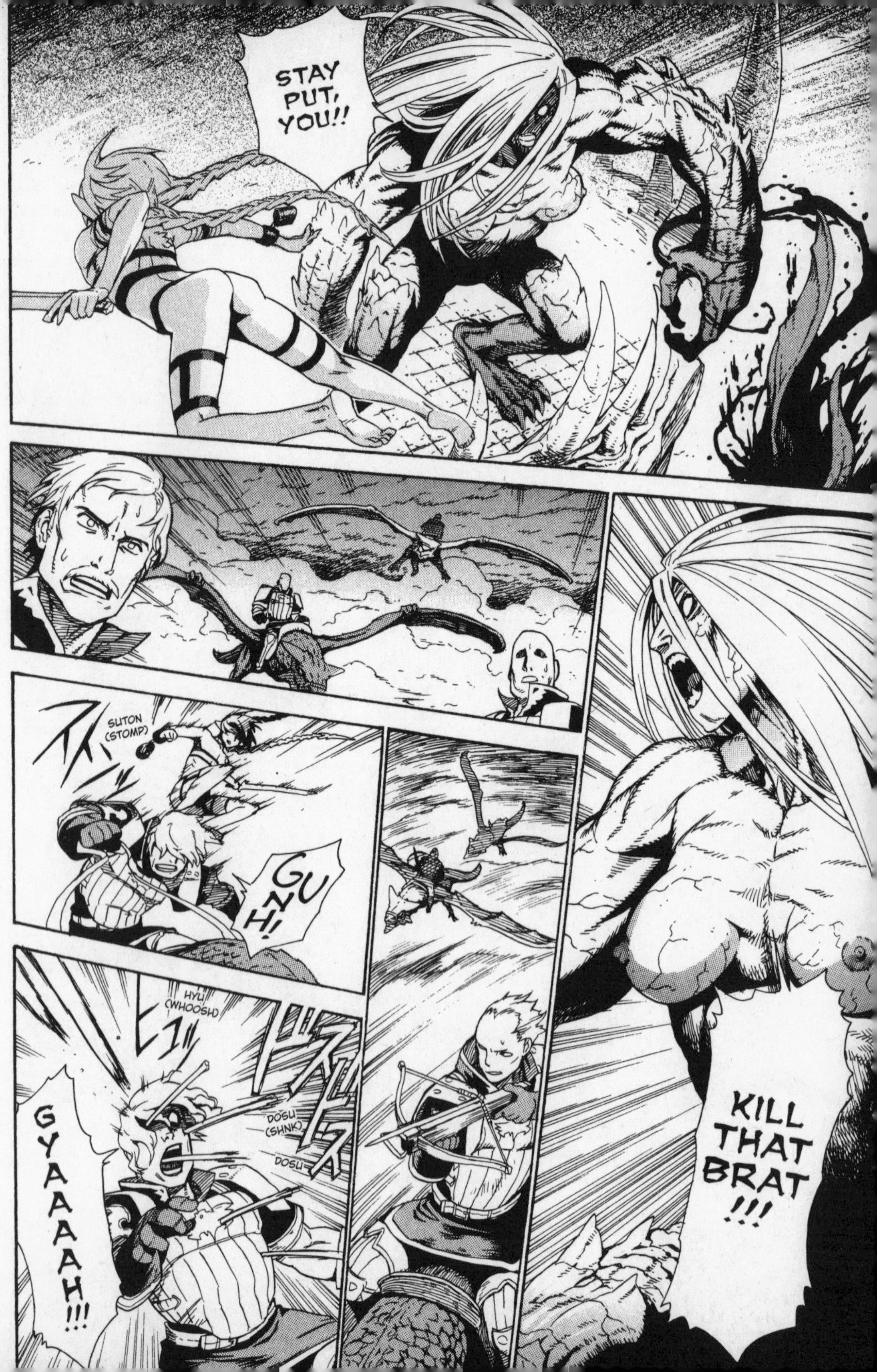
STAY PUT, YOU!!
KILL THAT BRAT!!!
SUTON (STOMP)
GUNH!
HYU (WHOOSH)
DOSU (SHNK)
DOSU
GYAAAAH!!!

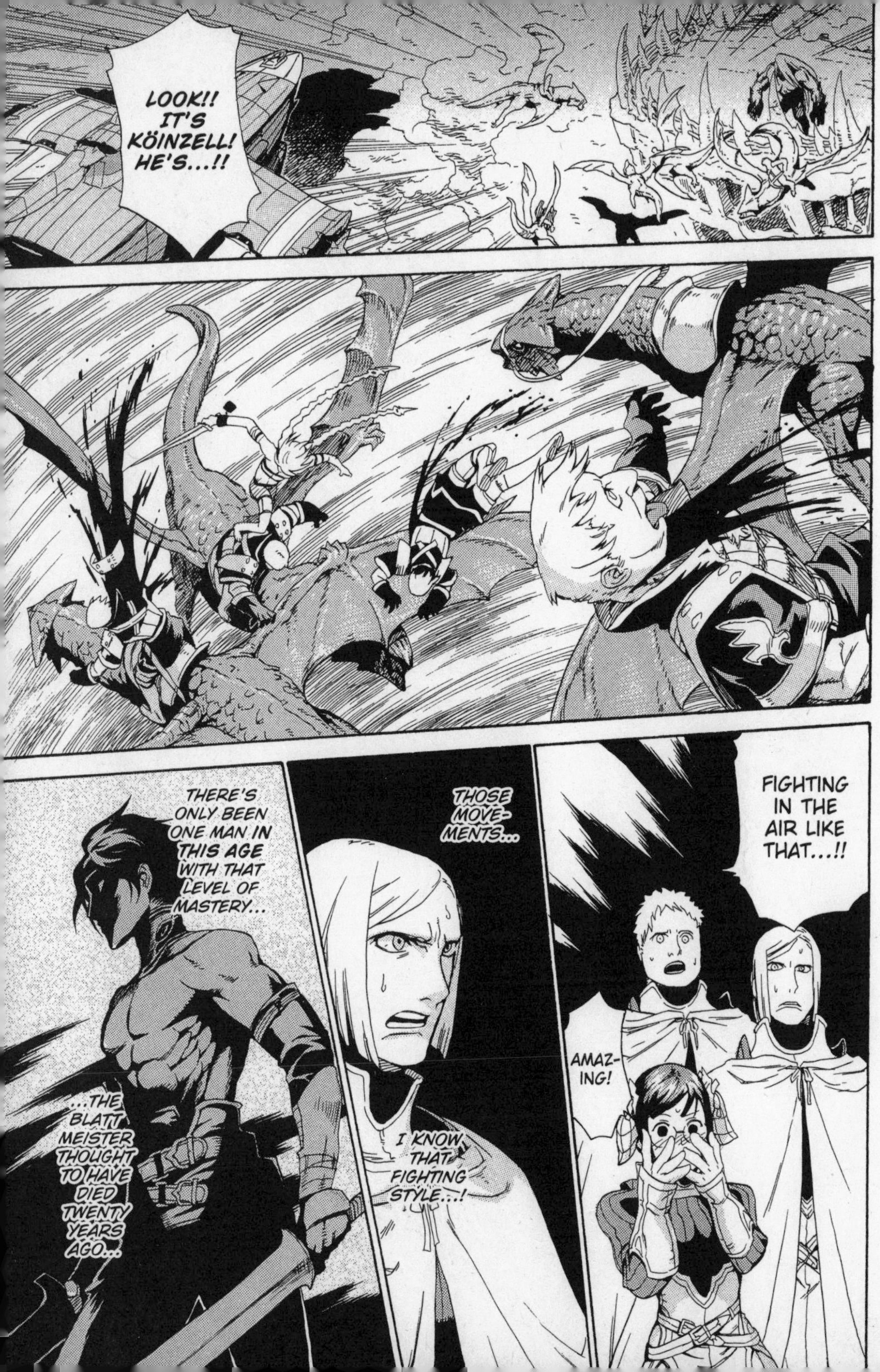
LOOK!! IT'S KÖINZELL! HE'S...!!
FIGHTING IN THE AIR LIKE THAT...!!
AMAZING!
THOSE MOVEMENTS...
I KNOW THAT FIGHTING STYLE...!
THERE'S ONLY BEEN ONE MAN IN THIS AGE WITH THAT LEVEL OF MASTERY...
...THE BLATT MEISTER THOUGHT TO HAVE DIED TWENTY YEARS AGO...

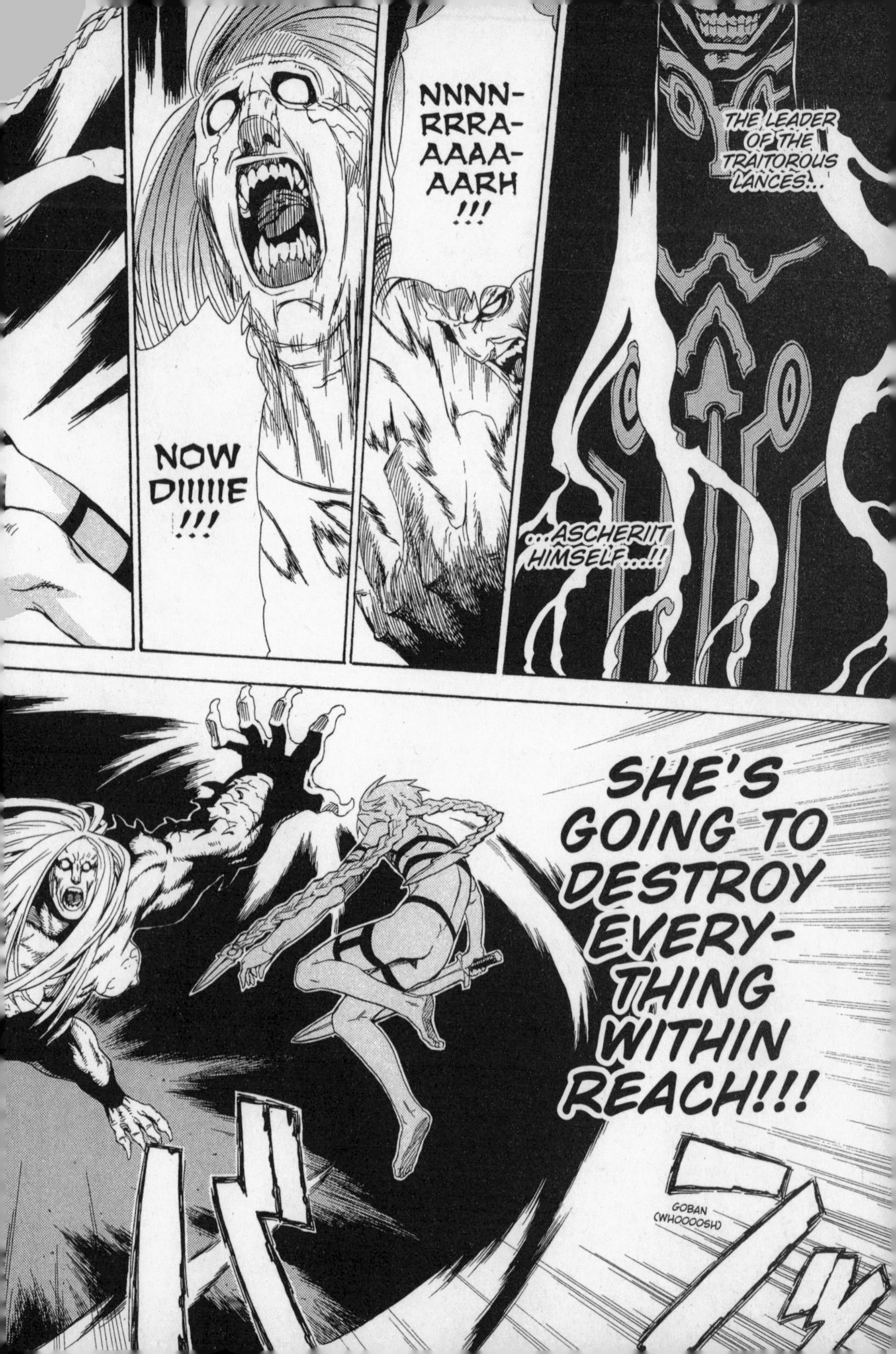
THE LEADER OF THE TRAITOROUS LANCES...
...ASCHERIIT HIMSELF...!!
NNNN-RRRA-AAAA-AARH!!!
NOW DIIIIIE!!!
SHE'S GOING TO DESTROY EVERY-THING WITHIN REACH!!!
GOBAN (WHOOOOSH)

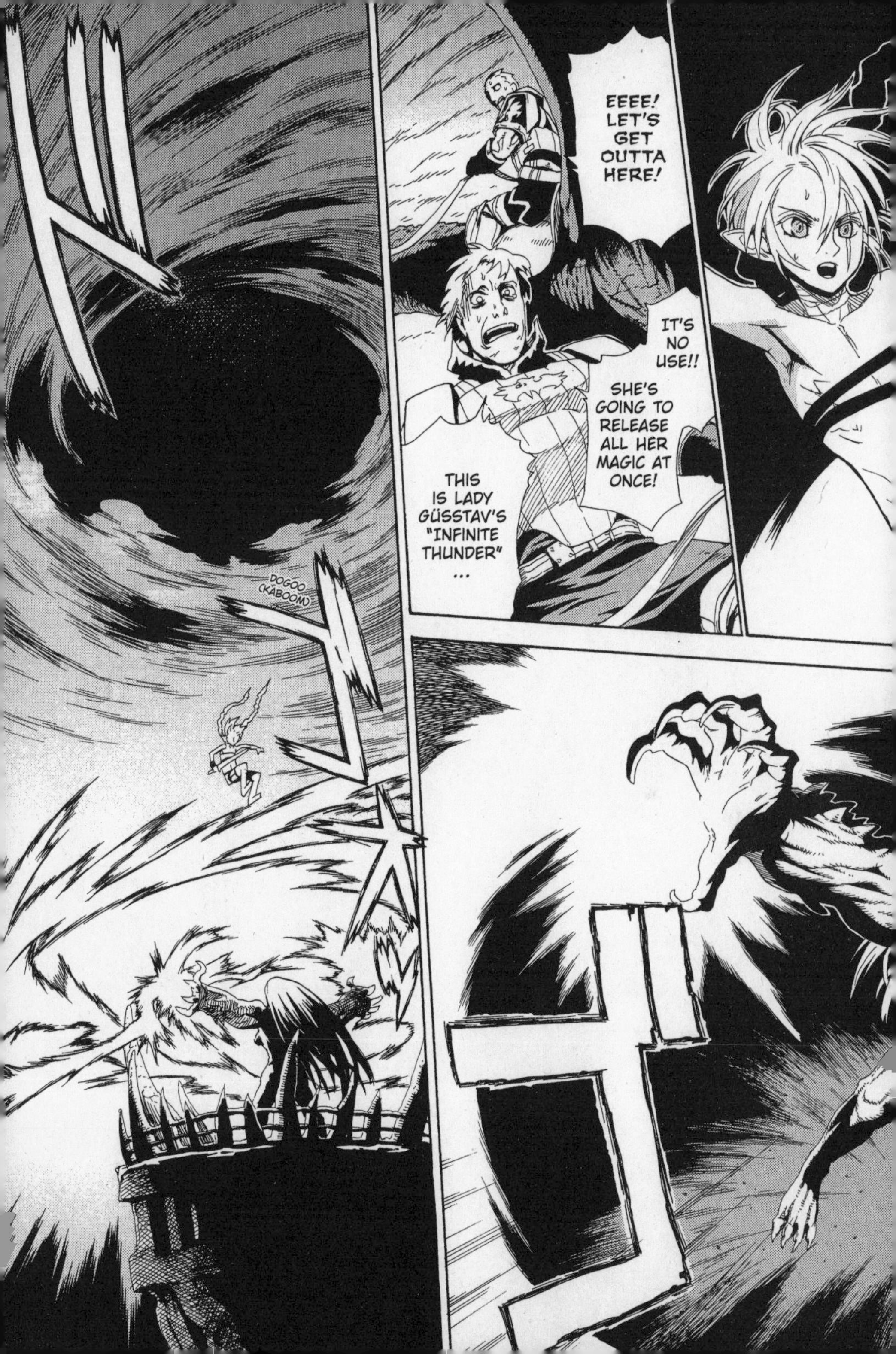
EEEE! LET'S GET OUTTA HERE!
IT'S NO USE!!
SHE'S GOING TO RELEASE ALL HER MAGIC AT ONCE!
THIS IS LADY GÜSSTAV'S "INFINITE THUNDER"...
DOGOO (KABOOM)

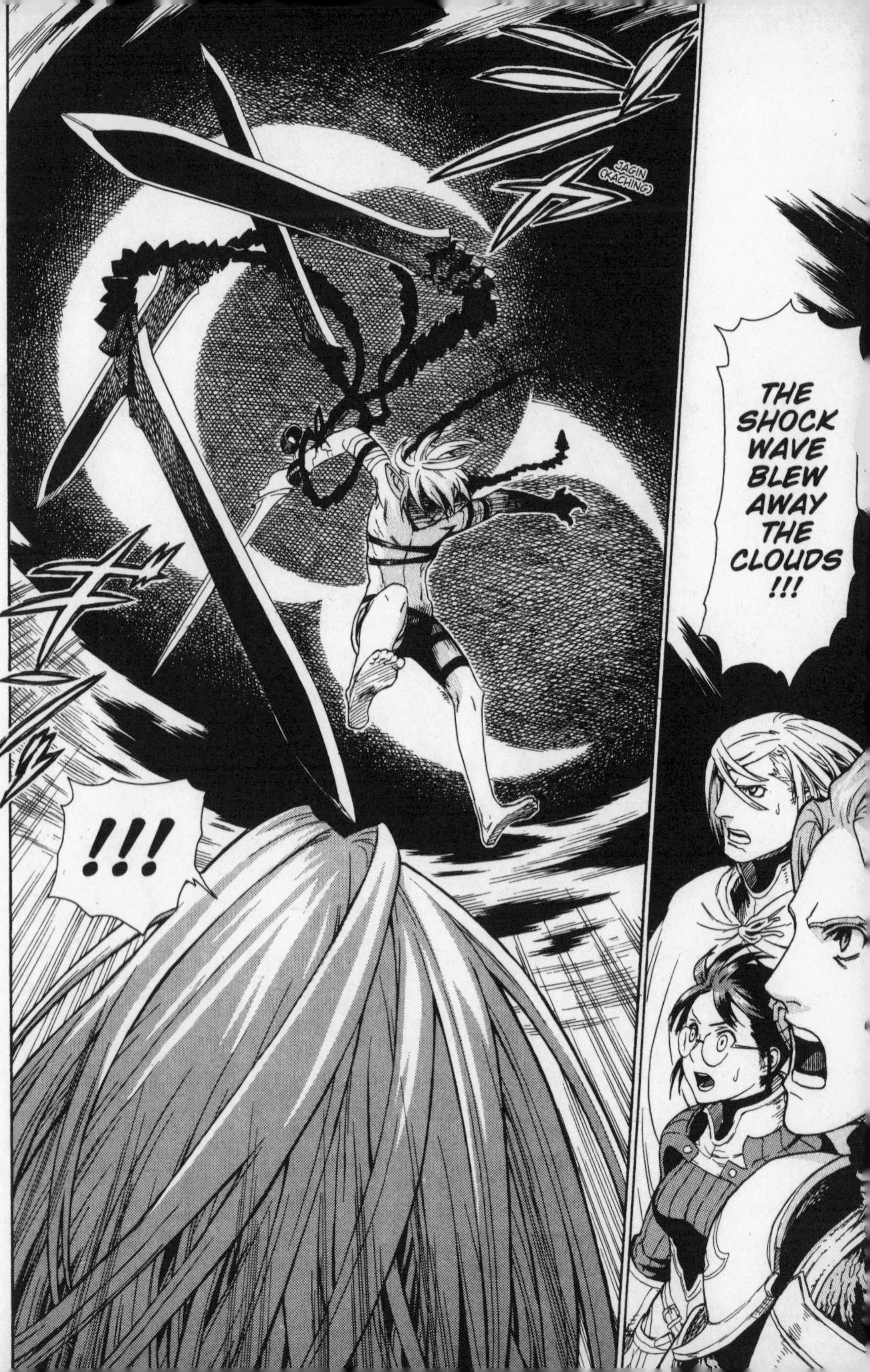
THE SHOCK WAVE BLEW AWAY THE CLOUDS!!!
JAGIN (KACHING)
!!!

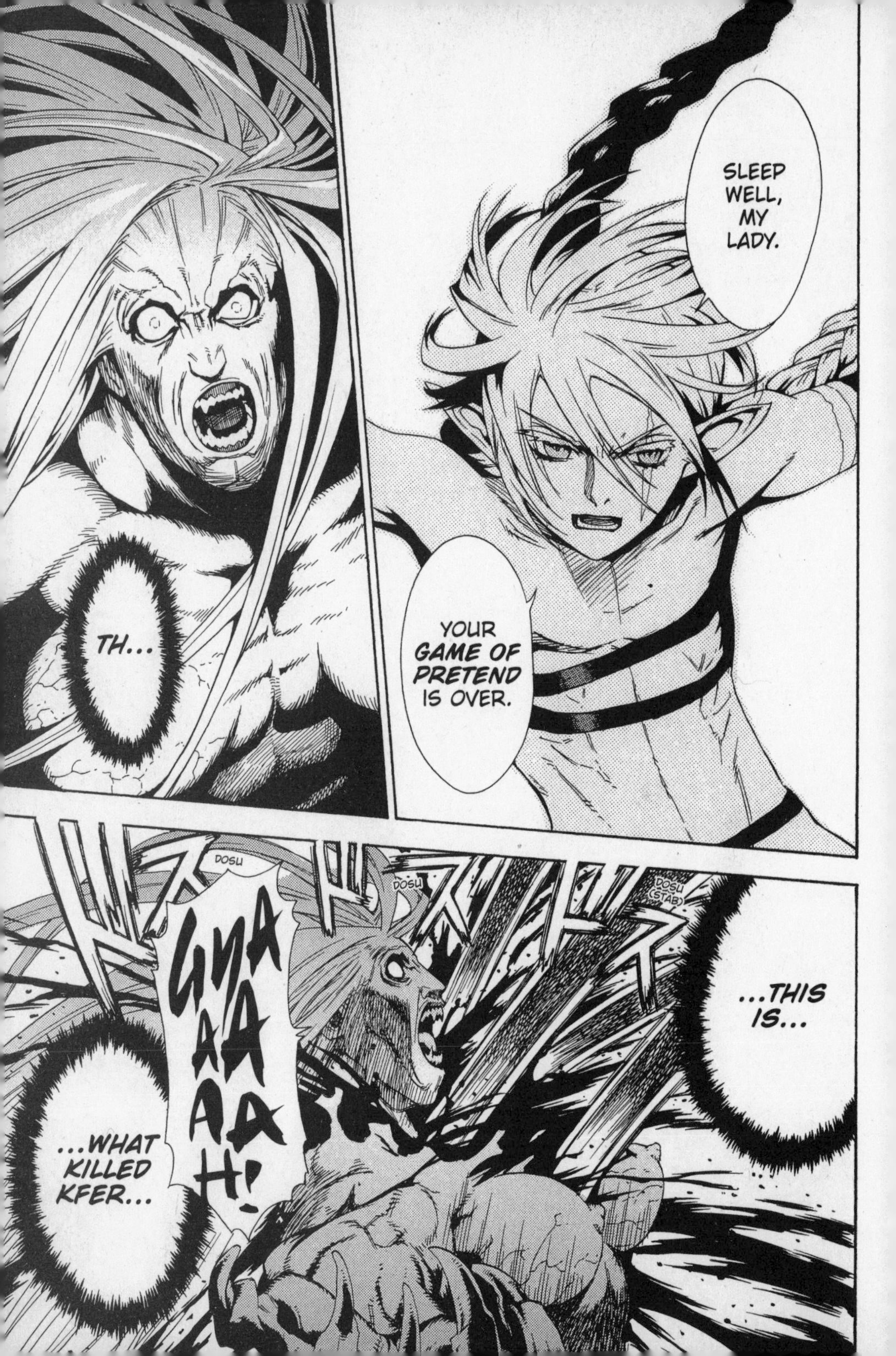
SLEEP WELL, MY LADY.
YOUR GAME OF PRETEND IS OVER.
TH...
DOSU (STAB)
DOSU
DOSU
...THIS IS...
GYAAAAAAH!
...WHAT KILLED KFER...

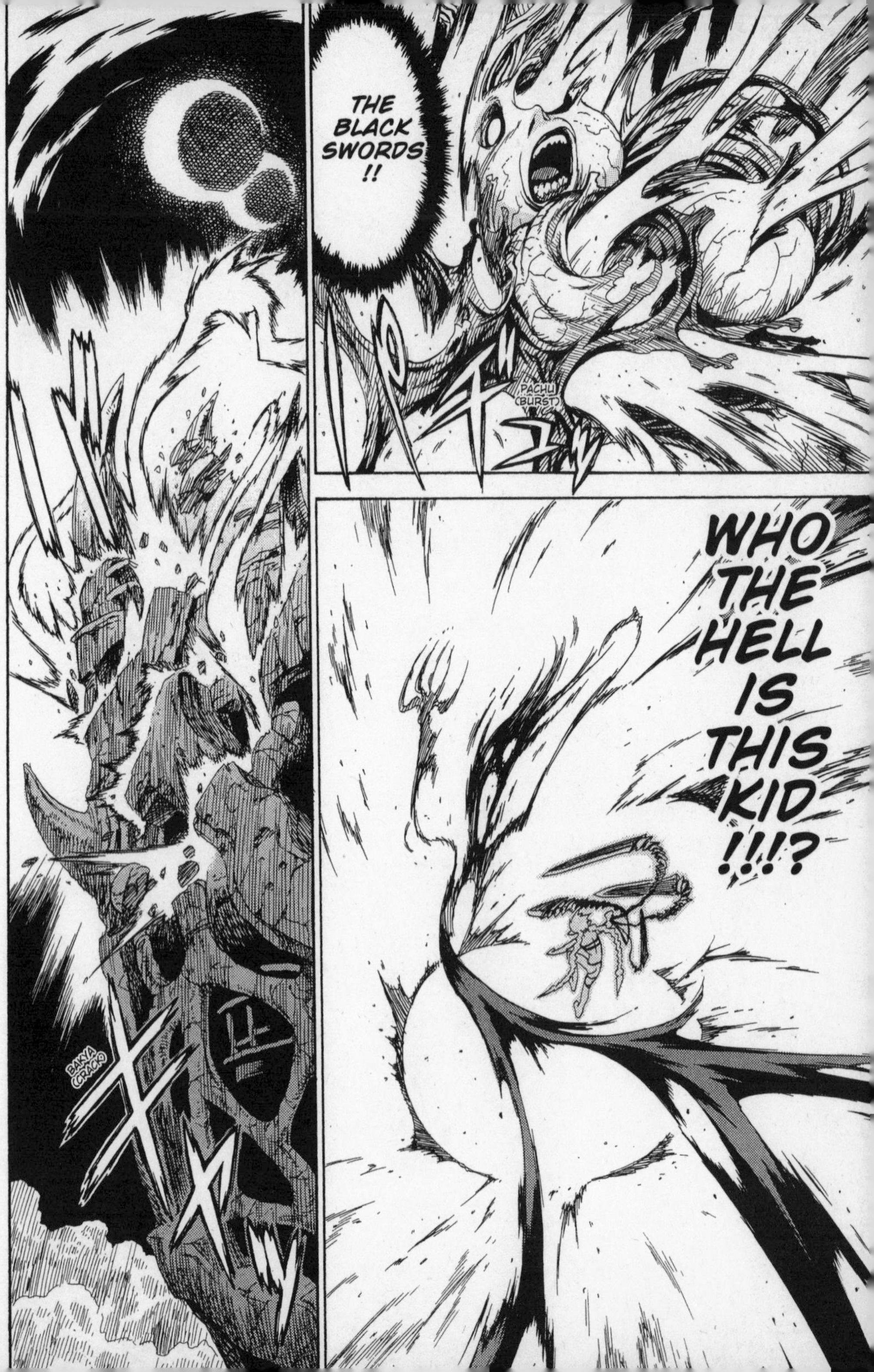
THE BLACK SWORDS !!
PACHU (BURST)
WHO THE HELL IS THIS KID !!!?
BAKYA (CRACK)

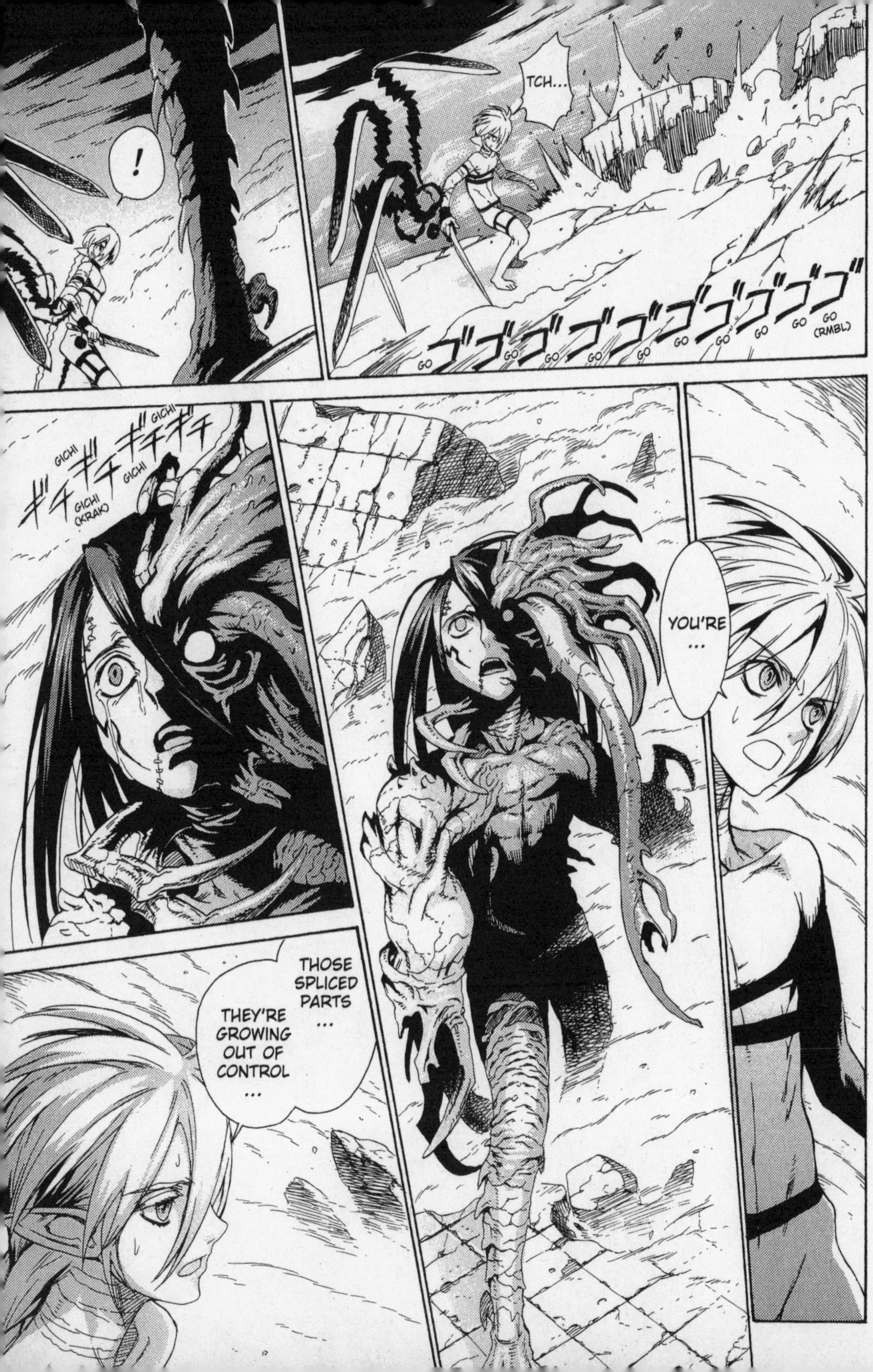
TCH...
GO GO GO GO GO GO GO GO GO GO (RMBL)
!
YOU'RE ...
GICHI GICHI GICHI GICHI (KRAK)
THOSE SPLICED PARTS ...
THEY'RE GROWING OUT OF CONTROL ...

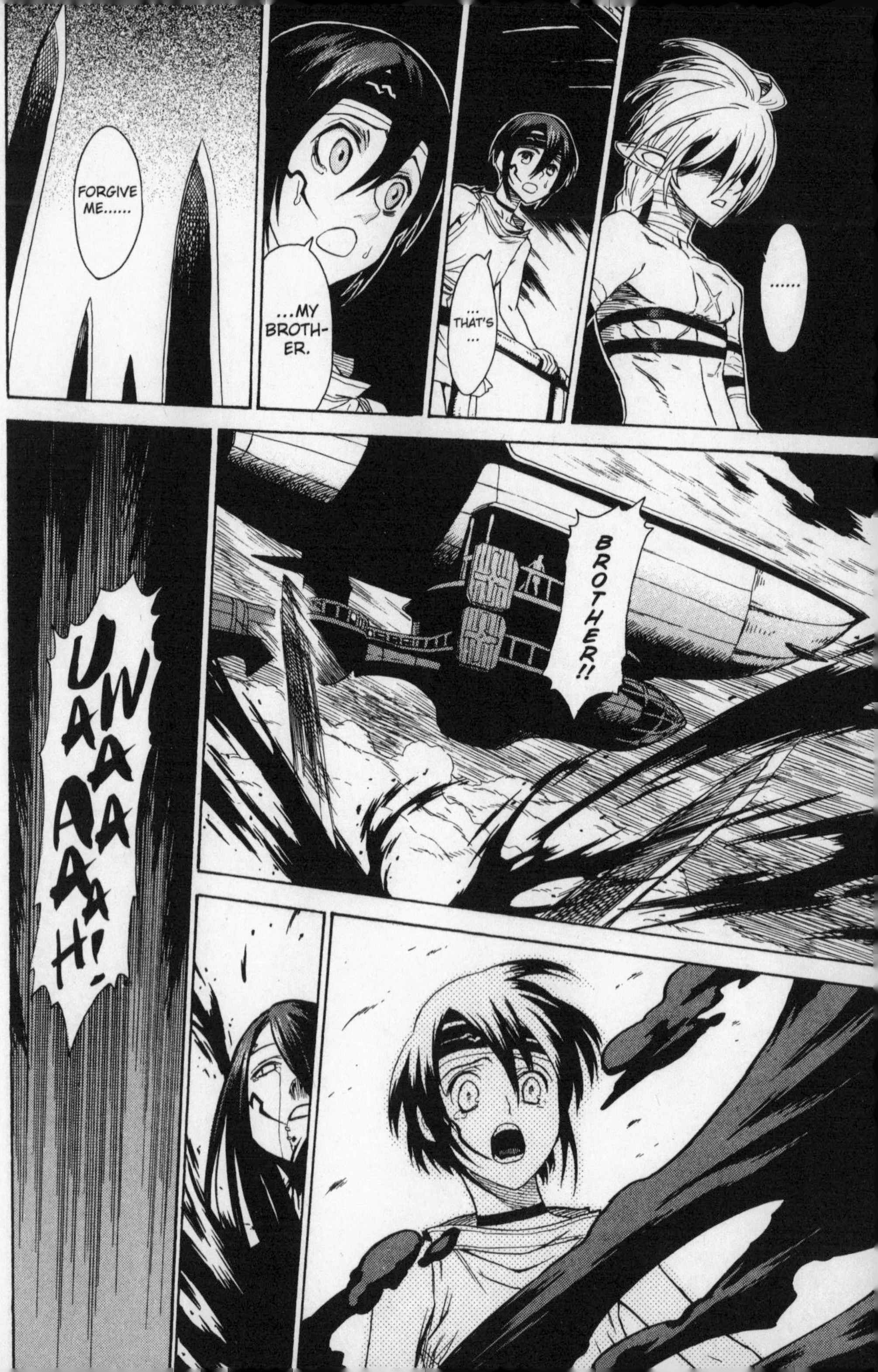
......
...THAT'S...
...MY BROTHER.
FORGIVE ME......
BROTHER!!
UWAAAAAAAH!

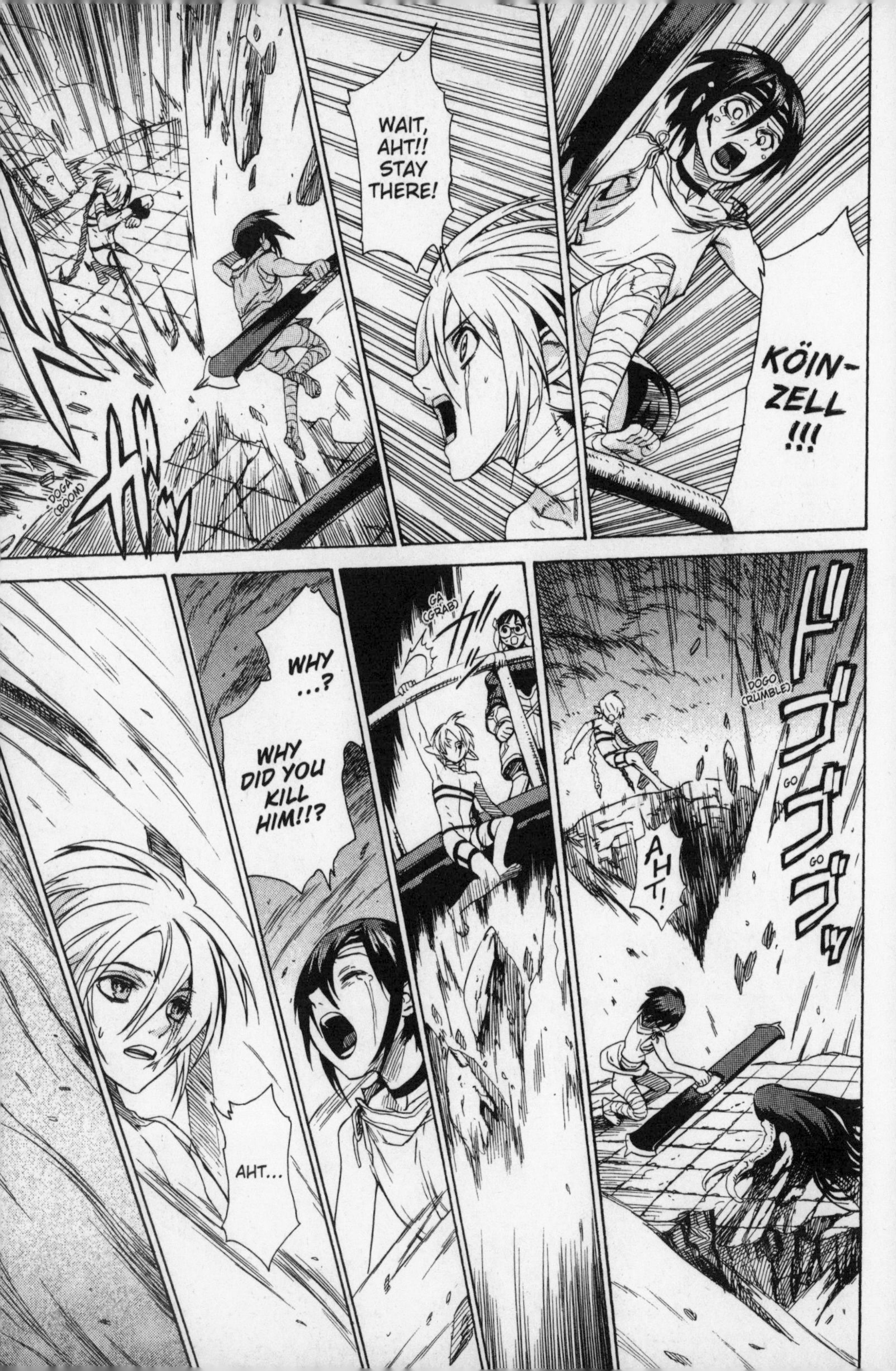
KÖIN-ZELL!!!
WAIT, AHT!! STAY THERE!
DOGA (BOOM)
DOGO (RUMBLE)
GO
GO
AHT!
GA (GRAB)
WHY ...?
WHY DID YOU KILL HIM!!?
AHT...

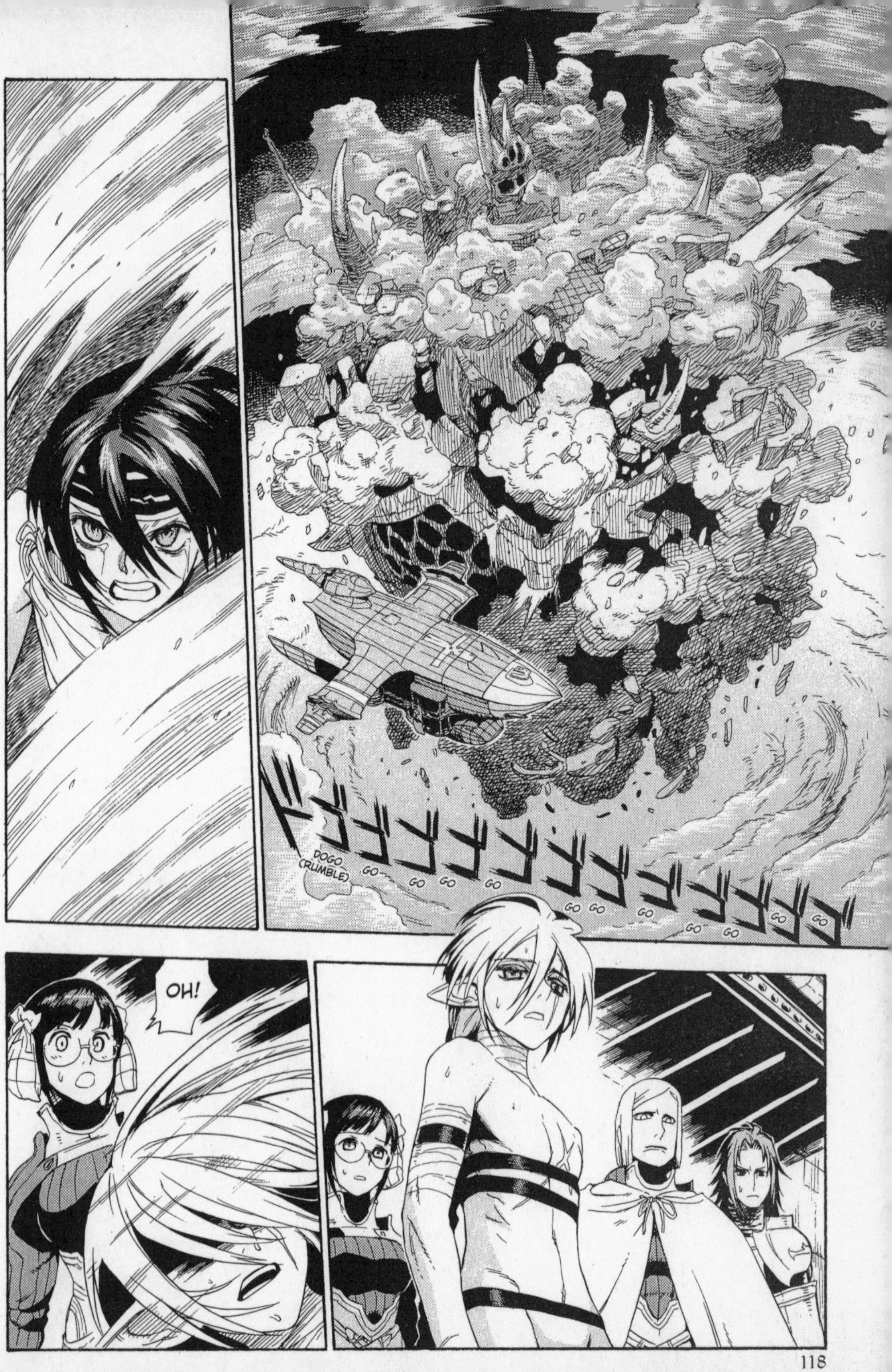
DOGO (RUMBLE) GO GO GO GO GO GO GO GO GO GO GO
OH!

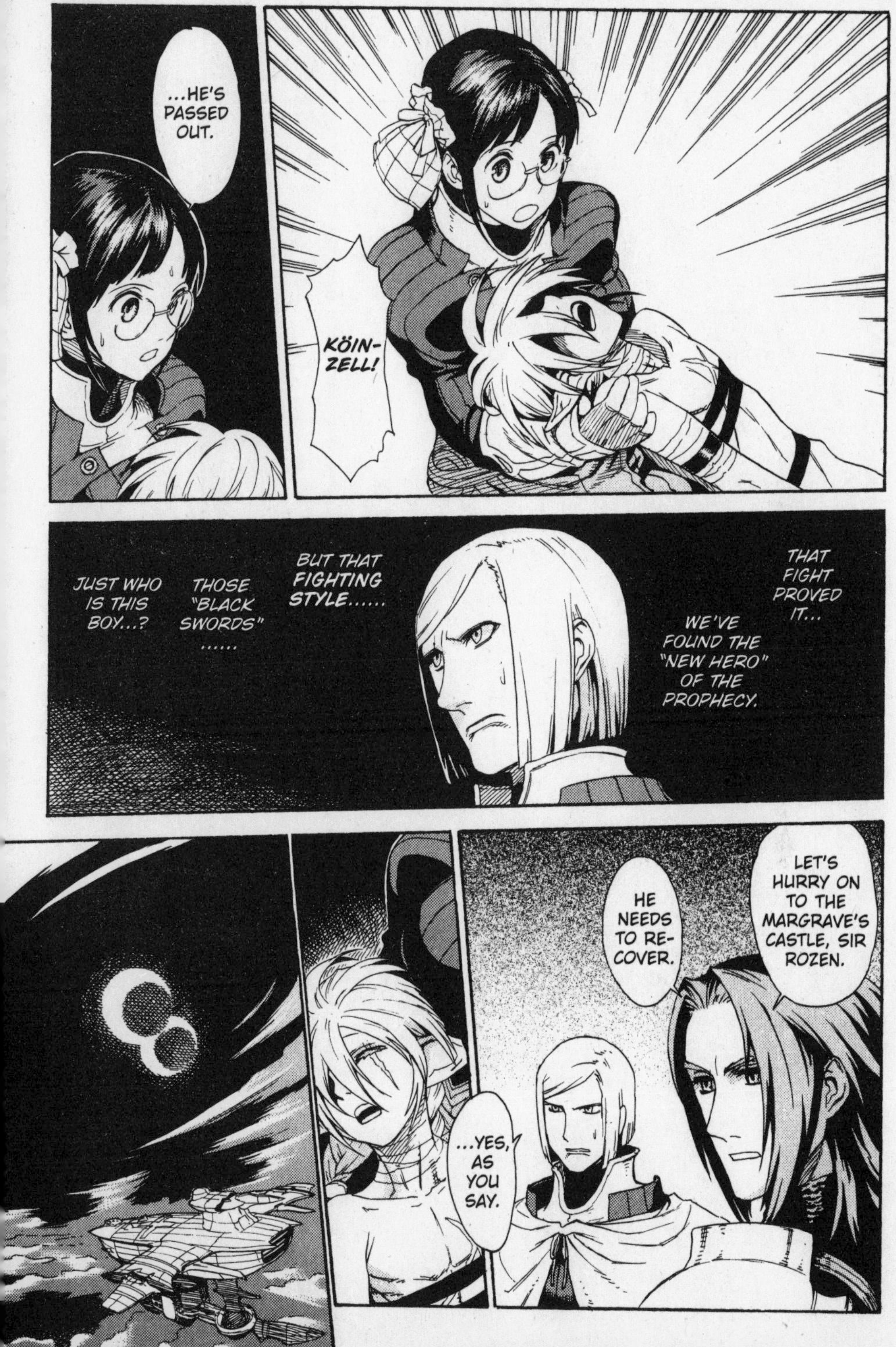
KÖIN-ZELL!
...HE'S PASSED OUT.
THAT FIGHT PROVED IT...
WE'VE FOUND THE "NEW HERO" OF THE PROPHECY.
BUT THAT FIGHTING STYLE......
THOSE "BLACK SWORDS"......
JUST WHO IS THIS BOY...?
LET'S HURRY ON TO THE MARGRAVE'S CASTLE, SIR ROZEN.
HE NEEDS TO RE-COVER.
...YES, AS YOU SAY.

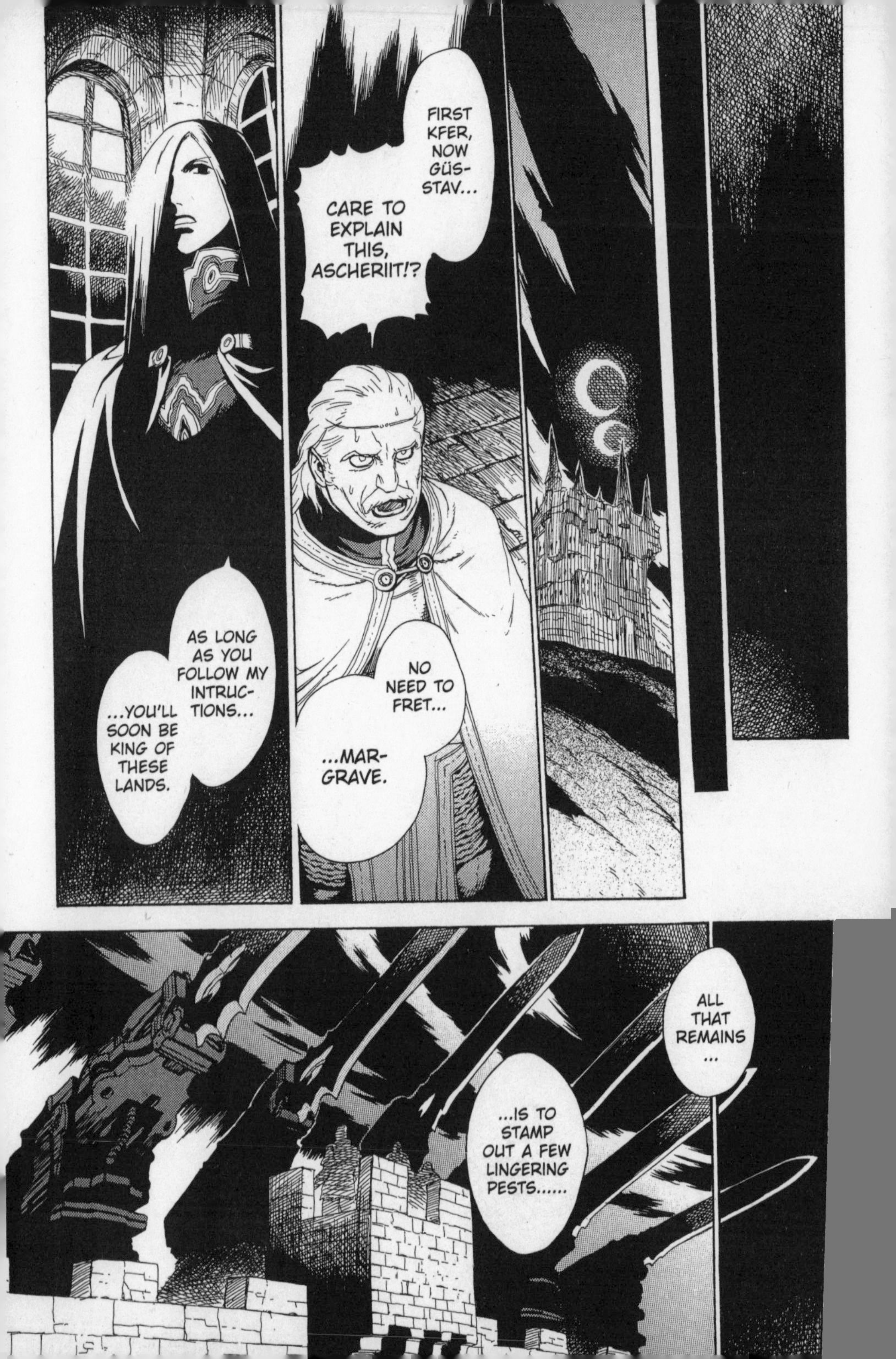
FIRST KFER, NOW GÜS-STAV...
CARE TO EXPLAIN THIS, ASCHERIIT!?
NO NEED TO FRET...
...MAR-GRAVE.
AS LONG AS YOU FOLLOW MY INTRUC-TIONS...
...YOU'LL SOON BE KING OF THESE LANDS.
ALL THAT REMAINS ...
...IS TO STAMP OUT A FEW LINGERING PESTS......

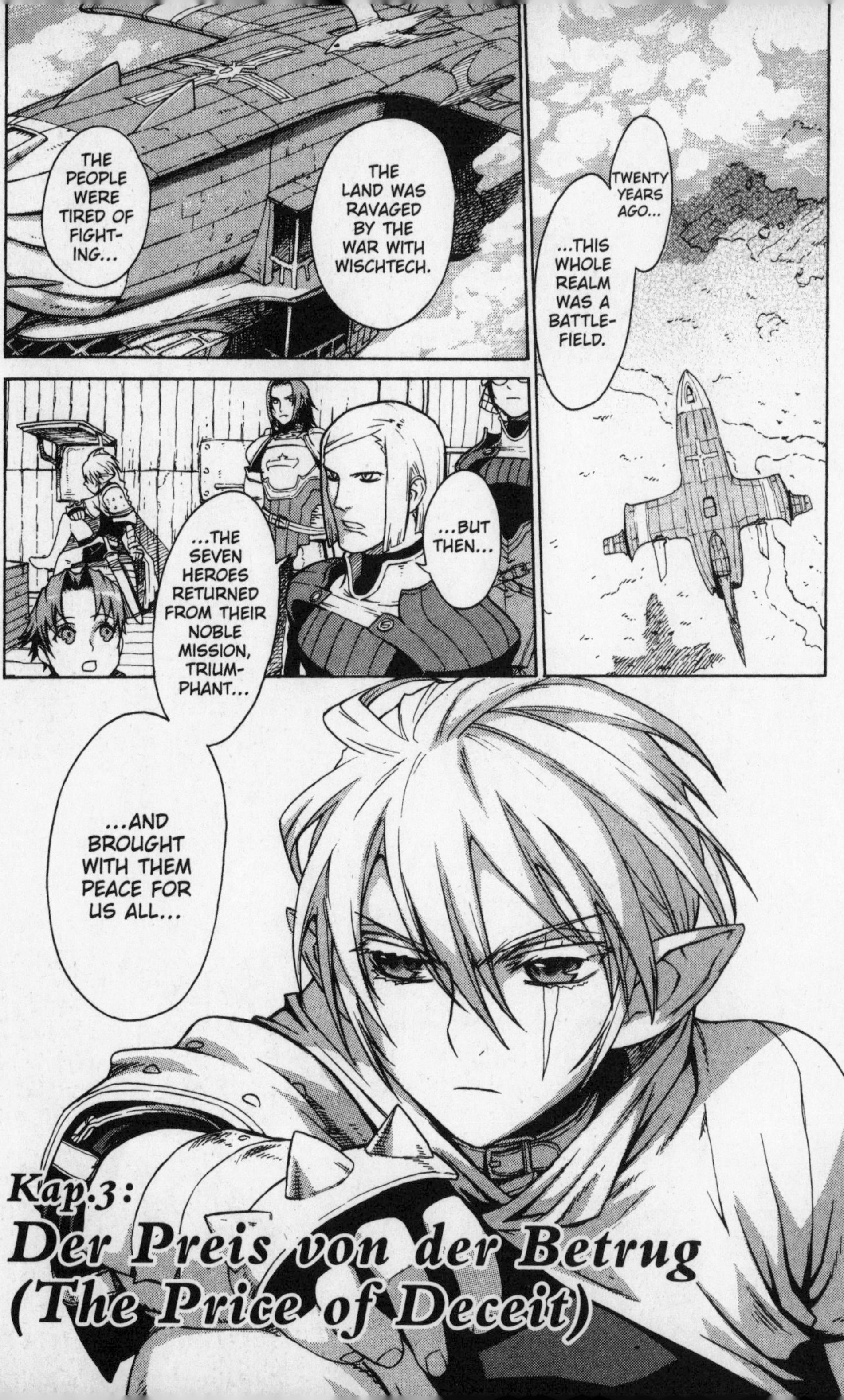
TWENTY YEARS AGO...
...THIS WHOLE REALM WAS A BATTLE-FIELD.
THE LAND WAS RAVAGED BY THE WAR WITH WISCHTECH.
THE PEOPLE WERE TIRED OF FIGHT-ING...
...BUT THEN...
...THE SEVEN HEROES RETURNED FROM THEIR NOBLE MISSION, TRIUM-PHANT...
...AND BROUGHT WITH THEM PEACE FOR US ALL...

Kap.3: Der Preis von der Betrug (The Price of Deceit)

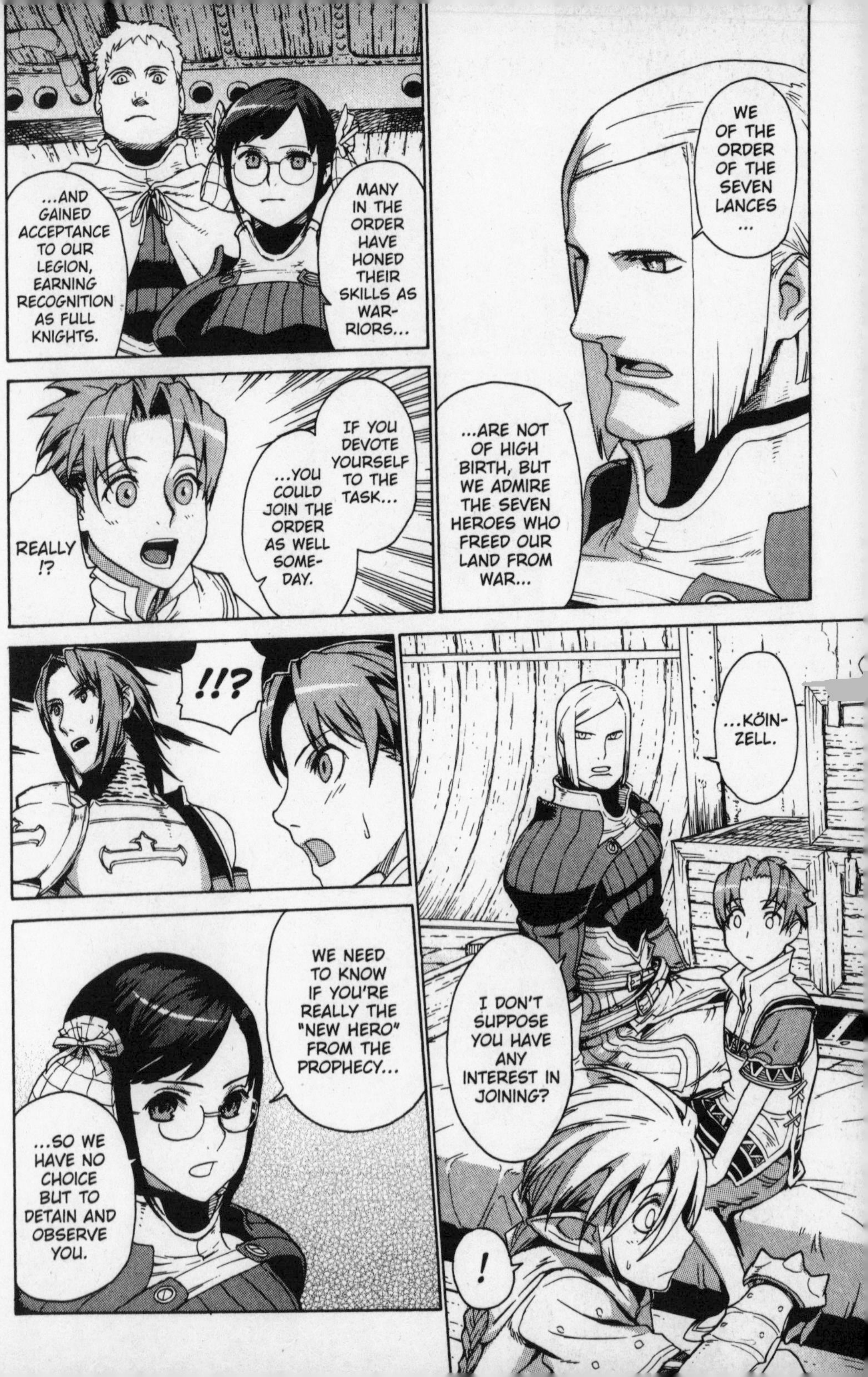
WE OF THE ORDER OF THE SEVEN LANCES...
...ARE NOT OF HIGH BIRTH, BUT WE ADMIRE THE SEVEN HEROES WHO FREED OUR LAND FROM WAR...
MANY IN THE ORDER HAVE HONED THEIR SKILLS AS WAR-RIORS...
...AND GAINED ACCEPTANCE TO OUR LEGION, EARNING RECOGNITION AS FULL KNIGHTS.
IF YOU DEVOTE YOURSELF TO THE TASK...
...YOU COULD JOIN THE ORDER AS WELL SOME-DAY.
REALLY!?
...KÖIN-ZELL.
I DON'T SUPPOSE YOU HAVE ANY INTEREST IN JOINING?
!
!!?
WE NEED TO KNOW IF YOU'RE REALLY THE "NEW HERO" FROM THE PROPHECY...
...SO WE HAVE NO CHOICE BUT TO DETAIN AND OBSERVE YOU.

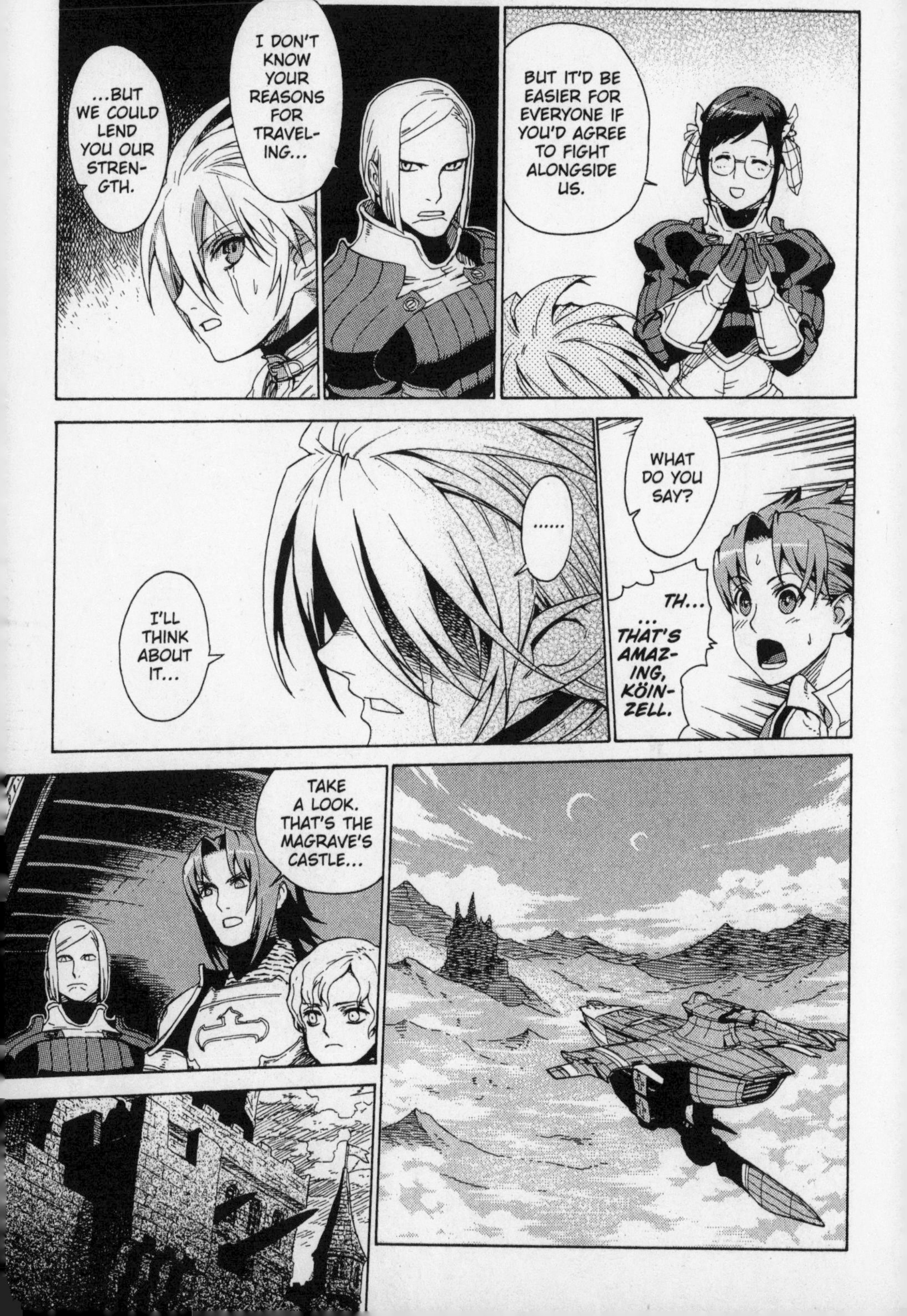
BUT IT'D BE EASIER FOR EVERYONE IF YOU'D AGREE TO FIGHT ALONGSIDE US.
I DON'T KNOW YOUR REASONS FOR TRAVEL-ING...
...BUT WE COULD LEND YOU OUR STREN-GTH.
WHAT DO YOU SAY?
TH... ...THAT'S AMAZ-ING, KÖIN-ZELL.
......
I'LL THINK ABOUT IT...
TAKE A LOOK. THAT'S THE MAGRAVE'S CASTLE...

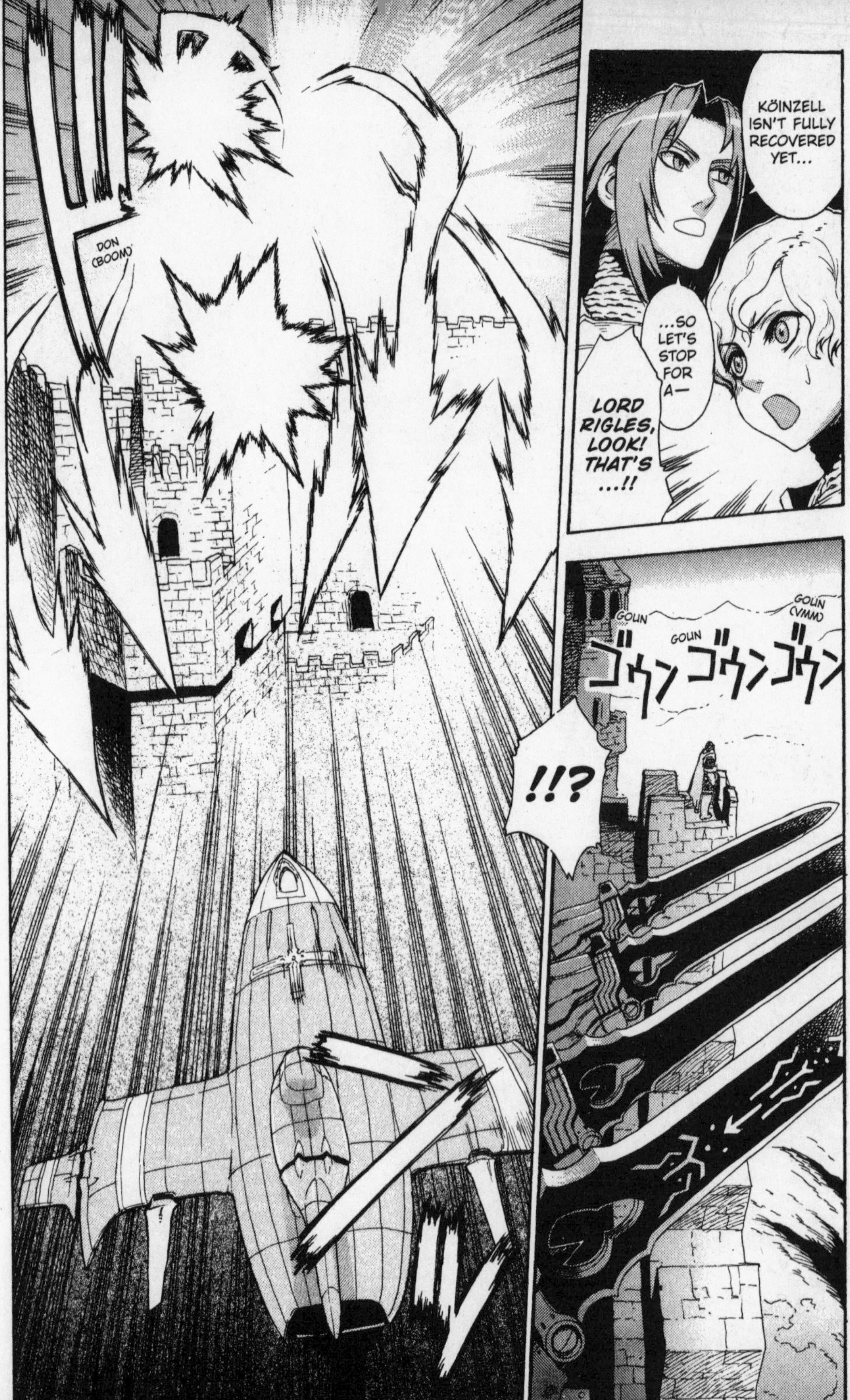
KÖINZELL ISN'T FULLY RECOVERED YET...
...SO LET'S STOP FOR A—
LORD RIGLES, LOOK! THAT'S ...!!
GOUN (VMM)
GOUN
GOUN
ゴウンゴウンゴウン
!!?
DON (BOOM)

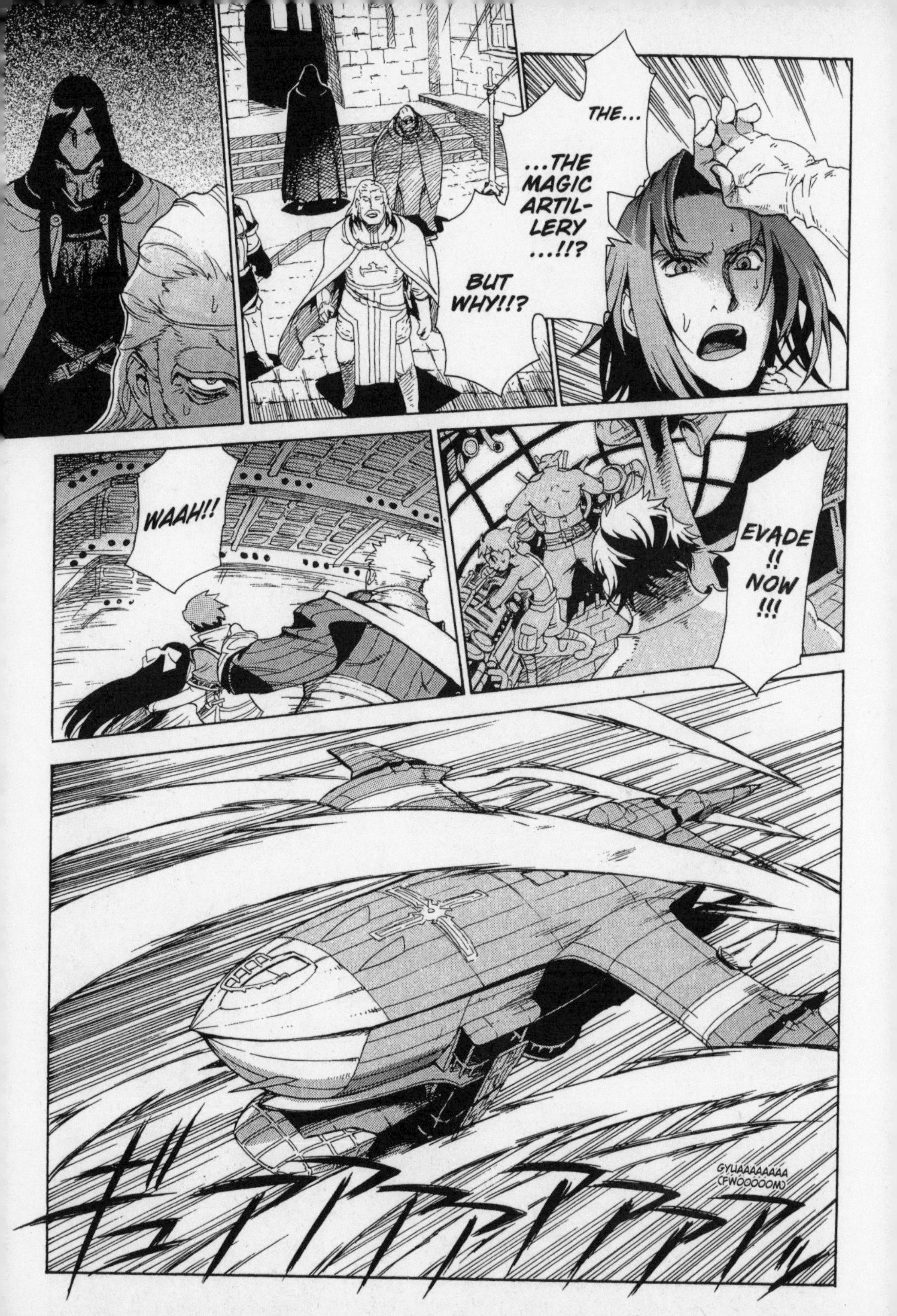
THE...
...THE MAGIC ARTIL-LERY ...!!?
BUT WHY!!?
EVADE!! NOW!!!
WAAH!!
GYUAAAAAAAAA (FWOOOOOM)

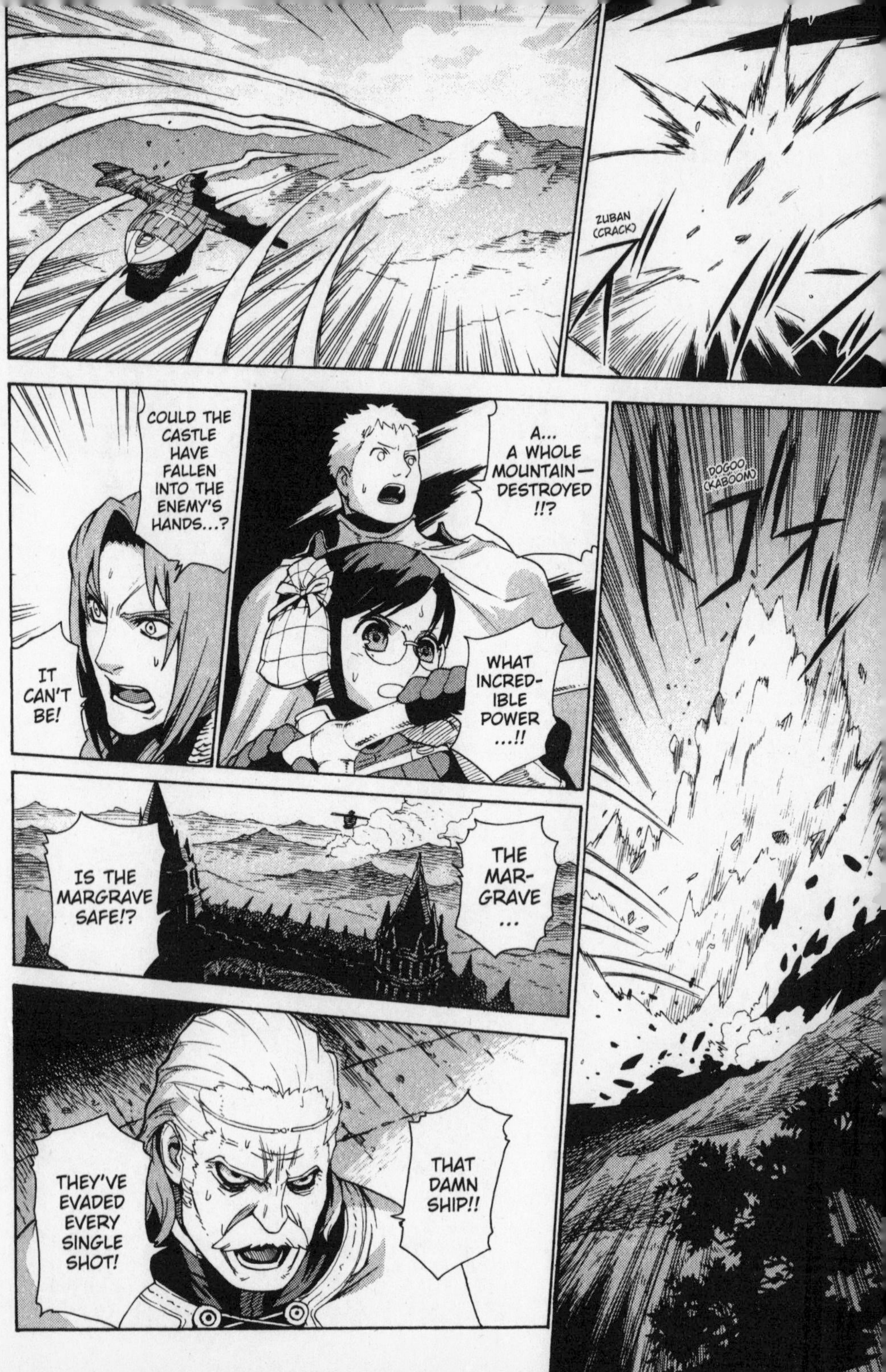
ZUBAN (CRACK)
DOGOO (KABOOM)
A... A WHOLE MOUNTAIN—DESTROYED!!?
WHAT INCRED-IBLE POWER ...!!
COULD THE CASTLE HAVE FALLEN INTO THE ENEMY'S HANDS...?
IT CAN'T BE!
THE MAR-GRAVE ...
IS THE MARGRAVE SAFE!?
THAT DAMN SHIP!!
THEY'VE EVADED EVERY SINGLE SHOT!

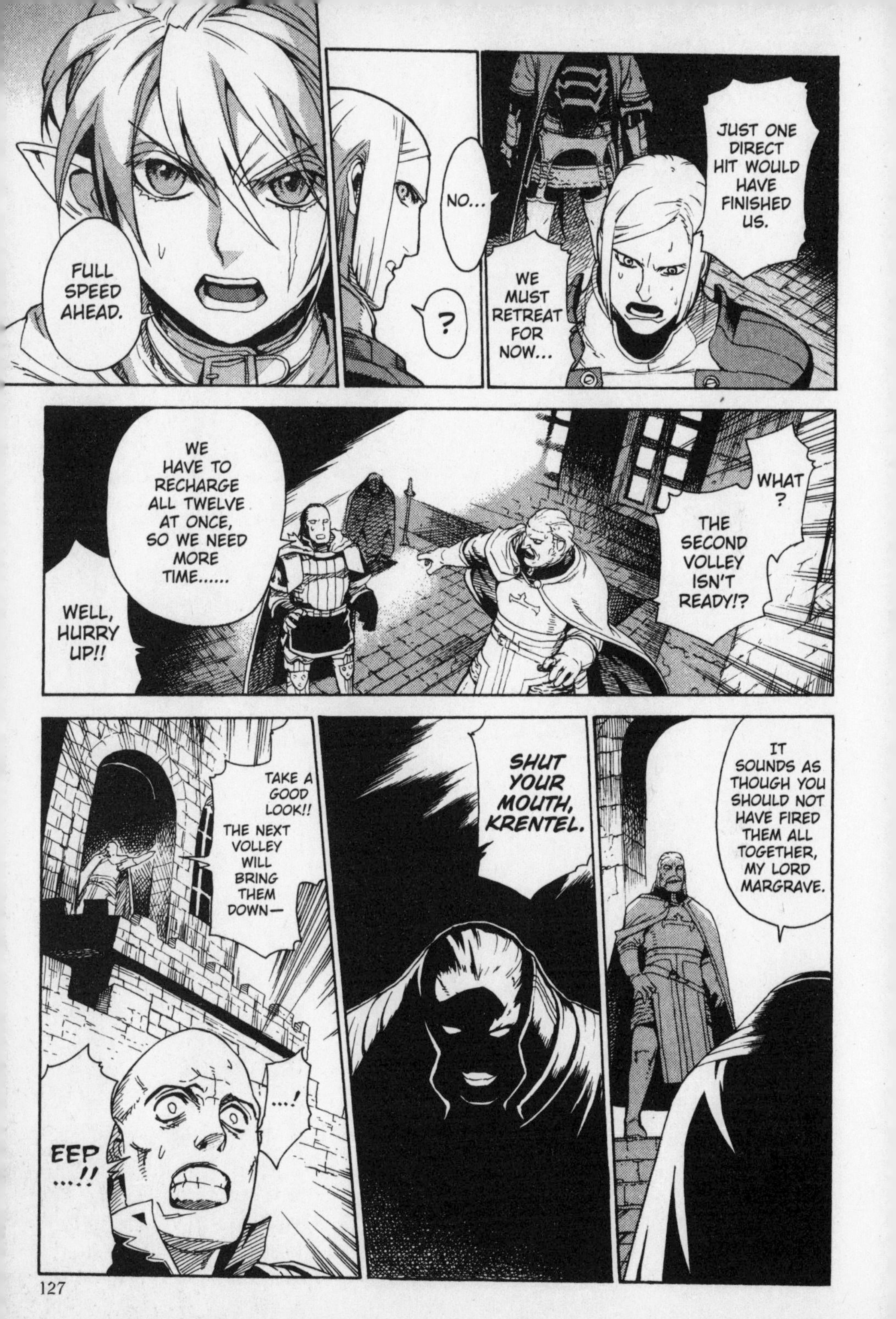
JUST ONE DIRECT HIT WOULD HAVE FINISHED US.
WE MUST RETREAT FOR NOW...
NO...
?
FULL SPEED AHEAD.
WHAT?
THE SECOND VOLLEY ISN'T READY!?
WE HAVE TO RECHARGE ALL TWELVE AT ONCE, SO WE NEED MORE TIME......
WELL, HURRY UP!!
IT SOUNDS AS THOUGH YOU SHOULD NOT HAVE FIRED THEM ALL TOGETHER, MY LORD MARGRAVE.
SHUT YOUR MOUTH, KRENTEL.
TAKE A GOOD LOOK!!
THE NEXT VOLLEY WILL BRING THEM DOWN—
...!
EEP ...!!

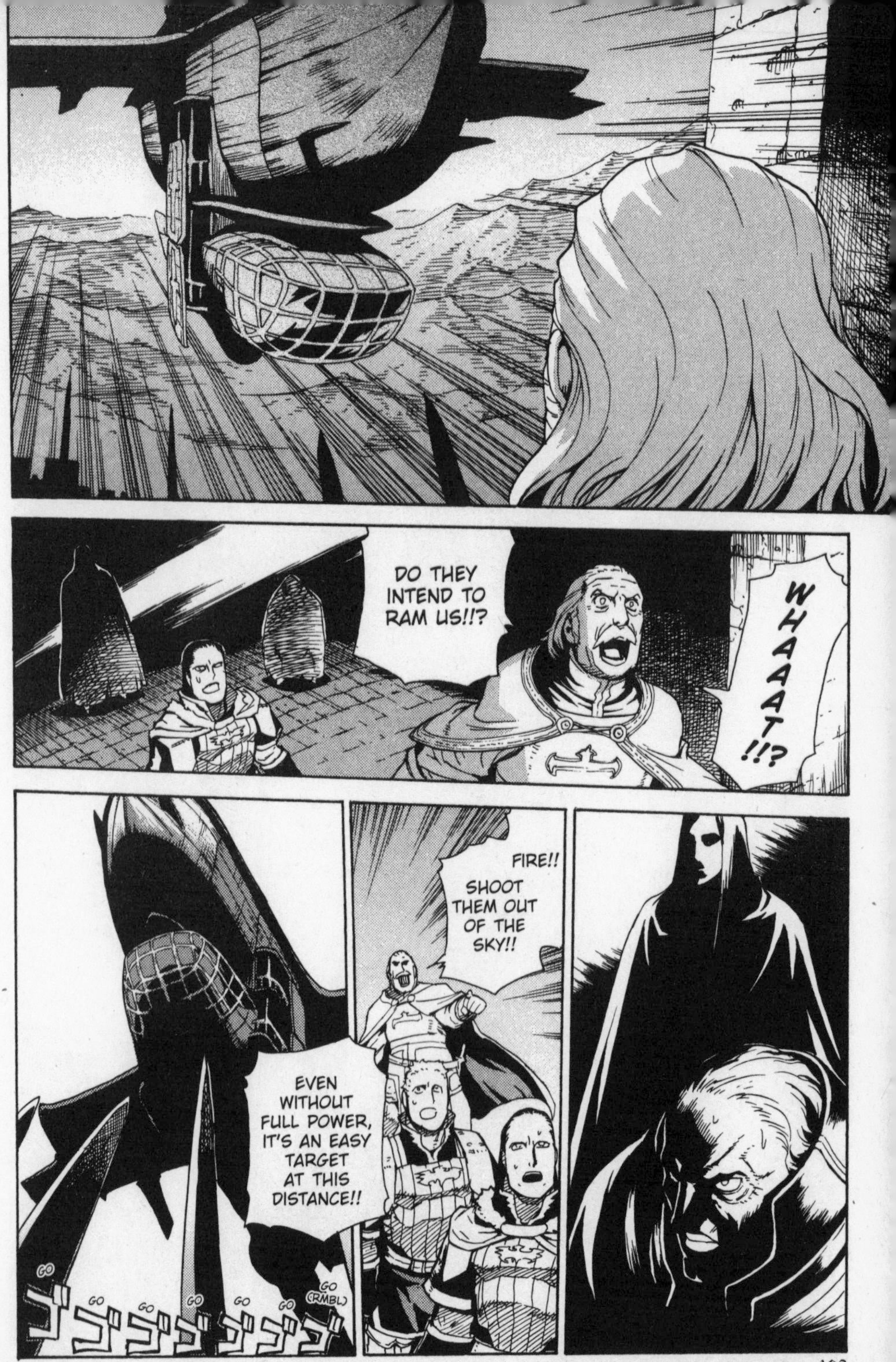

WHAAAAT!!?
DO THEY INTEND TO RAM US!!?
FIRE!!
SHOOT THEM OUT OF THE SKY!!
EVEN WITHOUT FULL POWER, IT'S AN EASY TARGET AT THIS DISTANCE!!
GO GO GO GO GO GO GO (RMBL)

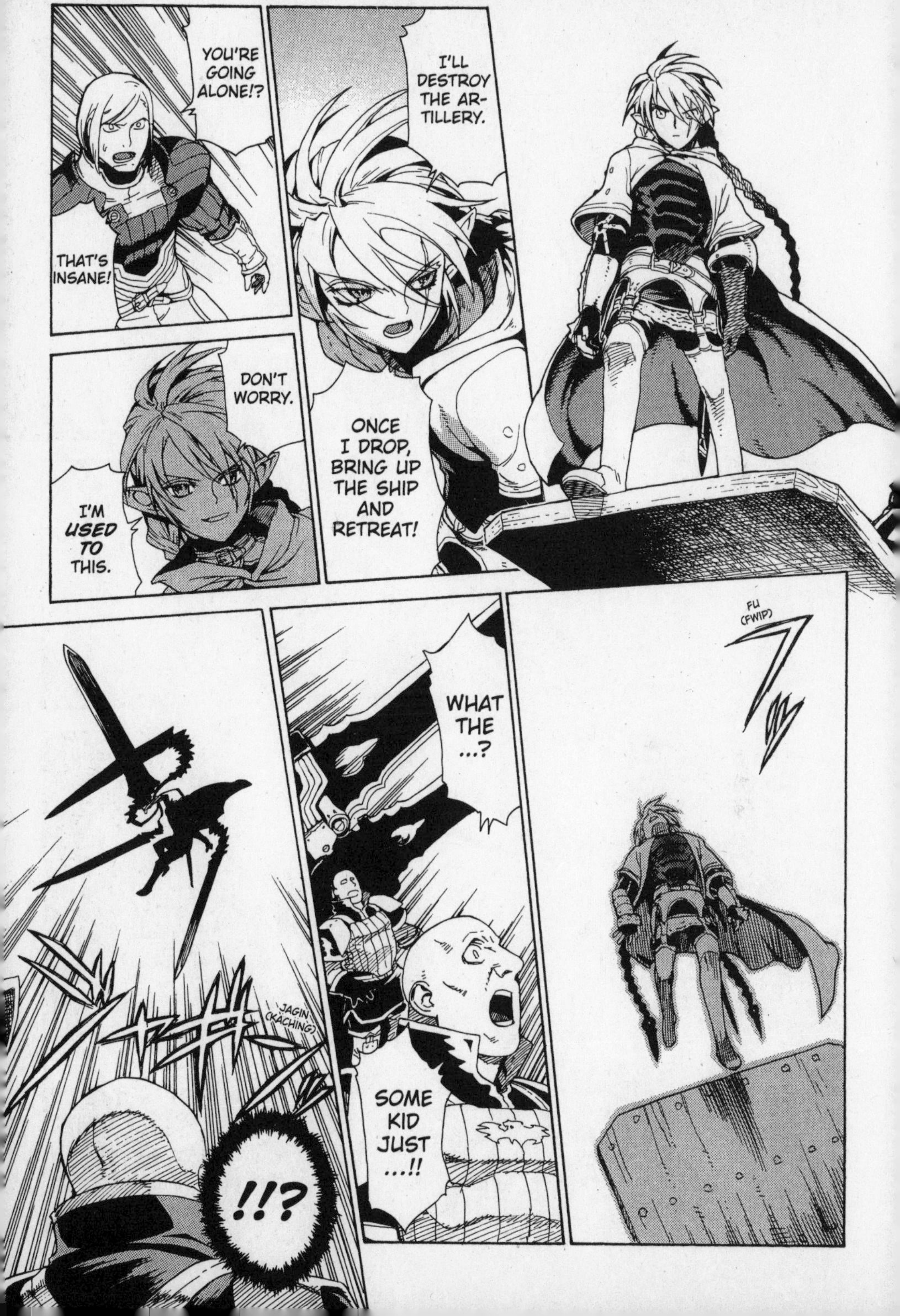
I'LL DESTROY THE AR-TILLERY.
ONCE I DROP, BRING UP THE SHIP AND RETREAT!
YOU'RE GOING ALONE!?
THAT'S INSANE!
DON'T WORRY.
I'M *USED TO* THIS.
FU (FWIP)
WHAT THE ...?
SOME KID JUST ...!!
JAGIN (KACHING)
!!?

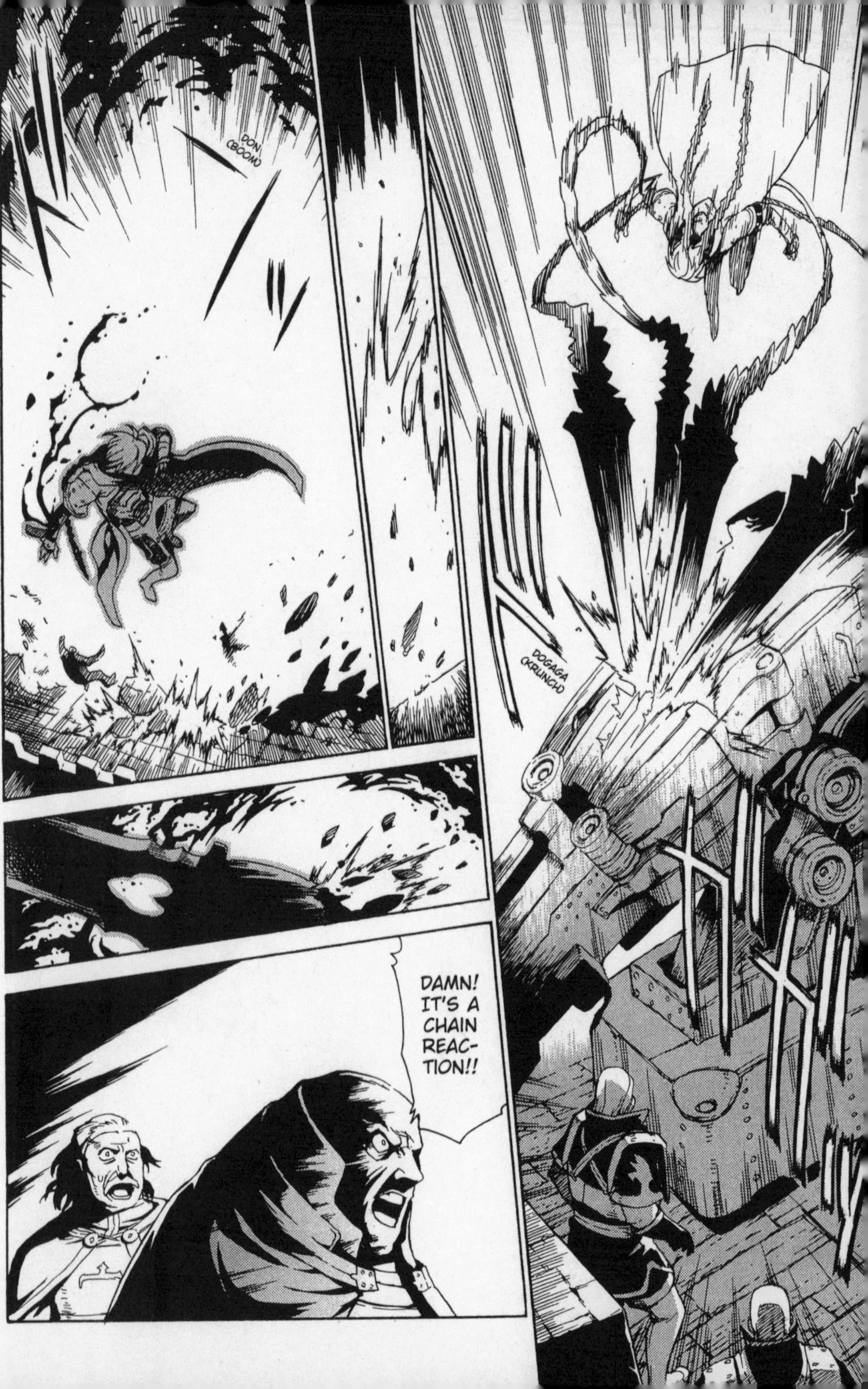
DOGAGA (KRUNCH)
DON (BOOM)
DAMN! IT'S A CHAIN REAC-TION!!

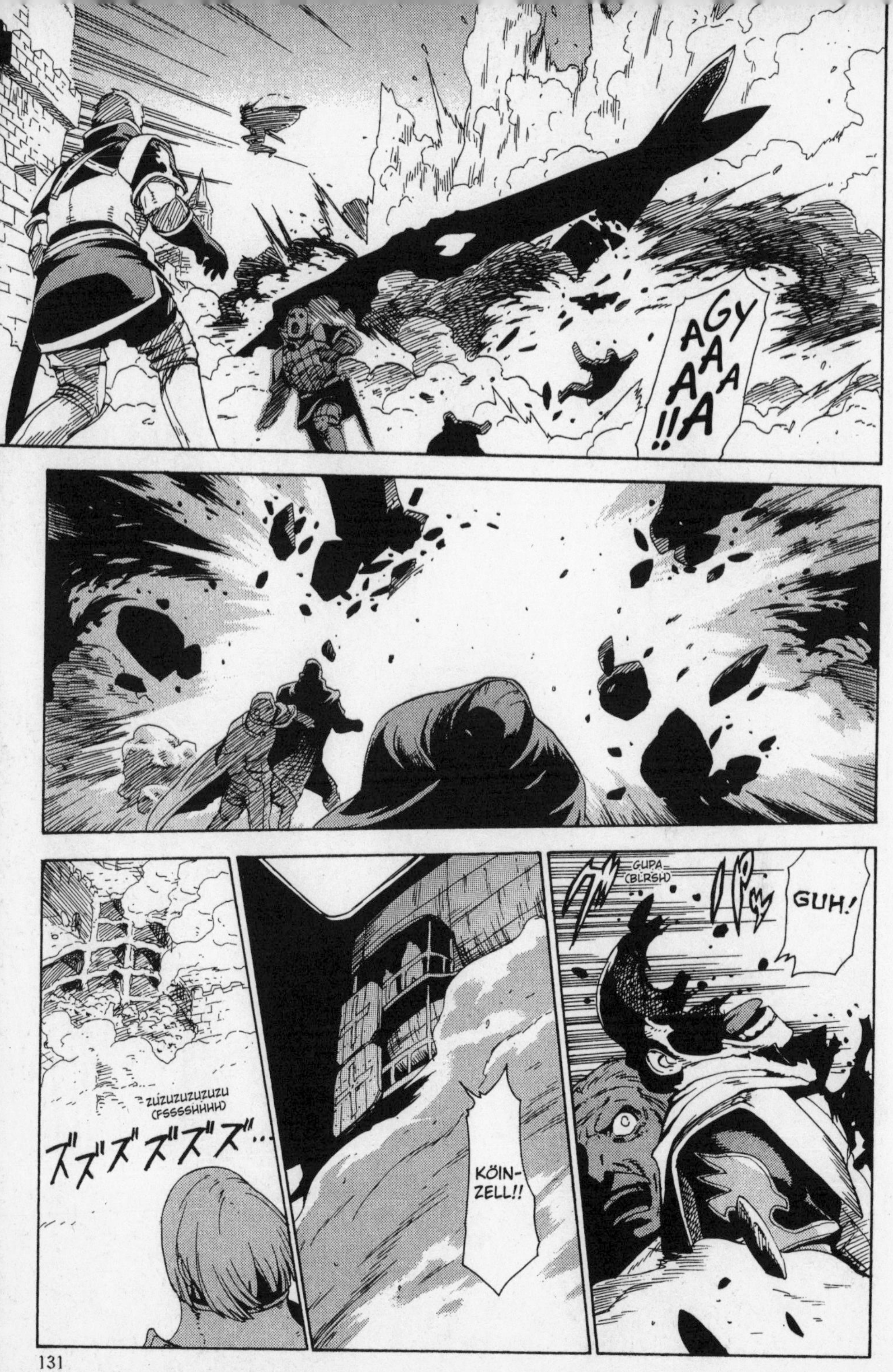
AGYAAAAA!!
GUPA
(BLRSH)
GUH!
KÖIN-
ZELL!!
ZUZUZUZUZUZU
(FSSSSHHHH)
ズズズズズ…

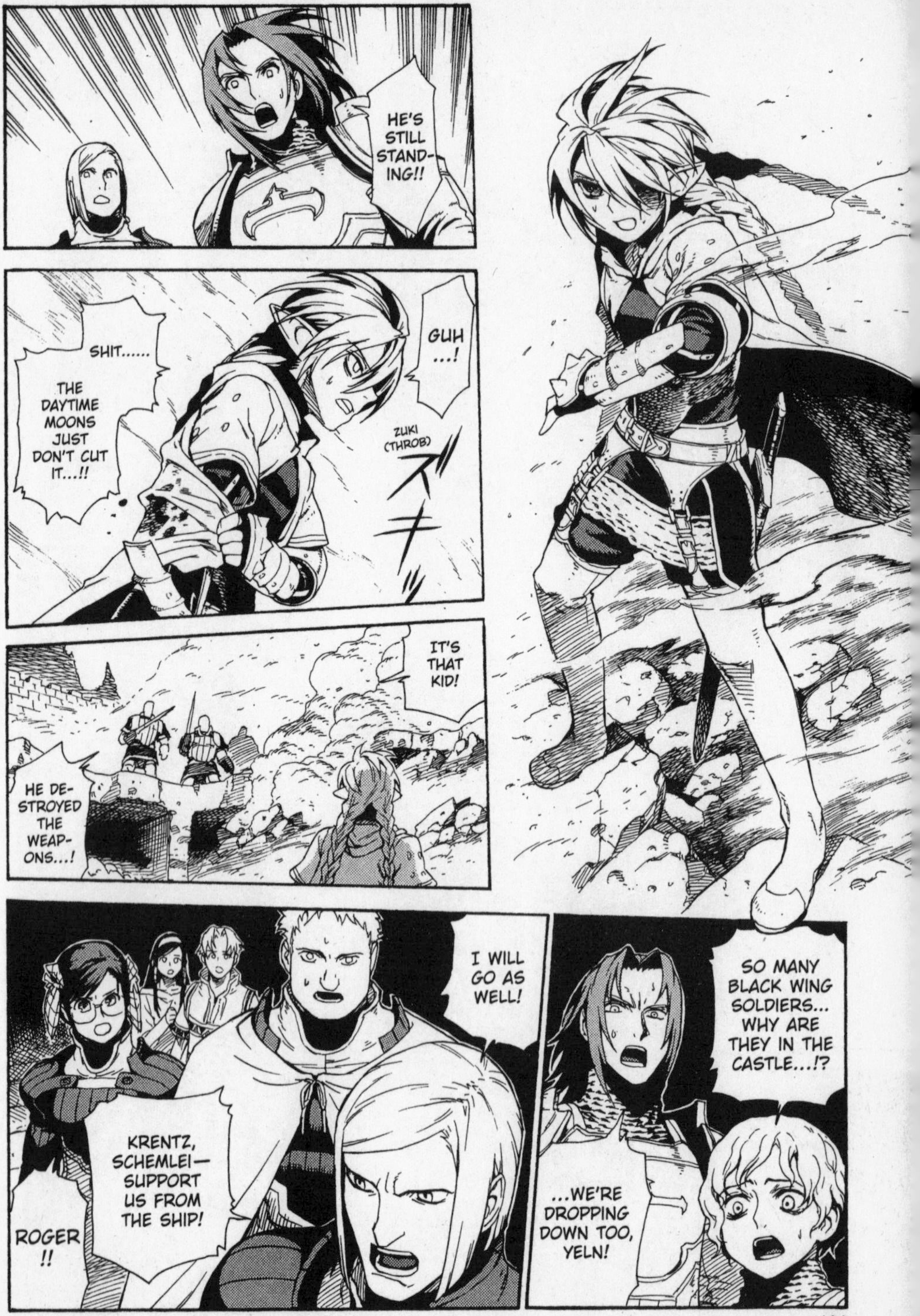
HE'S STILL STANDING!!
GUH...!
ZUKI (THROB)
SHIT......
THE DAYTIME MOONS JUST DON'T CUT IT...!!
IT'S THAT KID!
HE DESTROYED THE WEAPONS...!
SO MANY BLACK WING SOLDIERS... WHY ARE THEY IN THE CASTLE...!?
...WE'RE DROPPING DOWN TOO, YELN!
I WILL GO AS WELL!
KRENTZ, SCHEMLEI—SUPPORT US FROM THE SHIP!
ROGER!!

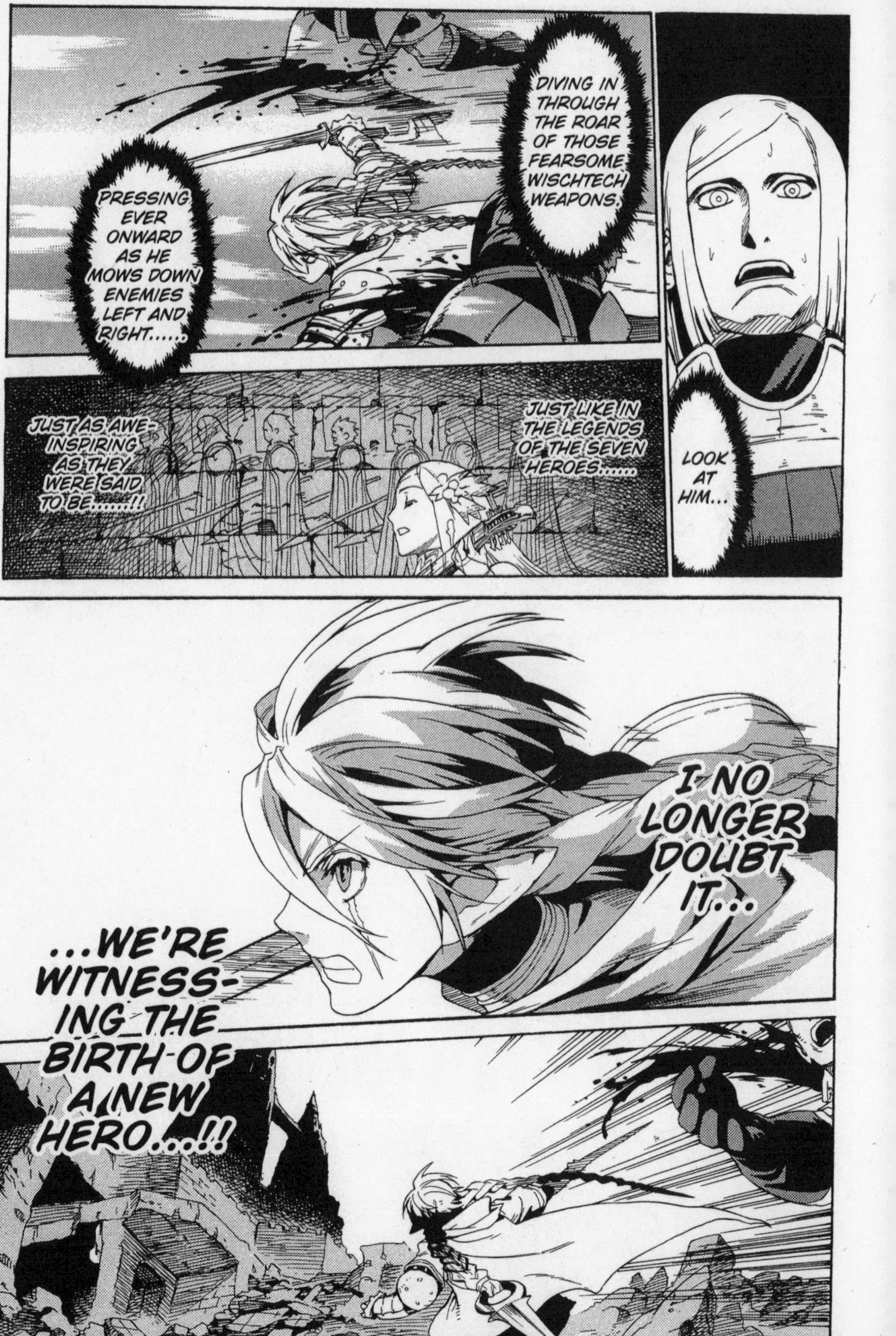
LOOK AT HIM...
DIVING IN THROUGH THE ROAR OF THOSE FEARSOME WISCHTECH WEAPONS.
PRESSING EVER ONWARD AS HE MOWS DOWN ENEMIES LEFT AND RIGHT......
JUST LIKE IN THE LEGENDS OF THE SEVEN HEROES......
JUST AS AWE-INSPIRING AS THEY WERE SAID TO BE......!!
I NO LONGER DOUBT IT...
...WE'RE WITNESSING THE BIRTH OF A NEW HERO...!!

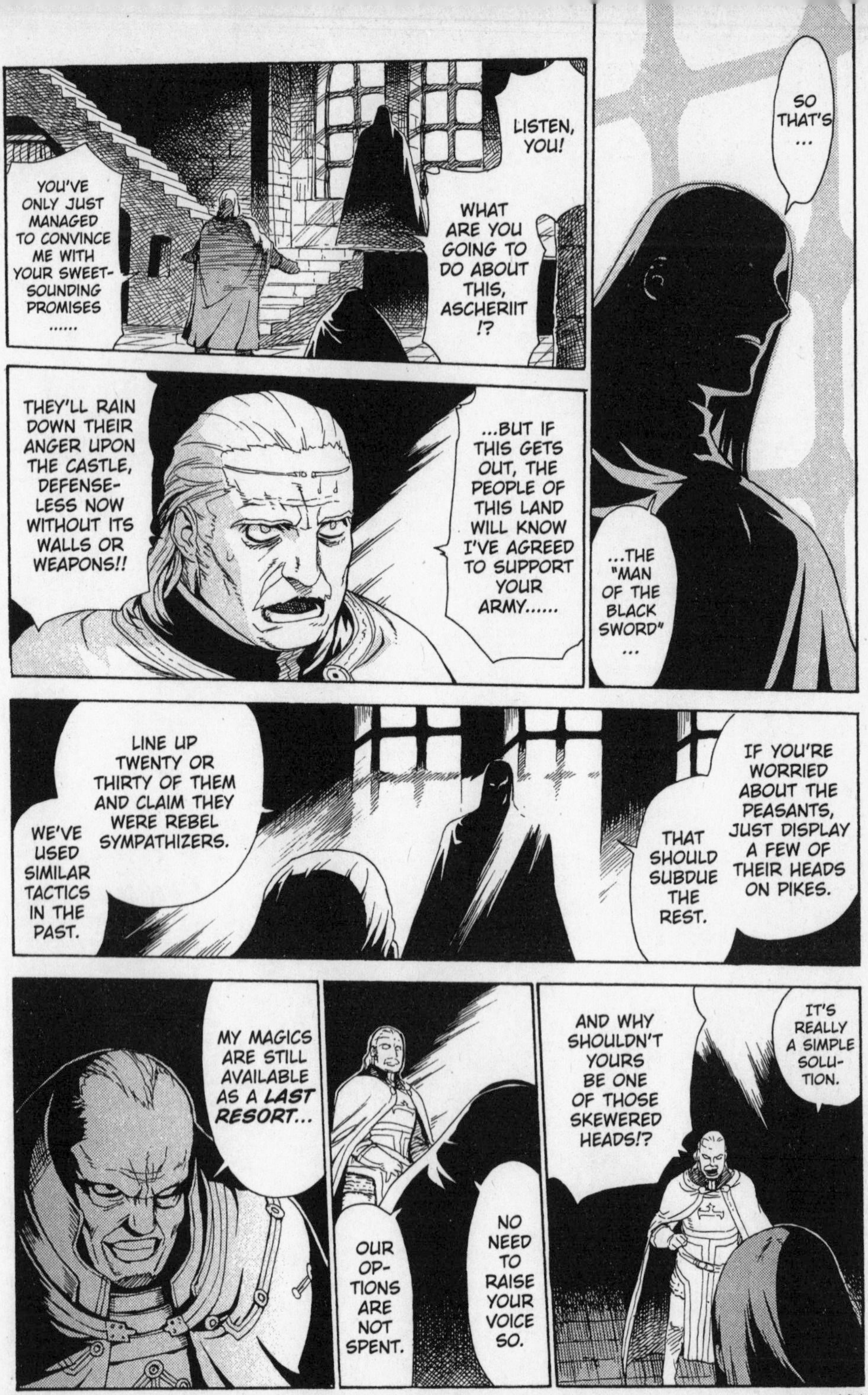
SO THAT'S ...
...THE "MAN OF THE BLACK SWORD" ...
LISTEN, YOU!
WHAT ARE YOU GOING TO DO ABOUT THIS, ASCHERIIT!?
YOU'VE ONLY JUST MANAGED TO CONVINCE ME WITH YOUR SWEET-SOUNDING PROMISES ......
...BUT IF THIS GETS OUT, THE PEOPLE OF THIS LAND WILL KNOW I'VE AGREED TO SUPPORT YOUR ARMY......
THEY'LL RAIN DOWN THEIR ANGER UPON THE CASTLE, DEFENSE-LESS NOW WITHOUT ITS WALLS OR WEAPONS!!
IF YOU'RE WORRIED ABOUT THE PEASANTS, JUST DISPLAY A FEW OF THEIR HEADS ON PIKES.
THAT SHOULD SUBDUE THE REST.
LINE UP TWENTY OR THIRTY OF THEM AND CLAIM THEY WERE REBEL SYMPATHIZERS.
WE'VE USED SIMILAR TACTICS IN THE PAST.
IT'S REALLY A SIMPLE SOLU-TION.
AND WHY SHOULDN'T YOURS BE ONE OF THOSE SKEWERED HEADS!?
NO NEED TO RAISE YOUR VOICE SO.
OUR OP-TIONS ARE NOT SPENT.
MY MAGICS ARE STILL AVAILABLE AS A ***LAST RESORT***...

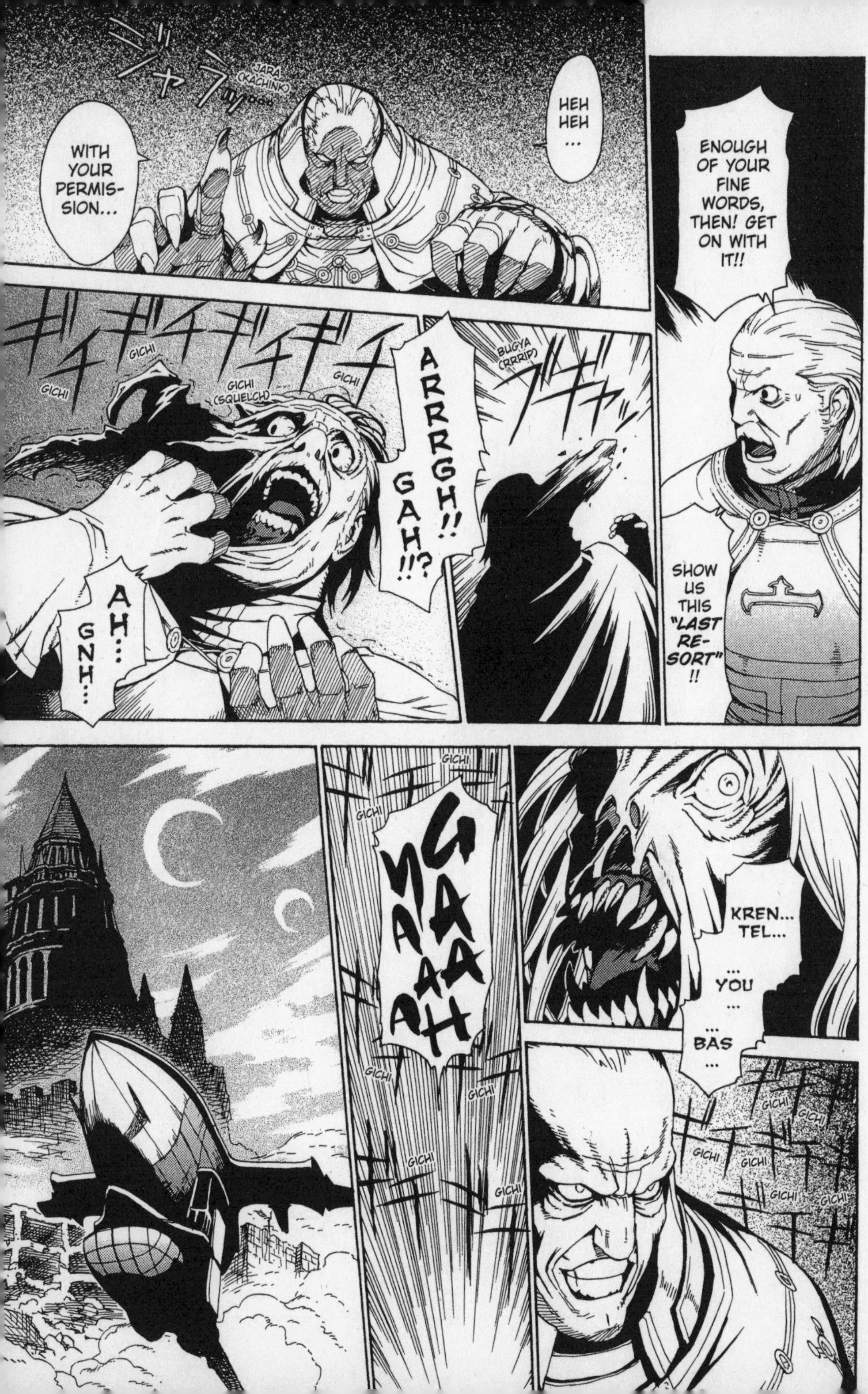

ENOUGH OF YOUR FINE WORDS, THEN! GET ON WITH IT!!
SHOW US THIS "LAST RESORT"!!
HEH HEH ...
JARA (KACHINK)
WITH YOUR PERMIS-SION...
BUGYA (RRRIP)
ARRRGH!! GAH!!?
GICHI
GICHI
GICHI (SQUELCH)
GICHI
AH... GNH...
KREN... TEL... ... YOU ... ... BAS ...
GICHI GICHI GICHI GICHI GICHI GICHI
GICHI
GICHI
NGAAAAAAH
GICHI
GICHI
GICHI
GICHI

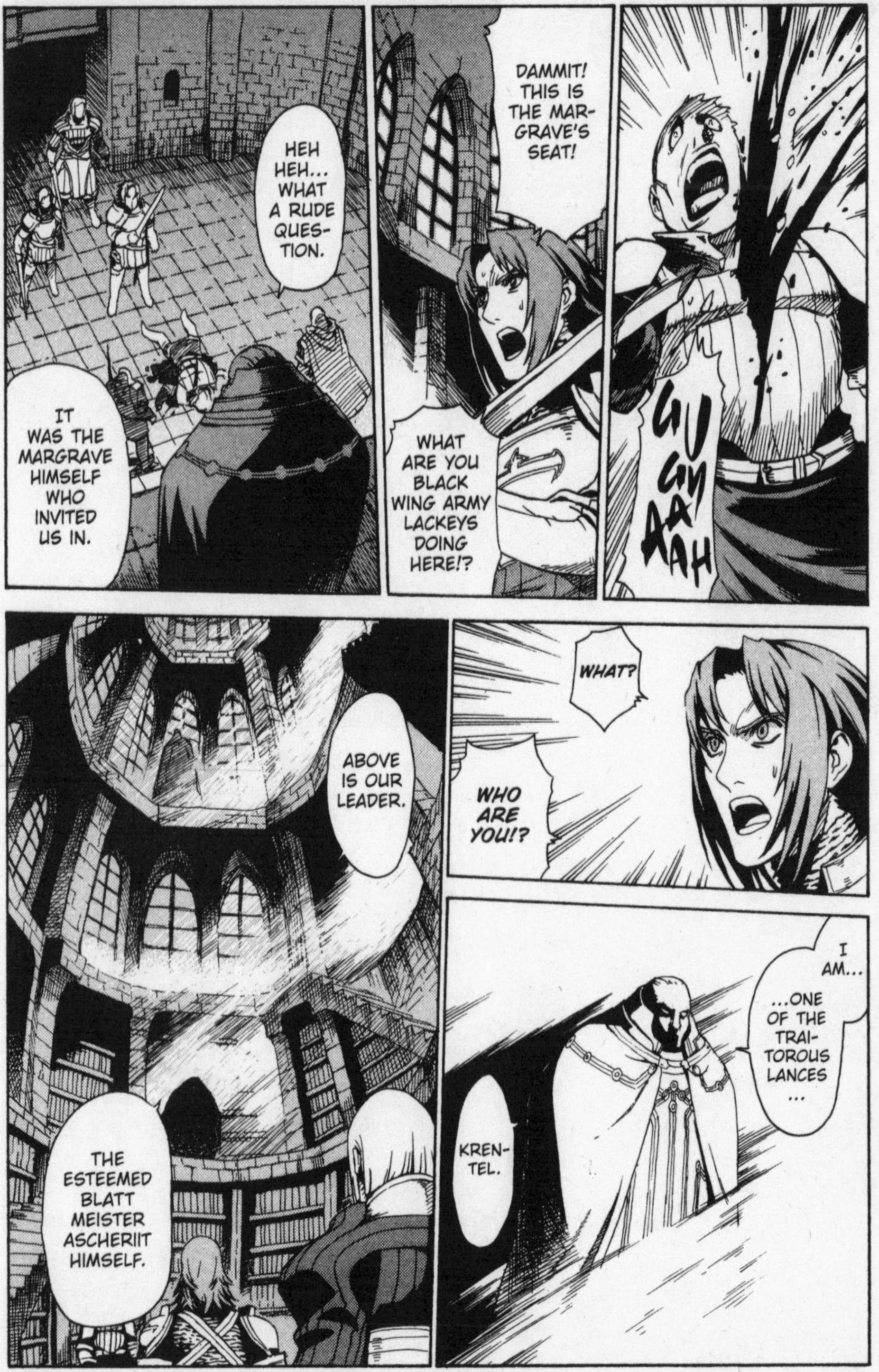
GUGYAAAAH
DAMMIT! THIS IS THE MARGRAVE'S SEAT!
WHAT ARE YOU BLACK WING ARMY LACKEYS DOING HERE!?
HEH HEH... WHAT A RUDE QUESTION.
IT WAS THE MARGRAVE HIMSELF WHO INVITED US IN.
WHAT?
WHO ARE YOU!?
I AM...
...ONE OF THE TRAITOROUS LANCES...
KRENTEL.
ABOVE IS OUR LEADER.
THE ESTEEMED BLATT MEISTER ASCHERIIT HIMSELF.

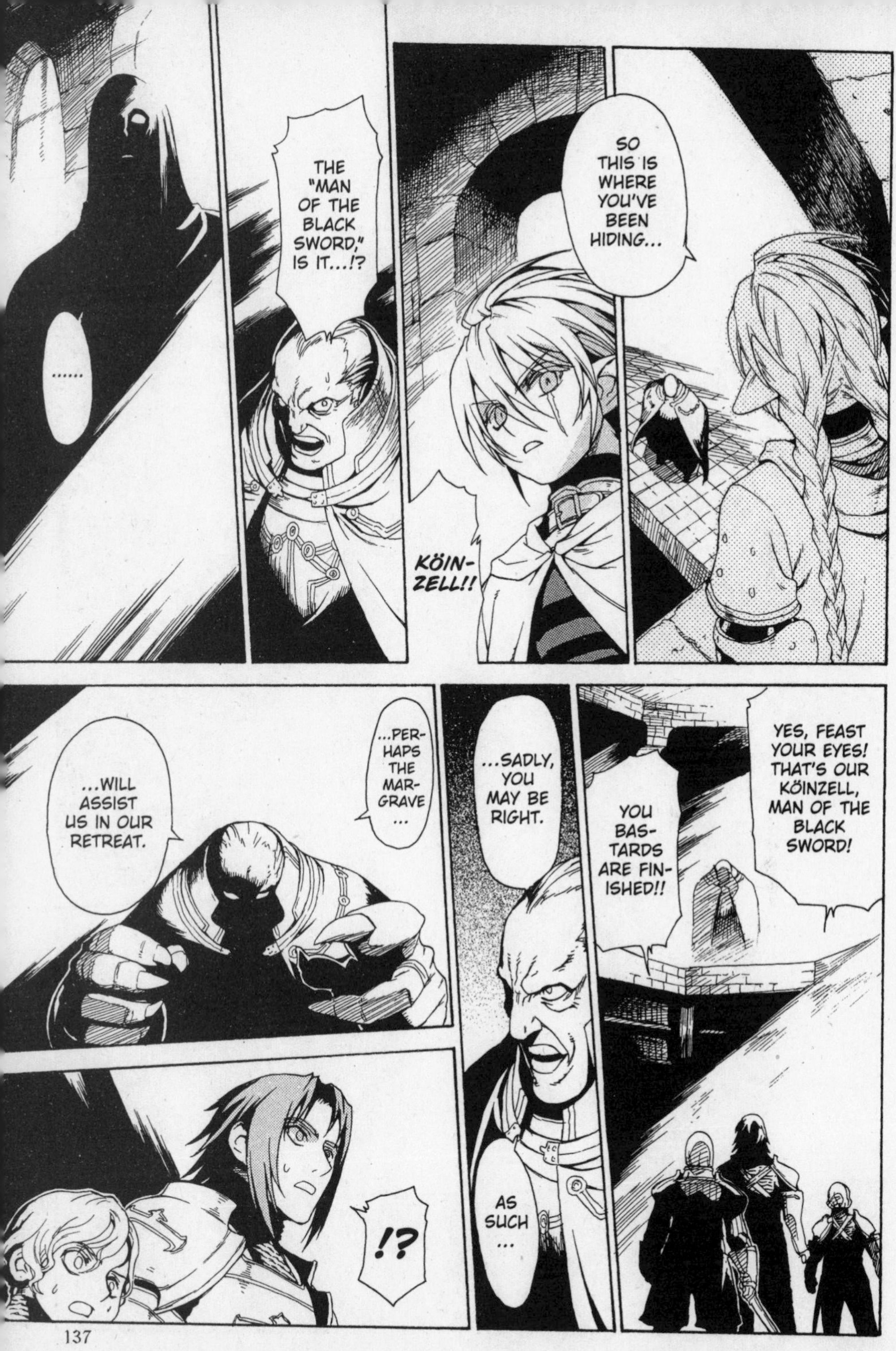
SO THIS IS WHERE YOU'VE BEEN HIDING...
KÖIN-ZELL!!
THE "MAN OF THE BLACK SWORD," IS IT...!?
......
YES, FEAST YOUR EYES! THAT'S OUR KÖINZELL, MAN OF THE BLACK SWORD!
YOU BAS-TARDS ARE FIN-ISHED!!
...SADLY, YOU MAY BE RIGHT.
AS SUCH ...
...PER-HAPS THE MAR-GRAVE ...
...WILL ASSIST US IN OUR RETREAT.
!?

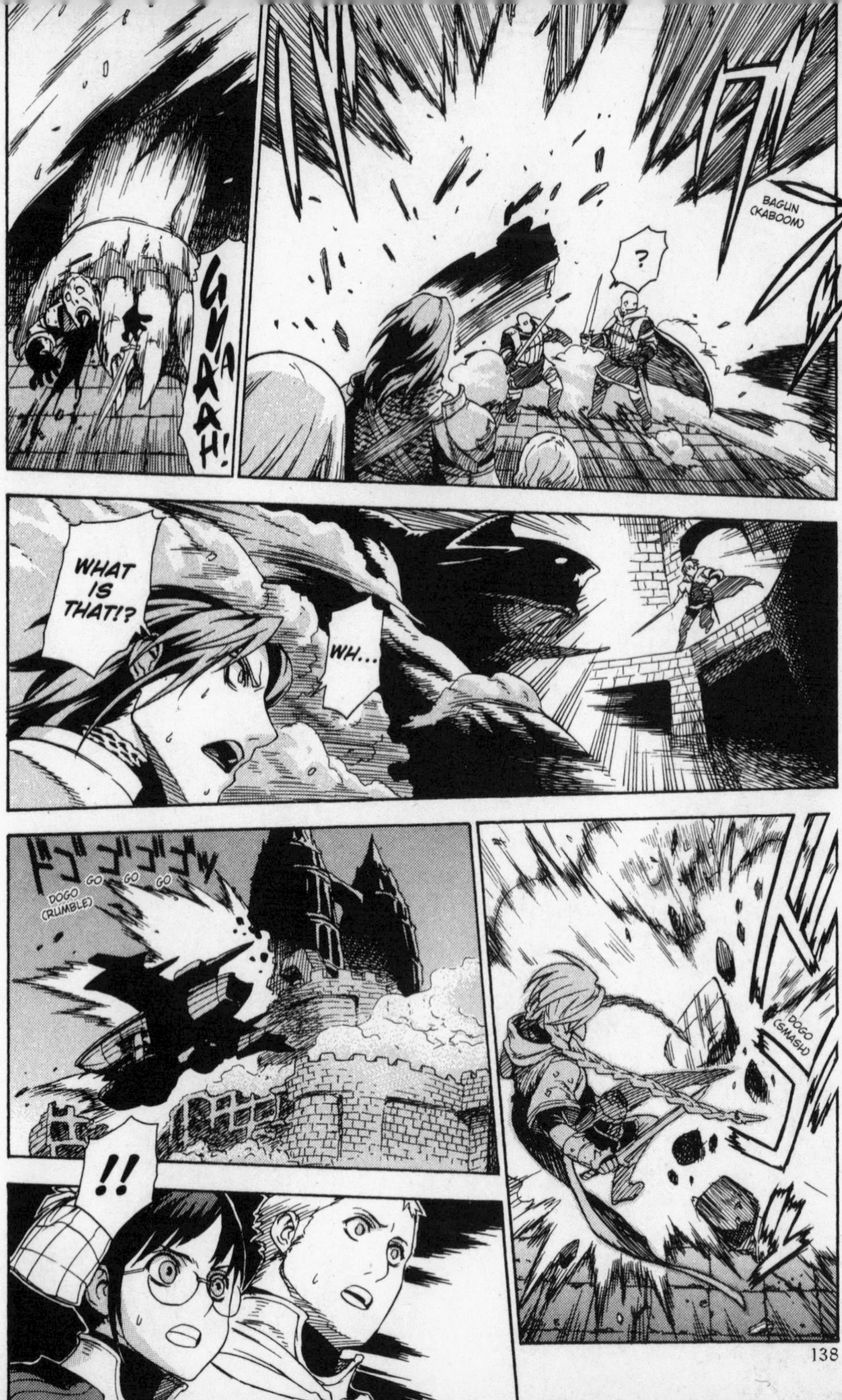
BAGUN (KABOOM)
?
UWAAAAH!
WH...
WHAT IS THAT!?
DOGO (SMASH)
DOGO (RUMBLE)
GO GO GO
!!

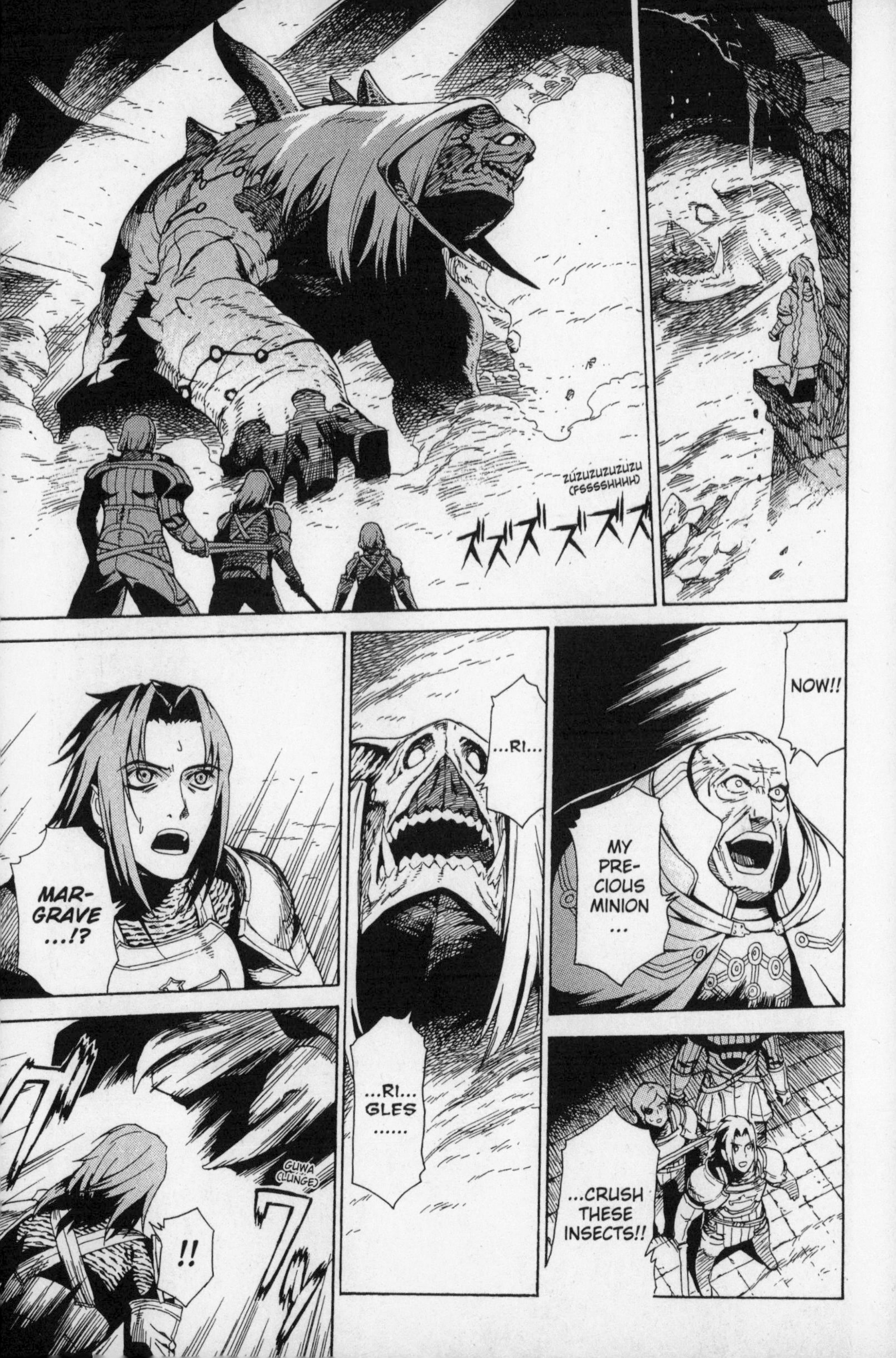
zúzuzuzuzuzu
(FSSSSHHHH)
ズズズズズズ
NOW!!
MY PRECIOUS MINION ...
...CRUSH THESE INSECTS!!
...RI...
...RI... GLES ......
MAR-GRAVE ...!?
GUWA (LUNGE)
!!

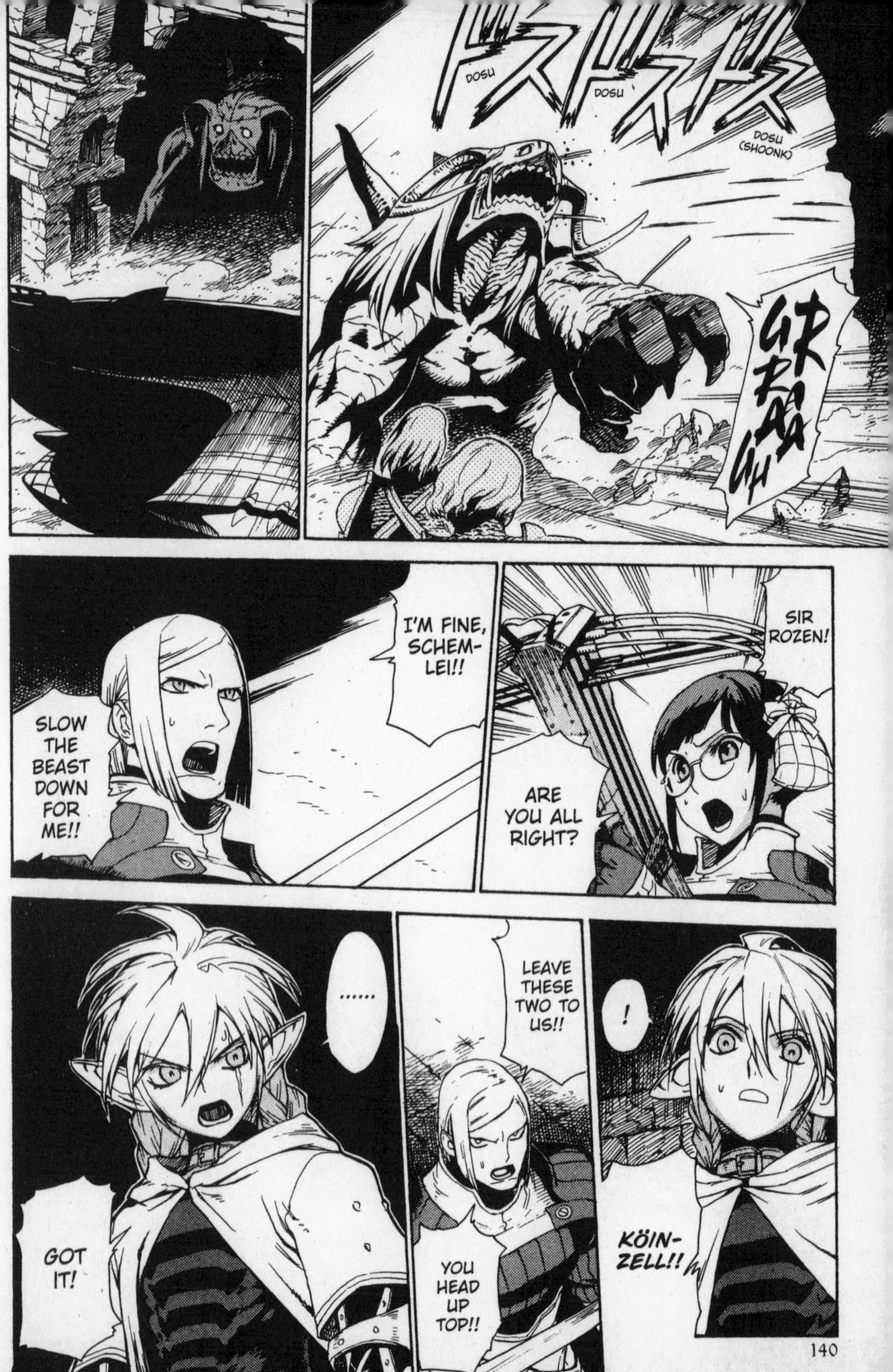
DOSU
DOSU
DOSU (SHOONK)
GRRAAAUH
SIR ROZEN!
ARE YOU ALL RIGHT?
I'M FINE, SCHEM-LEI!!
SLOW THE BEAST DOWN FOR ME!!
!
KÖIN-ZELL!!
LEAVE THESE TWO TO US!!
YOU HEAD UP TOP!!
......
GOT IT!

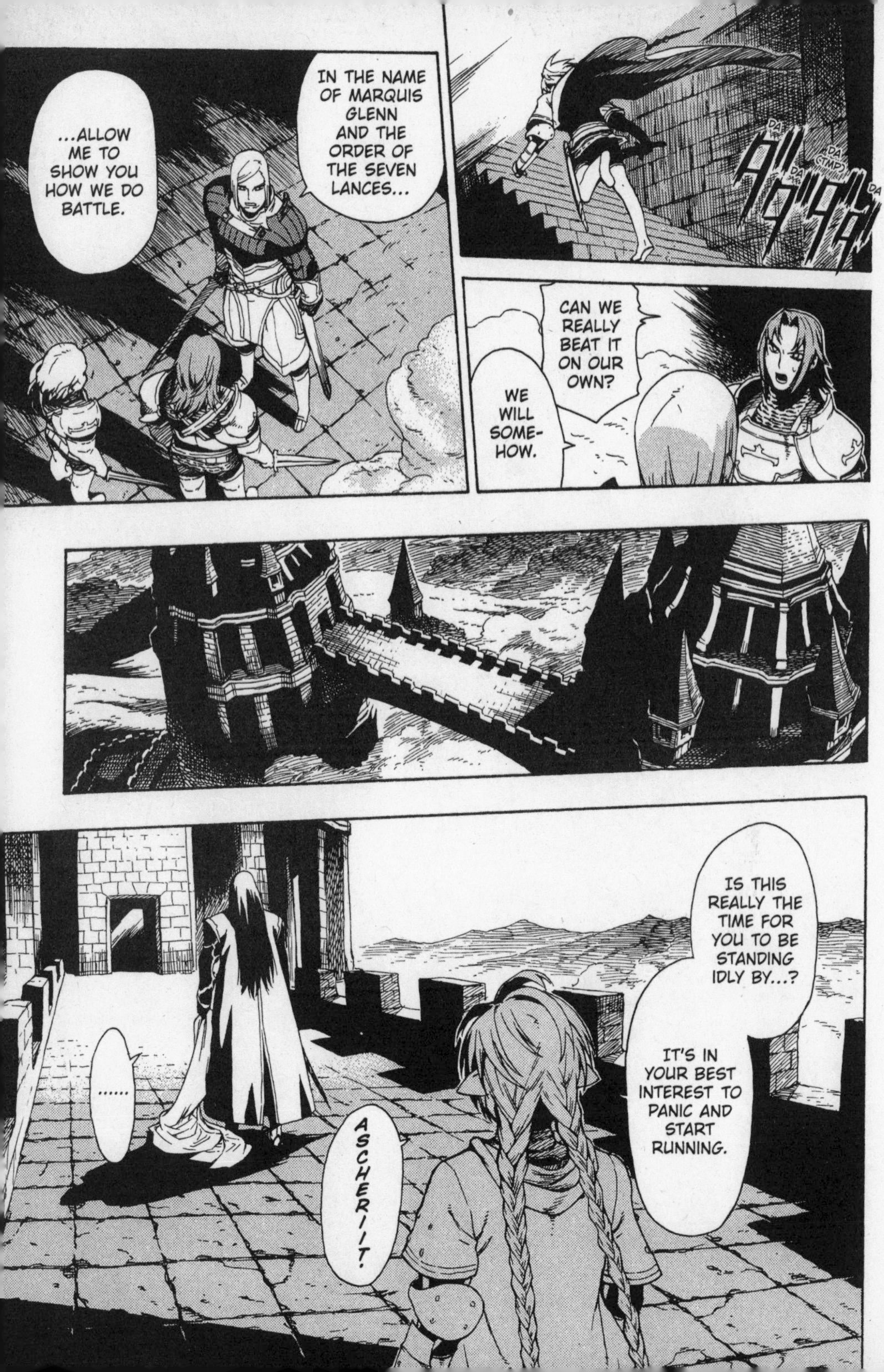
DA
DA (TMP)
DA
DA
CAN WE REALLY BEAT IT ON OUR OWN?
WE WILL SOMEHOW.
IN THE NAME OF MARQUIS GLENN AND THE ORDER OF THE SEVEN LANCES...
...ALLOW ME TO SHOW YOU HOW WE DO BATTLE.
IS THIS REALLY THE TIME FOR YOU TO BE STANDING IDLY BY...?
IT'S IN YOUR BEST INTEREST TO PANIC AND START RUNNING.
ASCHERIIT!
......

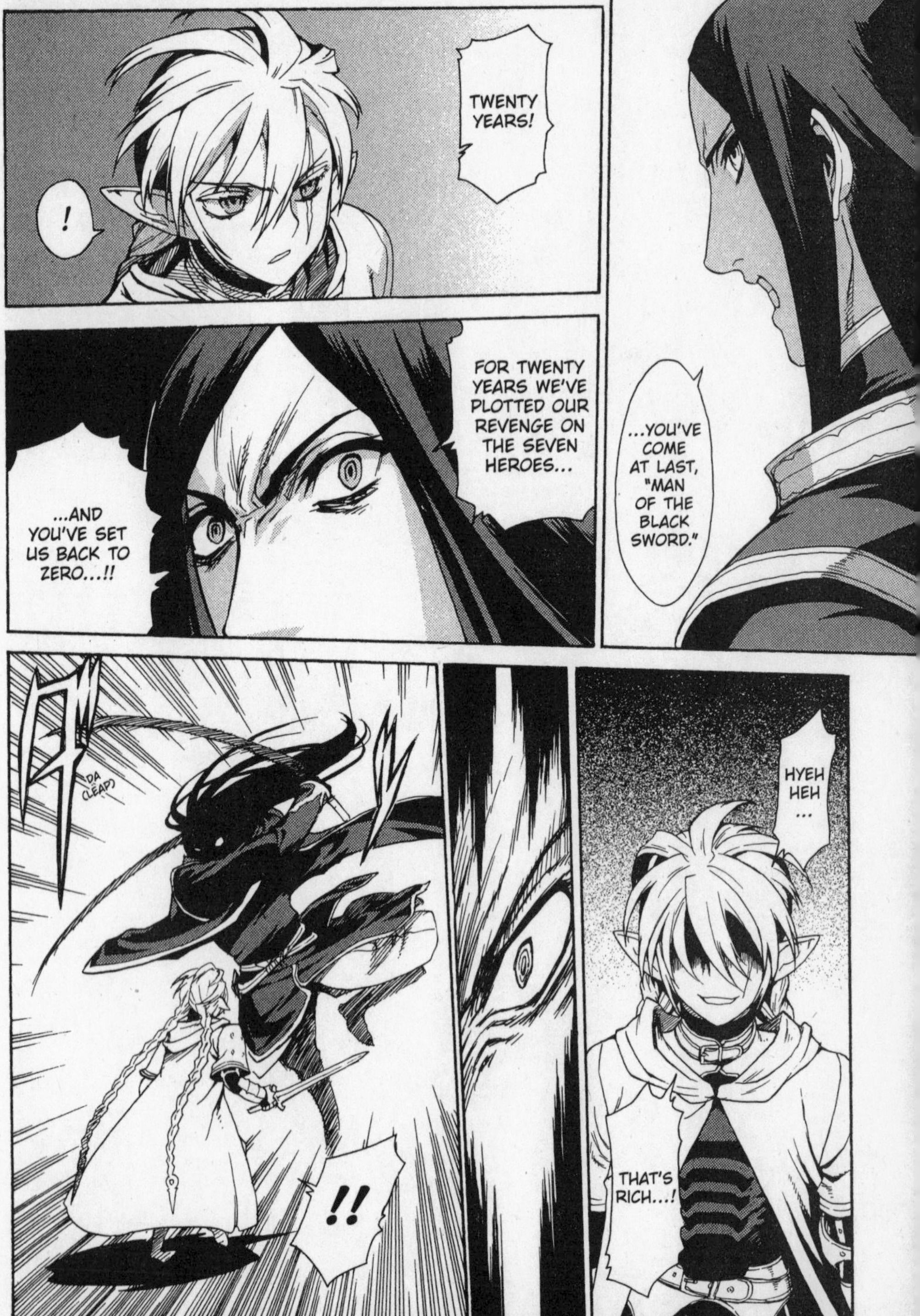
...YOU'VE COME AT LAST, "MAN OF THE BLACK SWORD."
TWENTY YEARS!
!
FOR TWENTY YEARS WE'VE PLOTTED OUR REVENGE ON THE SEVEN HEROES...
...AND YOU'VE SET US BACK TO ZERO...!!
HYEH HEH ...
THAT'S RICH...!
DA (LEAP)
!!

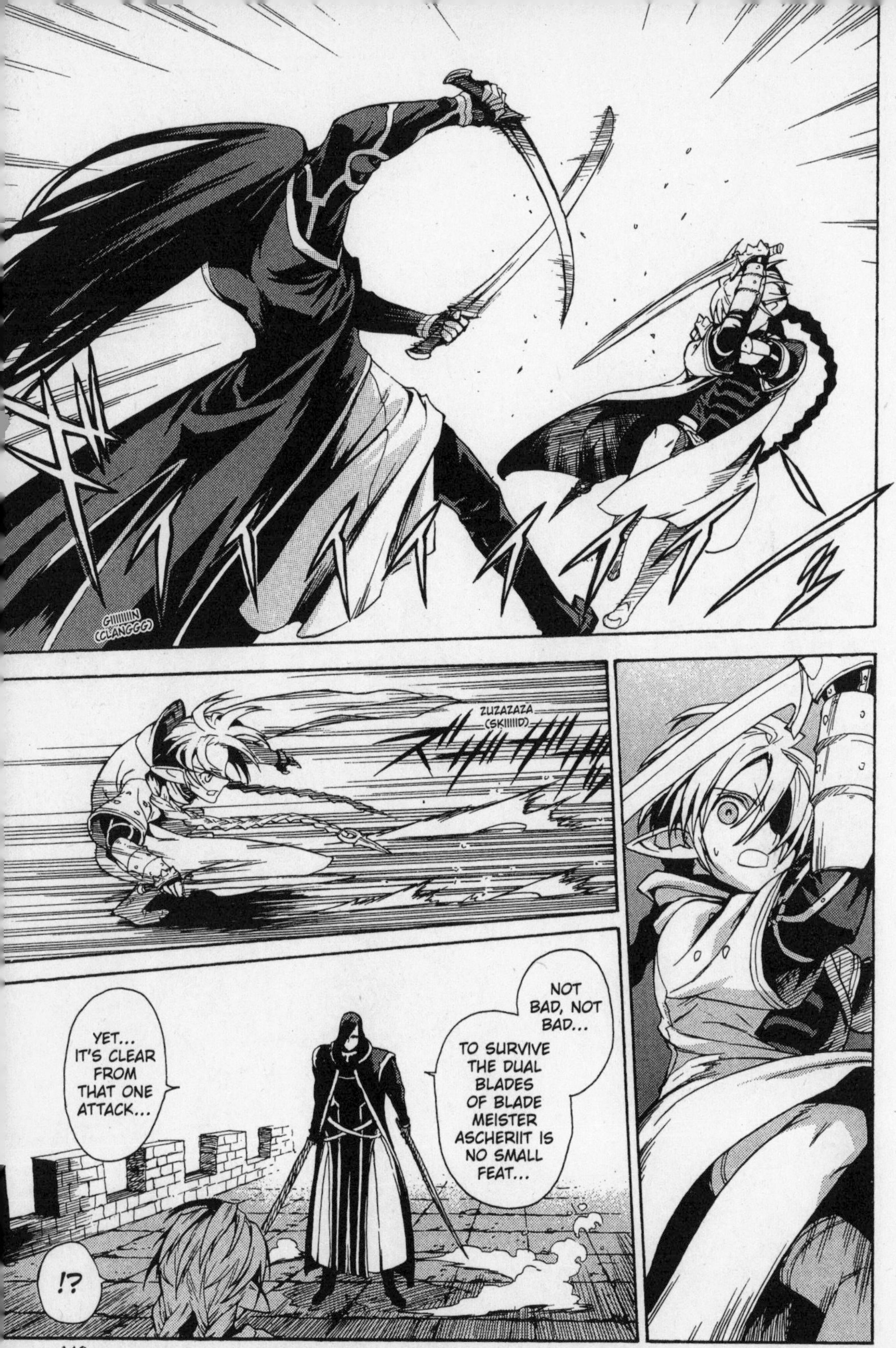
GIIIIIIIN
(CLANGGG)
ZUZAZAZA
(SKIIIIIID)
NOT BAD, NOT BAD...
TO SURVIVE THE DUAL BLADES OF BLADE MEISTER ASCHERIIT IS NO SMALL FEAT...
YET... IT'S CLEAR FROM THAT ONE ATTACK...
!?

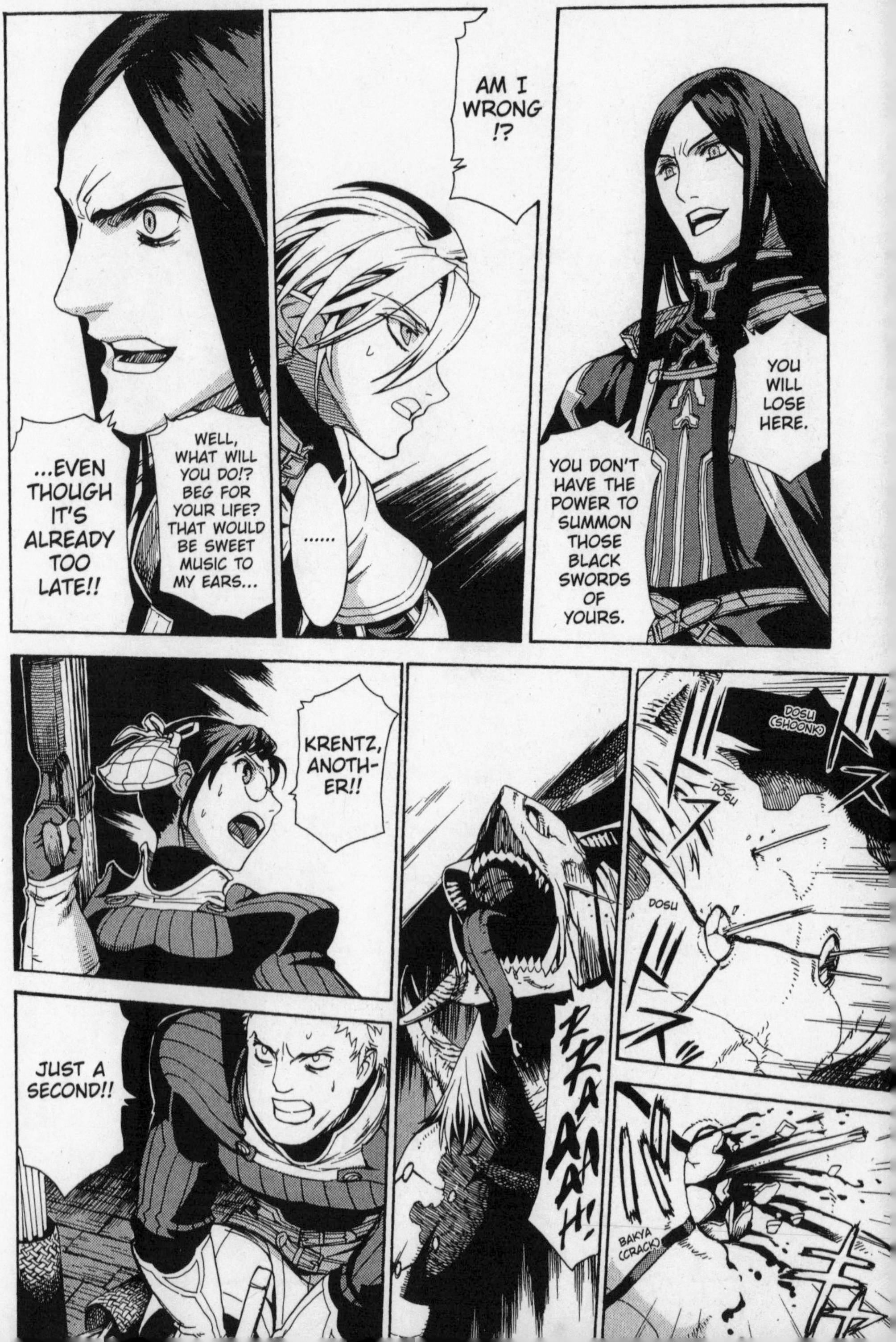
YOU WILL LOSE HERE.
YOU DON'T HAVE THE POWER TO SUMMON THOSE BLACK SWORDS OF YOURS.
AM I WRONG !?
......
WELL, WHAT WILL YOU DO!? BEG FOR YOUR LIFE? THAT WOULD BE SWEET MUSIC TO MY EARS...
...EVEN THOUGH IT'S ALREADY TOO LATE!!
DOSU (SHOONK)
DOSU
DOSU
BAKYA (CRACK)
GRAAAAH!
KRENTZ, ANOTHER!!
JUST A SECOND!!

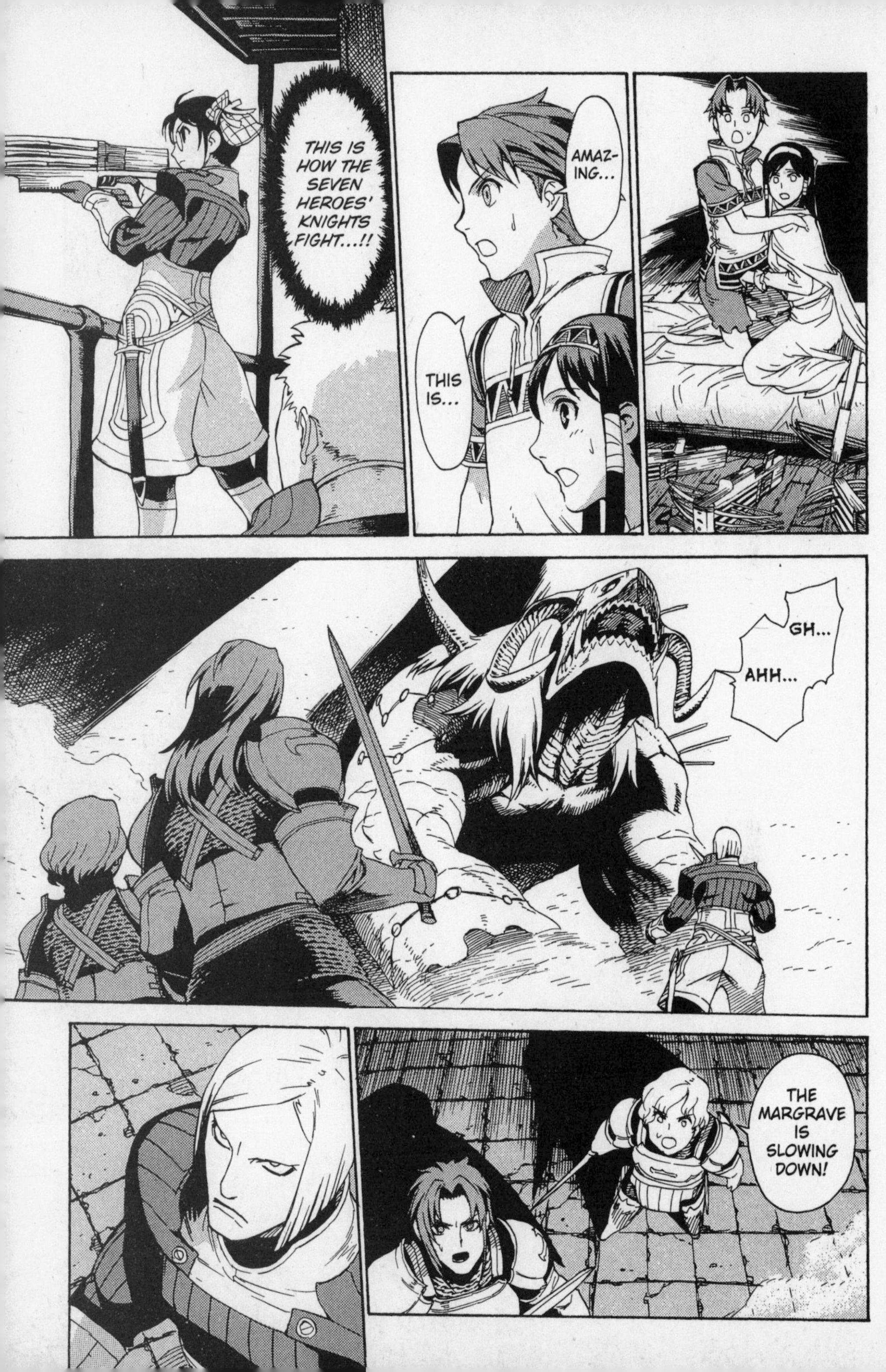
AMAZ-ING...
THIS IS...
THIS IS HOW THE SEVEN HEROES' KNIGHTS FIGHT...!!
GH...
AHH...
THE MARGRAVE IS SLOWING DOWN!

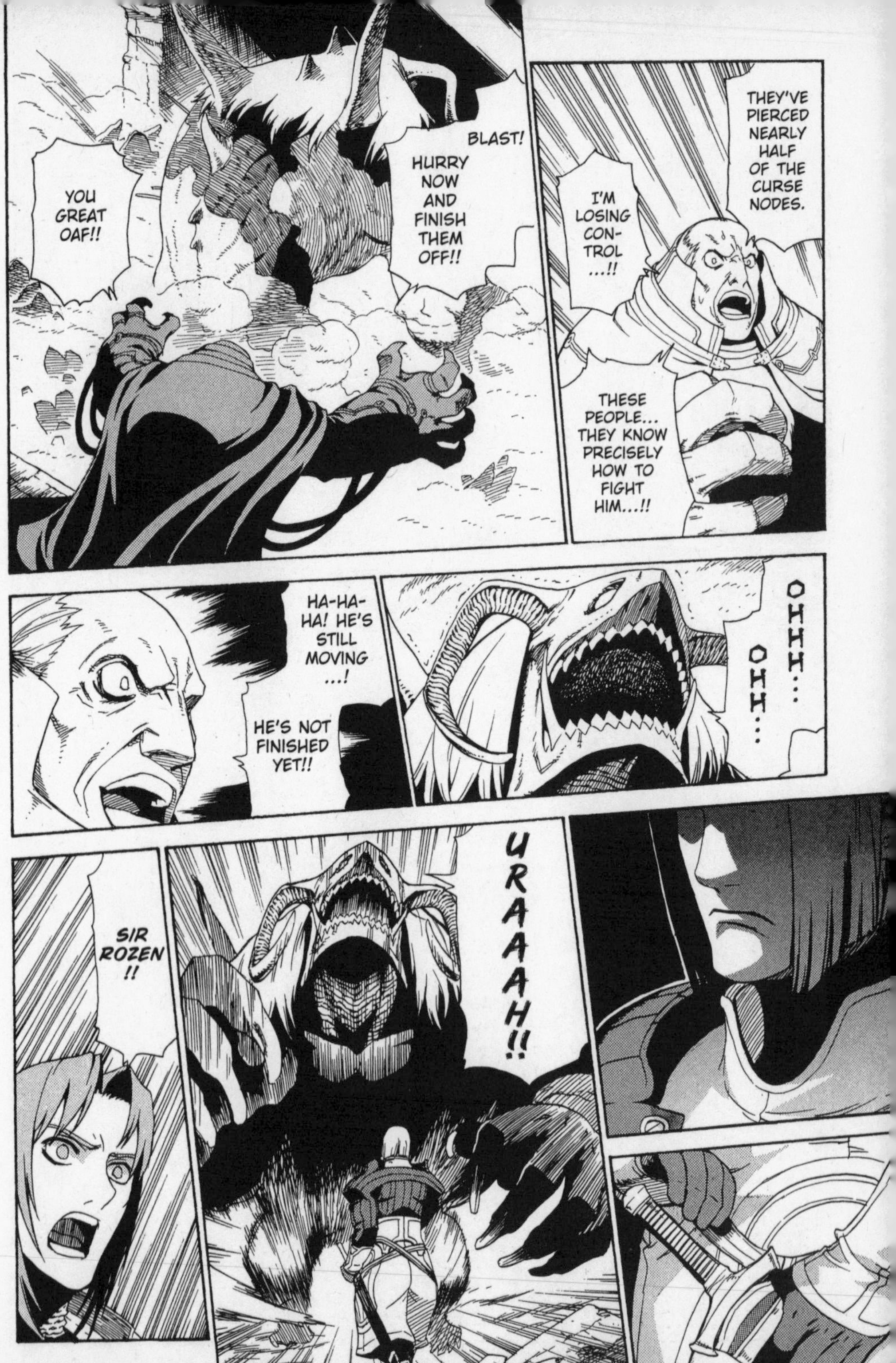
THEY'VE PIERCED NEARLY HALF OF THE CURSE NODES.
I'M LOSING CONTROL...!!
THESE PEOPLE... THEY KNOW PRECISELY HOW TO FIGHT HIM...!!
BLAST!
HURRY NOW AND FINISH THEM OFF!!
YOU GREAT OAF!!
OHHH...
OHH...
HA-HA-HA! HE'S STILL MOVING...!
HE'S NOT FINISHED YET!!
URAAAAH!!
SIR ROZEN!!

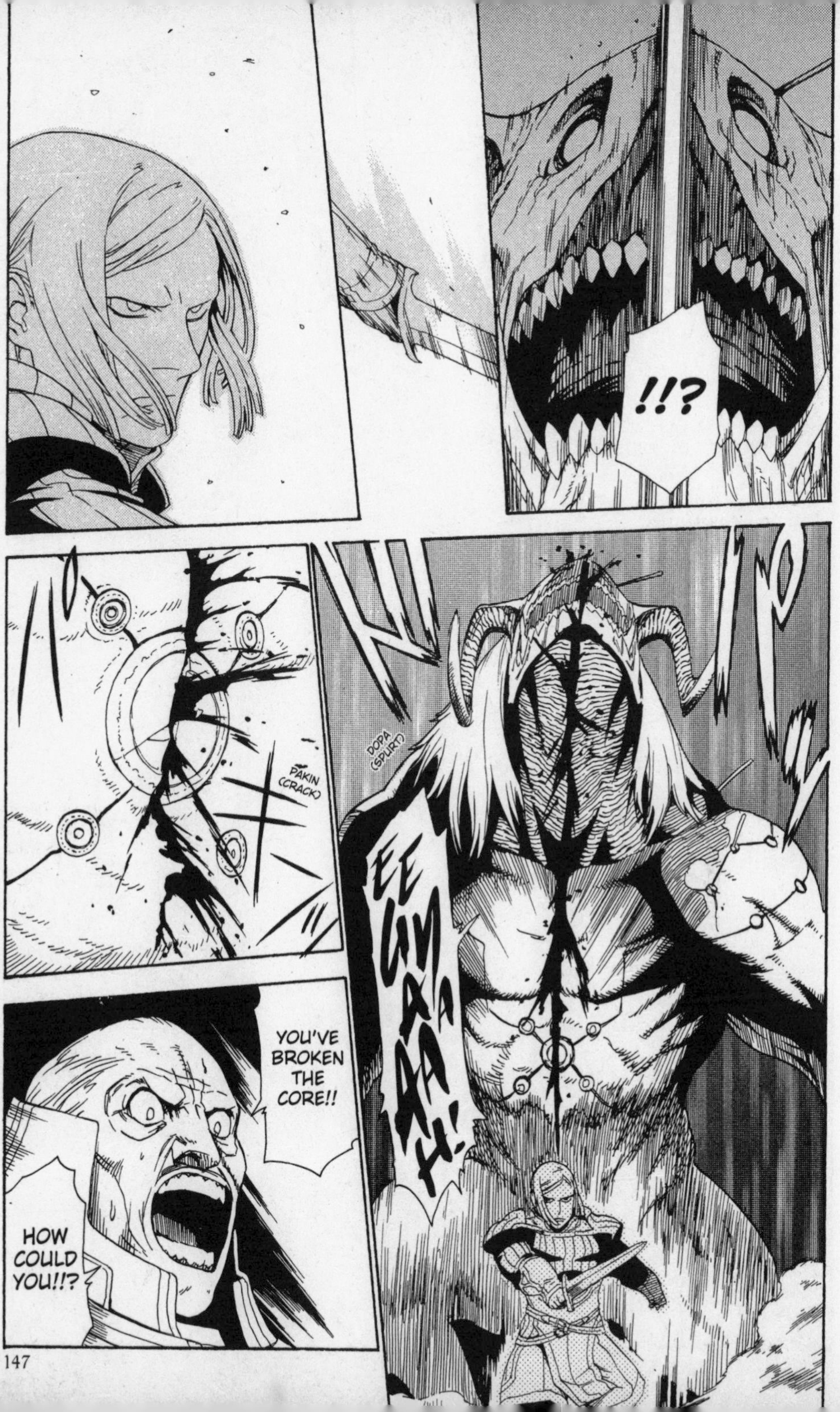
!!?
DOPA (SPURT)
EEUWAAAAAH!
PAKIN (CRACK)
YOU'VE BROKEN THE CORE!!
HOW COULD YOU!!?

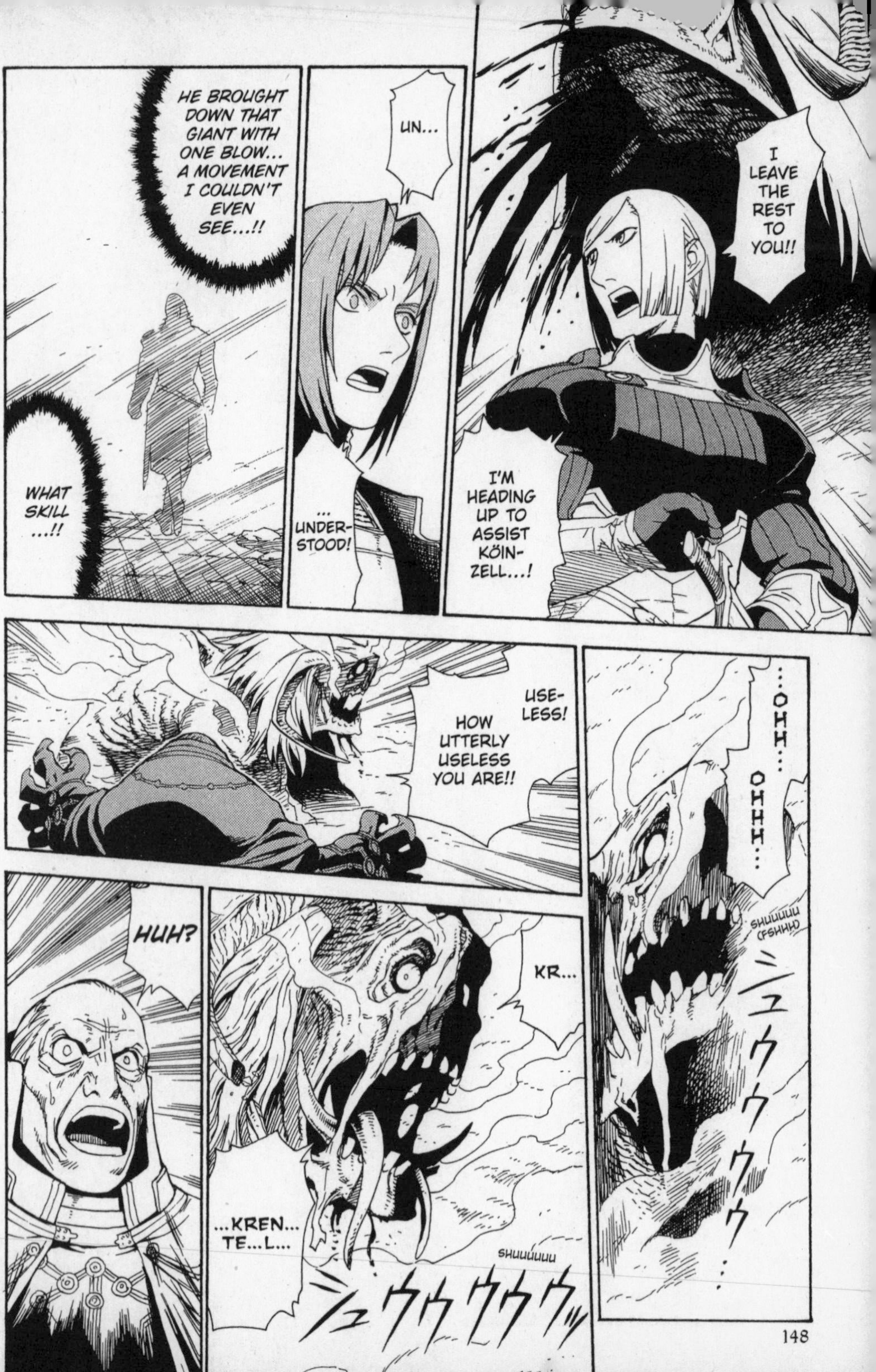
I LEAVE THE REST TO YOU!!
I'M HEADING UP TO ASSIST KÖIN-ZELL...!
UN...
...UNDER-STOOD!
HE BROUGHT DOWN THAT GIANT WITH ONE BLOW... A MOVEMENT I COULDN'T EVEN SEE...!!
WHAT SKILL...!!
...OHH... OHHH...
SHUUUUUU (FSHHH)
USE-LESS!
HOW UTTERLY USELESS YOU ARE!!
KR...
...KREN... TE...L...
SHUUUUUU
HUH?

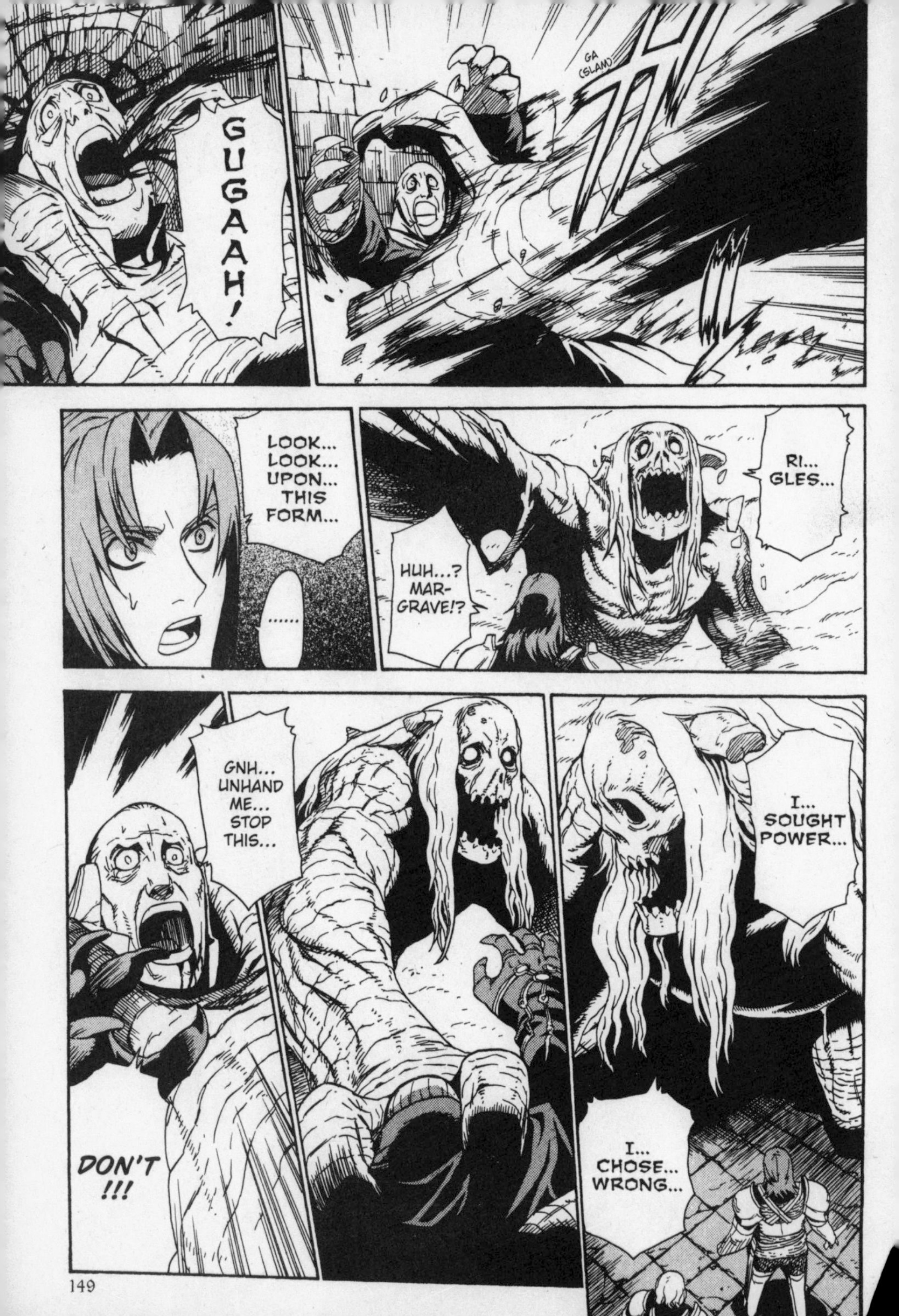
GA (SLAM)
GUGAAH!
RI... GLES...
HUH...? MAR-GRAVE!?
LOOK... LOOK... UPON... THIS FORM...
......
I... SOUGHT POWER...
I... CHOSE... WRONG...
GNH... UNHAND ME... STOP THIS...
DON'T!!!

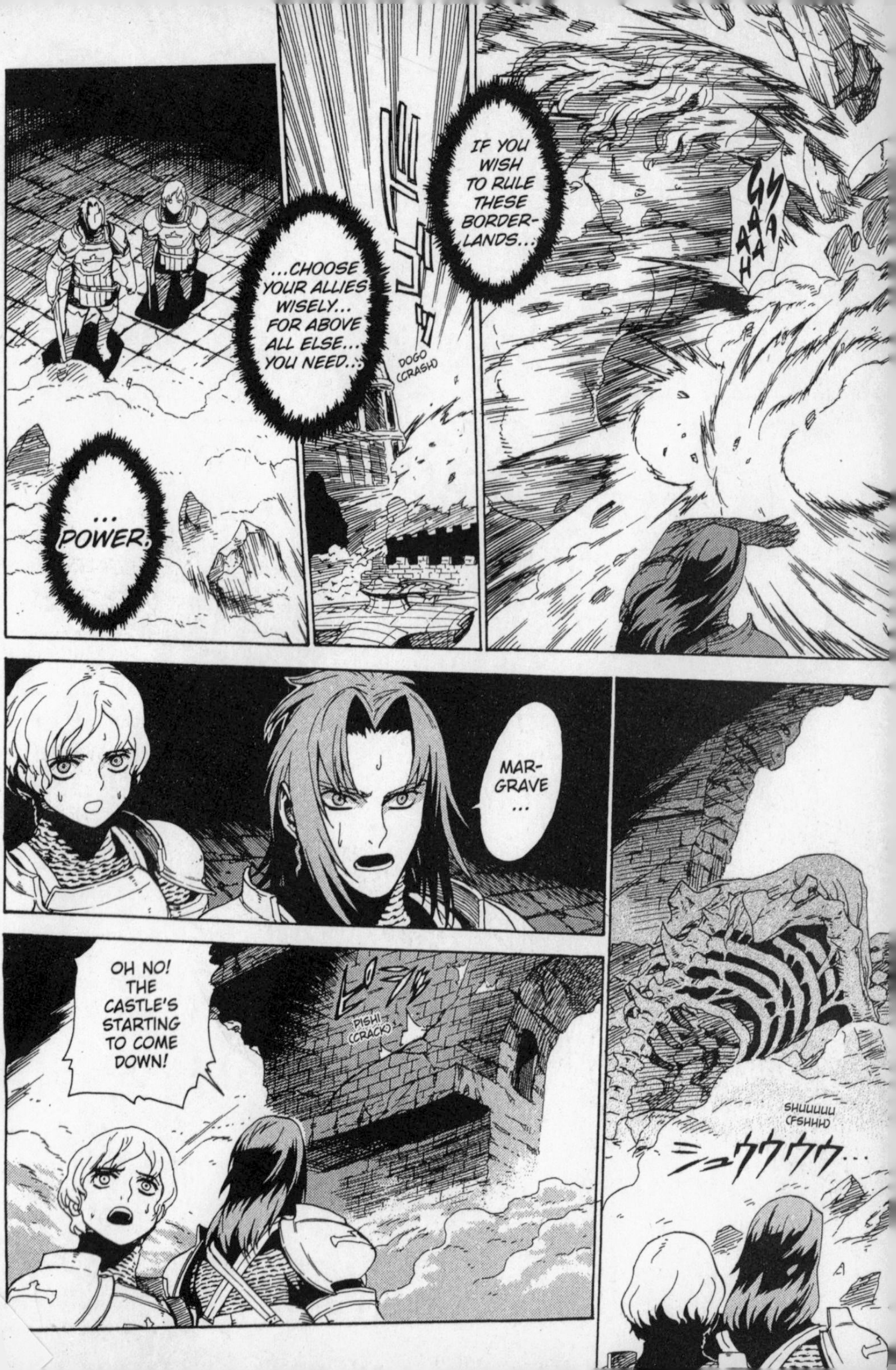
IF YOU WISH TO RULE THESE BORDER-LANDS...
...CHOOSE YOUR ALLIES WISELY... FOR ABOVE ALL ELSE... YOU NEED...
DOGO (CRASH)
... POWER.
SHUUUUU (FSHHH)
MAR-GRAVE ...
OH NO! THE CASTLE'S STARTING TO COME DOWN!
PISHI (CRACK)

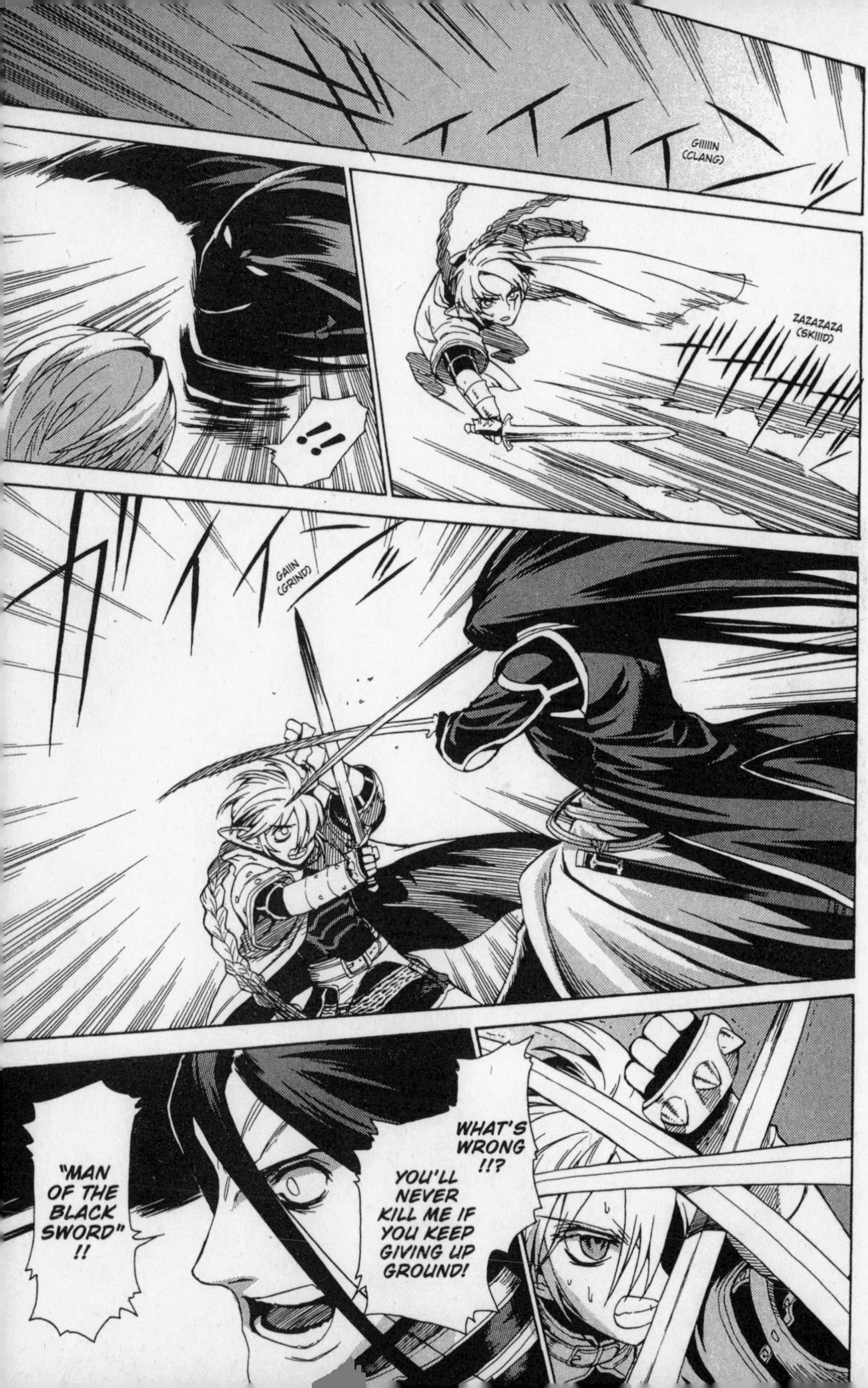
GIIIIN
(CLANG)
ZAZAZAZA
(SKIIID)
!!
GAIIN
(GRIND)
WHAT'S WRONG!!?
YOU'LL NEVER KILL ME IF YOU KEEP GIVING UP GROUND!
"MAN OF THE BLACK SWORD"!!

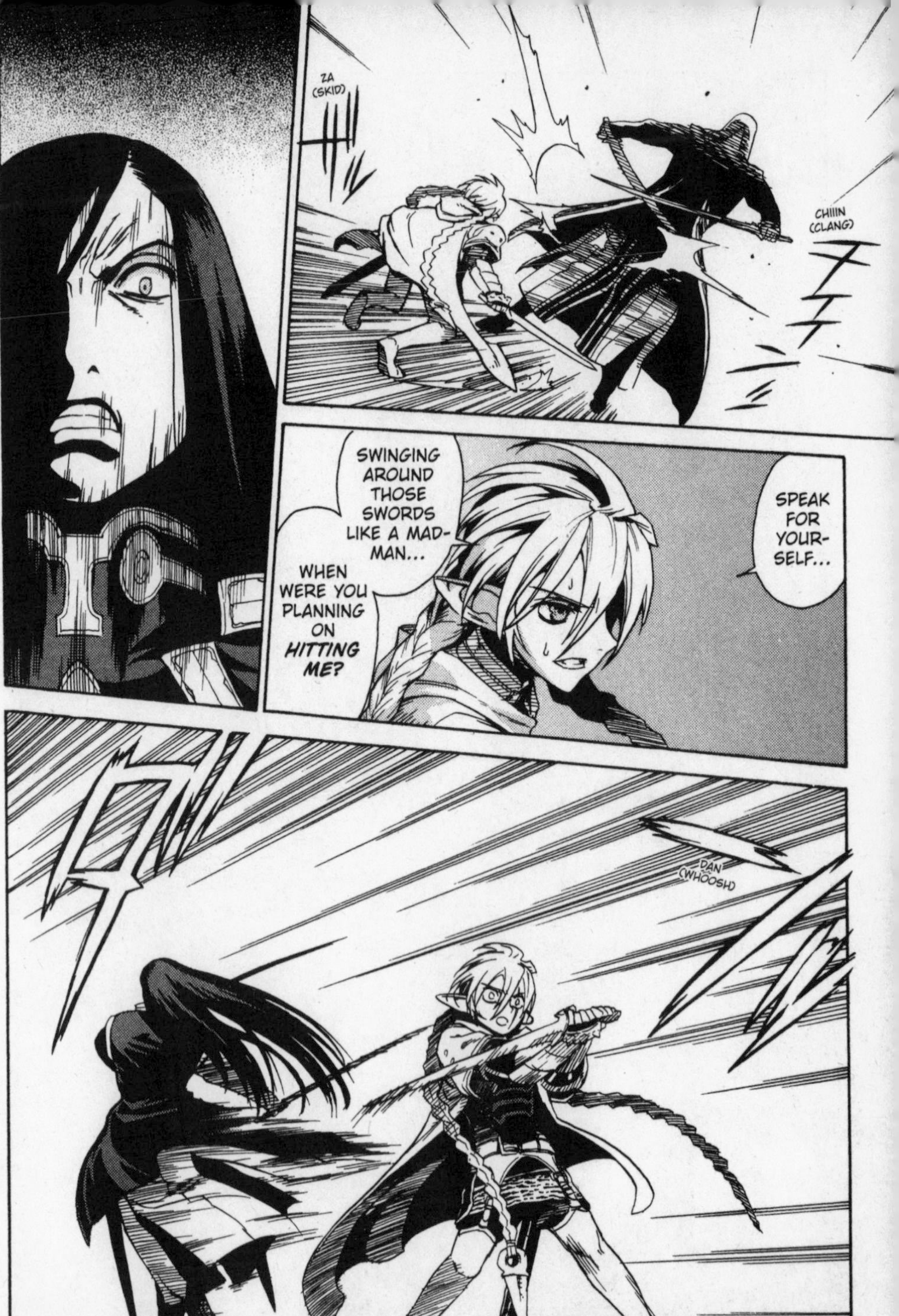
CHIIIN (CLANG)
ZA (SKID)
SPEAK FOR YOUR-SELF...
SWINGING AROUND THOSE SWORDS LIKE A MAD-MAN...
WHEN WERE YOU PLANNING ON *HITTING* ME?
DAN (WHOOSH)

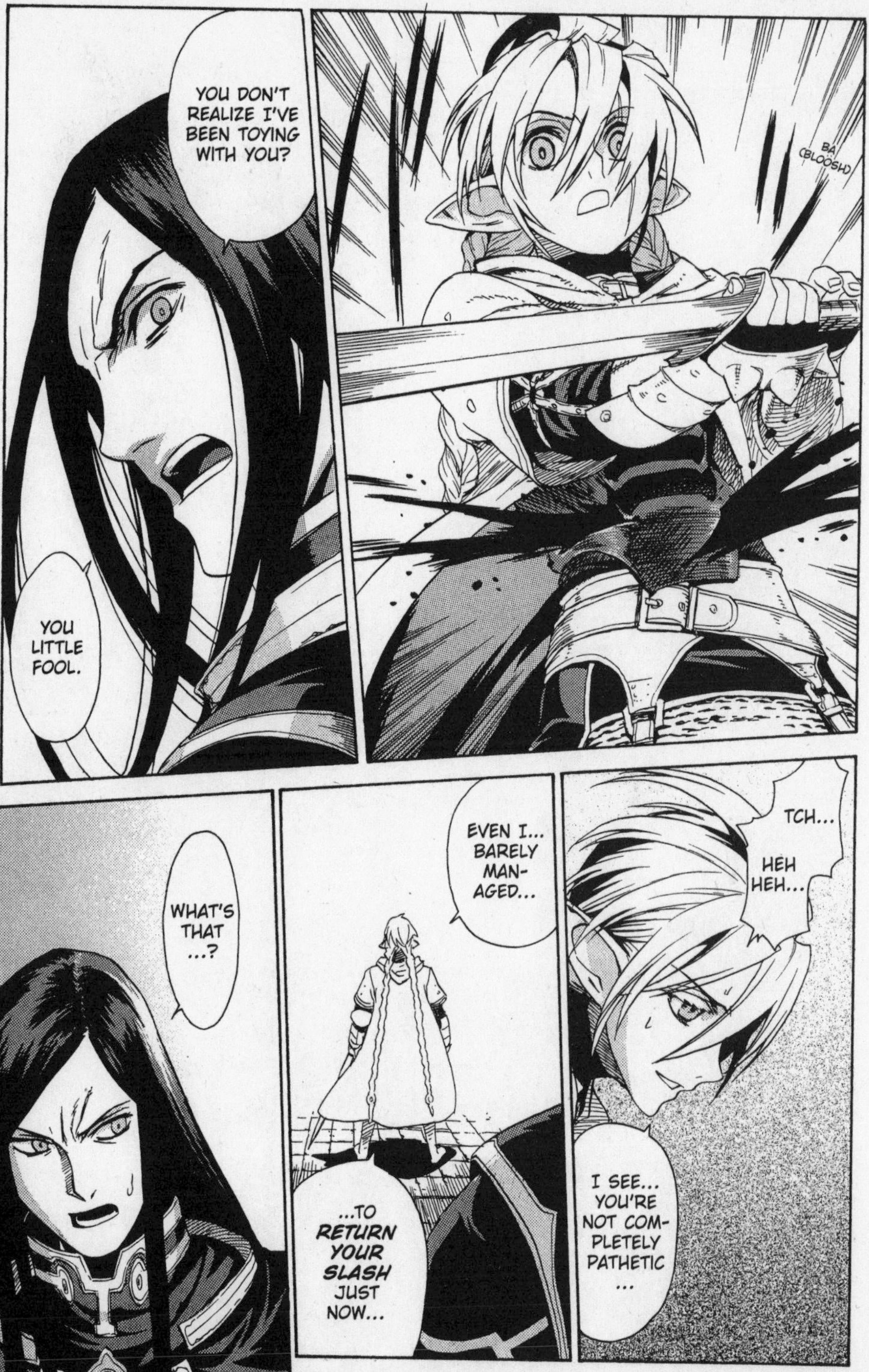
BA (BLOOSH)
YOU DON'T REALIZE I'VE BEEN TOYING WITH YOU?
YOU LITTLE FOOL.
TCH...
HEH HEH...
I SEE... YOU'RE NOT COM-PLETELY PATHETIC ...
EVEN I... BARELY MAN-AGED...
...TO *RETURN YOUR SLASH* JUST NOW...
WHAT'S THAT ...?

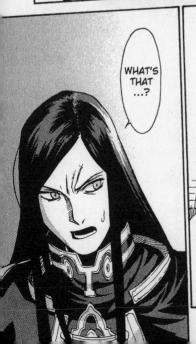

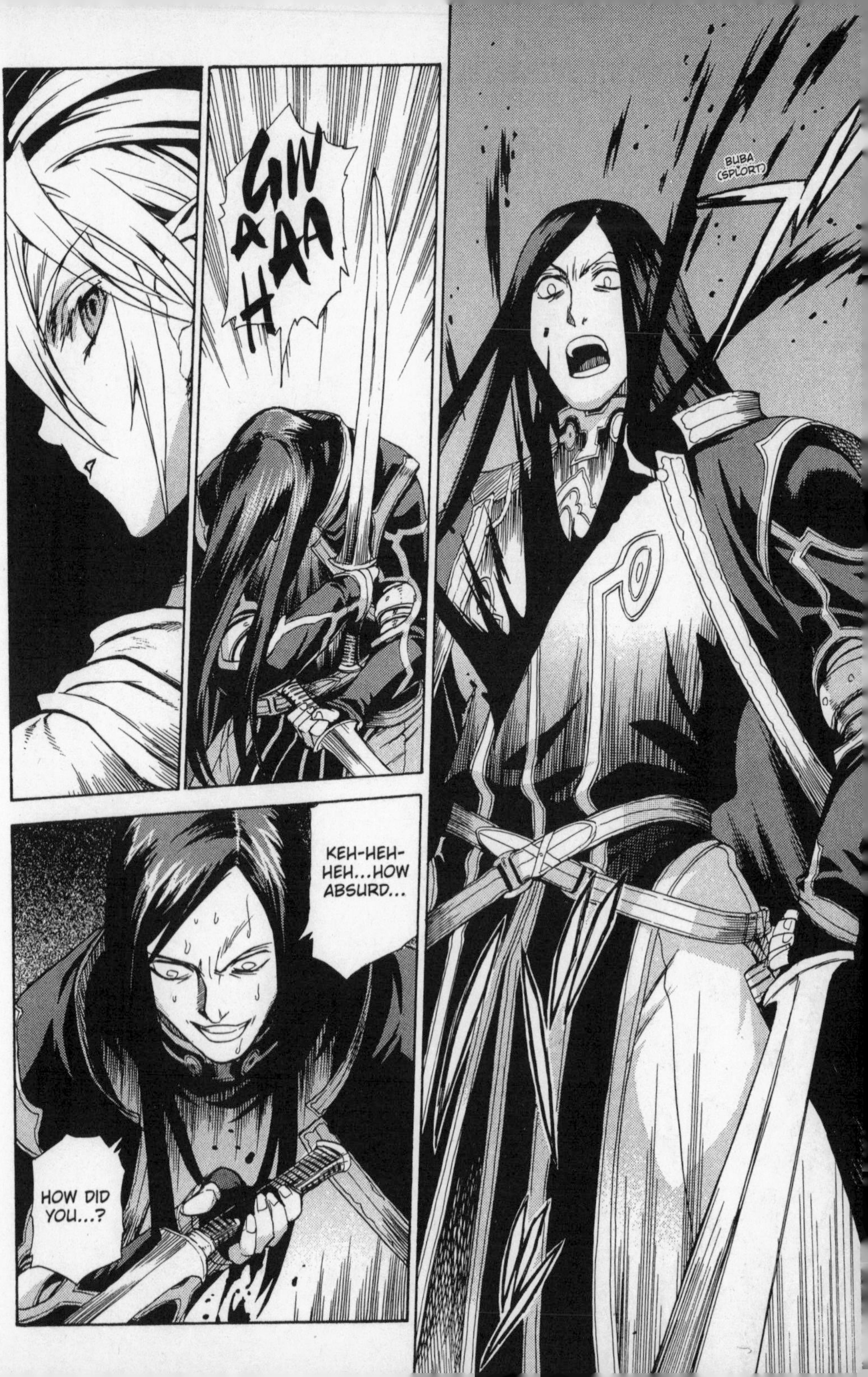
BUBA (SPLORT)
GWAAAH
KEH-HEH-HEH...HOW ABSURD...
HOW DID YOU...?

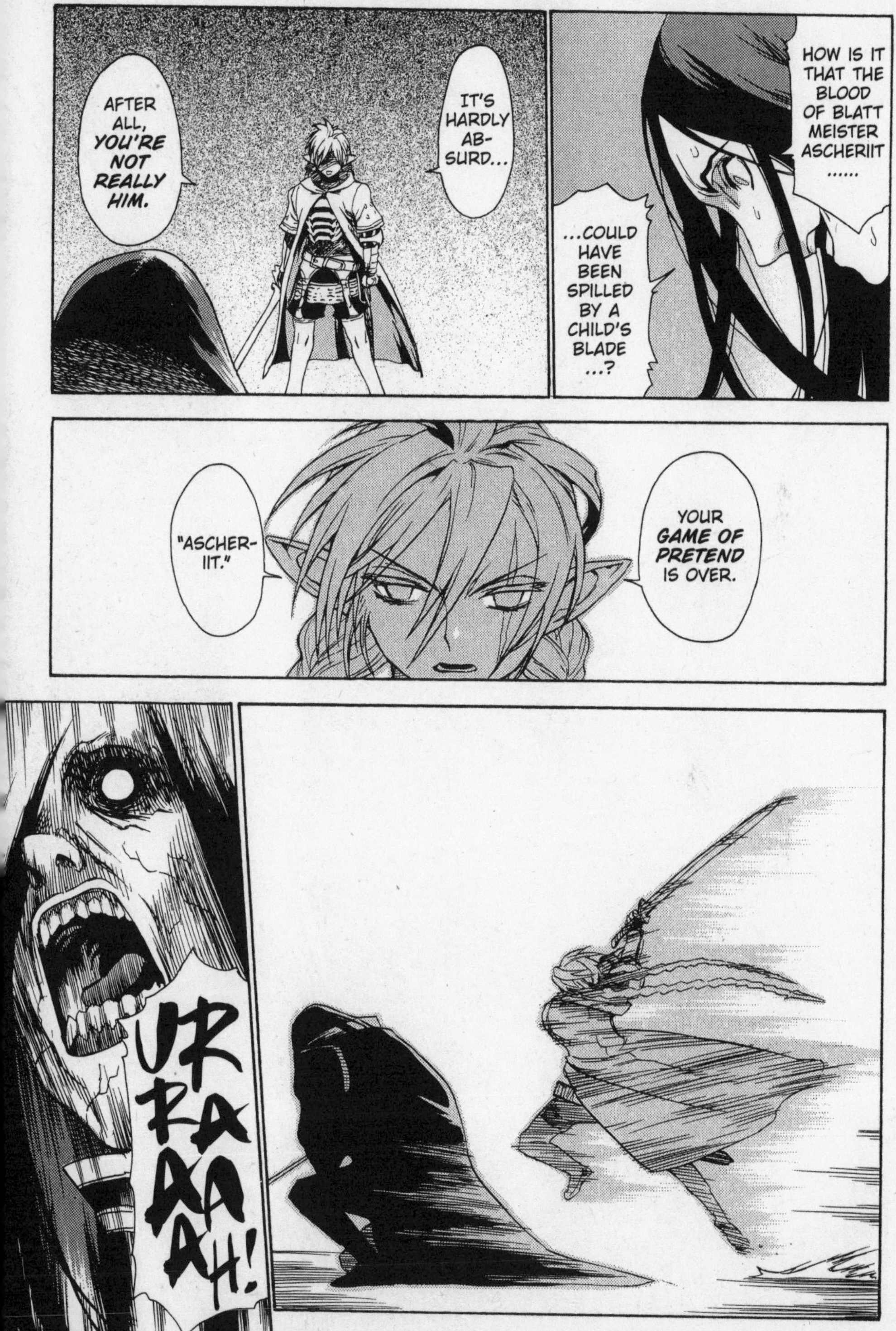
HOW IS IT THAT THE BLOOD OF BLATT MEISTER ASCHERIIT ......
...COULD HAVE BEEN SPILLED BY A CHILD'S BLADE ...?
IT'S HARDLY AB-SURD...
AFTER ALL, *YOU'RE NOT REALLY HIM.*
YOUR *GAME OF PRETEND* IS OVER.
"ASCHER-IIT."
URRAAAAH!

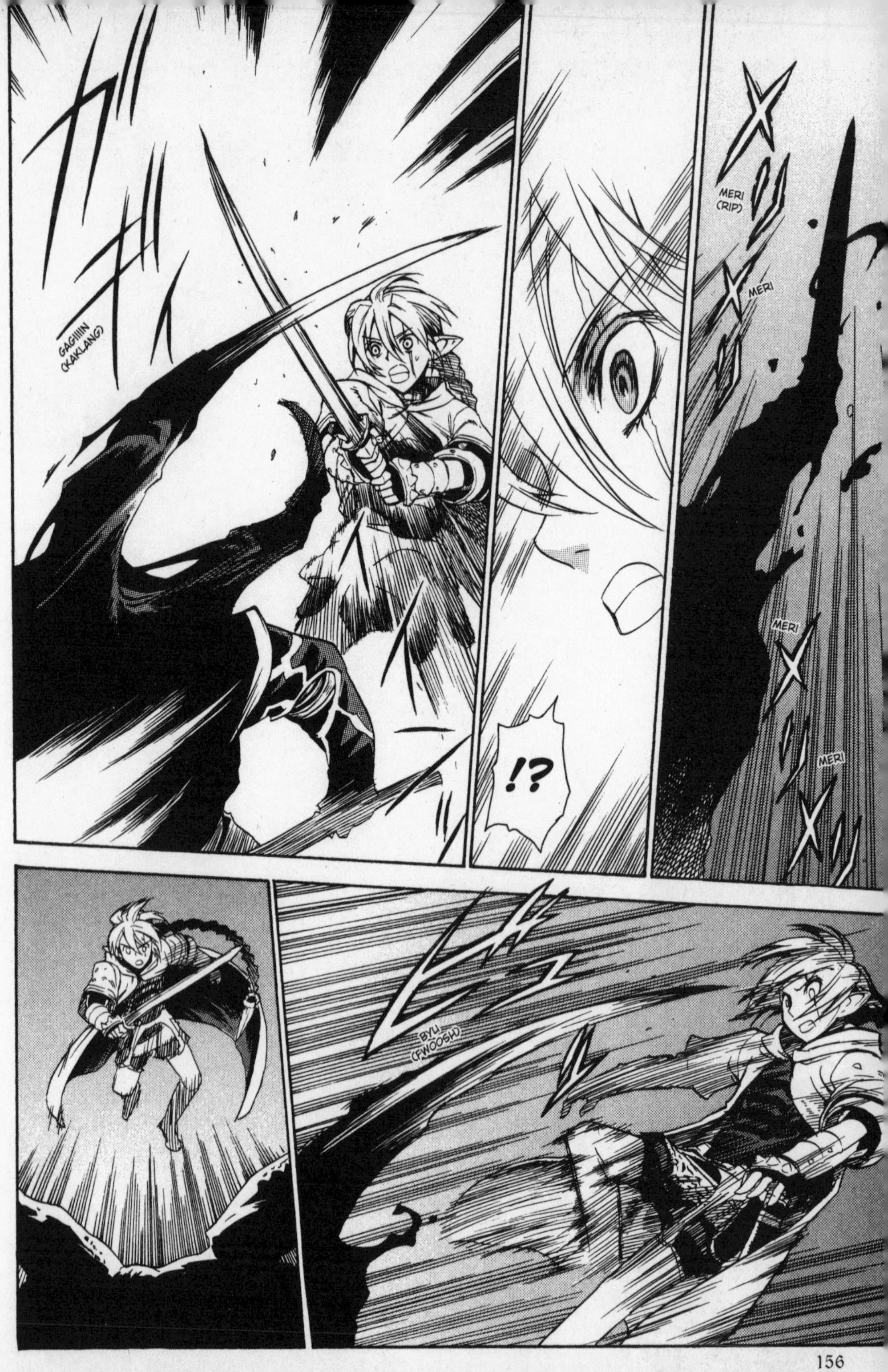
MERI (RIP)
MERI
MERI
MERI
!?
GAGIIIN (KAKLANG)
BYU (FWOOSH)

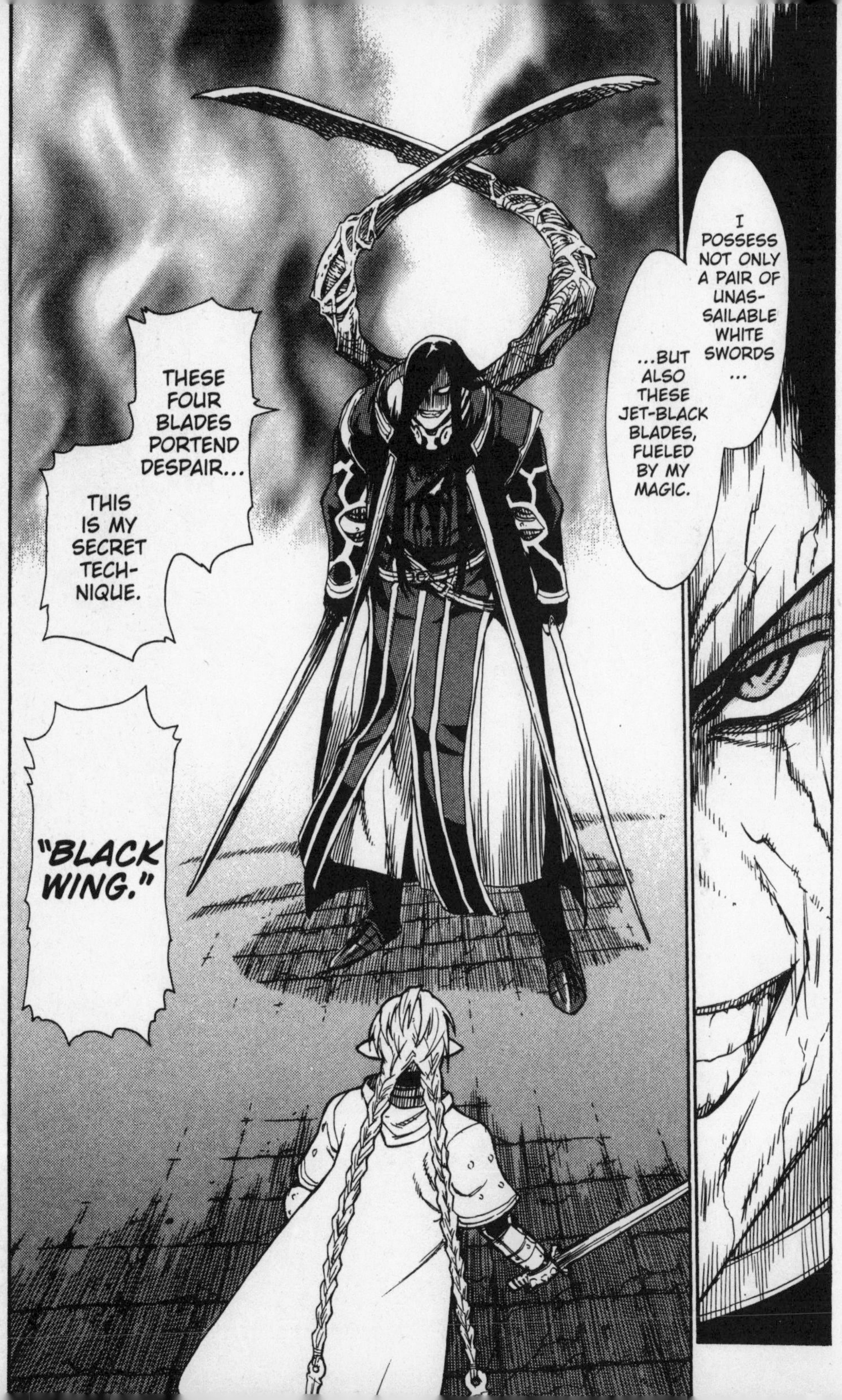
I POSSESS NOT ONLY A PAIR OF UNASSAILABLE WHITE SWORDS...
...BUT ALSO THESE JET-BLACK BLADES, FUELED BY MY MAGIC.
THESE FOUR BLADES PORTEND DESPAIR...
THIS IS MY SECRET TECHNIQUE.
"BLACK WING."

KA
KA
KA (TAK)
GA (CLANG)
GA
GA
GA
GA
GA
GA
HA-HA-HA-HA-HA-HA!!
WHERE'S YOUR ARROGANCE FROM BEFORE!?
KA
KA
KA
KA

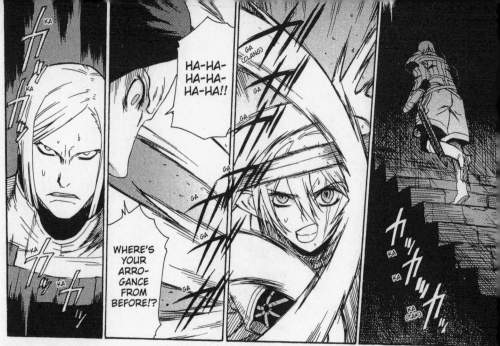

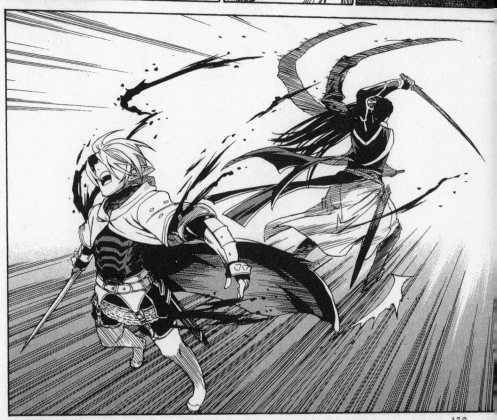

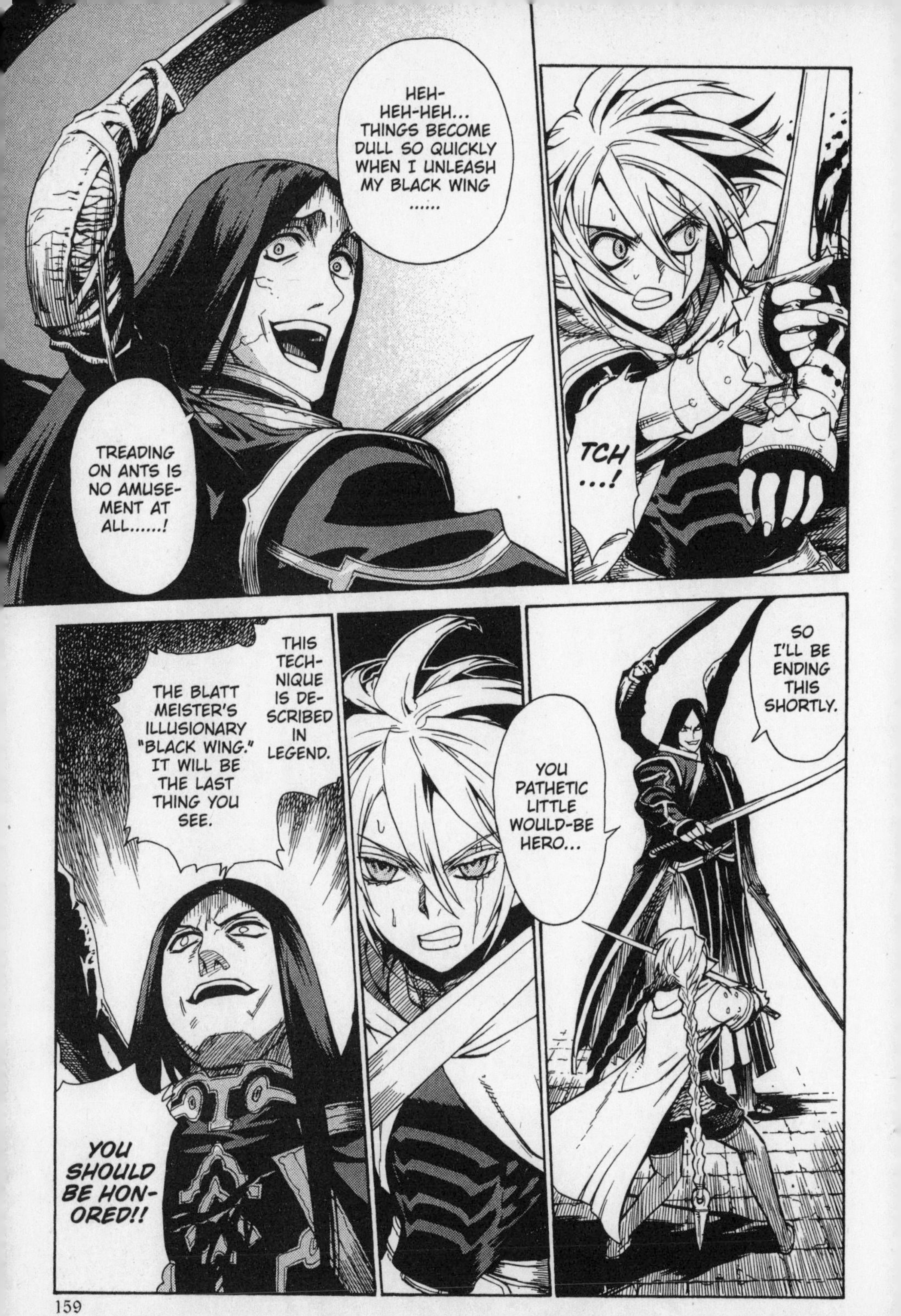
TCH ...!
HEH-HEH-HEH... THINGS BECOME DULL SO QUICKLY WHEN I UNLEASH MY BLACK WING ......
TREADING ON ANTS IS NO AMUSEMENT AT ALL......!
SO I'LL BE ENDING THIS SHORTLY.
YOU PATHETIC LITTLE WOULD-BE HERO...
THIS TECHNIQUE IS DESCRIBED IN LEGEND.
THE BLATT MEISTER'S ILLUSIONARY "BLACK WING." IT WILL BE THE LAST THING YOU SEE.
YOU SHOULD BE HONORED!!

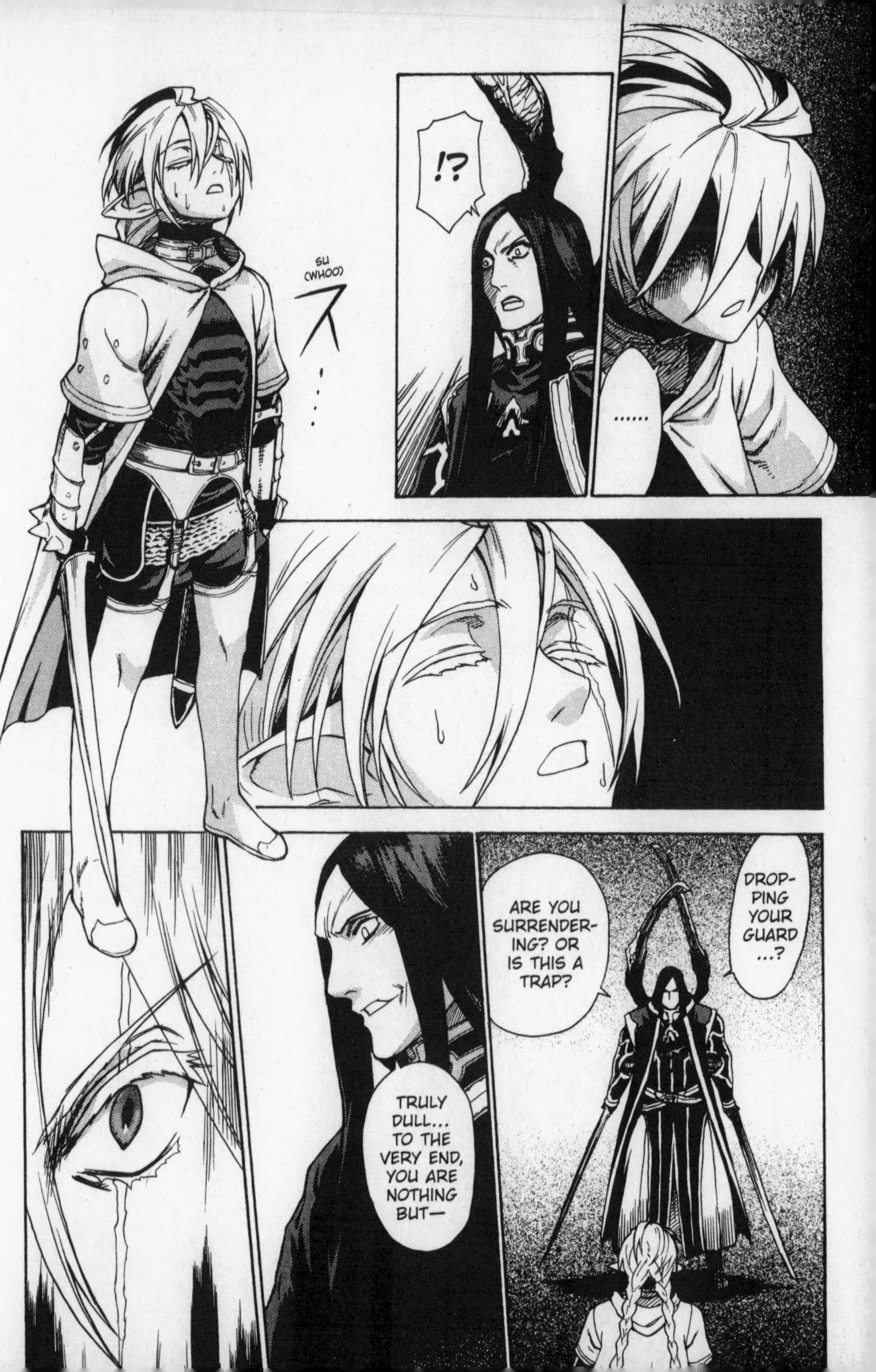
......
!?
SU
(WHOO)
DROP-PING YOUR GUARD ...?
ARE YOU SURRENDER-ING? OR IS THIS A TRAP?
TRULY DULL... TO THE VERY END, YOU ARE NOTHING BUT—

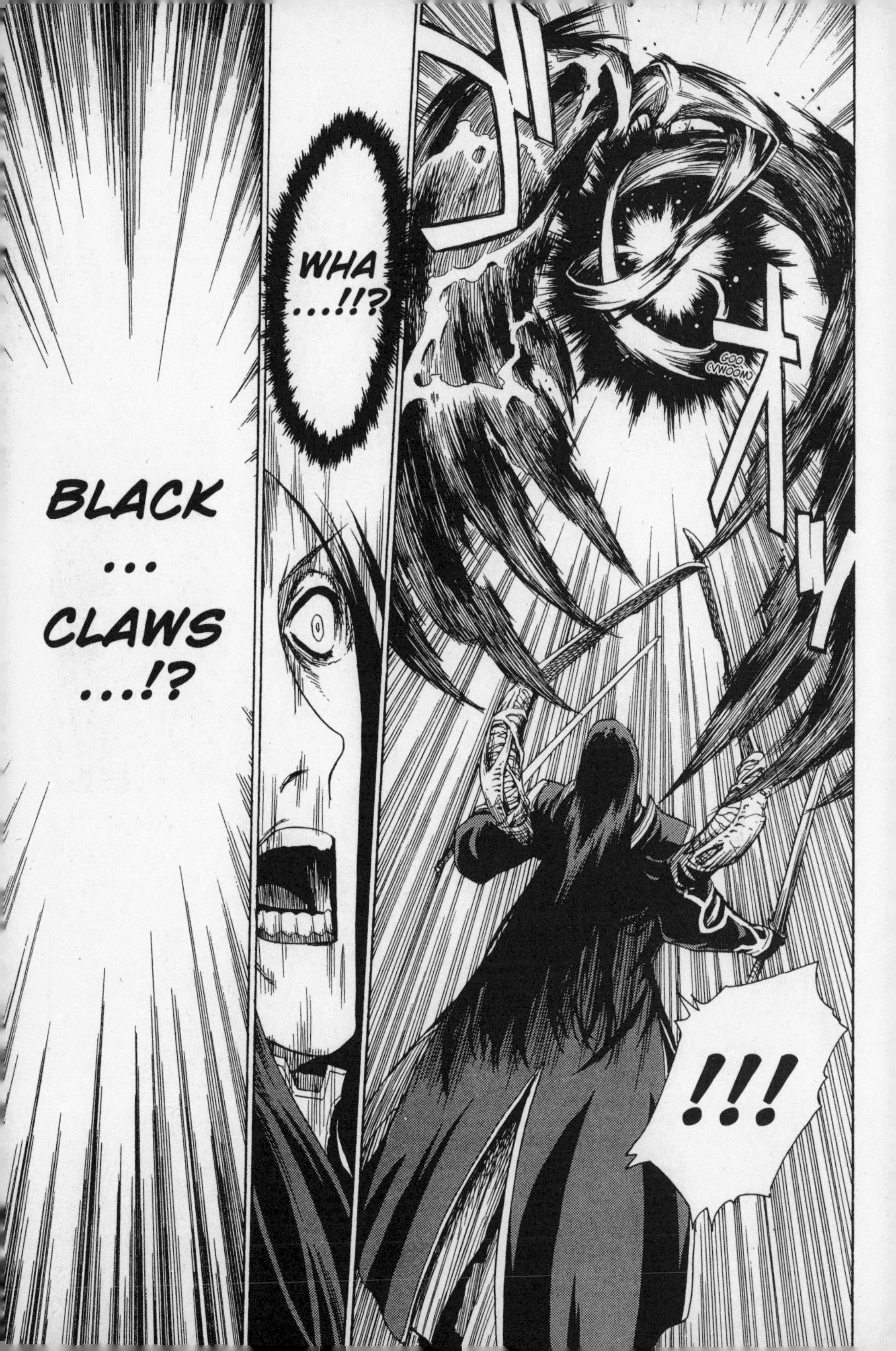
GOO (VWOOM)
!!!
WHA ...!!?
BLACK ... CLAWS ...!?

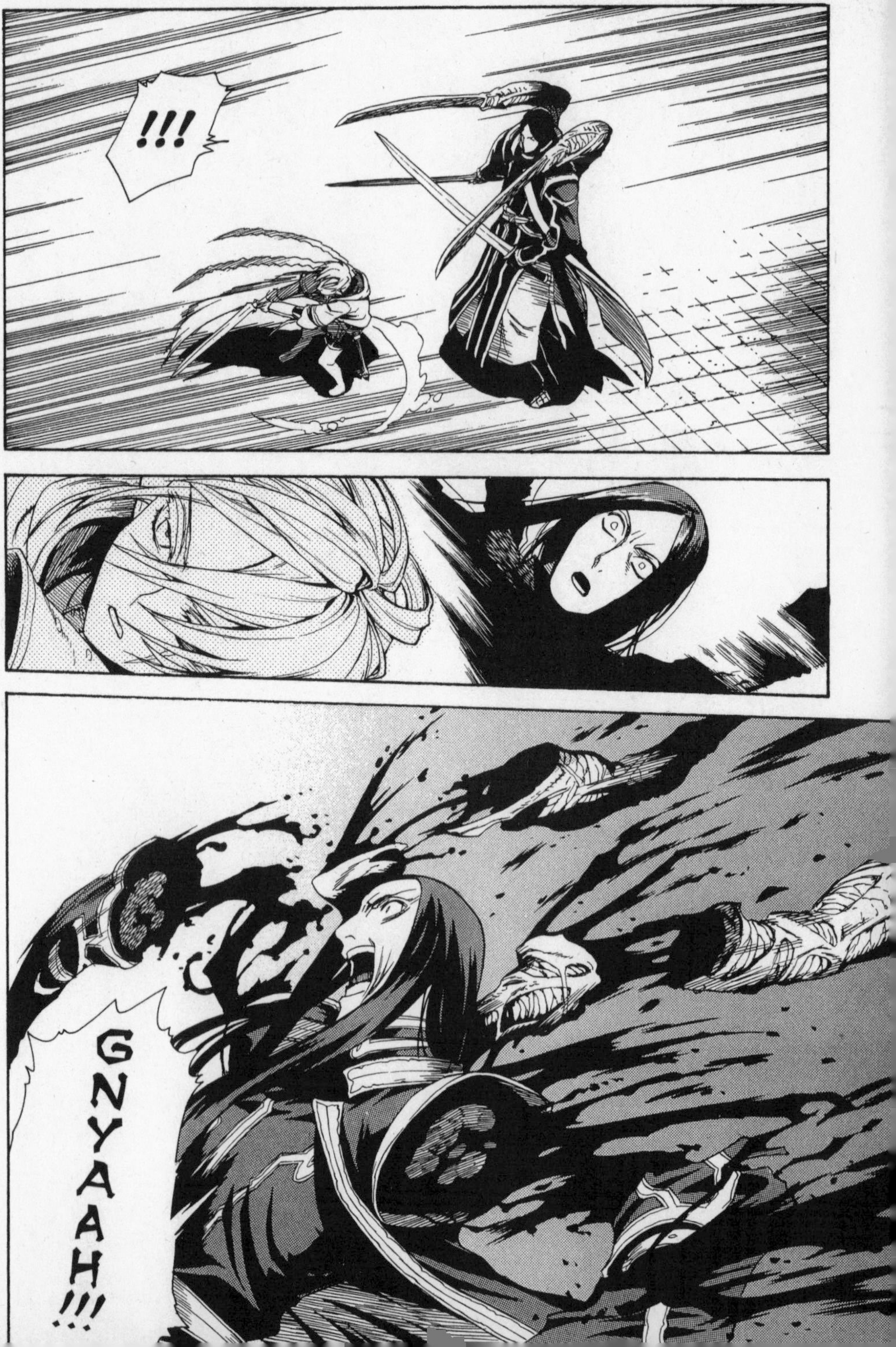
!!!
GNYAAH!!!

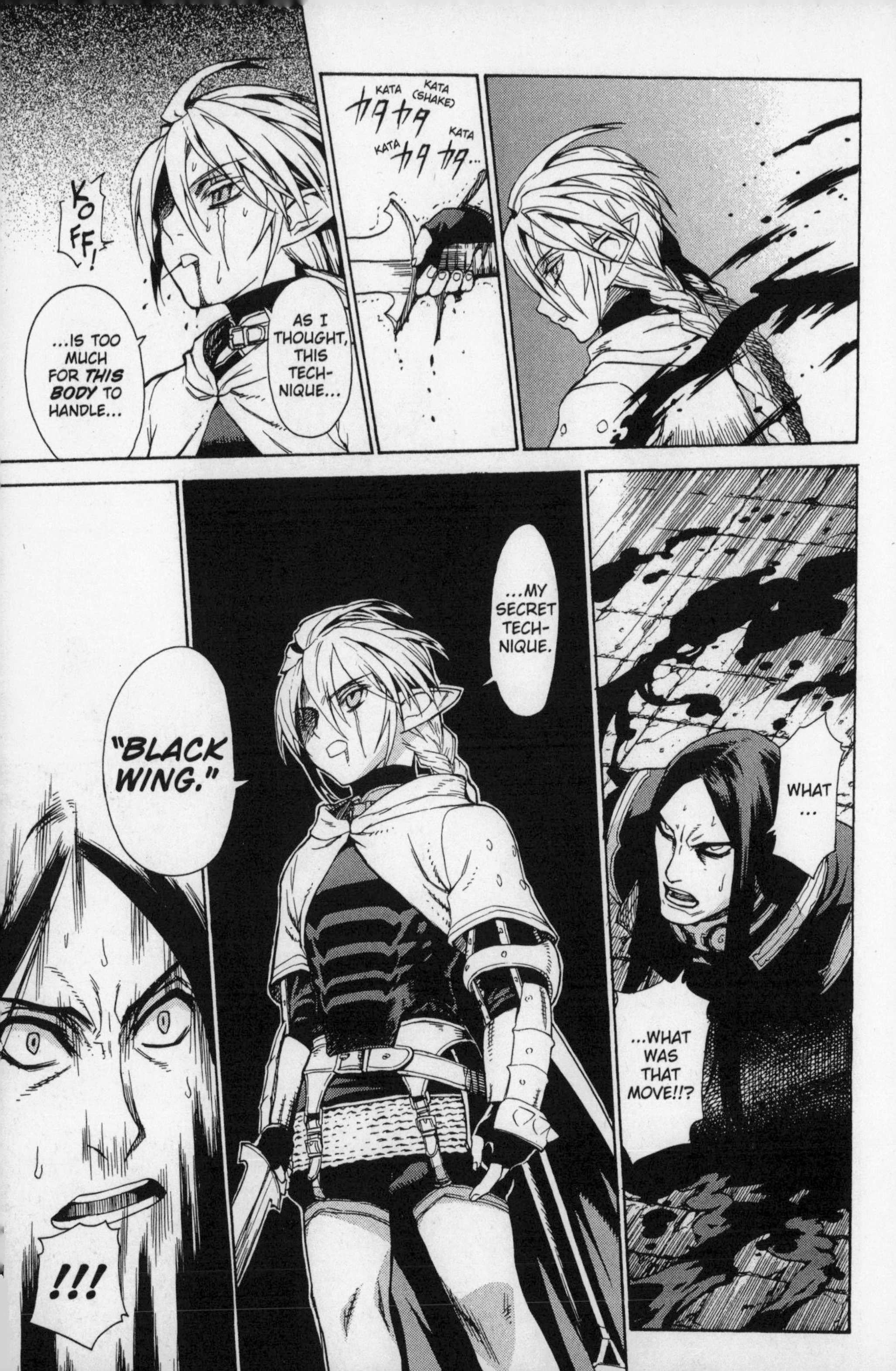
KATA KATA (SHAKE)
カタカタ
KATA KATA
カタカタ...
AS I THOUGHT, THIS TECHNIQUE...
KOFF!
...IS TOO MUCH FOR *THIS BODY* TO HANDLE...
WHAT...
...WHAT WAS THAT MOVE!!?
...MY SECRET TECHNIQUE.
"BLACK WING."
!!!

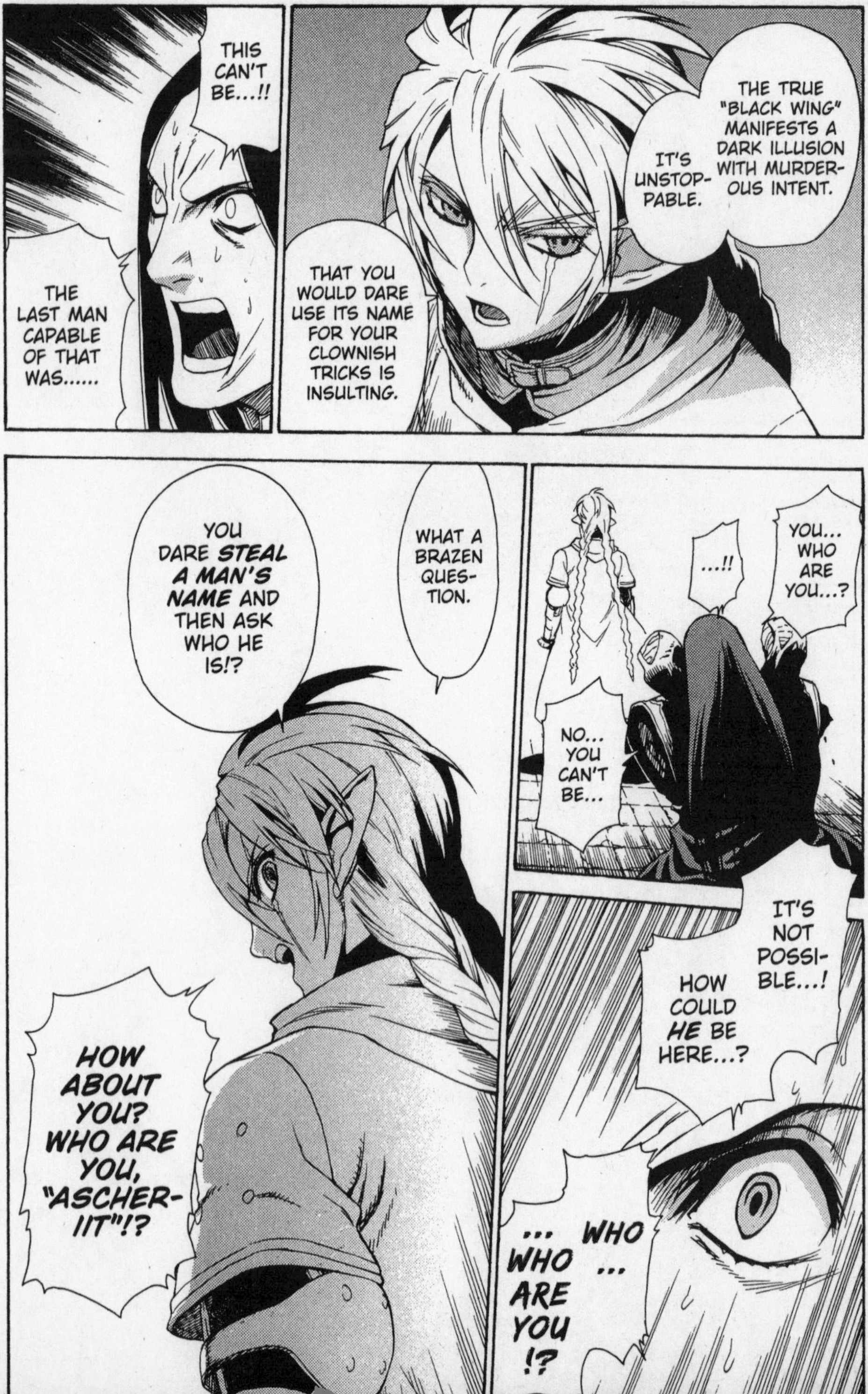
THE TRUE "BLACK WING" MANIFESTS A DARK ILLUSION WITH MURDER-OUS INTENT.
IT'S UNSTOP-PABLE.
THAT YOU WOULD DARE USE ITS NAME FOR YOUR CLOWNISH TRICKS IS INSULTING.
THIS CAN'T BE...!!
THE LAST MAN CAPABLE OF THAT WAS......
YOU... WHO ARE YOU...?
...!!
NO... YOU CAN'T BE...
IT'S NOT POSSI-BLE...!
HOW COULD *HE* BE HERE...?
... WHO ... WHO ARE YOU !?
WHAT A BRAZEN QUES-TION.
YOU DARE ***STEAL A MAN'S NAME*** AND THEN ASK WHO HE IS!?
HOW ABOUT YOU? WHO ARE YOU, "ASCHER-IIT"!?

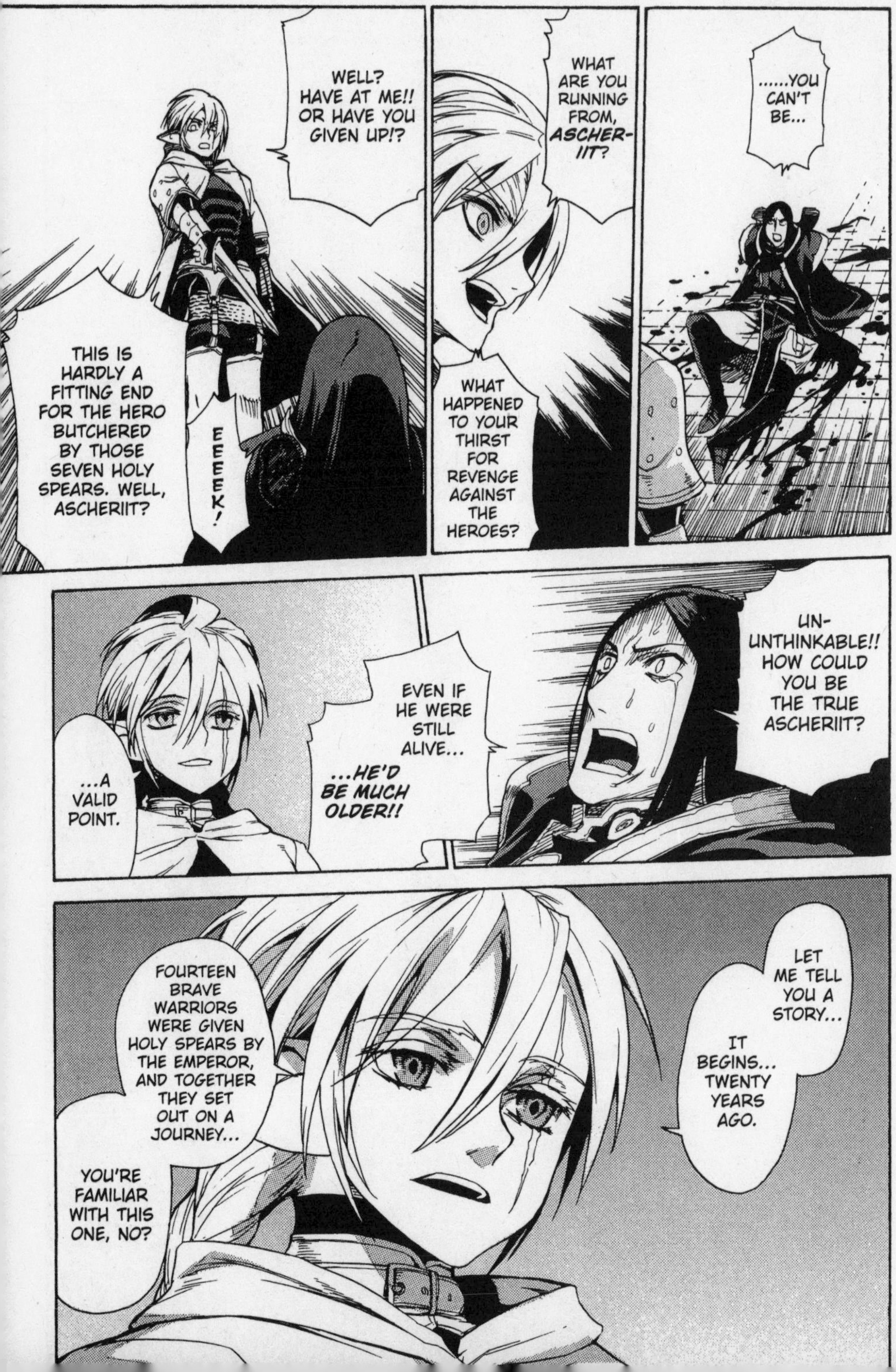
......YOU CAN'T BE...
WHAT ARE YOU RUNNING FROM, ASCHER-IIT?
WHAT HAPPENED TO YOUR THIRST FOR REVENGE AGAINST THE HEROES?
WELL? HAVE AT ME!! OR HAVE YOU GIVEN UP!?
EEEEK!
THIS IS HARDLY A FITTING END FOR THE HERO BUTCHERED BY THOSE SEVEN HOLY SPEARS. WELL, ASCHERIIT?
UN-UNTHINKABLE!! HOW COULD YOU BE THE TRUE ASCHERIIT?
EVEN IF HE WERE STILL ALIVE...
...HE'D BE MUCH OLDER!!
...A VALID POINT.
LET ME TELL YOU A STORY...
IT BEGINS... TWENTY YEARS AGO.
FOURTEEN BRAVE WARRIORS WERE GIVEN HOLY SPEARS BY THE EMPEROR, AND TOGETHER THEY SET OUT ON A JOURNEY...
YOU'RE FAMILIAR WITH THIS ONE, NO?

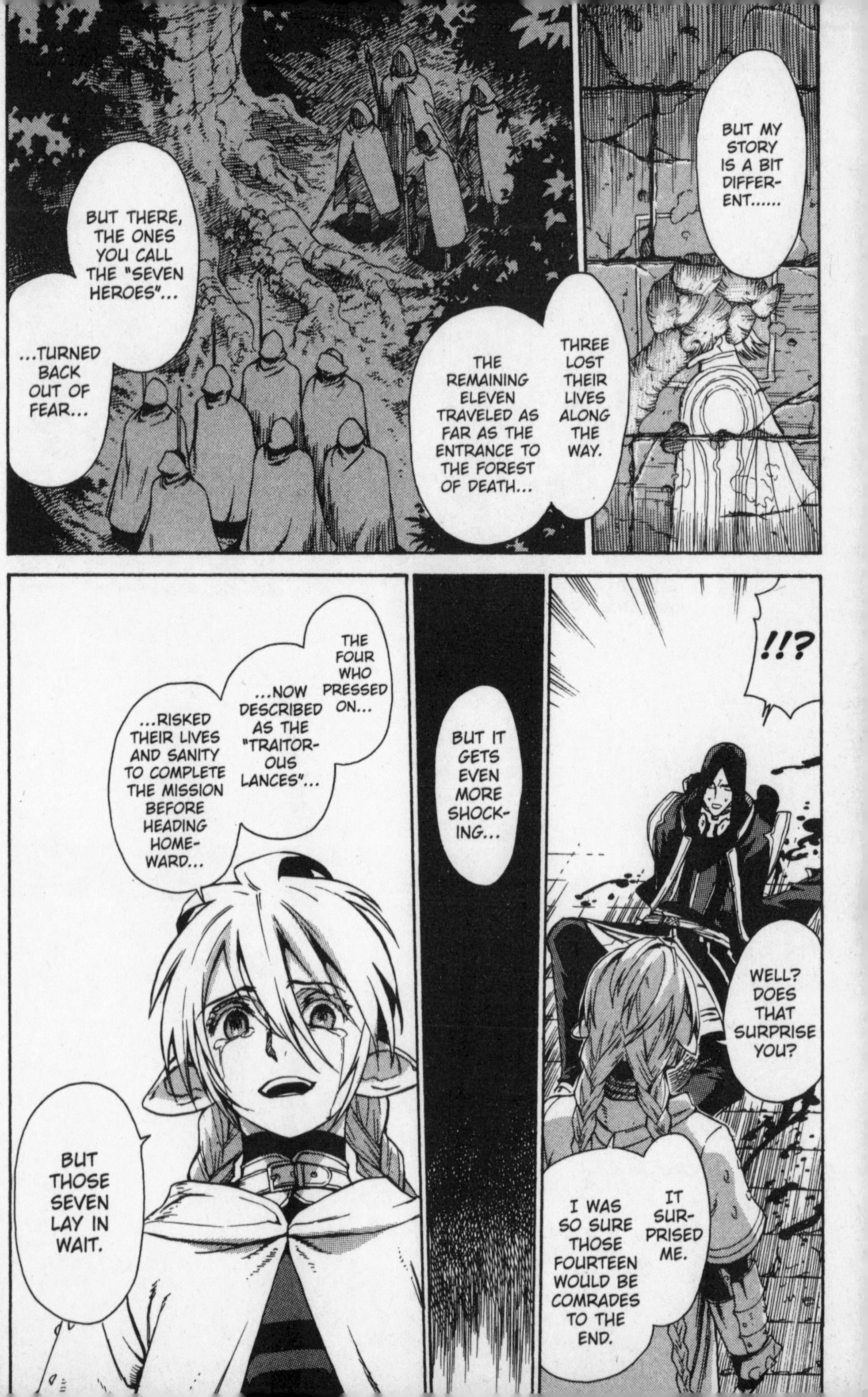
BUT MY STORY IS A BIT DIFFERENT......
THREE LOST THEIR LIVES ALONG THE WAY.
THE REMAINING ELEVEN TRAVELED AS FAR AS THE ENTRANCE TO THE FOREST OF DEATH...
BUT THERE, THE ONES YOU CALL THE "SEVEN HEROES"...
...TURNED BACK OUT OF FEAR...
!!?
WELL? DOES THAT SURPRISE YOU?
IT SURPRISED ME.
I WAS SO SURE THOSE FOURTEEN WOULD BE COMRADES TO THE END.
BUT IT GETS EVEN MORE SHOCKING...
THE FOUR WHO PRESSED ON...
...NOW DESCRIBED AS THE "TRAITOROUS LANCES"...
...RISKED THEIR LIVES AND SANITY TO COMPLETE THE MISSION BEFORE HEADING HOMEWARD...
BUT THOSE SEVEN LAY IN WAIT.

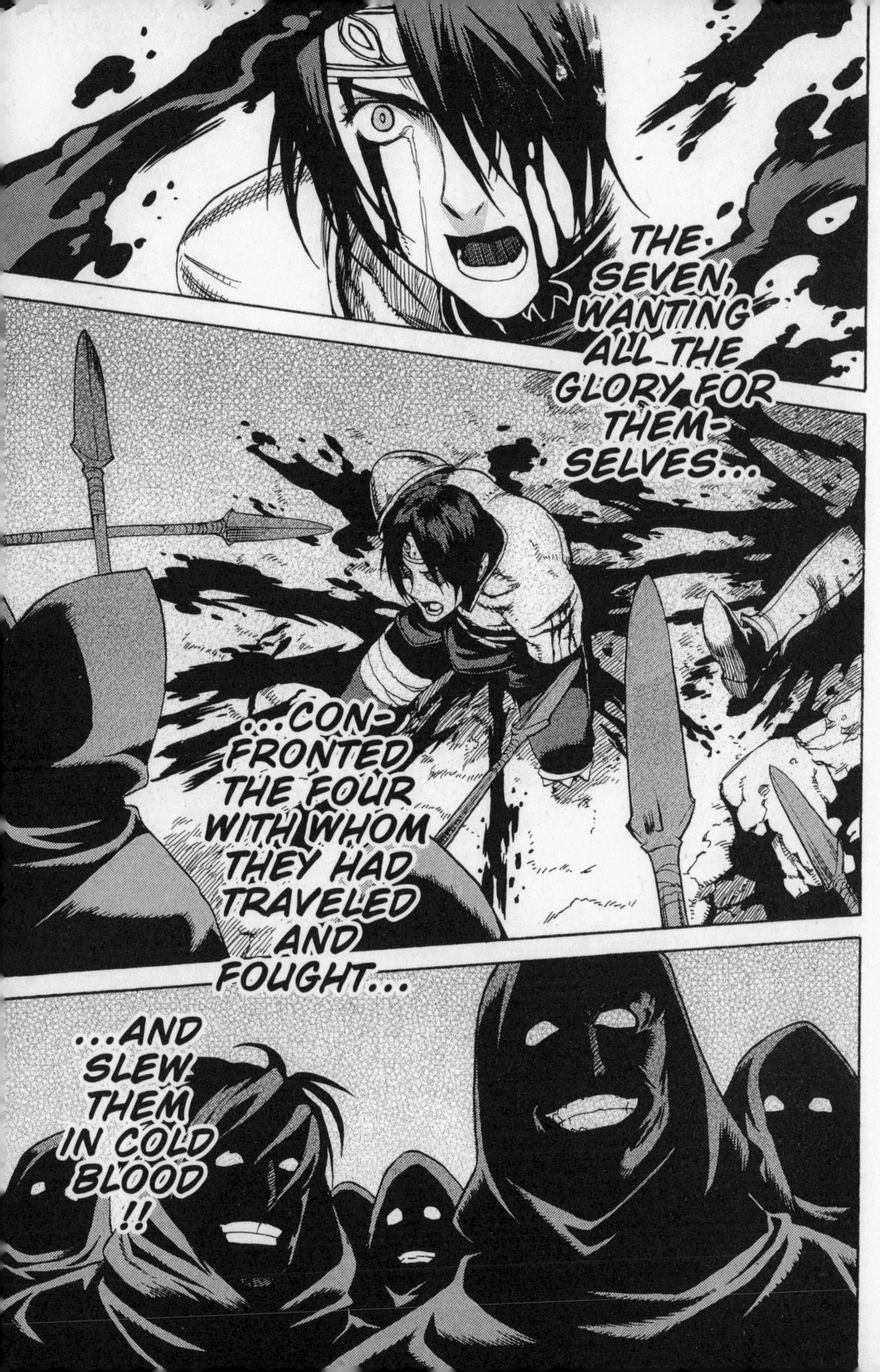
THE SEVEN, WANTING ALL THE GLORY FOR THEM-SELVES...
...CON-FRONTED THE FOUR WITH WHOM THEY HAD TRAVELED AND FOUGHT...
...AND SLEW THEM IN COLD BLOOD!!

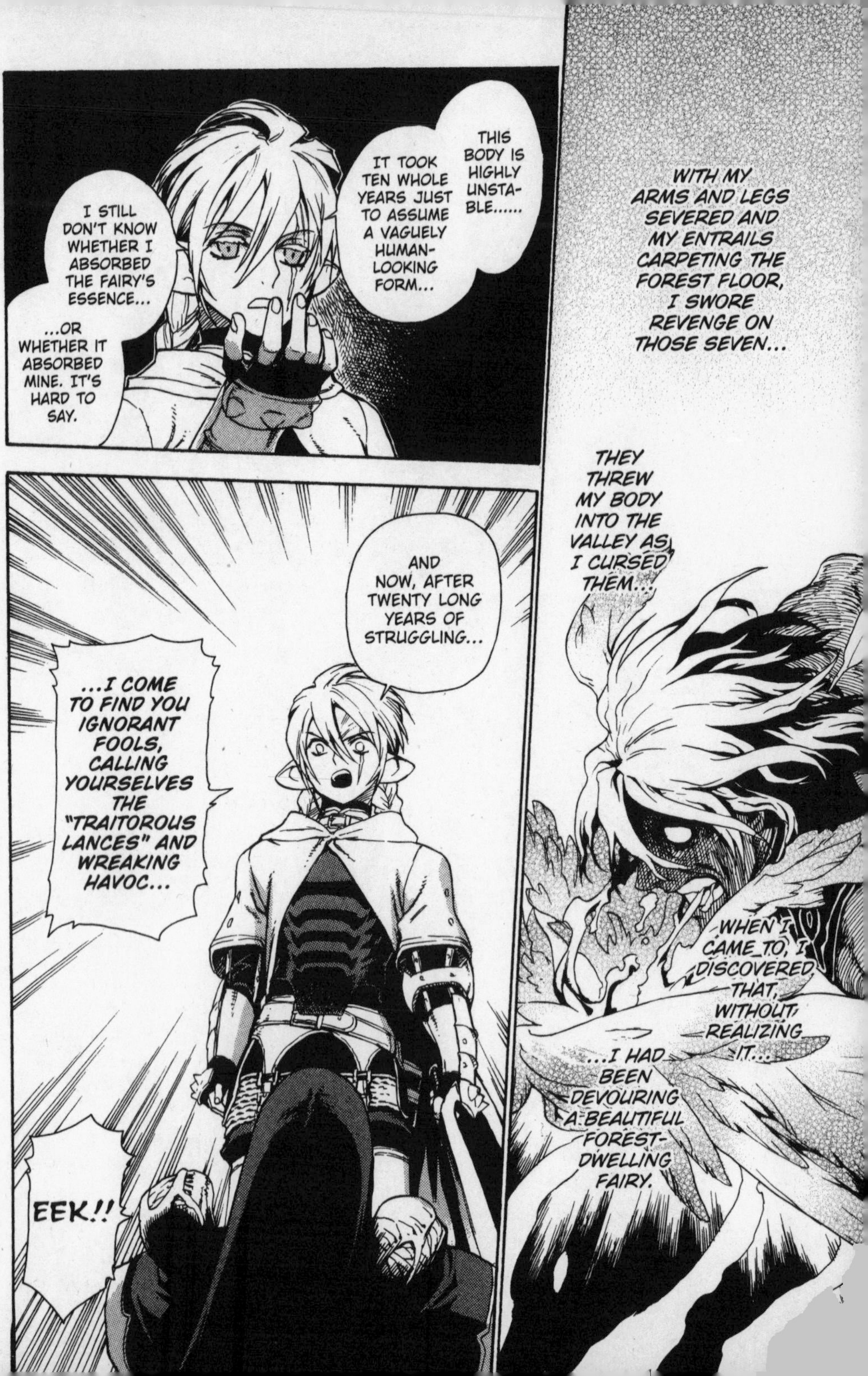
WITH MY ARMS AND LEGS SEVERED AND MY ENTRAILS CARPETING THE FOREST FLOOR, I SWORE REVENGE ON THOSE SEVEN...
THEY THREW MY BODY INTO THE VALLEY AS I CURSED THEM...
WHEN I CAME TO, I DISCOVERED THAT, WITHOUT REALIZING IT...
...I HAD BEEN DEVOURING A BEAUTIFUL FOREST-DWELLING FAIRY.
THIS BODY IS HIGHLY UNSTABLE......
IT TOOK TEN WHOLE YEARS JUST TO ASSUME A VAGUELY HUMAN-LOOKING FORM...
I STILL DON'T KNOW WHETHER I ABSORBED THE FAIRY'S ESSENCE...
...OR WHETHER IT ABSORBED MINE. IT'S HARD TO SAY.
AND NOW, AFTER TWENTY LONG YEARS OF STRUGGLING...
...I COME TO FIND YOU IGNORANT FOOLS, CALLING YOURSELVES THE "TRAITOROUS LANCES" AND WREAKING HAVOC...
EEK!!

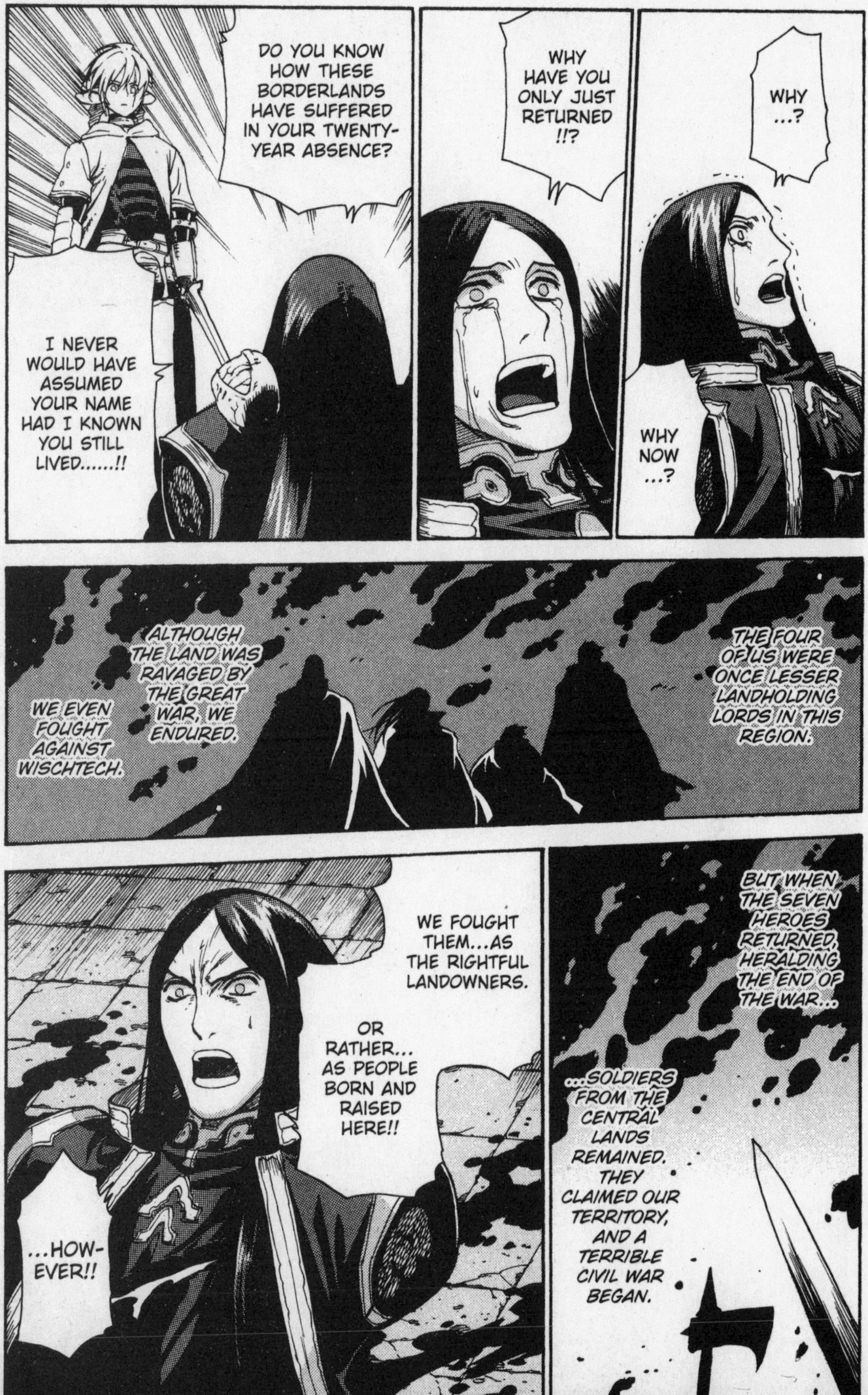
WHY ...?
WHY NOW ...?
WHY HAVE YOU ONLY JUST RETURNED !!?
DO YOU KNOW HOW THESE BORDERLANDS HAVE SUFFERED IN YOUR TWENTY-YEAR ABSENCE?
I NEVER WOULD HAVE ASSUMED YOUR NAME HAD I KNOWN YOU STILL LIVED......!!
THE FOUR OF US WERE ONCE LESSER LANDHOLDING LORDS IN THIS REGION.
ALTHOUGH THE LAND WAS RAVAGED BY THE GREAT WAR, WE ENDURED.
WE EVEN FOUGHT AGAINST WISCHTECH.
BUT WHEN THE SEVEN HEROES RETURNED, HERALDING THE END OF THE WAR...
...SOLDIERS FROM THE CENTRAL LANDS REMAINED. THEY CLAIMED OUR TERRITORY, AND A TERRIBLE CIVIL WAR BEGAN.
WE FOUGHT THEM...AS THE RIGHTFUL LANDOWNERS.
OR RATHER... AS PEOPLE BORN AND RAISED HERE!!
...HOW-EVER!!

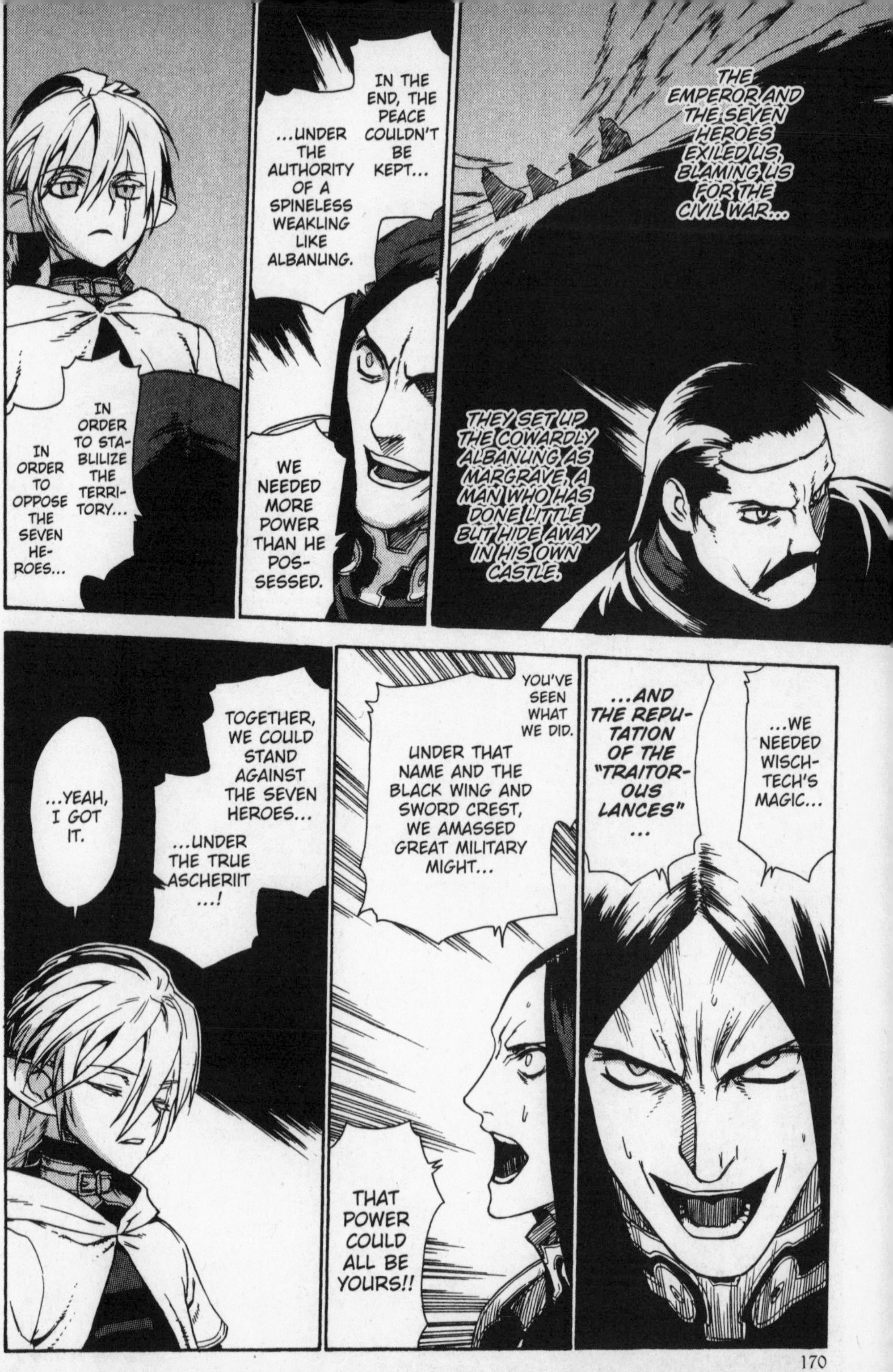
THE EMPEROR AND THE SEVEN HEROES EXILED US, BLAMING US FOR THE CIVIL WAR...
THEY SET UP THE COWARDLY ALBANUNG AS MARGRAVE, A MAN WHO HAS DONE LITTLE BUT HIDE AWAY IN HIS OWN CASTLE.
IN THE END, THE PEACE COULDN'T BE KEPT...
...UNDER THE AUTHORITY OF A SPINELESS WEAKLING LIKE ALBANUNG.
WE NEEDED MORE POWER THAN HE POSSESSED.
IN ORDER TO STABLILIZE THE TERRITORY...
IN ORDER TO OPPOSE THE SEVEN HEROES...
...WE NEEDED WISCHTECH'S MAGIC...
...AND THE REPUTATION OF THE "TRAITOROUS LANCES"...
YOU'VE SEEN WHAT WE DID.
UNDER THAT NAME AND THE BLACK WING AND SWORD CREST, WE AMASSED GREAT MILITARY MIGHT...
THAT POWER COULD ALL BE YOURS!!
TOGETHER, WE COULD STAND AGAINST THE SEVEN HEROES...
...UNDER THE TRUE ASCHERIIT ...!
...YEAH, I GOT IT.

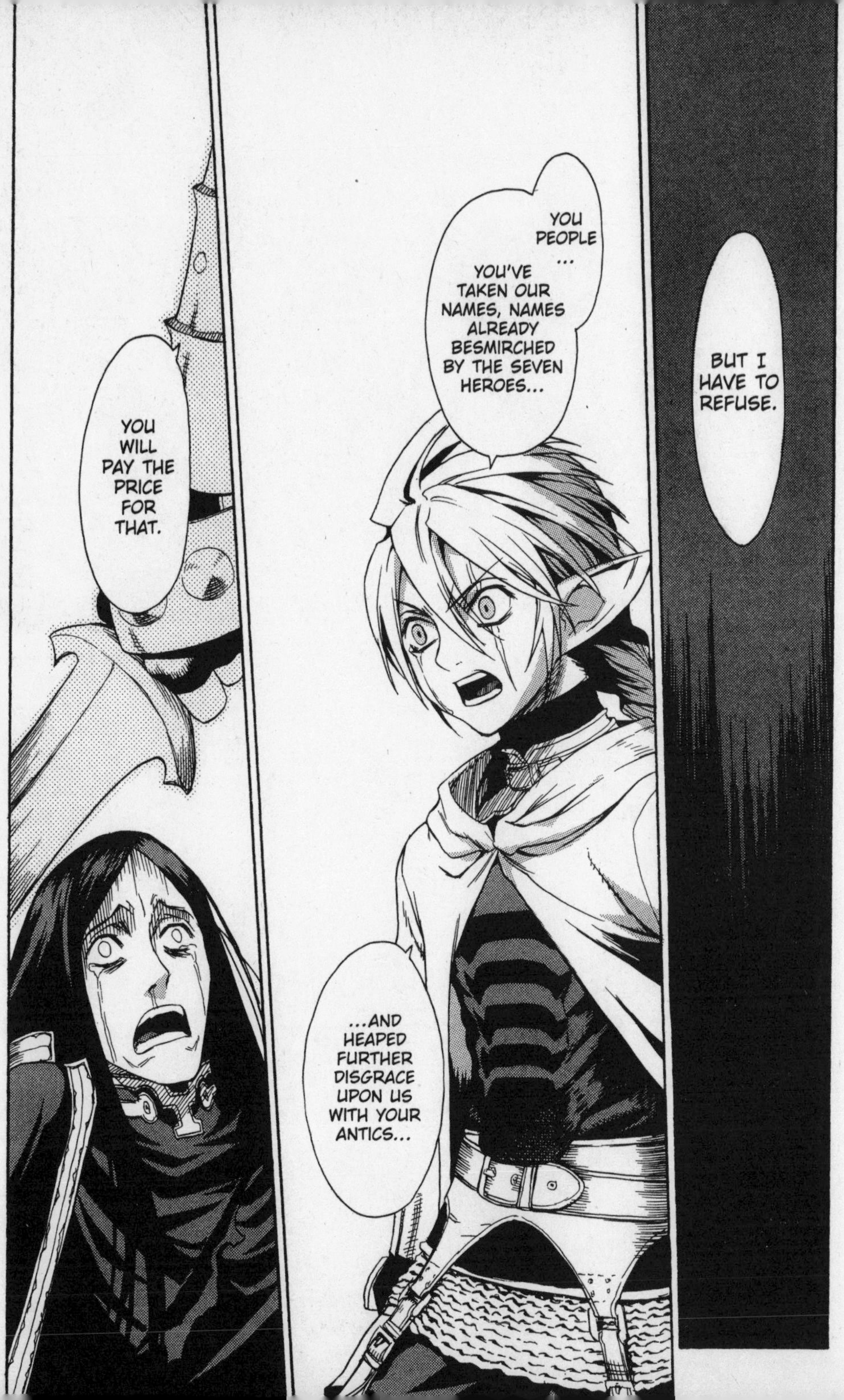
BUT I HAVE TO REFUSE.
YOU PEOPLE ... YOU'VE TAKEN OUR NAMES, NAMES ALREADY BESMIRCHED BY THE SEVEN HEROES...
...AND HEAPED FURTHER DISGRACE UPON US WITH YOUR ANTICS...
YOU WILL PAY THE PRICE FOR THAT.

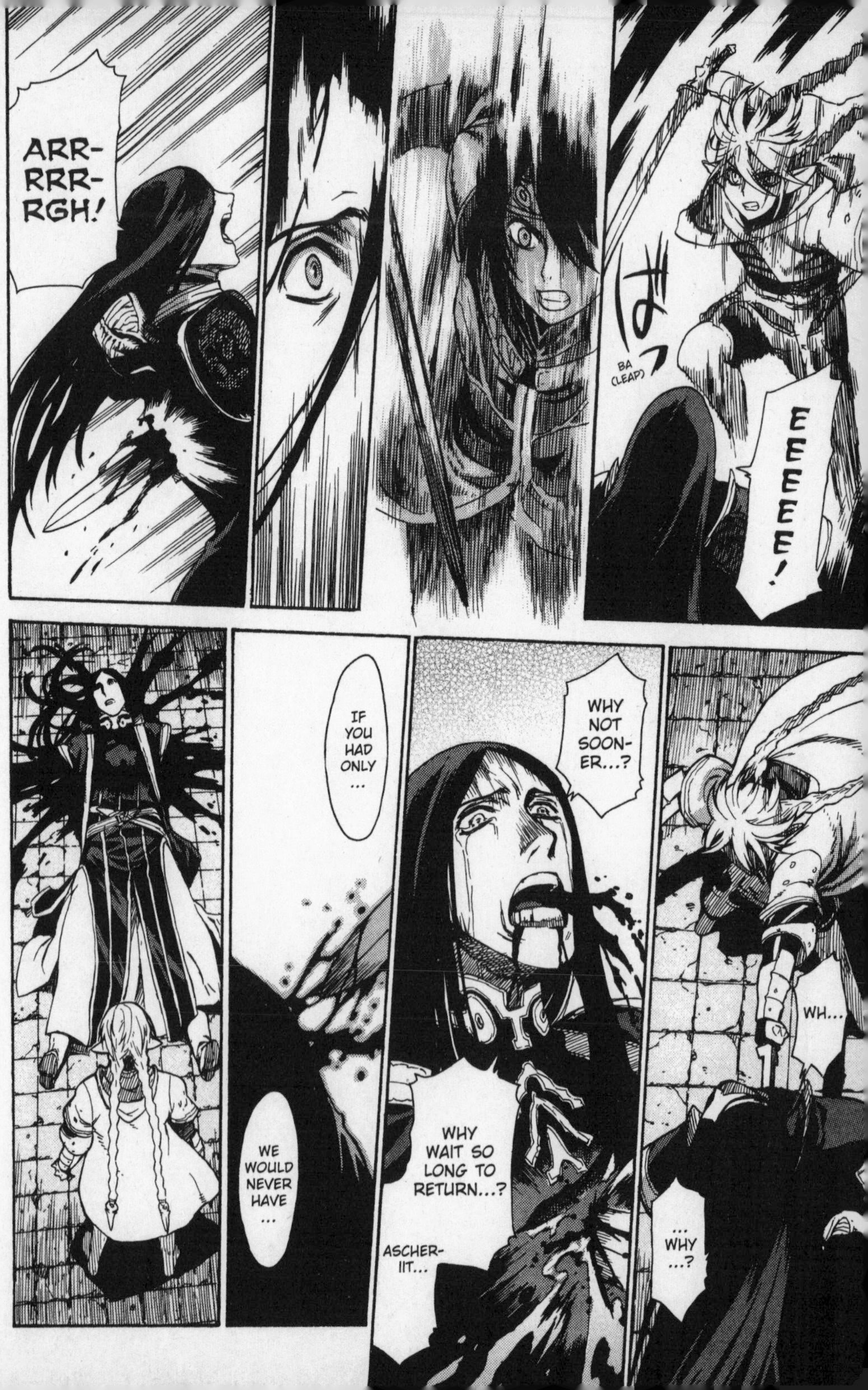
ばっ
BA (LEAP)
EEEEEE!
ARR-RRR-RGH!
WH...
...WHY...?
WHY NOT SOON-ER...?
WHY WAIT SO LONG TO RETURN...?
ASCHER-IIT...
IF YOU HAD ONLY...
WE WOULD NEVER HAVE...

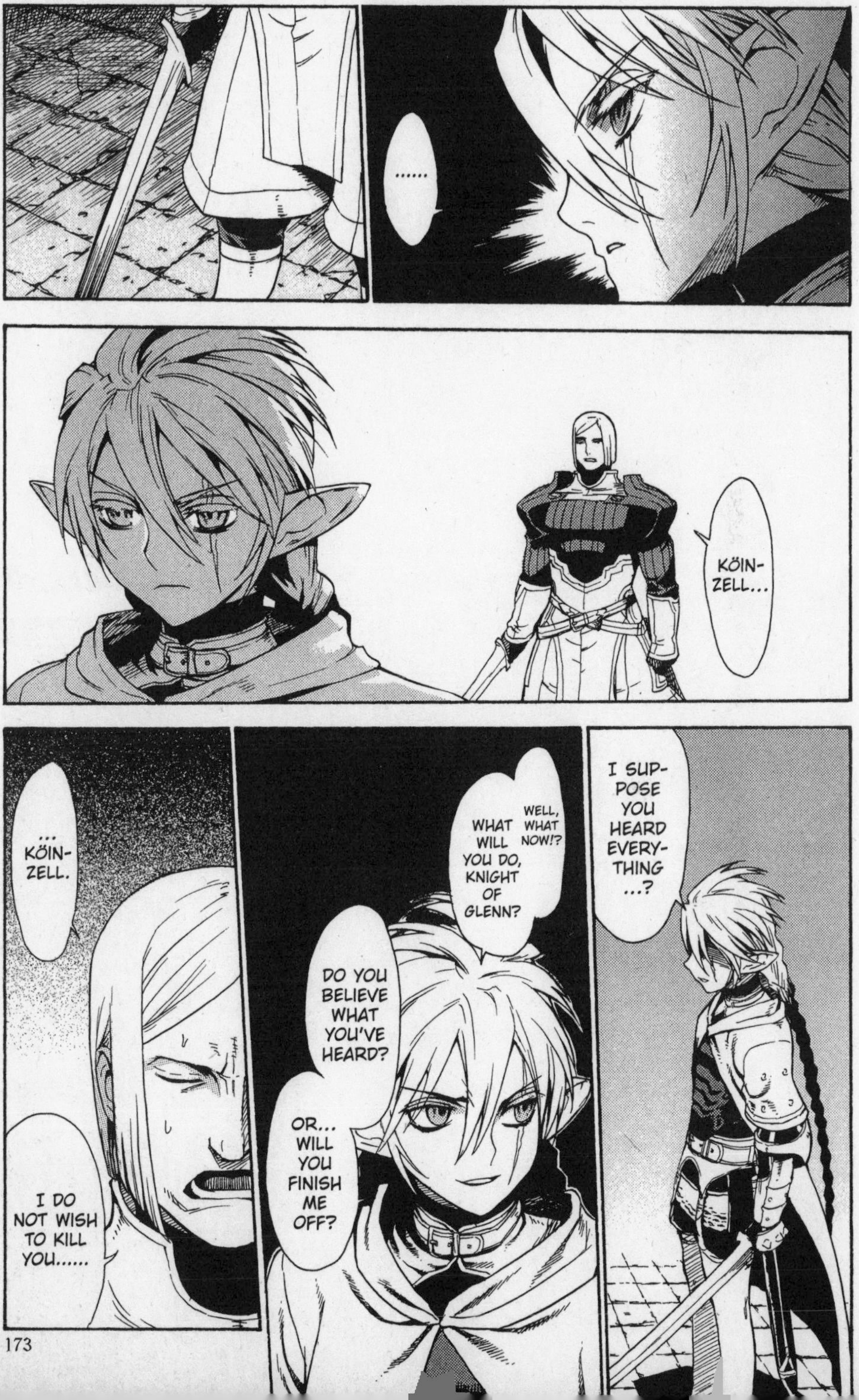
......
KÖIN-ZELL...
I SUP-POSE YOU HEARD EVERY-THING ...?
WELL, WHAT NOW!?
WHAT WILL YOU DO, KNIGHT OF GLENN?
DO YOU BELIEVE WHAT YOU'VE HEARD?
OR... WILL YOU FINISH ME OFF?
... KÖIN-ZELL.
I DO NOT WISH TO KILL YOU......

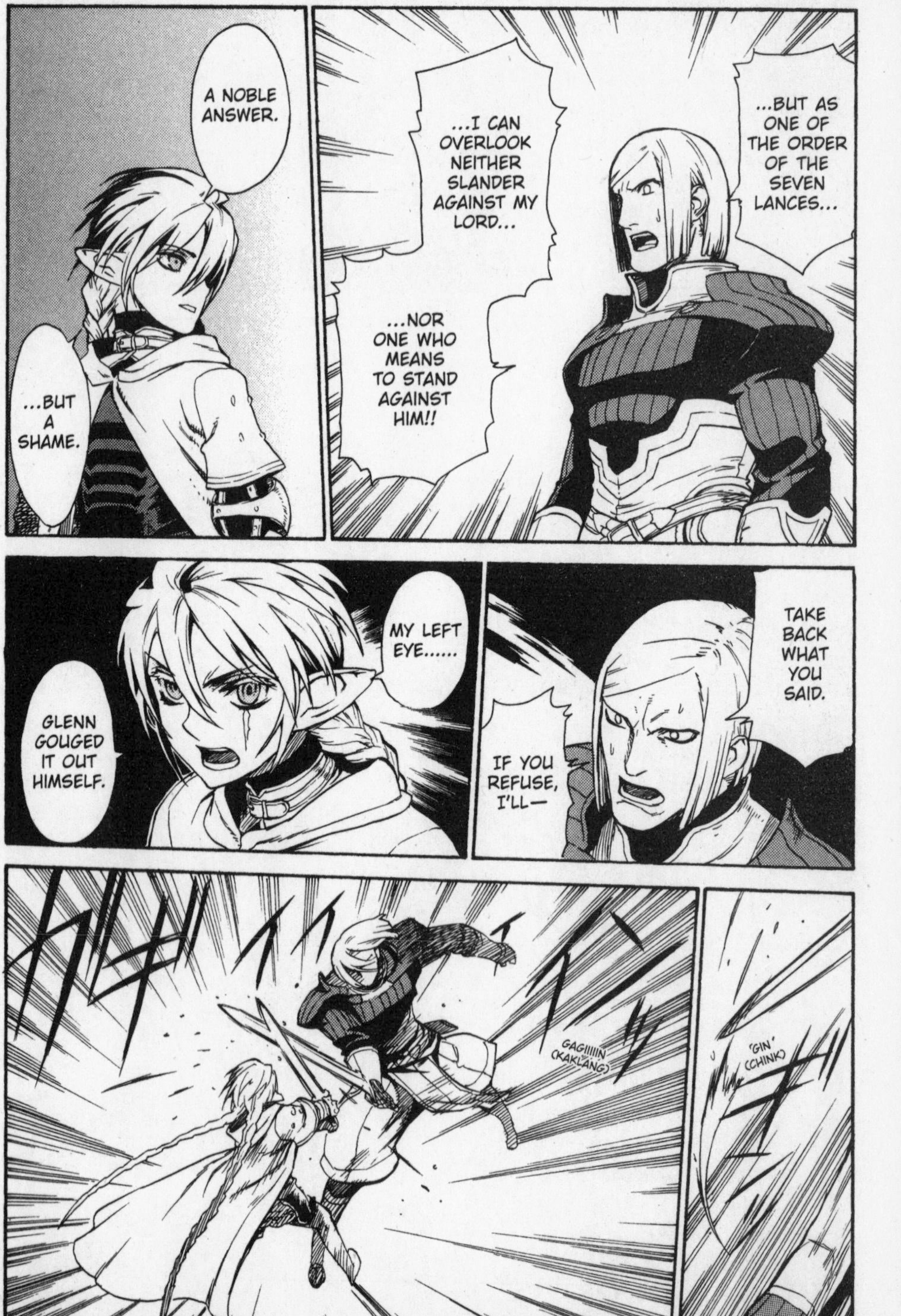
...BUT AS ONE OF THE ORDER OF THE SEVEN LANCES...
...I CAN OVERLOOK NEITHER SLANDER AGAINST MY LORD...
...NOR ONE WHO MEANS TO STAND AGAINST HIM!!
A NOBLE ANSWER.
...BUT A SHAME.
TAKE BACK WHAT YOU SAID.
IF YOU REFUSE, I'LL—
MY LEFT EYE......
GLENN GOUGED IT OUT HIMSELF.
'GIN' (CHINK)
GAGIIIIIN (KAKLANG)

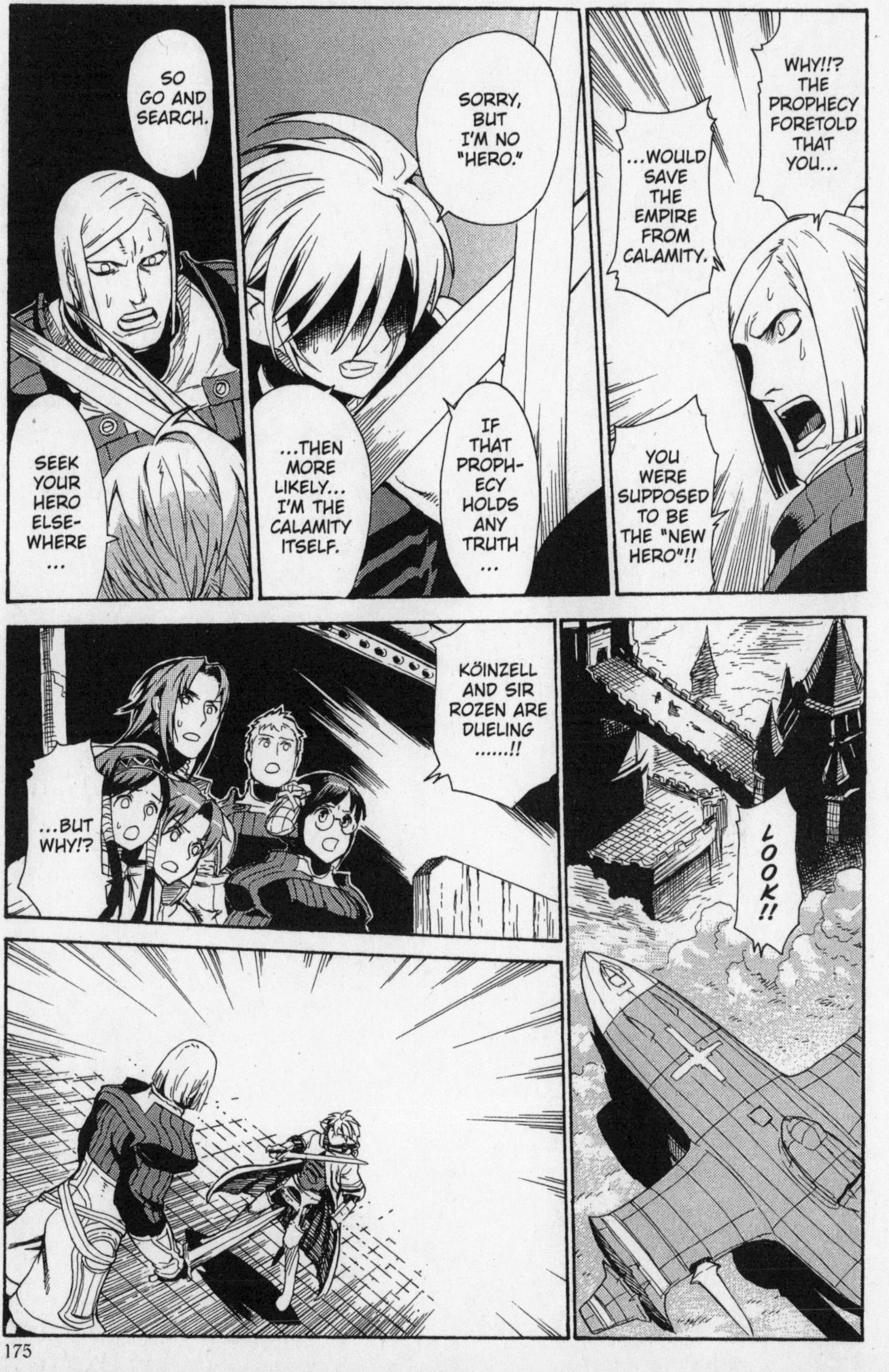
WHY!!? THE PROPHECY FORETOLD THAT YOU...
...WOULD SAVE THE EMPIRE FROM CALAMITY.
YOU WERE SUPPOSED TO BE THE "NEW HERO"!!
SORRY, BUT I'M NO "HERO."
IF THAT PROPHECY HOLDS ANY TRUTH...
...THEN MORE LIKELY... I'M THE CALAMITY ITSELF.
SEEK YOUR HERO ELSEWHERE...
SO GO AND SEARCH.
LOOK!!
KÖINZELL AND SIR ROZEN ARE DUELING ......!!
...BUT WHY!?

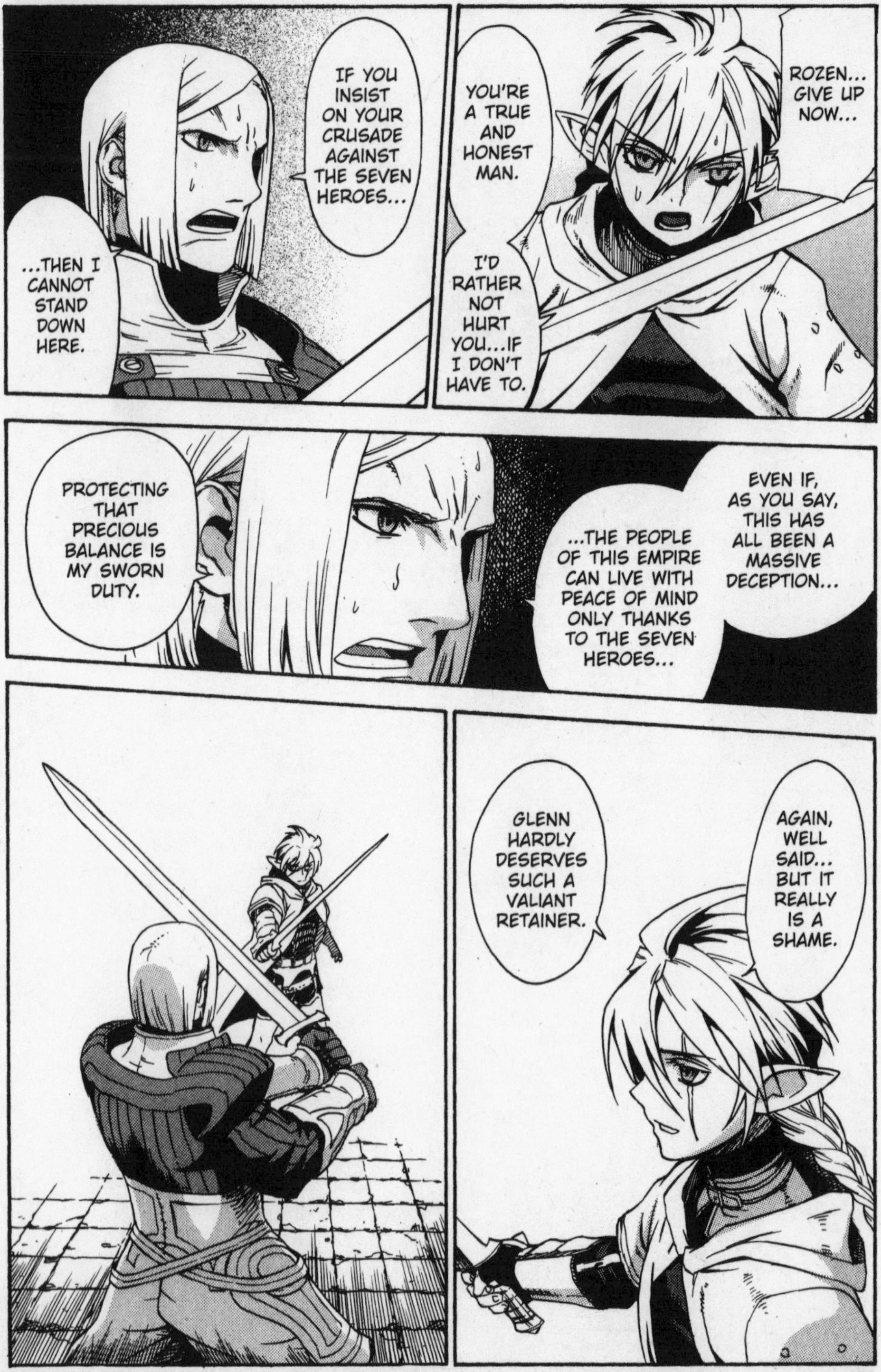
ROZEN... GIVE UP NOW...
YOU'RE A TRUE AND HONEST MAN.
I'D RATHER NOT HURT YOU...IF I DON'T HAVE TO.
IF YOU INSIST ON YOUR CRUSADE AGAINST THE SEVEN HEROES...
...THEN I CANNOT STAND DOWN HERE.
EVEN IF, AS YOU SAY, THIS HAS ALL BEEN A MASSIVE DECEPTION...
...THE PEOPLE OF THIS EMPIRE CAN LIVE WITH PEACE OF MIND ONLY THANKS TO THE SEVEN HEROES...
PROTECTING THAT PRECIOUS BALANCE IS MY SWORN DUTY.
AGAIN, WELL SAID... BUT IT REALLY IS A SHAME.
GLENN HARDLY DESERVES SUCH A VALIANT RETAINER.

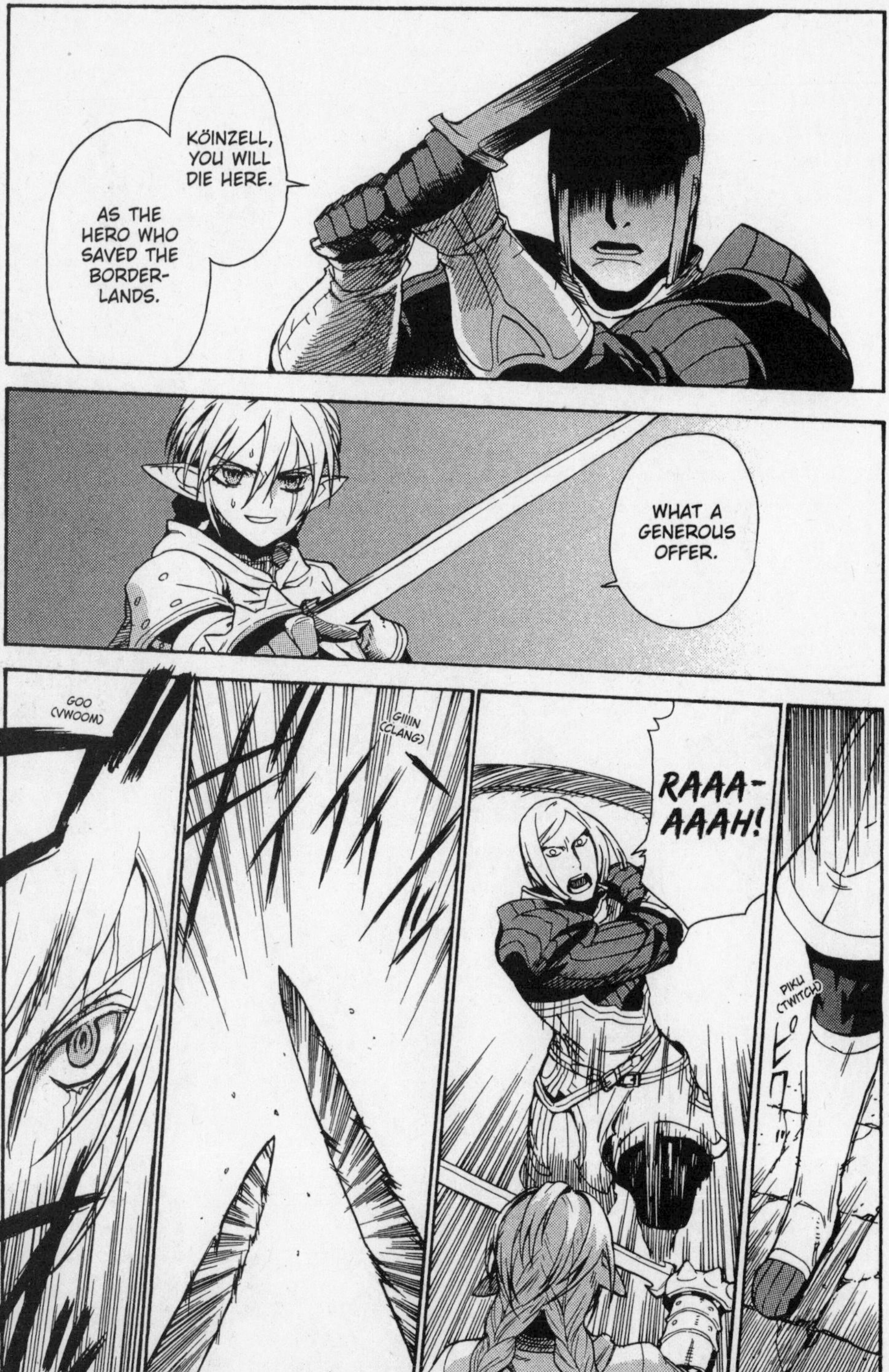
KÖINZELL, YOU WILL DIE HERE.
AS THE HERO WHO SAVED THE BORDER-LANDS.
WHAT A GENEROUS OFFER.
PIKU (TWITCH)
RAAA-AAAH!
GIIIN (CLANG)
GOO (VWOOM)

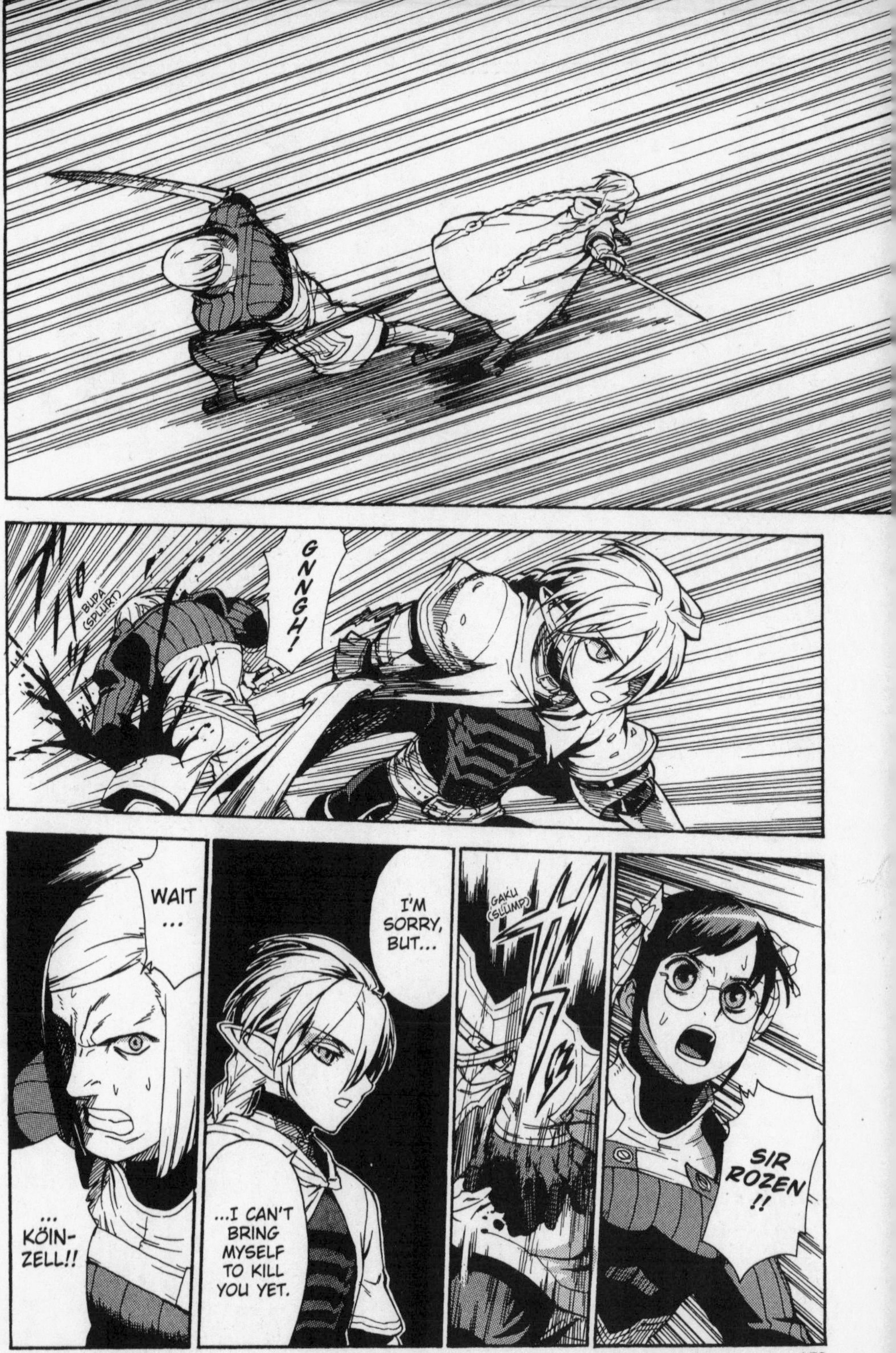
GNNGH!
BUPA (SPLURT)
SIR ROZEN!!
GAKU (SLUMP)
I'M SORRY, BUT...
...I CAN'T BRING MYSELF TO KILL YOU YET.
WAIT...
...KÖIN-ZELL!!

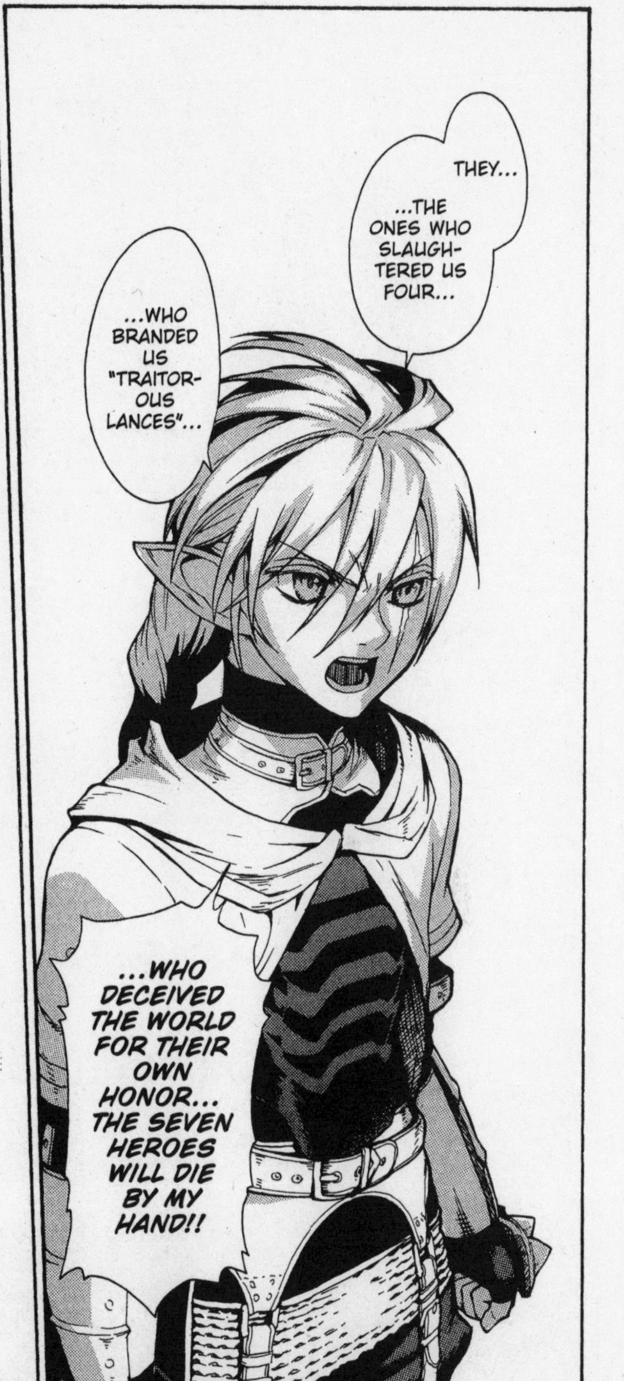
THEY...
...THE ONES WHO SLAUGHTERED US FOUR...
...WHO BRANDED US "TRAITOROUS LANCES"...
...WHO DECEIVED THE WORLD FOR THEIR OWN HONOR... THE SEVEN HEROES WILL DIE BY MY HAND!!
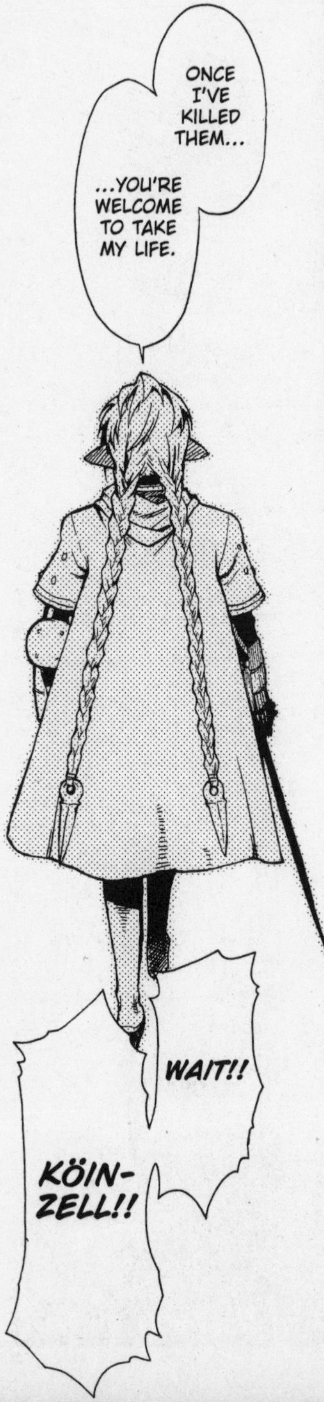
ONCE I'VE KILLED THEM...
...YOU'RE WELCOME TO TAKE MY LIFE.
WAIT!!
KÖIN-ZELL!!

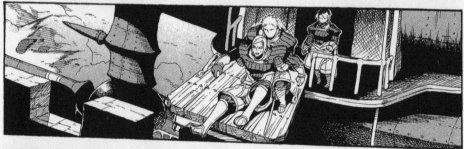

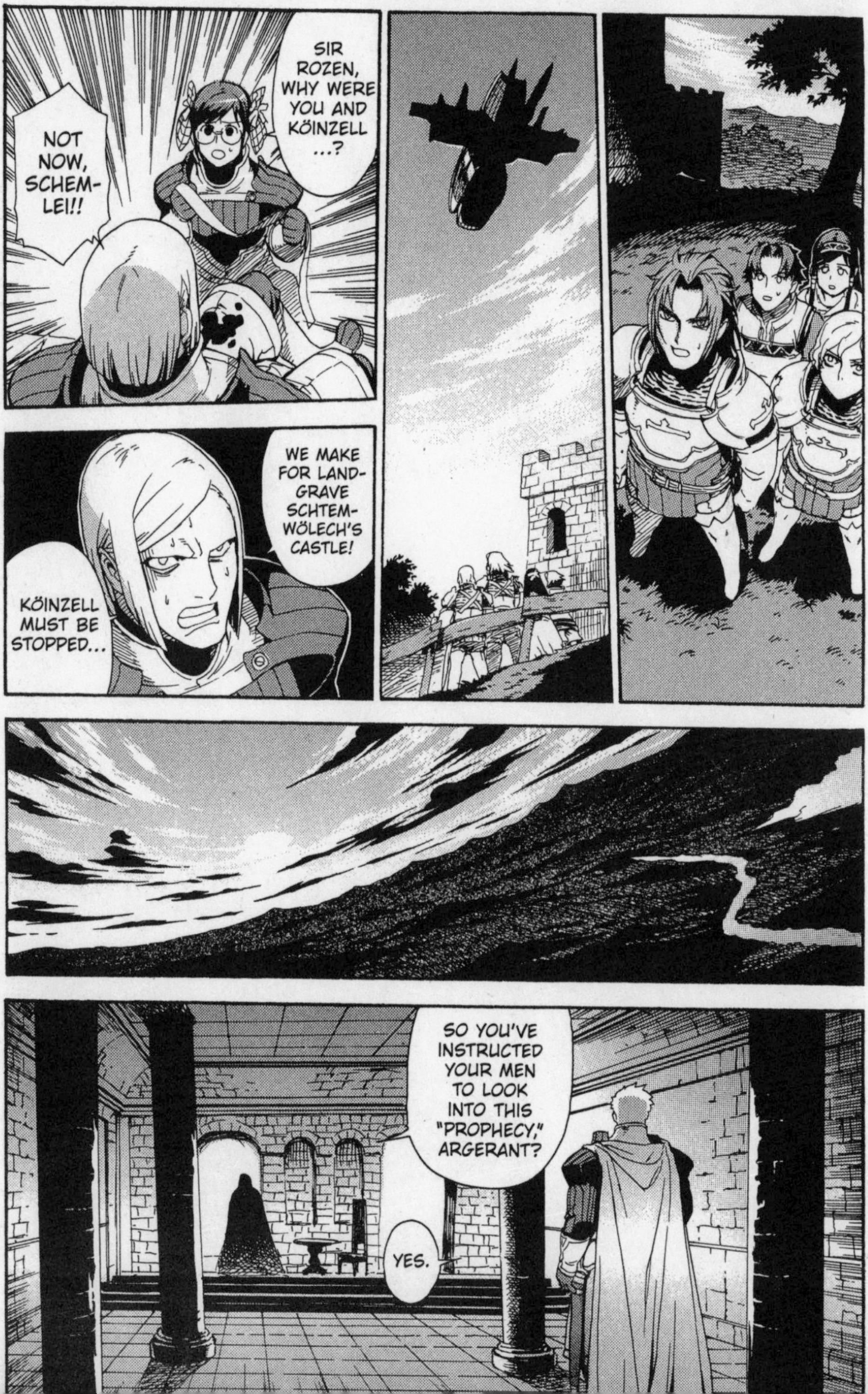
SIR ROZEN, WHY WERE YOU AND KÖINZELL ...?
NOT NOW, SCHEMLEI!!
WE MAKE FOR LANDGRAVE SCHTEMWÖLECH'S CASTLE!
KÖINZELL MUST BE STOPPED...
SO YOU'VE INSTRUCTED YOUR MEN TO LOOK INTO THIS "PROPHECY," ARGERANT?
YES.

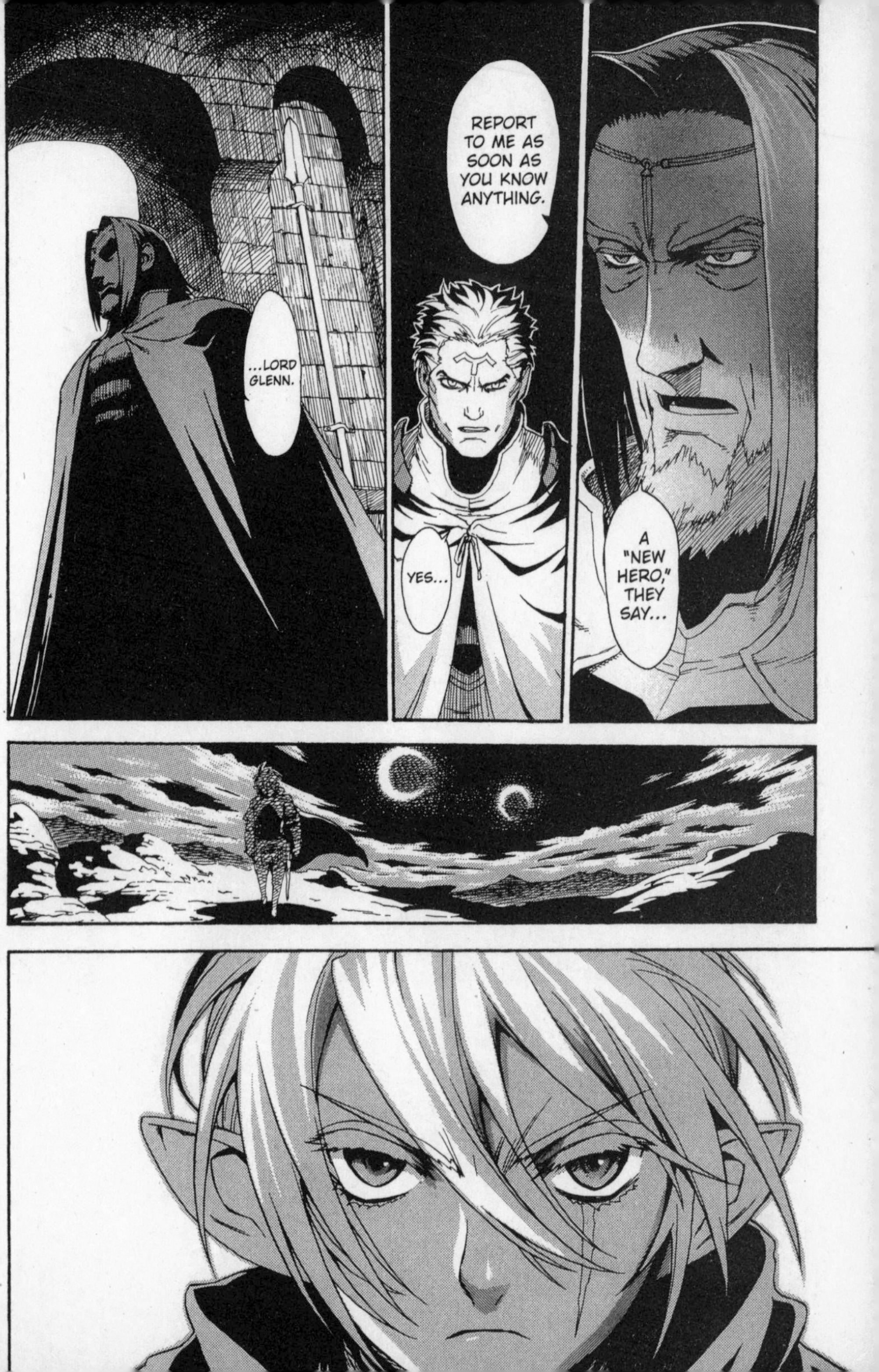
A "NEW HERO," THEY SAY...
REPORT TO ME AS SOON AS YOU KNOW ANYTHING.
YES...
...LORD GLENN.

Side Story: Blatt Meister (Blade Master) Part 1

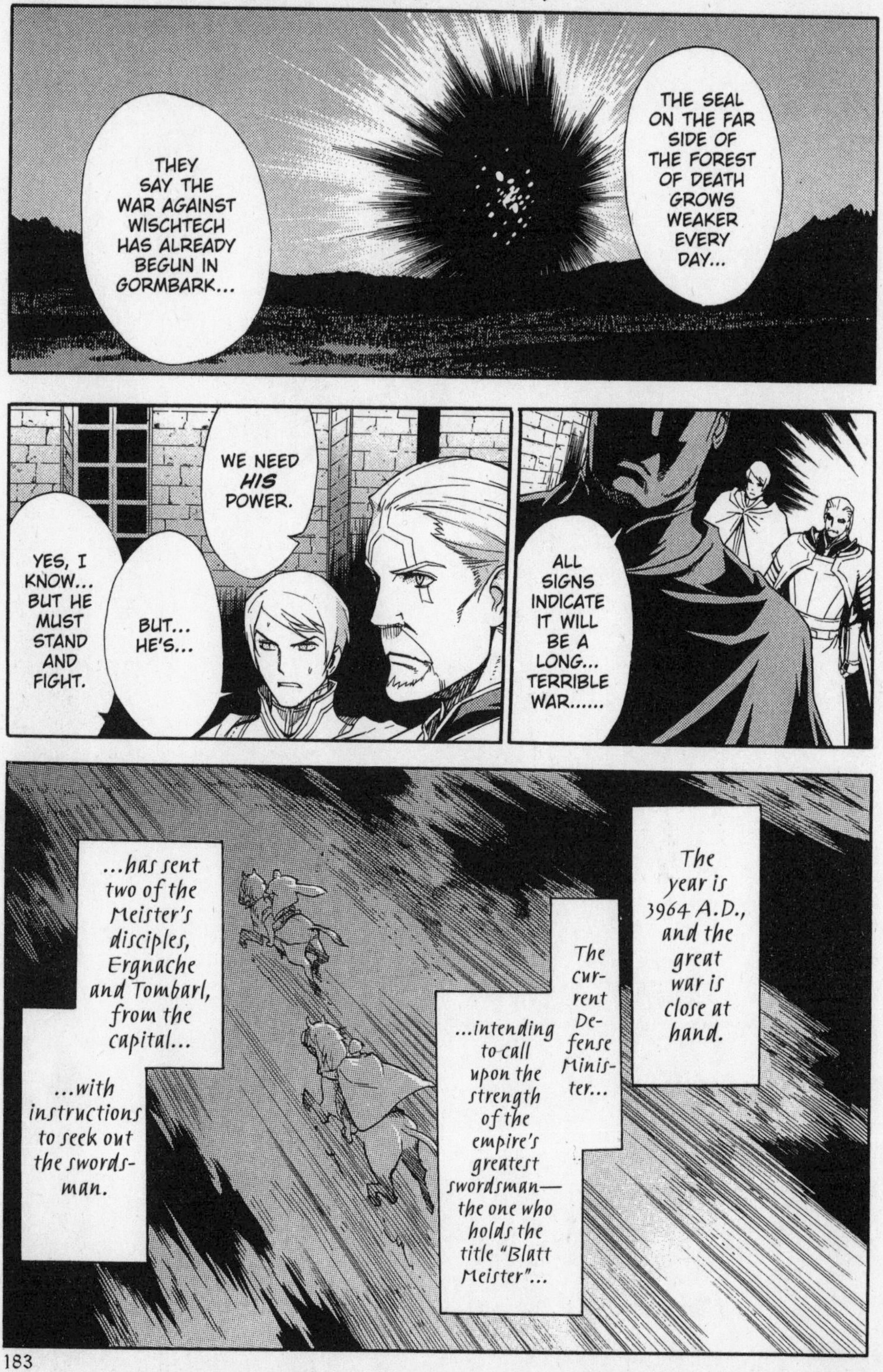
THE SEAL ON THE FAR SIDE OF THE FOREST OF DEATH GROWS WEAKER EVERY DAY...
THEY SAY THE WAR AGAINST WISCHTECH HAS ALREADY BEGUN IN GORMBARK...
ALL SIGNS INDICATE IT WILL BE A LONG... TERRIBLE WAR......
WE NEED HIS POWER.
BUT... HE'S...
YES, I KNOW... BUT HE MUST STAND AND FIGHT.
The year is 3964 A.D., and the great war is close at hand.
The current Defense Minister...
...intending to call upon the strength of the empire's greatest swordsman—the one who holds the title "Blatt Meister"...
...has sent two of the Meister's disciples, Ergnache and Tombarl, from the capital...
...with instructions to seek out the swordsman.

Side Story:

Blatt Meister (Blade Master) Part 1

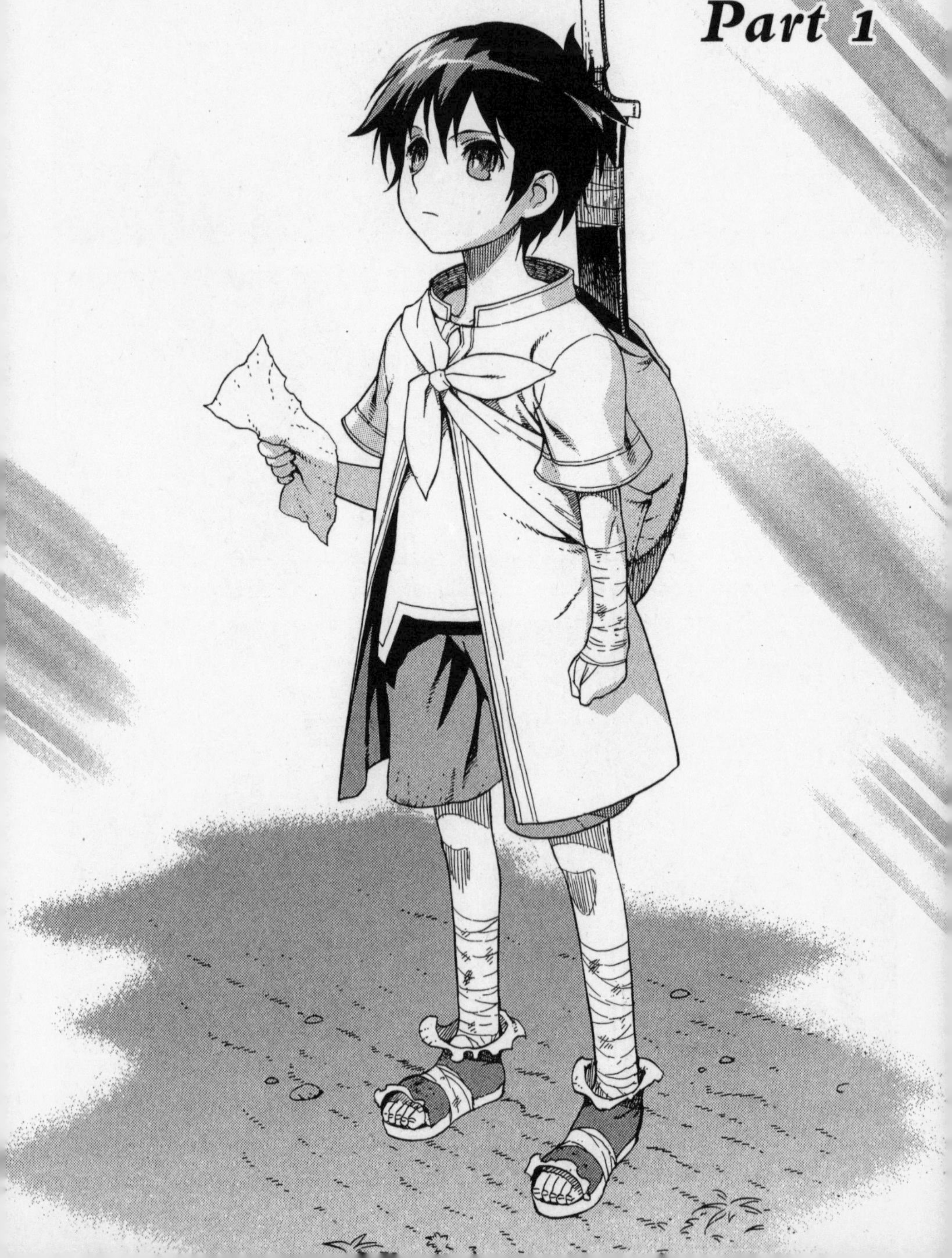

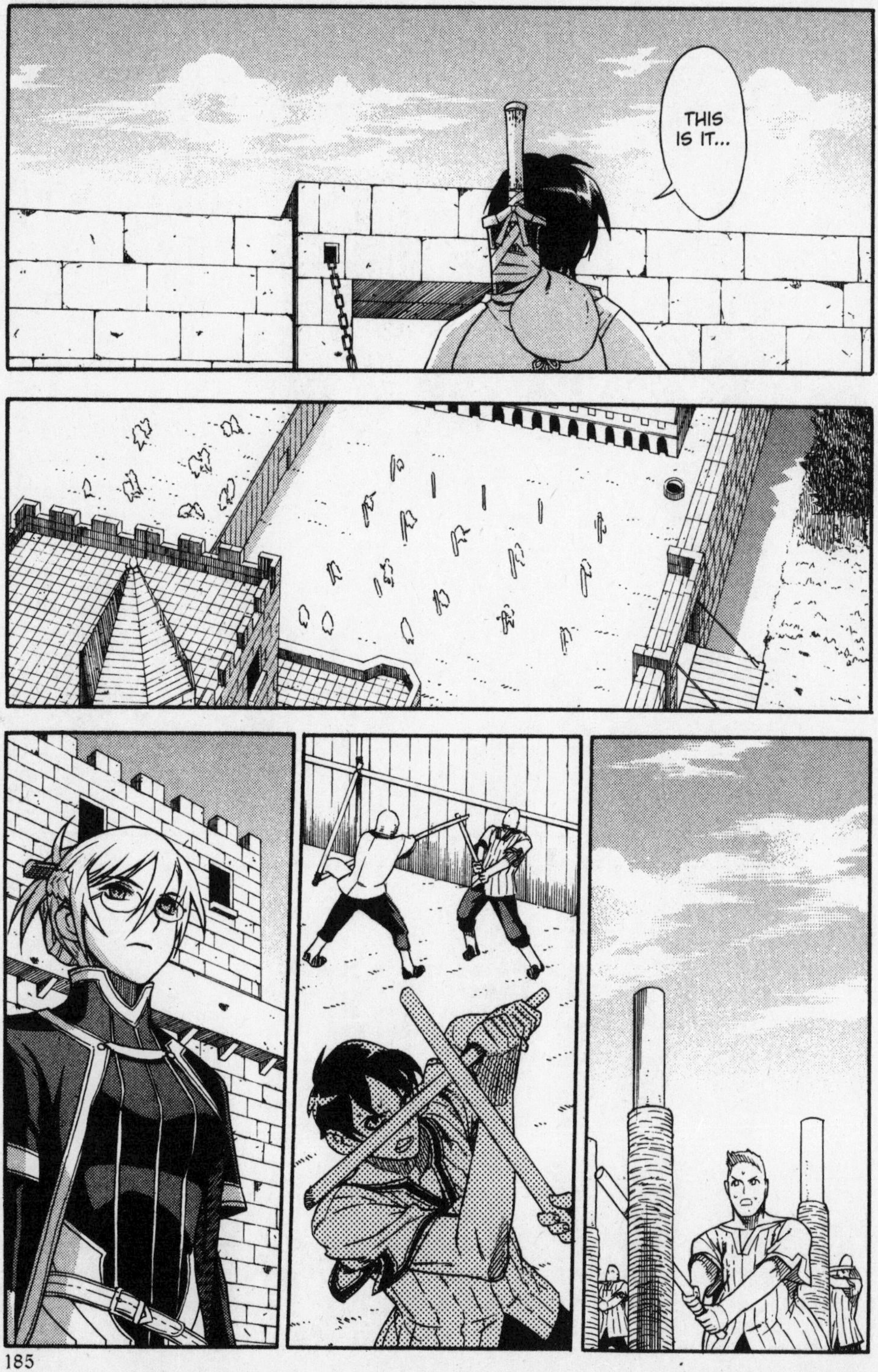
THIS IS IT...

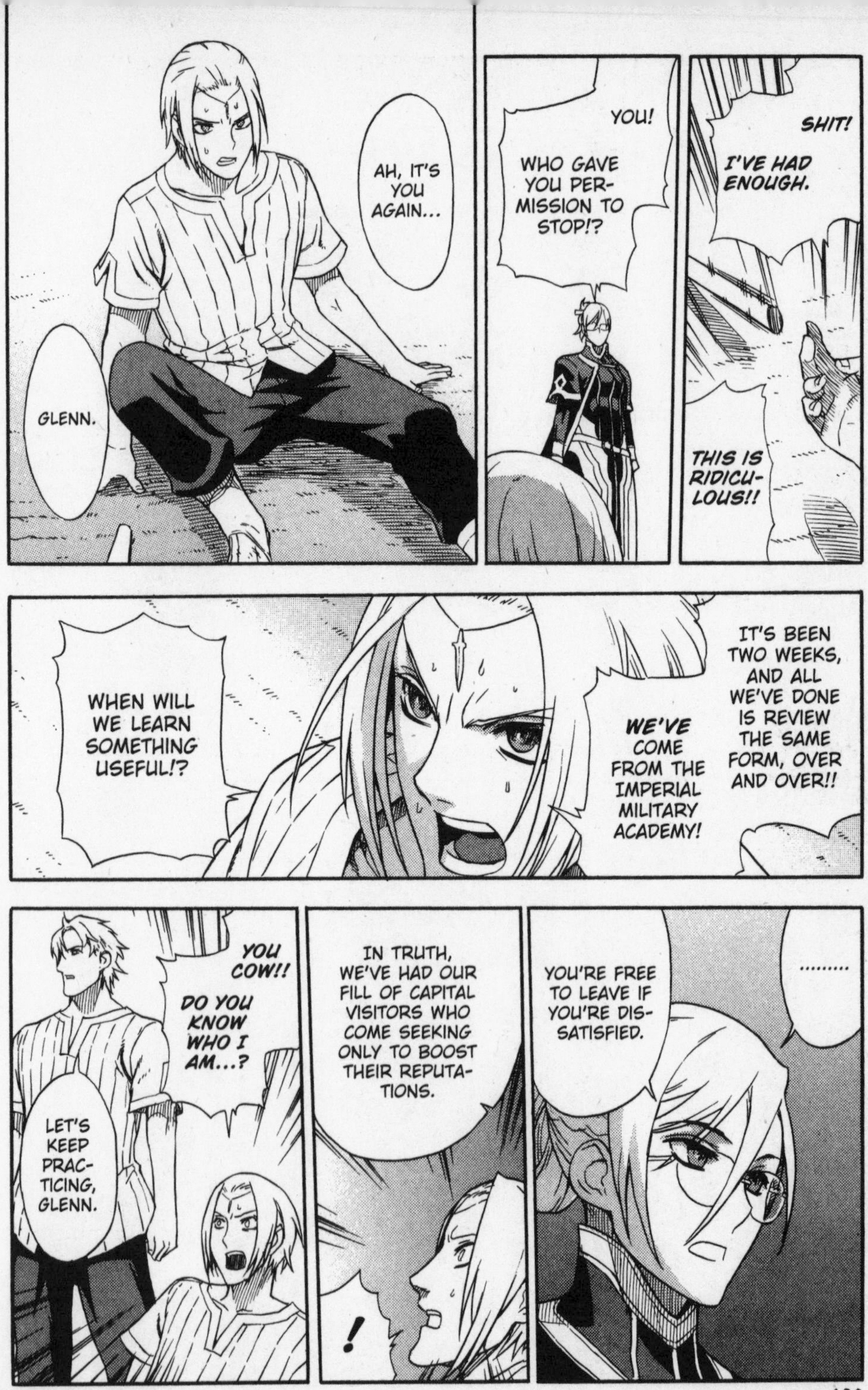
SHIT!
I'VE HAD ENOUGH.
THIS IS RIDICULOUS!!
YOU!
WHO GAVE YOU PERMISSION TO STOP!?
AH, IT'S YOU AGAIN...
GLENN.
IT'S BEEN TWO WEEKS, AND ALL WE'VE DONE IS REVIEW THE SAME FORM, OVER AND OVER!!
WE'VE COME FROM THE IMPERIAL MILITARY ACADEMY!
WHEN WILL WE LEARN SOMETHING USEFUL!?
....
YOU'RE FREE TO LEAVE IF YOU'RE DISSATISFIED.
IN TRUTH, WE'VE HAD OUR FILL OF CAPITAL VISITORS WHO COME SEEKING ONLY TO BOOST THEIR REPUTATIONS.
!
YOU COW!!
DO YOU KNOW WHO I AM...?
LET'S KEEP PRACTICING, GLENN.

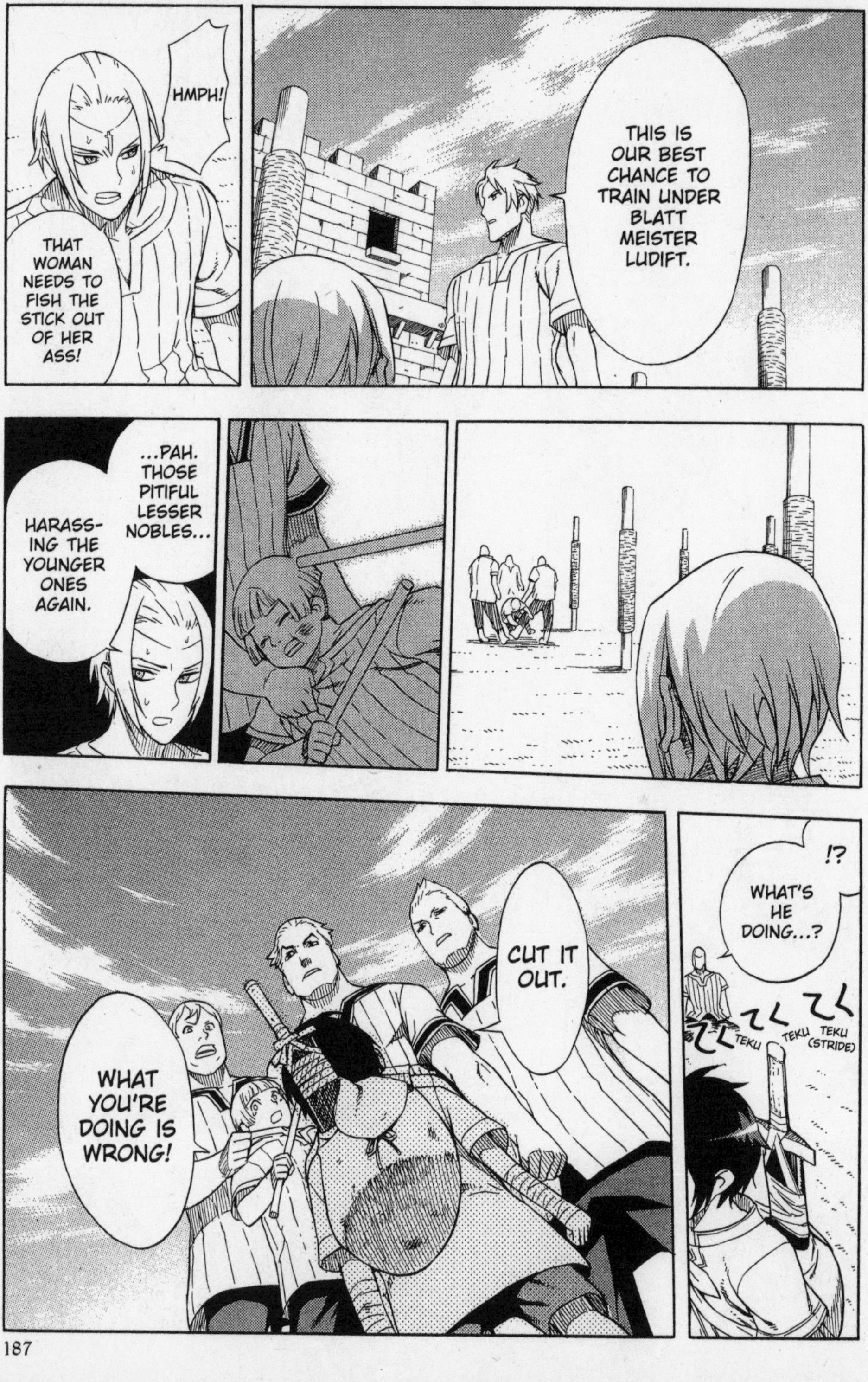
THIS IS OUR BEST CHANCE TO TRAIN UNDER BLATT MEISTER LUDIFT.
HMPH!
THAT WOMAN NEEDS TO FISH THE STICK OUT OF HER ASS!
...PAH. THOSE PITIFUL LESSER NOBLES...
HARASSING THE YOUNGER ONES AGAIN.
!?
WHAT'S HE DOING...?
TEKU TEKU TEKU (STRIDE)
CUT IT OUT.
WHAT YOU'RE DOING IS WRONG!

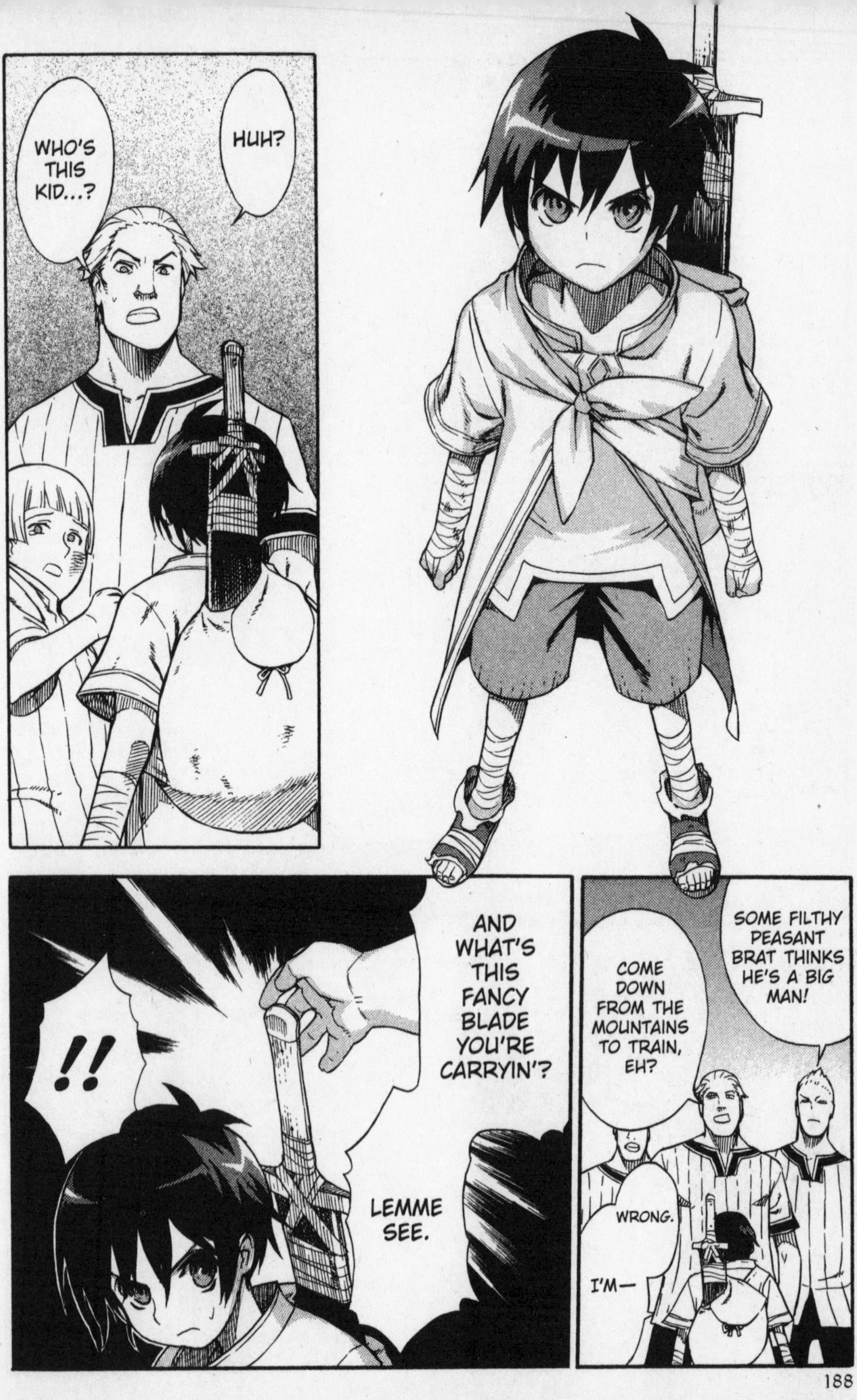
HUH?
WHO'S THIS KID...?
SOME FILTHY PEASANT BRAT THINKS HE'S A BIG MAN!
COME DOWN FROM THE MOUNTAINS TO TRAIN, EH?
WRONG.
I'M—
AND WHAT'S THIS FANCY BLADE YOU'RE CARRYIN'?
LEMME SEE.
!!

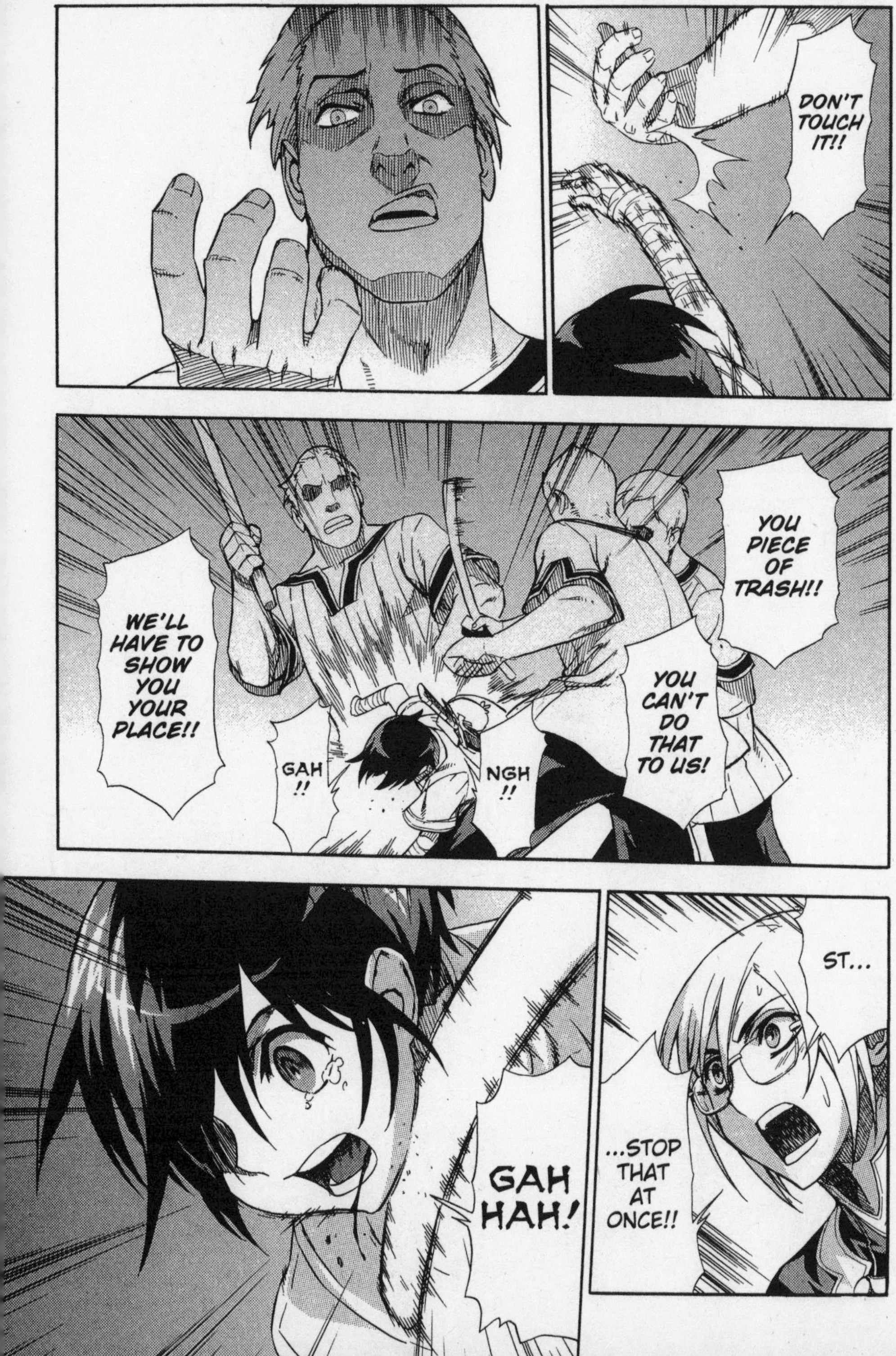

DON'T TOUCH IT!!
YOU PIECE OF TRASH!!
YOU CAN'T DO THAT TO US!
NGH!!
GAH!!
WE'LL HAVE TO SHOW YOU YOUR PLACE!!
ST...
...STOP THAT AT ONCE!!
GAH HAH!

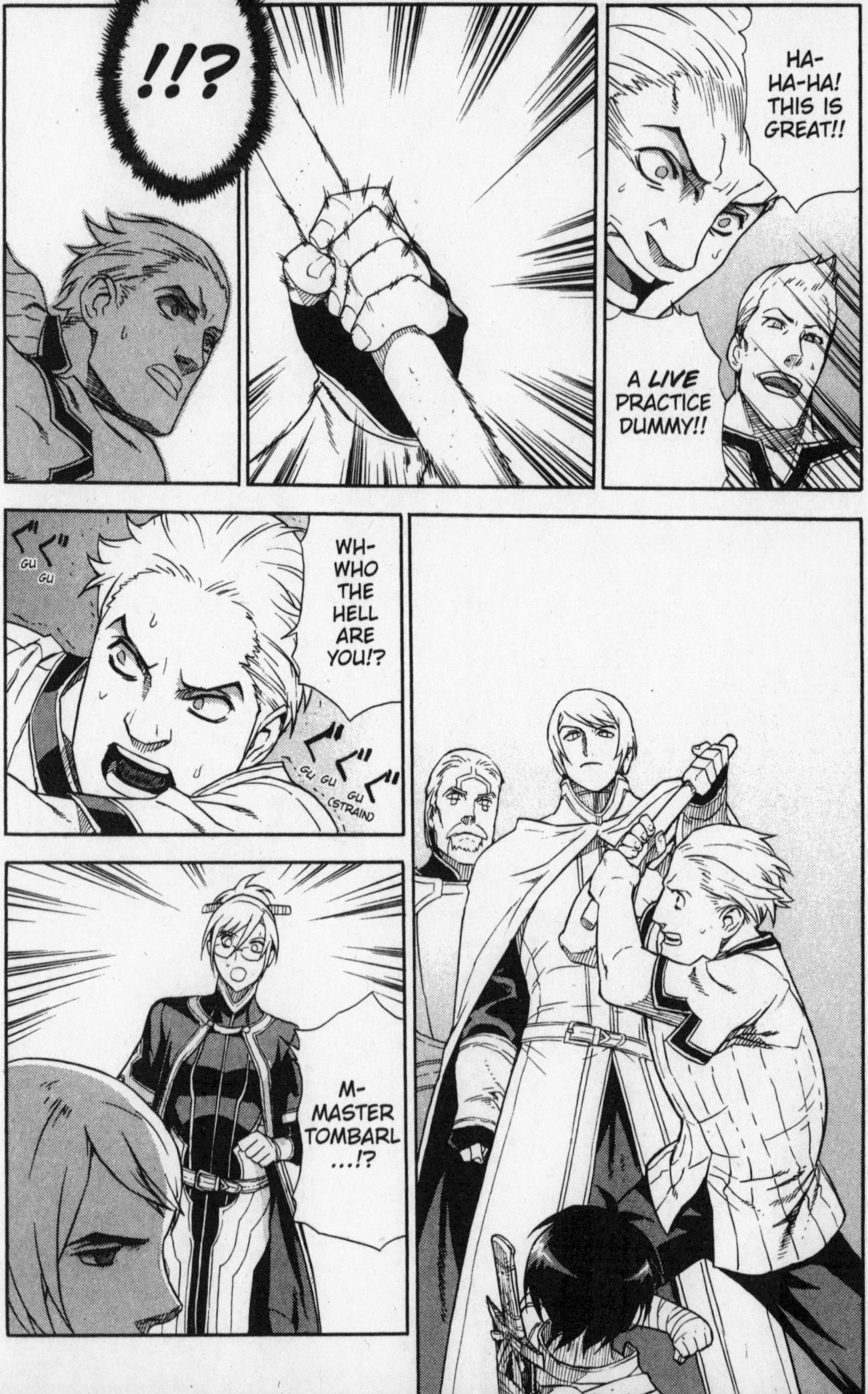
HA-HA-HA! THIS IS GREAT!!
A LIVE PRACTICE DUMMY!!
!!?
WH-WHO THE HELL ARE YOU!?
ぐぐ
GU GU
ぐぐぐ
GU GU GU (STRAIN)
M-MASTER TOMBARL ...!?

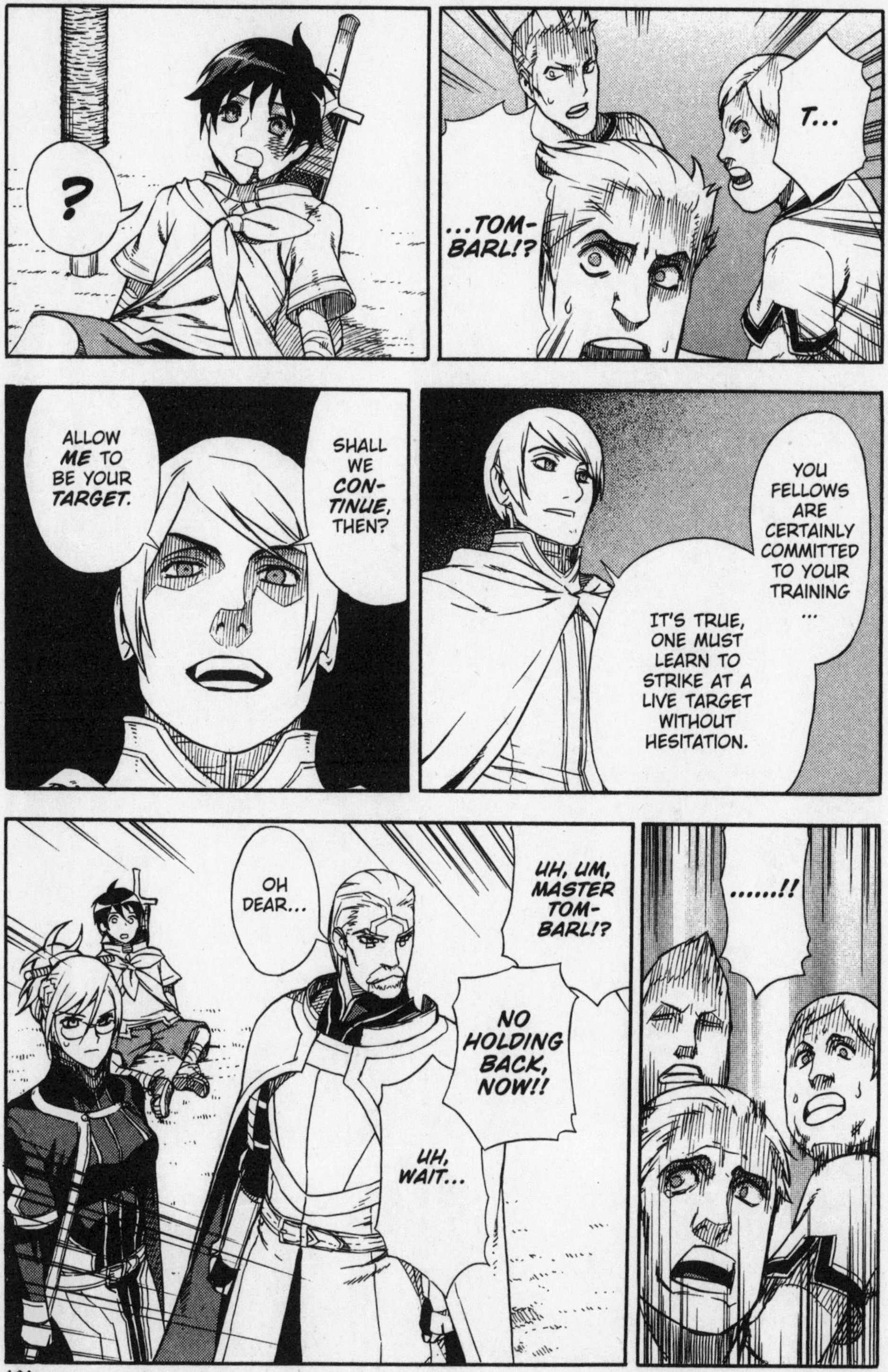
T...
...TOM-BARL!?
?
YOU FELLOWS ARE CERTAINLY COMMITTED TO YOUR TRAINING...
IT'S TRUE, ONE MUST LEARN TO STRIKE AT A LIVE TARGET WITHOUT HESITATION.
SHALL WE CON-TINUE, THEN?
ALLOW *ME* TO BE YOUR *TARGET*.
......!!
UH, UM, MASTER TOM-BARL!?
OH DEAR...
NO HOLDING BACK, NOW!!
UH, WAIT...

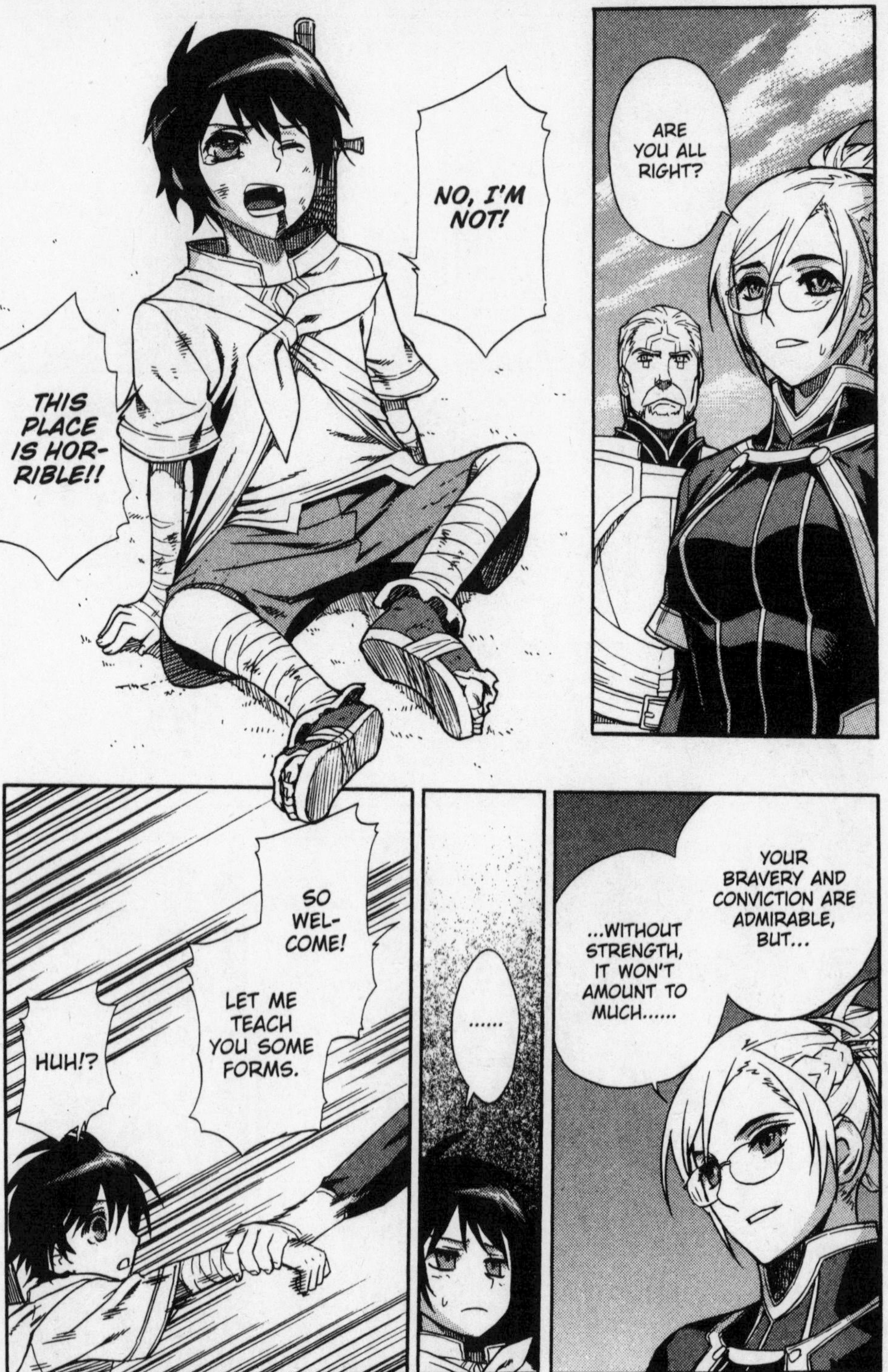
ARE YOU ALL RIGHT?
NO, I'M NOT!
THIS PLACE IS HOR-RIBLE!!
YOUR BRAVERY AND CONVICTION ARE ADMIRABLE, BUT...
...WITHOUT STRENGTH, IT WON'T AMOUNT TO MUCH......
......
SO WEL-COME!
LET ME TEACH YOU SOME FORMS.
HUH!?

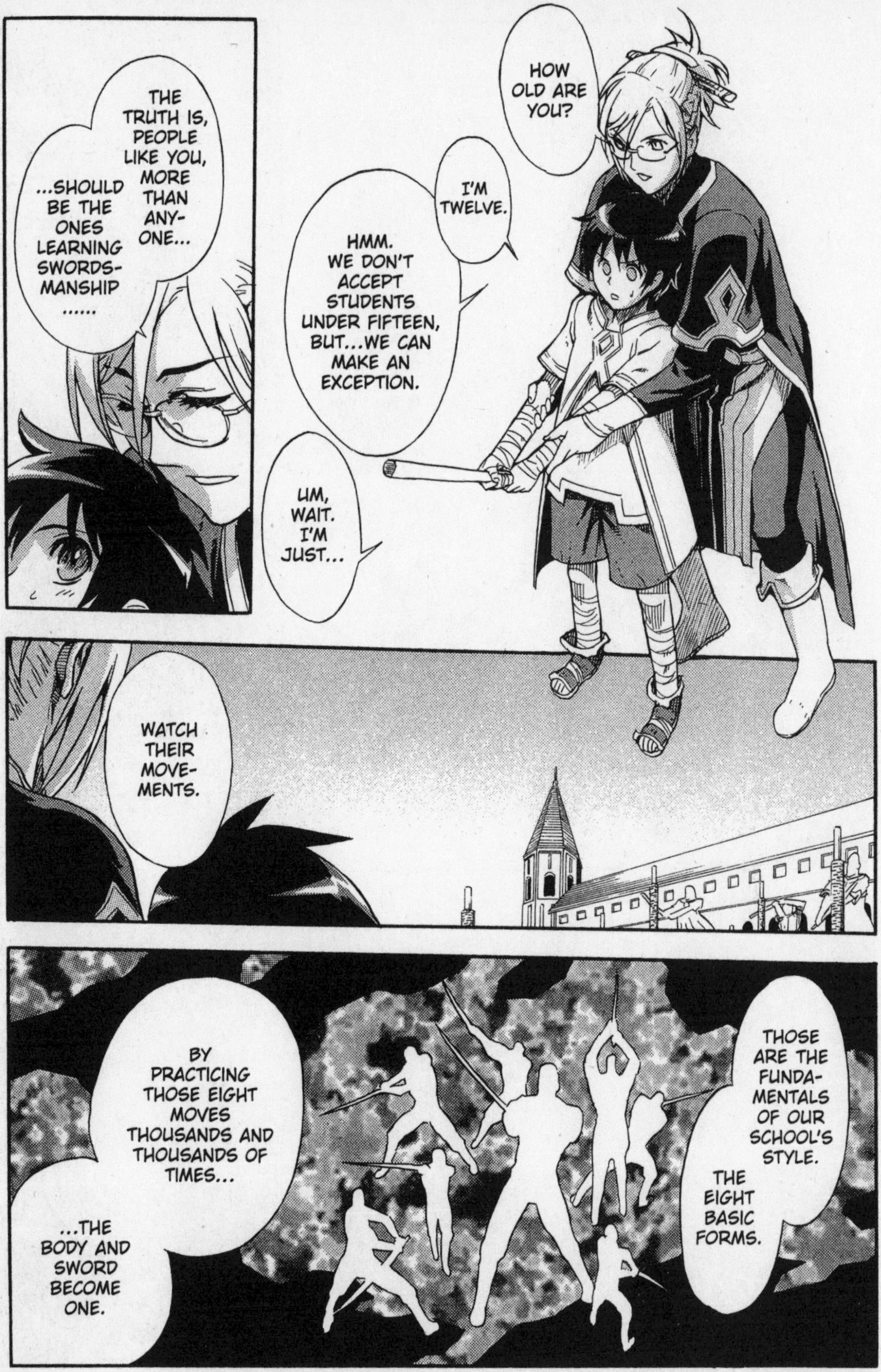
HOW OLD ARE YOU?
I'M TWELVE.
HMM. WE DON'T ACCEPT STUDENTS UNDER FIFTEEN, BUT...WE CAN MAKE AN EXCEPTION.
UM, WAIT. I'M JUST...
THE TRUTH IS, PEOPLE LIKE YOU, MORE THAN ANYONE...
...SHOULD BE THE ONES LEARNING SWORDSMANSHIP......
WATCH THEIR MOVEMENTS.
THOSE ARE THE FUNDAMENTALS OF OUR SCHOOL'S STYLE.
THE EIGHT BASIC FORMS.
BY PRACTICING THOSE EIGHT MOVES THOUSANDS AND THOUSANDS OF TIMES...
...THE BODY AND SWORD BECOME ONE.

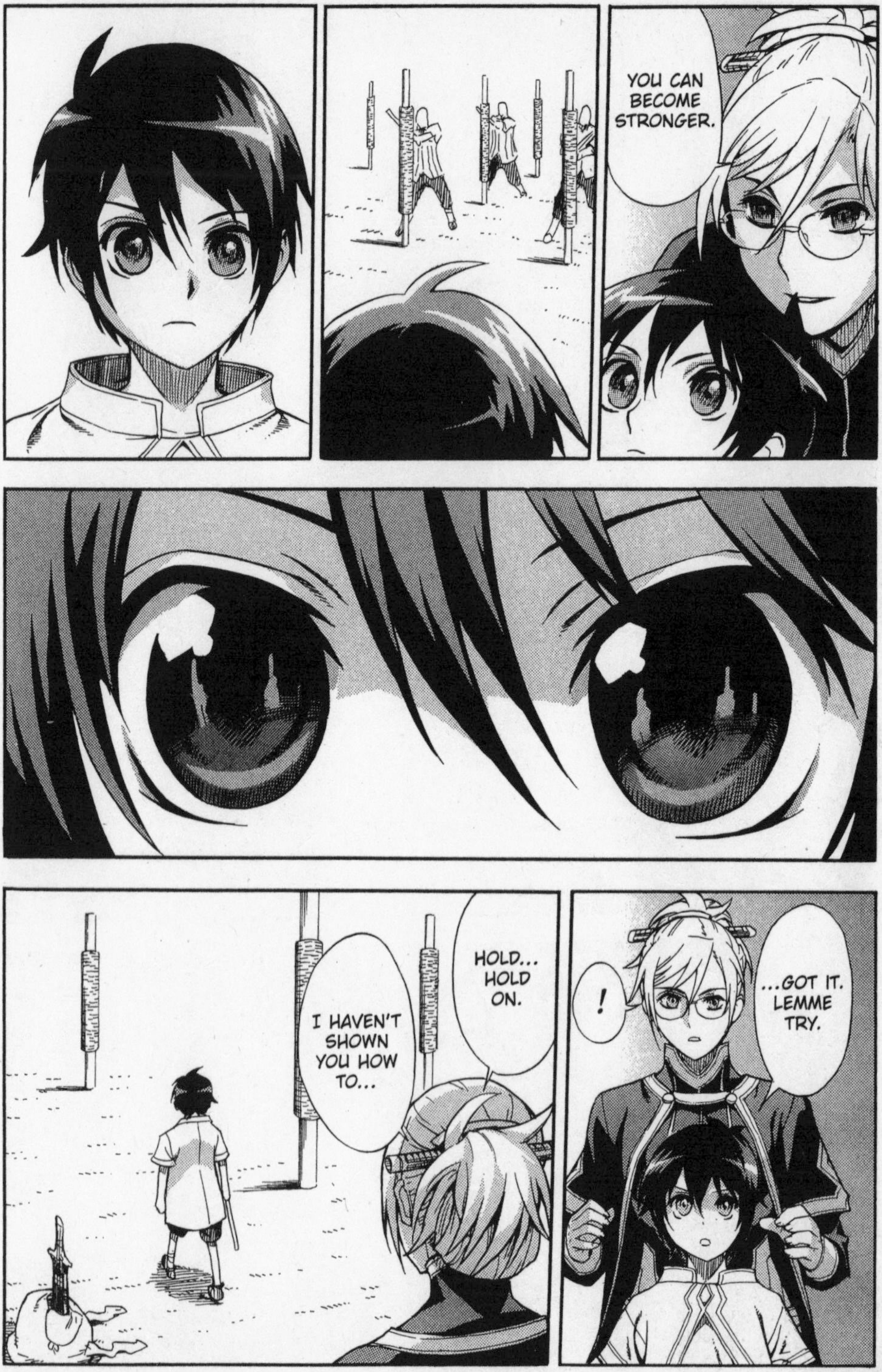
YOU CAN BECOME STRONGER.
...GOT IT. LEMME TRY.
!
HOLD... HOLD ON.
I HAVEN'T SHOWN YOU HOW TO...

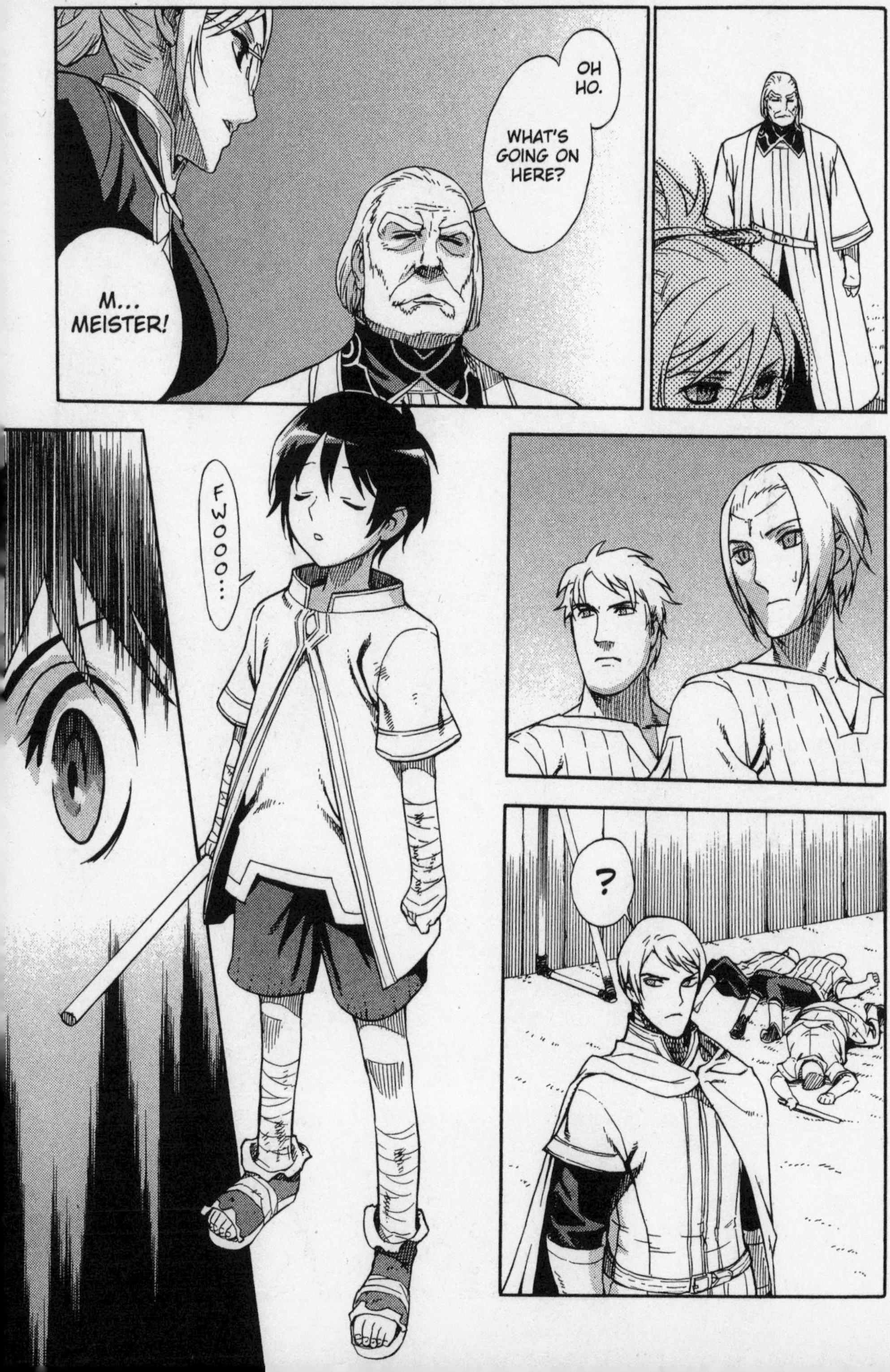
OH HO.
WHAT'S GOING ON HERE?
M... MEISTER!
?
FWOOO...

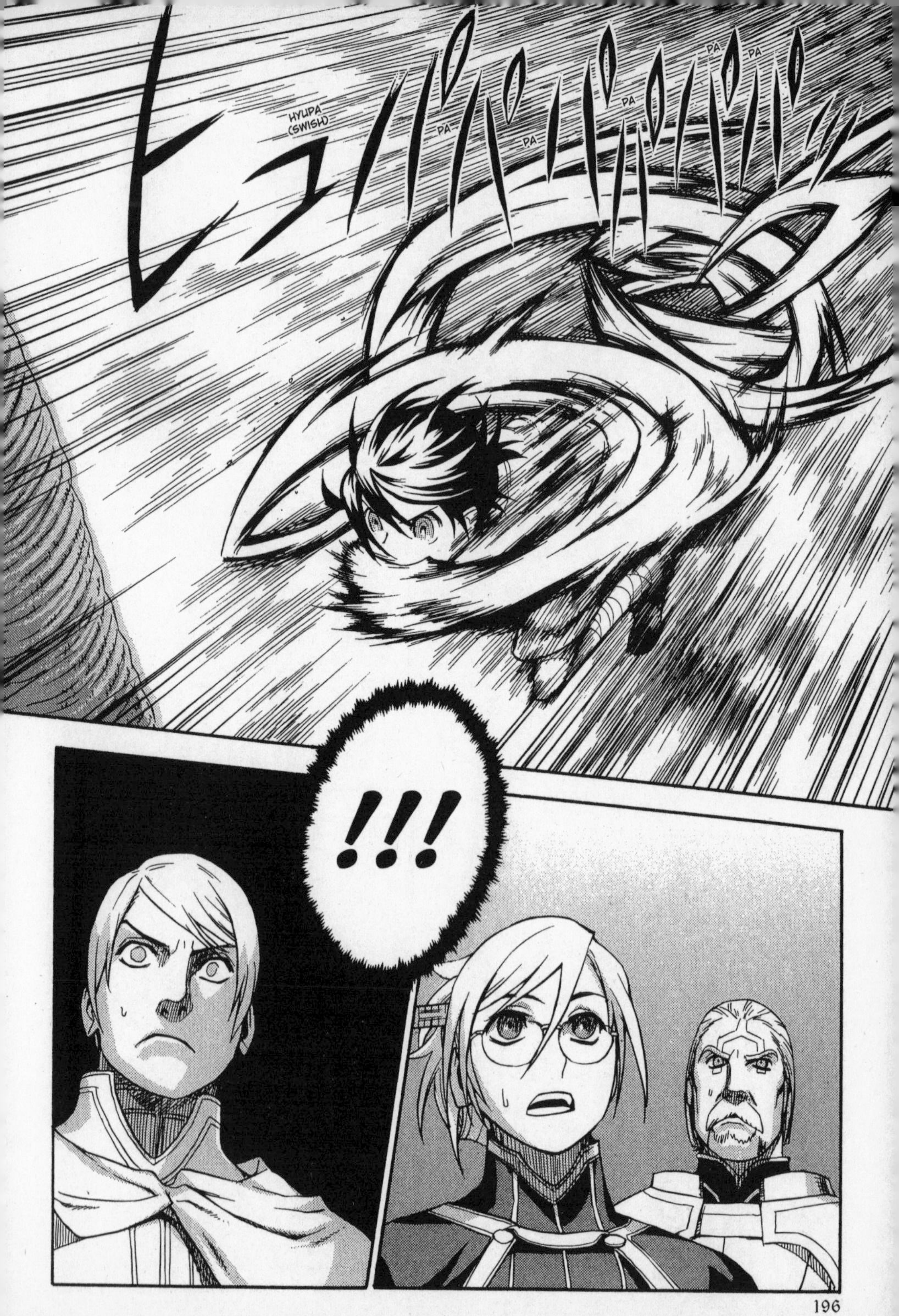
HYUPA (SWISH)
PA
PA
PA
PA
PA
!!!

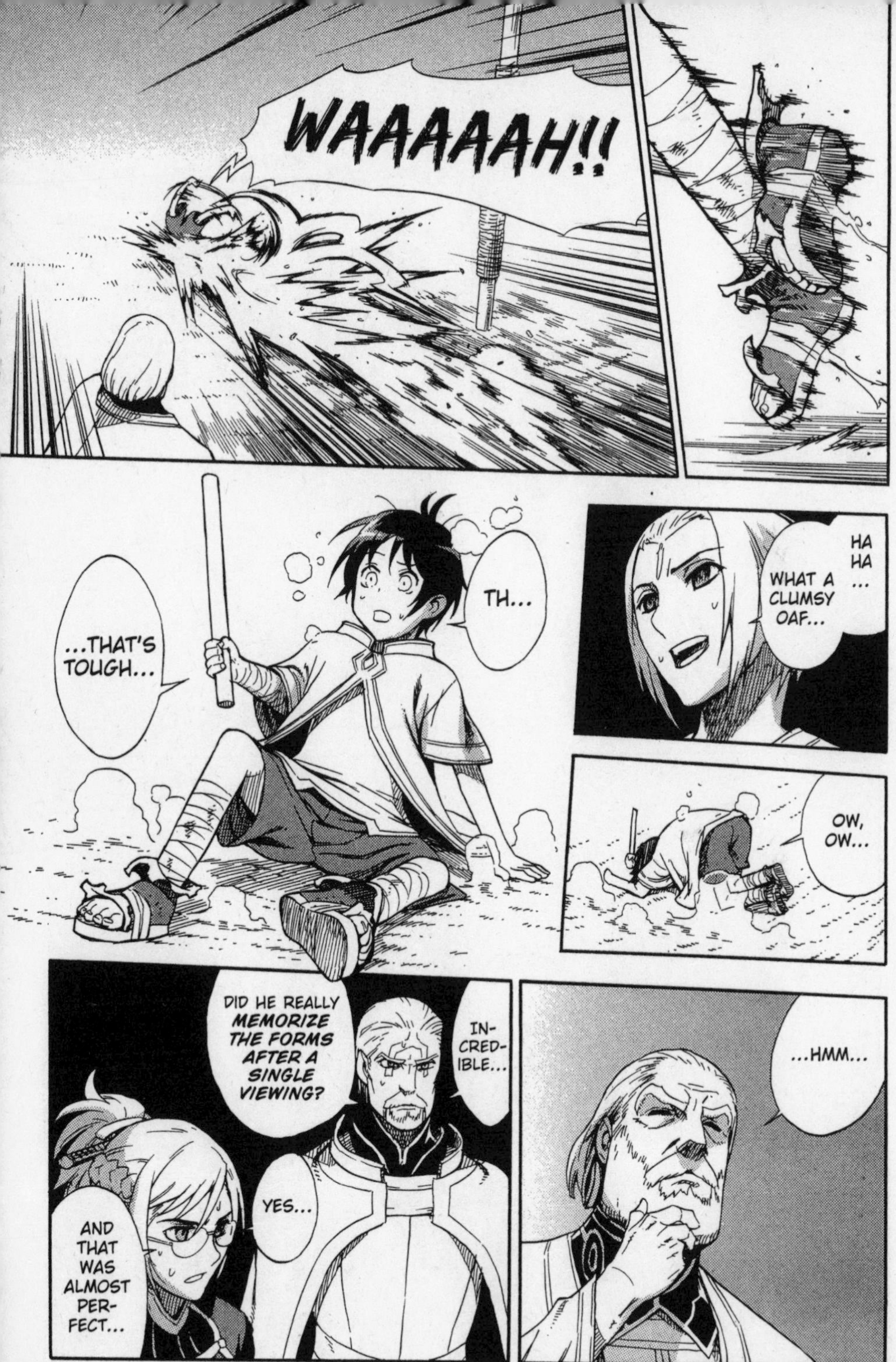
WAAAAAH!!
HA HA...
WHAT A CLUMSY OAF...
OW, OW...
TH...
...THAT'S TOUGH...
...HMM...
IN-CRED-IBLE...
DID HE REALLY MEMORIZE THE FORMS AFTER A SINGLE VIEWING?
YES...
AND THAT WAS ALMOST PER-FECT...

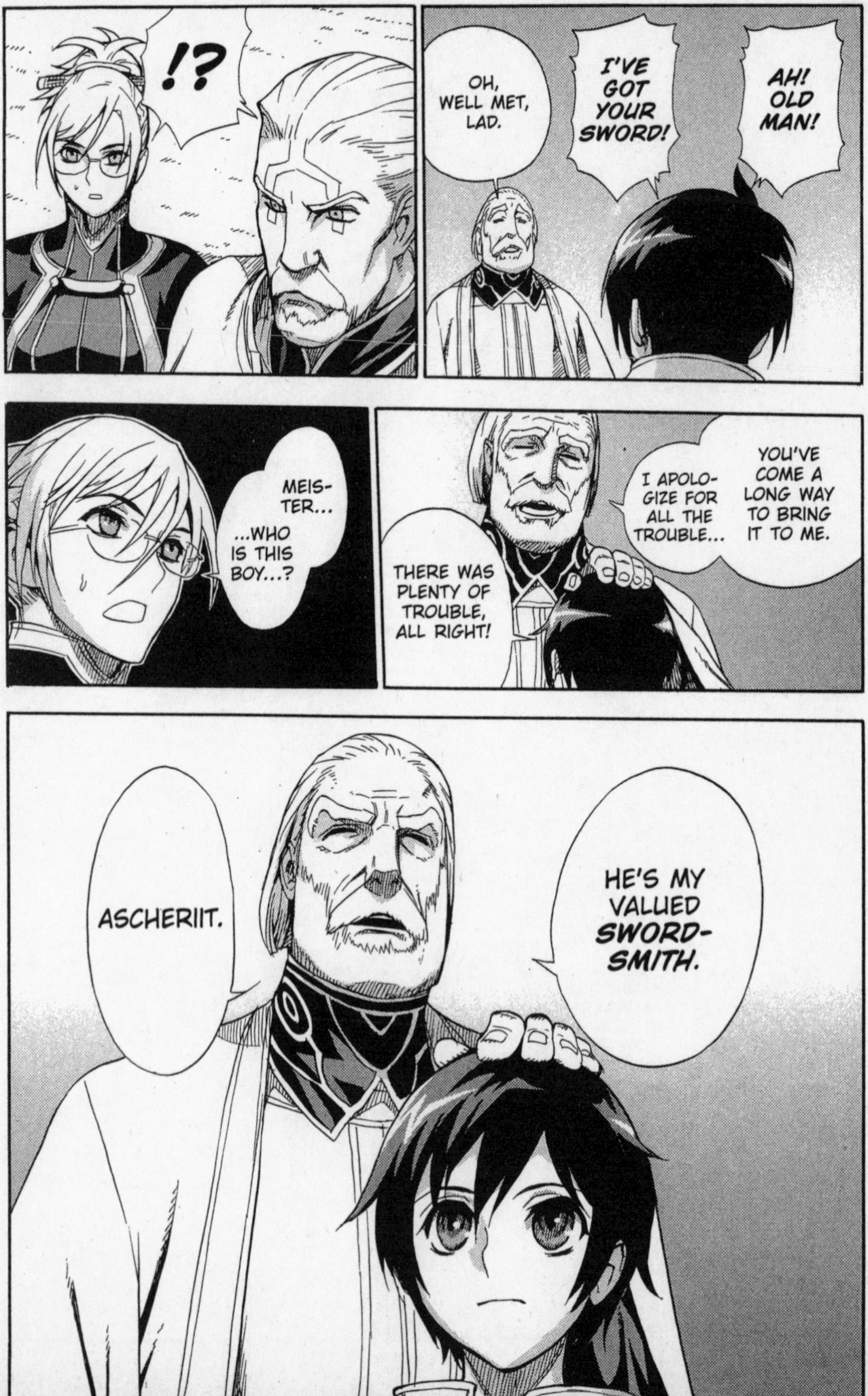
AH! OLD MAN!
I'VE GOT YOUR SWORD!
OH, WELL MET, LAD.
!?
YOU'VE COME A LONG WAY TO BRING IT TO ME.
I APOLO-GIZE FOR ALL THE TROUBLE...
THERE WAS PLENTY OF TROUBLE, ALL RIGHT!
MEIS-TER...
...WHO IS THIS BOY...?
HE'S MY VALUED SWORD-SMITH.
ASCHERIIT.

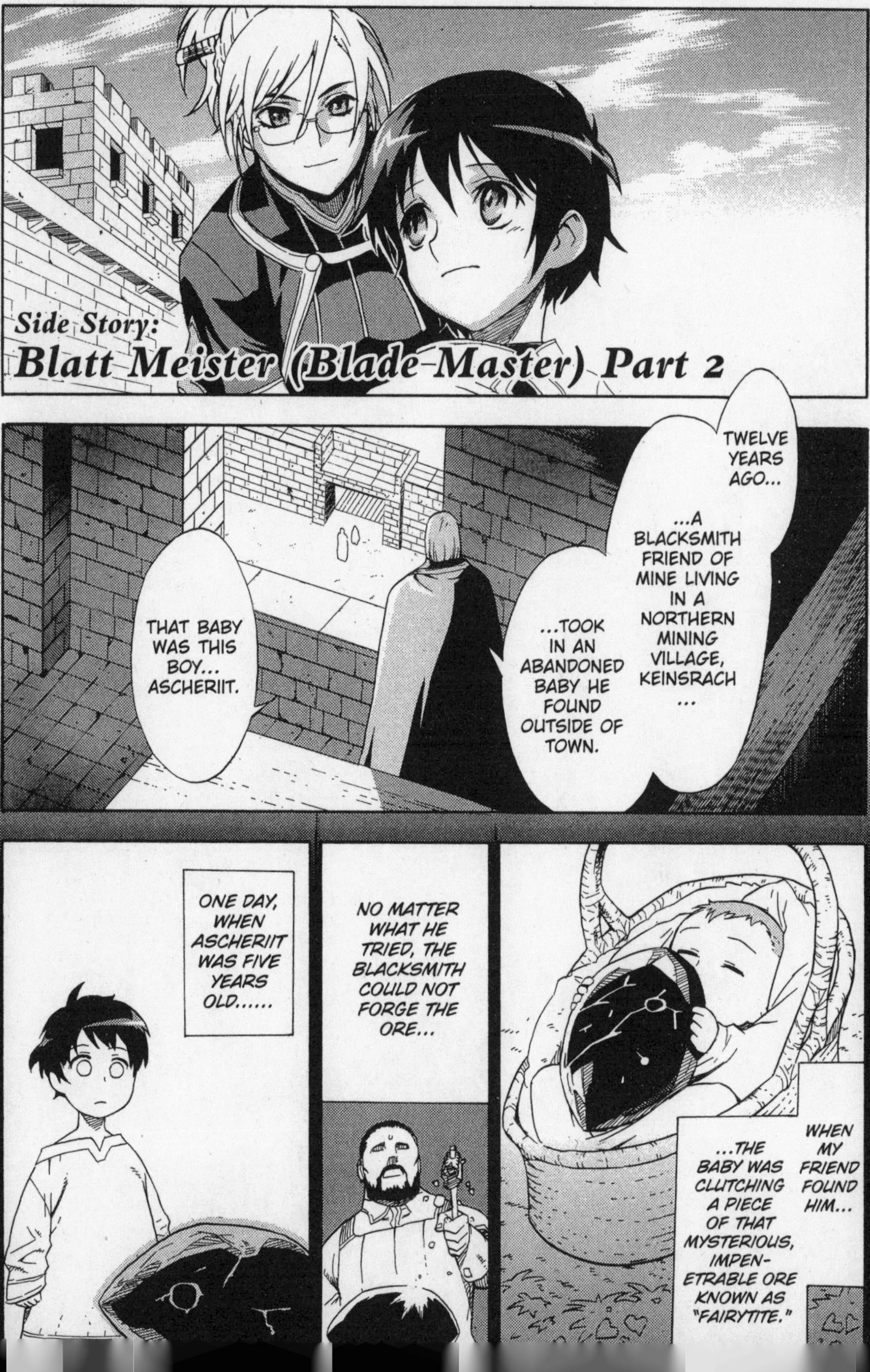
Side Story:
Blatt Meister (Blade Master) Part 2
TWELVE YEARS AGO...
...A BLACKSMITH FRIEND OF MINE LIVING IN A NORTHERN MINING VILLAGE, KEINSRACH ...
...TOOK IN AN ABANDONED BABY HE FOUND OUTSIDE OF TOWN.
THAT BABY WAS THIS BOY... ASCHERIIT.
WHEN MY FRIEND FOUND HIM...
...THE BABY WAS CLUTCHING A PIECE OF THAT MYSTERIOUS, IMPEN-ETRABLE ORE KNOWN AS "FAIRYTITE."
NO MATTER WHAT HE TRIED, THE BLACKSMITH COULD NOT FORGE THE ORE...
ONE DAY, WHEN ASCHERIIT WAS FIVE YEARS OLD......

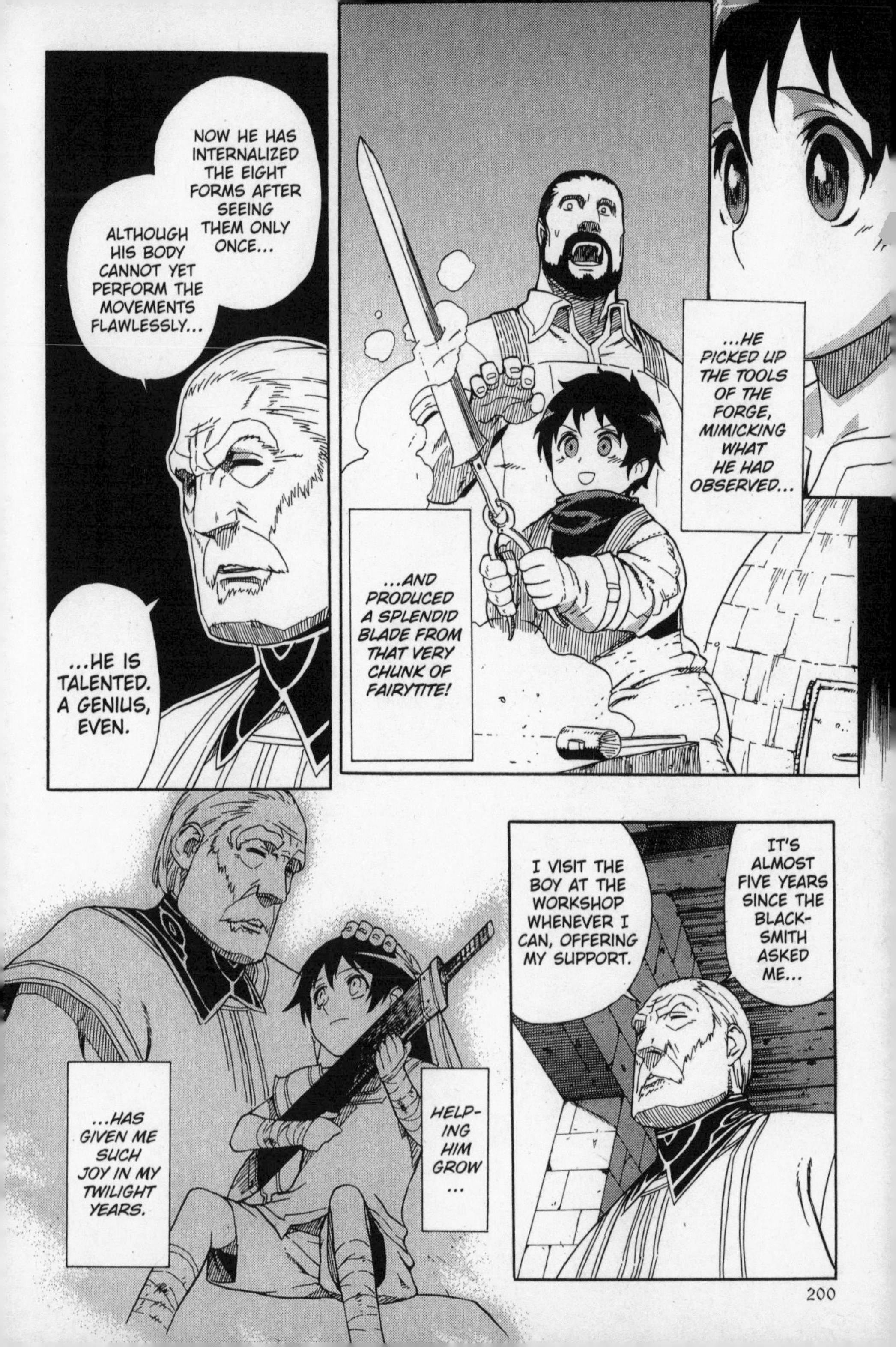
...HE PICKED UP THE TOOLS OF THE FORGE, MIMICKING WHAT HE HAD OBSERVED...
...AND PRODUCED A SPLENDID BLADE FROM THAT VERY CHUNK OF FAIRYTITE!
NOW HE HAS INTERNALIZED THE EIGHT FORMS AFTER SEEING THEM ONLY ONCE...
ALTHOUGH HIS BODY CANNOT YET PERFORM THE MOVEMENTS FLAWLESSLY...
...HE IS TALENTED. A GENIUS, EVEN.
IT'S ALMOST FIVE YEARS SINCE THE BLACK-SMITH ASKED ME...
I VISIT THE BOY AT THE WORKSHOP WHENEVER I CAN, OFFERING MY SUPPORT.
HELP-ING HIM GROW...
...HAS GIVEN ME SUCH JOY IN MY TWILIGHT YEARS.

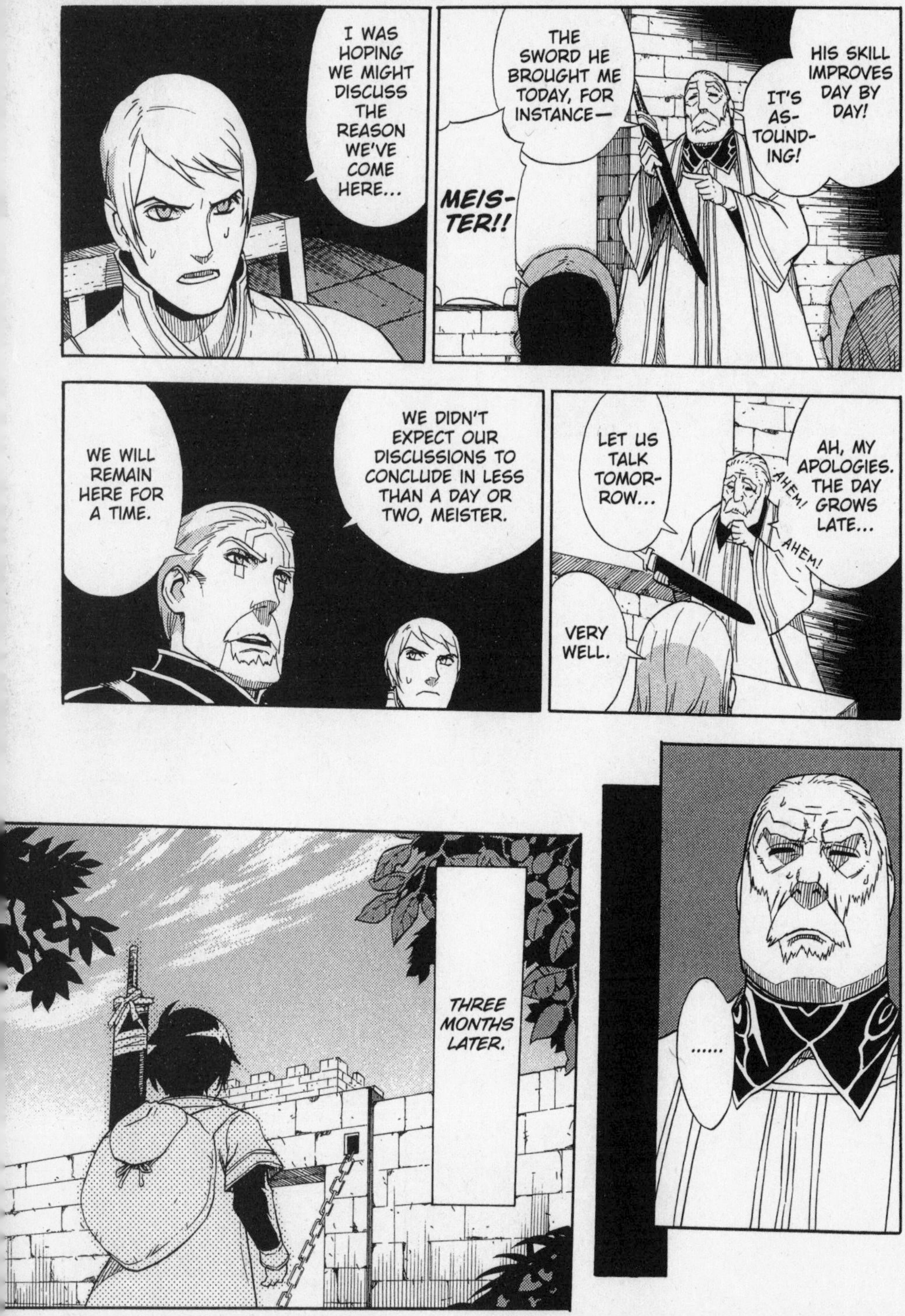
HIS SKILL IMPROVES DAY BY DAY!
IT'S AS-TOUNDING!
THE SWORD HE BROUGHT ME TODAY, FOR INSTANCE—
MEIS-TER!!
I WAS HOPING WE MIGHT DISCUSS THE REASON WE'VE COME HERE...
AH, MY APOLOGIES. THE DAY GROWS LATE...
AHEM!
AHEM!
LET US TALK TOMOR-ROW...
VERY WELL.
WE DIDN'T EXPECT OUR DISCUSSIONS TO CONCLUDE IN LESS THAN A DAY OR TWO, MEISTER.
WE WILL REMAIN HERE FOR A TIME.
......
THREE MONTHS LATER.

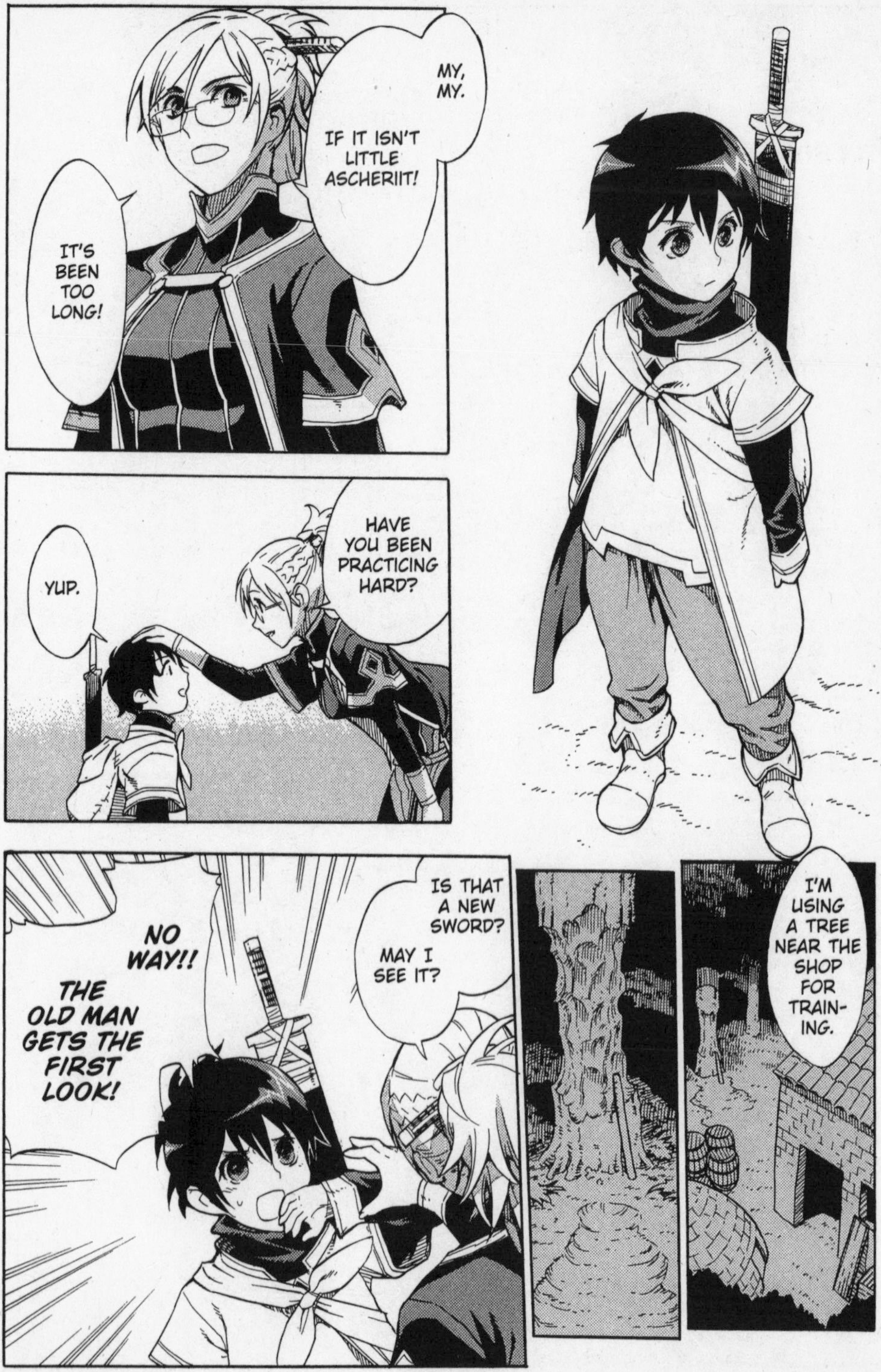
MY, MY.
IF IT ISN'T LITTLE ASCHERIIT!
IT'S BEEN TOO LONG!
HAVE YOU BEEN PRACTICING HARD?
YUP.
I'M USING A TREE NEAR THE SHOP FOR TRAIN-ING.
IS THAT A NEW SWORD?
MAY I SEE IT?
NO WAY!!
THE OLD MAN GETS THE FIRST LOOK!

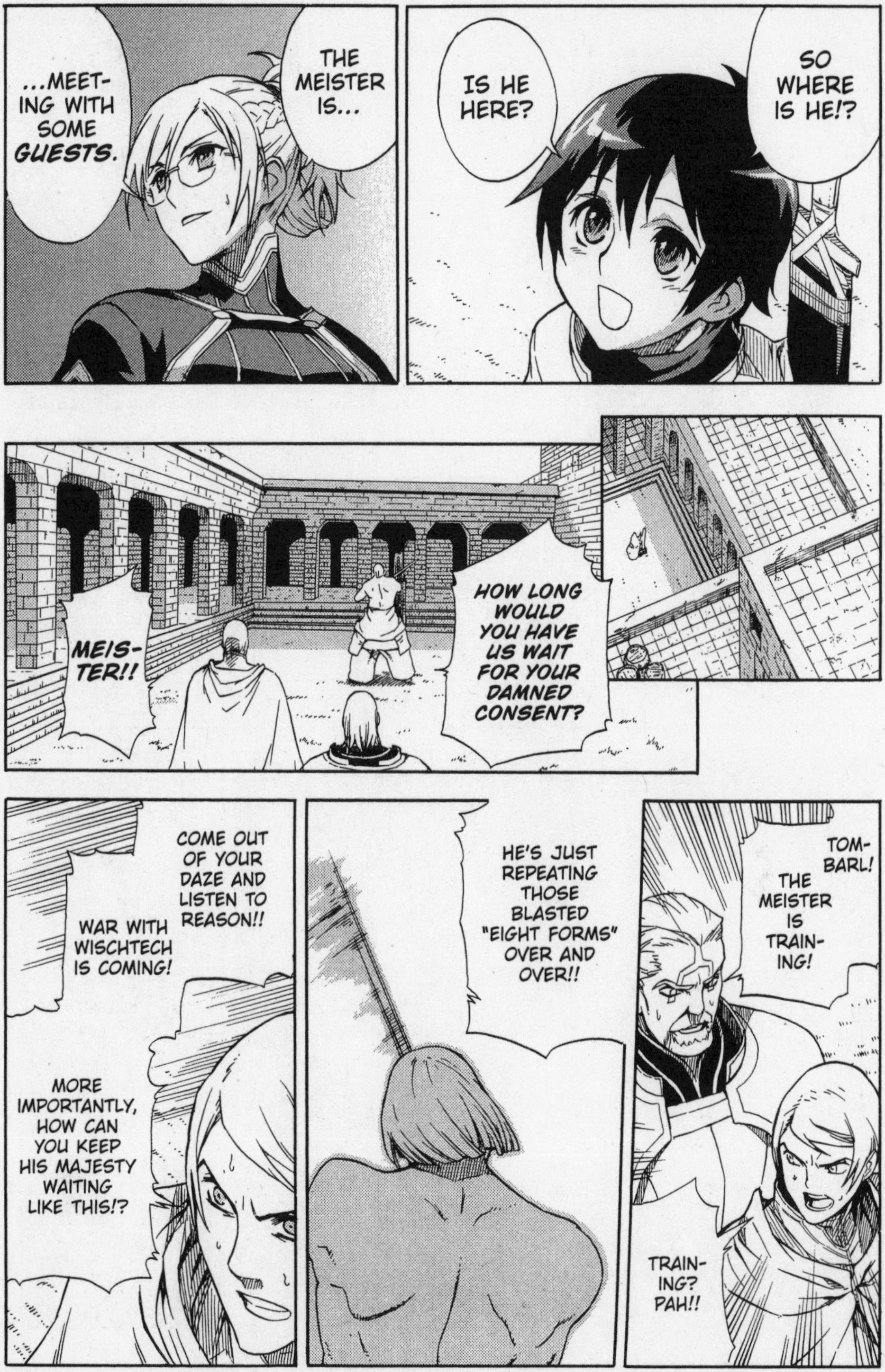
SO WHERE IS HE!?
IS HE HERE?
THE MEISTER IS...
...MEETING WITH SOME *GUESTS*.
HOW LONG WOULD YOU HAVE US WAIT FOR YOUR DAMNED CONSENT?
MEISTER!!
TOMBARL!
THE MEISTER IS TRAINING!
TRAINING? PAH!!
HE'S JUST REPEATING THOSE BLASTED "EIGHT FORMS" OVER AND OVER!!
COME OUT OF YOUR DAZE AND LISTEN TO REASON!!
WAR WITH WISCHTECH IS COMING!
MORE IMPORTANTLY, HOW CAN YOU KEEP HIS MAJESTY WAITING LIKE THIS!?

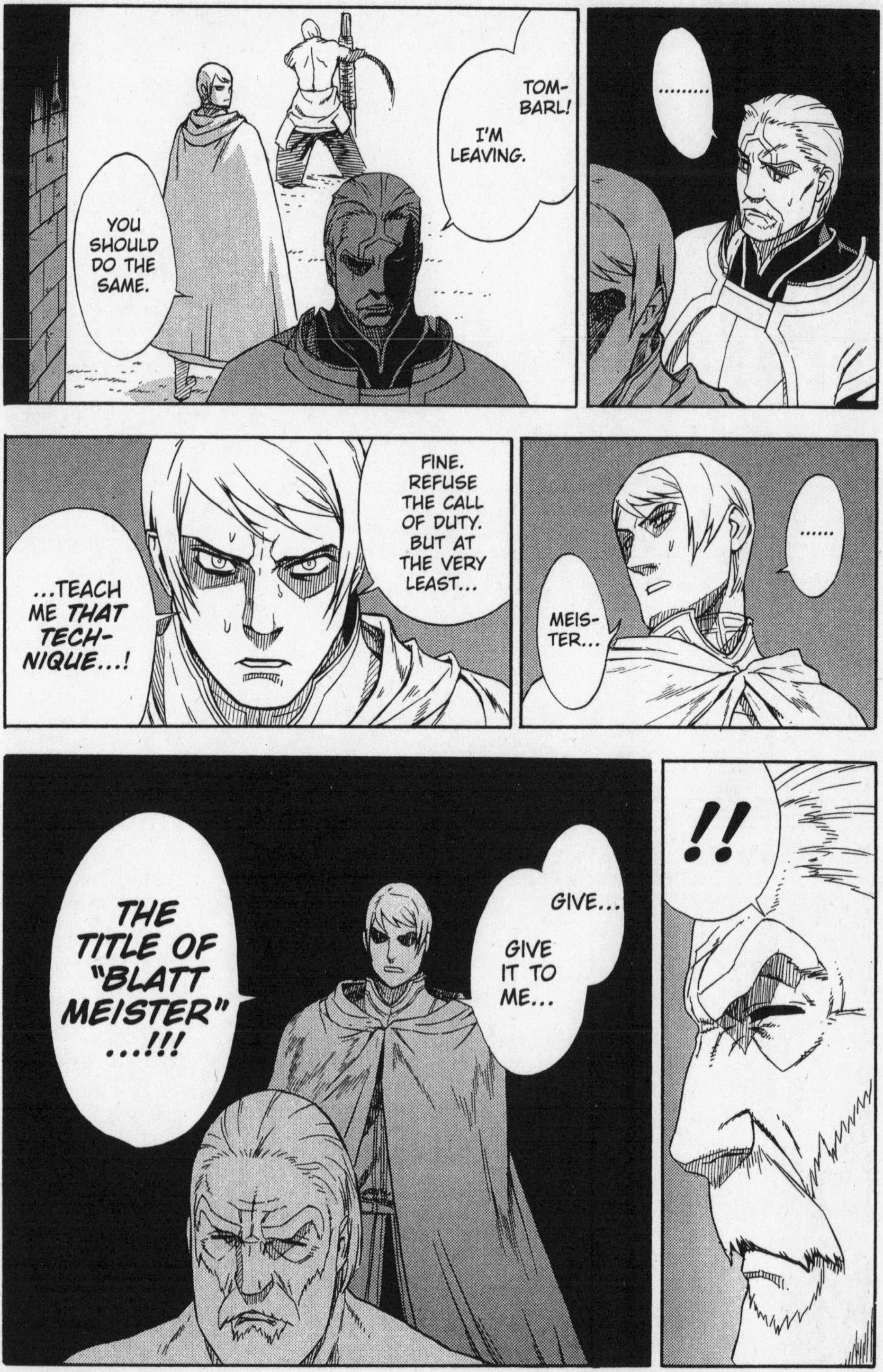
....
TOM-BARL!
I'M LEAVING.
YOU SHOULD DO THE SAME.
......
MEIS-TER...
FINE. REFUSE THE CALL OF DUTY. BUT AT THE VERY LEAST...
...TEACH ME *THAT* TECH-NIQUE...!
!!
GIVE...
GIVE IT TO ME...
THE TITLE OF "BLATT MEISTER" ...!!!

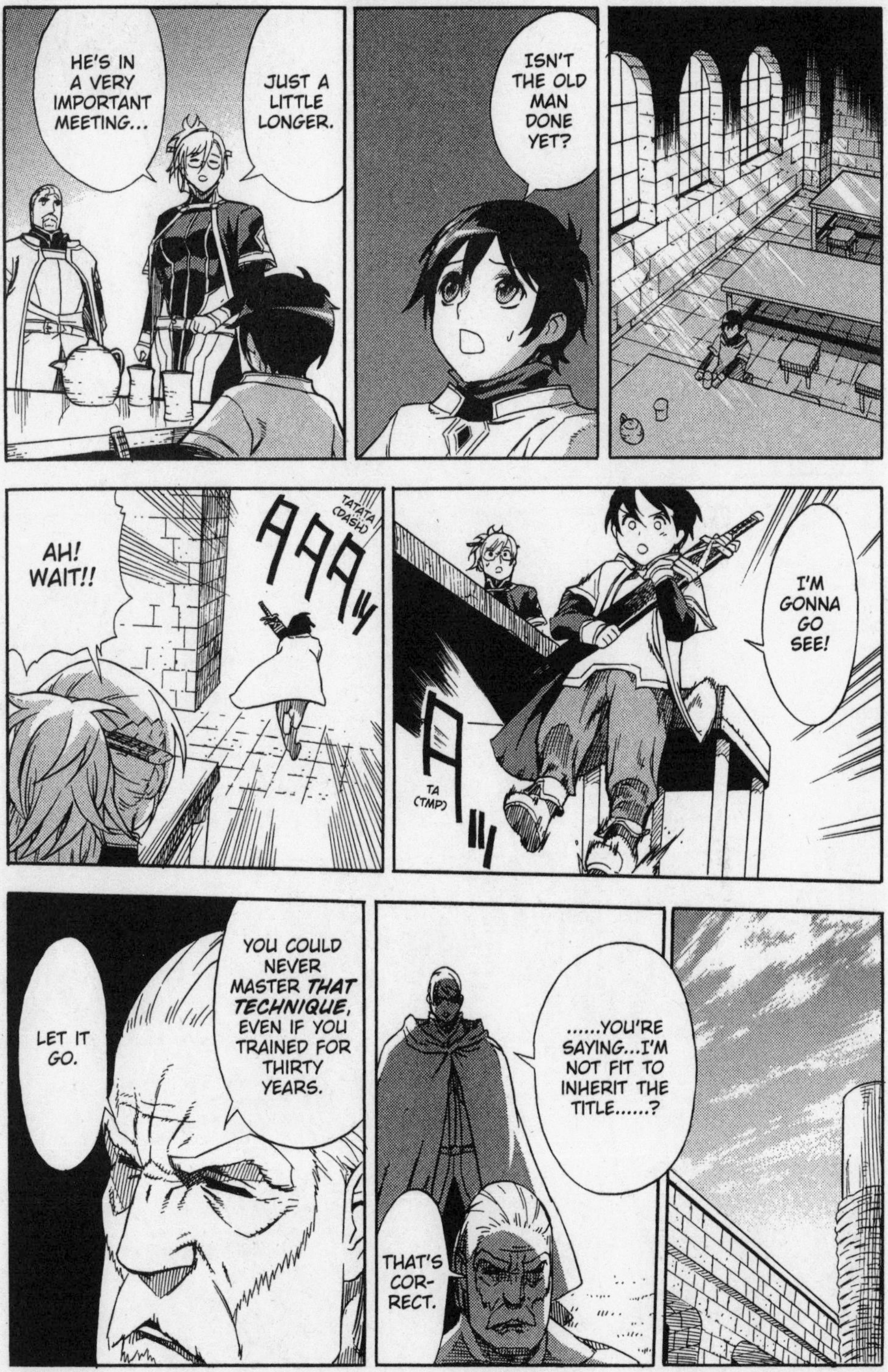
ISN'T THE OLD MAN DONE YET?
JUST A LITTLE LONGER.
HE'S IN A VERY IMPORTANT MEETING...
I'M GONNA GO SEE!
TA (TMP)
TATATA (DASH)
AH! WAIT!!
......YOU'RE SAYING...I'M NOT FIT TO INHERIT THE TITLE......?
THAT'S COR-RECT.
YOU COULD NEVER MASTER *THAT TECHNIQUE*, EVEN IF YOU TRAINED FOR THIRTY YEARS.
LET IT GO.

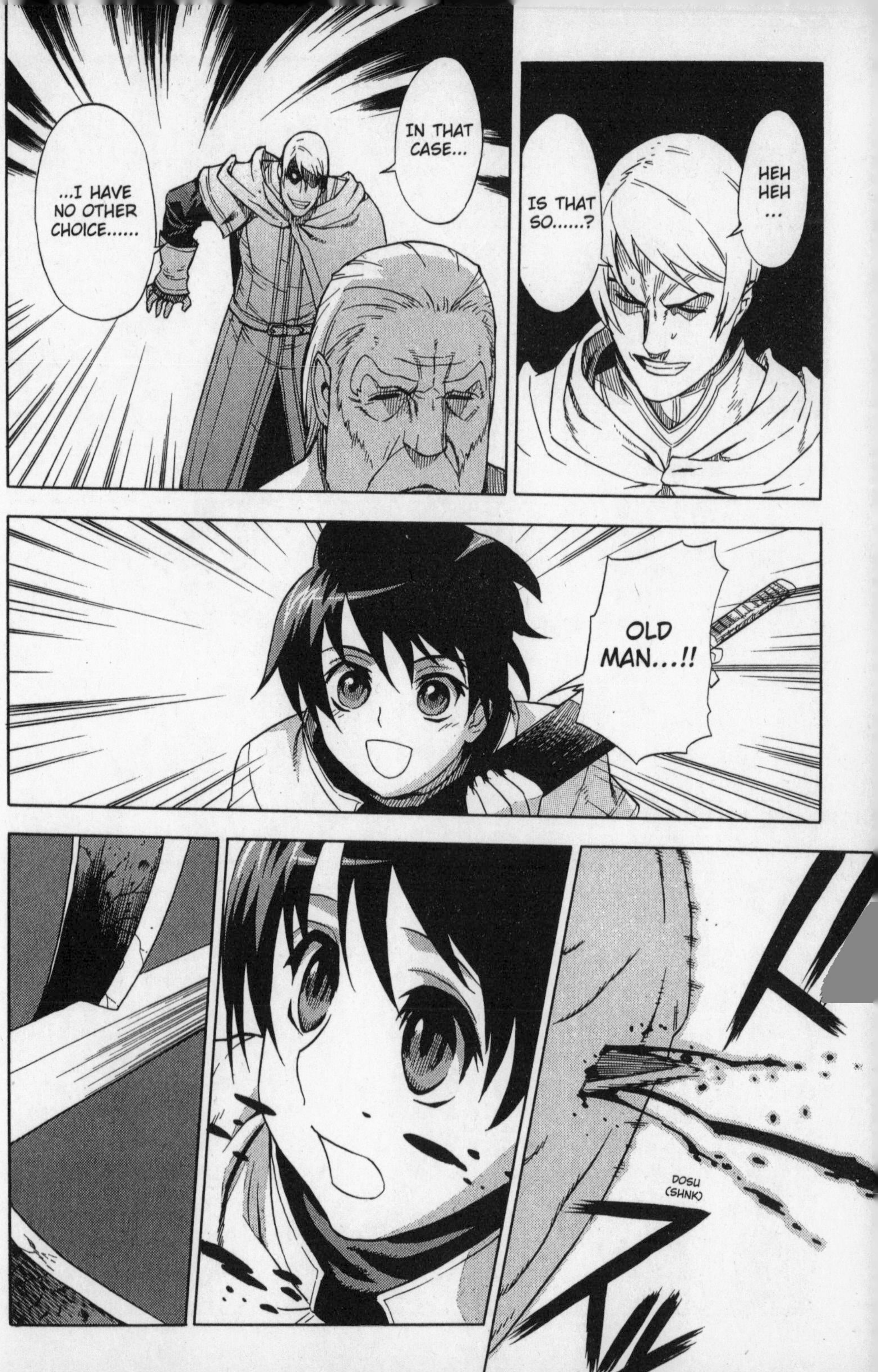
HEH HEH ...
IS THAT SO......?
IN THAT CASE...
...I HAVE NO OTHER CHOICE......
OLD MAN...!!
DOSU (SHNK)

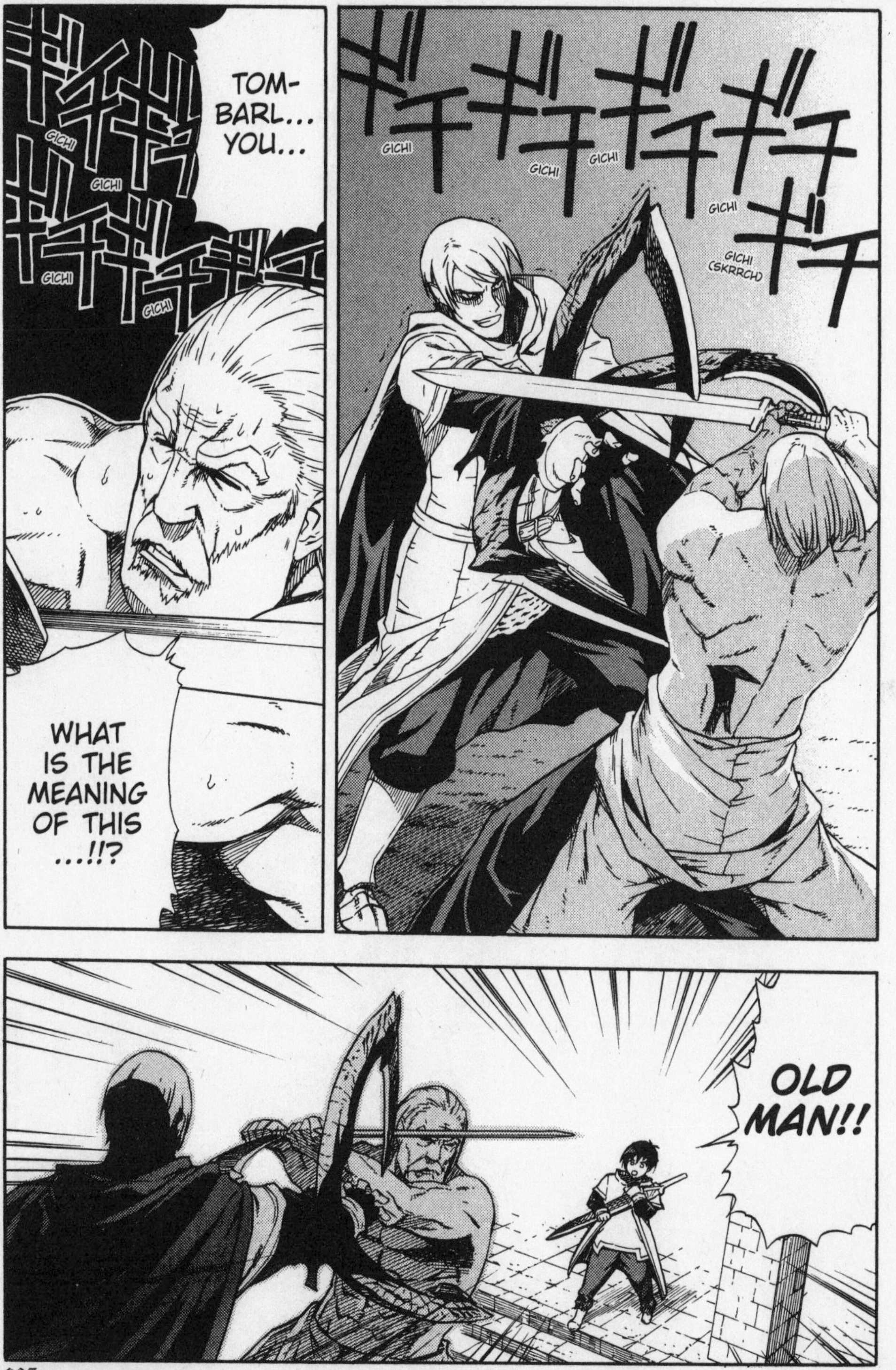
GICHI
GICHI
GICHI
GICHI
GICHI (SKRRCH)
GICHI
GICHI
GICHI
GICHI
TOM-BARL... YOU...
WHAT IS THE MEANING OF THIS ...!!?
OLD MAN!!

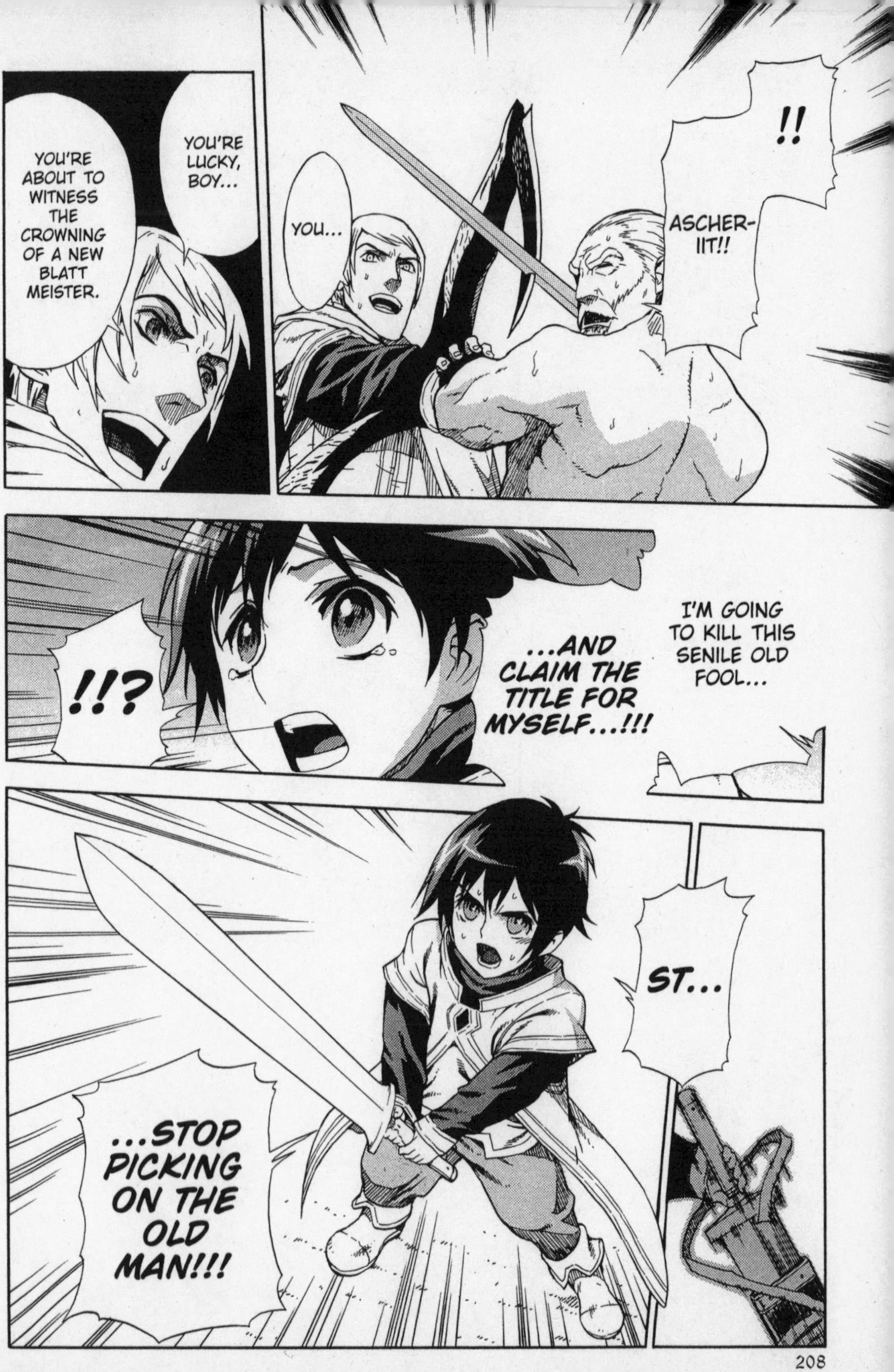
!!
ASCHER-IIT!!
YOU...
YOU'RE LUCKY, BOY...
YOU'RE ABOUT TO WITNESS THE CROWNING OF A NEW BLATT MEISTER.
I'M GOING TO KILL THIS SENILE OLD FOOL...
...AND CLAIM THE TITLE FOR MYSELF...!!!
!!?
ST...
...STOP PICKING ON THE OLD MAN!!!

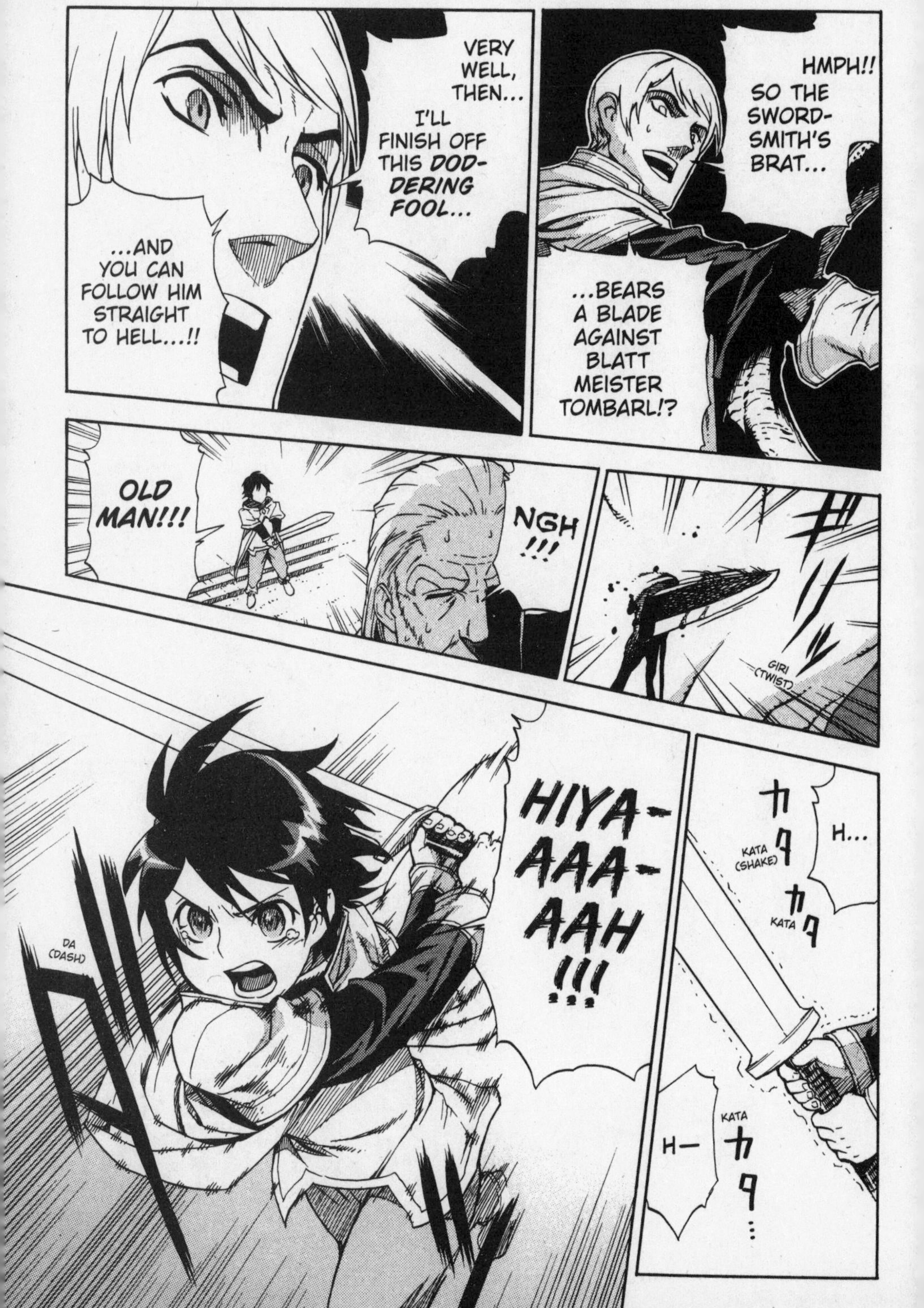
HMPH!!
SO THE SWORD-SMITH'S BRAT...
...BEARS A BLADE AGAINST BLATT MEISTER TOMBARL!?
VERY WELL, THEN...
I'LL FINISH OFF THIS *DODDERING FOOL*...
...AND YOU CAN FOLLOW HIM STRAIGHT TO HELL...!!
GIRI (TWIST)
NGH !!!
OLD MAN!!!
H...
カタ
KATA (SHAKE)
カタ
KATA
H—
カタ
KATA
HIYA-AAA-AAH!!!
DA (DASH)

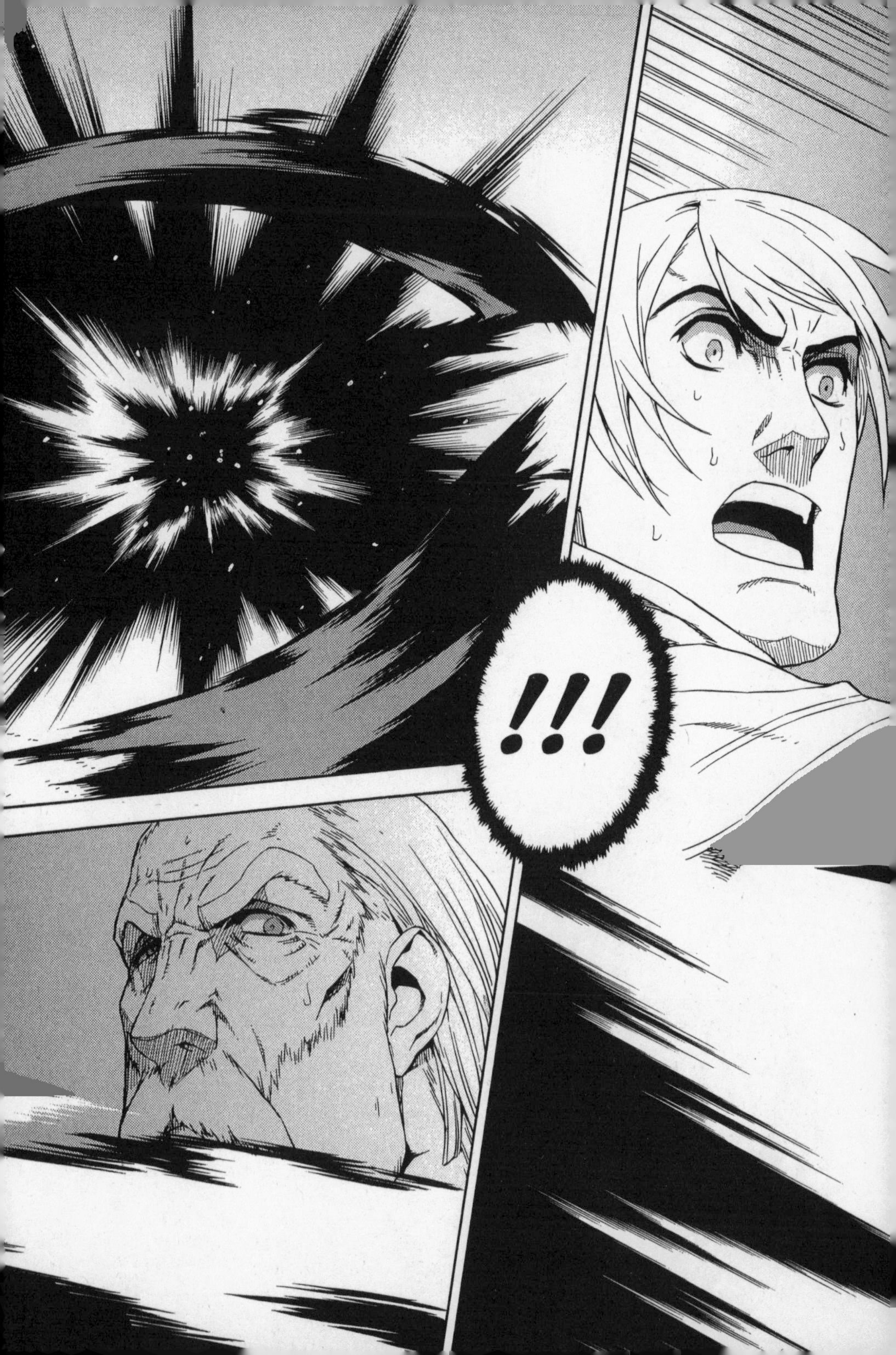
!!!

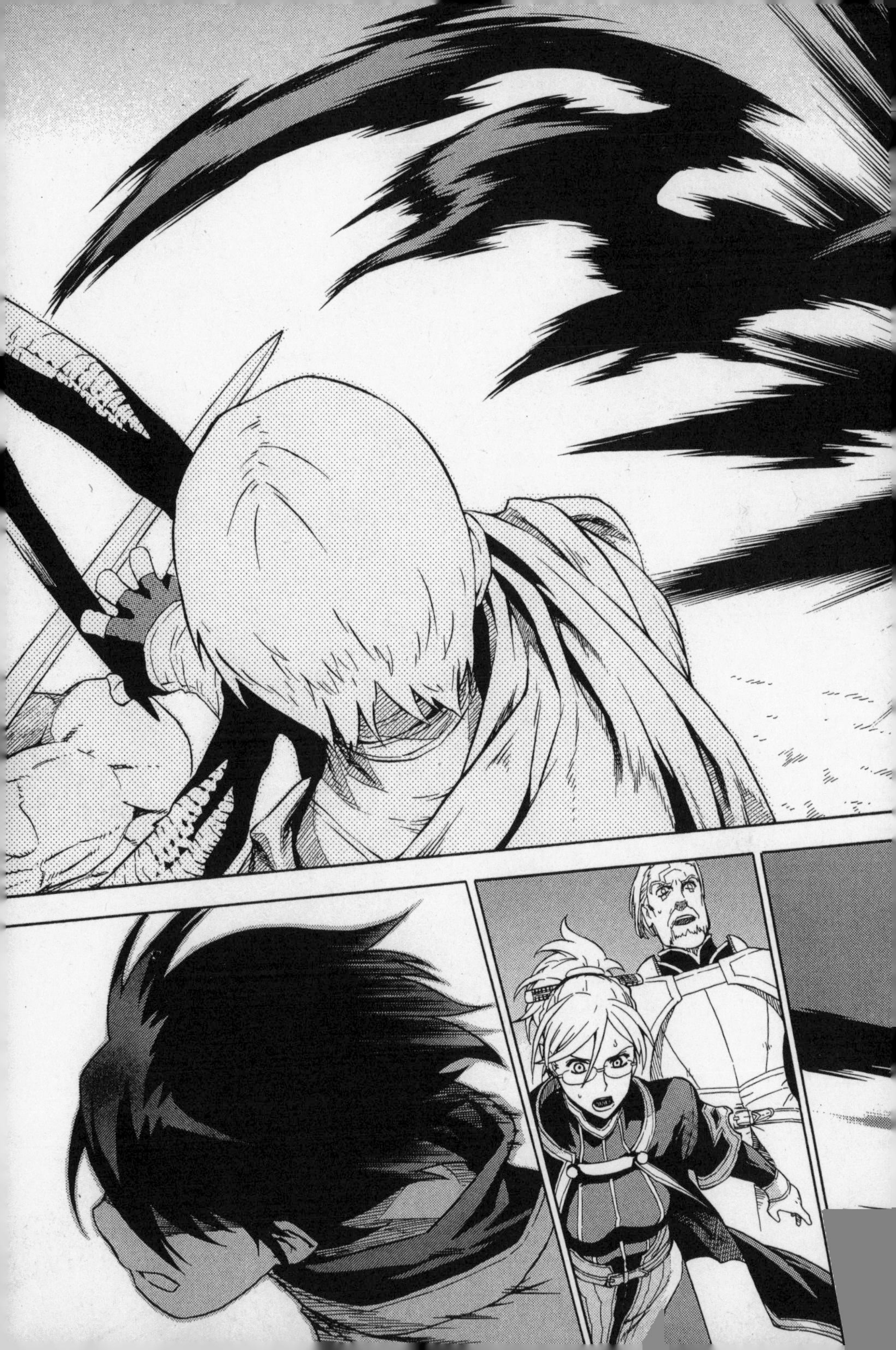

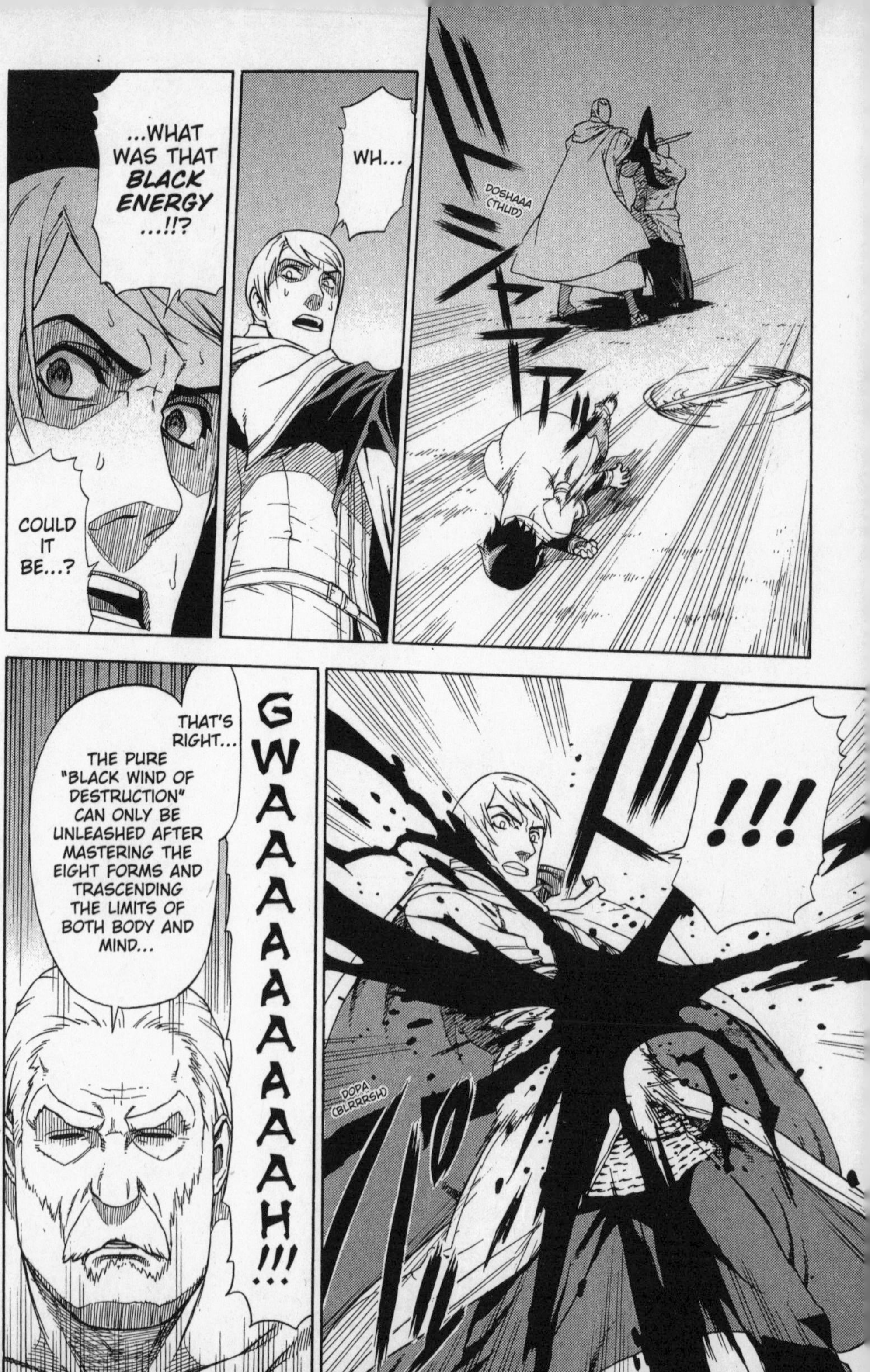
DOSHAAA (THUD)
WH...
...WHAT WAS THAT BLACK ENERGY ...!!?
COULD IT BE...?
!!!
GWAAAAAAAAAAH!!!
DOPA (BLRRRSH)
THAT'S RIGHT... THE PURE "BLACK WIND OF DESTRUCTION" CAN ONLY BE UNLEASHED AFTER MASTERING THE EIGHT FORMS AND TRASCENDING THE LIMITS OF BOTH BODY AND MIND...

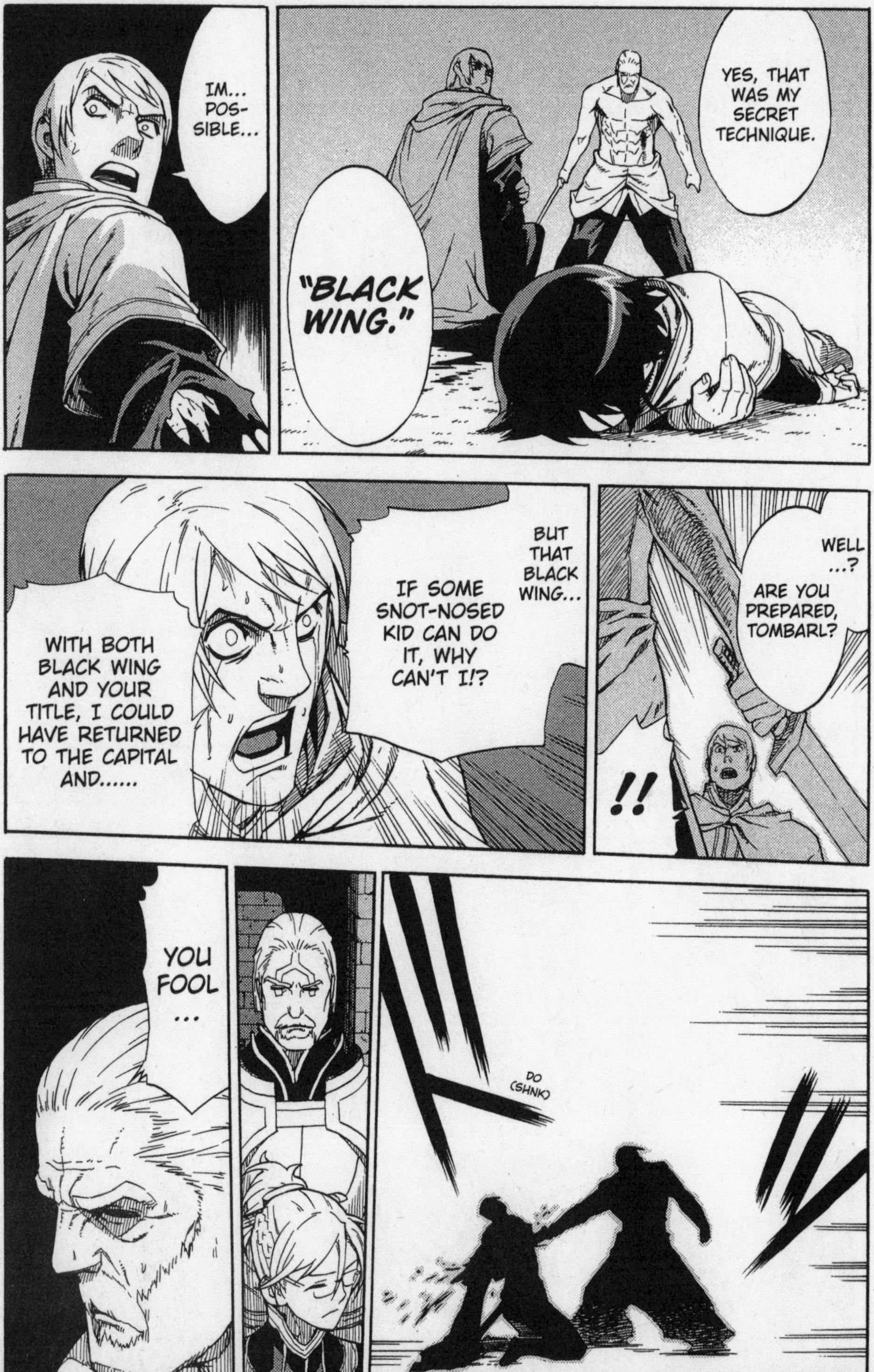
YES, THAT WAS MY SECRET TECHNIQUE.
"BLACK WING."
IM... POS-SIBLE...
WELL ...? ARE YOU PREPARED, TOMBARL?
!!
BUT THAT BLACK WING...
IF SOME SNOT-NOSED KID CAN DO IT, WHY CAN'T I!?
WITH BOTH BLACK WING AND YOUR TITLE, I COULD HAVE RETURNED TO THE CAPITAL AND......
DO (SHNK)
YOU FOOL ...

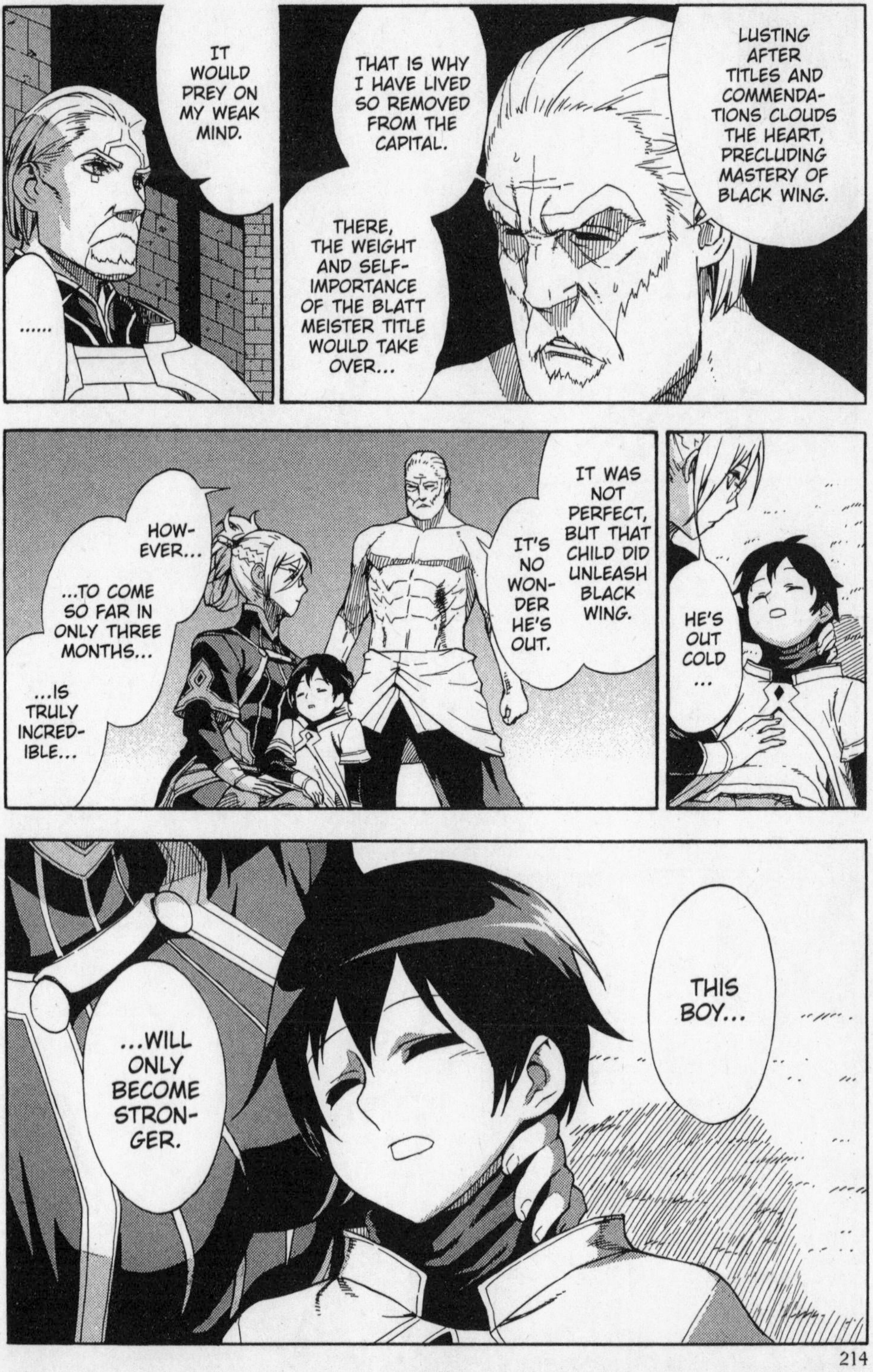
LUSTING AFTER TITLES AND COMMENDATIONS CLOUDS THE HEART, PRECLUDING MASTERY OF BLACK WING.
THAT IS WHY I HAVE LIVED SO REMOVED FROM THE CAPITAL.
THERE, THE WEIGHT AND SELF-IMPORTANCE OF THE BLATT MEISTER TITLE WOULD TAKE OVER...
IT WOULD PREY ON MY WEAK MIND.
......
HE'S OUT COLD...
IT WAS NOT PERFECT, BUT THAT CHILD DID UNLEASH BLACK WING.
IT'S NO WONDER HE'S OUT.
HOWEVER...
...TO COME SO FAR IN ONLY THREE MONTHS...
...IS TRULY INCREDIBLE...
THIS BOY...
...WILL ONLY BECOME STRONGER.

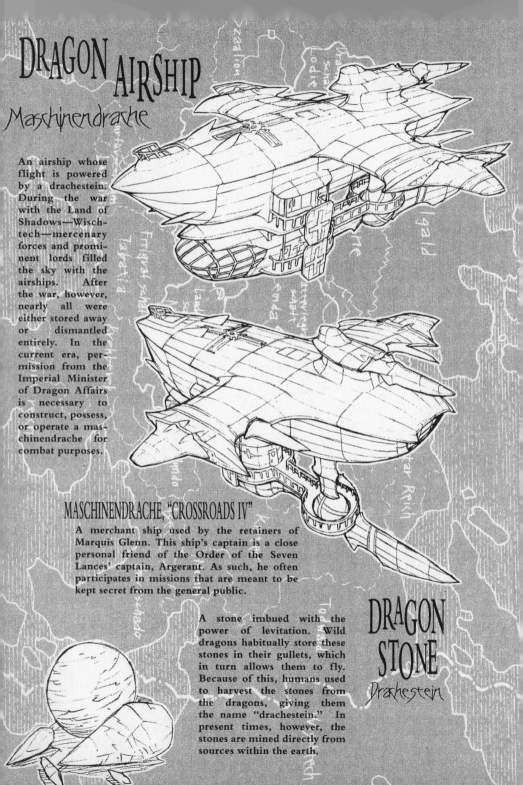

DRAGON AIRSHIP

Maschinendrache

An airship whose flight is powered by a drachestein. During the war with the Land of Shadows—Wischtech—mercenary forces and prominent lords filled the sky with the airships. After the war, however, nearly all were either stored away or dismantled entirely. In the current era, permission from the Imperial Minister of Dragon Affairs is necessary to construct, possess, or operate a maschinendrache for combat purposes.

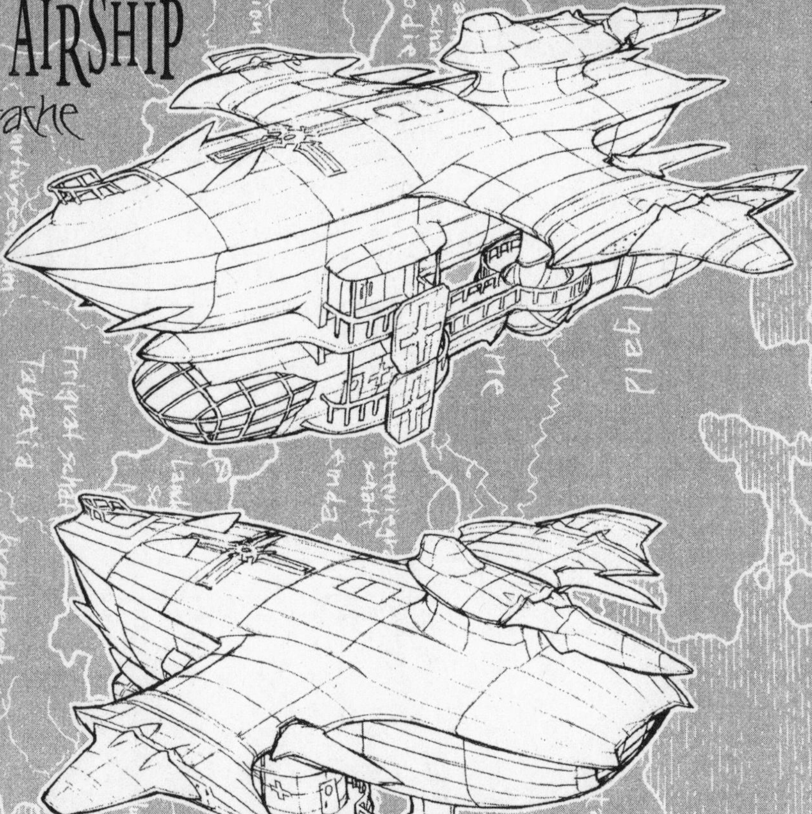

MASCHINENDRACHE, "CROSSROADS IV"

A merchant ship used by the retainers of Marquis Glenn. This ship's captain is a close personal friend of the Order of the Seven Lances' captain, Argerant. As such, he often participates in missions that are meant to be kept secret from the general public.

DRAGON STONE

Drachestein

A stone imbued with the power of levitation. Wild dragons habitually store these stones in their gullets, which in turn allows them to fly. Because of this, humans used to harvest the stones from the dragons, giving them the name "drachestein." In present times, however, the stones are mined directly from sources within the earth.

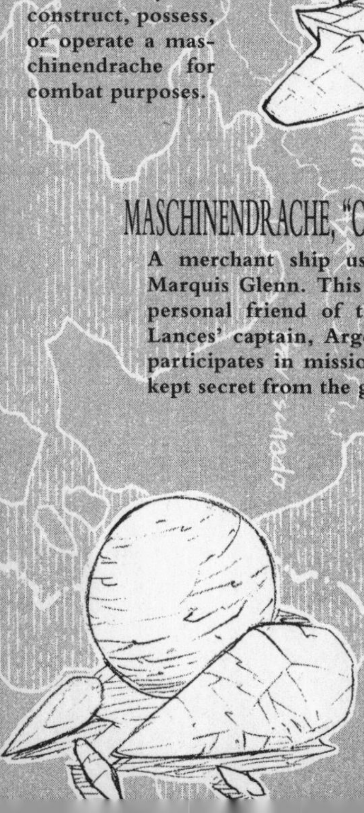

CRESTS
Sinnbild

MARQUIS GLENN'S CREST

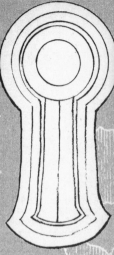

The crest worn by Marquis Glenn and his loyal followers in the Order of the Seven Lances.

Created for Glenn at the end of the great war, this crest doesn't have a very long history, but it is already one of the more well-known and easily-recognized crests among the people of the empire.

BLACK WING & SWORD CREST

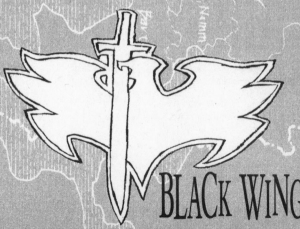

A crest granted to generations of Blatt Meisters by the emperor. The previous Blatt Meister, Ludift, returned the crest upon leaving the imperial capital. There is currently no successor to this crest.

It was once regarded with respect, but ever since Ascheriit, who was meant to be the next Blatt Meister, betrayed the empire, the people have viewed it as a bad omen.

Order Of The SEVEN SPEARS

Sieben Spießen Orden

A unit of warriors serving under Marquis Glenn, one of the Seven Heroes. Nowadays they are regarded less as an official unit of knights and more as Marquis Glenn's private army. It is said that they are the kingdom's strongest military force.

The unit was founded in 3988 A.D. when the current captain, Argerant, and a number of his followers called upon Marquis Glenn, whose domain had recently been relocated by the emperor. Glenn invited them into his employ.

There is no formal ranking system within the Order, but divisions do exist. There is the elite brigade that guards Marquis Glenn (about twenty members), the main brigade (about fifty members), and the knights-in-training (about eighty members). It is expected that once the unit receives official recognition from the imperial capital, these three divisions will remain largely intact and turned into formal ranks.

The Order's ranks have swelled as of late, thanks to an influx of young members who either look up to Marquis Glenn or the Order itself, whose noble actions in warring regions throughout the empire have won the hearts and minds of the people.

However, now that twenty years have passed since the end of the great war, there are many lords and ministers in the capital who feel uneasy about Marquis Glenn's quickly-expanding military force, especially considering that his own domain is so close to the capital and so far removed from Wischtech.

Übel Blatt

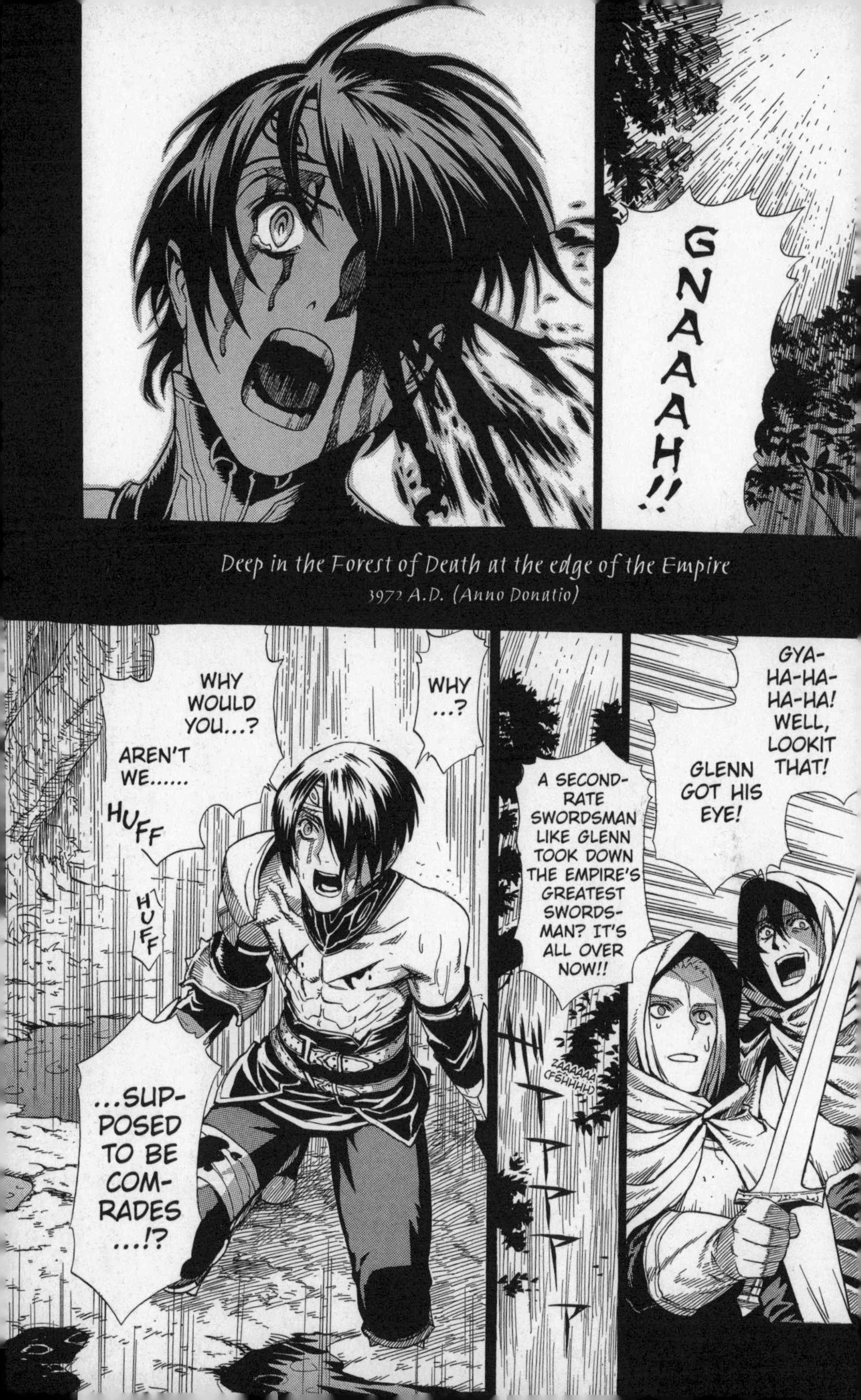
GNAAAH!!
Deep in the Forest of Death at the edge of the Empire
3972 A.D. (Anno Donatio)
GYA-HA-HA-HA-HA! WELL, LOOKIT THAT!
GLENN GOT HIS EYE!
A SECOND-RATE SWORDSMAN LIKE GLENN TOOK DOWN THE EMPIRE'S GREATEST SWORDS-MAN? IT'S ALL OVER NOW!!
ZAAAAAA CFSHHHHH
WHY ...?
WHY WOULD YOU...?
AREN'T WE......
HUFF
HUFF
...SUP-POSED TO BE COM-RADES ...!?

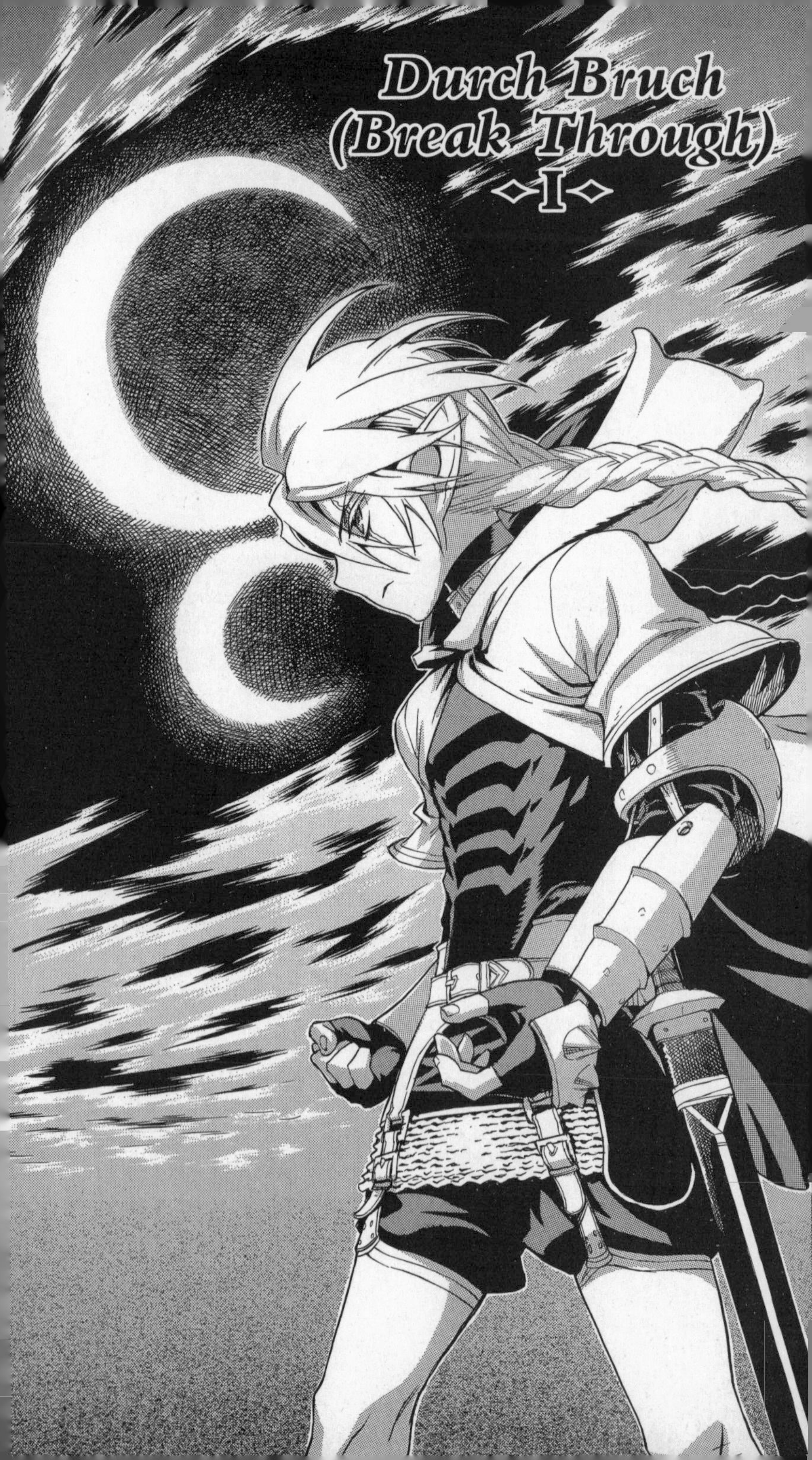
Durch Bruch
(Break Through)
-I-

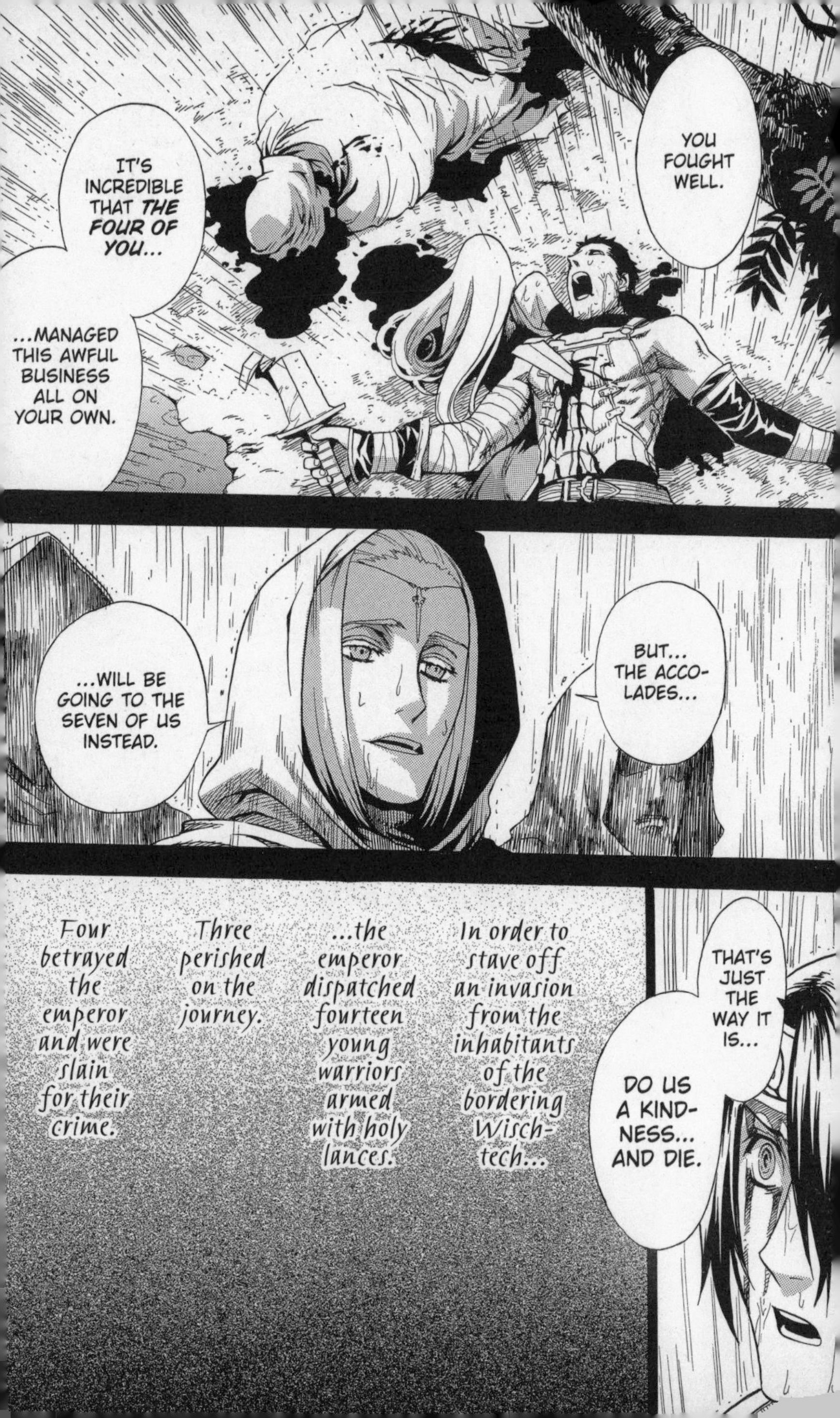

YOU FOUGHT WELL.
IT'S INCREDIBLE THAT *THE FOUR OF YOU*...
...MANAGED THIS AWFUL BUSINESS ALL ON YOUR OWN.
BUT... THE ACCOLADES...
...WILL BE GOING TO THE SEVEN OF US INSTEAD.
THAT'S JUST THE WAY IT IS...
DO US A KINDNESS... AND DIE.
In order to stave off an invasion from the inhabitants of the bordering Wischtech...
...the emperor dispatched fourteen young warriors armed with holy lances.
Three perished on the journey.
Four betrayed the emperor and were slain for their crime.

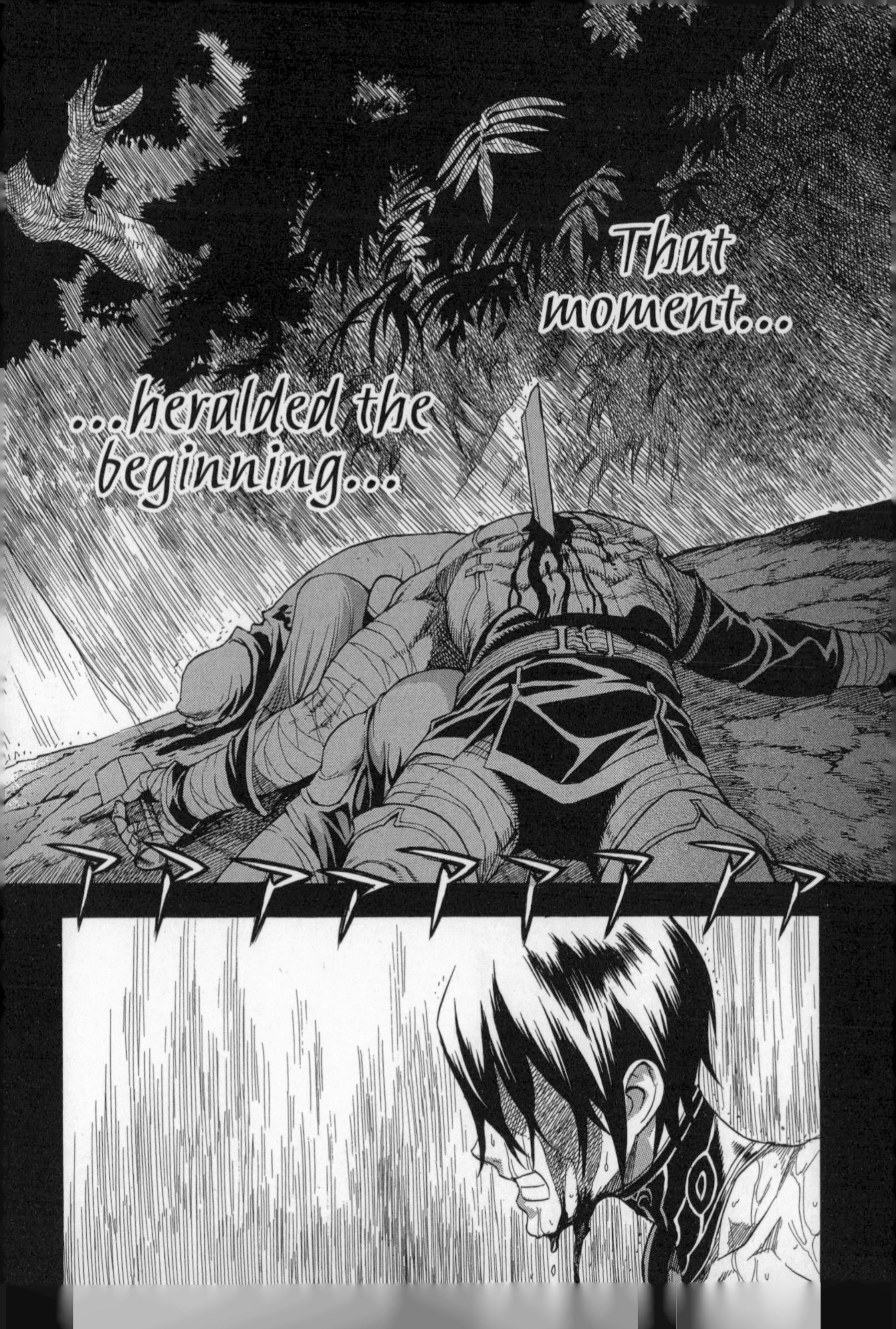
That moment...
...heralded the beginning...

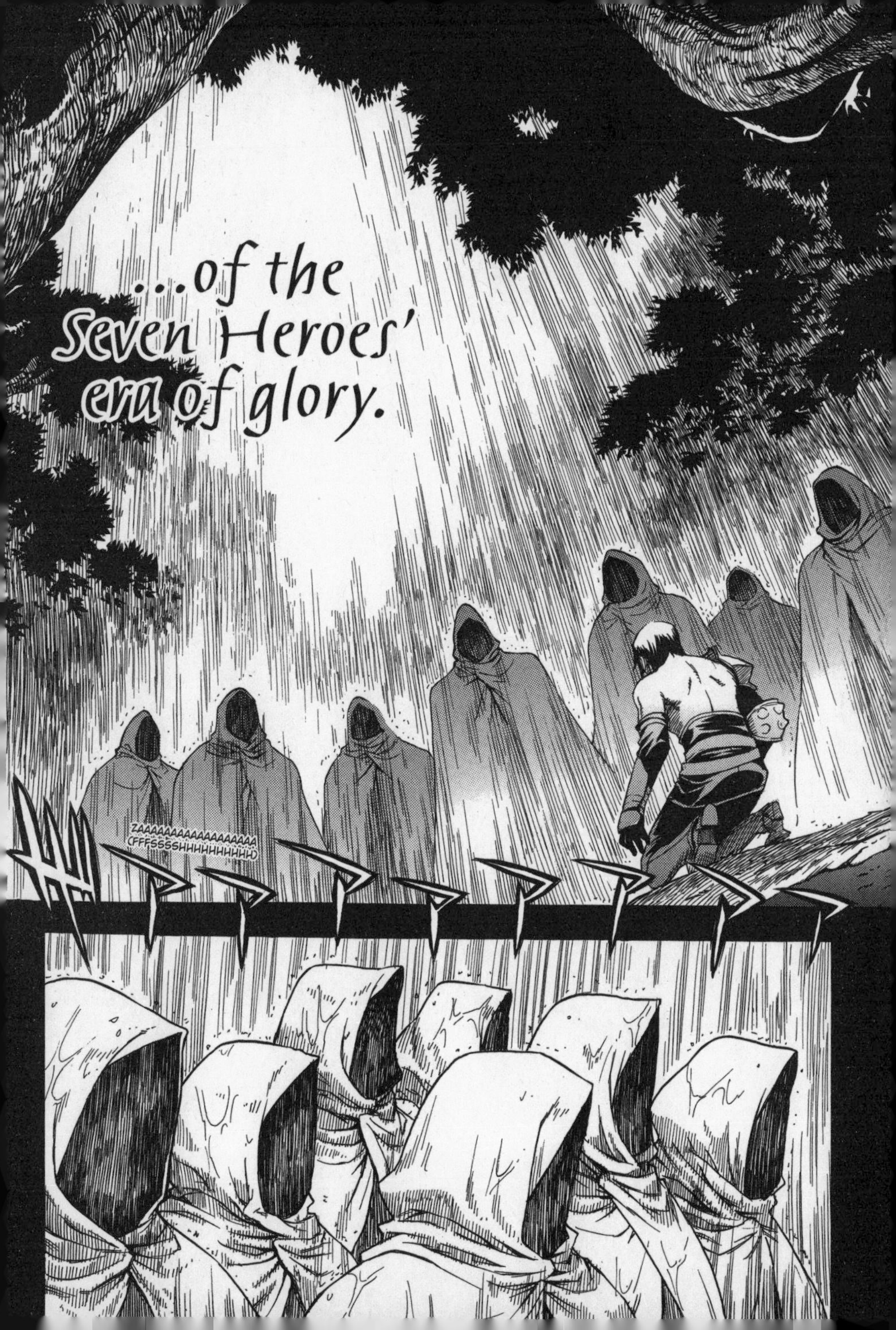
...of the Seven Heroes' era of glory.
ZAAAAAAAAAAAAAAAAAAA
(FFFSSSSHHHHHHHHHHHH)

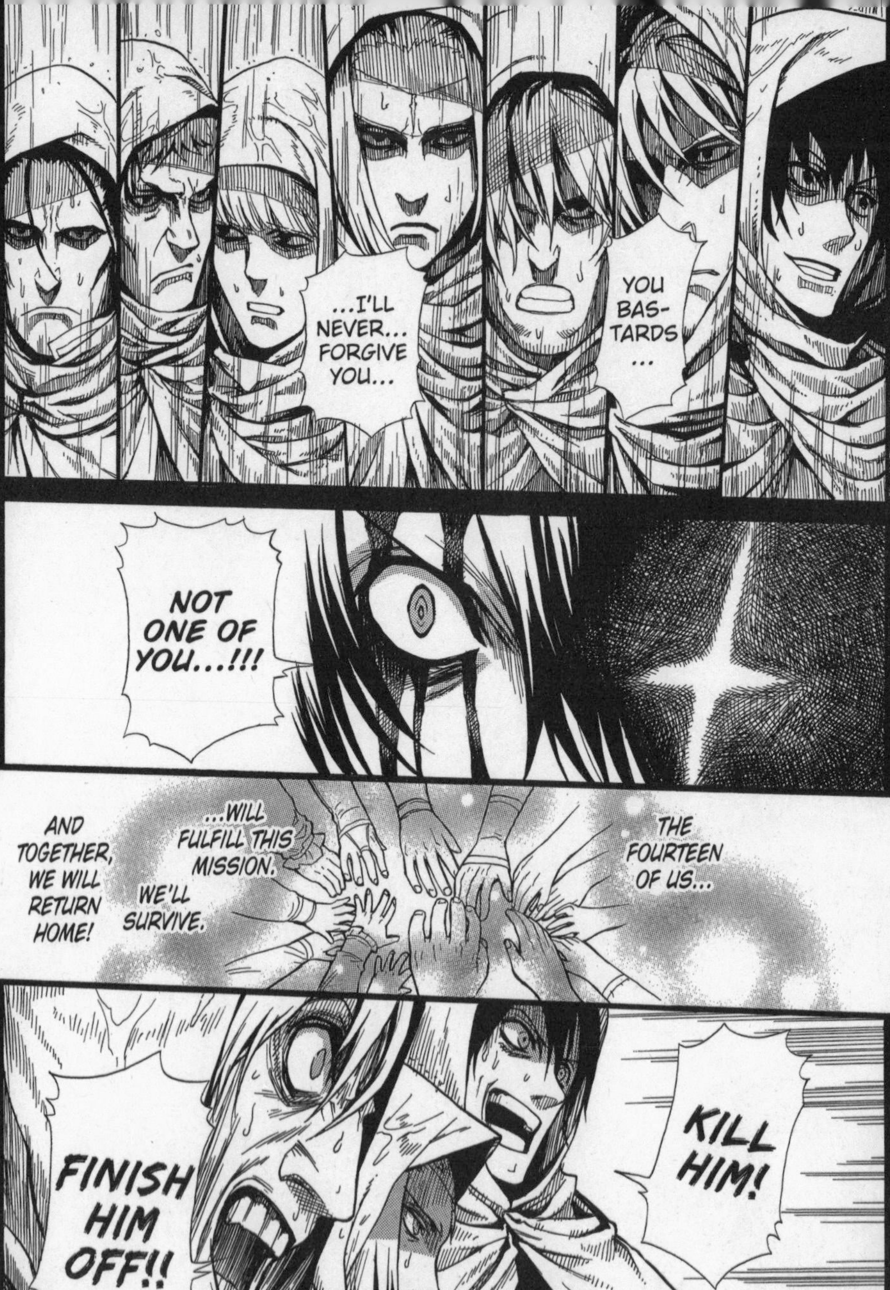
YOU BAS-TARDS ...
...I'LL NEVER... FORGIVE YOU...
NOT ONE OF YOU...!!!
THE FOURTEEN OF US...
...WILL FULFILL THIS MISSION.
WE'LL SURVIVE.
AND TOGETHER, WE WILL RETURN HOME!
KILL HIM!
FINISH HIM OFF!!

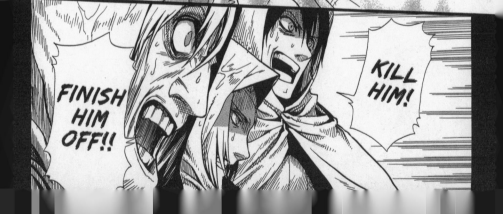

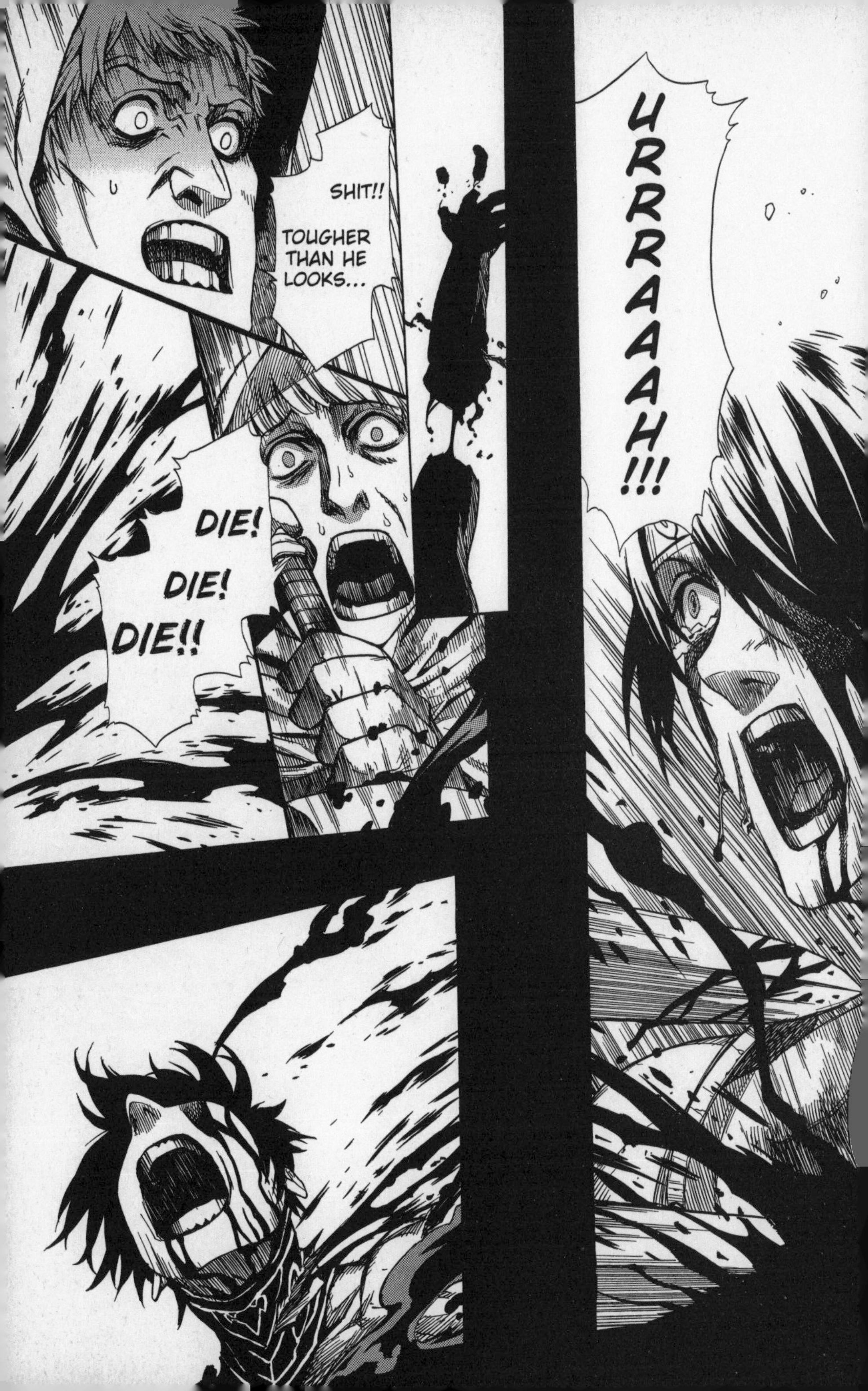
URRRAAAAH!!!
SHIT!!
TOUGHER THAN HE LOOKS...
DIE! DIE! DIE!!

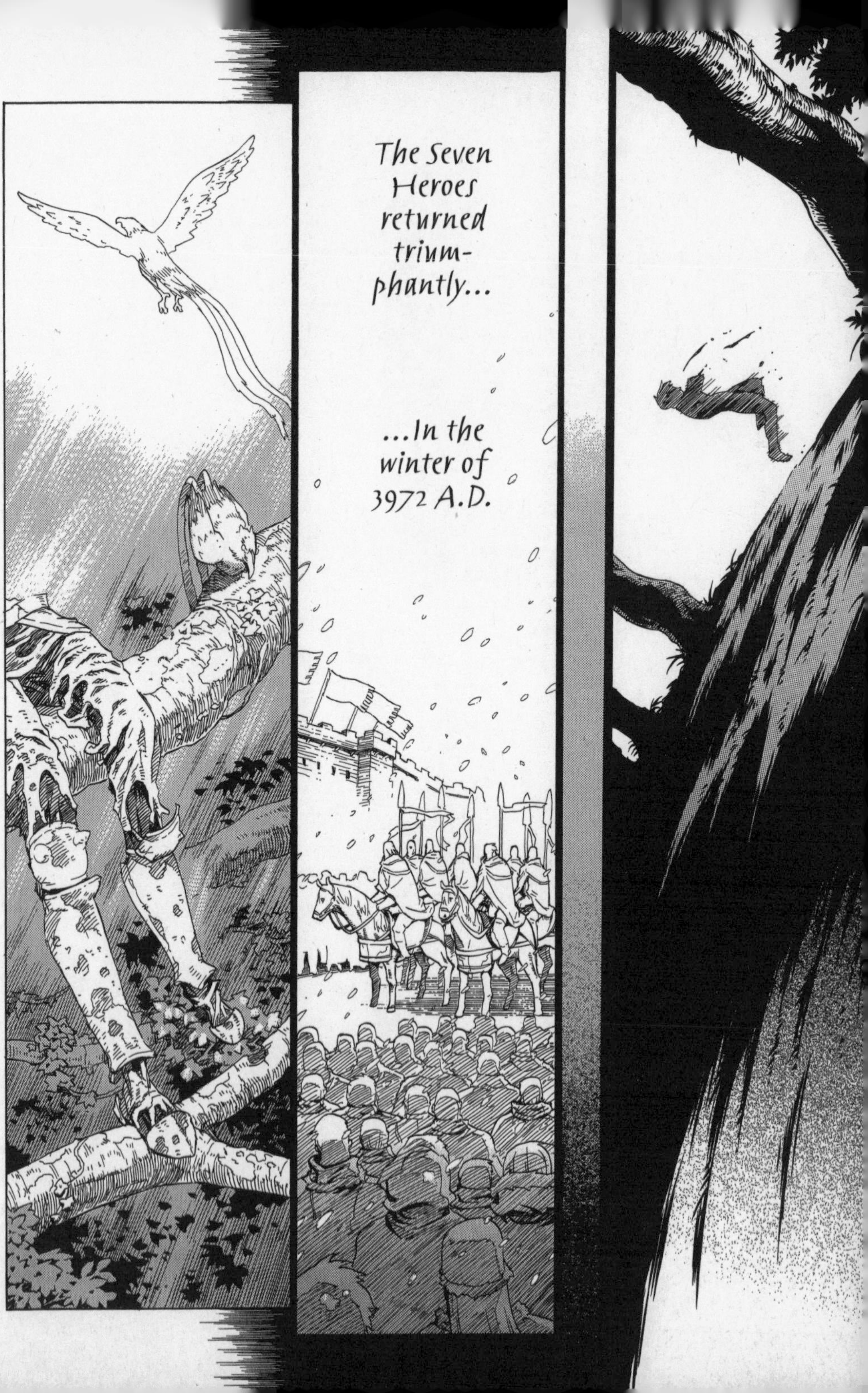
The Seven Heroes returned trium-phantly...
...In the winter of 3972 A.D.

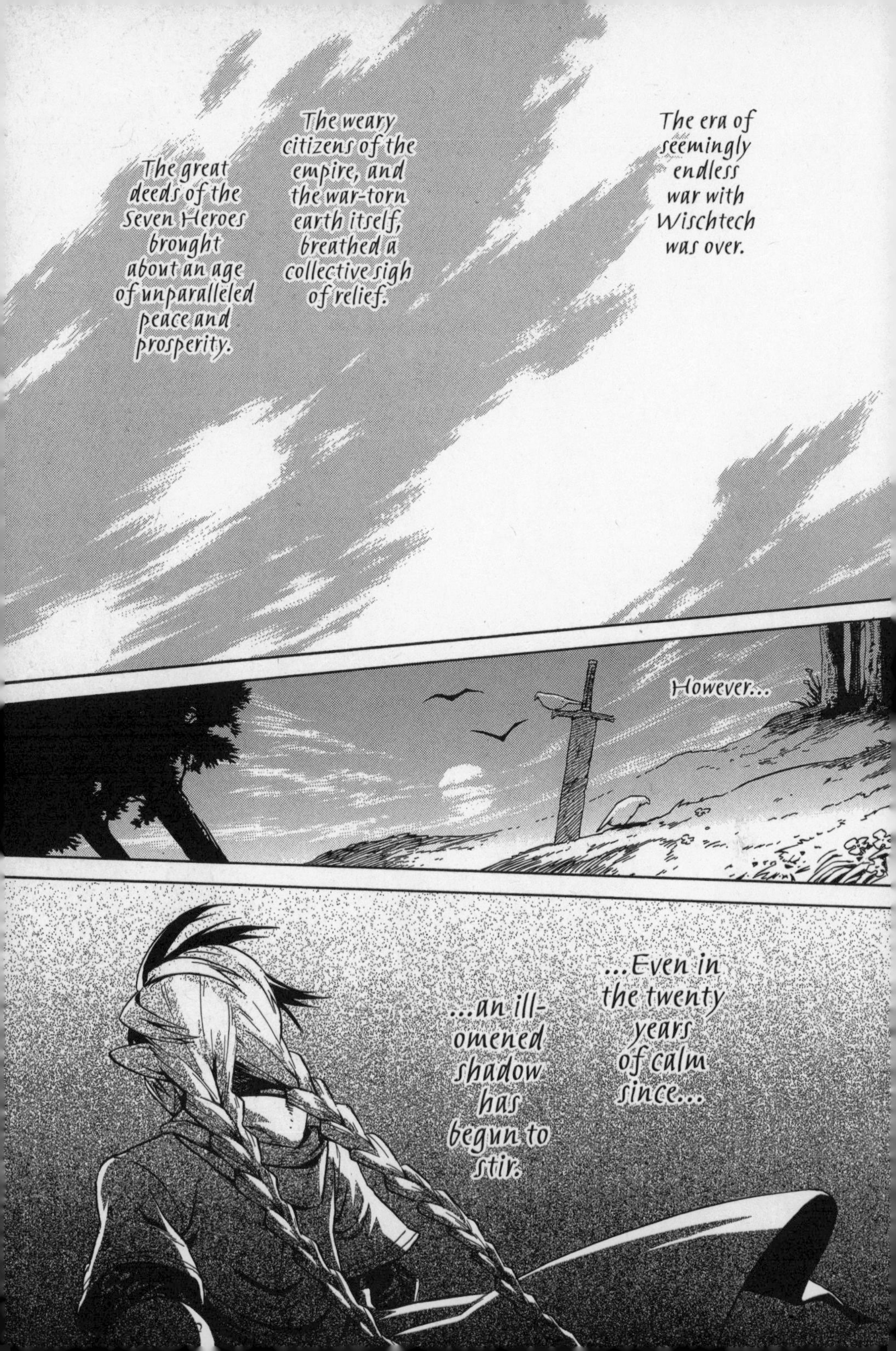
The era of seemingly endless war with Wischtech was over.
The weary citizens of the empire, and the war-torn earth itself, breathed a collective sigh of relief.
The great deeds of the Seven Heroes brought about an age of unparalleled peace and prosperity.
However...
...Even in the twenty years of calm since...
...an ill-omened shadow has begun to stir.

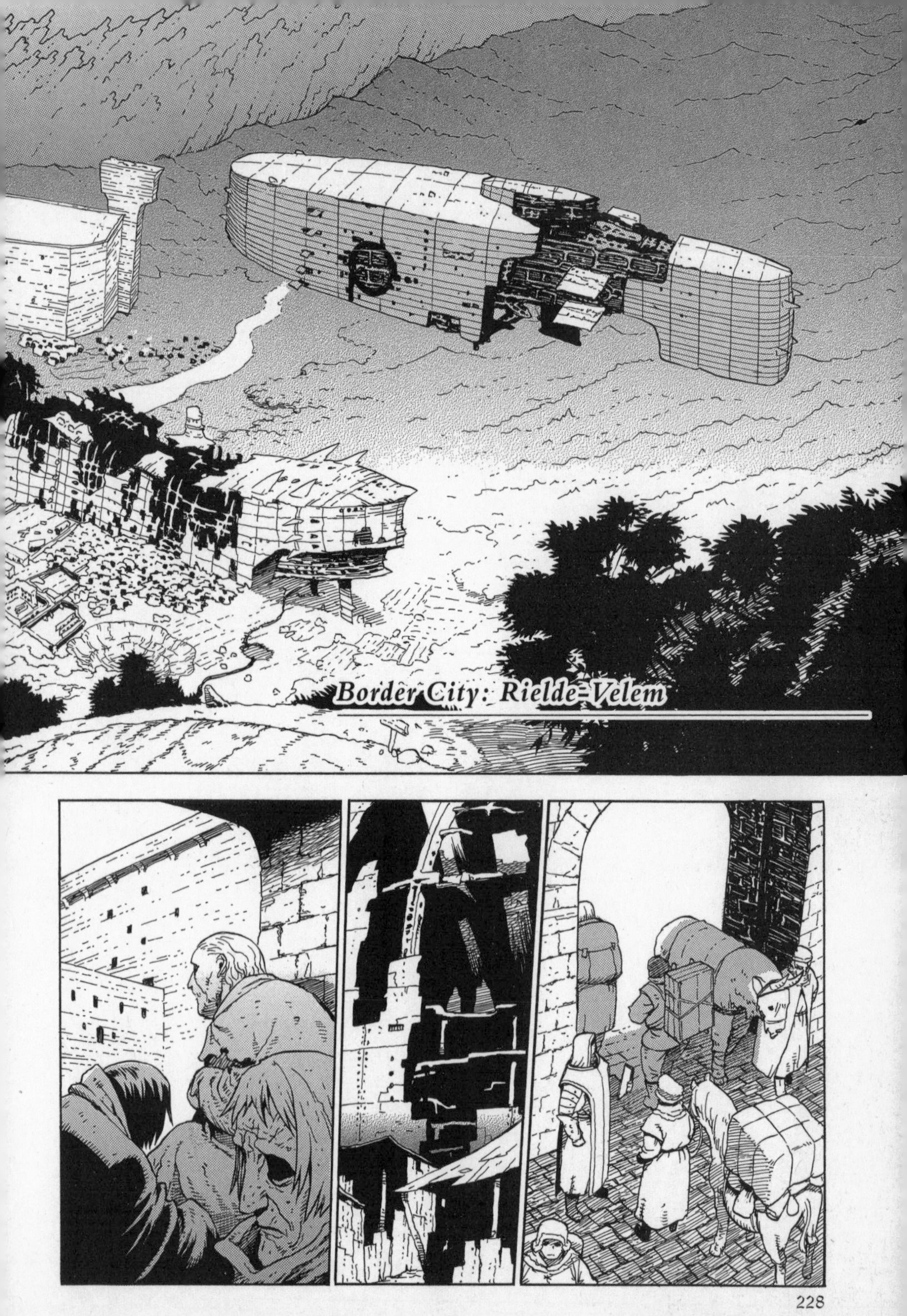
Border City: Rielde-Velem

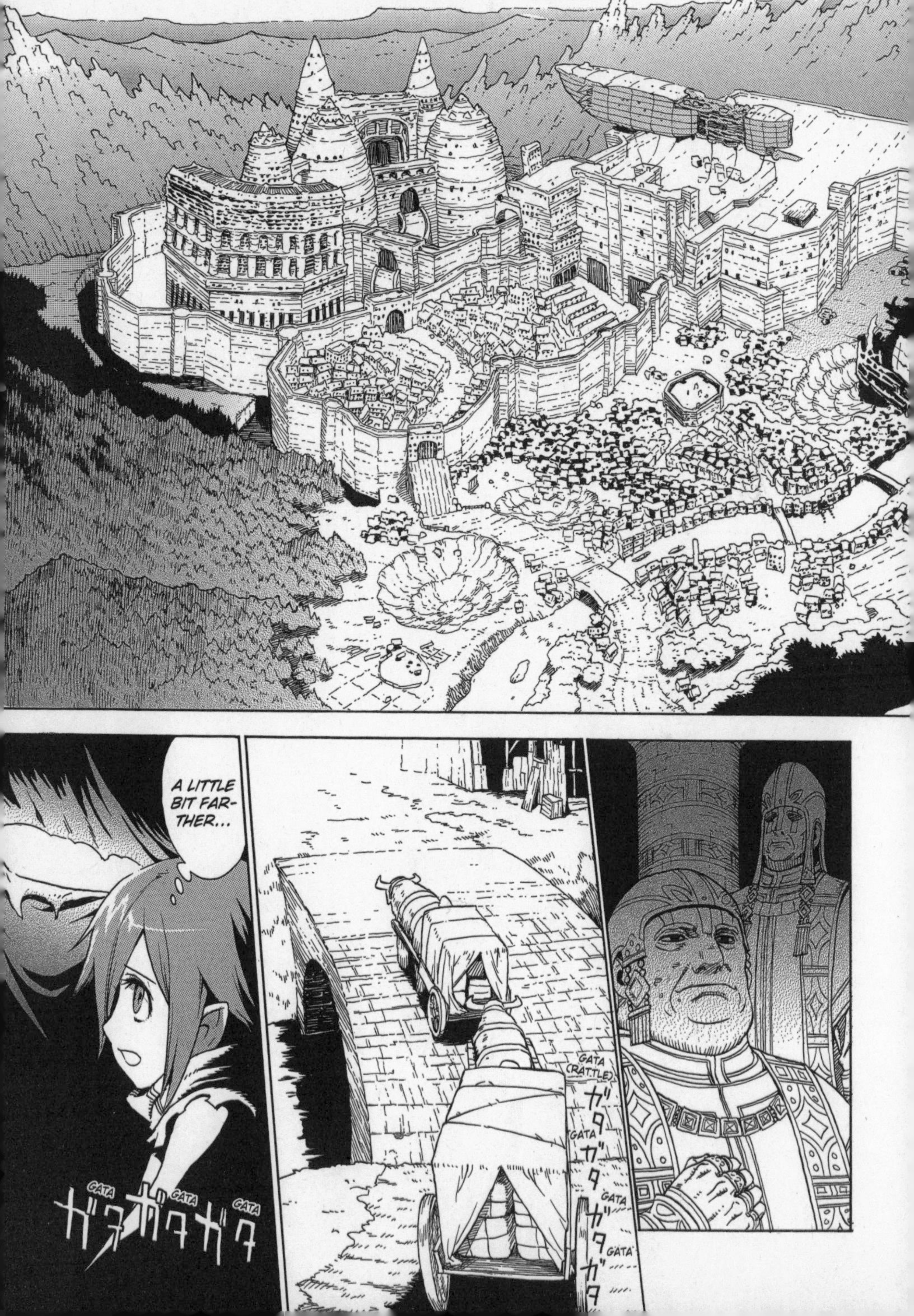
GATA (RATTLE)
ガタ
GATA
ガタ
GATA
ガタ
GATA
ガタ
A LITTLE BIT FAR-THER...
GATA GATA GATA
ガタガタガタ

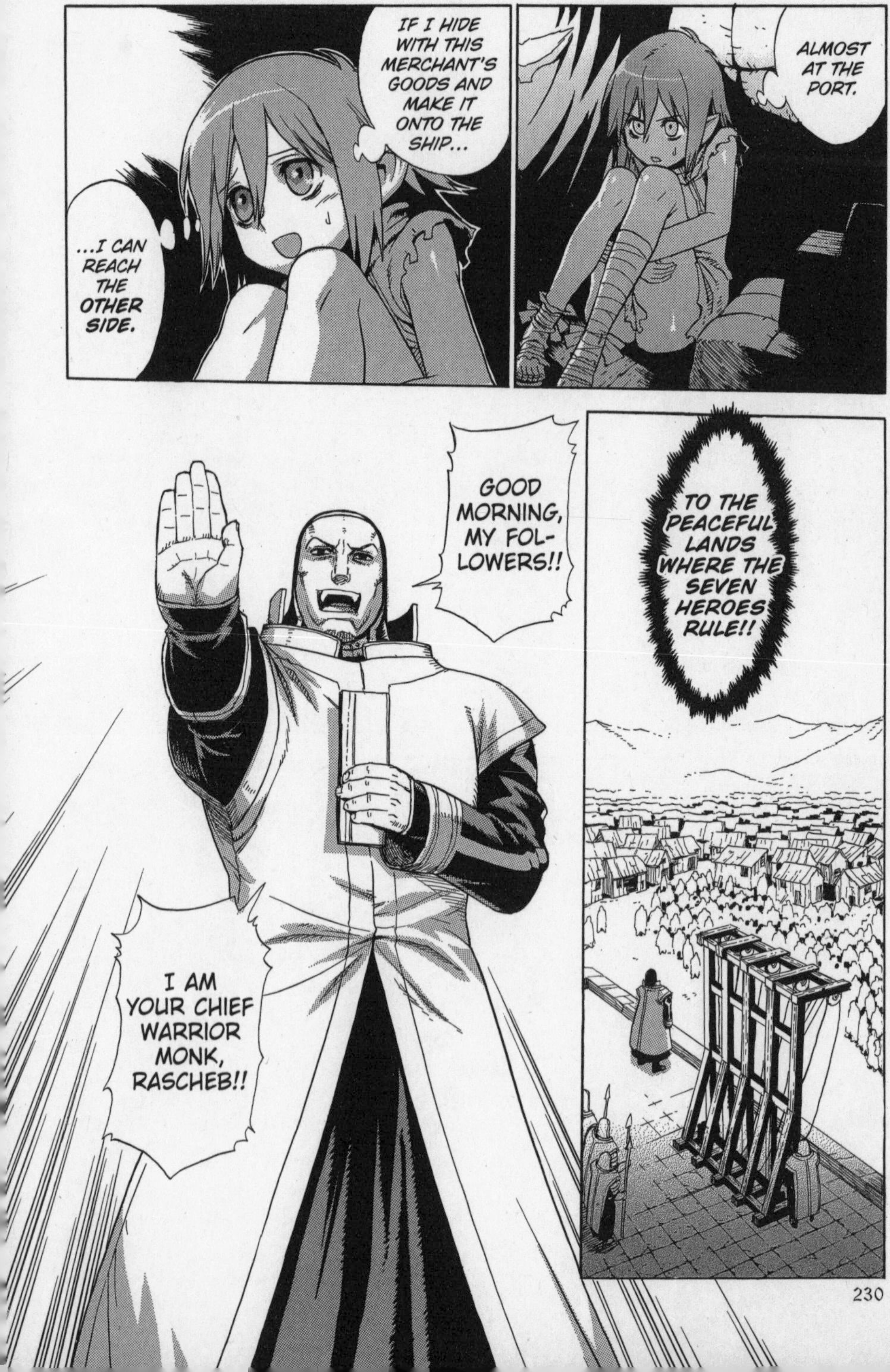
ALMOST AT THE PORT.
IF I HIDE WITH THIS MERCHANT'S GOODS AND MAKE IT ONTO THE SHIP...
...I CAN REACH THE OTHER SIDE.
TO THE PEACEFUL LANDS WHERE THE SEVEN HEROES RULE!!
GOOD MORNING, MY FOL-LOWERS!!
I AM YOUR CHIEF WARRIOR MONK, RASCHEB!!

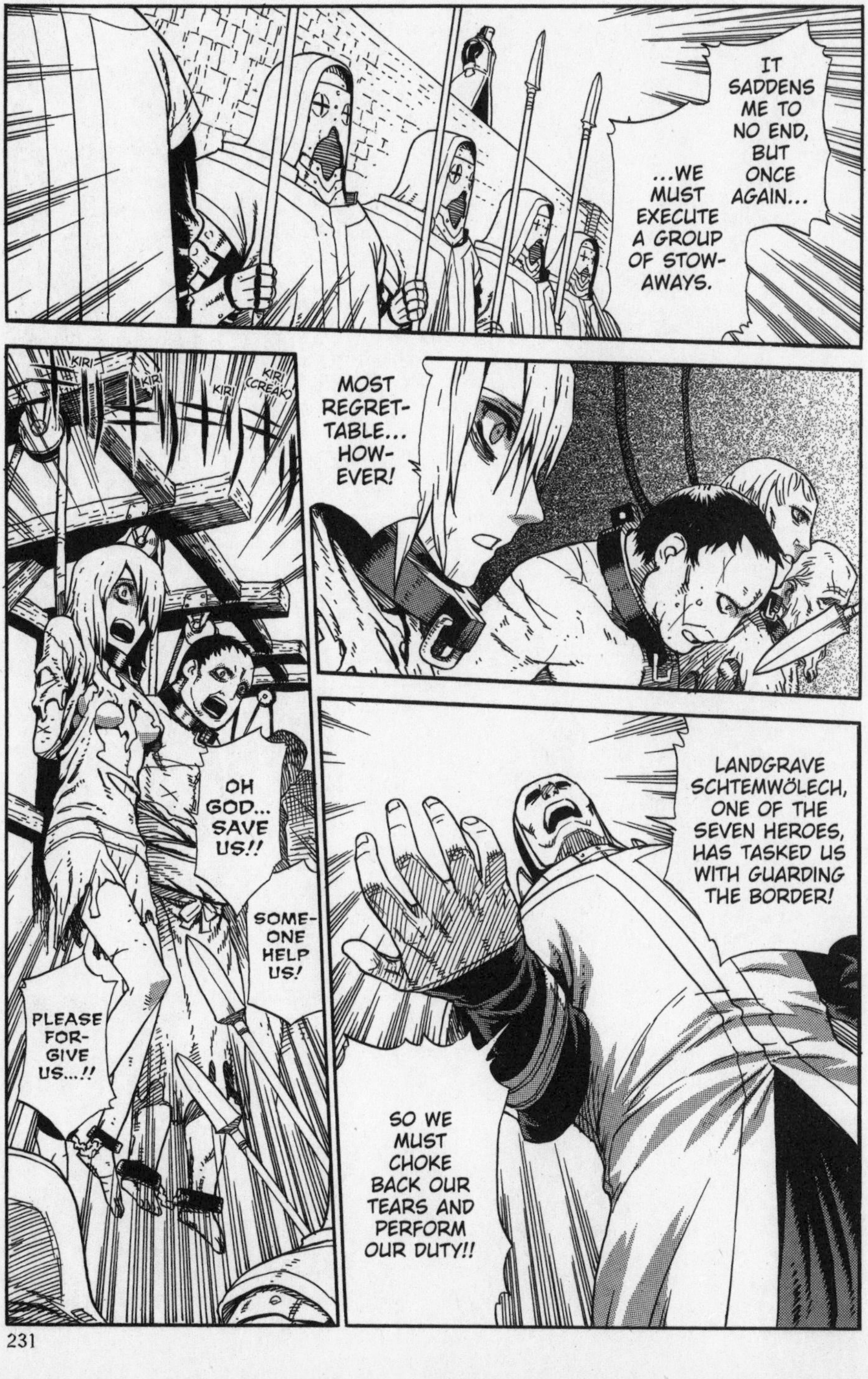
IT SADDENS ME TO NO END, BUT ONCE AGAIN...
...WE MUST EXECUTE A GROUP OF STOW-AWAYS.
MOST REGRET-TABLE... HOW-EVER!
LANDGRAVE SCHTEMWÖLECH, ONE OF THE SEVEN HEROES, HAS TASKED US WITH GUARDING THE BORDER!
SO WE MUST CHOKE BACK OUR TEARS AND PERFORM OUR DUTY!!
KIRI (CREAK)
KIRI
KIRI
KIRI
OH GOD... SAVE US!!
SOME-ONE HELP US!
PLEASE FOR-GIVE US...!!

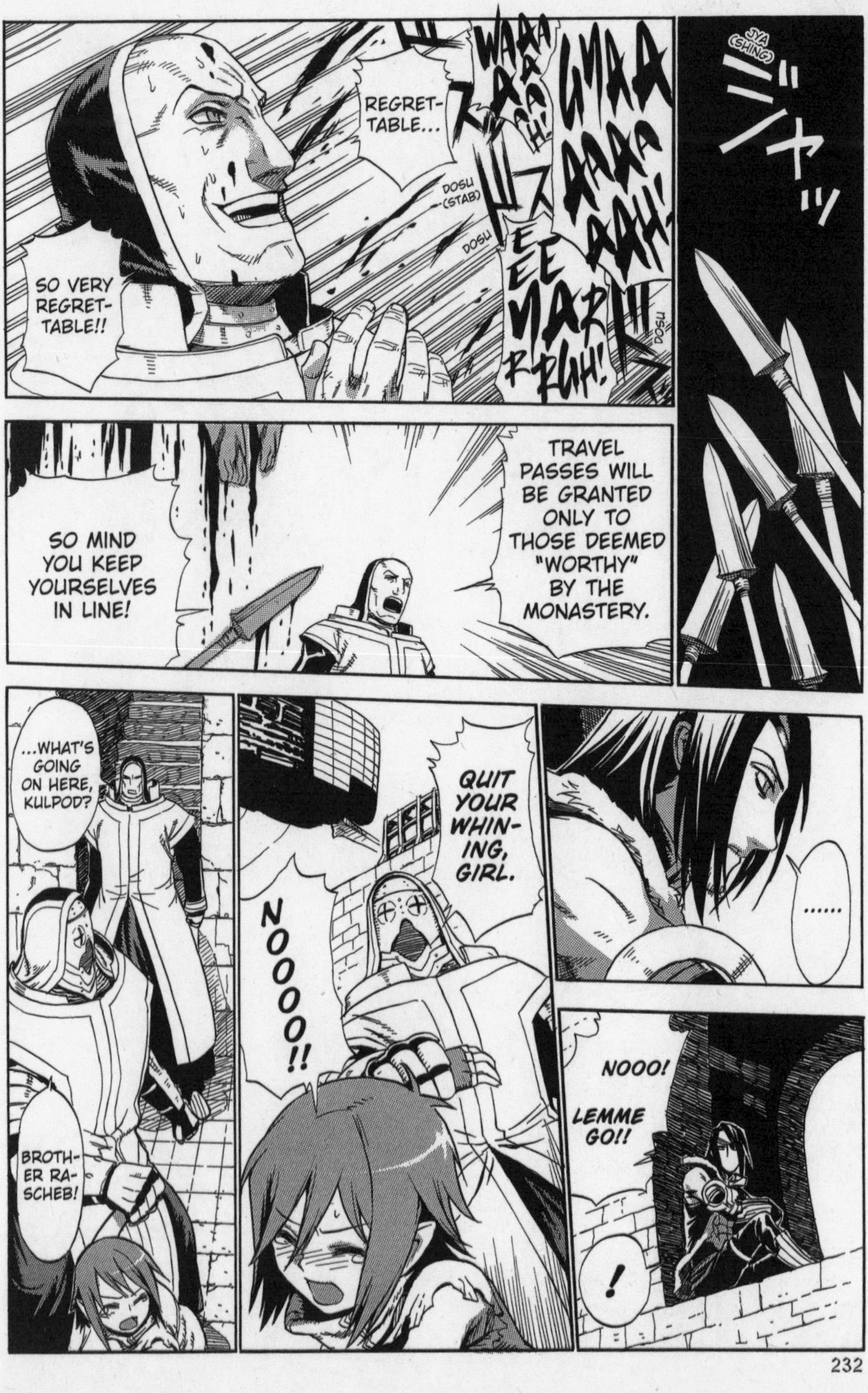
JYA (SHING)
GWAAAAAAAAAH!!
WAAAAAH!
REGRET-TABLE...
DOSU (STAB)
DOSU
EEEMARRRUH!!
DOSU
SO VERY REGRET-TABLE!!
TRAVEL PASSES WILL BE GRANTED ONLY TO THOSE DEEMED "WORTHY" BY THE MONASTERY.
SO MIND YOU KEEP YOURSELVES IN LINE!
......
NOOO!
LEMME GO!!
!
QUIT YOUR WHIN-ING, GIRL.
NOOOOO!!
...WHAT'S GOING ON HERE, KULPOD?
BROTH-ER RA-SCHEB!

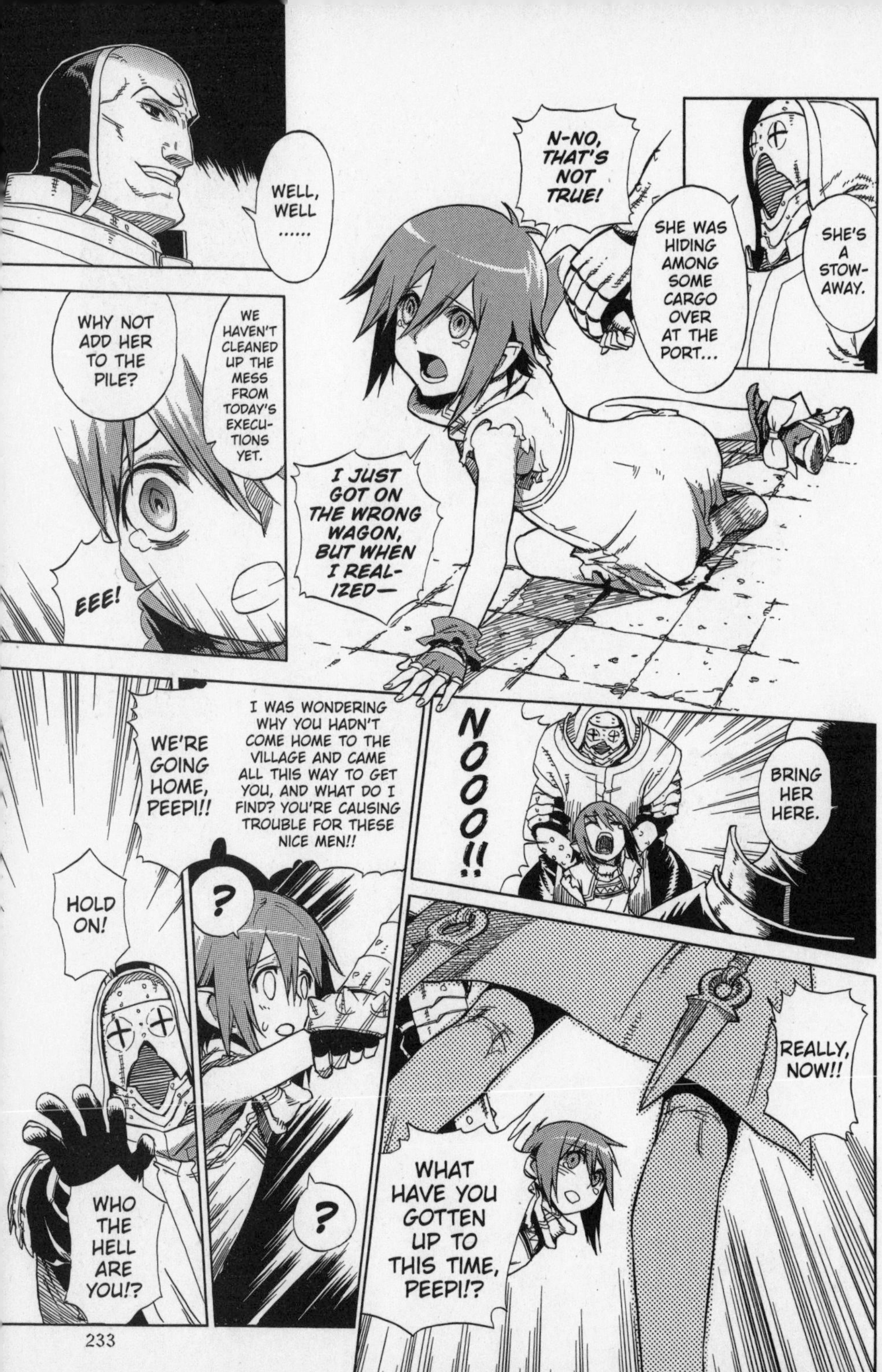
SHE'S A STOW-AWAY.
SHE WAS HIDING AMONG SOME CARGO OVER AT THE PORT...
N-NO, THAT'S NOT TRUE!
WELL, WELL ......
WE HAVEN'T CLEANED UP THE MESS FROM TODAY'S EXECU-TIONS YET.
WHY NOT ADD HER TO THE PILE?
EEE!
I JUST GOT ON THE WRONG WAGON, BUT WHEN I REAL-IZED—
BRING HER HERE.
NOOOO!!
I WAS WONDERING WHY YOU HADN'T COME HOME TO THE VILLAGE AND CAME ALL THIS WAY TO GET YOU, AND WHAT DO I FIND? YOU'RE CAUSING TROUBLE FOR THESE NICE MEN!!
WE'RE GOING HOME, PEEPI!!
REALLY, NOW!!
WHAT HAVE YOU GOTTEN UP TO THIS TIME, PEEPI!?
?
?
HOLD ON!
WHO THE HELL ARE YOU!?

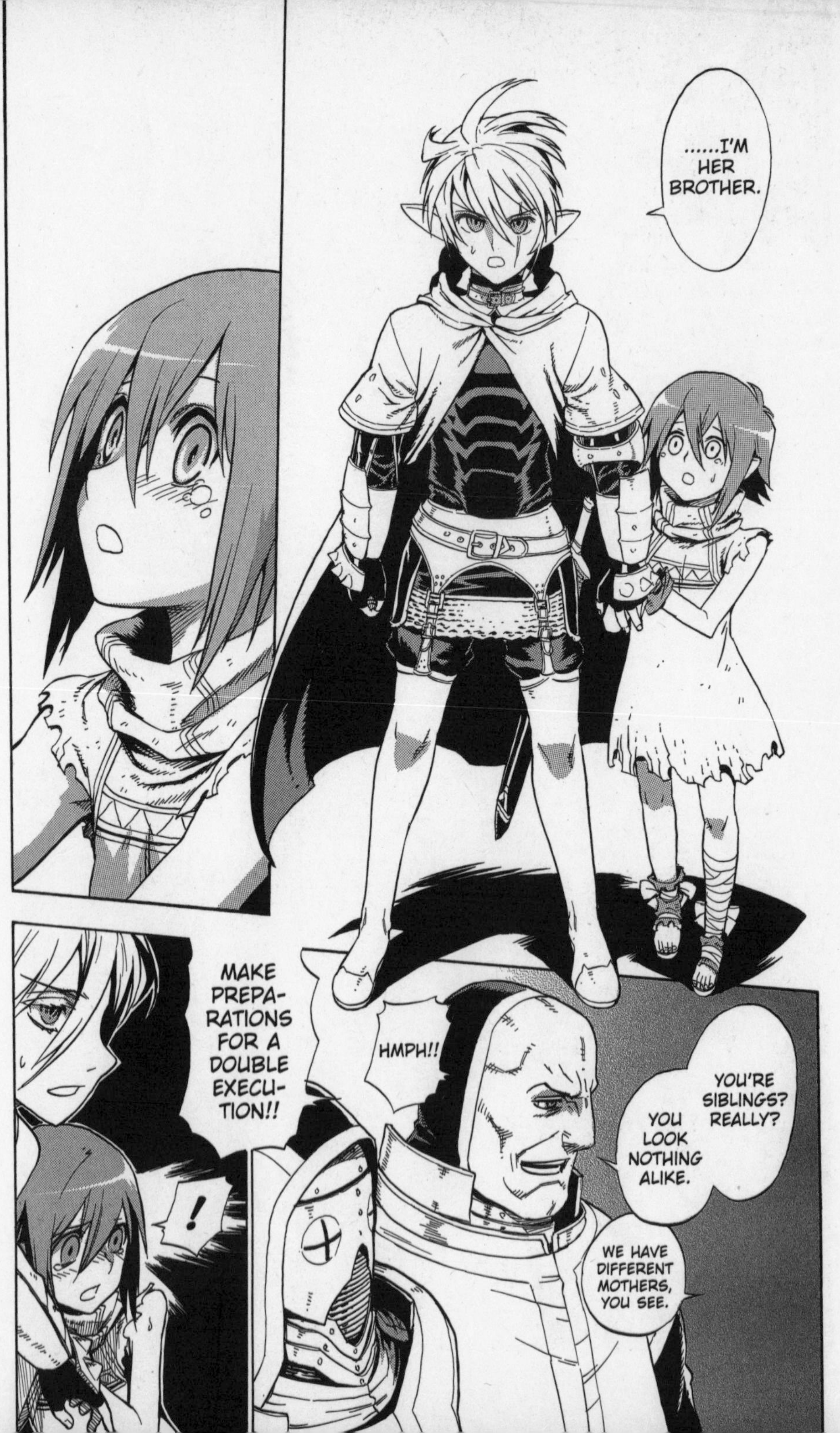
......I'M HER BROTHER.
YOU'RE SIBLINGS? REALLY? YOU LOOK NOTHING ALIKE.
WE HAVE DIFFERENT MOTHERS, YOU SEE.
HMPH!!
MAKE PREPARATIONS FOR A DOUBLE EXECUTION!!
!

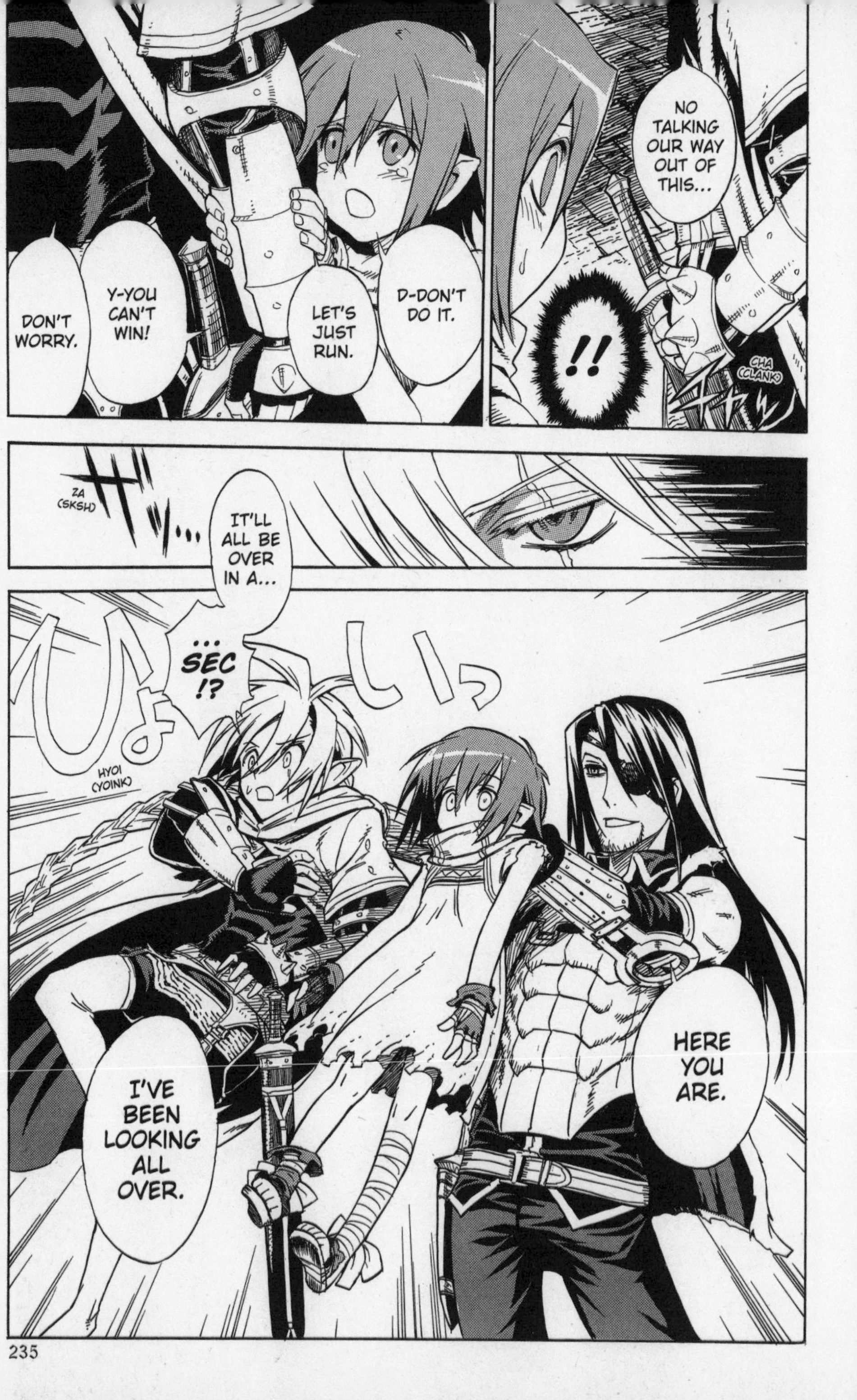
NO TALKING OUR WAY OUT OF THIS...
!!
CHA (CLANK)
D-DON'T DO IT.
LET'S JUST RUN.
Y-YOU CAN'T WIN!
DON'T WORRY.
ZA (SKSH)
IT'LL ALL BE OVER IN A...
...SEC!?
ひょいっ
HYOI (YOINK)
HERE YOU ARE.
I'VE BEEN LOOKING ALL OVER.

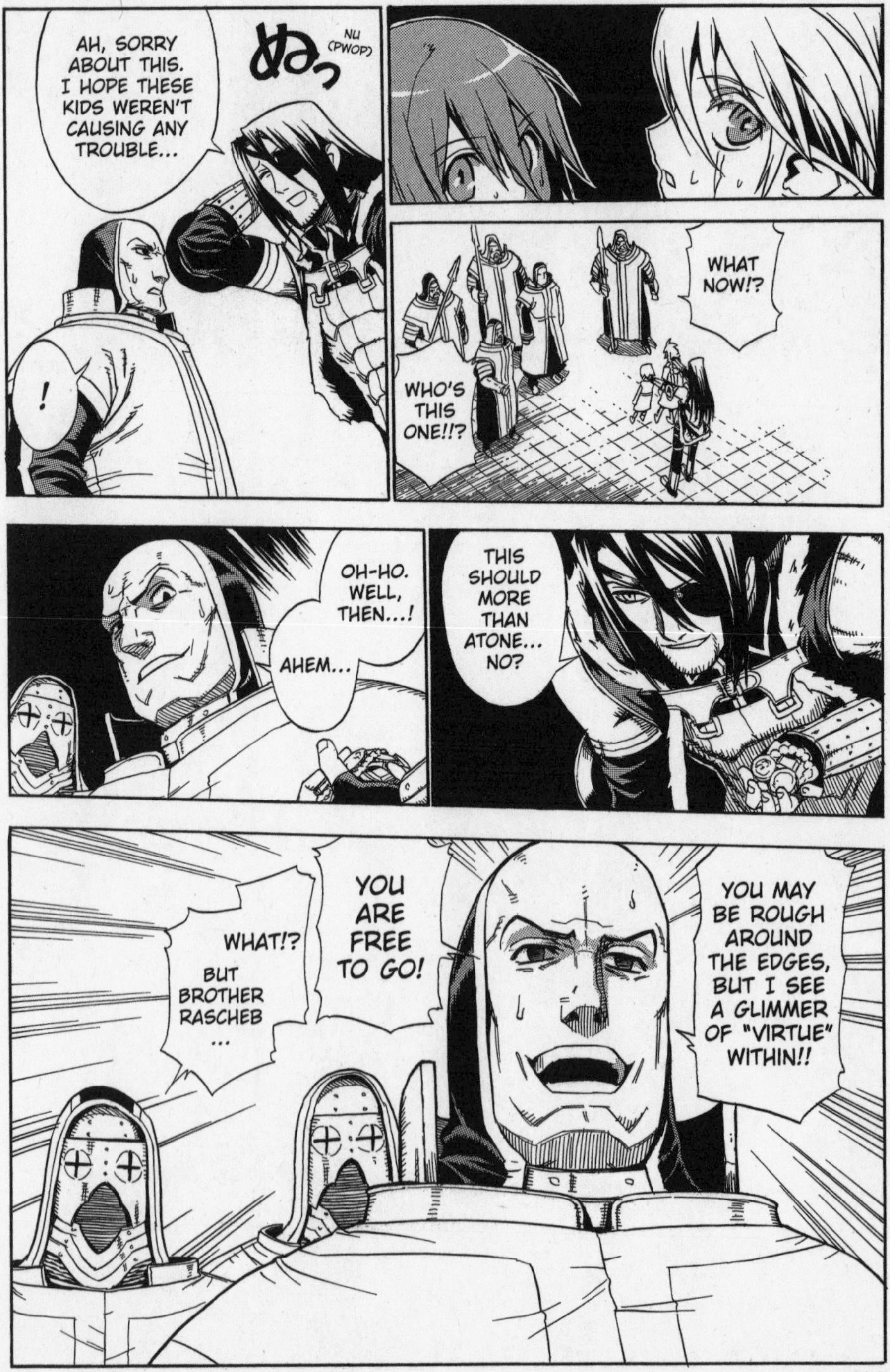
WHAT NOW!?
WHO'S THIS ONE!?
AH, SORRY ABOUT THIS. I HOPE THESE KIDS WEREN'T CAUSING ANY TROUBLE...
ぬっ
NU (PWOP)
!
THIS SHOULD MORE THAN ATONE... NO?
OH-HO. WELL, THEN...!
AHEM...
YOU MAY BE ROUGH AROUND THE EDGES, BUT I SEE A GLIMMER OF "VIRTUE" WITHIN!!
YOU ARE FREE TO GO!
WHAT!?
BUT BROTHER RASCHEB ...

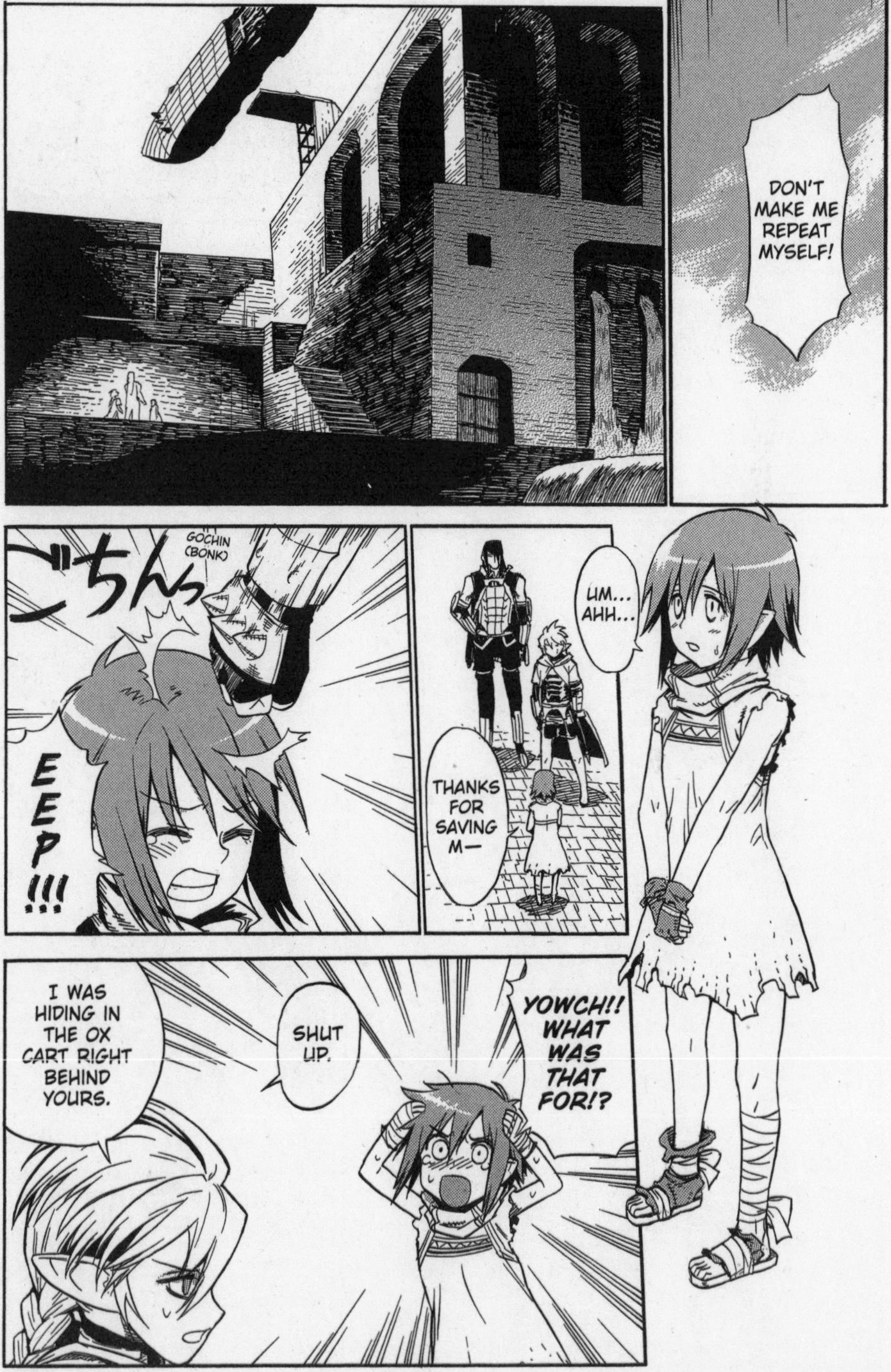
DON'T MAKE ME REPEAT MYSELF!
UM... AHH...
THANKS FOR SAVING M—
ごちんっ
GOCHIN (BONK)
EEP!!!
YOWCH!! WHAT WAS THAT FOR!?
SHUT UP.
I WAS HIDING IN THE OX CART RIGHT BEHIND YOURS.

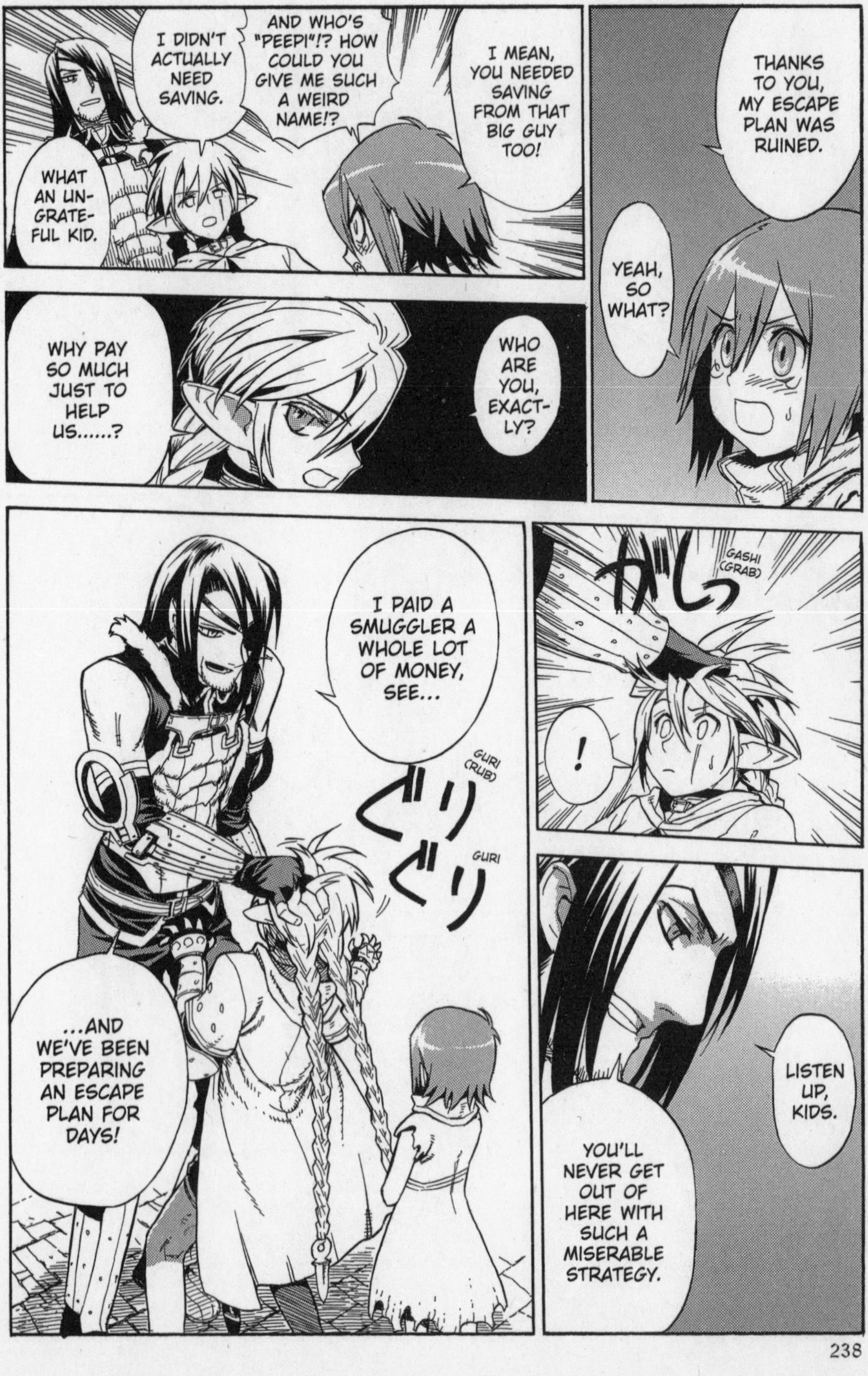
THANKS TO YOU, MY ESCAPE PLAN WAS RUINED.
YEAH, SO WHAT?
I MEAN, YOU NEEDED SAVING FROM THAT BIG GUY TOO!
AND WHO'S "PEEPI"!? HOW COULD YOU GIVE ME SUCH A WEIRD NAME!?
I DIDN'T ACTUALLY NEED SAVING.
WHAT AN UN-GRATE-FUL KID.
WHO ARE YOU, EXACT-LY?
WHY PAY SO MUCH JUST TO HELP US......?
がしっ
GASHI (GRAB)
!
LISTEN UP, KIDS.
YOU'LL NEVER GET OUT OF HERE WITH SUCH A MISERABLE STRATEGY.
I PAID A SMUGGLER A WHOLE LOT OF MONEY, SEE...
ぐり
GURI (RUB)
ぐり
GURI
...AND WE'VE BEEN PREPARING AN ESCAPE PLAN FOR DAYS!

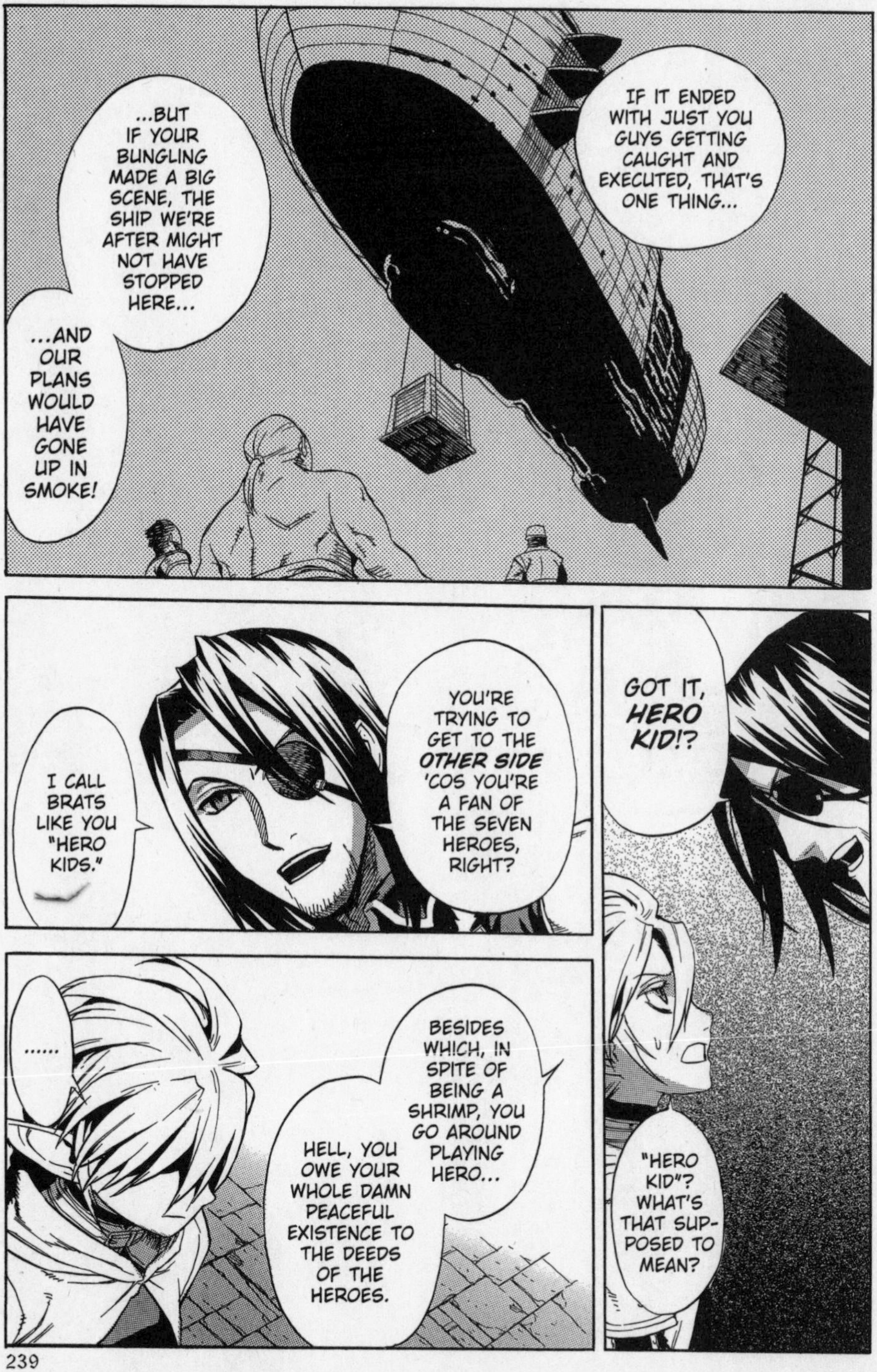
IF IT ENDED WITH JUST YOU GUYS GETTING CAUGHT AND EXECUTED, THAT'S ONE THING...
...BUT IF YOUR BUNGLING MADE A BIG SCENE, THE SHIP WE'RE AFTER MIGHT NOT HAVE STOPPED HERE...
...AND OUR PLANS WOULD HAVE GONE UP IN SMOKE!
GOT IT, **HERO KID**!?
"HERO KID"? WHAT'S THAT SUP-POSED TO MEAN?
YOU'RE TRYING TO GET TO THE **OTHER SIDE** 'COS YOU'RE A FAN OF THE SEVEN HEROES, RIGHT?
I CALL BRATS LIKE YOU "HERO KIDS."
BESIDES WHICH, IN SPITE OF BEING A SHRIMP, YOU GO AROUND PLAYING HERO...
HELL, YOU OWE YOUR WHOLE DAMN PEACEFUL EXISTENCE TO THE DEEDS OF THE HEROES.
......

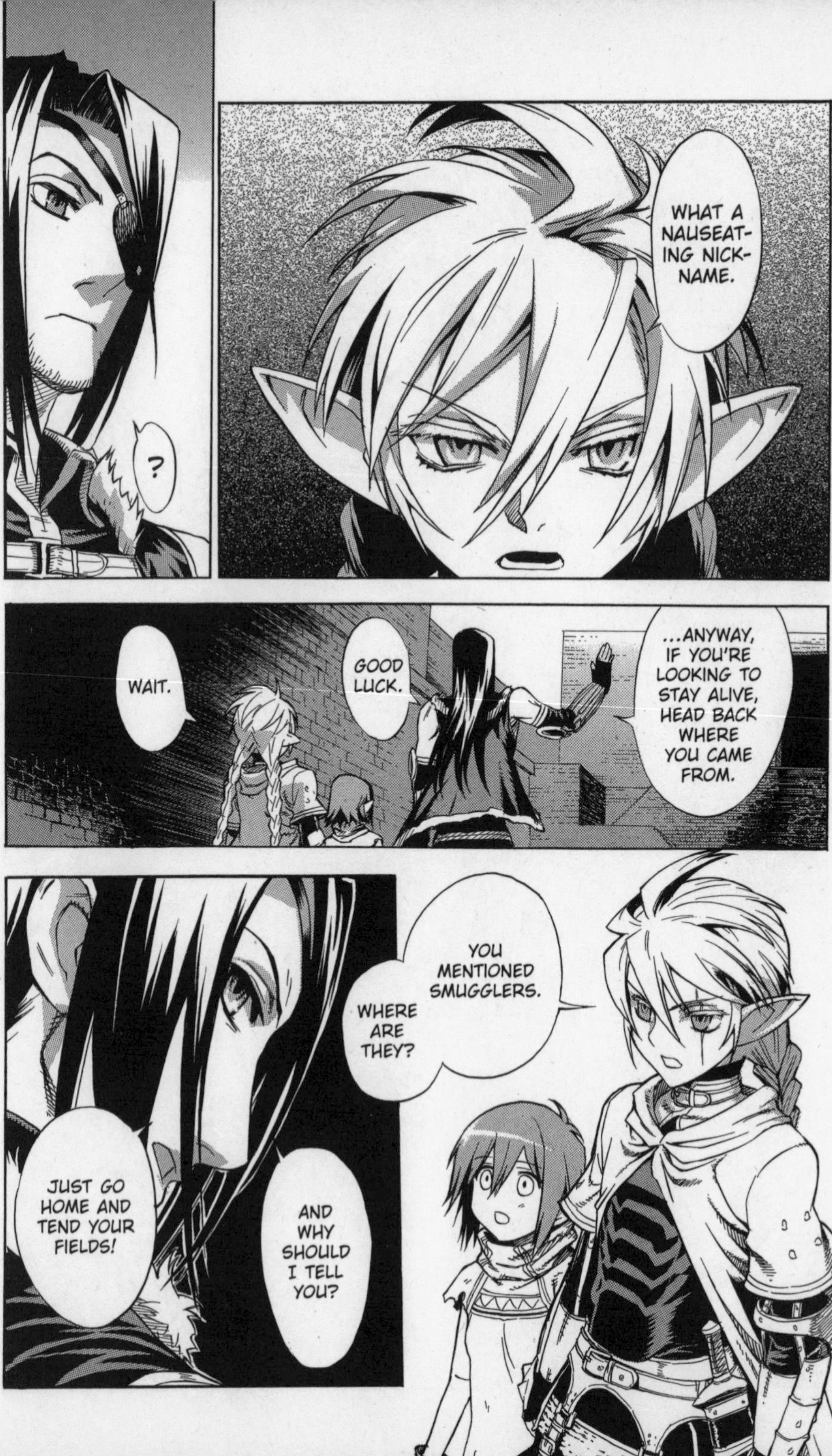
WHAT A NAUSEATING NICK-NAME.
?
...ANYWAY, IF YOU'RE LOOKING TO STAY ALIVE, HEAD BACK WHERE YOU CAME FROM.
GOOD LUCK.
WAIT.
YOU MENTIONED SMUGGLERS.
WHERE ARE THEY?
AND WHY SHOULD I TELL YOU?
JUST GO HOME AND TEND YOUR FIELDS!

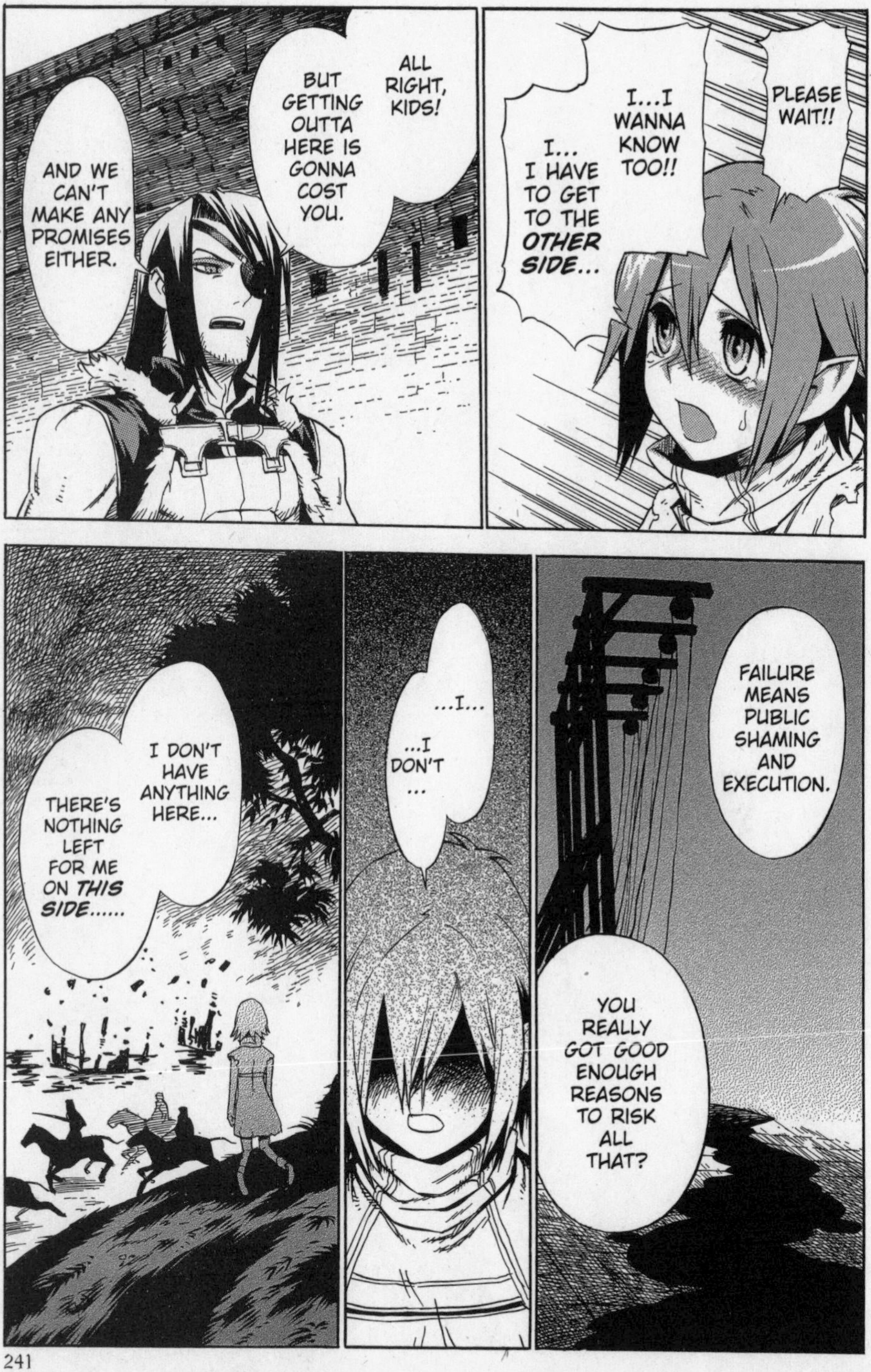
PLEASE WAIT!!
I...I WANNA KNOW TOO!!
I... I HAVE TO GET TO THE *OTHER SIDE*...
ALL RIGHT, KIDS!
BUT GETTING OUTTA HERE IS GONNA COST YOU.
AND WE CAN'T MAKE ANY PROMISES EITHER.
FAILURE MEANS PUBLIC SHAMING AND EXECUTION.
YOU REALLY GOT GOOD ENOUGH REASONS TO RISK ALL THAT?
...I...
...I DON'T ...
I DON'T HAVE ANYTHING HERE...
THERE'S NOTHING LEFT FOR ME ON *THIS SIDE*......

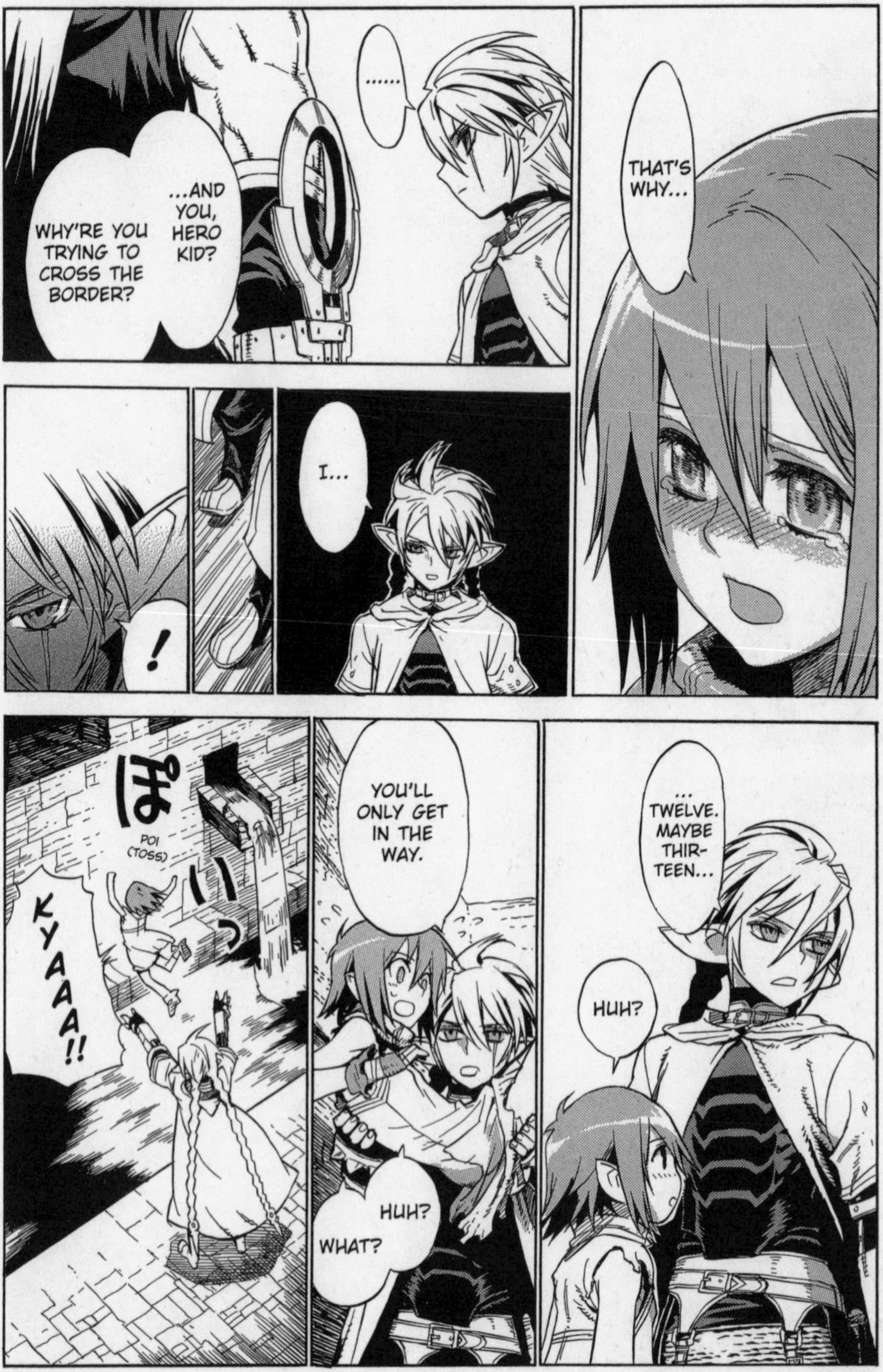
THAT'S WHY...
......
...AND YOU, HERO KID?
WHY'RE YOU TRYING TO CROSS THE BORDER?
I...
!
... TWELVE. MAYBE THIR-TEEN...
HUH?
YOU'LL ONLY GET IN THE WAY.
HUH?
WHAT?
ぽいっ
POI (TOSS)
KYAAAA!!

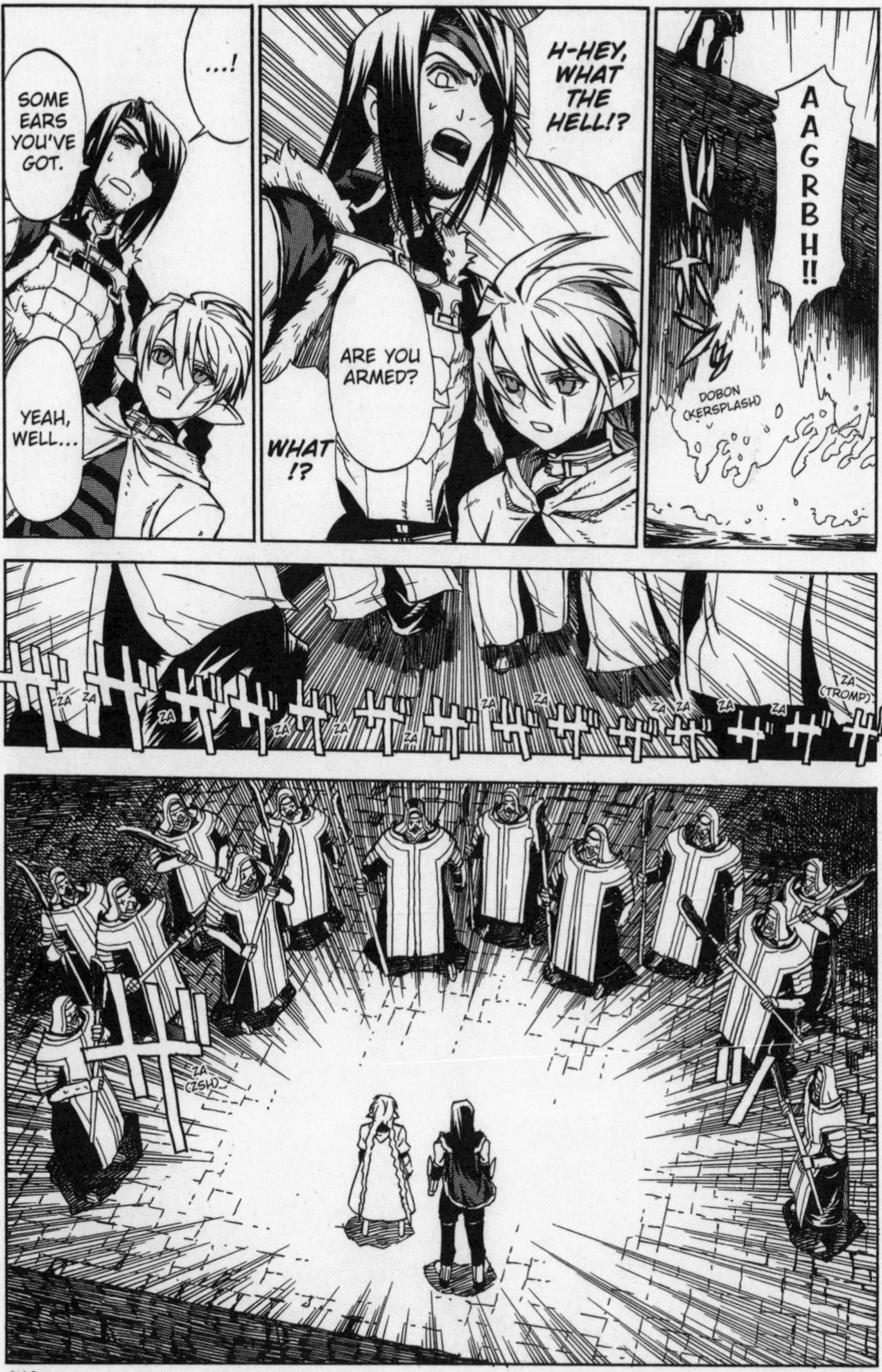

AAGRBH!!
DOBON (KERSPLASH)
H-HEY, WHAT THE HELL!?
ARE YOU ARMED?
WHAT!?
...!
SOME EARS YOU'VE GOT.
YEAH, WELL...
ZA (TROMP)
ZA (ZSH)

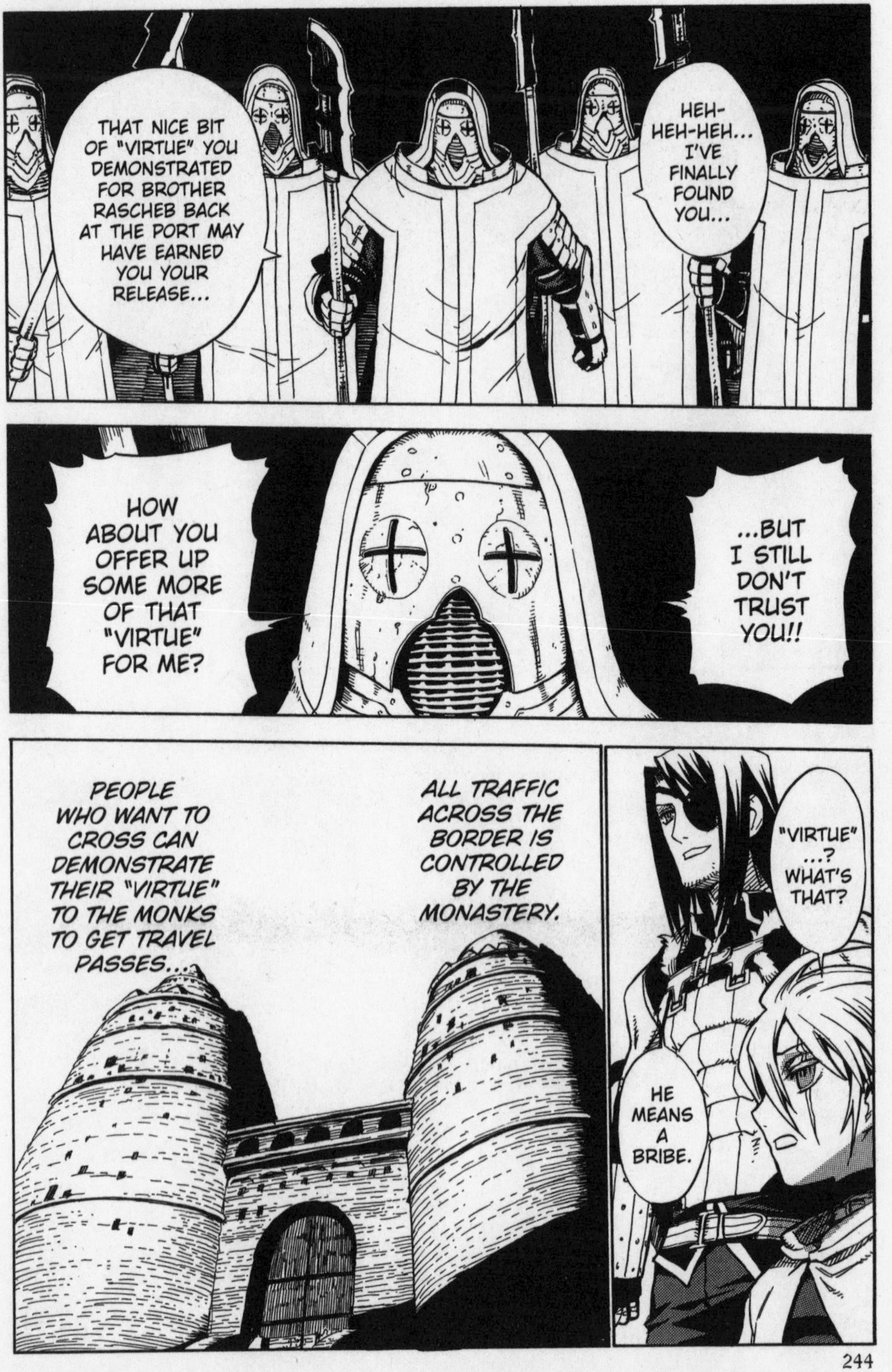
HEH-HEH-HEH... I'VE FINALLY FOUND YOU...
THAT NICE BIT OF "VIRTUE" YOU DEMONSTRATED FOR BROTHER RASCHEB BACK AT THE PORT MAY HAVE EARNED YOU YOUR RELEASE...
...BUT I STILL DON'T TRUST YOU!!
HOW ABOUT YOU OFFER UP SOME MORE OF THAT "VIRTUE" FOR ME?
"VIRTUE" ...? WHAT'S THAT?
HE MEANS A BRIBE.
ALL TRAFFIC ACROSS THE BORDER IS CONTROLLED BY THE MONASTERY.
PEOPLE WHO WANT TO CROSS CAN DEMONSTRATE THEIR "VIRTUE" TO THE MONKS TO GET TRAVEL PASSES...

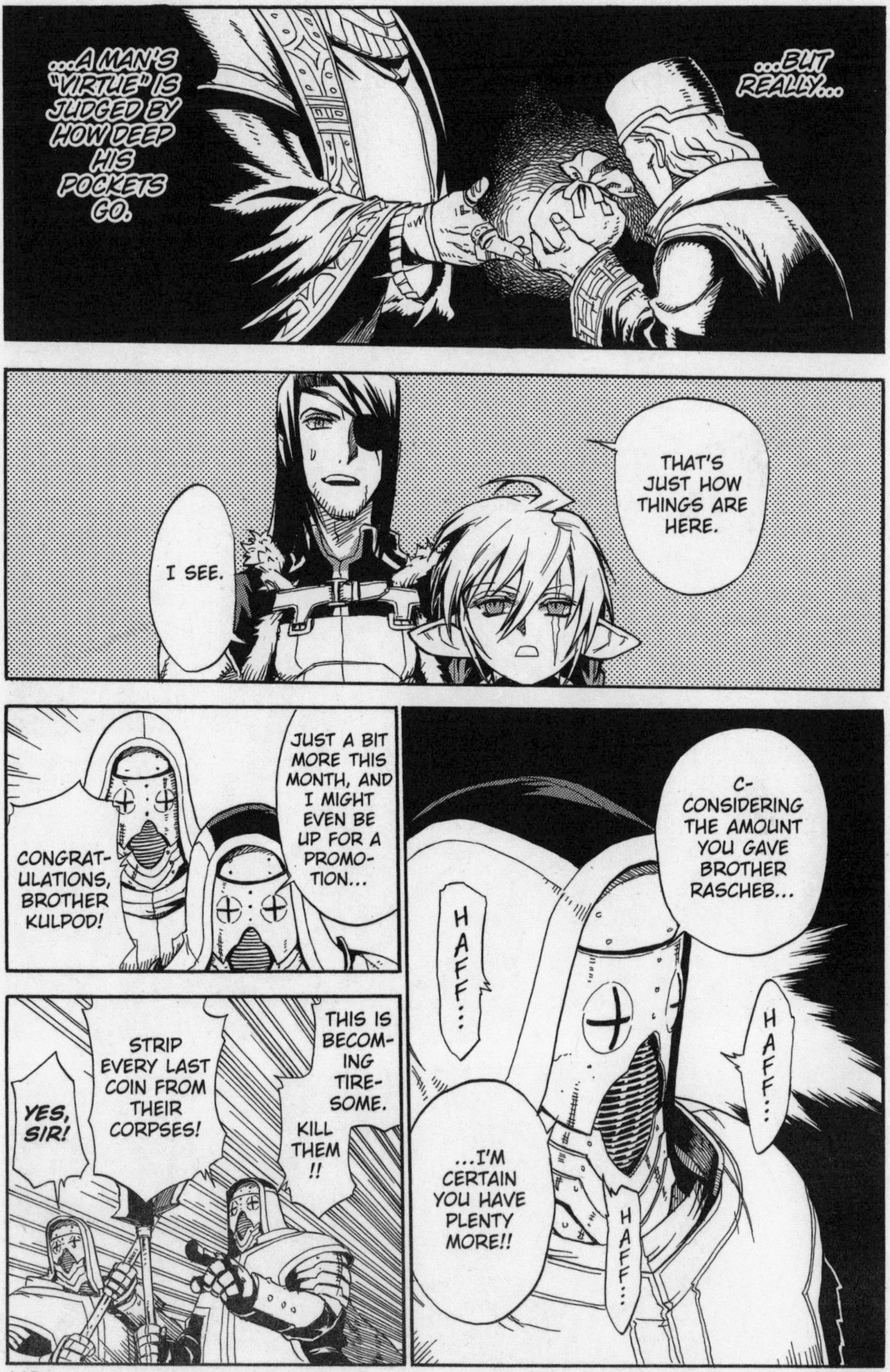
...BUT REALLY...
...A MAN'S "VIRTUE" IS JUDGED BY HOW DEEP HIS POCKETS GO.
THAT'S JUST HOW THINGS ARE HERE.
I SEE.
C-CONSIDERING THE AMOUNT YOU GAVE BROTHER RASCHEB...
HAFF...
HAFF...
...I'M CERTAIN YOU HAVE PLENTY MORE!!
HAFF...
JUST A BIT MORE THIS MONTH, AND I MIGHT EVEN BE UP FOR A PROMOTION...
CONGRATULATIONS, BROTHER KULPOD!
THIS IS BECOMING TIRESOME.
KILL THEM!!
STRIP EVERY LAST COIN FROM THEIR CORPSES!
YES, SIR!

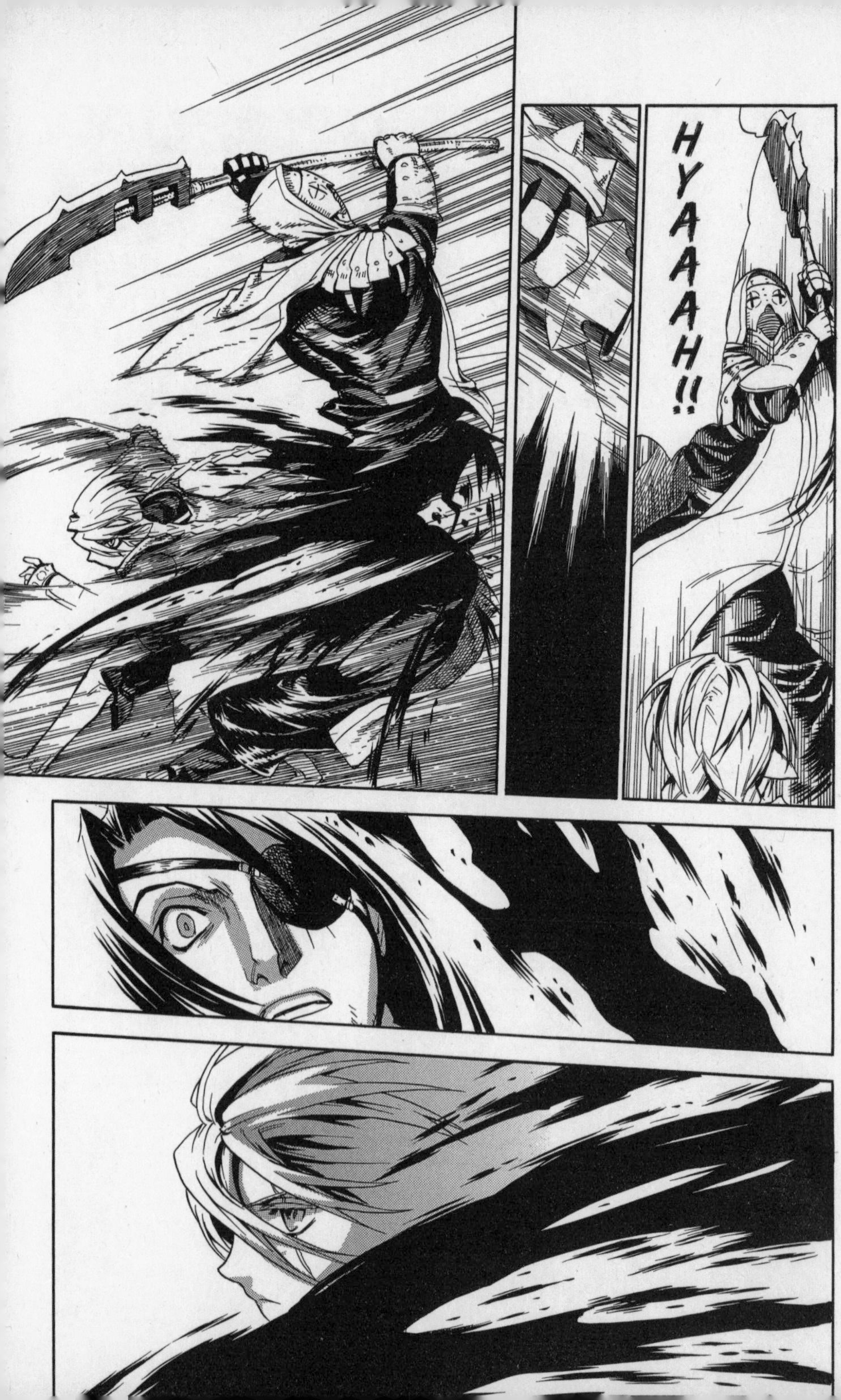
HYAAAAH!!

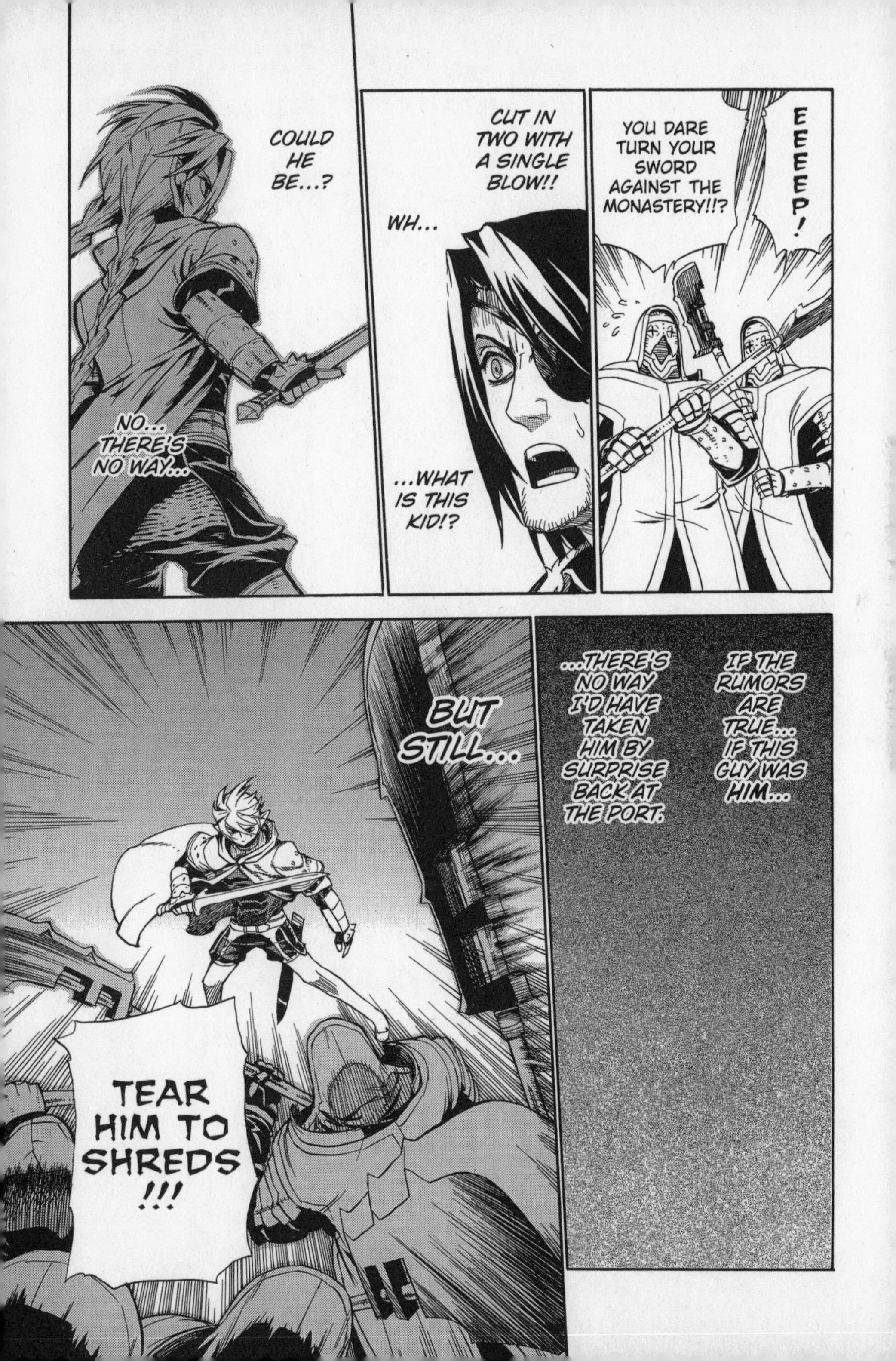

EEEEP!
YOU DARE TURN YOUR SWORD AGAINST THE MONASTERY!!?
CUT IN TWO WITH A SINGLE BLOW!!
WH...
...WHAT IS THIS KID!?
COULD HE BE...?
NO... THERE'S NO WAY...
IF THE RUMORS ARE TRUE... IF THIS GUY WAS HIM...
...THERE'S NO WAY I'D HAVE TAKEN HIM BY SURPRISE BACK AT THE PORT.
BUT STILL...
TEAR HIM TO SHREDS!!!

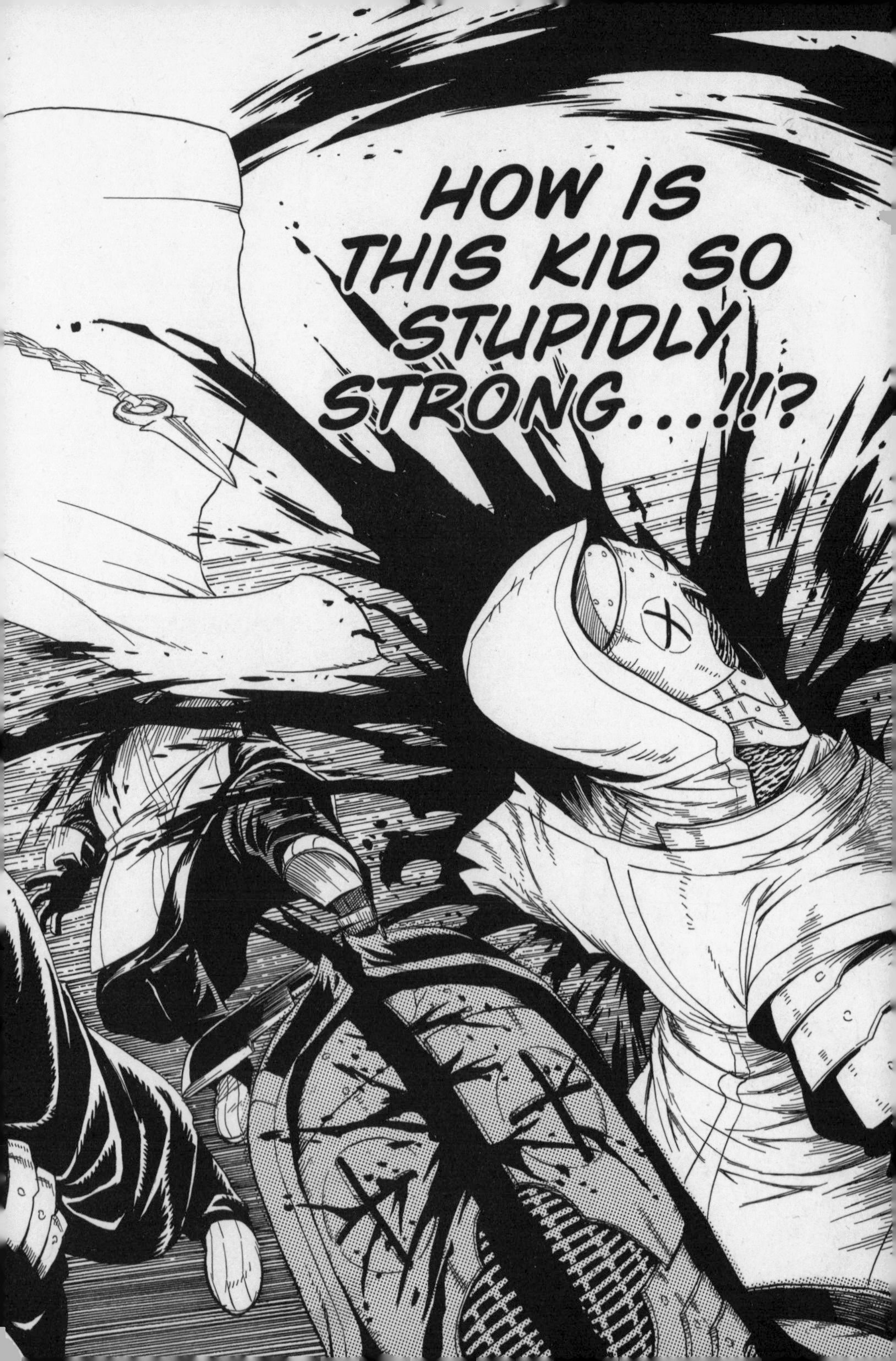
HOW IS THIS KID SO STUPIDLY STRONG...!!?

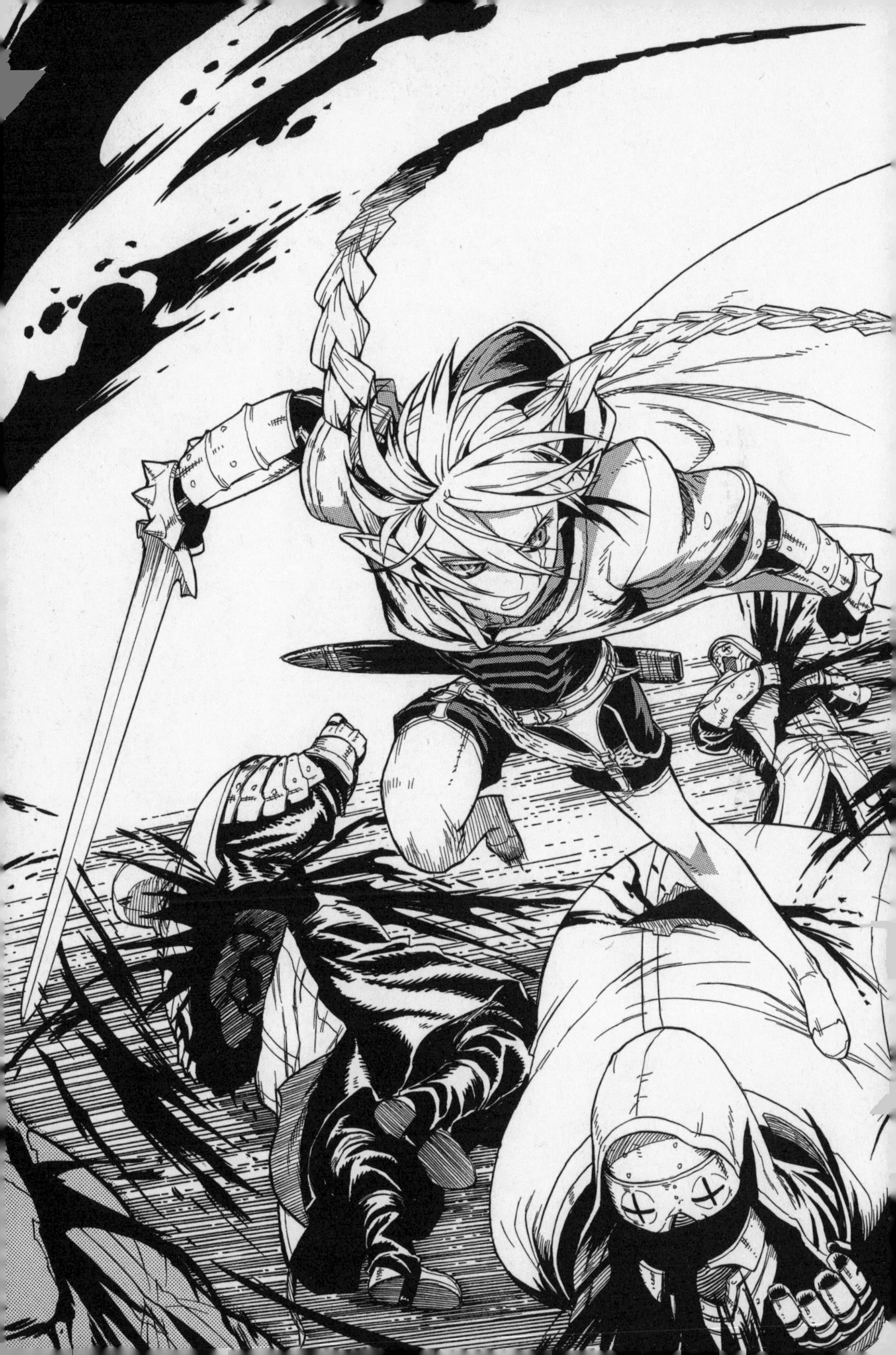

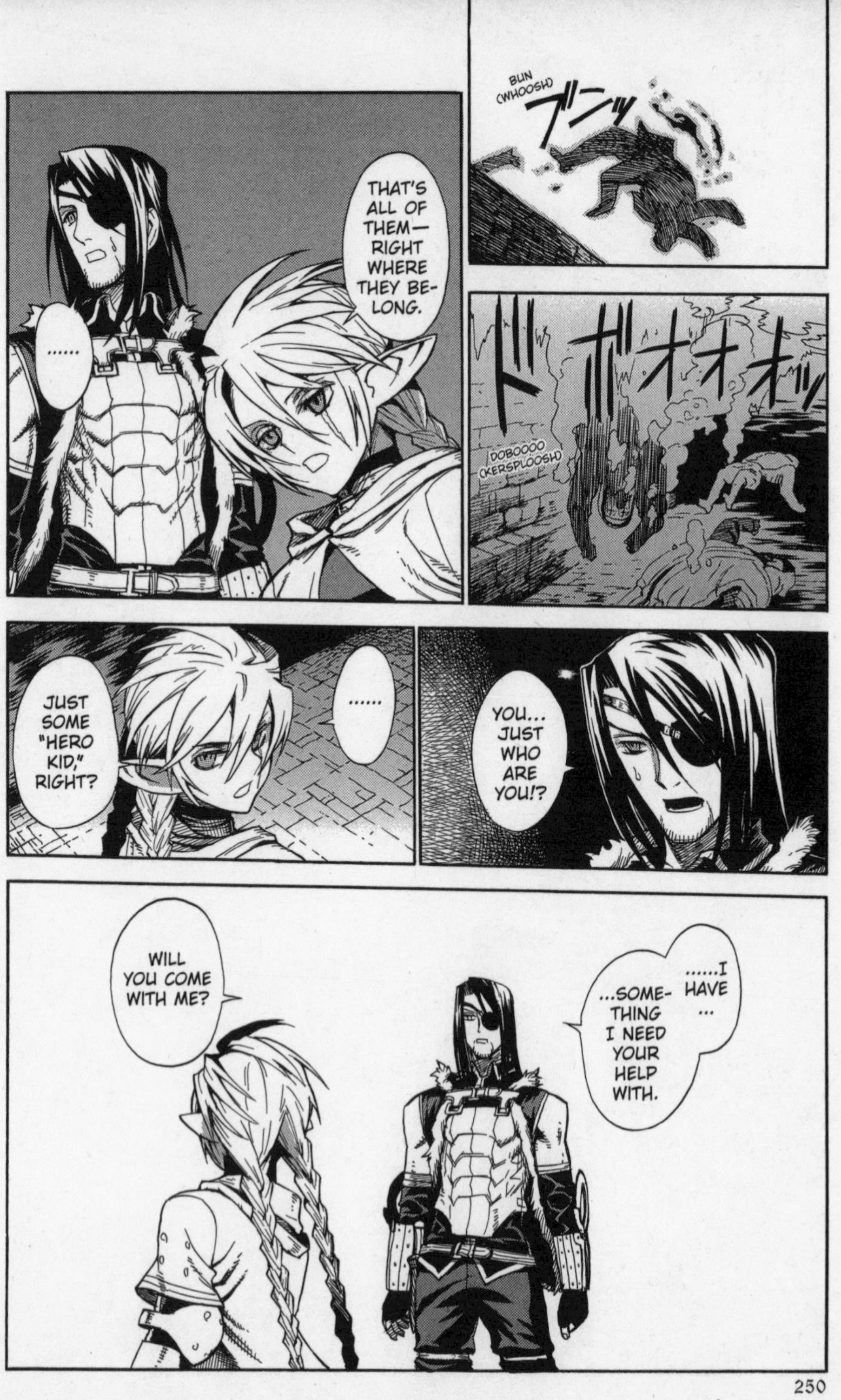
BUN (WHOOSH)
DOBOOOO (KERSPLOOSH)
THAT'S ALL OF THEM— RIGHT WHERE THEY BE- LONG.
......
YOU... JUST WHO ARE YOU!?
......
JUST SOME "HERO KID," RIGHT?
......I HAVE ...
...SOME- THING I NEED YOUR HELP WITH.
WILL YOU COME WITH ME?

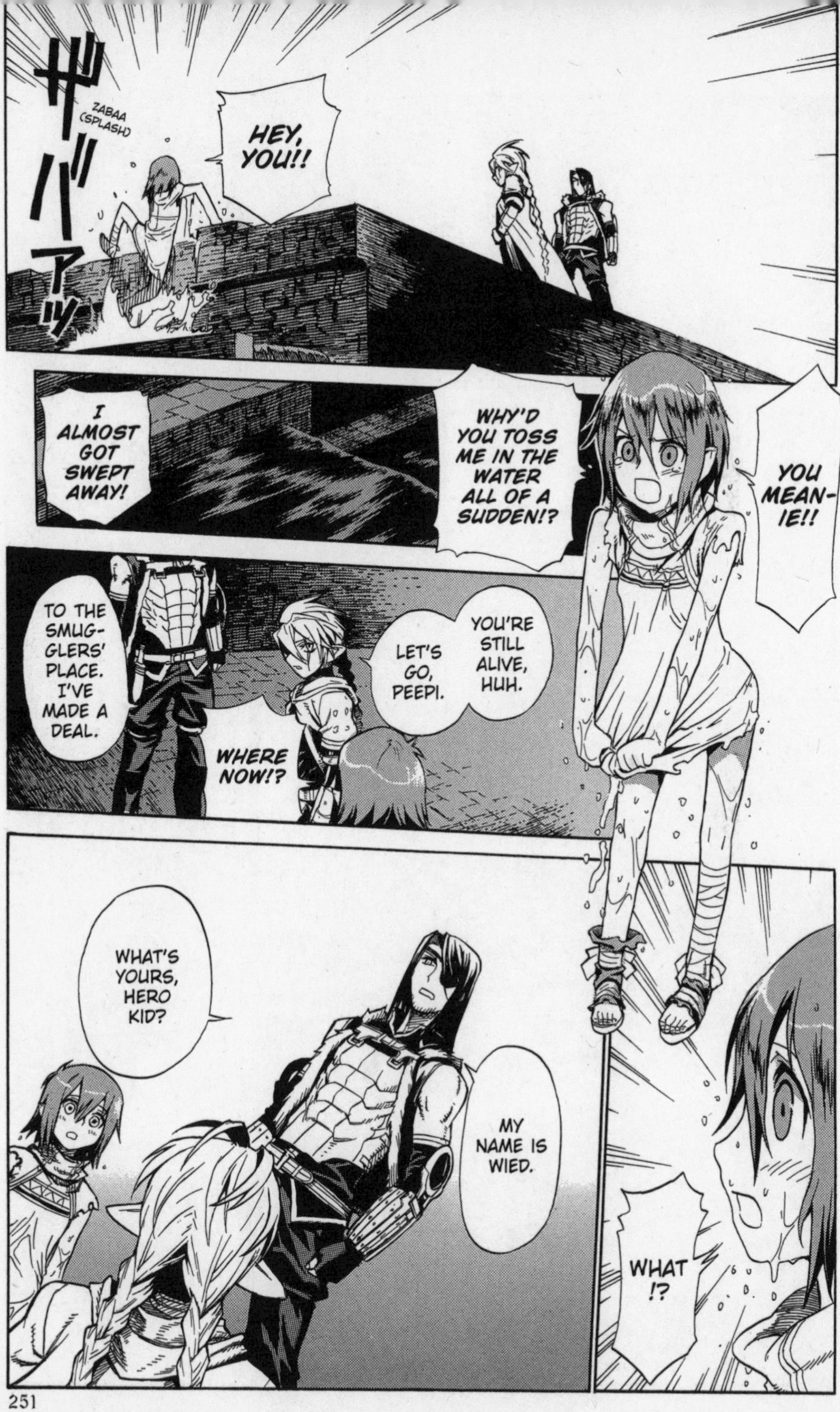
HEY, YOU!!
ザバァッ
ZABAA (SPLASH)
YOU MEAN-IE!!
WHY'D YOU TOSS ME IN THE WATER ALL OF A SUDDEN!?
I ALMOST GOT SWEPT AWAY!
YOU'RE STILL ALIVE, HUH.
LET'S GO, PEEPI.
WHERE NOW!?
TO THE SMUG-GLERS' PLACE. I'VE MADE A DEAL.
WHAT !?
MY NAME IS WIED.
WHAT'S YOURS, HERO KID?

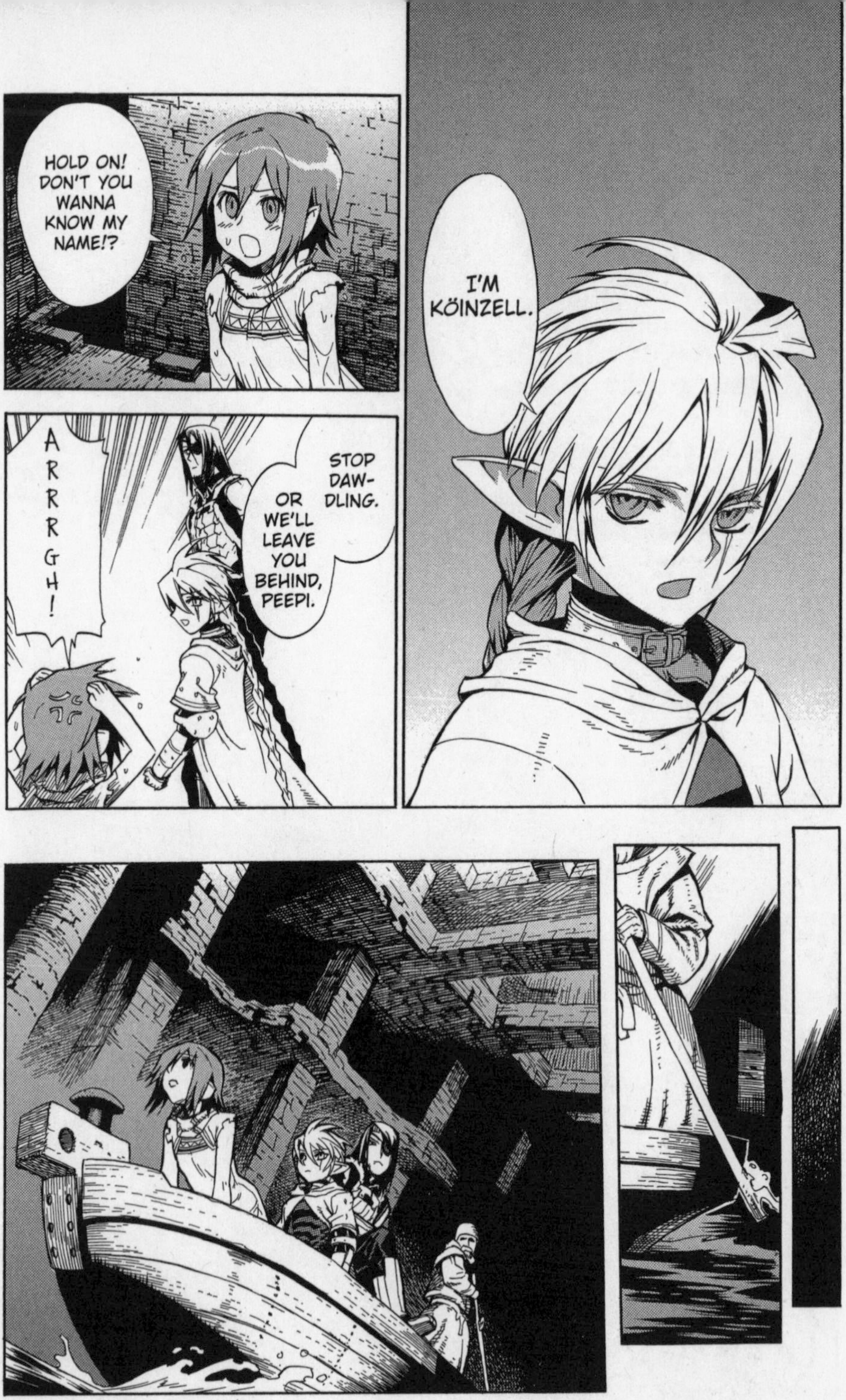
I'M KÖINZELL.
HOLD ON! DON'T YOU WANNA KNOW MY NAME!?
STOP DAWDLING. OR WE'LL LEAVE YOU BEHIND, PEEPI.
ARRRGH!

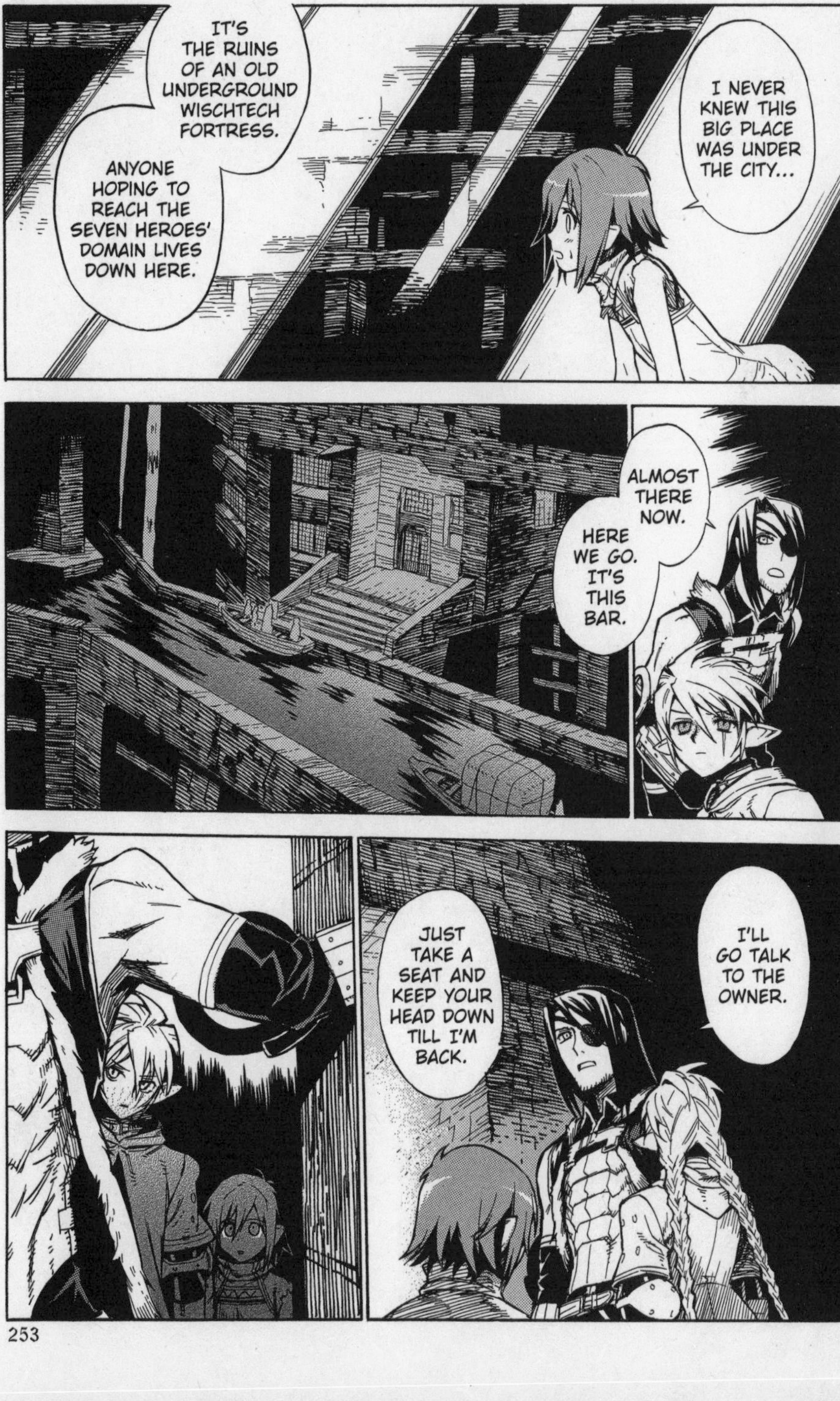
I NEVER KNEW THIS BIG PLACE WAS UNDER THE CITY...
IT'S THE RUINS OF AN OLD UNDERGROUND WISCHTECH FORTRESS.
ANYONE HOPING TO REACH THE SEVEN HEROES' DOMAIN LIVES DOWN HERE.
ALMOST THERE NOW.
HERE WE GO. IT'S THIS BAR.
I'LL GO TALK TO THE OWNER.
JUST TAKE A SEAT AND KEEP YOUR HEAD DOWN TILL I'M BACK.

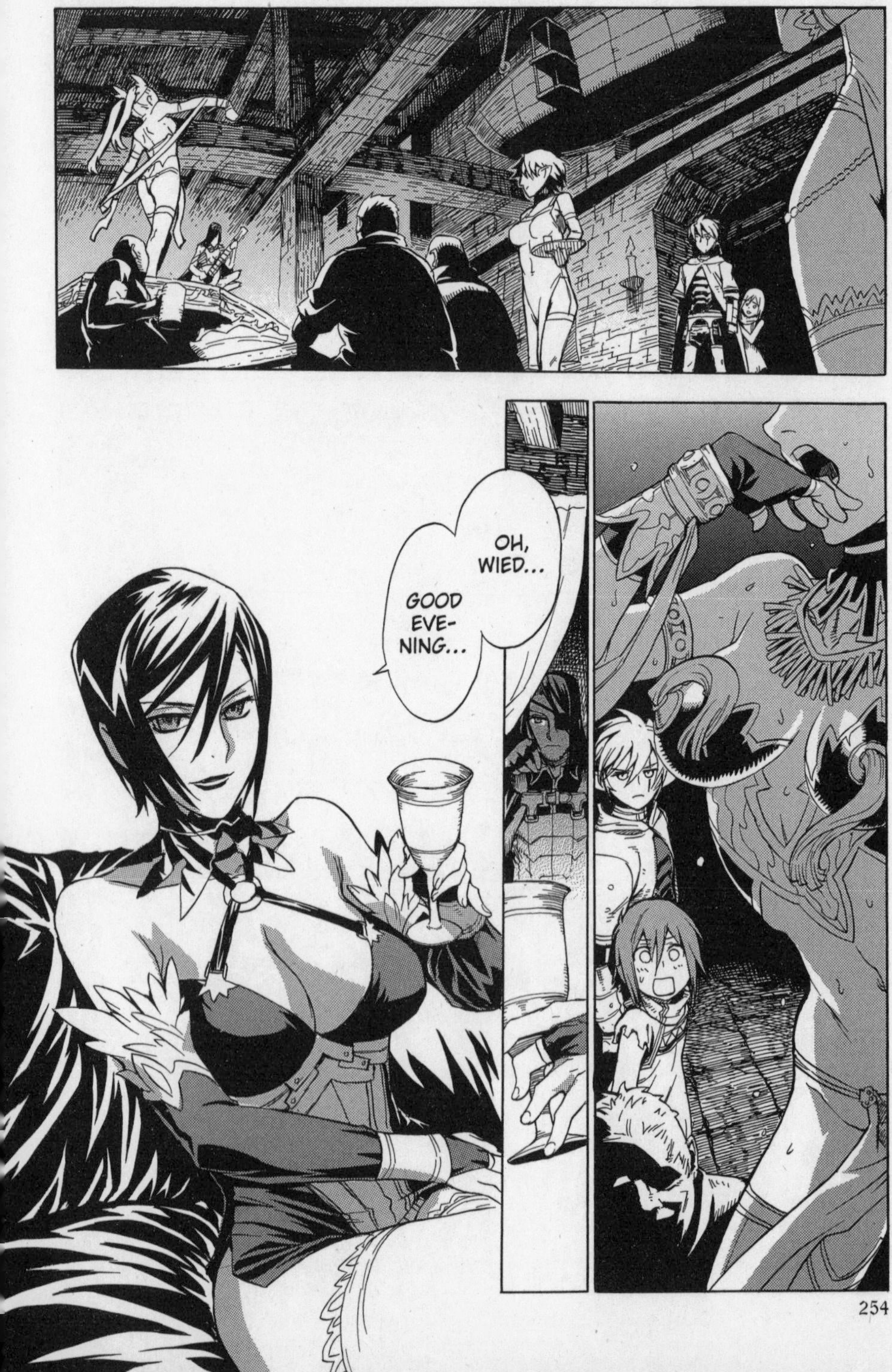
OH, WIED... GOOD EVE-NING...

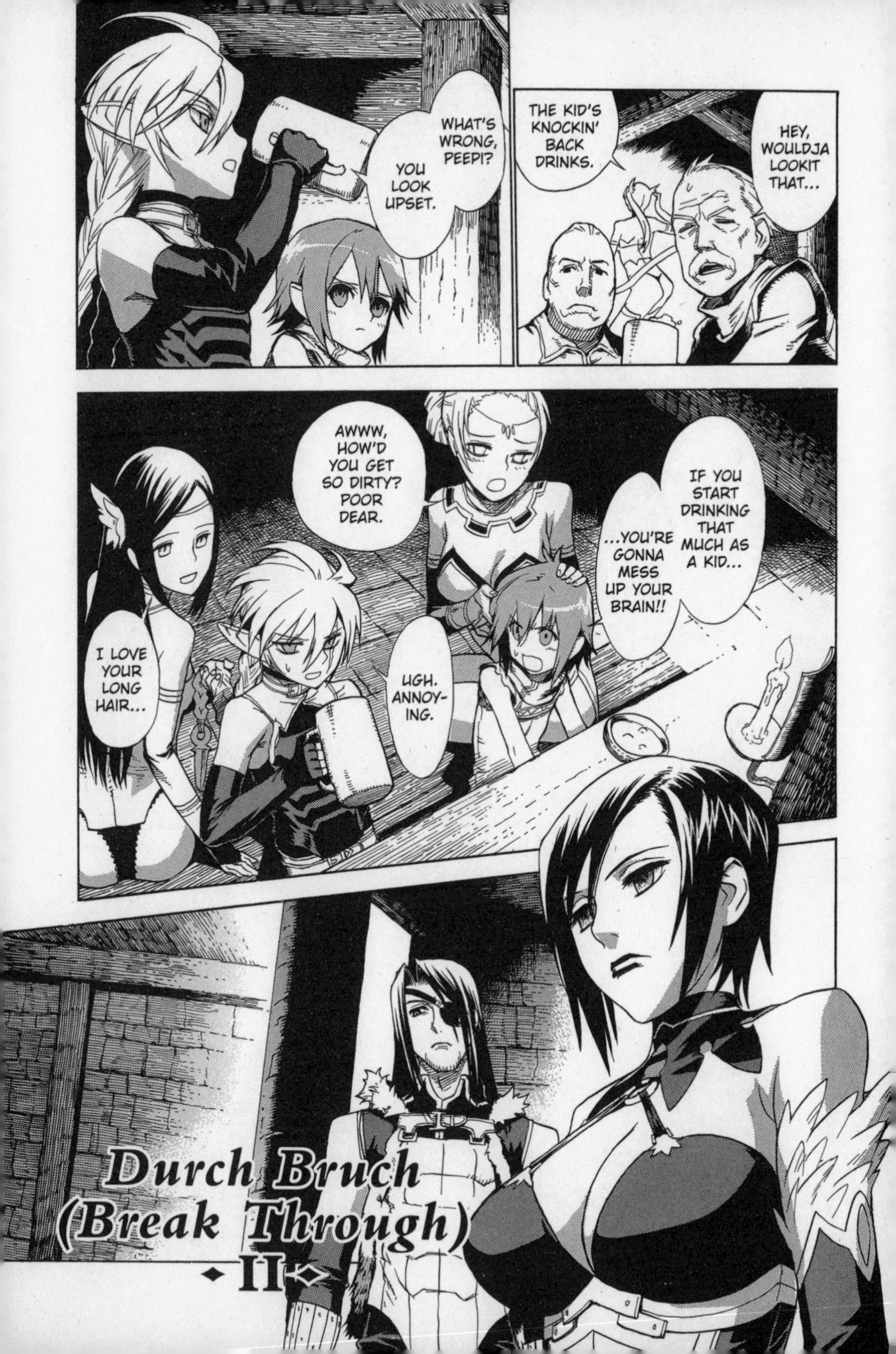
HEY, WOULDJA LOOKIT THAT...
THE KID'S KNOCKIN' BACK DRINKS.
WHAT'S WRONG, PEEPI?
YOU LOOK UPSET.
IF YOU START DRINKING THAT MUCH AS A KID...
...YOU'RE GONNA MESS UP YOUR BRAIN!!
AWWW, HOW'D YOU GET SO DIRTY? POOR DEAR.
UGH. ANNOY-ING.
I LOVE YOUR LONG HAIR...
Durch Bruch (Break Through)
II

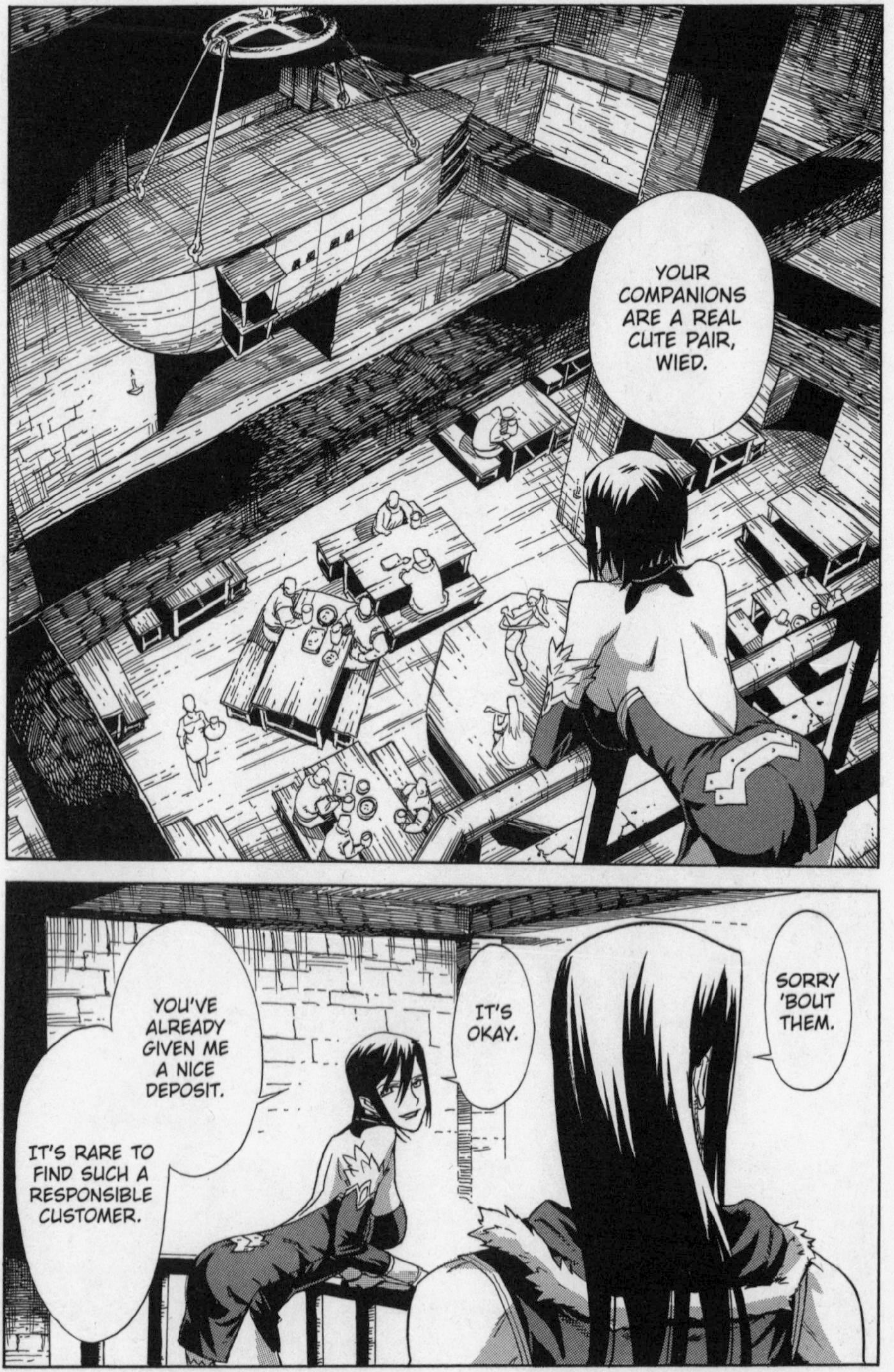
YOUR COMPANIONS ARE A REAL CUTE PAIR, WIED.
SORRY 'BOUT THEM.
IT'S OKAY.
YOU'VE ALREADY GIVEN ME A NICE DEPOSIT.
IT'S RARE TO FIND SUCH A RESPONSIBLE CUSTOMER.

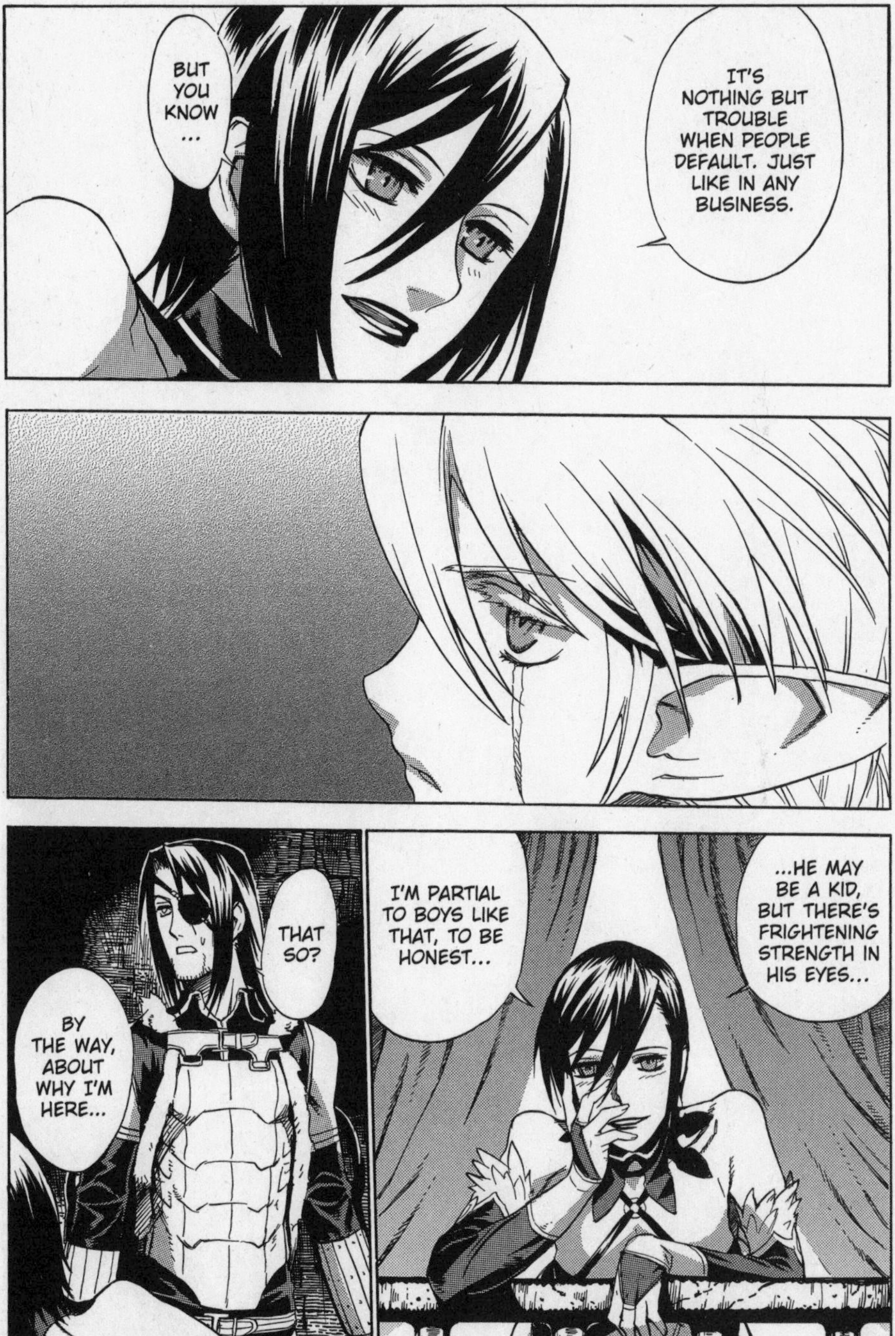
IT'S NOTHING BUT TROUBLE WHEN PEOPLE DEFAULT. JUST LIKE IN ANY BUSINESS.
BUT YOU KNOW ...
...HE MAY BE A KID, BUT THERE'S FRIGHTENING STRENGTH IN HIS EYES...
I'M PARTIAL TO BOYS LIKE THAT, TO BE HONEST...
THAT SO?
BY THE WAY, ABOUT WHY I'M HERE...

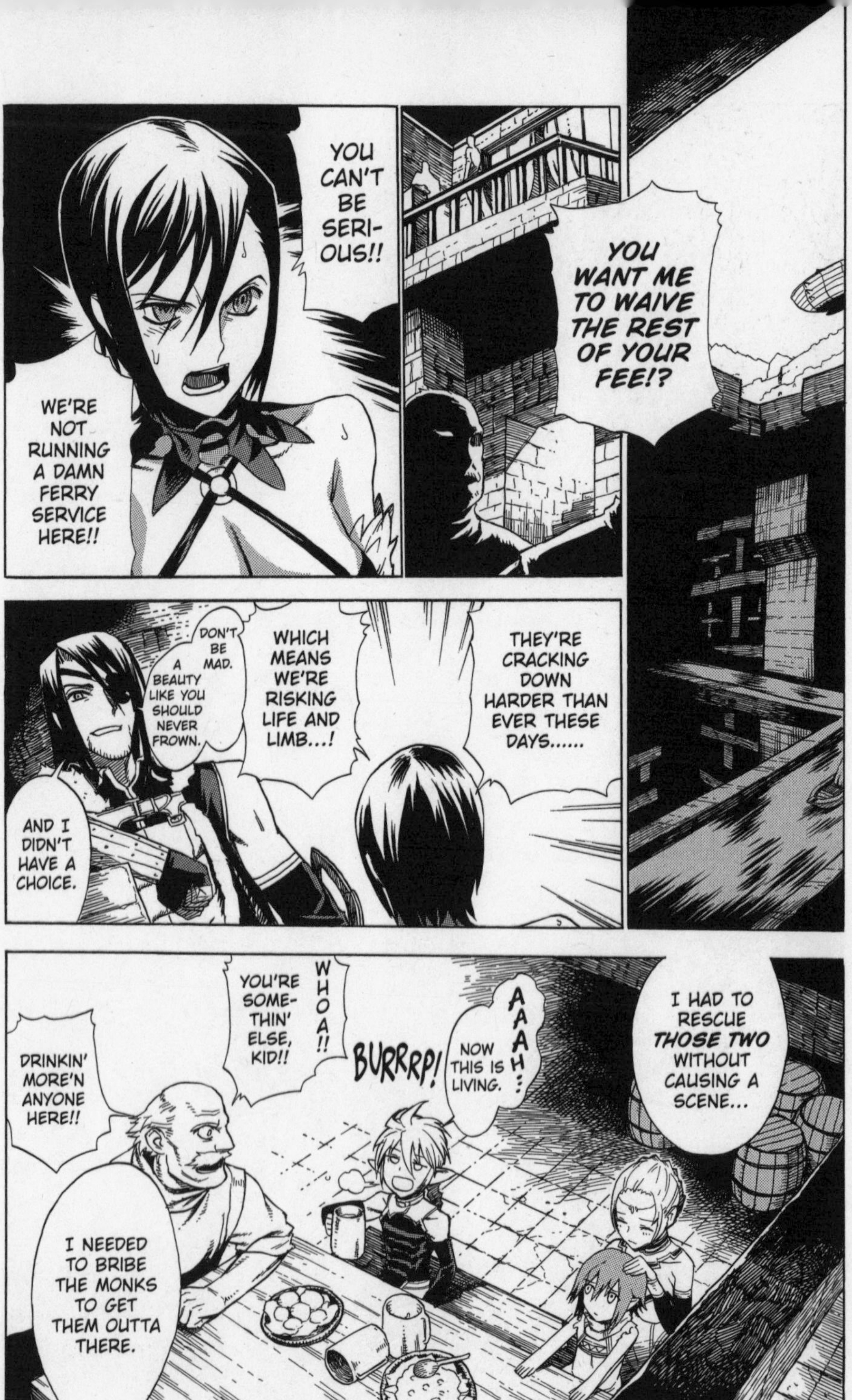
YOU WANT ME TO WAIVE THE REST OF YOUR FEE!?
YOU CAN'T BE SERIOUS!!
WE'RE NOT RUNNING A DAMN FERRY SERVICE HERE!!
THEY'RE CRACKING DOWN HARDER THAN EVER THESE DAYS......
WHICH MEANS WE'RE RISKING LIFE AND LIMB...!
DON'T BE MAD.
A BEAUTY LIKE YOU SHOULD NEVER FROWN.
AND I DIDN'T HAVE A CHOICE.
I HAD TO RESCUE *THOSE TWO* WITHOUT CAUSING A SCENE...
AAAH...
NOW THIS IS LIVING.
BURRRP!
WHOA!!
YOU'RE SOMETHIN' ELSE, KID!!
DRINKIN' MORE'N ANYONE HERE!!
I NEEDED TO BRIBE THE MONKS TO GET THEM OUTTA THERE.

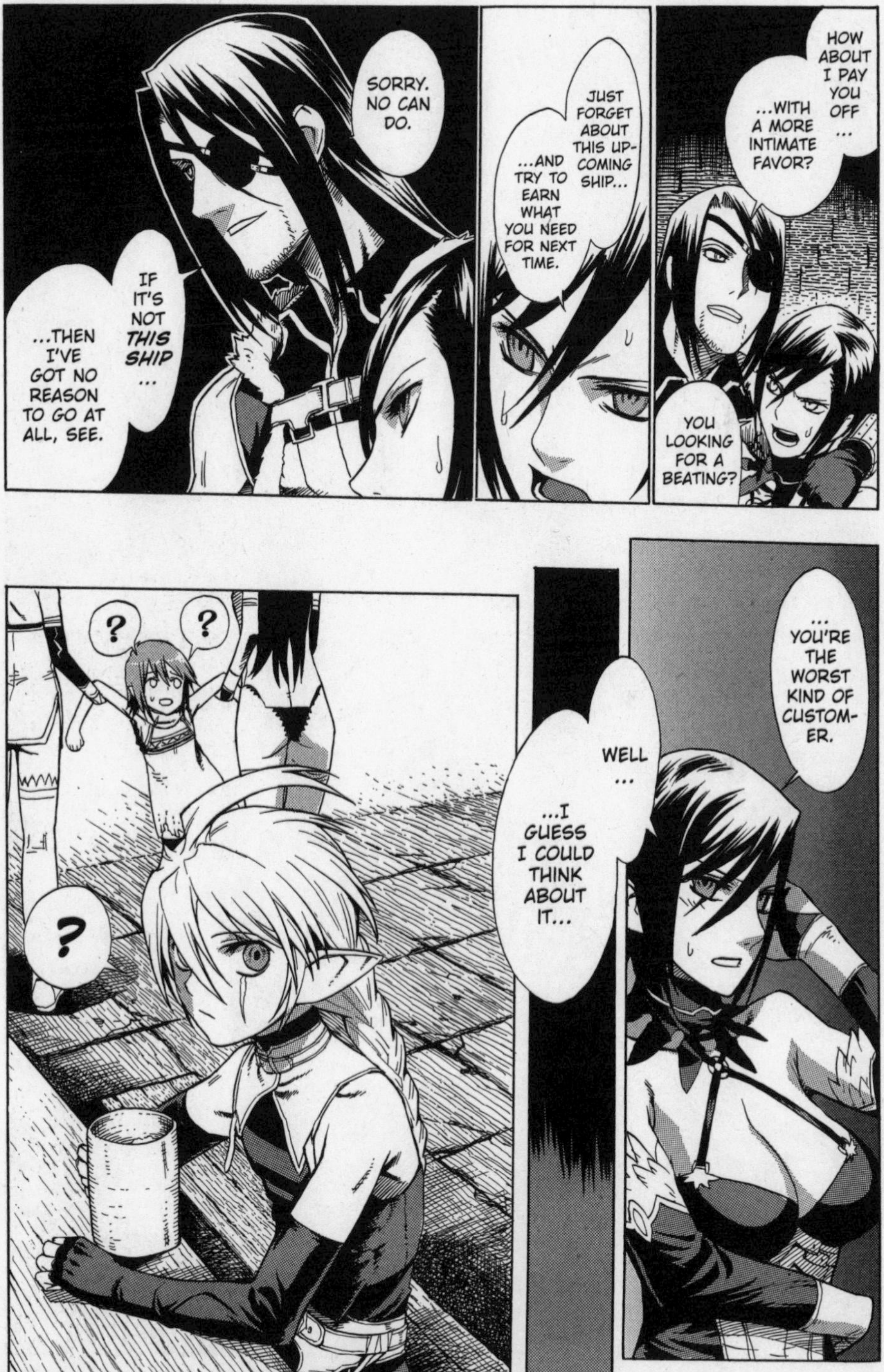
HOW ABOUT I PAY YOU OFF ...
...WITH A MORE INTIMATE FAVOR?
YOU LOOKING FOR A BEATING?
JUST FORGET ABOUT THIS UP-COMING SHIP...
...AND TRY TO EARN WHAT YOU NEED FOR NEXT TIME.
SORRY. NO CAN DO.
IF IT'S NOT *THIS SHIP* ...
...THEN I'VE GOT NO REASON TO GO AT ALL, SEE.
... YOU'RE THE WORST KIND OF CUSTOM-ER.
WELL ...
...I GUESS I COULD THINK ABOUT IT...
?
?
?

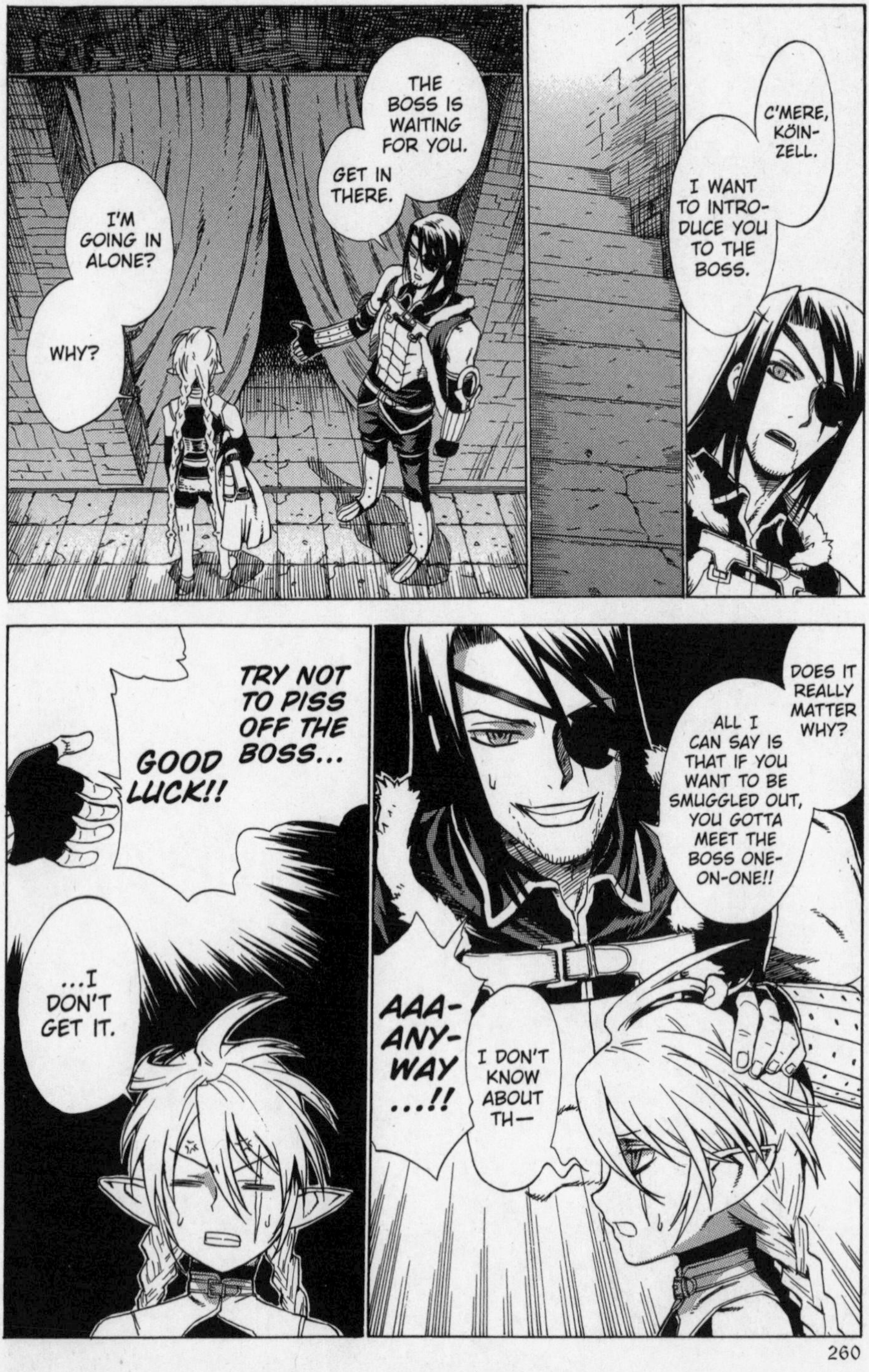
C'MERE, KÖIN-ZELL.
I WANT TO INTRO-DUCE YOU TO THE BOSS.
THE BOSS IS WAITING FOR YOU.
GET IN THERE.
I'M GOING IN ALONE?
WHY?
DOES IT REALLY MATTER WHY?
ALL I CAN SAY IS THAT IF YOU WANT TO BE SMUGGLED OUT, YOU GOTTA MEET THE BOSS ONE-ON-ONE!!
I DON'T KNOW ABOUT TH—
AAA-ANY-WAY...!!
TRY NOT TO PISS OFF THE BOSS...
GOOD LUCK!!
...I DON'T GET IT.

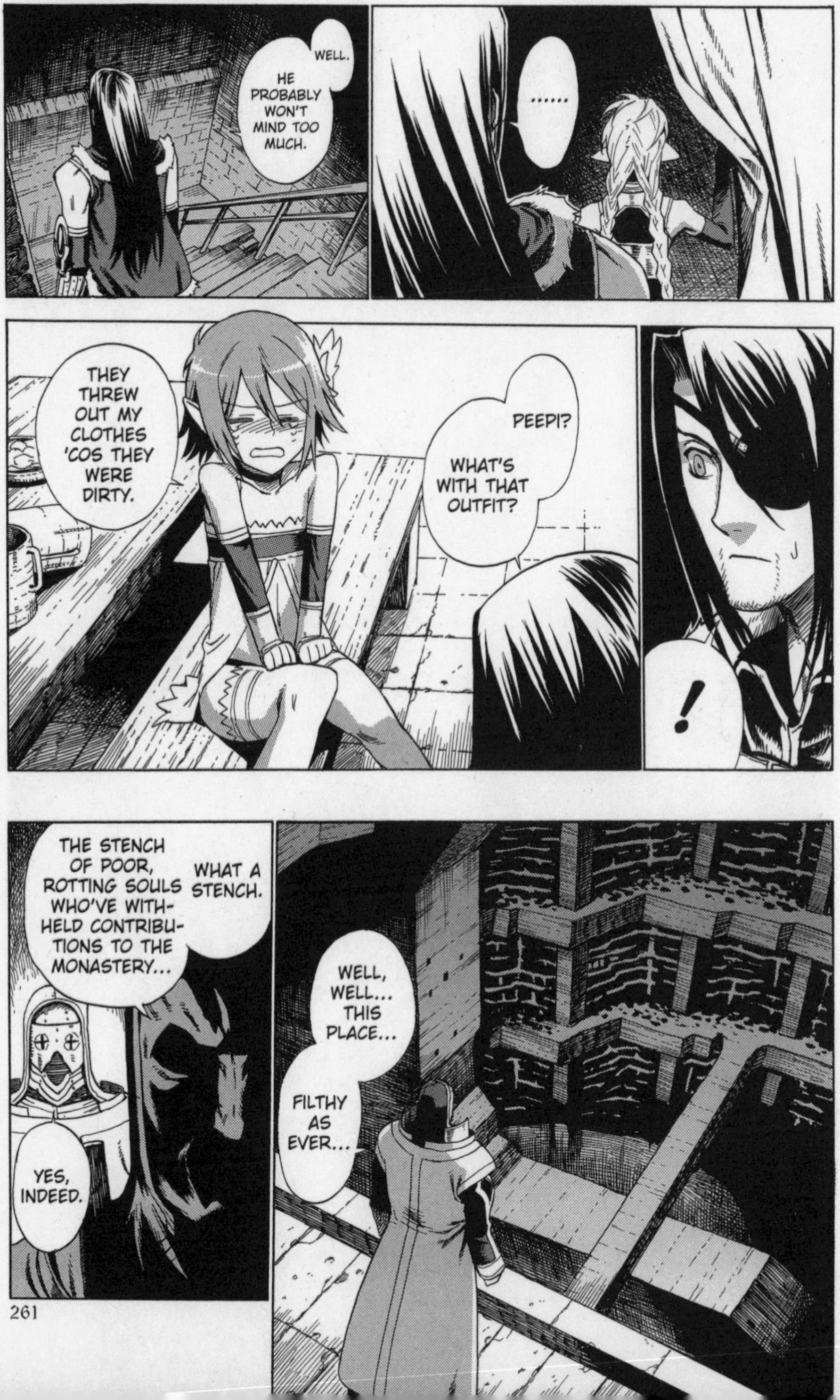
......
WELL.
HE PROBABLY WON'T MIND TOO MUCH.
!
PEEPI?
WHAT'S WITH THAT OUTFIT?
THEY THREW OUT MY CLOTHES 'COS THEY WERE DIRTY.
WELL, WELL... THIS PLACE...
FILTHY AS EVER...
WHAT A STENCH.
THE STENCH OF POOR, ROTTING SOULS WHO'VE WITH-HELD CONTRIBU-TIONS TO THE MONASTERY...
YES, INDEED.

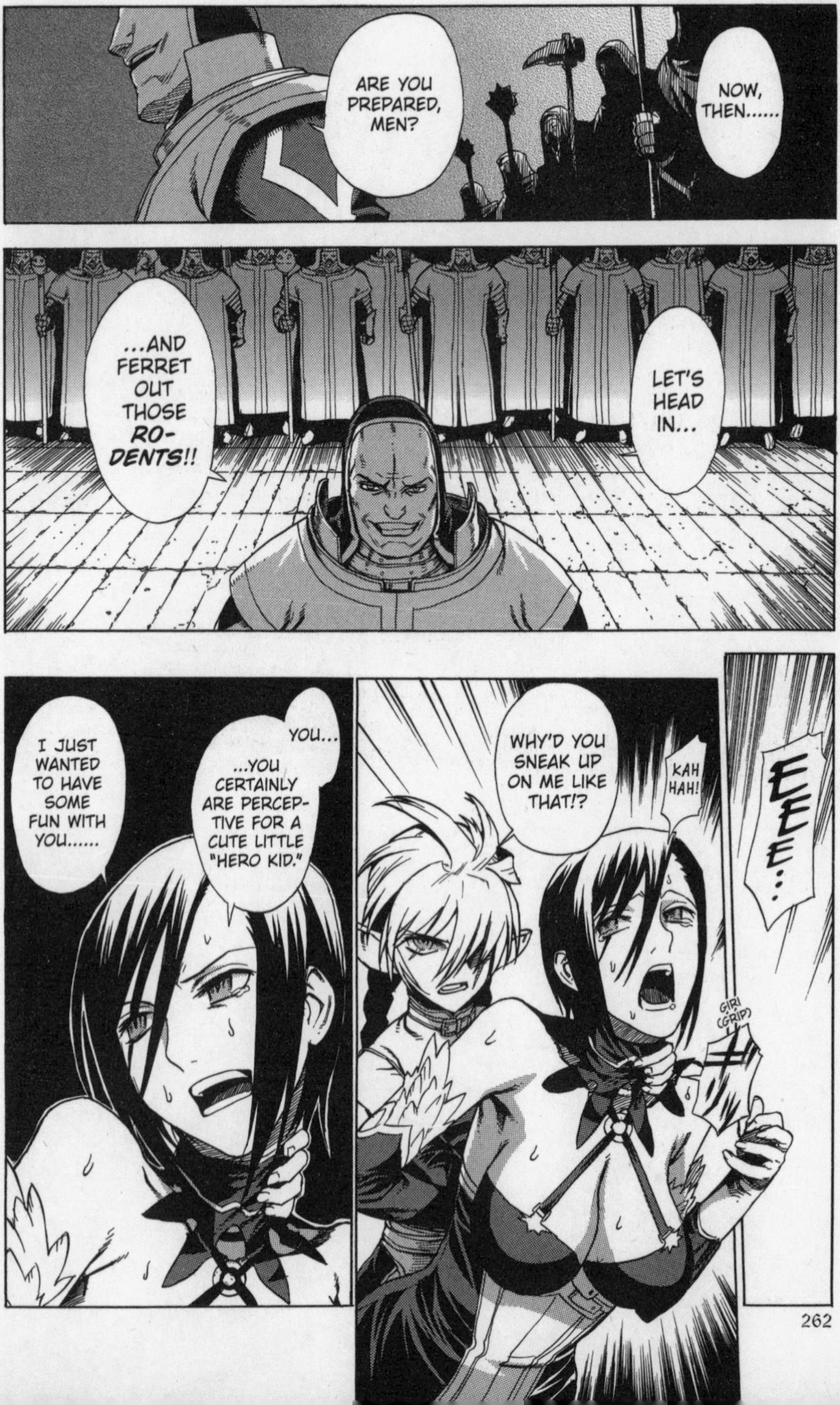
NOW, THEN......
ARE YOU PREPARED, MEN?
LET'S HEAD IN...
...AND FERRET OUT THOSE RO-DENTS!!
EEE...
KAH HAH!
WHY'D YOU SNEAK UP ON ME LIKE THAT!?
GIRI (GRIP)
YOU...
...YOU CERTAINLY ARE PERCEP-TIVE FOR A CUTE LITTLE "HERO KID."
I JUST WANTED TO HAVE SOME FUN WITH YOU......

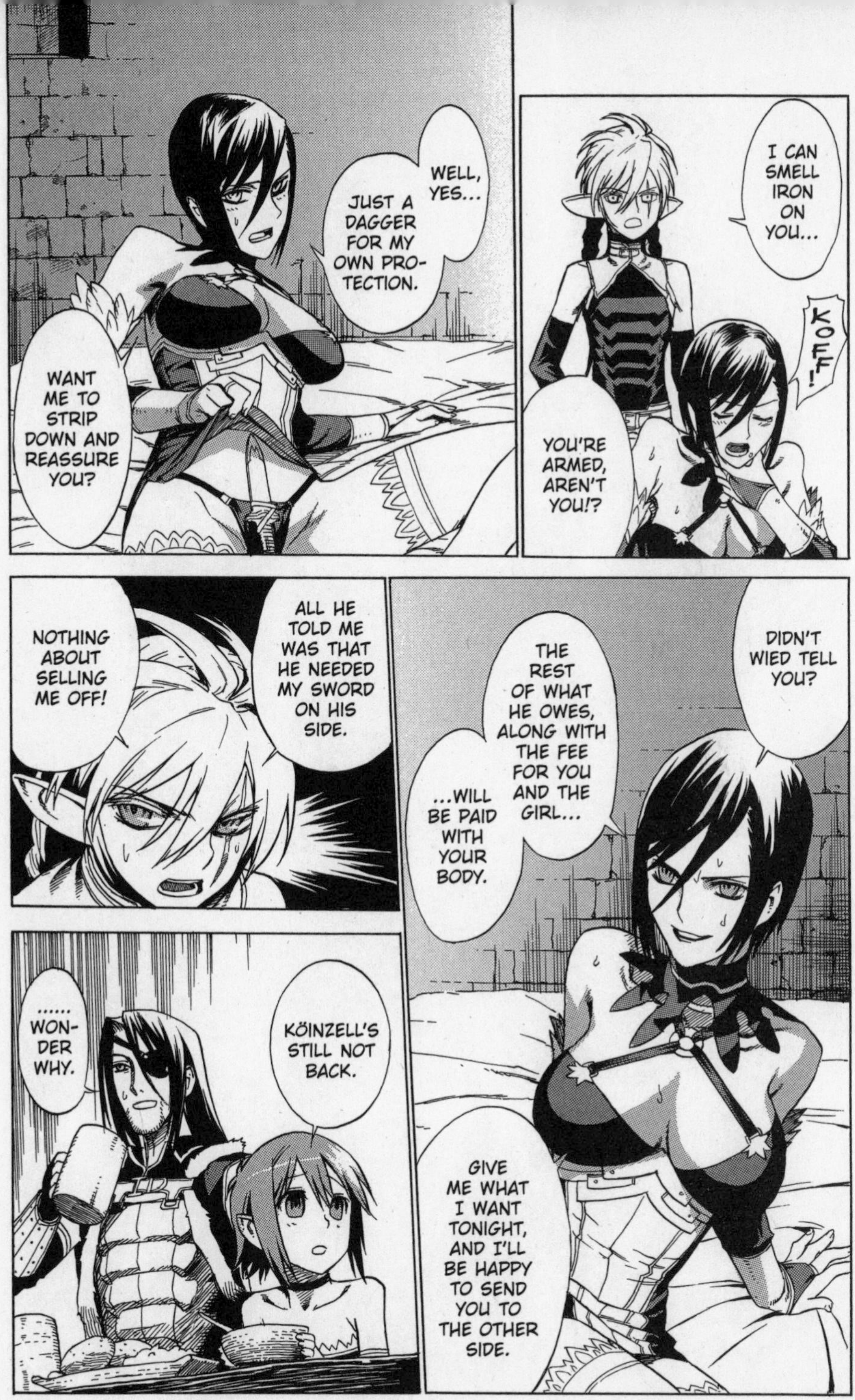
I CAN SMELL IRON ON YOU...
KOFF!
YOU'RE ARMED, AREN'T YOU!?
WELL, YES...
JUST A DAGGER FOR MY OWN PROTECTION.
WANT ME TO STRIP DOWN AND REASSURE YOU?
DIDN'T WIED TELL YOU?
THE REST OF WHAT HE OWES, ALONG WITH THE FEE FOR YOU AND THE GIRL...
...WILL BE PAID WITH YOUR BODY.
GIVE ME WHAT I WANT TONIGHT, AND I'LL BE HAPPY TO SEND YOU TO THE OTHER SIDE.
ALL HE TOLD ME WAS THAT HE NEEDED MY SWORD ON HIS SIDE.
NOTHING ABOUT SELLING ME OFF!
KÖINZELL'S STILL NOT BACK.
......WONDER WHY.

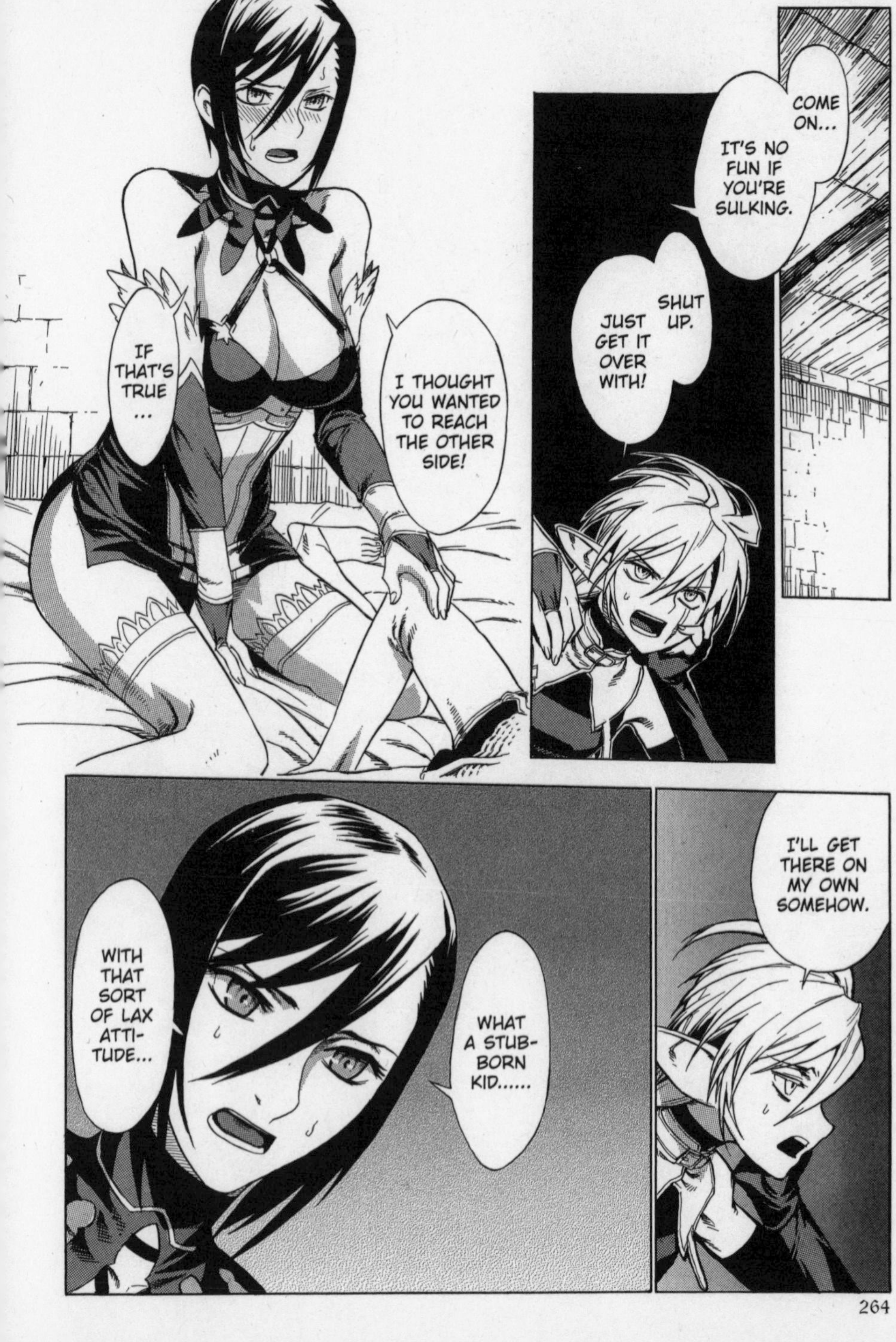
COME ON... IT'S NO FUN IF YOU'RE SULKING.
SHUT UP. JUST GET IT OVER WITH!
I THOUGHT YOU WANTED TO REACH THE OTHER SIDE!
IF THAT'S TRUE ...
I'LL GET THERE ON MY OWN SOMEHOW.
WHAT A STUB-BORN KID......
WITH THAT SORT OF LAX ATTI-TUDE...

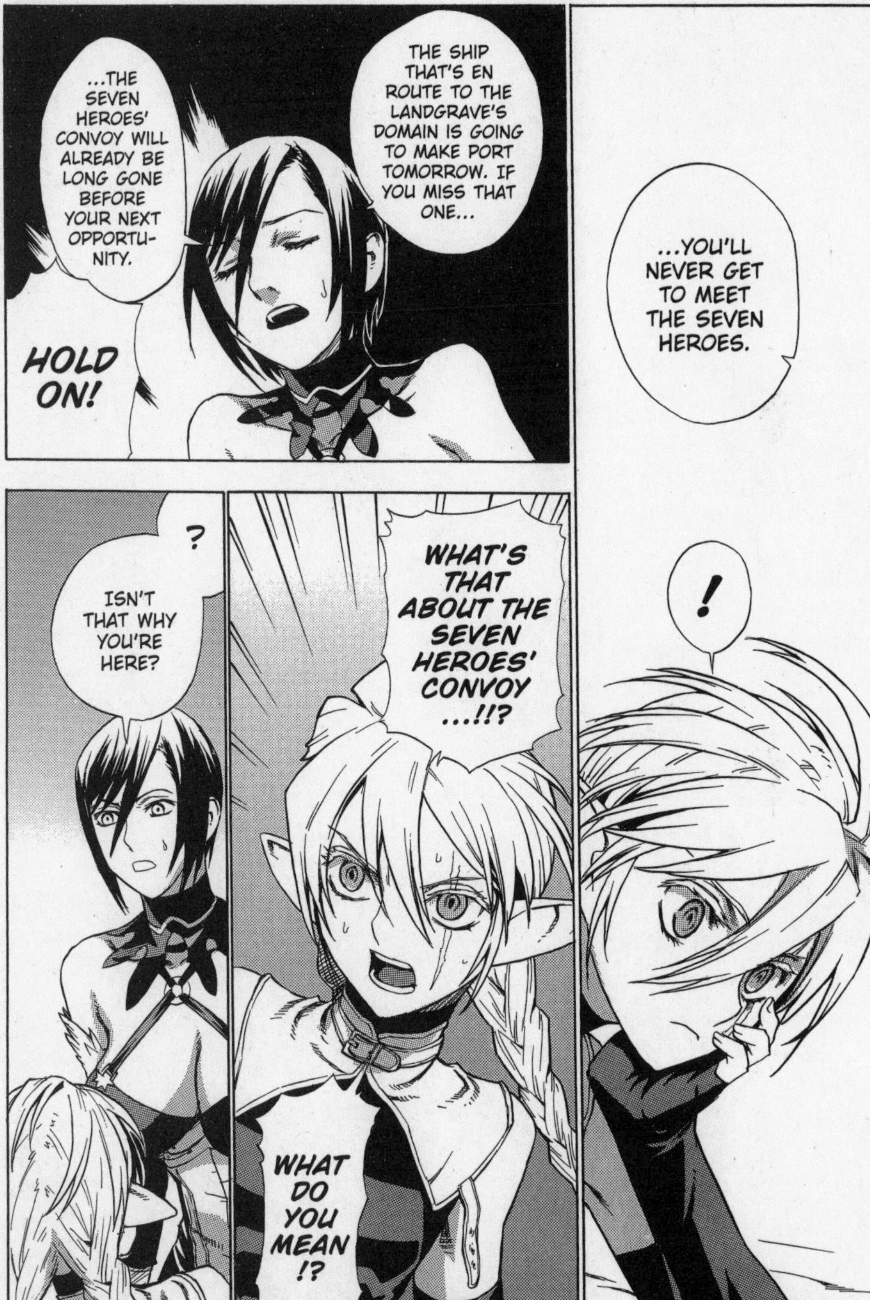
...YOU'LL NEVER GET TO MEET THE SEVEN HEROES.
THE SHIP THAT'S EN ROUTE TO THE LANDGRAVE'S DOMAIN IS GOING TO MAKE PORT TOMORROW. IF YOU MISS THAT ONE...
...THE SEVEN HEROES' CONVOY WILL ALREADY BE LONG GONE BEFORE YOUR NEXT OPPORTU-NITY.
HOLD ON!
!
WHAT'S THAT ABOUT THE SEVEN HEROES' CONVOY ...!!?
WHAT DO YOU MEAN !?
?
ISN'T THAT WHY YOU'RE HERE?

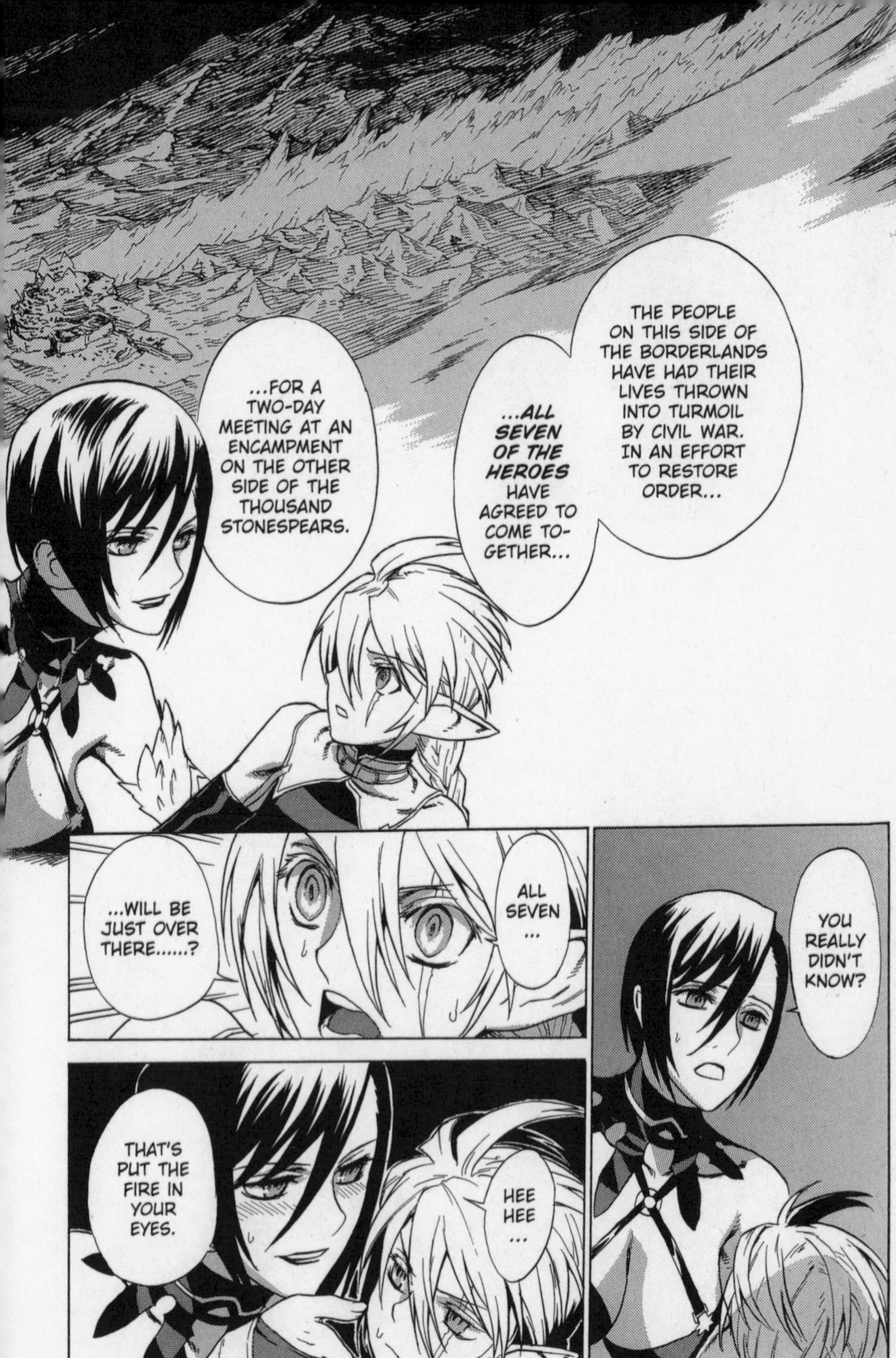
THE PEOPLE ON THIS SIDE OF THE BORDERLANDS HAVE HAD THEIR LIVES THROWN INTO TURMOIL BY CIVIL WAR. IN AN EFFORT TO RESTORE ORDER...
...ALL SEVEN OF THE HEROES HAVE AGREED TO COME TO-GETHER...
...FOR A TWO-DAY MEETING AT AN ENCAMPMENT ON THE OTHER SIDE OF THE THOUSAND STONESPEARS.
YOU REALLY DIDN'T KNOW?
ALL SEVEN ...
...WILL BE JUST OVER THERE......?
HEE HEE ...
THAT'S PUT THE FIRE IN YOUR EYES.

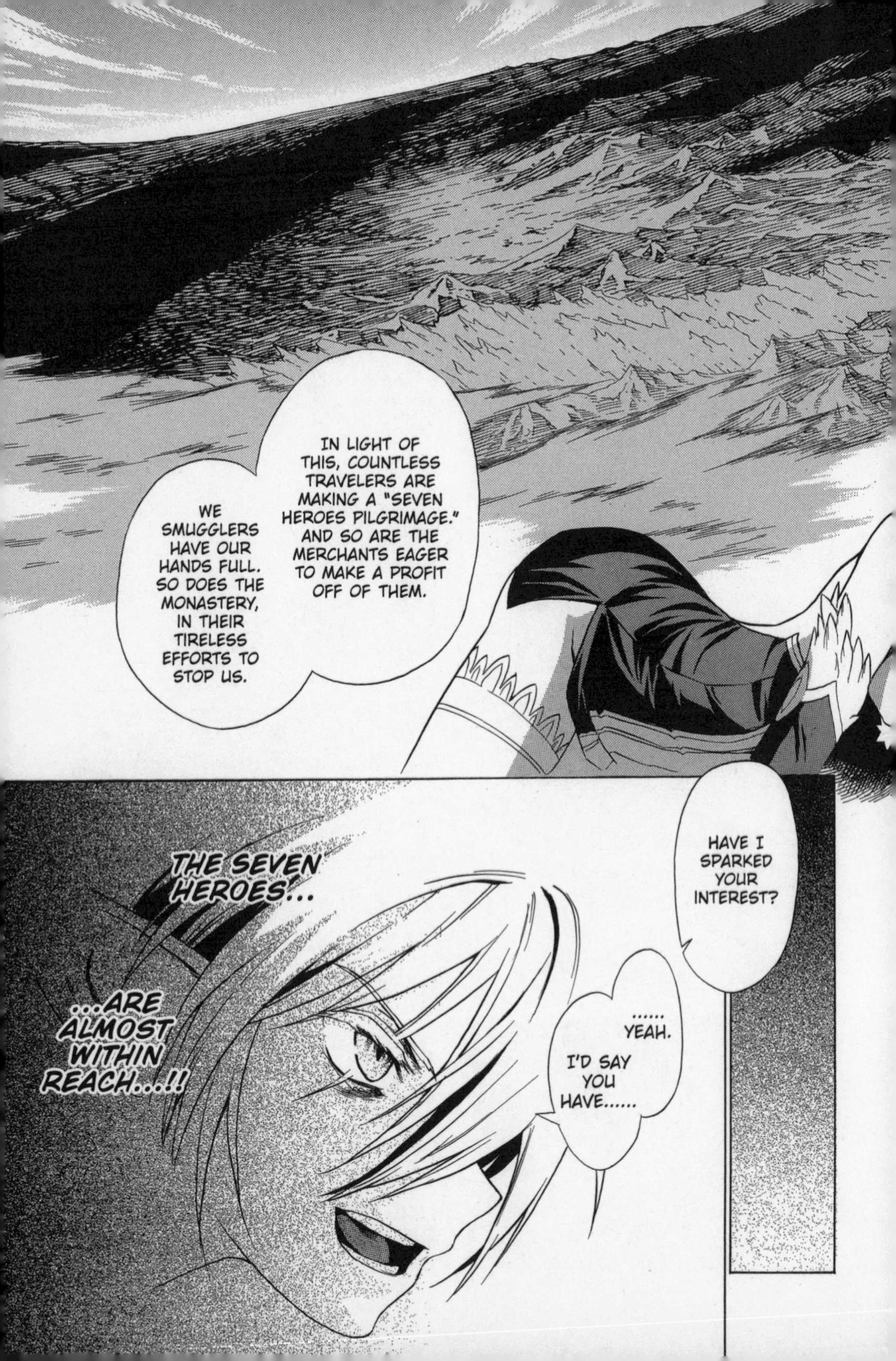
IN LIGHT OF THIS, COUNTLESS TRAVELERS ARE MAKING A "SEVEN HEROES PILGRIMAGE." AND SO ARE THE MERCHANTS EAGER TO MAKE A PROFIT OFF OF THEM.
WE SMUGGLERS HAVE OUR HANDS FULL. SO DOES THE MONASTERY, IN THEIR TIRELESS EFFORTS TO STOP US.
HAVE I SPARKED YOUR INTEREST?
...... YEAH.
I'D SAY YOU HAVE......
THE SEVEN HEROES'...
...ARE ALMOST WITHIN REACH...!!

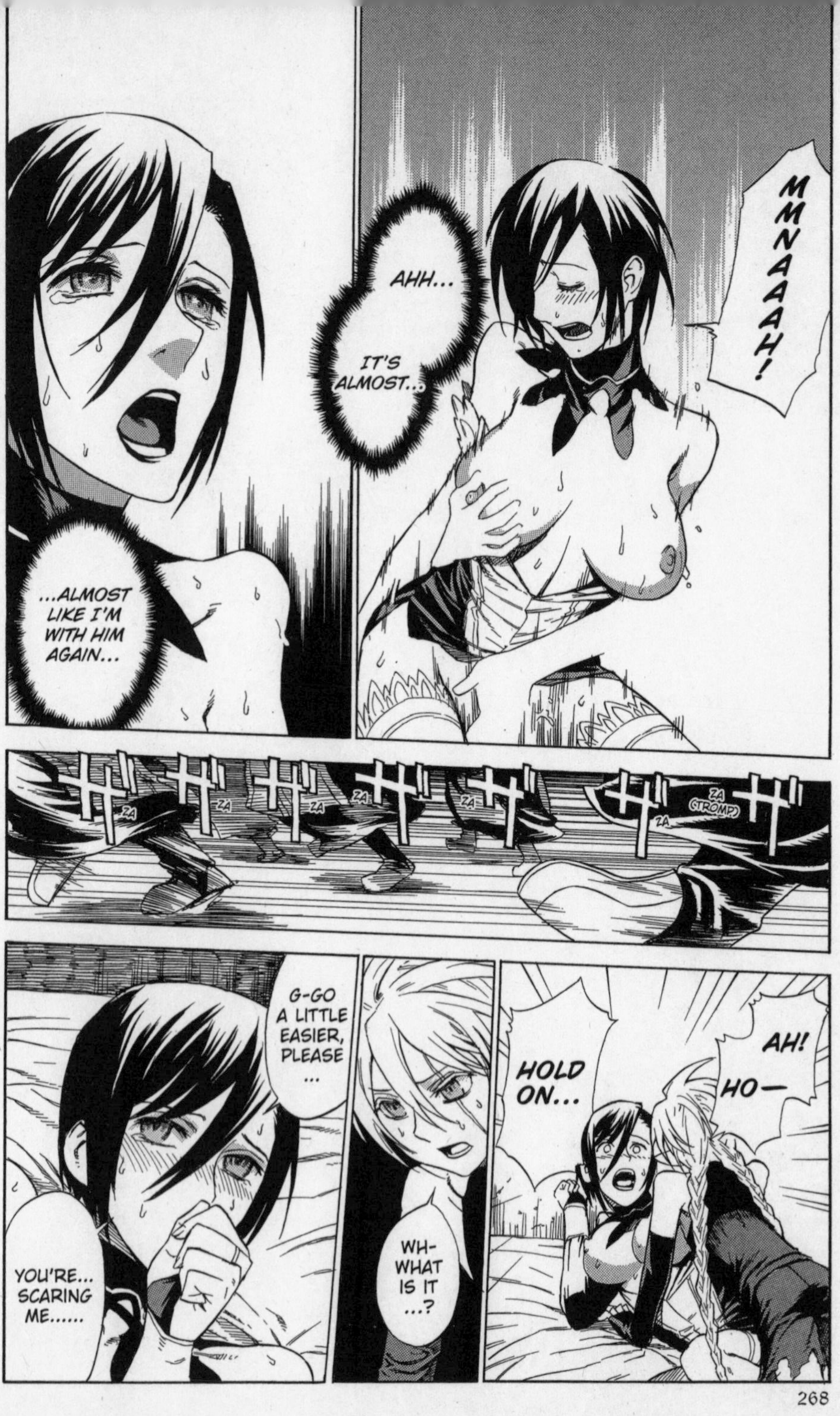
MMNAAAAH!
AHH...
IT'S ALMOST...
...ALMOST LIKE I'M WITH HIM AGAIN...
ザ ZA (TROMP)
ザ ZA
ザ ZA
ザ ZA
ザ ZA
ザ ZA
ザ ZA
AH!
HO—
HOLD ON...
WH-WHAT IS IT...?
G-GO A LITTLE EASIER, PLEASE...
YOU'RE... SCARING ME......

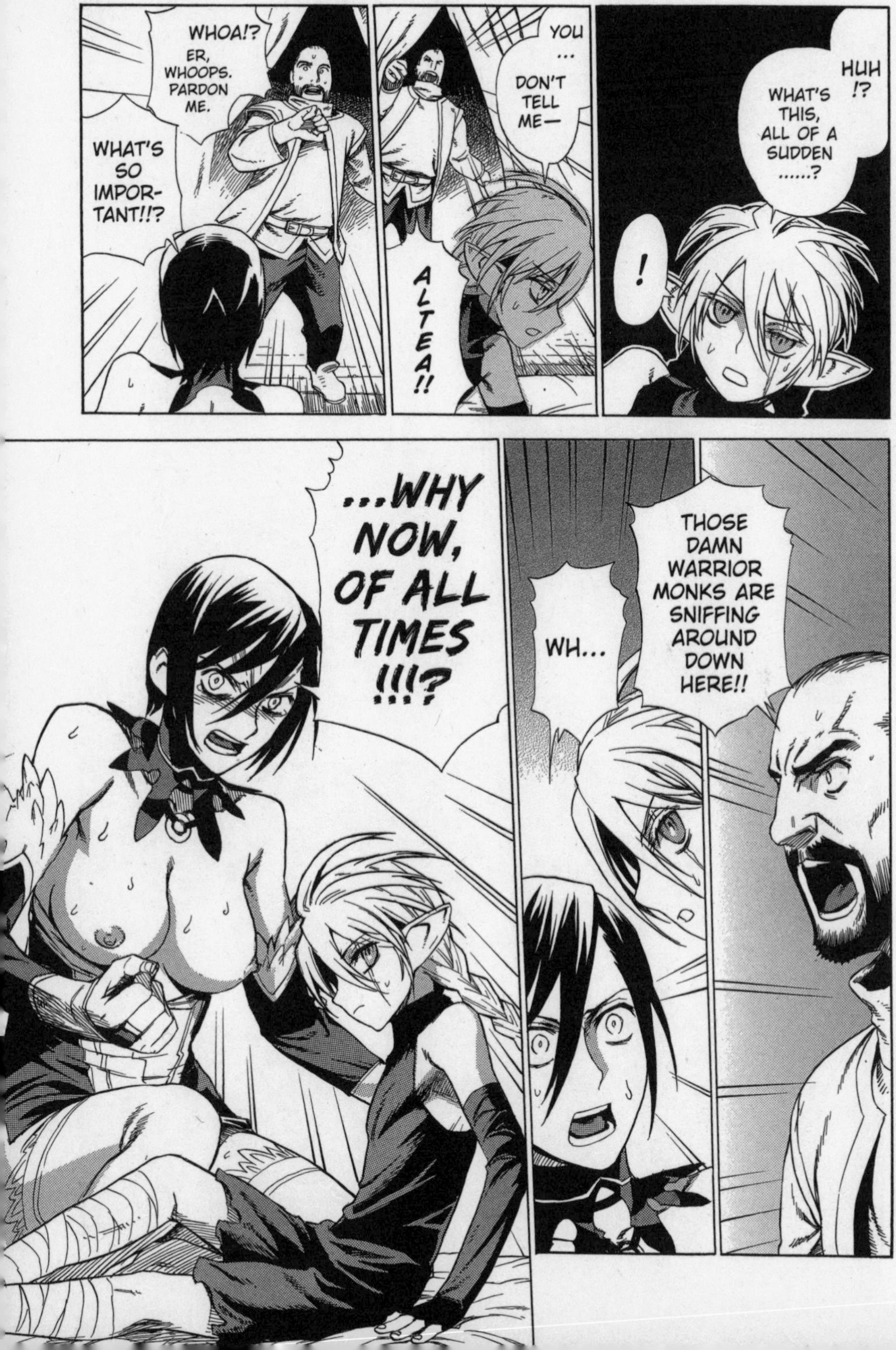
HUH!?
WHAT'S THIS, ALL OF A SUDDEN......?
!
YOU... DON'T TELL ME—
ALTEA!!
WHOA!?
ER, WHOOPS. PARDON ME.
WHAT'S SO IMPORTANT!!?
THOSE DAMN WARRIOR MONKS ARE SNIFFING AROUND DOWN HERE!!
WH...
...WHY NOW, OF ALL TIMES!!!?

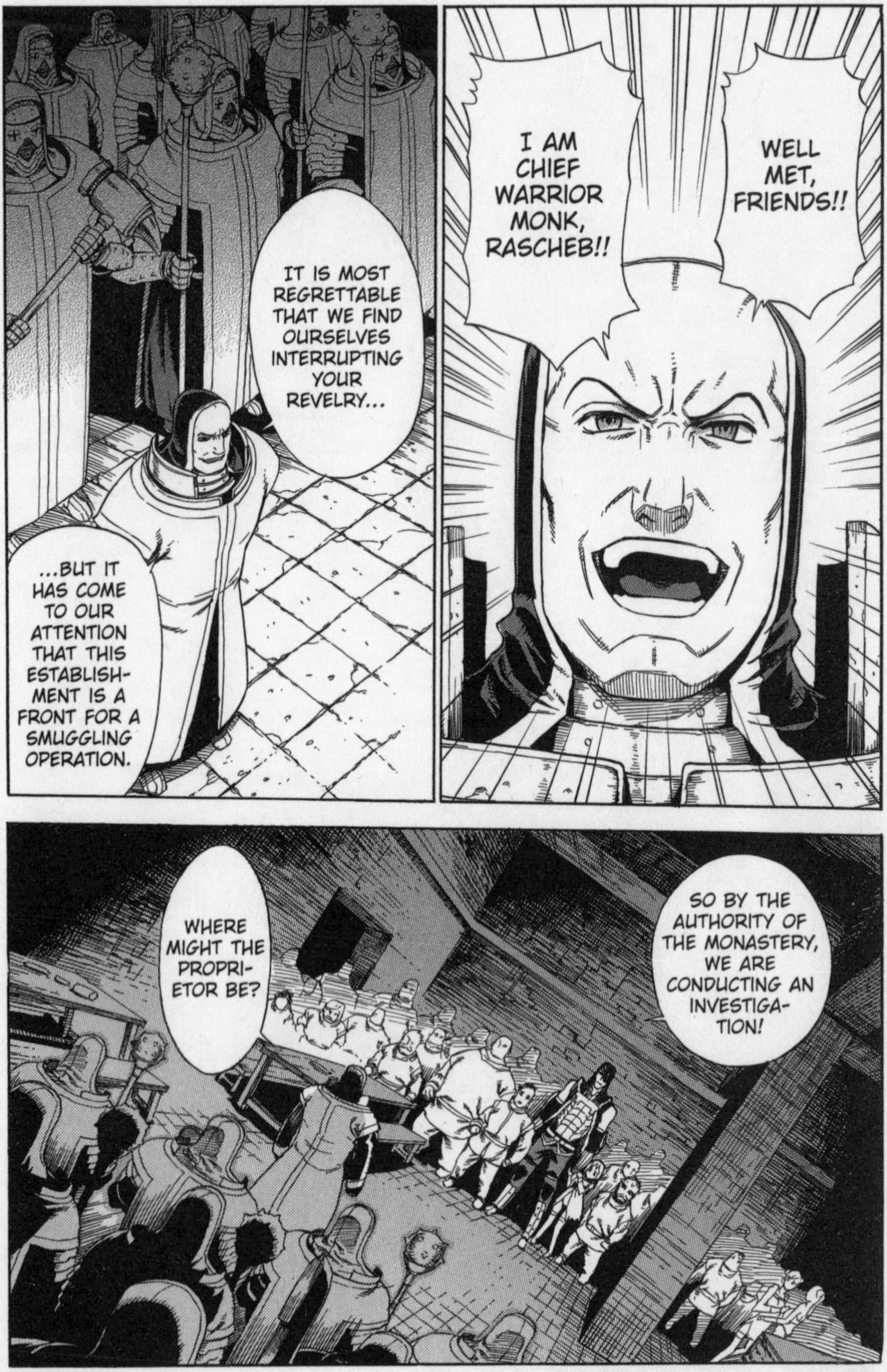
WELL MET, FRIENDS!!
I AM CHIEF WARRIOR MONK, RASCHEB!!
IT IS MOST REGRETTABLE THAT WE FIND OURSELVES INTERRUPTING YOUR REVELRY...
...BUT IT HAS COME TO OUR ATTENTION THAT THIS ESTABLISH-MENT IS A FRONT FOR A SMUGGLING OPERATION.
SO BY THE AUTHORITY OF THE MONASTERY, WE ARE CONDUCTING AN INVESTIGA-TION!
WHERE MIGHT THE PROPRI-ETOR BE?

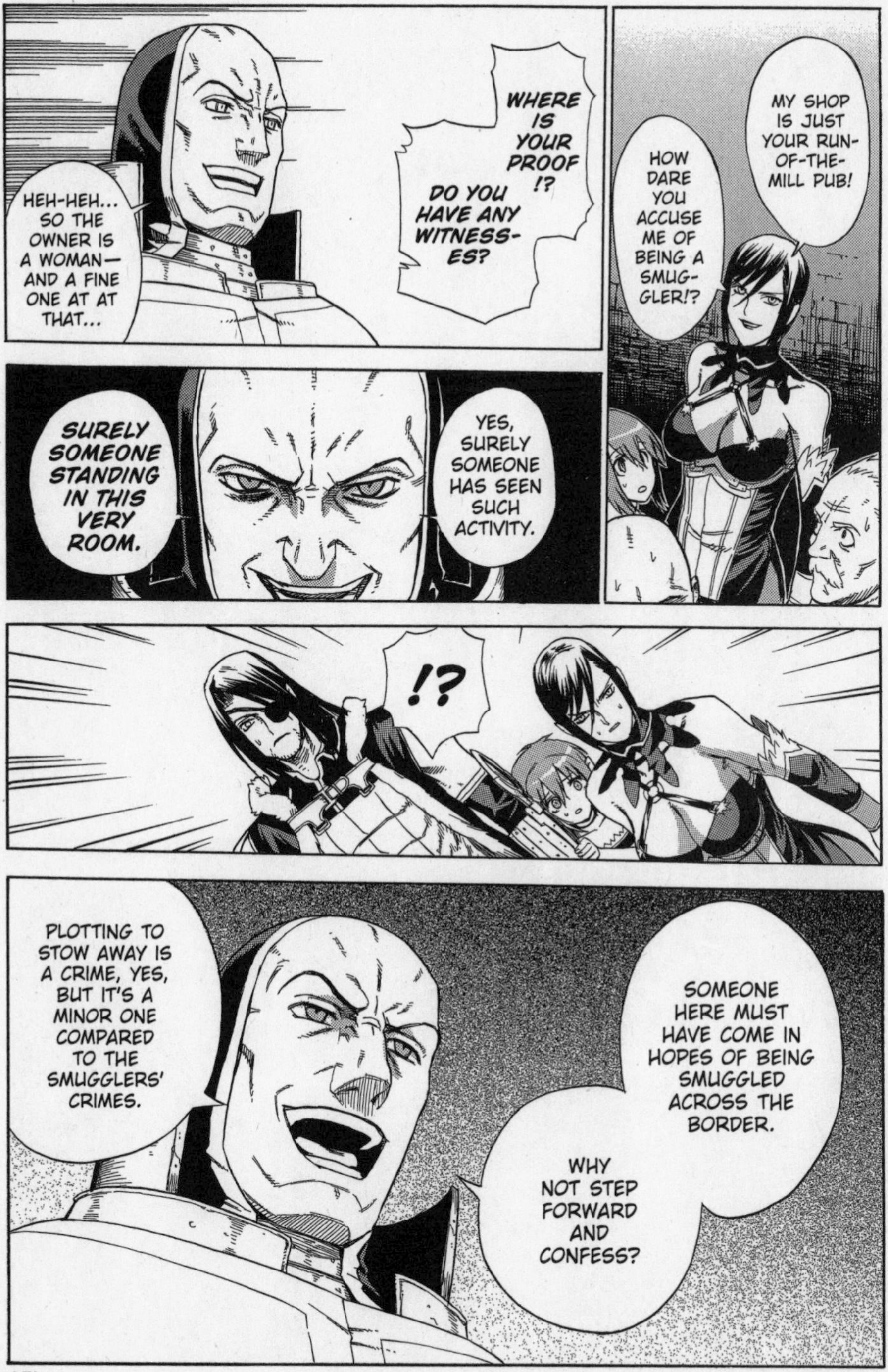
MY SHOP IS JUST YOUR RUN-OF-THE-MILL PUB!
HOW DARE YOU ACCUSE ME OF BEING A SMUGGLER!?
WHERE IS YOUR PROOF!?
DO YOU HAVE ANY WITNESSES?
HEH-HEH... SO THE OWNER IS A WOMAN—AND A FINE ONE AT AT THAT...
YES, SURELY SOMEONE HAS SEEN SUCH ACTIVITY.
SURELY SOMEONE STANDING IN THIS VERY ROOM.
!?
SOMEONE HERE MUST HAVE COME IN HOPES OF BEING SMUGGLED ACROSS THE BORDER.
WHY NOT STEP FORWARD AND CONFESS?
PLOTTING TO STOW AWAY IS A CRIME, YES, BUT IT'S A MINOR ONE COMPARED TO THE SMUGGLERS' CRIMES.

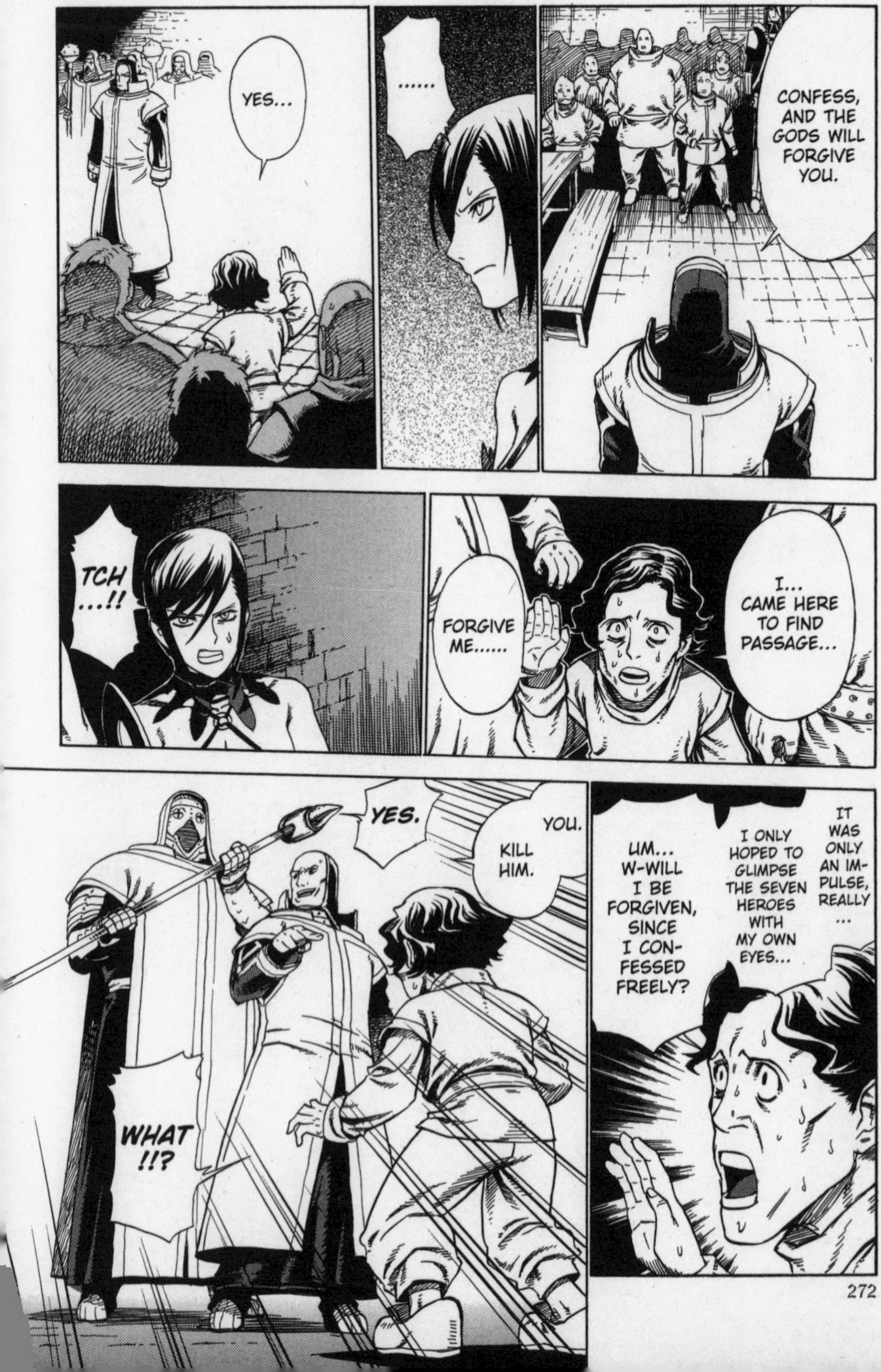
CONFESS, AND THE GODS WILL FORGIVE YOU.
......
YES...
I... CAME HERE TO FIND PASSAGE...
FORGIVE ME......
TCH...!!
IT WAS ONLY AN IMPULSE, REALLY...
I ONLY HOPED TO GLIMPSE THE SEVEN HEROES WITH MY OWN EYES...
UM... W-WILL I BE FORGIVEN, SINCE I CONFESSED FREELY?
YOU.
KILL HIM.
YES.
WHAT!!?

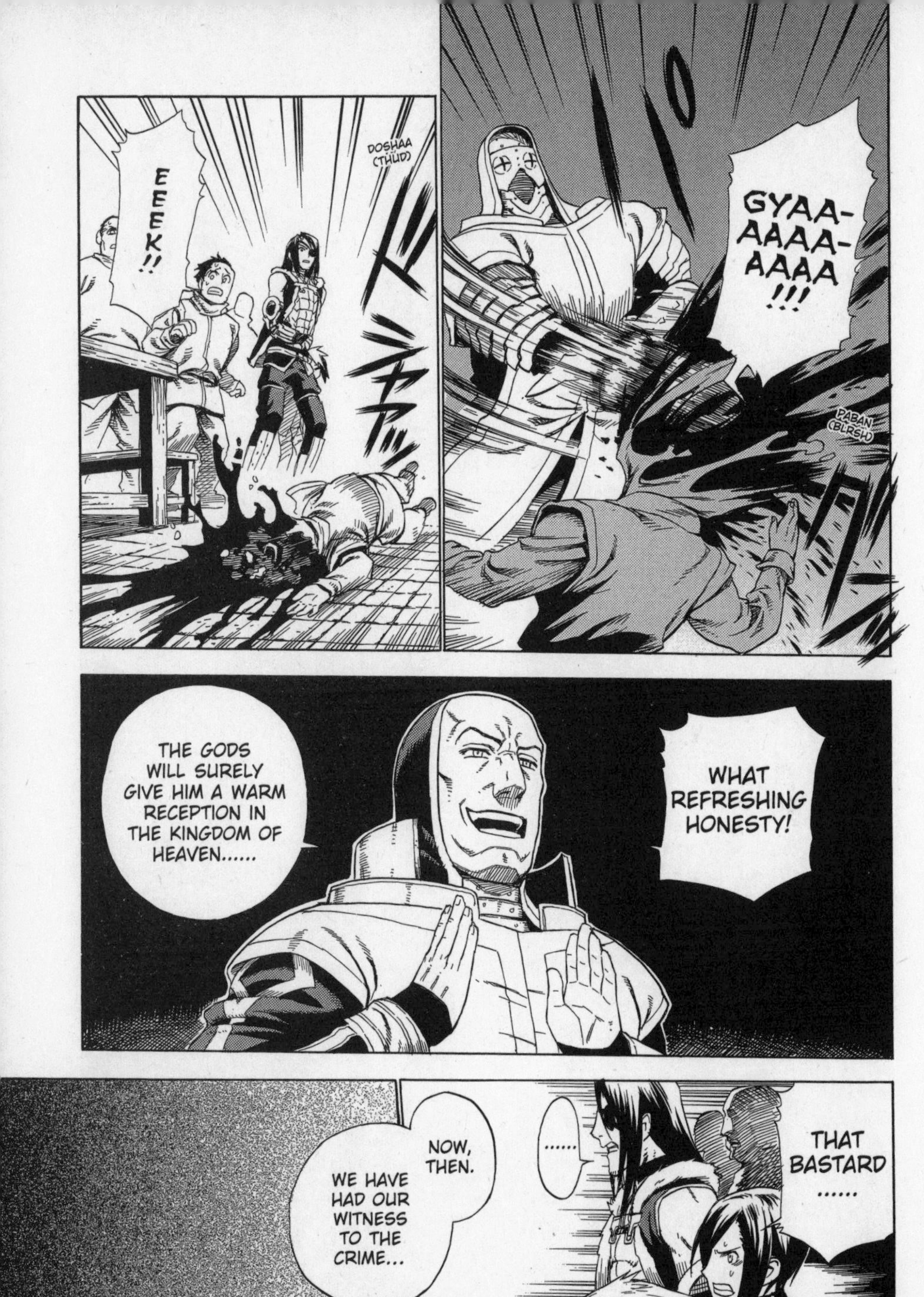
GYAA-AAAA-AAAA!!!
PABAN (BLRSH)
DOSHAA (THUD)
EEEK!!
WHAT REFRESHING HONESTY!
THE GODS WILL SURELY GIVE HIM A WARM RECEPTION IN THE KINGDOM OF HEAVEN......
THAT BASTARD......
......
NOW, THEN.
WE HAVE HAD OUR WITNESS TO THE CRIME...

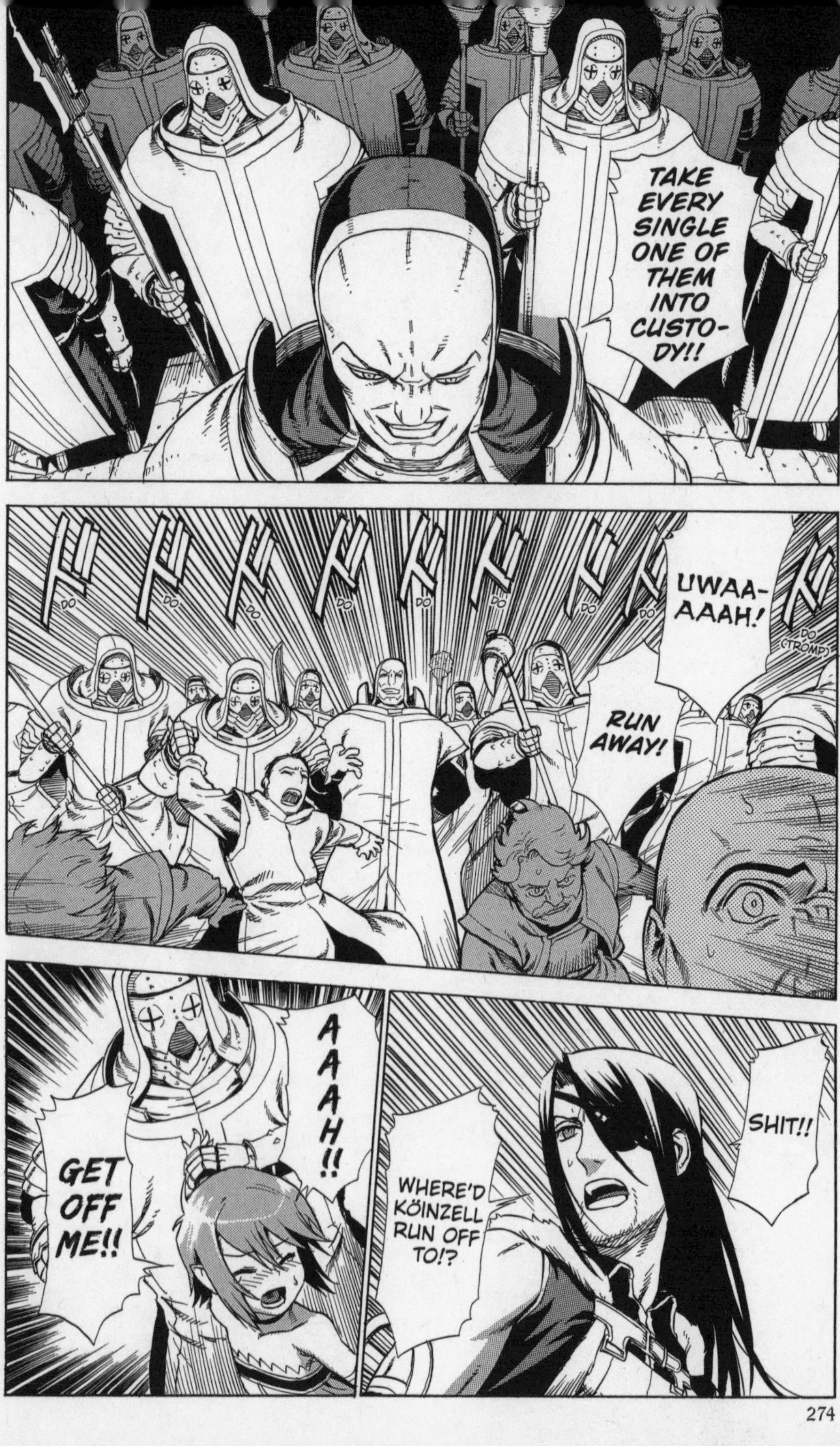
TAKE EVERY SINGLE ONE OF THEM INTO CUSTO-DY!!
ドドドドドドドドド
DO DO DO DO DO DO DO DO DO (TROMP)
UWAA-AAAH!
RUN AWAY!
SHIT!!
WHERE'D KÖINZELL RUN OFF TO!?
AAAAH!!
GET OFF ME!!

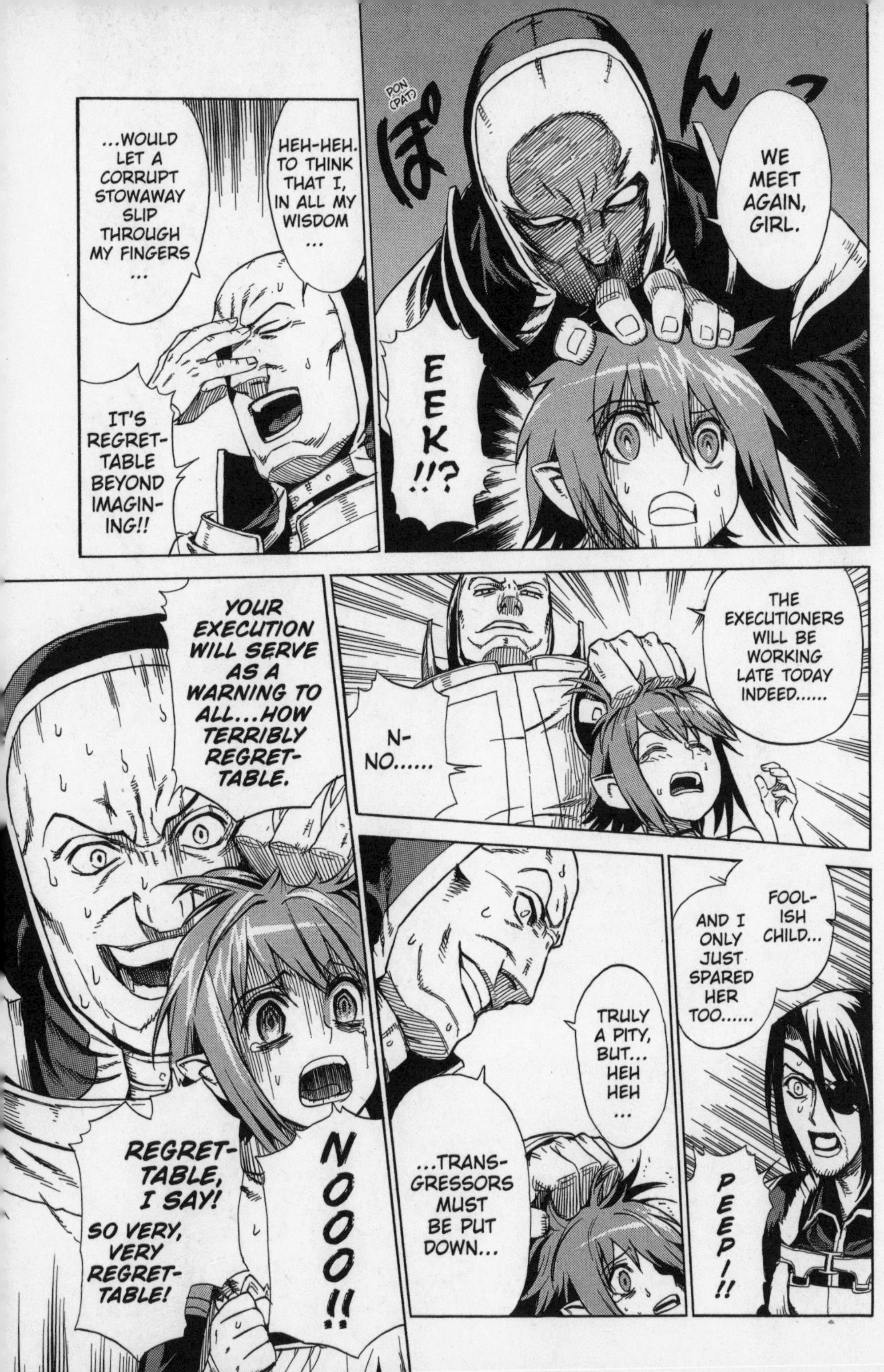
ぽんっ
PON (PAT)
WE MEET AGAIN, GIRL.
EEK!!?
HEH-HEH. TO THINK THAT I, IN ALL MY WISDOM...
...WOULD LET A CORRUPT STOWAWAY SLIP THROUGH MY FINGERS...
IT'S REGRETTABLE BEYOND IMAGINING!!
THE EXECUTIONERS WILL BE WORKING LATE TODAY INDEED......
N-NO......
FOOLISH CHILD...
AND I ONLY JUST SPARED HER TOO......
PEEP!!
TRULY A PITY, BUT... HEH HEH...
...TRANSGRESSORS MUST BE PUT DOWN...
YOUR EXECUTION WILL SERVE AS A WARNING TO ALL...HOW TERRIBLY REGRETTABLE.
REGRETTABLE, I SAY!
SO VERY, VERY REGRETTABLE!
NOOOO!!

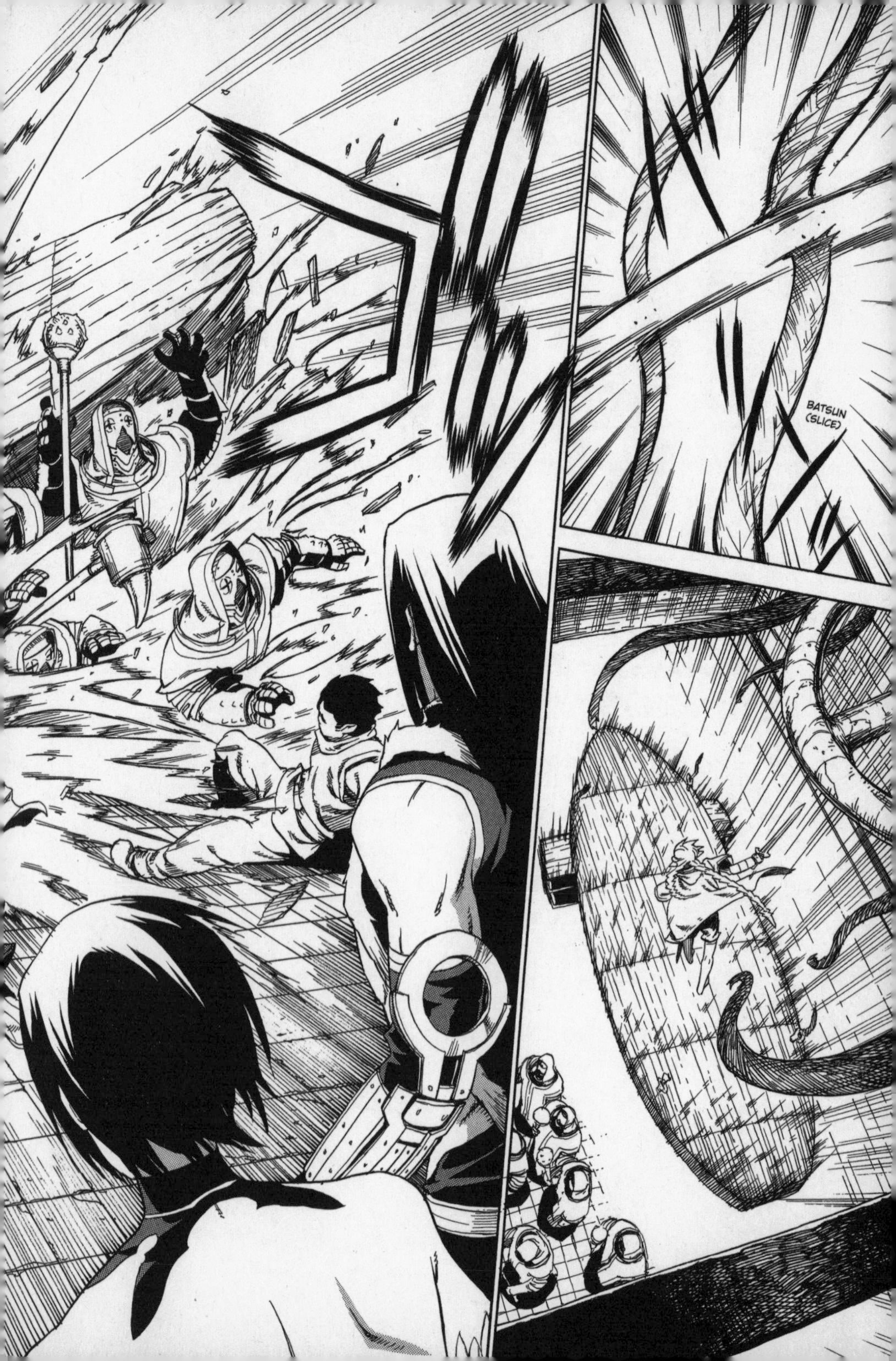
BATSUN
(SLICE)

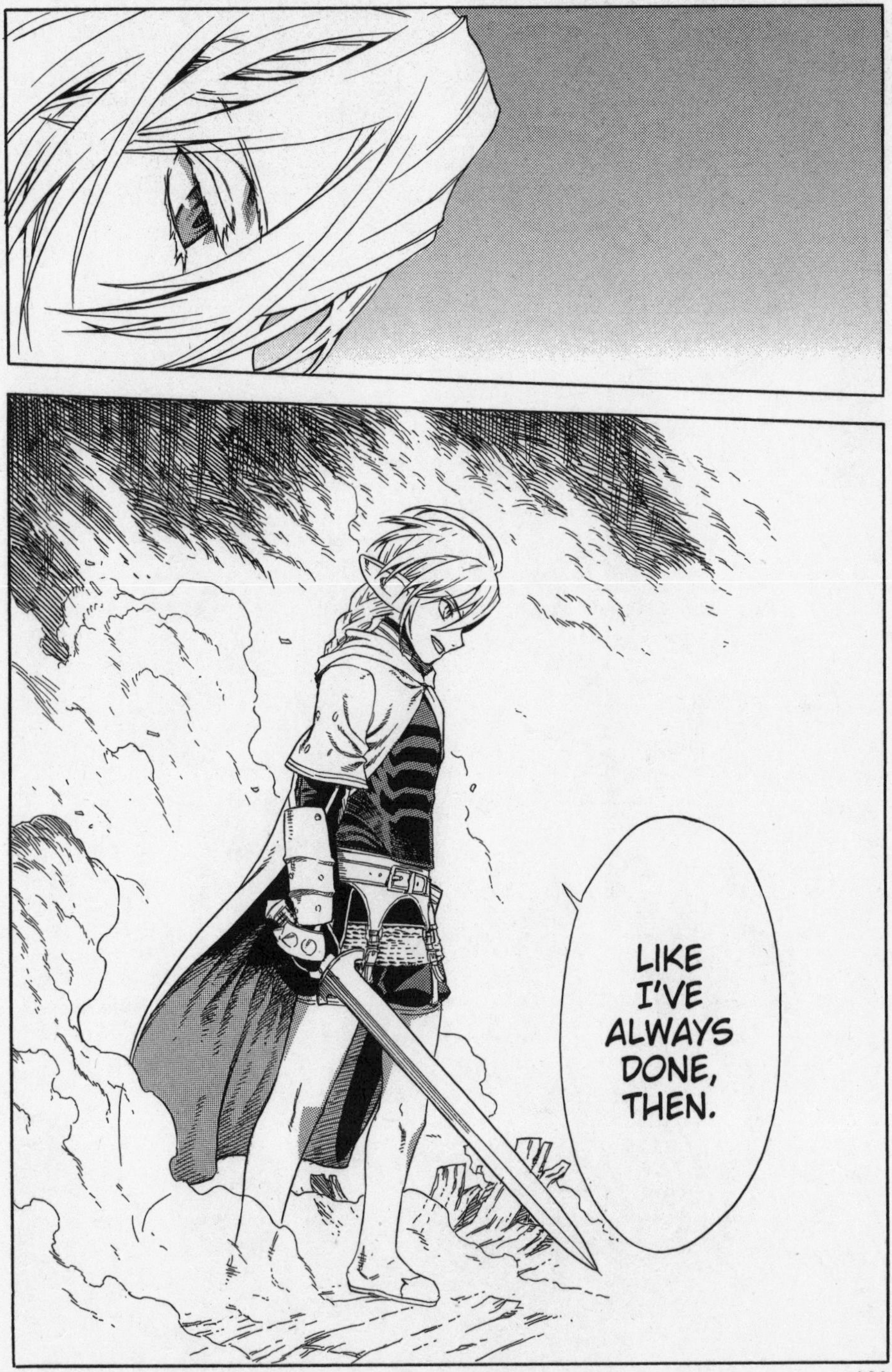
LIKE I'VE ALWAYS DONE, THEN.

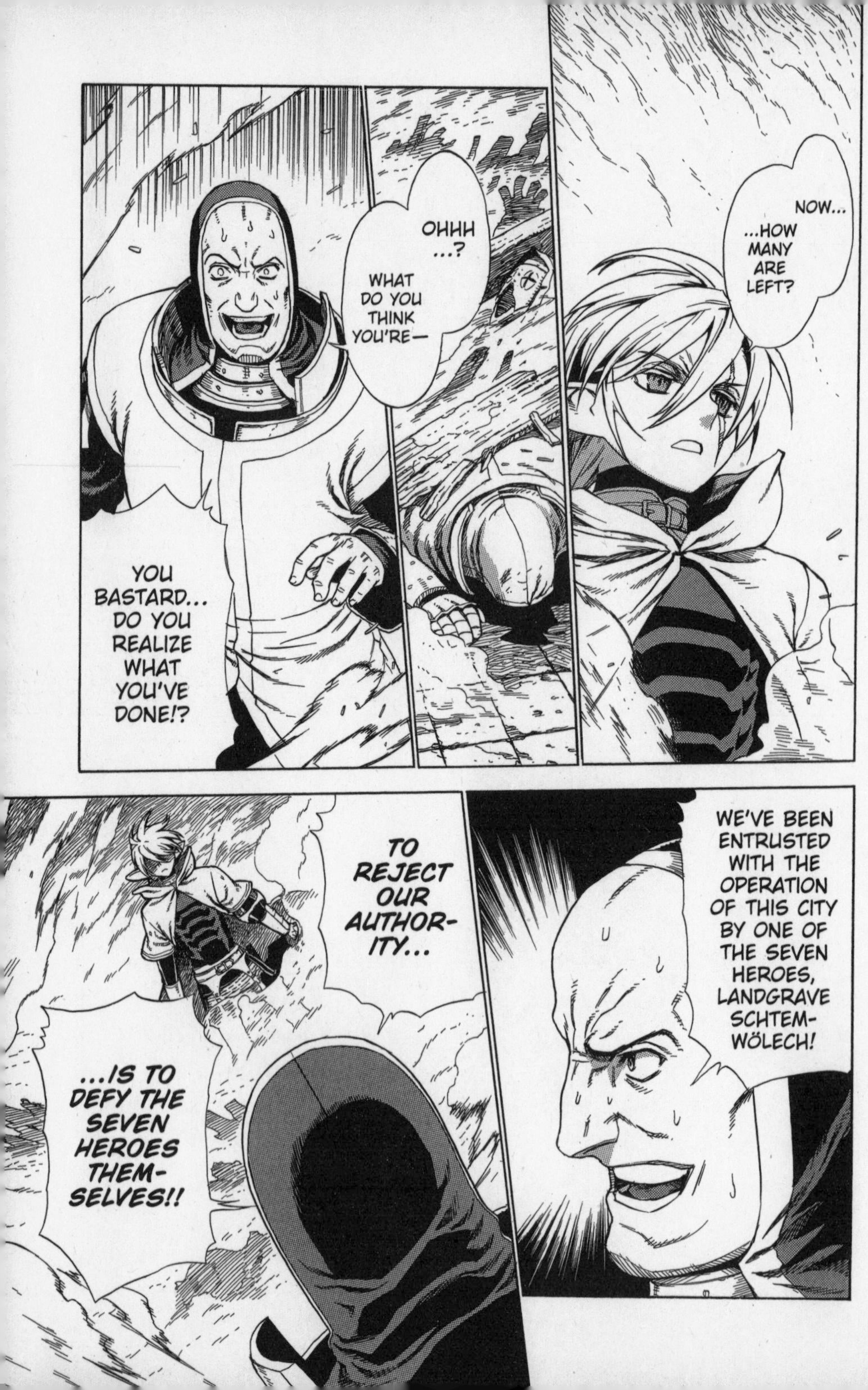
NOW... ...HOW MANY ARE LEFT?
OHHH ...?
WHAT DO YOU THINK YOU'RE—
YOU BASTARD... DO YOU REALIZE WHAT YOU'VE DONE!?
WE'VE BEEN ENTRUSTED WITH THE OPERATION OF THIS CITY BY ONE OF THE SEVEN HEROES, LANDGRAVE SCHTEM-WÖLECH!
TO REJECT OUR AUTHOR-ITY...
...IS TO DEFY THE SEVEN HEROES THEM-SELVES!!

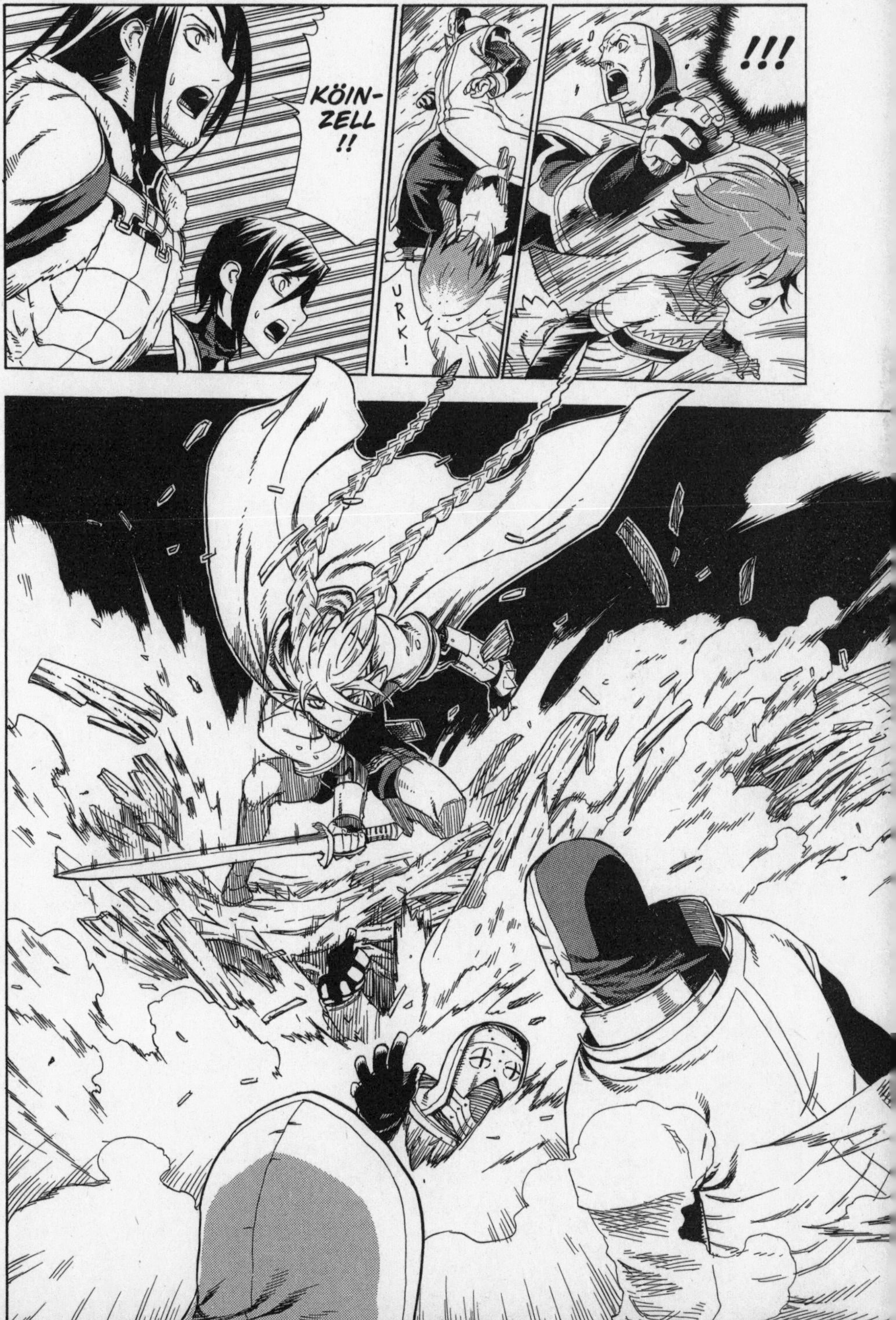
!!!
URK!
KÖIN-ZELL!!

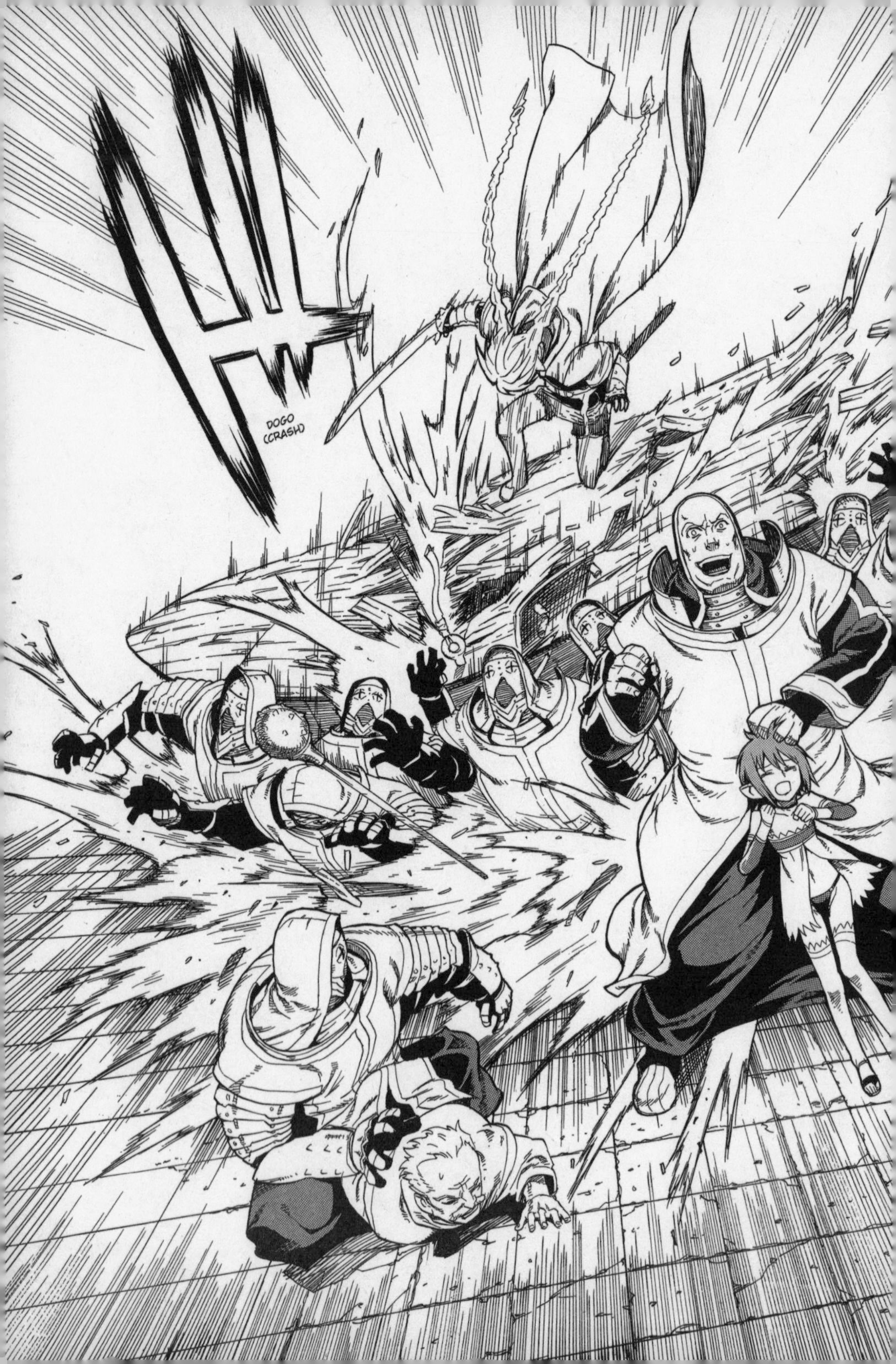
DOGO
(CRASH)

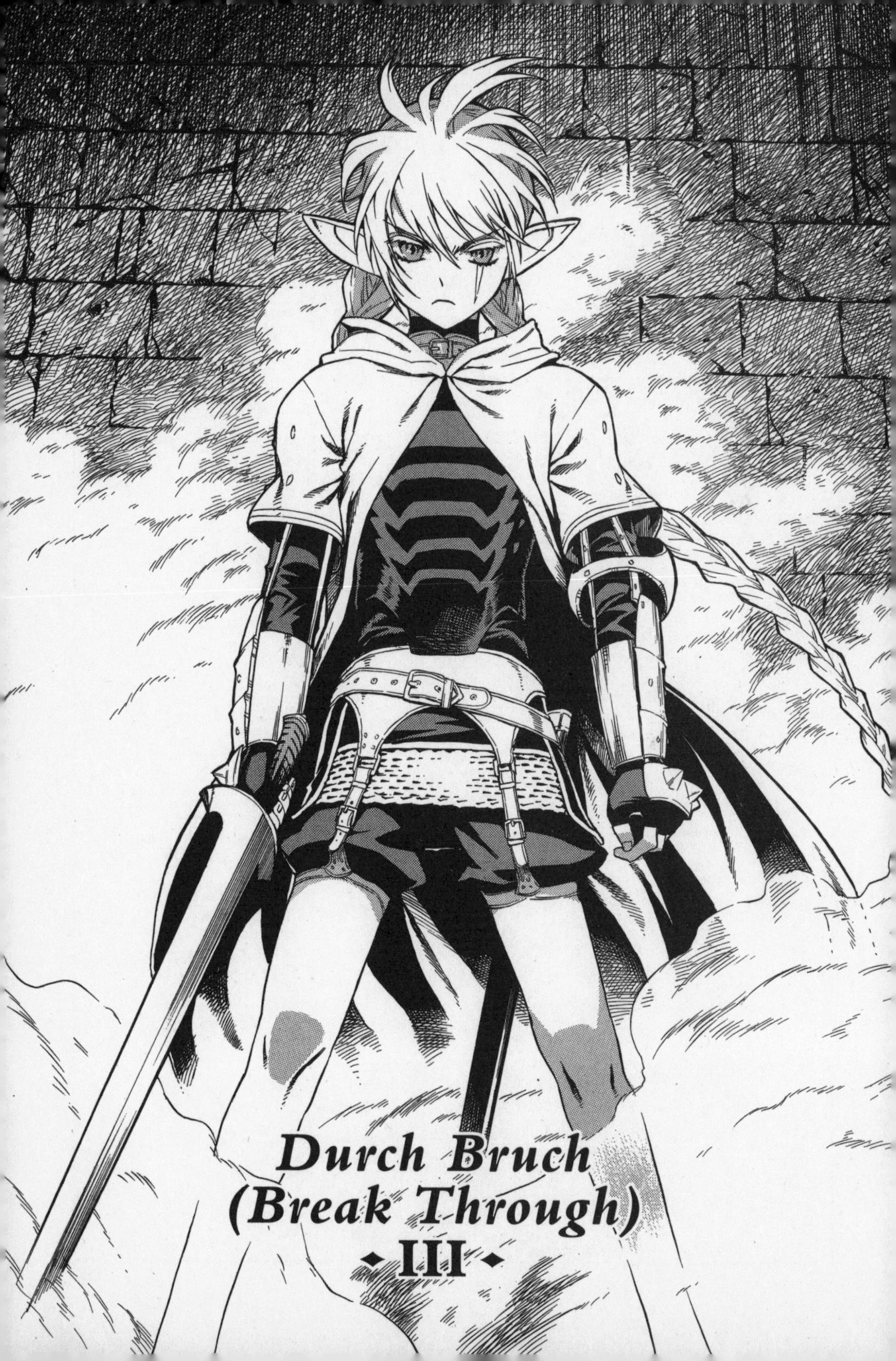
Durch Bruch
(Break Through)
III

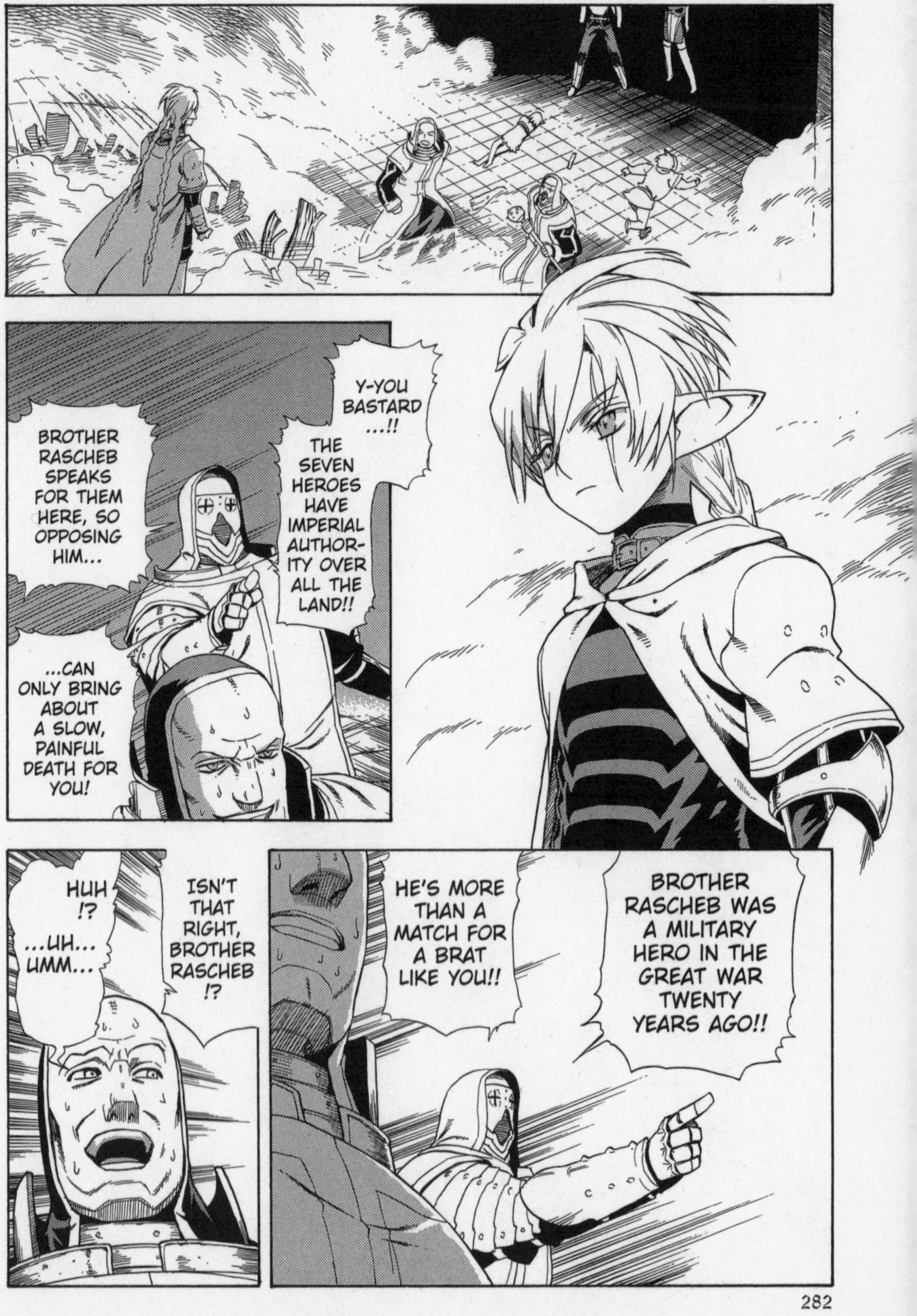
Y-YOU BASTARD...!!
THE SEVEN HEROES HAVE IMPERIAL AUTHORITY OVER ALL THE LAND!!
BROTHER RASCHEB SPEAKS FOR THEM HERE, SO OPPOSING HIM...
...CAN ONLY BRING ABOUT A SLOW, PAINFUL DEATH FOR YOU!
BROTHER RASCHEB WAS A MILITARY HERO IN THE GREAT WAR TWENTY YEARS AGO!!
HE'S MORE THAN A MATCH FOR A BRAT LIKE YOU!!
ISN'T THAT RIGHT, BROTHER RASCHEB!?
HUH!? ...UH... UMM...

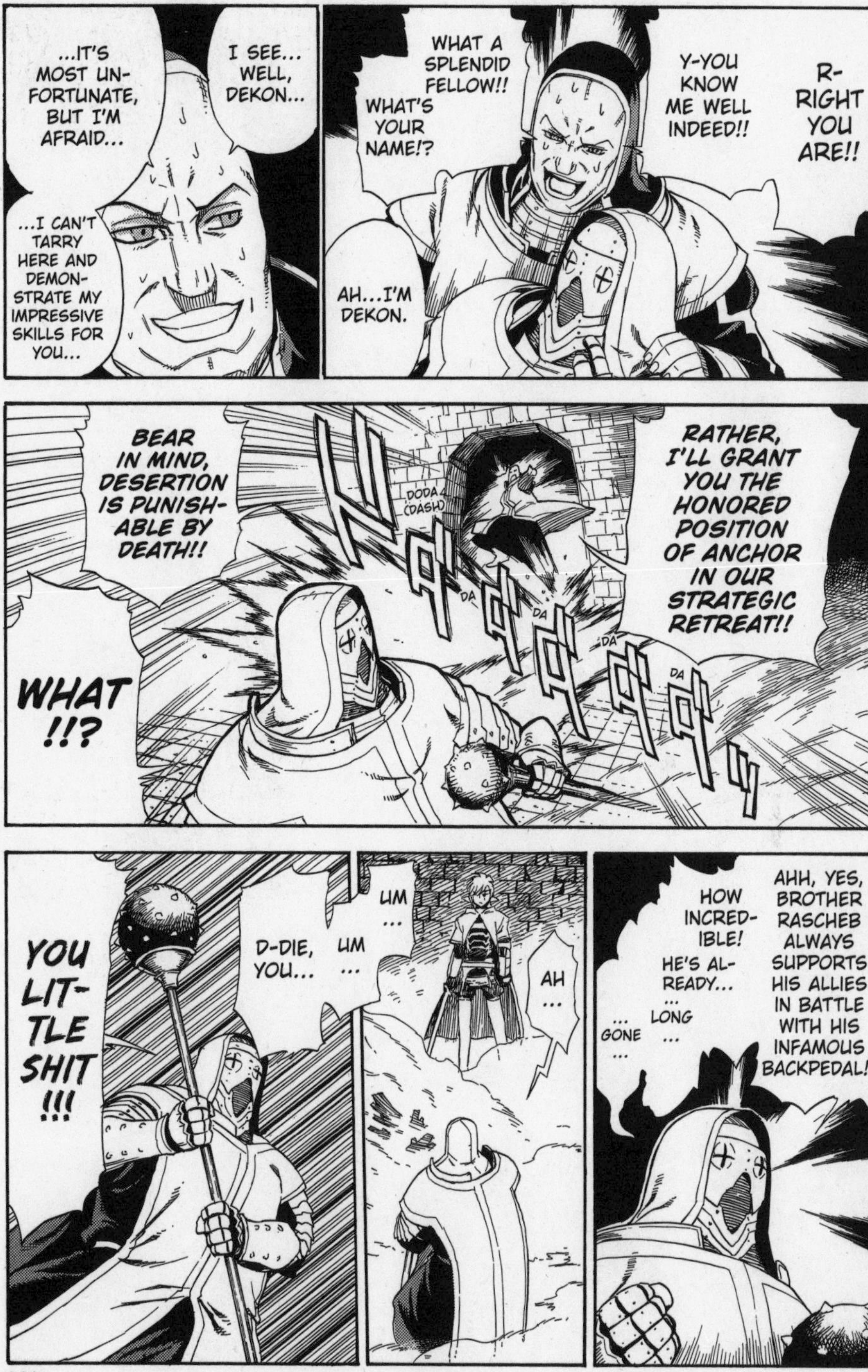
R-RIGHT YOU ARE!!
Y-YOU KNOW ME WELL INDEED!!
WHAT A SPLENDID FELLOW!!
WHAT'S YOUR NAME!?
AH...I'M DEKON.
I SEE... WELL, DEKON...
...IT'S MOST UNFORTUNATE, BUT I'M AFRAID...
...I CAN'T TARRY HERE AND DEMONSTRATE MY IMPRESSIVE SKILLS FOR YOU...
RATHER, I'LL GRANT YOU THE HONORED POSITION OF ANCHOR IN OUR STRATEGIC RETREAT!!
BEAR IN MIND, DESERTION IS PUNISHABLE BY DEATH!!
DODA (DASH)
DA
DA
DA
DA
WHAT!!?
AHH, YES, BROTHER RASCHEB ALWAYS SUPPORTS HIS ALLIES IN BATTLE WITH HIS INFAMOUS BACKPEDAL!!
HOW INCREDIBLE! HE'S ALREADY...
...LONG...
...GONE...
AH...
UM...
UM...
D-DIE, YOU...
YOU LITTLE SHIT!!!

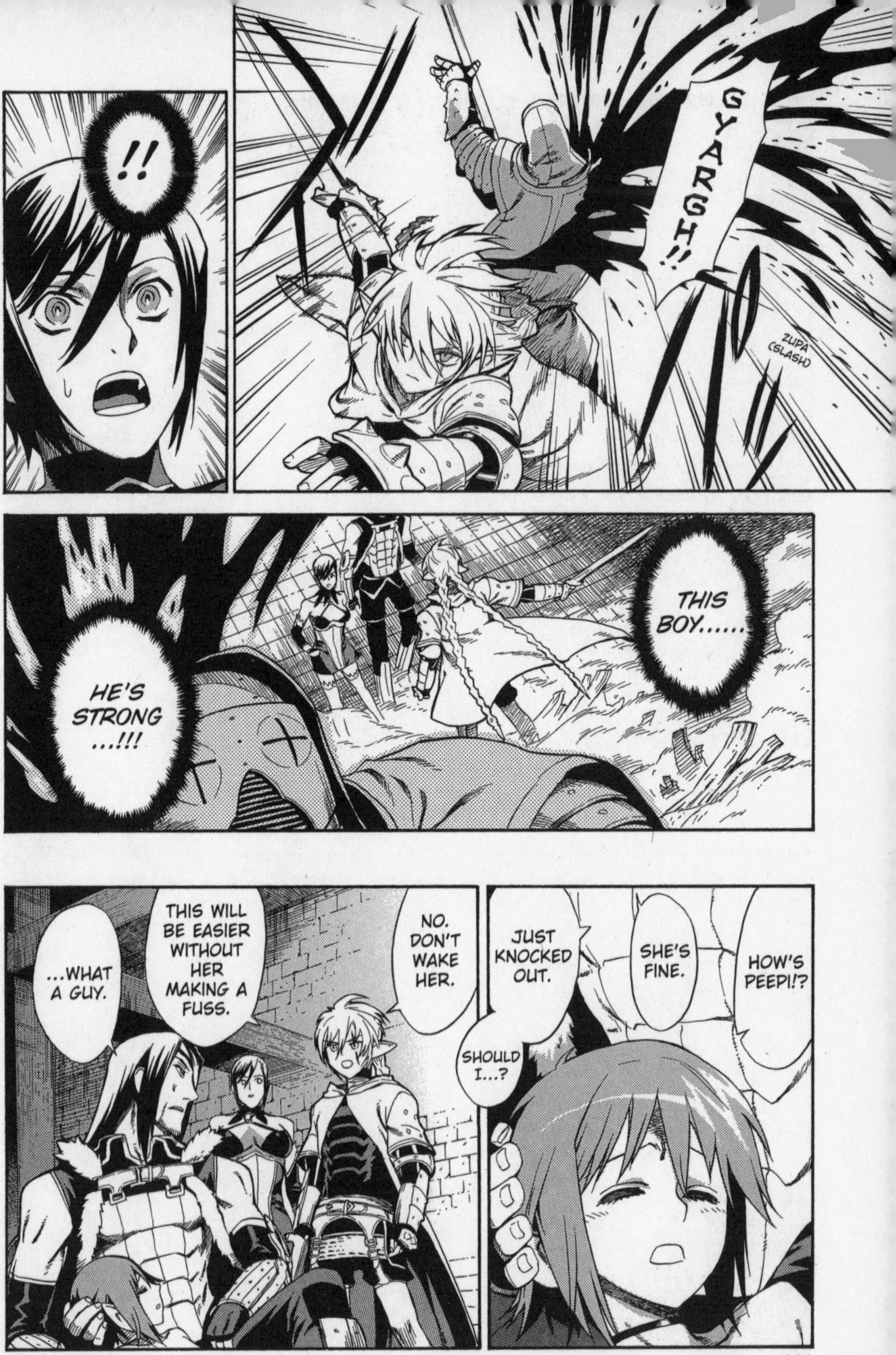
GYARGH!!
ZUPA (SLASH)
!!
THIS BOY......
HE'S STRONG ...!!!
HOW'S PEEPI!?
SHE'S FINE.
JUST KNOCKED OUT.
SHOULD I...?
NO. DON'T WAKE HER.
THIS WILL BE EASIER WITHOUT HER MAKING A FUSS.
...WHAT A GUY.

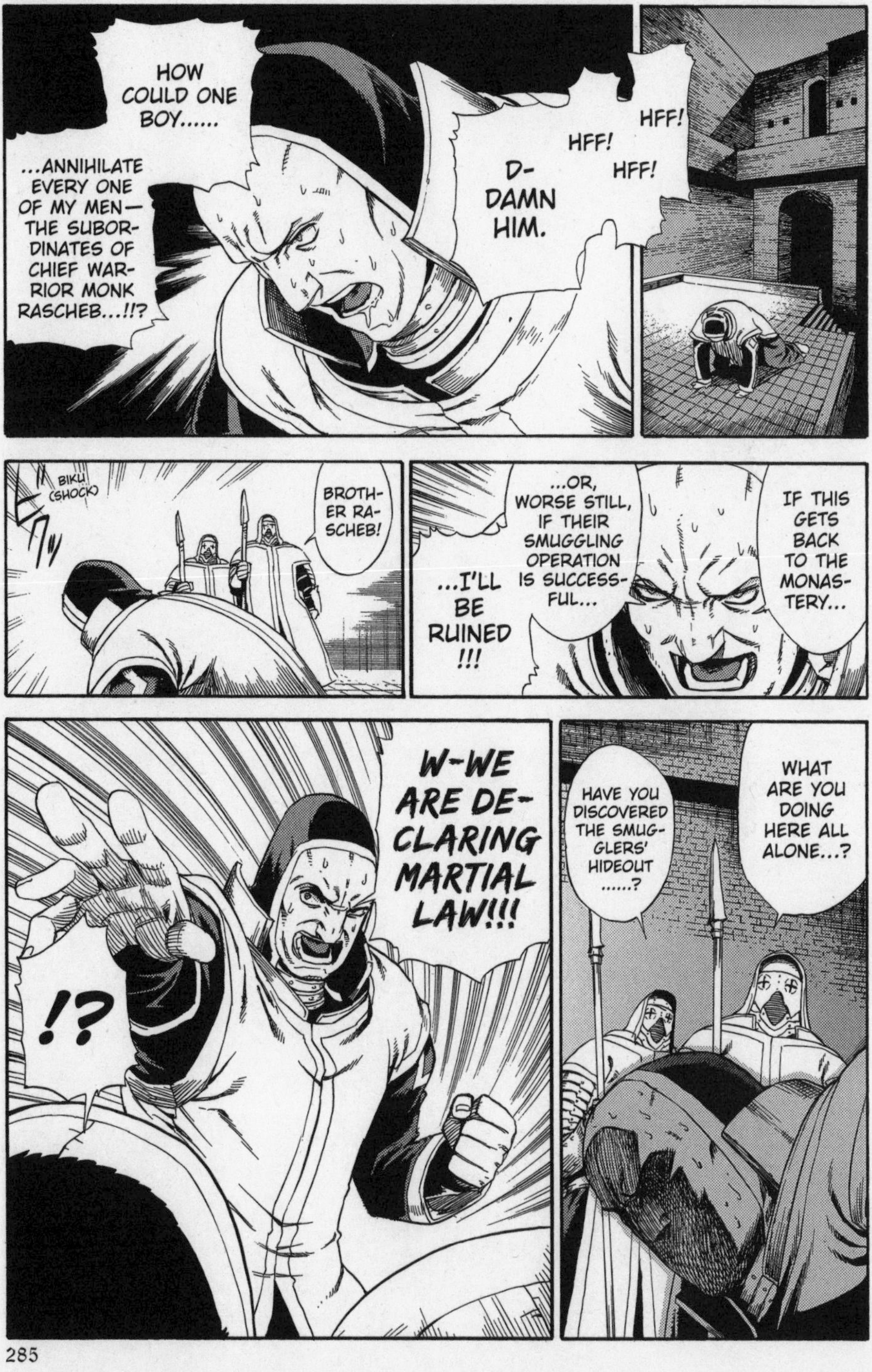
HFF! HFF! HFF!
D-DAMN HIM.
HOW COULD ONE BOY......
...ANNIHILATE EVERY ONE OF MY MEN—THE SUBORDINATES OF CHIEF WARRIOR MONK RASCHEB...!!?
IF THIS GETS BACK TO THE MONASTERY...
...OR, WORSE STILL, IF THEIR SMUGGLING OPERATION IS SUCCESSFUL...
...I'LL BE RUINED!!!
BROTHER RASCHEB!
BIKU (SHOCK)
WHAT ARE YOU DOING HERE ALL ALONE...?
HAVE YOU DISCOVERED THE SMUGGLERS' HIDEOUT......?
W-WE ARE DECLARING MARTIAL LAW!!!
!?

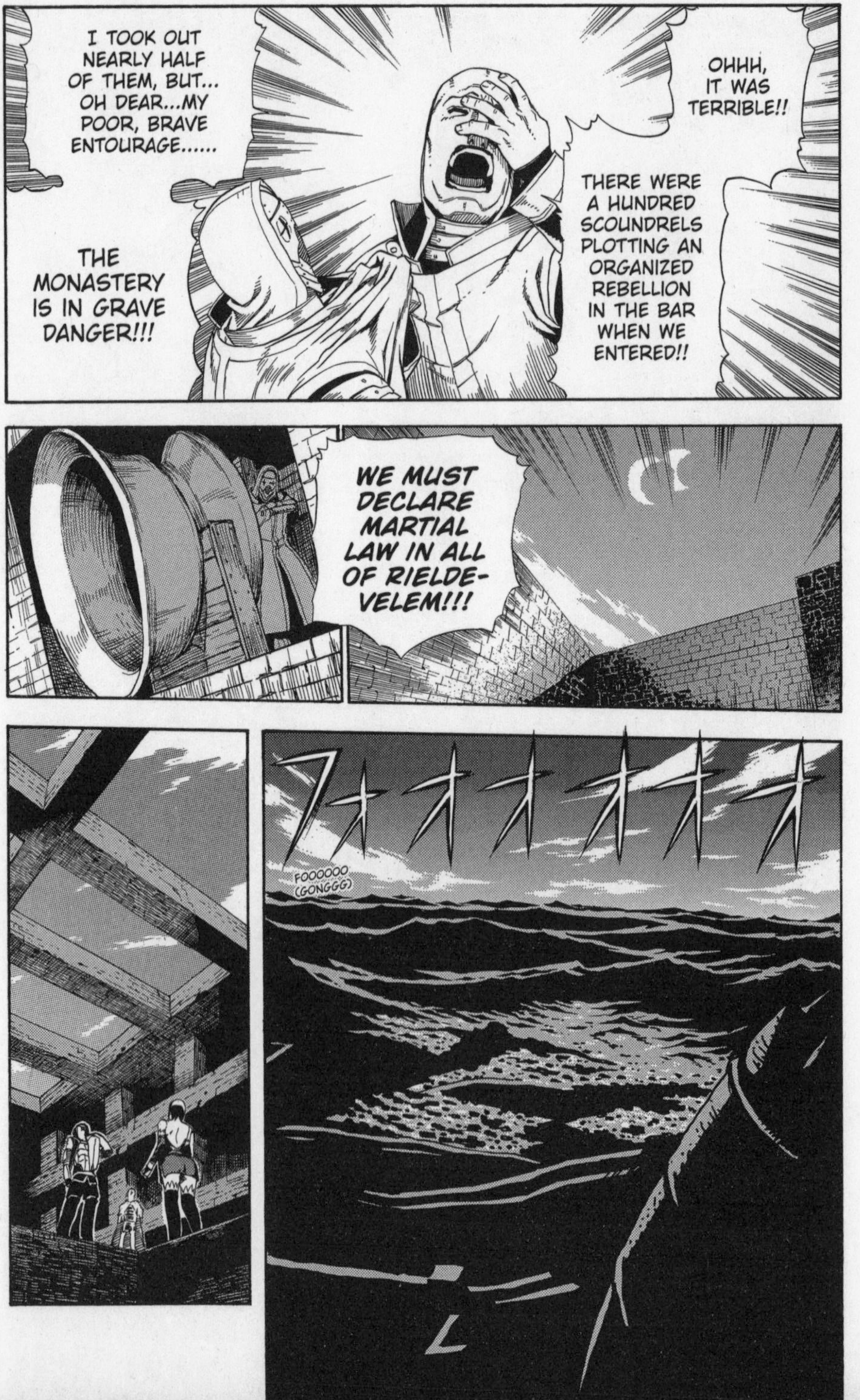
OHHH, IT WAS TERRIBLE!!
THERE WERE A HUNDRED SCOUNDRELS PLOTTING AN ORGANIZED REBELLION IN THE BAR WHEN WE ENTERED!!
I TOOK OUT NEARLY HALF OF THEM, BUT... OH DEAR...MY POOR, BRAVE ENTOURAGE......
THE MONASTERY IS IN GRAVE DANGER!!!
WE MUST DECLARE MARTIAL LAW IN ALL OF RIELDE-VELEM!!!
フォオオオオオ
FOOOOOO (GONGGG)

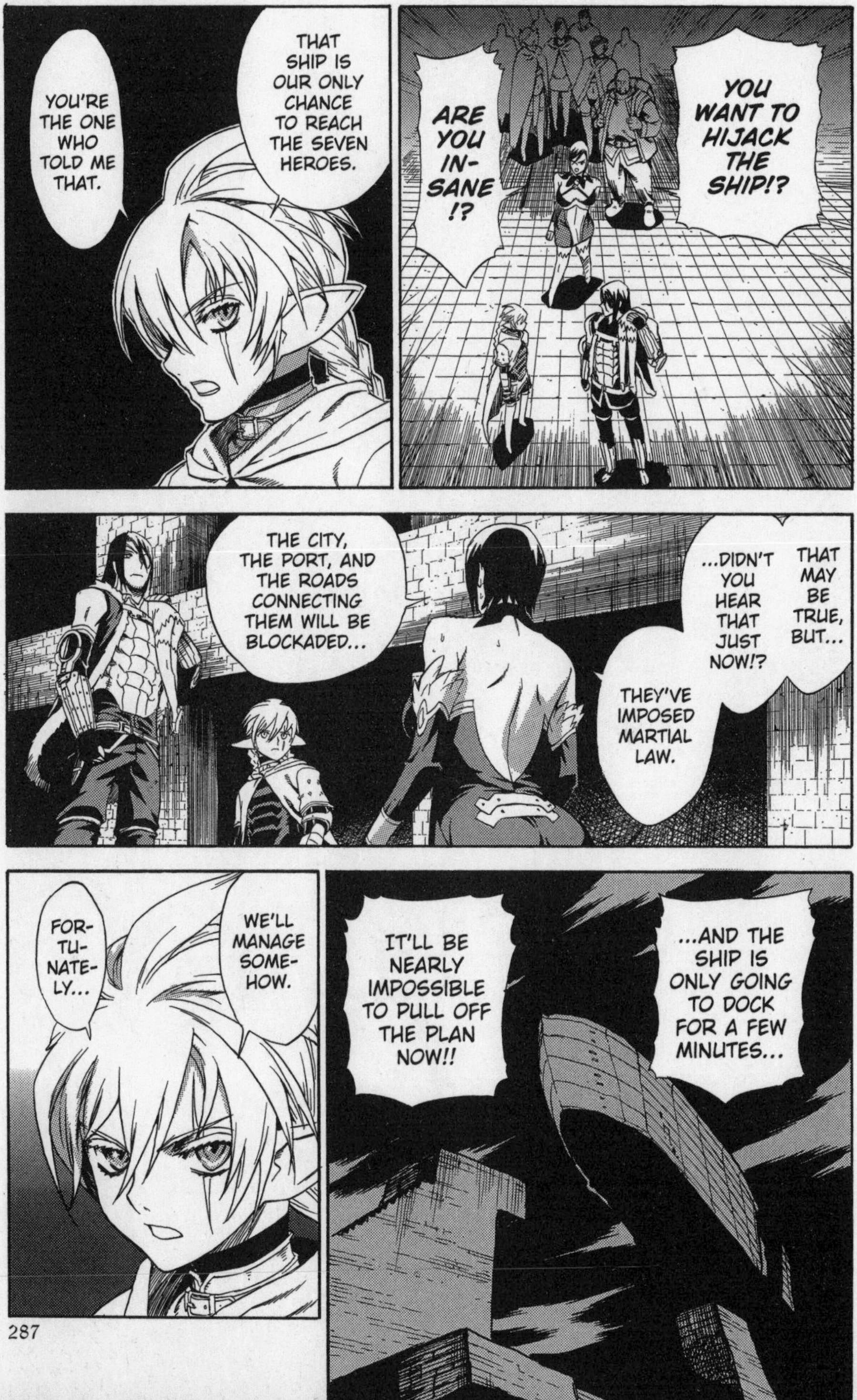
YOU WANT TO HIJACK THE SHIP!?
ARE YOU IN-SANE!?
THAT SHIP IS OUR ONLY CHANCE TO REACH THE SEVEN HEROES.
YOU'RE THE ONE WHO TOLD ME THAT.
THAT MAY BE TRUE, BUT...
...DIDN'T YOU HEAR THAT JUST NOW!?
THEY'VE IMPOSED MARTIAL LAW.
THE CITY, THE PORT, AND THE ROADS CONNECTING THEM WILL BE BLOCKADED...
...AND THE SHIP IS ONLY GOING TO DOCK FOR A FEW MINUTES...
IT'LL BE NEARLY IMPOSSIBLE TO PULL OFF THE PLAN NOW!!
WE'LL MANAGE SOME-HOW.
FOR-TU-NATE-LY...

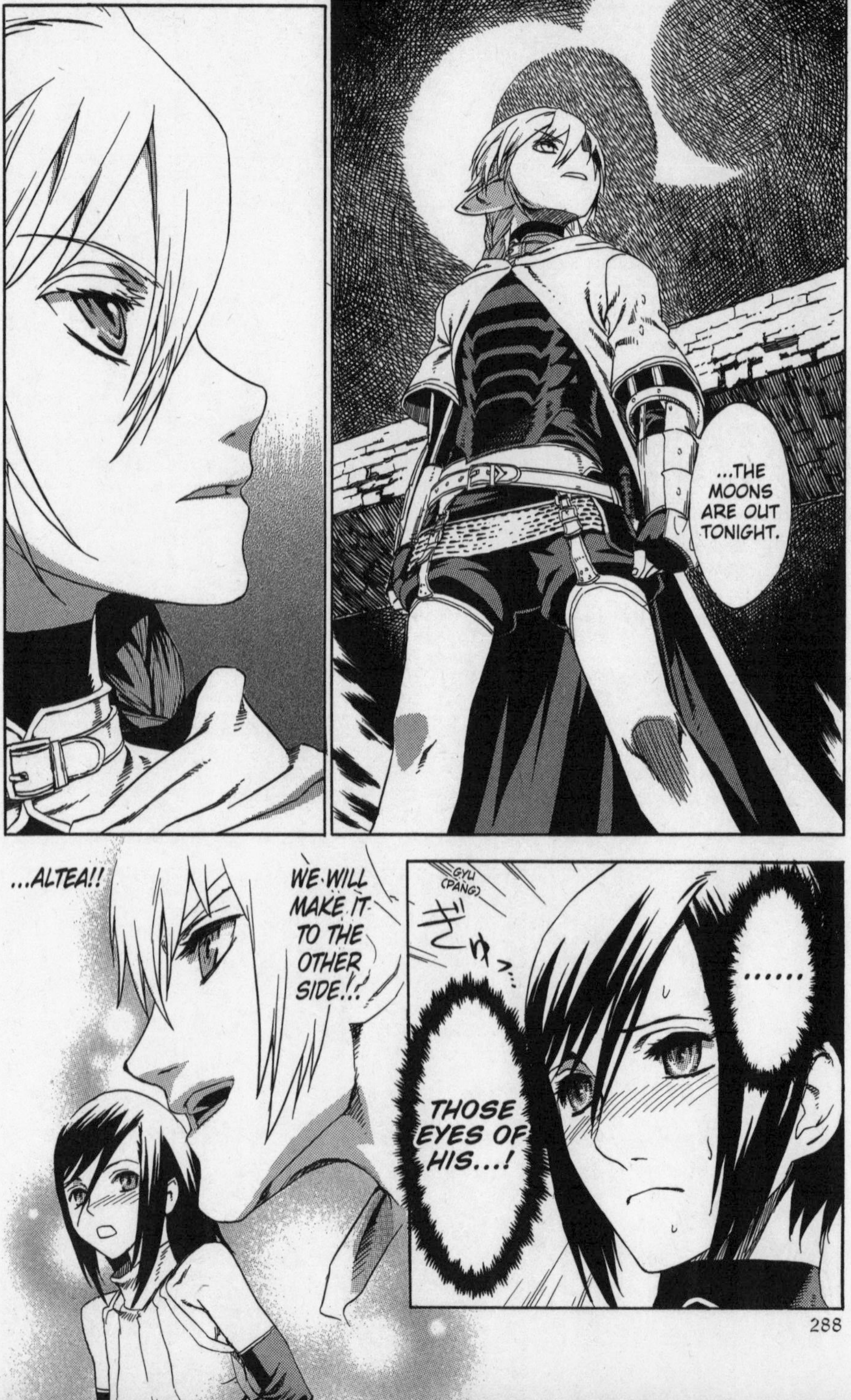
...THE MOONS ARE OUT TONIGHT.
......
GYU (PANG)
ぎゅっ
THOSE EYES OF HIS...!
WE WILL MAKE IT TO THE OTHER SIDE!!
...ALTEA!!

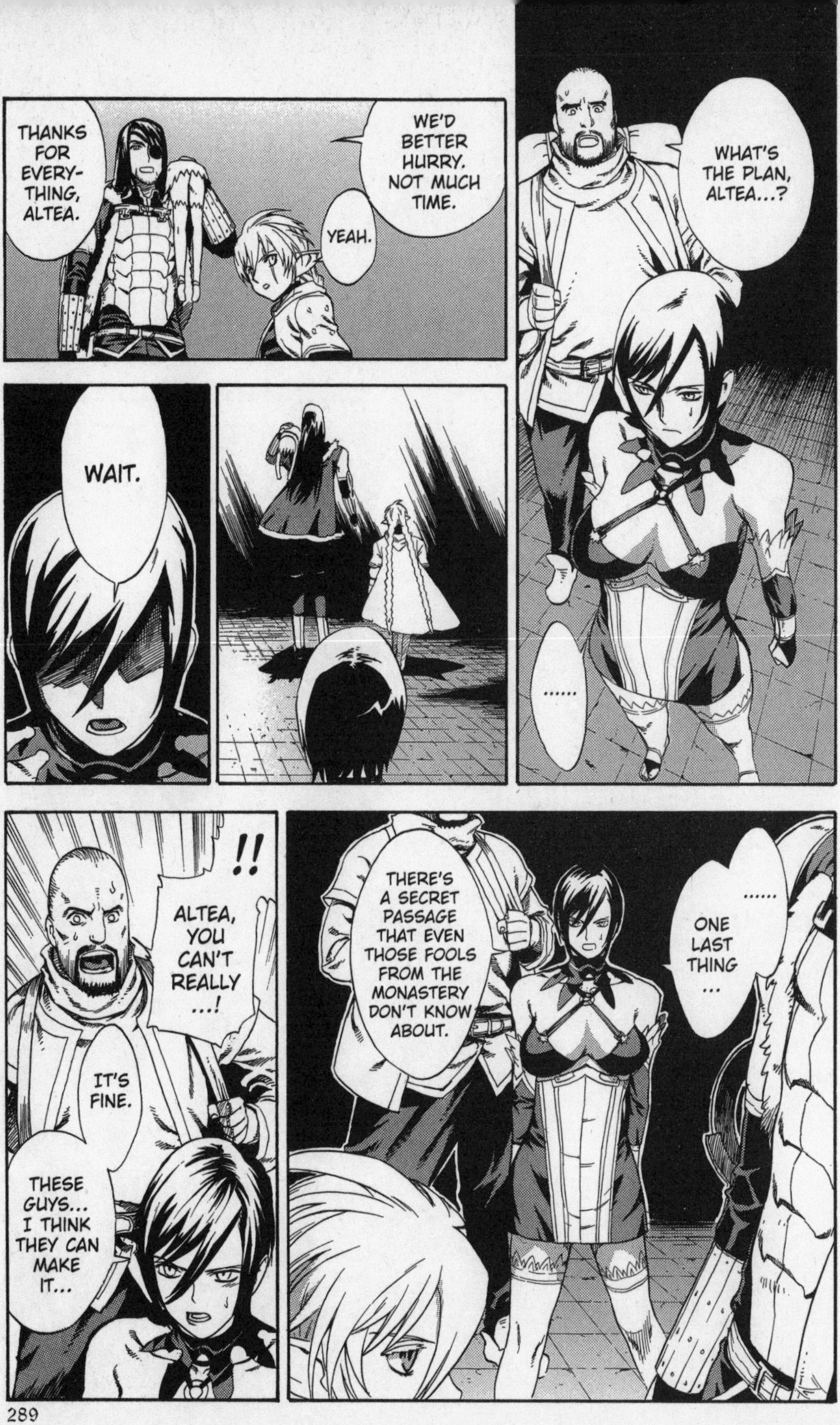
WHAT'S THE PLAN, ALTEA...?
......
WE'D BETTER HURRY. NOT MUCH TIME.
YEAH.
THANKS FOR EVERY-THING, ALTEA.
WAIT.
...... ONE LAST THING ...
THERE'S A SECRET PASSAGE THAT EVEN THOSE FOOLS FROM THE MONASTERY DON'T KNOW ABOUT.
!!
ALTEA, YOU CAN'T REALLY ...!
IT'S FINE.
THESE GUYS... I THINK THEY CAN MAKE IT...

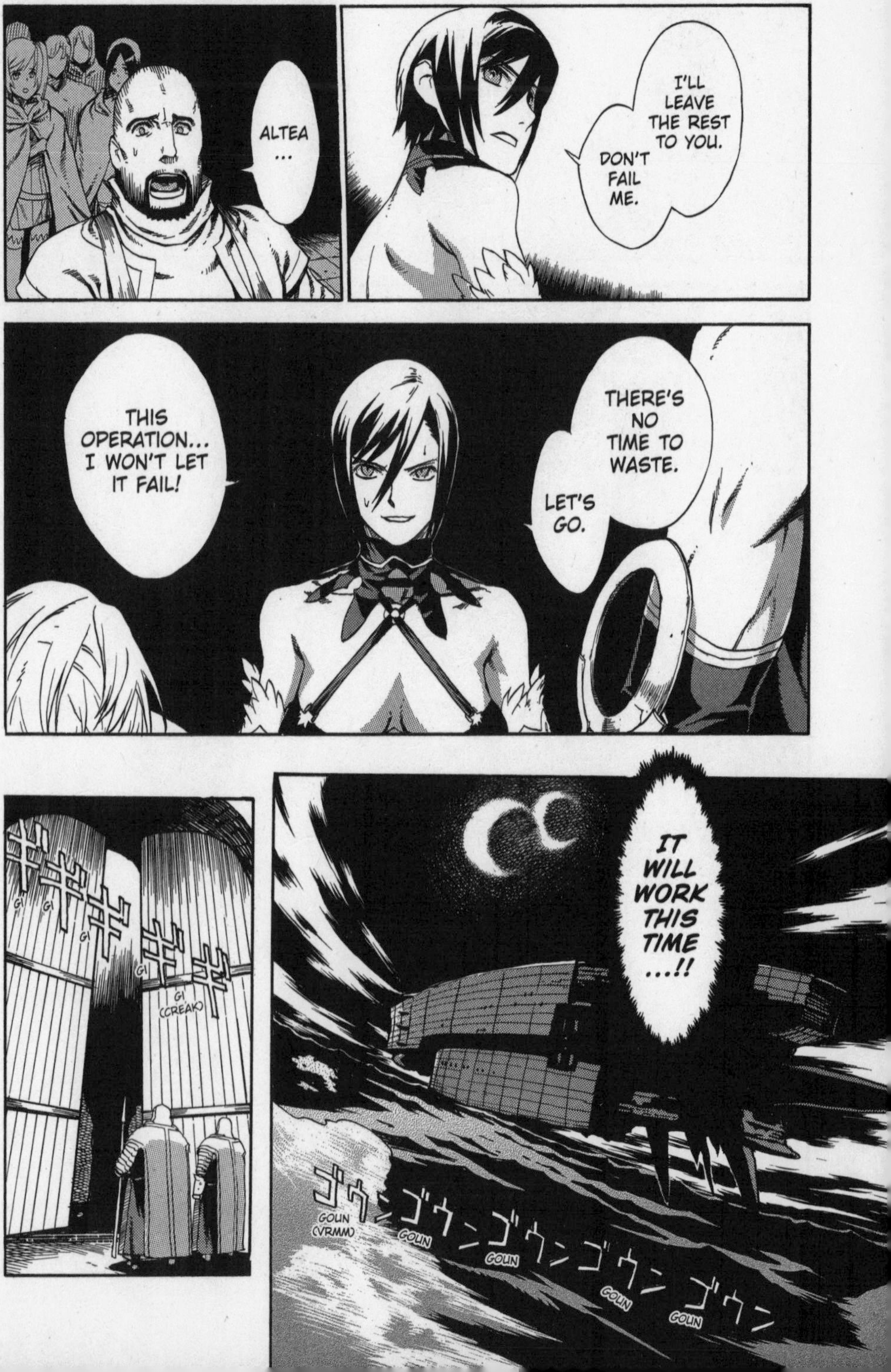
I'LL LEAVE THE REST TO YOU.
DON'T FAIL ME.
ALTEA ...
THERE'S NO TIME TO WASTE.
LET'S GO.
THIS OPERATION... I WON'T LET IT FAIL!
IT WILL WORK THIS TIME ...!!
ゴウンゴウンゴウンゴウンゴウン
GOUN (VRMM)
GOUN
GOUN
GOUN
GOUN
ギギギギギ
GI
GI
GI
GI
GI (CREAK)

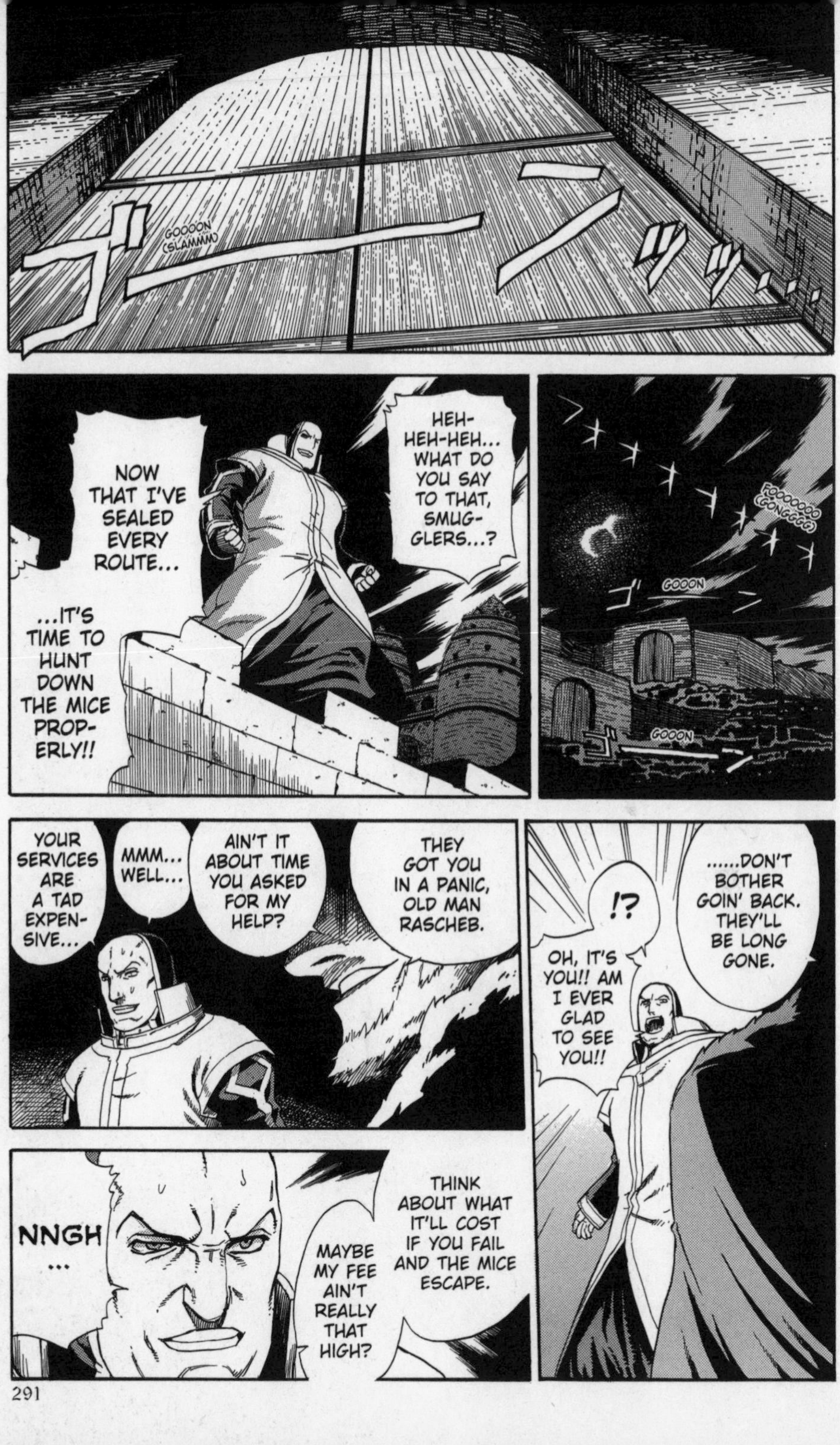
GOOOON (SLAMMM)
FOOOOOOO (GONGGGG)
GOOON
GOOON
HEH-HEH-HEH... WHAT DO YOU SAY TO THAT, SMUGGLERS...?
NOW THAT I'VE SEALED EVERY ROUTE...
...IT'S TIME TO HUNT DOWN THE MICE PROPERLY!!
......DON'T BOTHER GOIN' BACK. THEY'LL BE LONG GONE.
!?
OH, IT'S YOU!! AM I EVER GLAD TO SEE YOU!!
THEY GOT YOU IN A PANIC, OLD MAN RASCHEB.
AIN'T IT ABOUT TIME YOU ASKED FOR MY HELP?
MMM... WELL...
YOUR SERVICES ARE A TAD EXPENSIVE...
THINK ABOUT WHAT IT'LL COST IF YOU FAIL AND THE MICE ESCAPE.
MAYBE MY FEE AIN'T REALLY THAT HIGH?
NNGH...

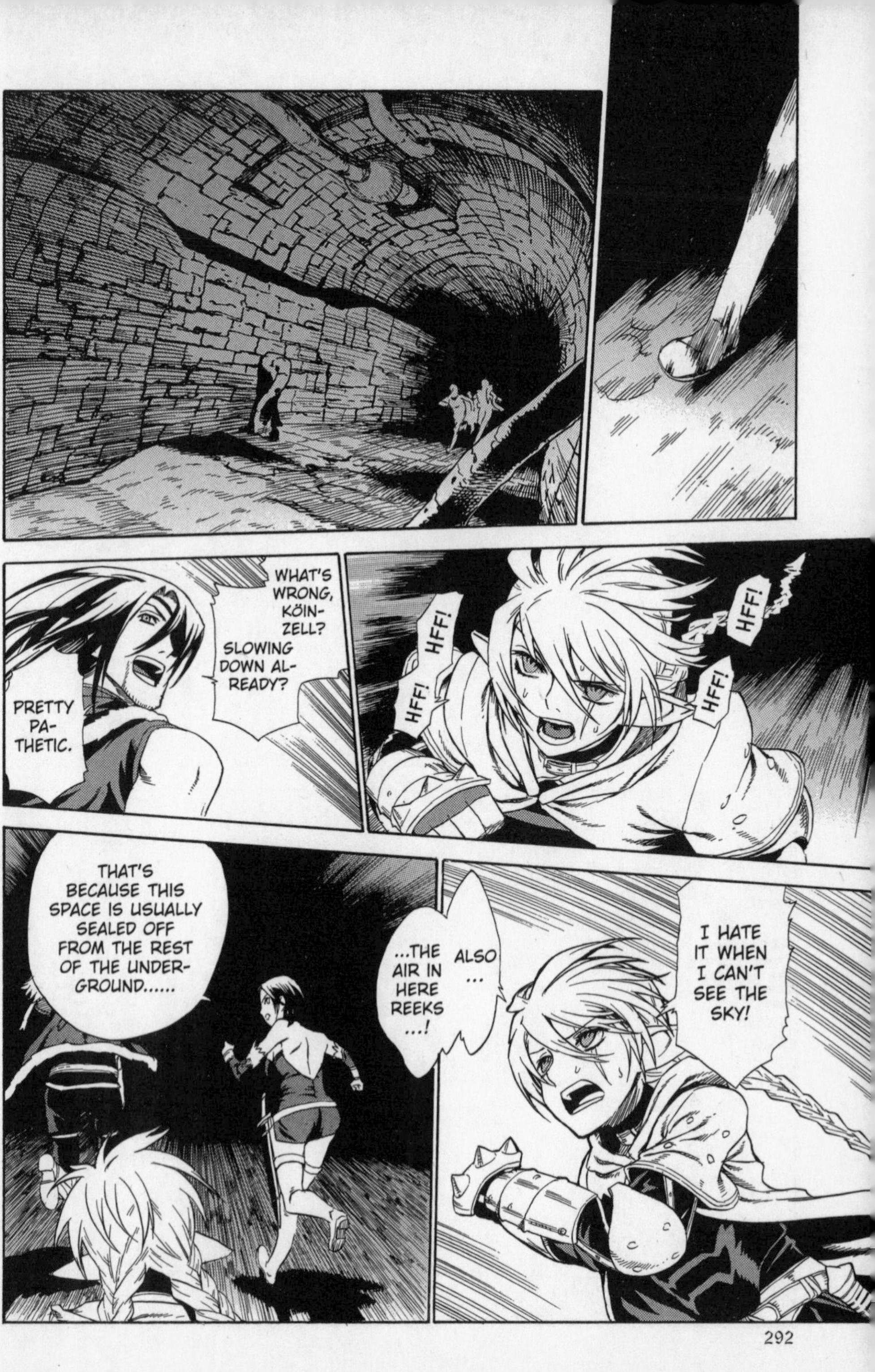
HFF!
HFF!
HFF!
HFF!
WHAT'S WRONG, KÖIN-ZELL? SLOWING DOWN AL-READY?
PRETTY PA-THETIC.
I HATE IT WHEN I CAN'T SEE THE SKY!
ALSO...
...THE AIR IN HERE REEKS...!
THAT'S BECAUSE THIS SPACE IS USUALLY SEALED OFF FROM THE REST OF THE UNDER-GROUND......

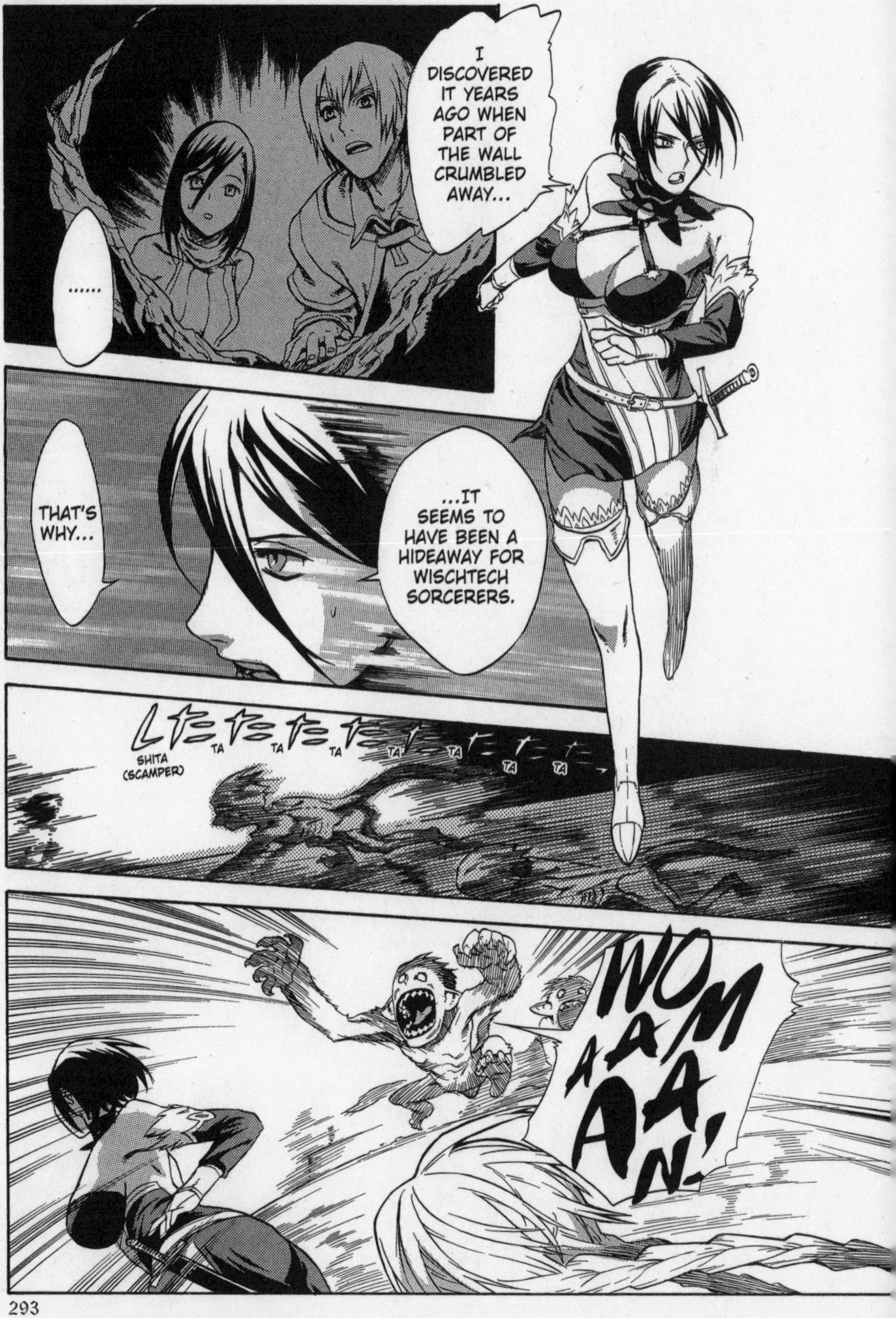
I DISCOVERED IT YEARS AGO WHEN PART OF THE WALL CRUMBLED AWAY...
......
...IT SEEMS TO HAVE BEEN A HIDEAWAY FOR WISCHTECH SORCERERS.
THAT'S WHY...
SHITA (SCAMPER)
TA TA TA TA TA TA TA
WOMAAAAAN!

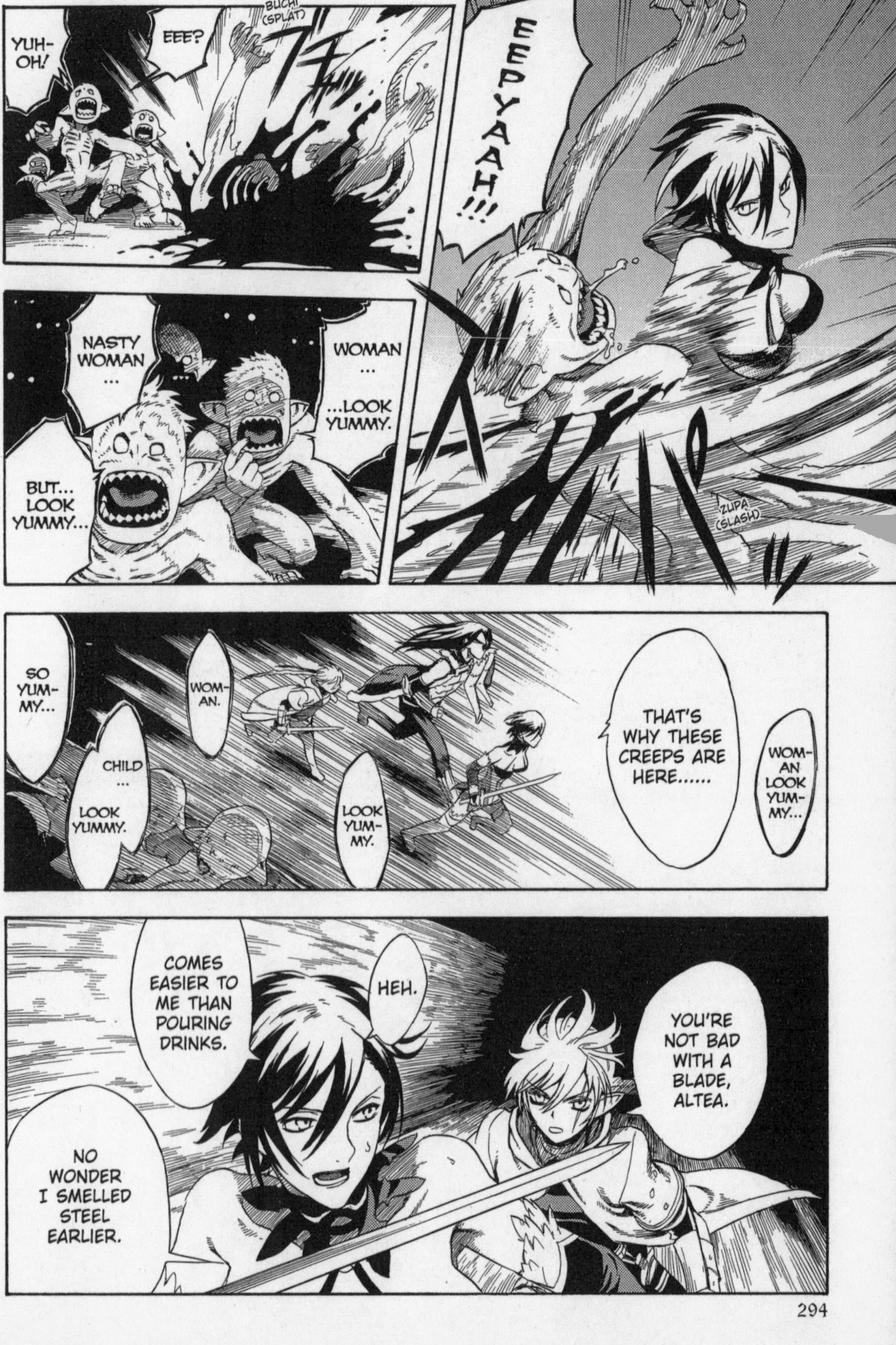
EEPYAAH!!!
ZUPA (SLASH)
BUCHI (SPLAT)
EEE?
YUH-OH!
WOMAN... ...LOOK YUMMY.
NASTY WOMAN...
BUT... LOOK YUMMY...
WOM-AN LOOK YUM-MY...
THAT'S WHY THESE CREEPS ARE HERE......
LOOK YUM-MY.
WOM-AN.
CHILD... LOOK YUMMY.
SO YUM-MY...
YOU'RE NOT BAD WITH A BLADE, ALTEA.
HEH.
COMES EASIER TO ME THAN POURING DRINKS.
NO WONDER I SMELLED STEEL EARLIER.

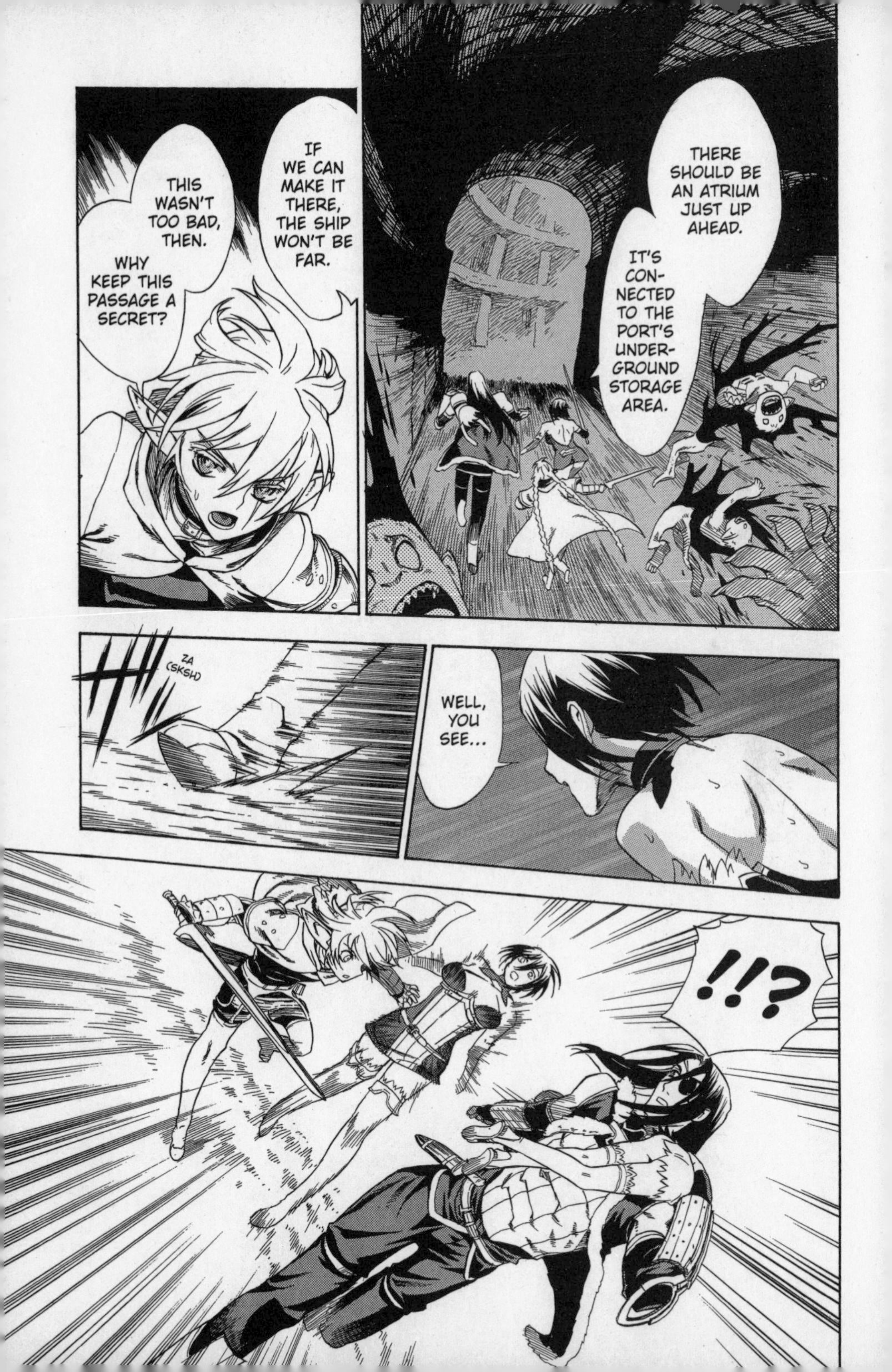
THERE SHOULD BE AN ATRIUM JUST UP AHEAD.
IT'S CON-NECTED TO THE PORT'S UNDER-GROUND STORAGE AREA.
IF WE CAN MAKE IT THERE, THE SHIP WON'T BE FAR.
THIS WASN'T TOO BAD, THEN.
WHY KEEP THIS PASSAGE A SECRET?
WELL, YOU SEE...
ZA (SKSH)
!!?

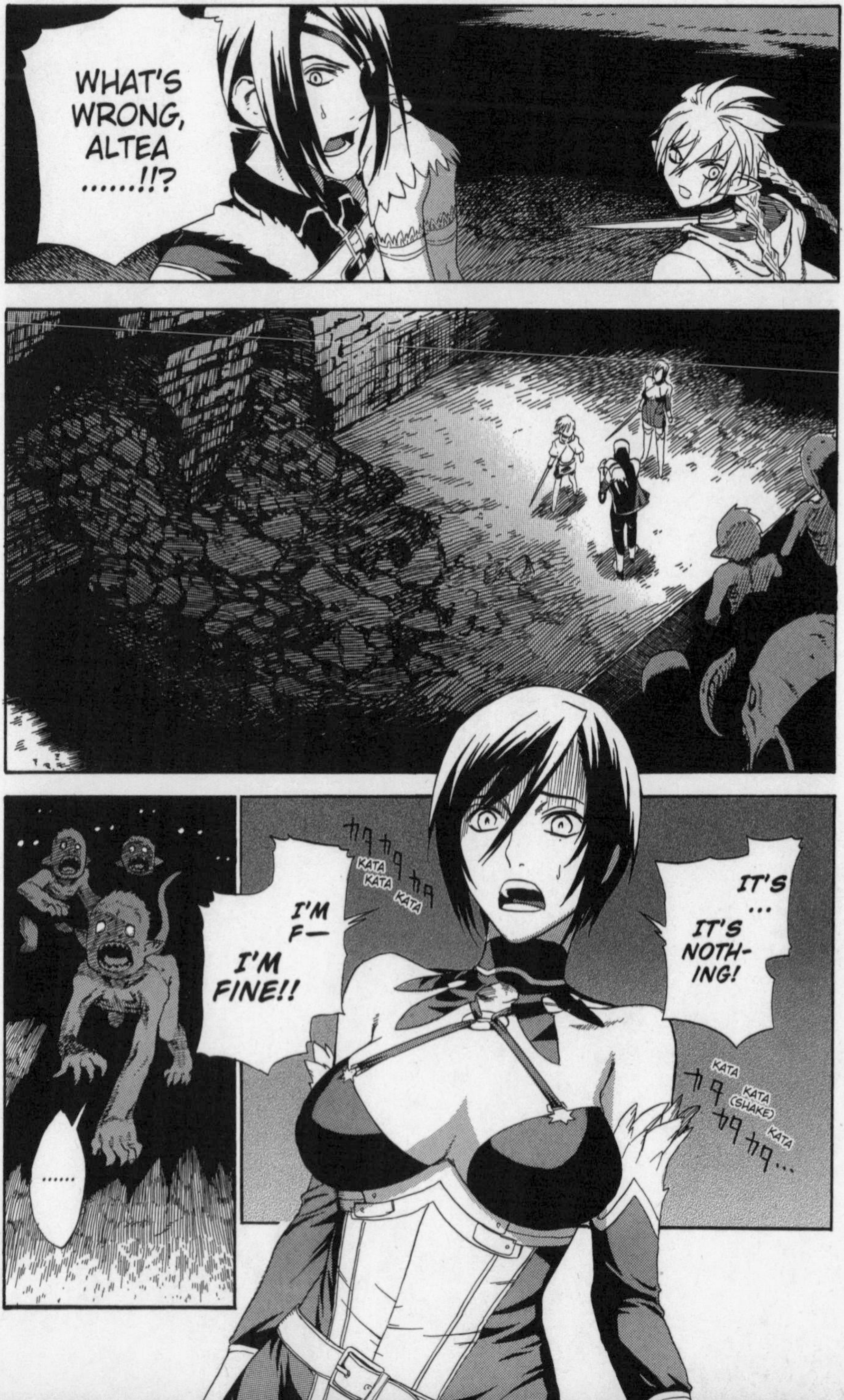
WHAT'S WRONG, ALTEA ......!!?
IT'S ... IT'S NOTHING!
カタカタカタ
KATA KATA KATA
I'M F— I'M FINE!!
カタカタカタ...
KATA KATA (SHAKE) KATA
......

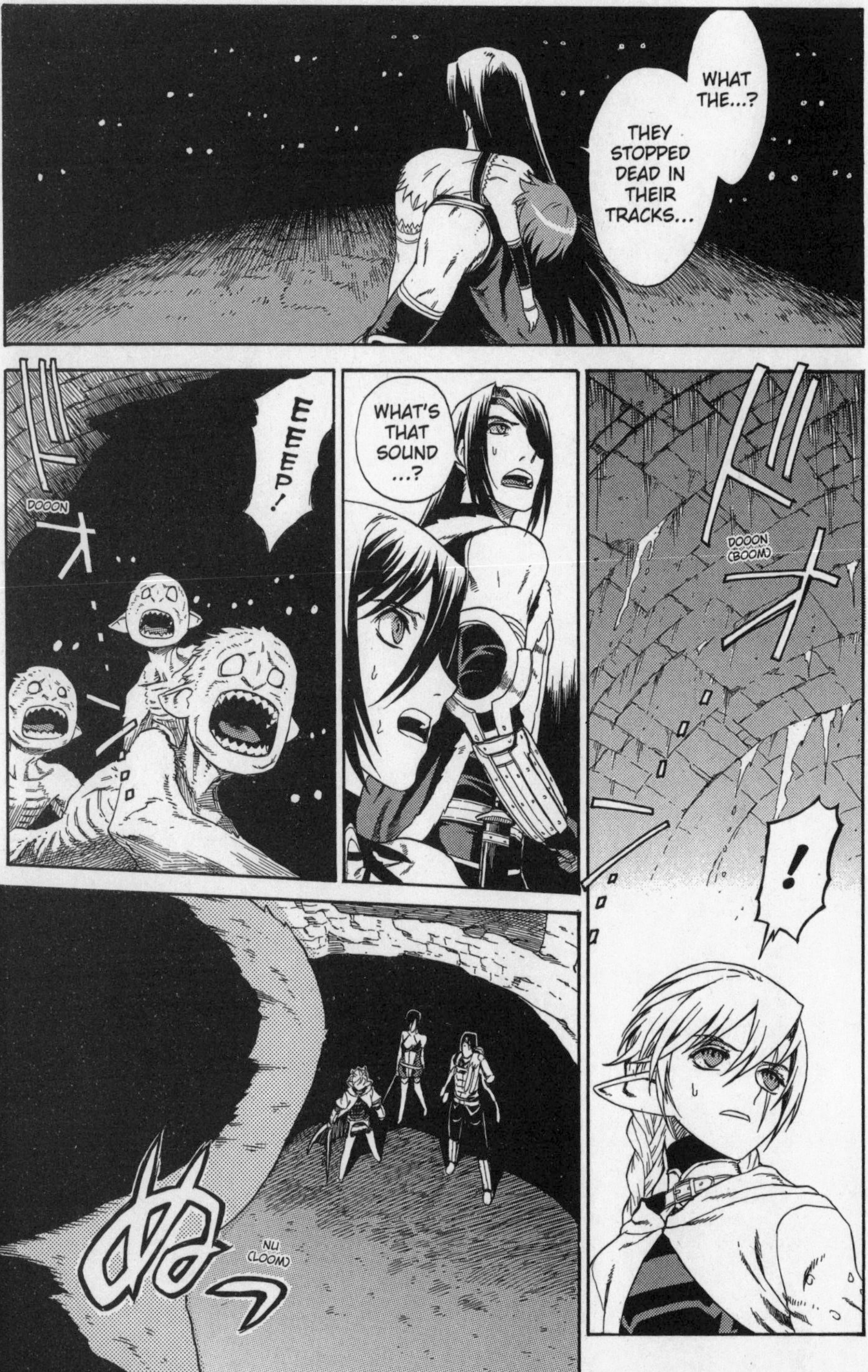
WHAT THE...?
THEY STOPPED DEAD IN THEIR TRACKS...
DOOON (BOOM)
WHAT'S THAT SOUND ...?
EEEP!
DOOON
!
NU (LOOM)

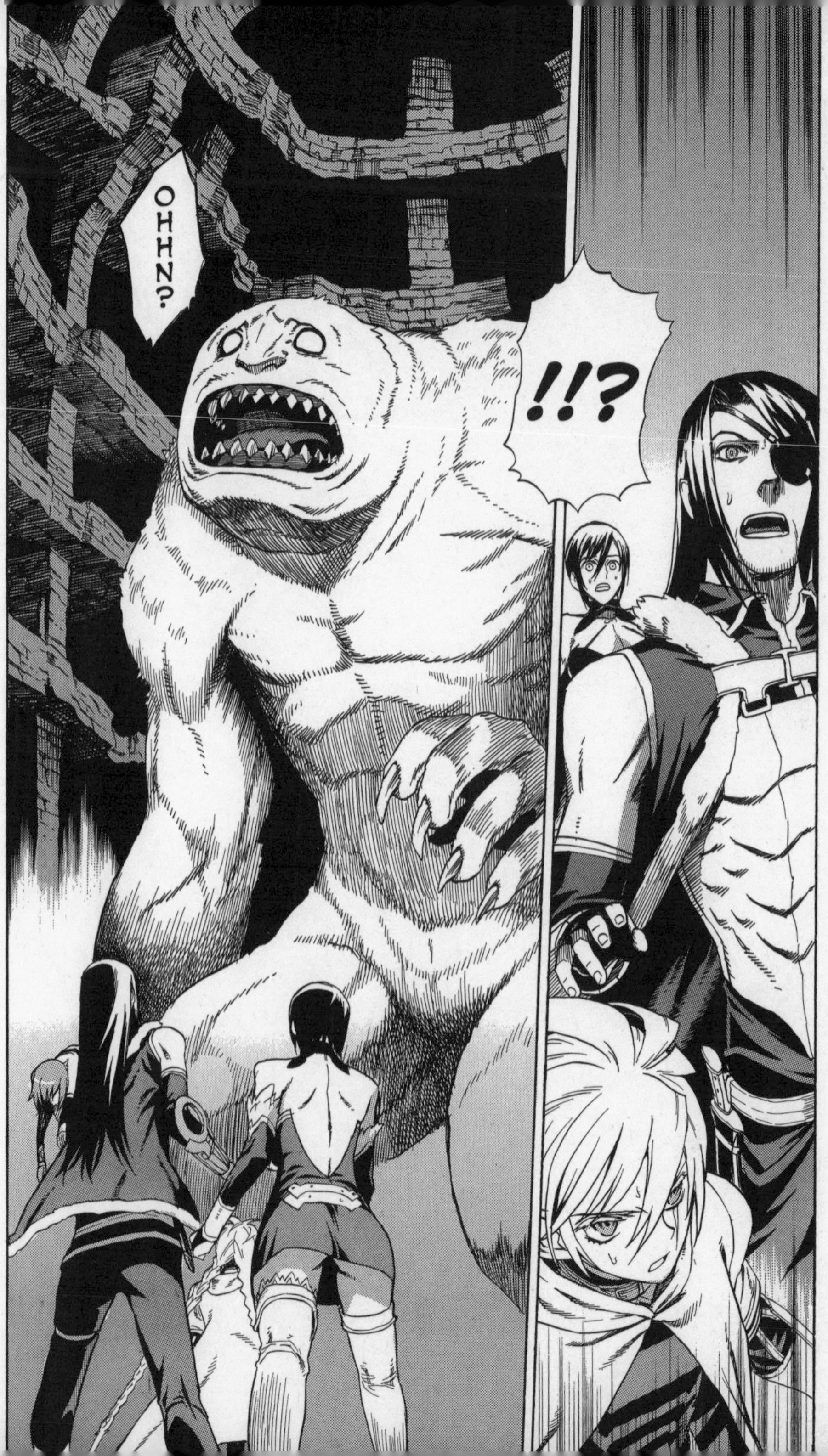
!!?
OHHN?

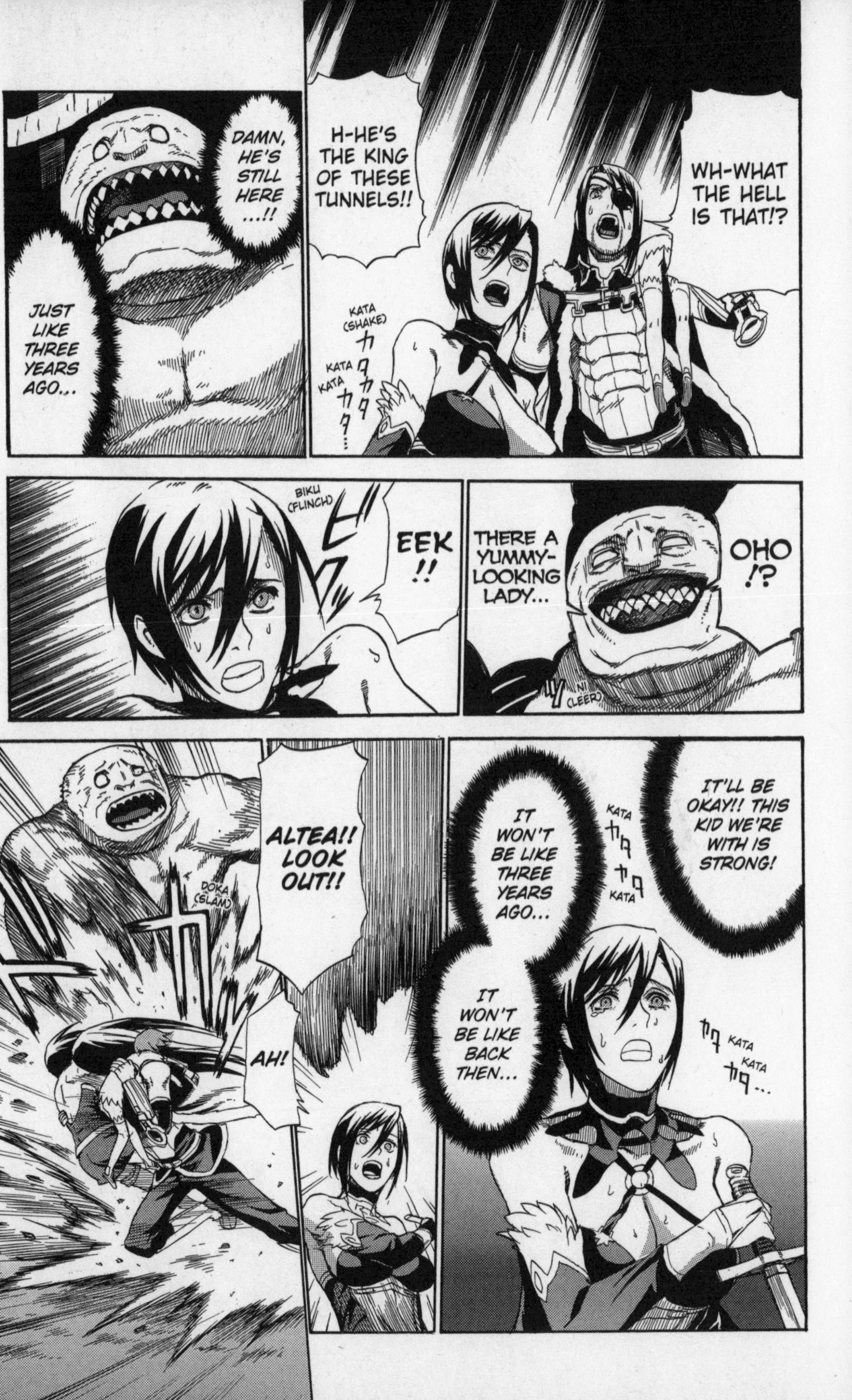
WH-WHAT THE HELL IS THAT!?
H-HE'S THE KING OF THESE TUNNELS!!
KATA (SHAKE) KATA KATA
DAMN, HE'S STILL HERE ...!!
JUST LIKE THREE YEARS AGO...
OHO !?
THERE A YUMMY-LOOKING LADY...
NI (LEER)
EEK !!
BIKU (FLINCH)
IT'LL BE OKAY!! THIS KID WE'RE WITH IS STRONG!
KATA KATA
IT WON'T BE LIKE THREE YEARS AGO...
IT WON'T BE LIKE BACK THEN...
KATA KATA...
ALTEA!! LOOK OUT!!
AH!
DOKA (SLAM)

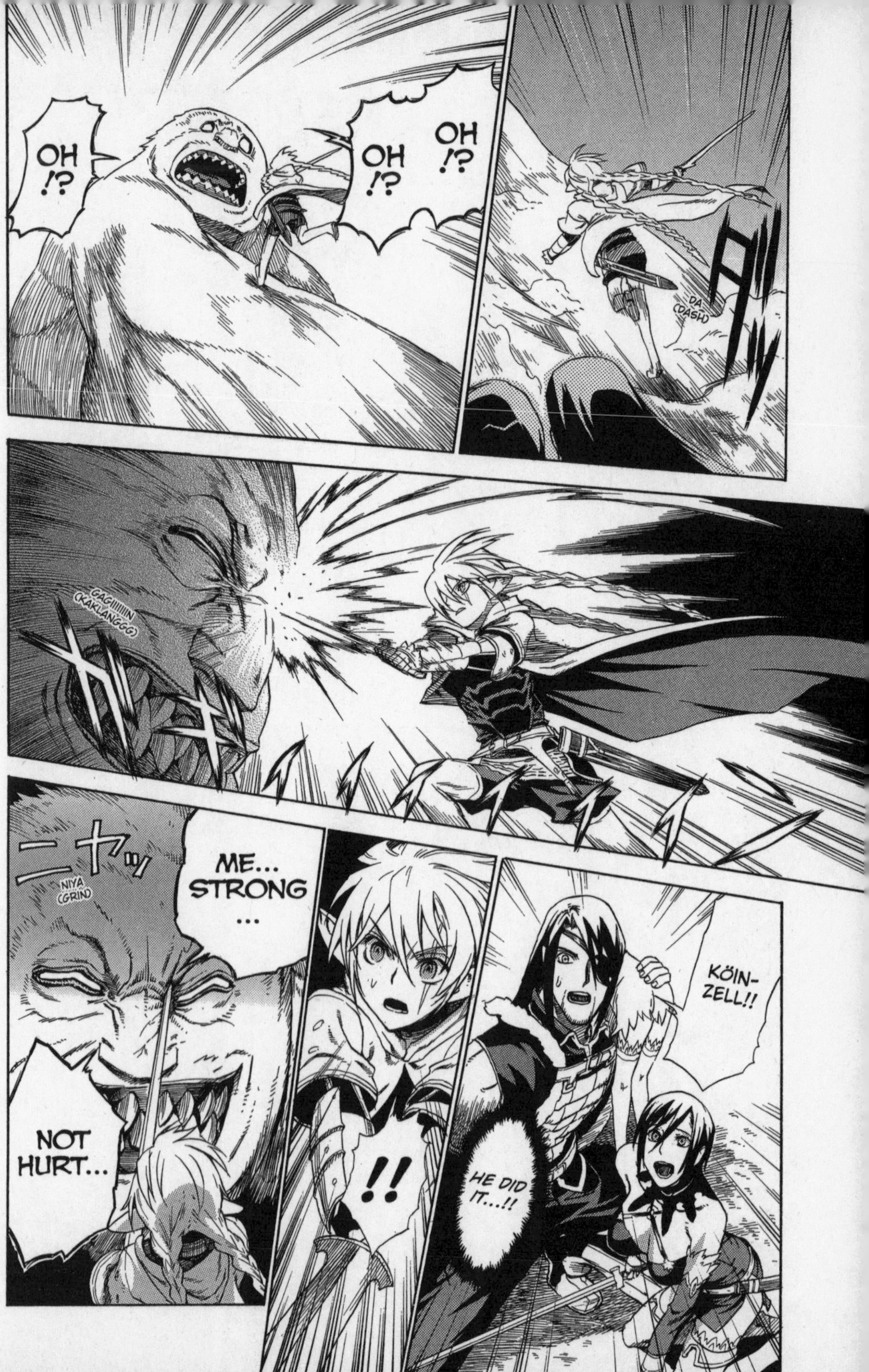
DA (DASH)
OH !?
OH !?
OH !?
GAGIIIIIN (KAKLANGGG)
KÖIN-ZELL!!
HE DID IT...!!
ME... STRONG ...
!!
NIYA (GRIN)
NOT HURT...

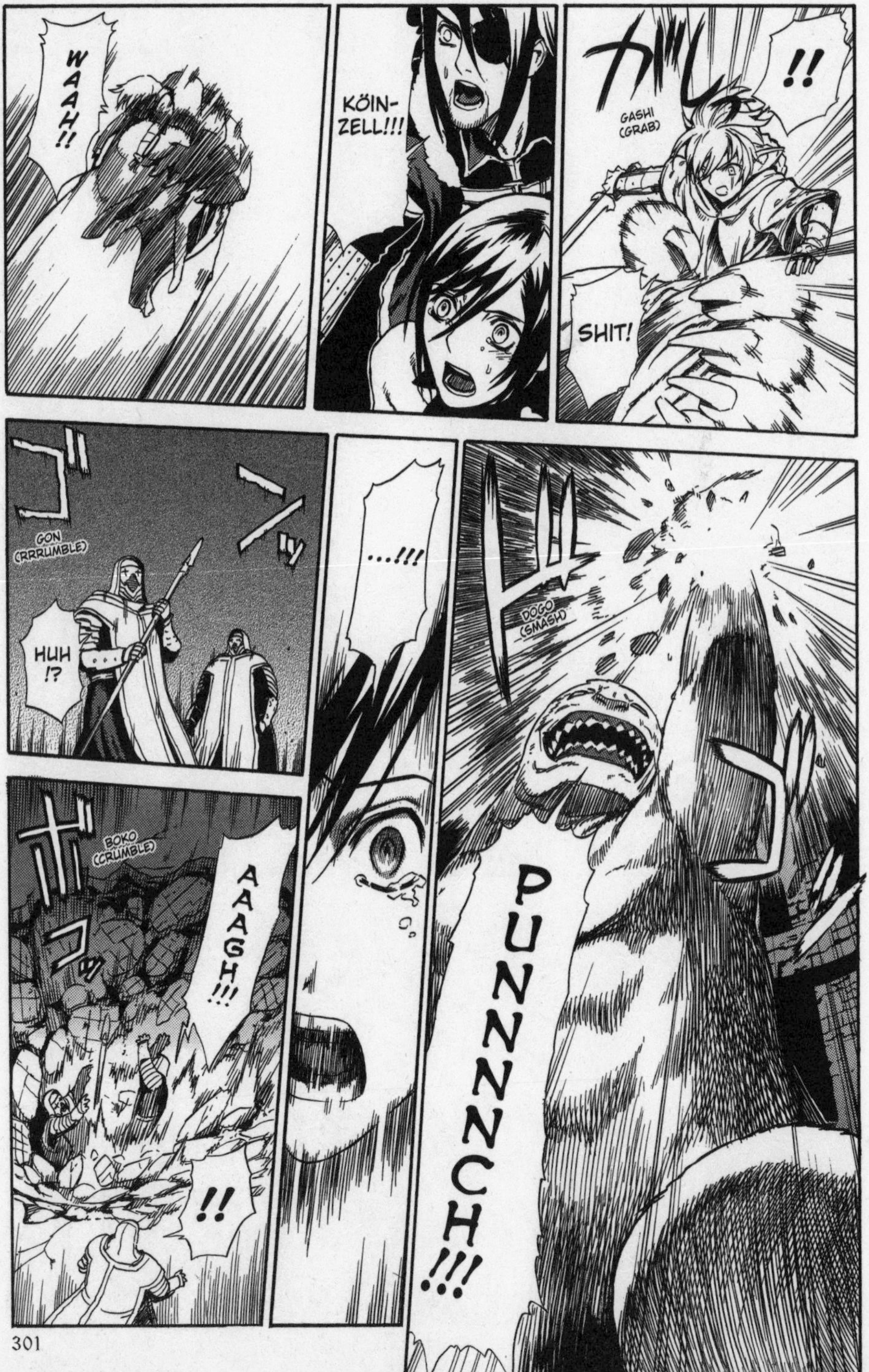
!!
GASHI (GRAB)
SHIT!
KÖIN-ZELL!!!
WAAH!!
DOGO (SMASH)
PUNNNNCH!!!
...!!!
GON (RRRUMBLE)
HUH!?
BOKO (CRUMBLE)
AAAGH!!!
!!

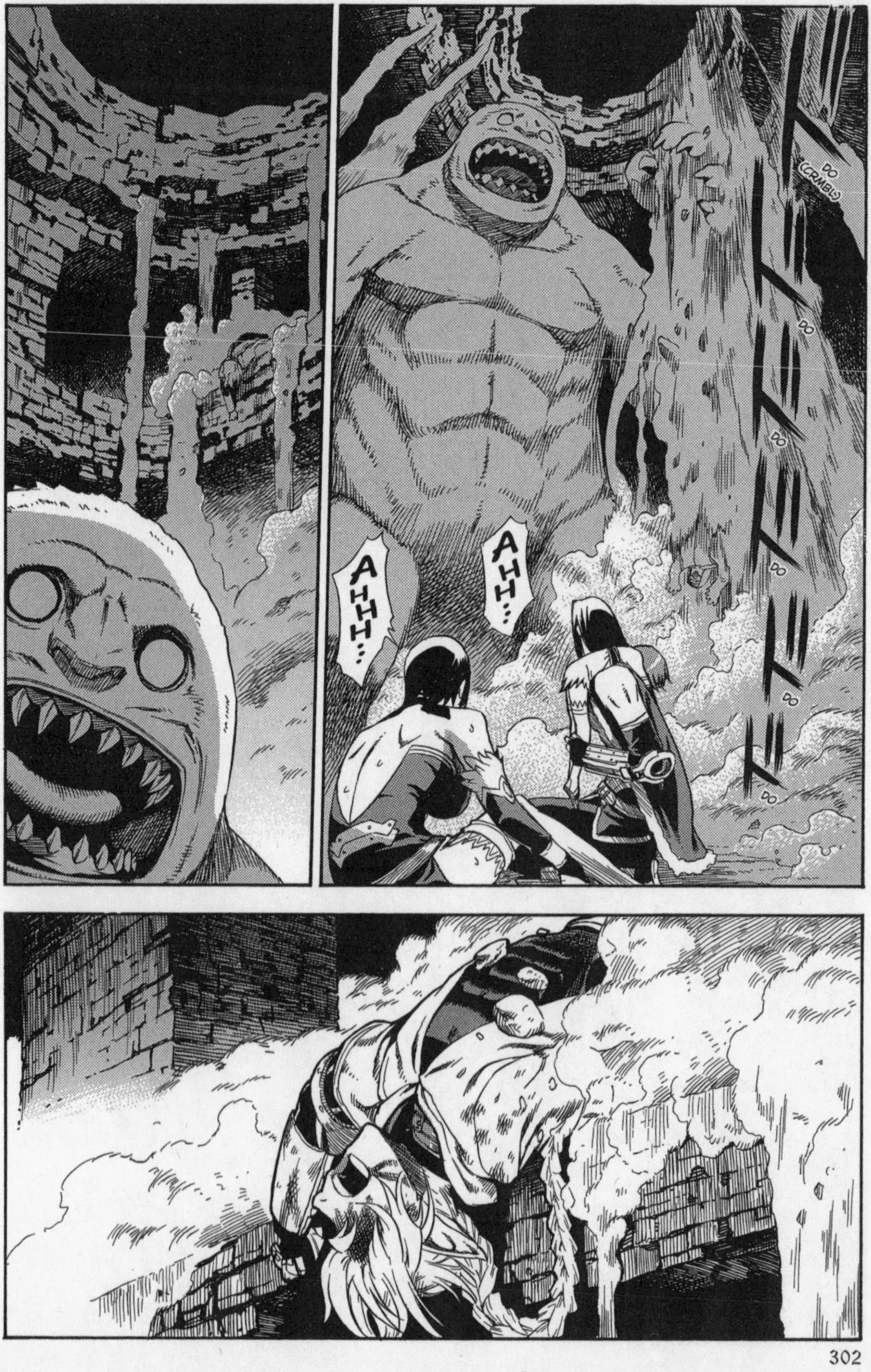
DO
(CRMBL)
DO
DO
DO
DO
DO
AHH...
AHHHH...

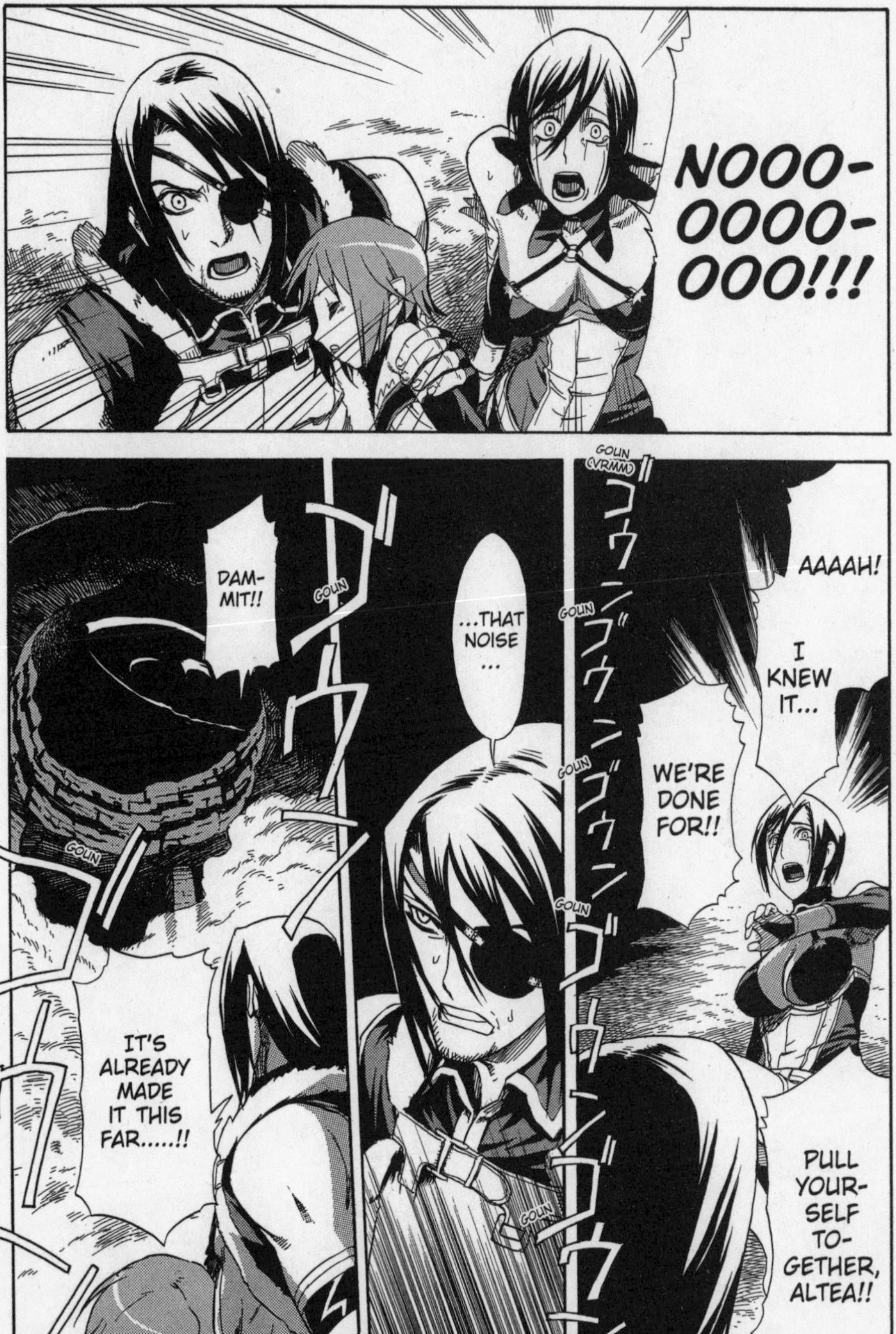
NOOOO-OOOO-OOO!!!
AAAAH!
I KNEW IT...
WE'RE DONE FOR!!
PULL YOURSELF TOGETHER, ALTEA!!
GOUN (VRMM)
GOUN
GOUN
GOUN
GOUN
...THAT NOISE...
DAMMIT!!
GOUN
GOUN
IT'S ALREADY MADE IT THIS FAR.....!!

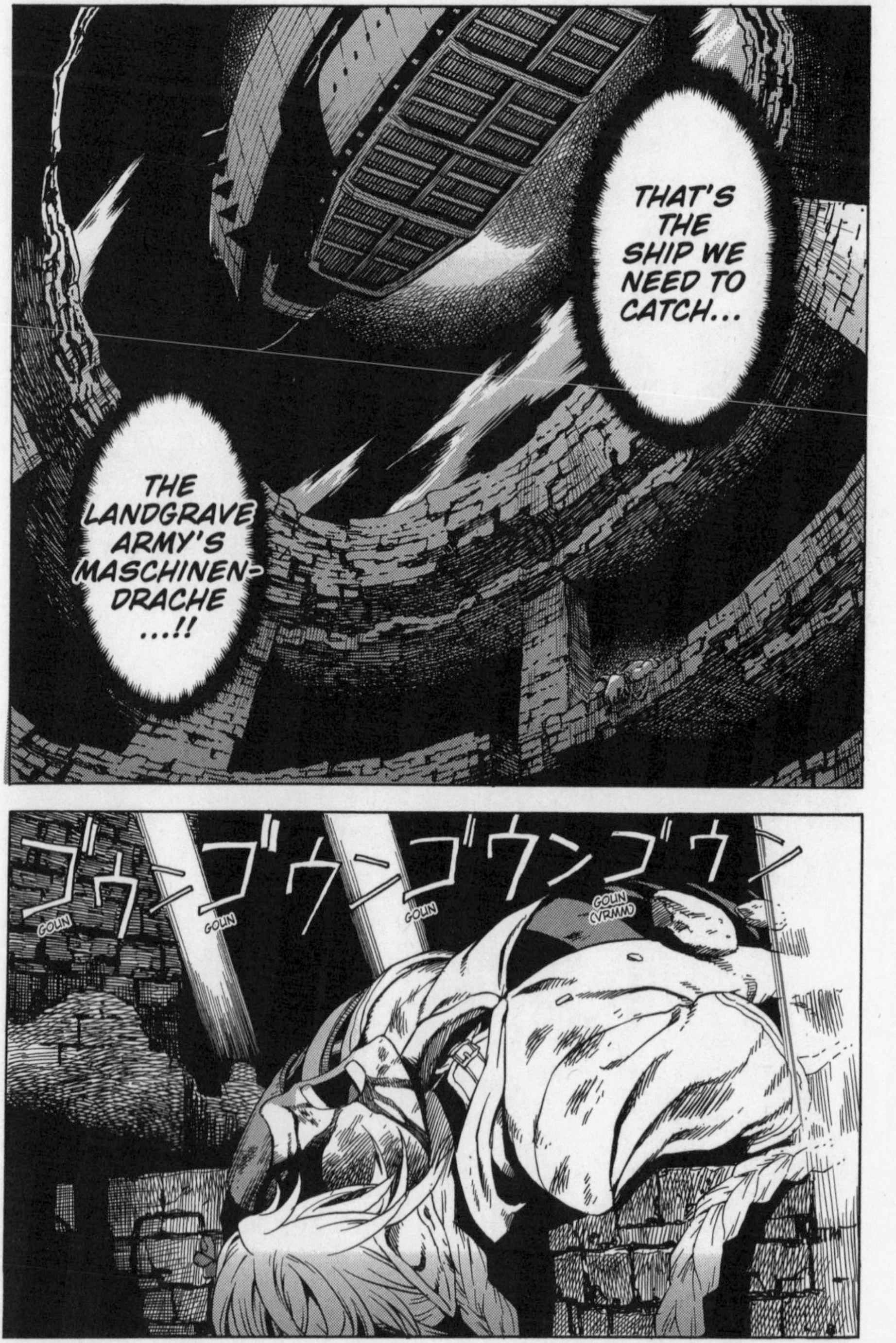
THAT'S THE SHIP WE NEED TO CATCH...
THE LANDGRAVE ARMY'S MASCHINEN-DRACHE ...!!
ゴウンゴウンゴウンゴウン
GOUN (VRMM)
GOUN
GOUN
GOUN

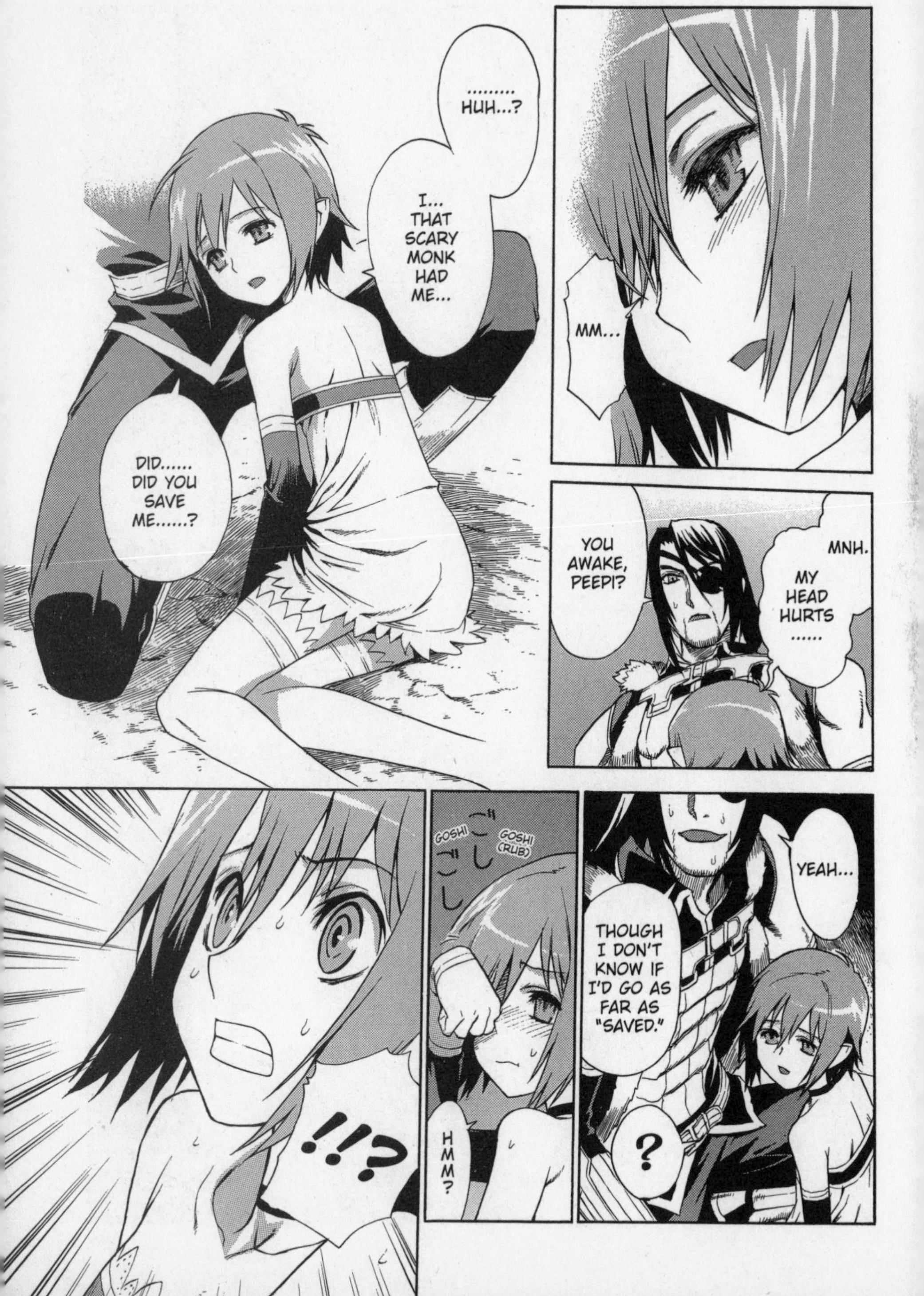
MM...
MNH. MY HEAD HURTS ......
YOU AWAKE, PEEPI?
.... HUH...?
I... THAT SCARY MONK HAD ME...
DID...... DID YOU SAVE ME......?
YEAH...
THOUGH I DON'T KNOW IF I'D GO AS FAR AS "SAVED."
?
ごし ごし
GOSHI GOSHI (RUB)
HMM?
!!?

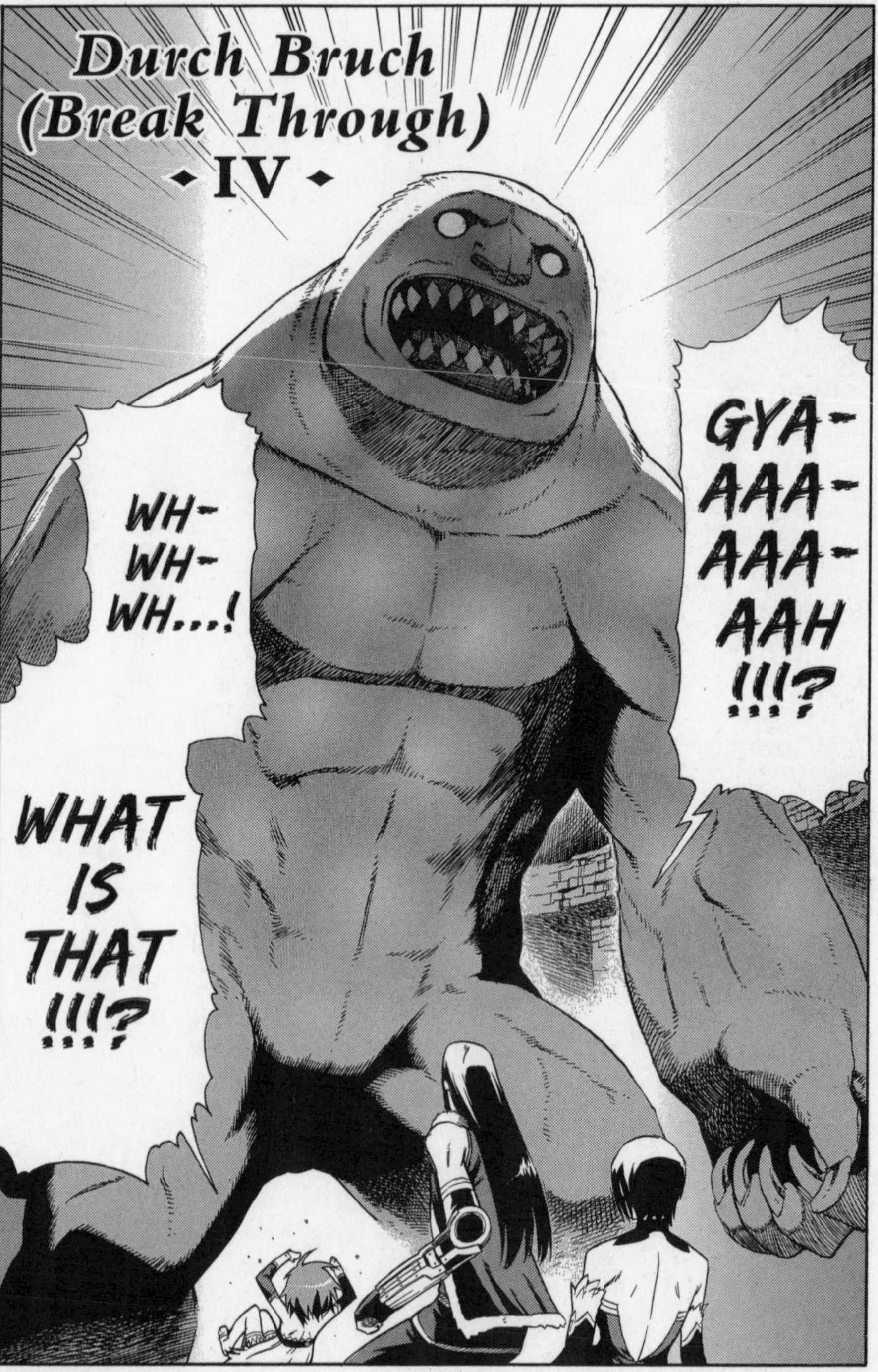
Durch Bruch (Break Through) •IV•
GYA-AAA-AAA-AAH!!!?
WH-WH-WH...!
WHAT IS THAT!!!?

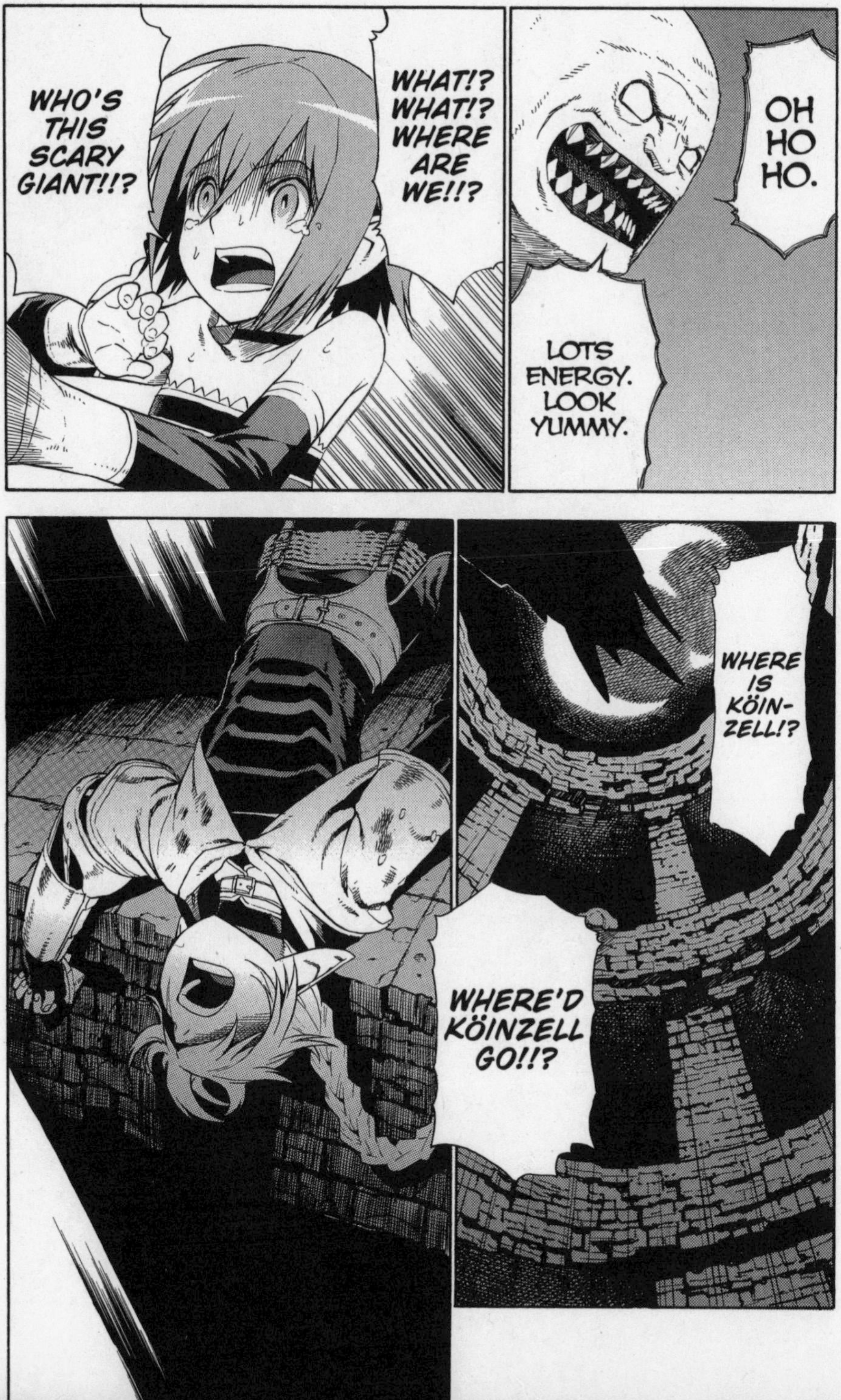
OH HO HO.
LOTS ENERGY. LOOK YUMMY.
WHAT!? WHAT!? WHERE ARE WE!!?
WHO'S THIS SCARY GIANT!!?
WHERE IS KÖIN-ZELL!?
WHERE'D KÖINZELL GO!!?

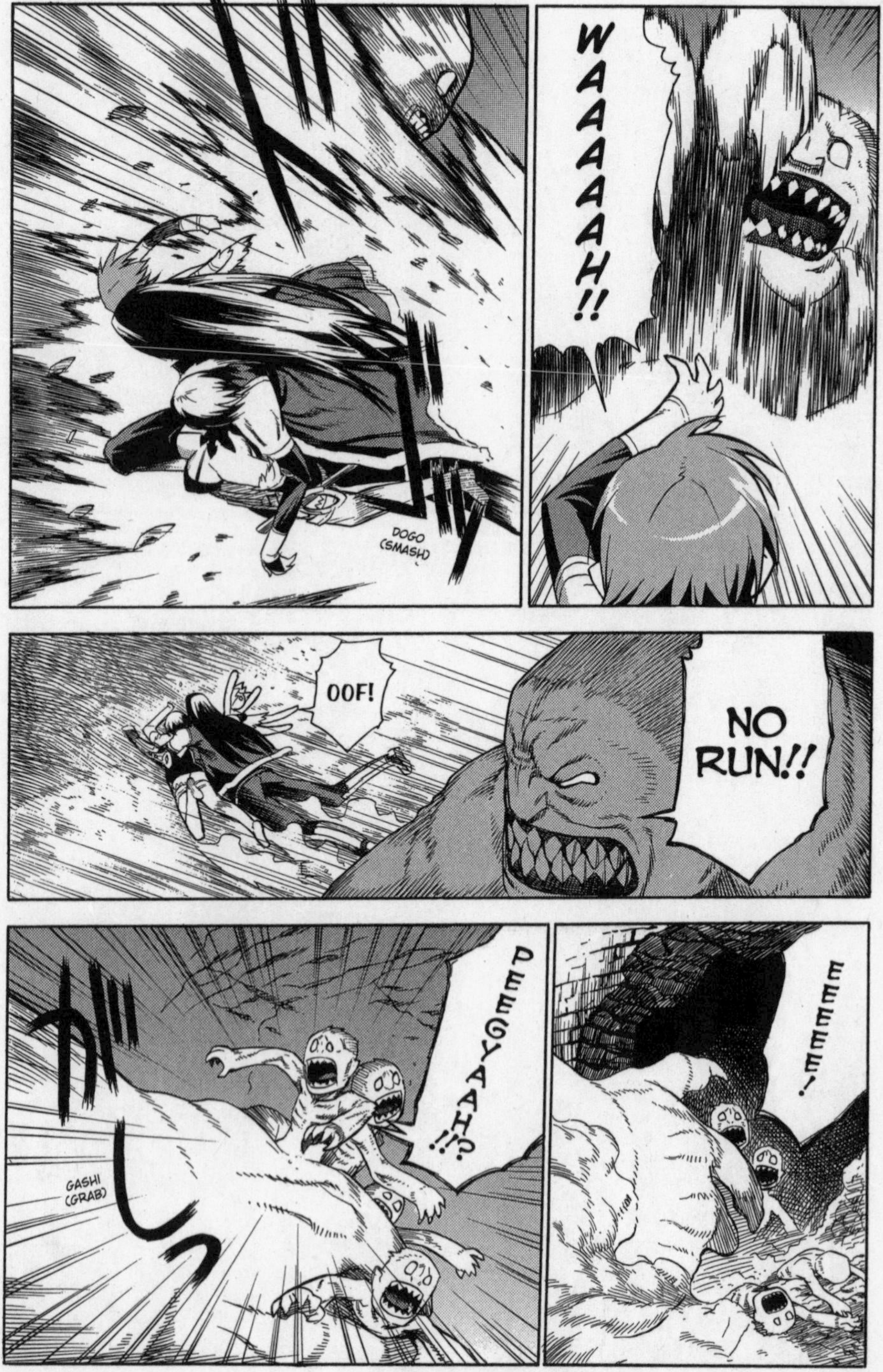
WAAAAAH!!
DOGO (SMASH)
NO RUN!!
OOF!
EEEEE!
PEEGYAAAH!!?
GASHI (GRAB)

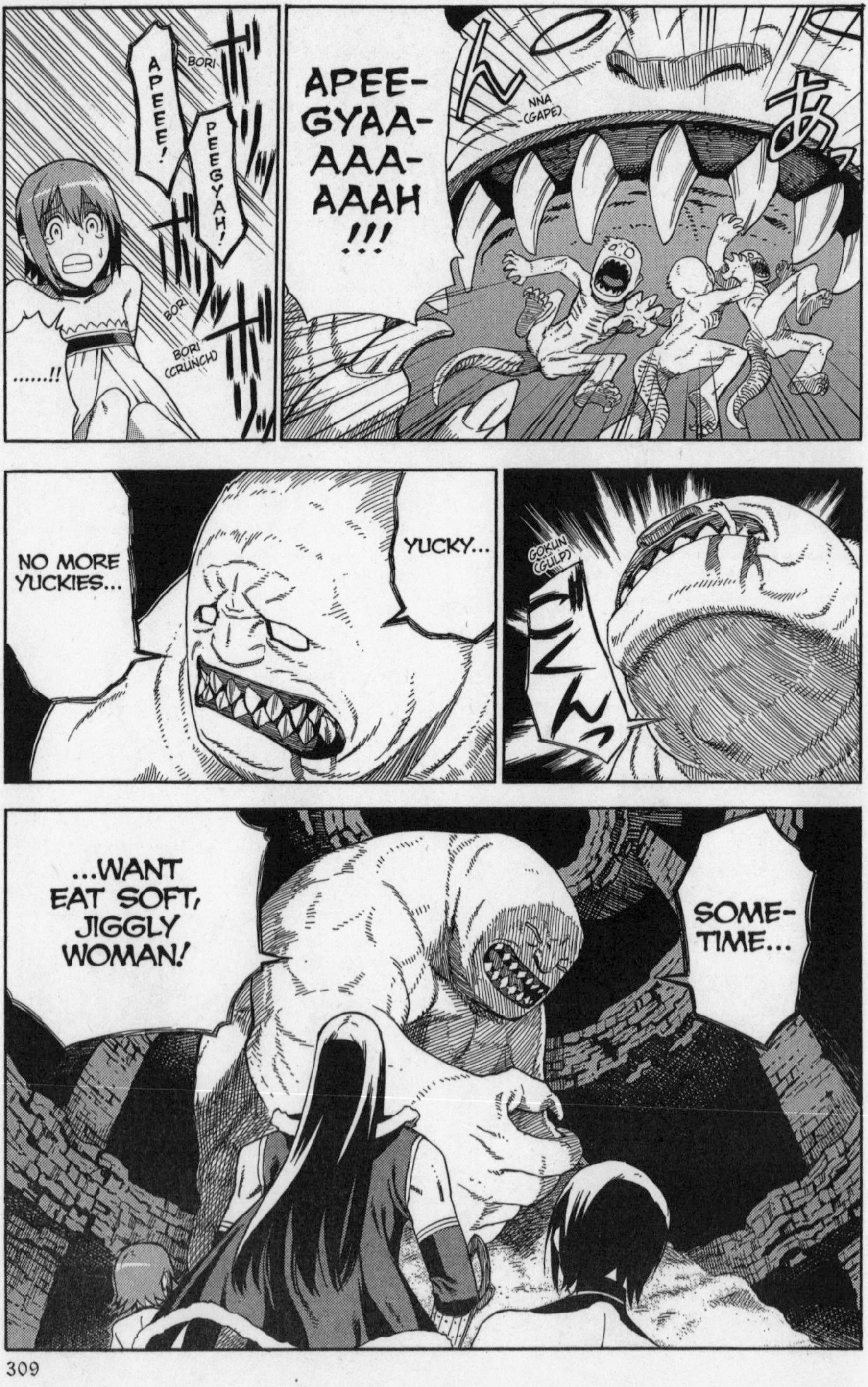
NNA (GAPE)
APEE-GYAA-AAA-AAAH!!!
APEEE!
PEEGYAH!
BORI
BORI
BORI (CRUNCH)
......!!
GOKUN (GULP)
YUCKY...
NO MORE YUCKIES...
SOME-TIME...
...WANT EAT SOFT, JIGGLY WOMAN!

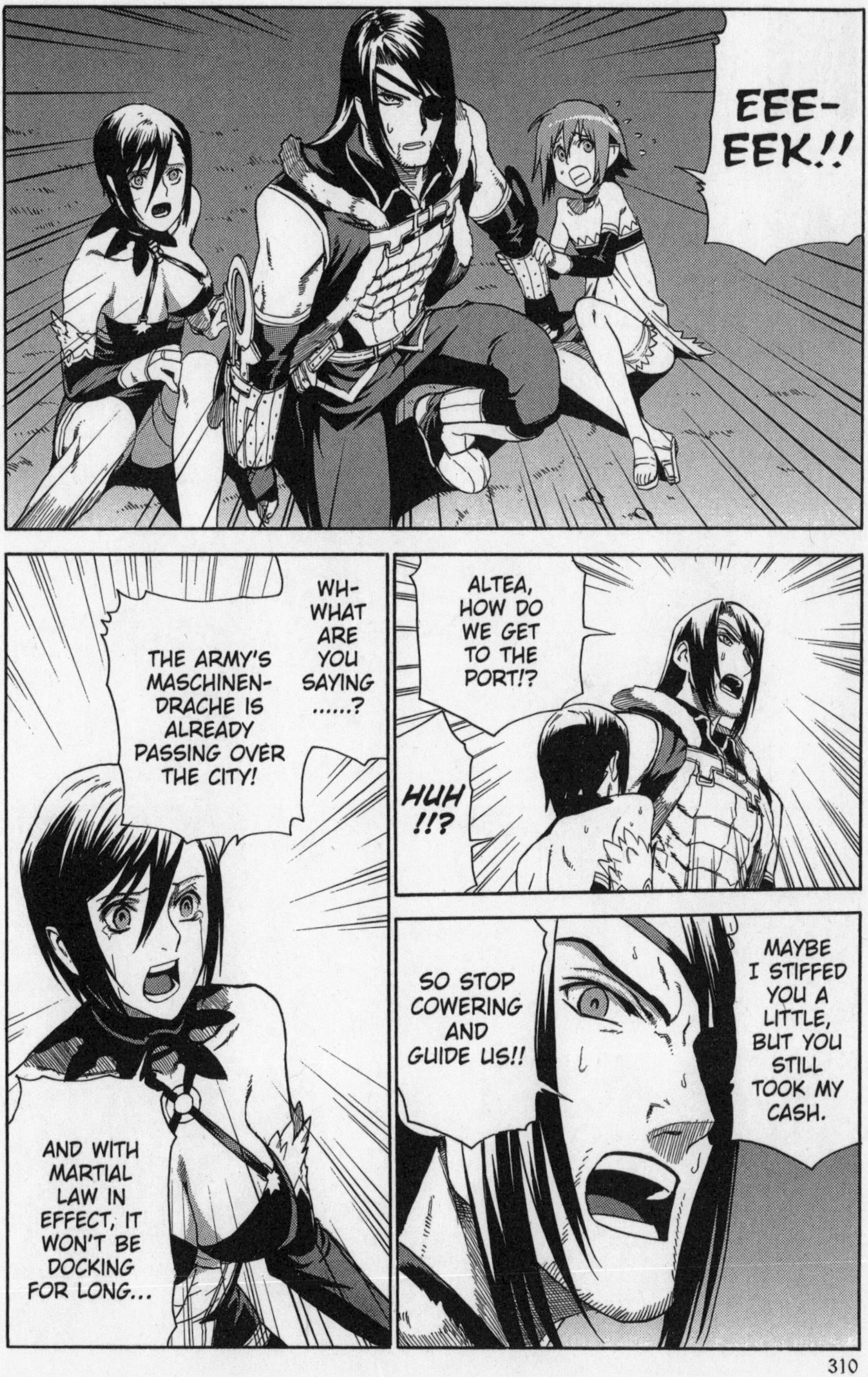
EEE-EEK!!
ALTEA, HOW DO WE GET TO THE PORT!?
HUH!!?
MAYBE I STIFFED YOU A LITTLE, BUT YOU STILL TOOK MY CASH.
SO STOP COWERING AND GUIDE US!!
WH-WHAT ARE YOU SAYING......?
THE ARMY'S MASCHINEN-DRACHE IS ALREADY PASSING OVER THE CITY!
AND WITH MARTIAL LAW IN EFFECT, IT WON'T BE DOCKING FOR LONG...

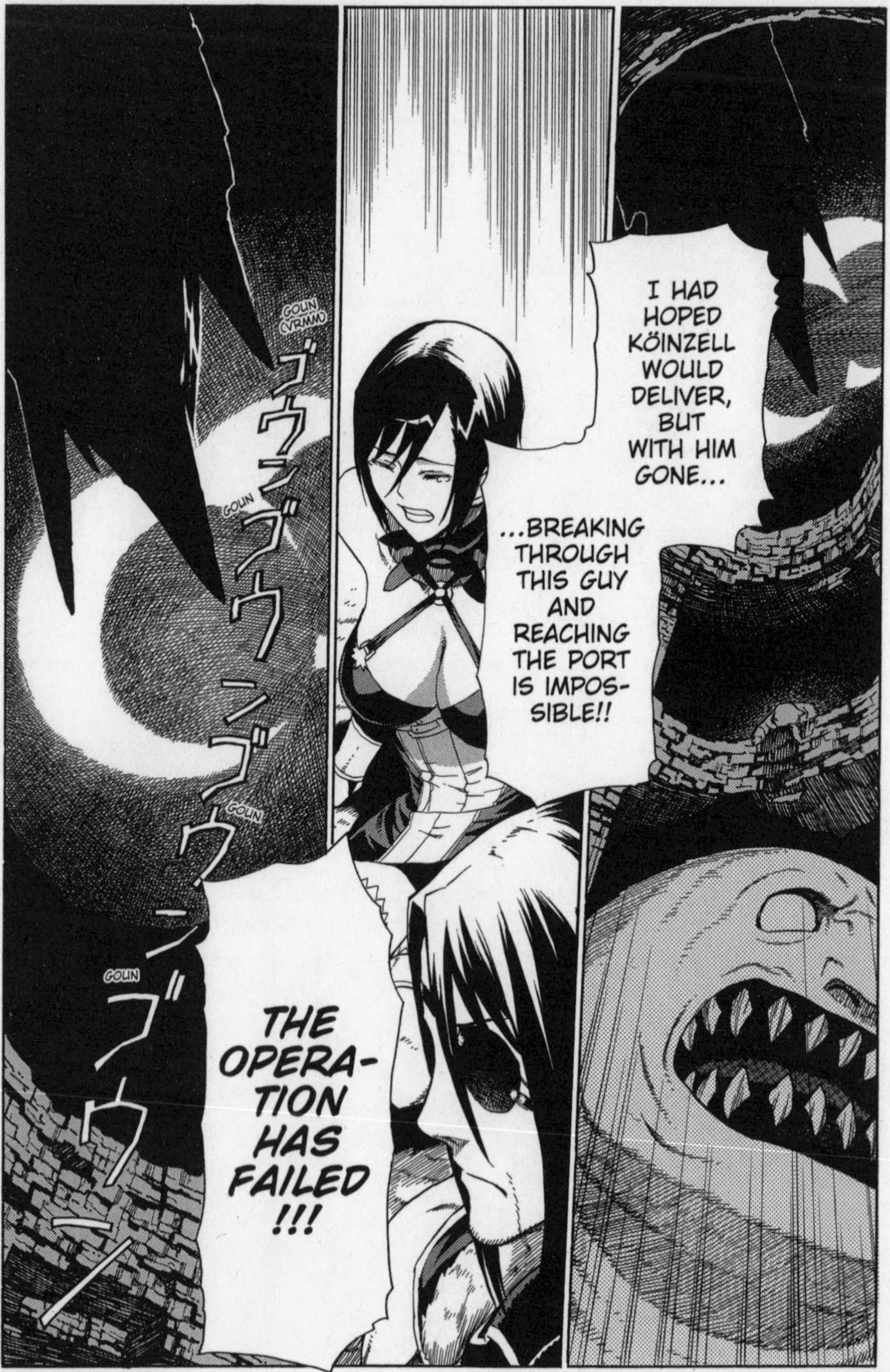
I HAD HOPED KÖINZELL WOULD DELIVER, BUT WITH HIM GONE...
...BREAKING THROUGH THIS GUY AND REACHING THE PORT IS IMPOSSIBLE!!
THE OPERATION HAS FAILED!!!
GOUN (VRMM)
GOUN
GOUN
GOUN

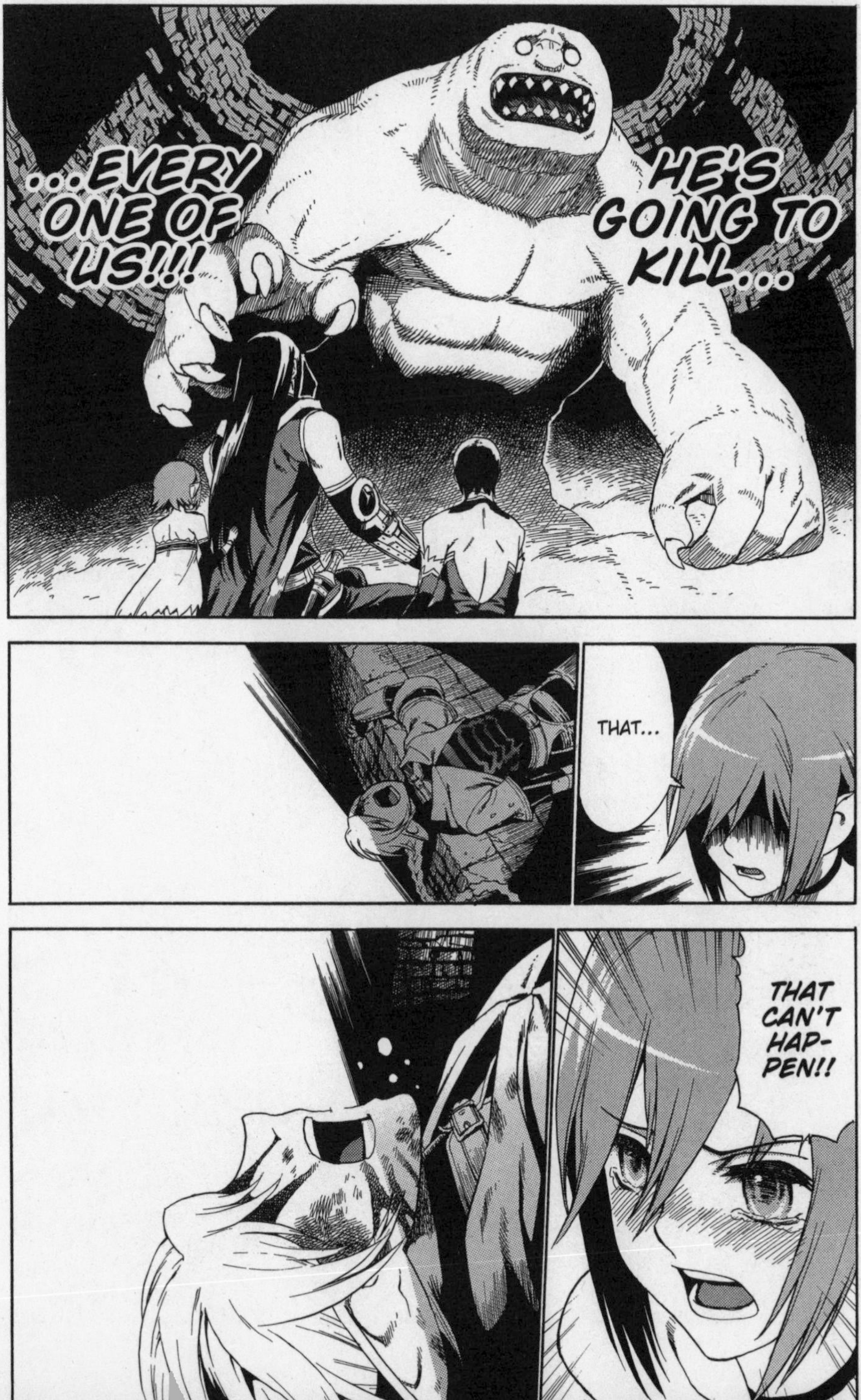
HE'S GOING TO KILL...
...EVERY ONE OF US!!!
THAT...
THAT CAN'T HAP-PEN!!

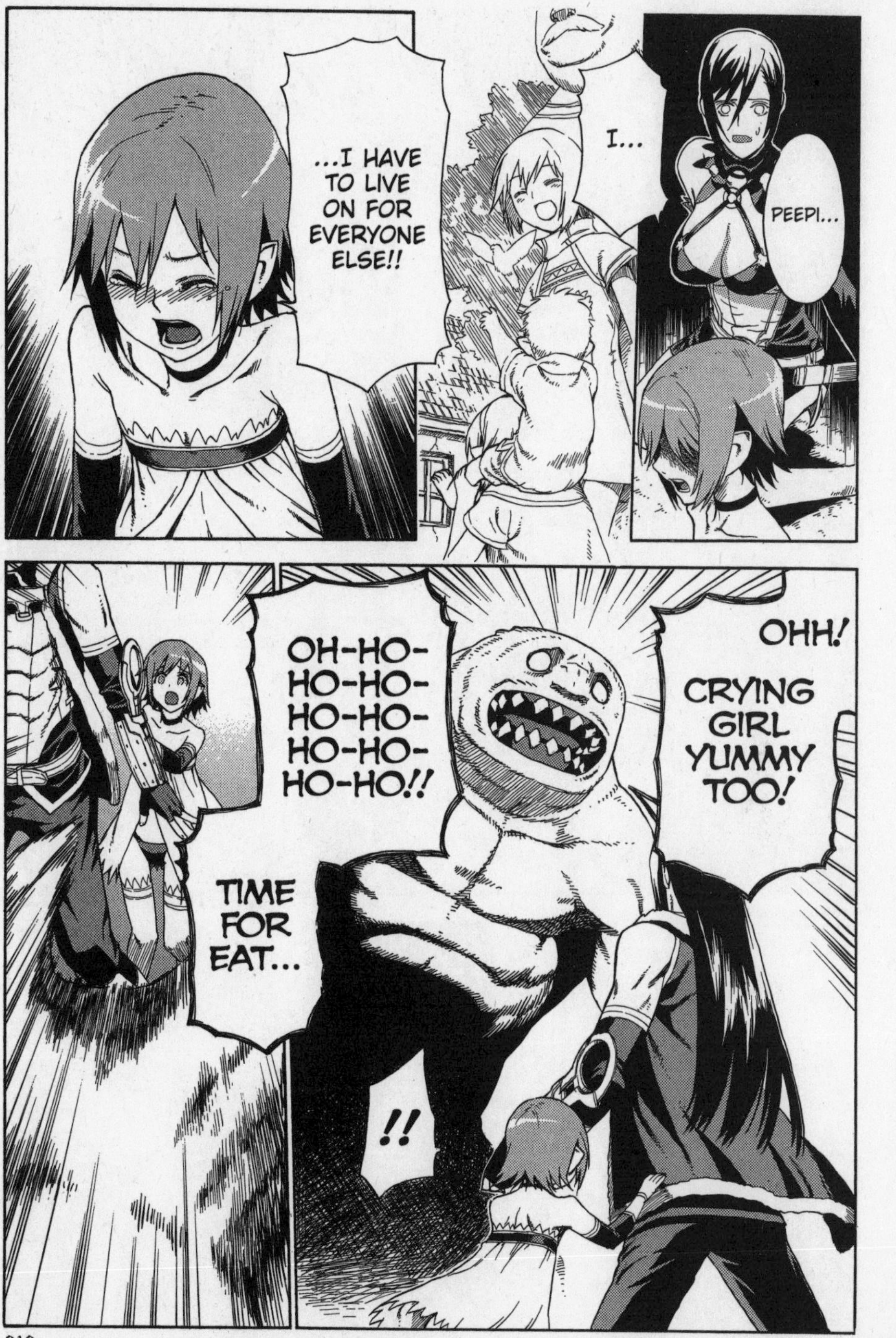
PEEPI...
I...
...I HAVE TO LIVE ON FOR EVERYONE ELSE!!
OHH!
CRYING GIRL YUMMY TOO!
OH-HO-HO-HO-HO-HO-HO-HO-HO-HO!!
TIME FOR EAT...
!!

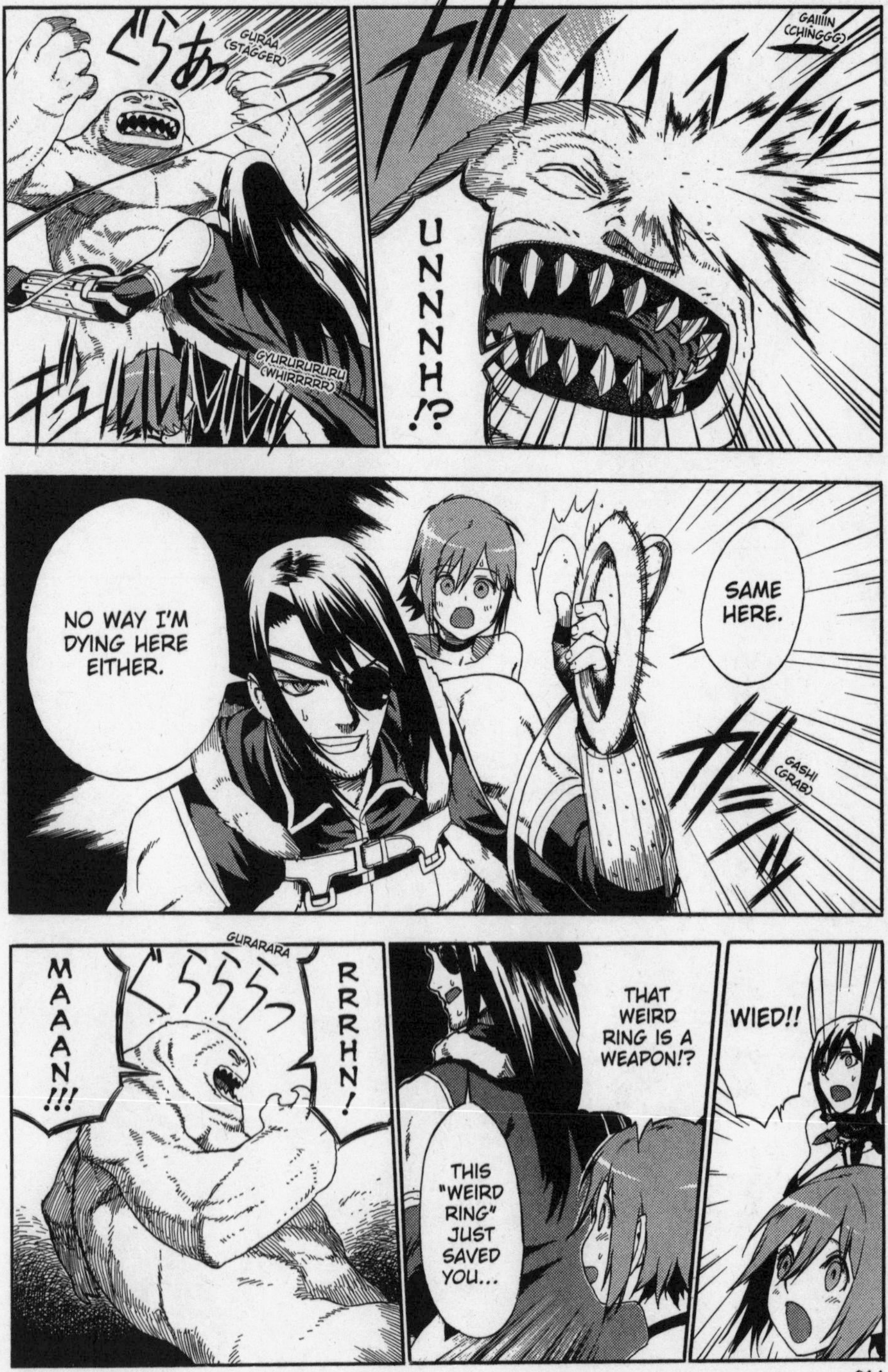
GAIIIIN (CHINGGG)
UNNNH!?
GURAA (STAGGER)
GYURURURURU (WHIRRRRR)
SAME HERE.
GASHI (GRAB)
NO WAY I'M DYING HERE EITHER.
WIED!!
THAT WEIRD RING IS A WEAPON!?
THIS "WEIRD RING" JUST SAVED YOU...
RRRHN!
GURARARA
MAAAN!!!

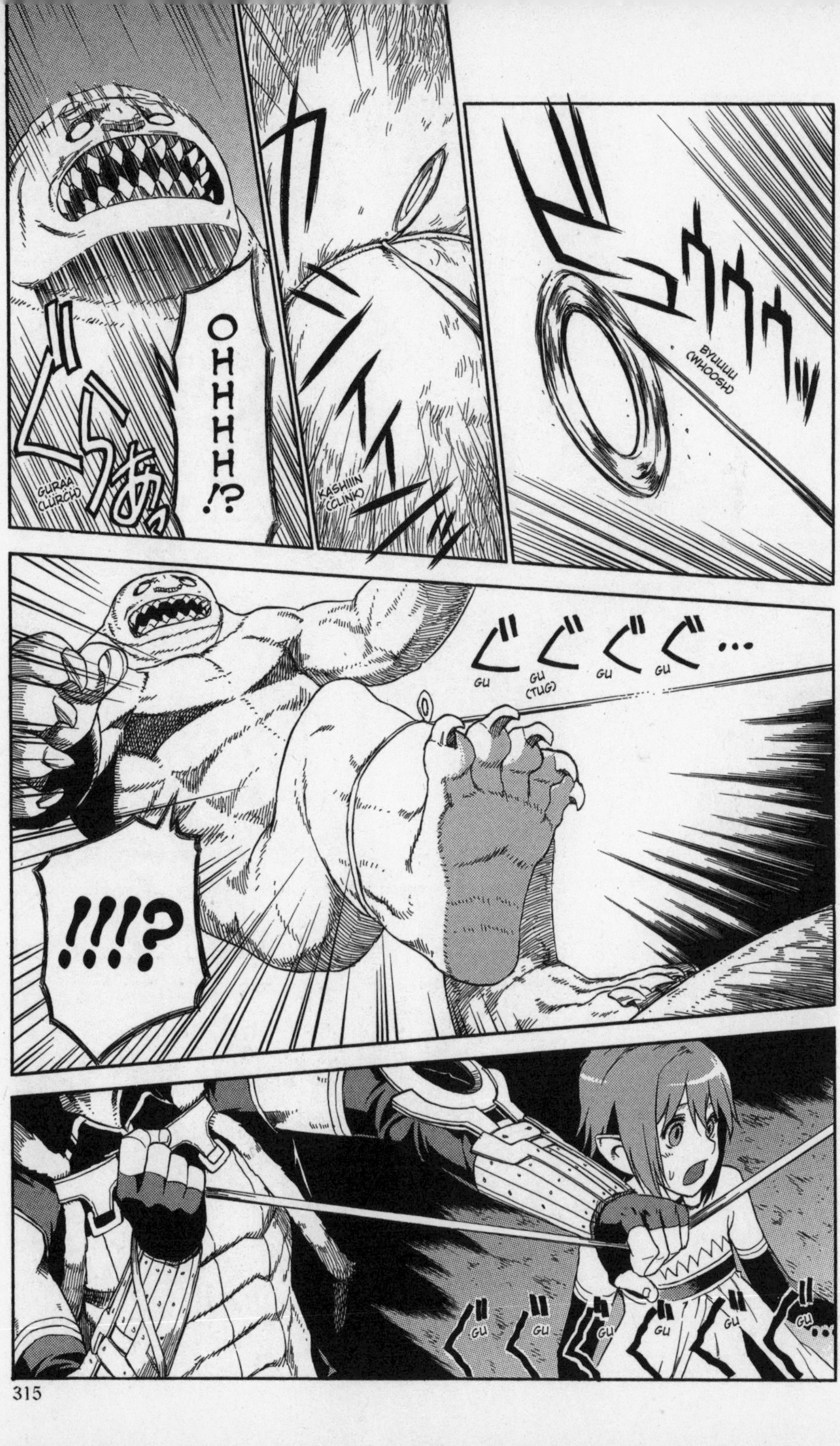
BYUUUU (WHOOSH)
KASHIIIN (CLINK)
ぐらぁっ
GURAA (LURCH)
OHHHHH!?
ぐぐぐぐ…
GU GU (TUG) GU GU
!!!?
GU GU GU GU GU GU...

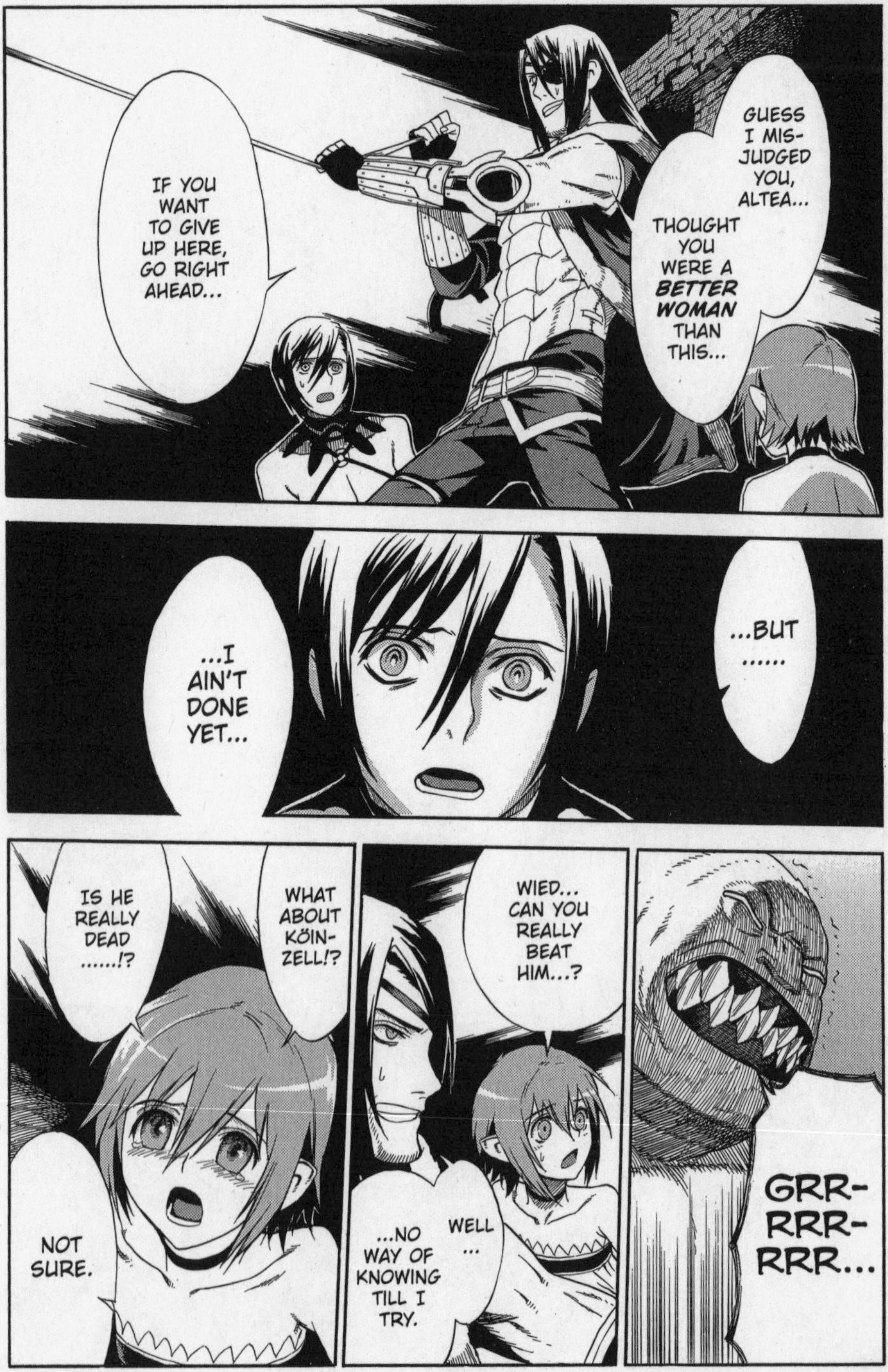
GUESS I MIS-JUDGED YOU, ALTEA...
THOUGHT YOU WERE A **BETTER WOMAN** THAN THIS...
IF YOU WANT TO GIVE UP HERE, GO RIGHT AHEAD...
...BUT ......
...I AIN'T DONE YET...
GRR-RRR-RRR...
WIED... CAN YOU REALLY BEAT HIM...?
WELL ...
...NO WAY OF KNOWING TILL I TRY.
WHAT ABOUT KÖIN-ZELL!?
IS HE REALLY DEAD ......!?
NOT SURE.

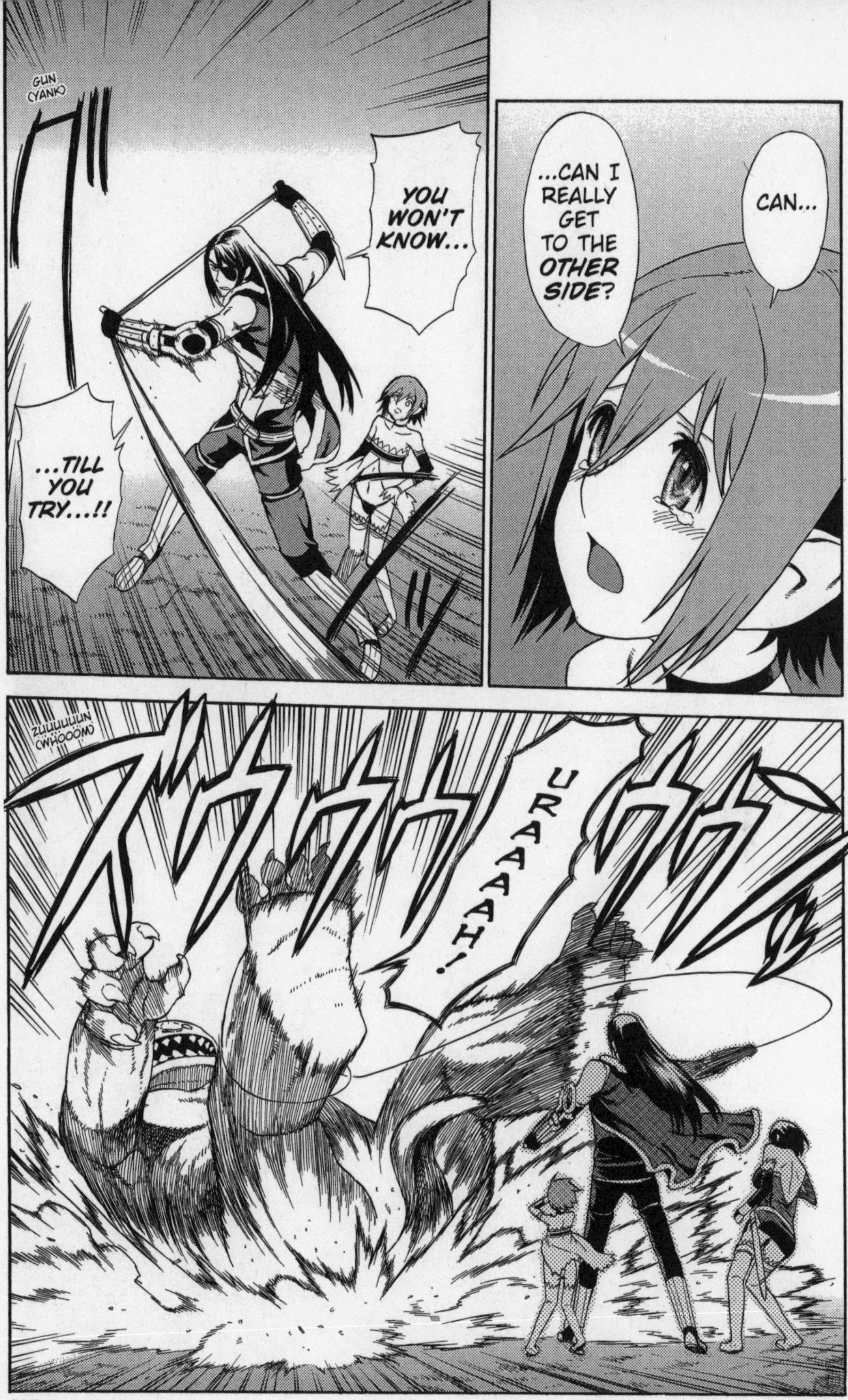
CAN...
...CAN I REALLY GET TO THE OTHER SIDE?
GUN (YANK)
YOU WON'T KNOW...
...TILL YOU TRY...!!
ZUUUUUUN (WHOOOM)
URAAAAAH!

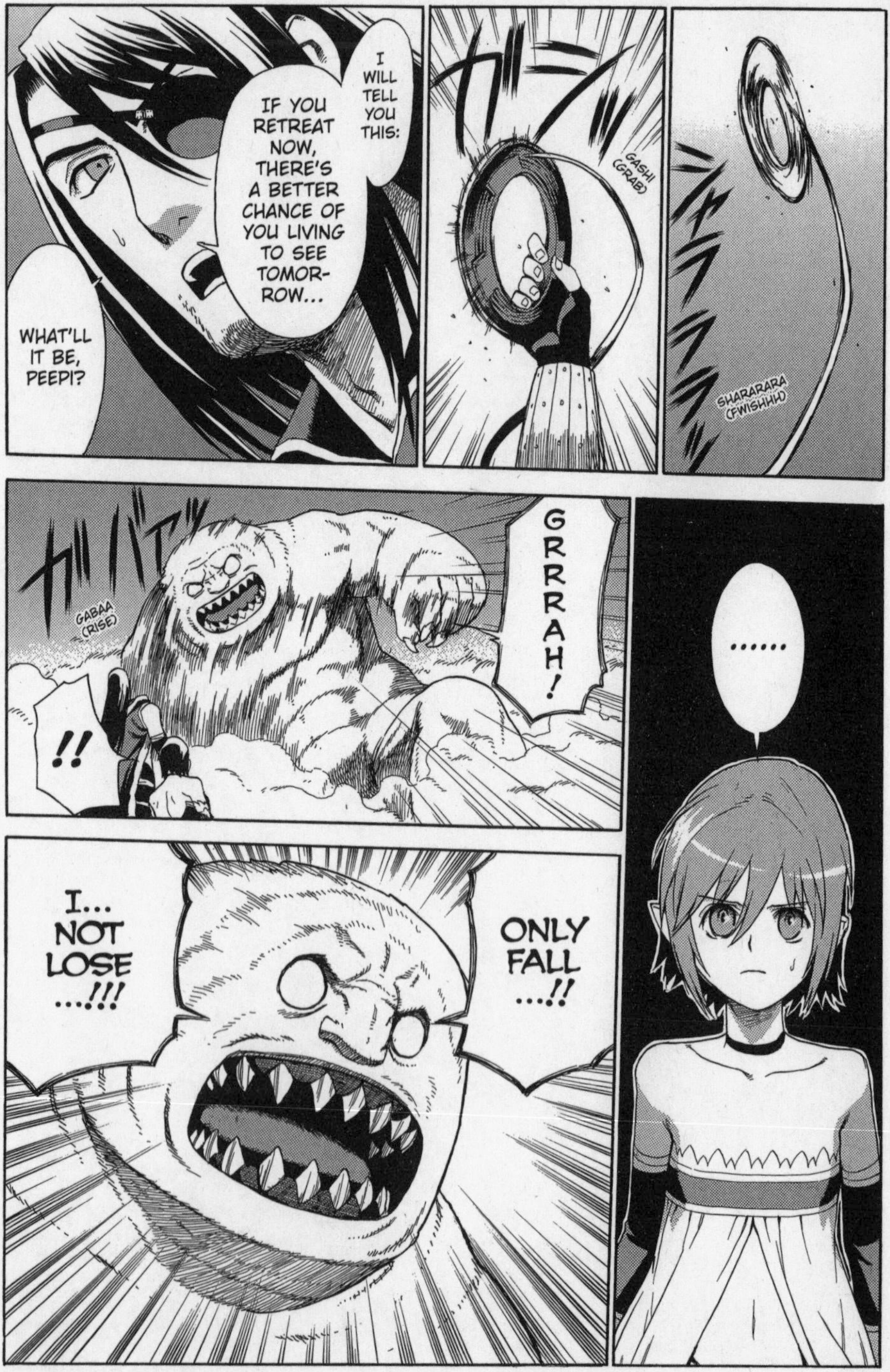
SHARARARA (FWISHHH)
GASHI (GRAB)
I WILL TELL YOU THIS:
IF YOU RETREAT NOW, THERE'S A BETTER CHANCE OF YOU LIVING TO SEE TOMORROW...
WHAT'LL IT BE, PEEPI?
......
GRRRAH!
GABAA (RISE)
!!
ONLY FALL ...!!
I... NOT LOSE ...!!!

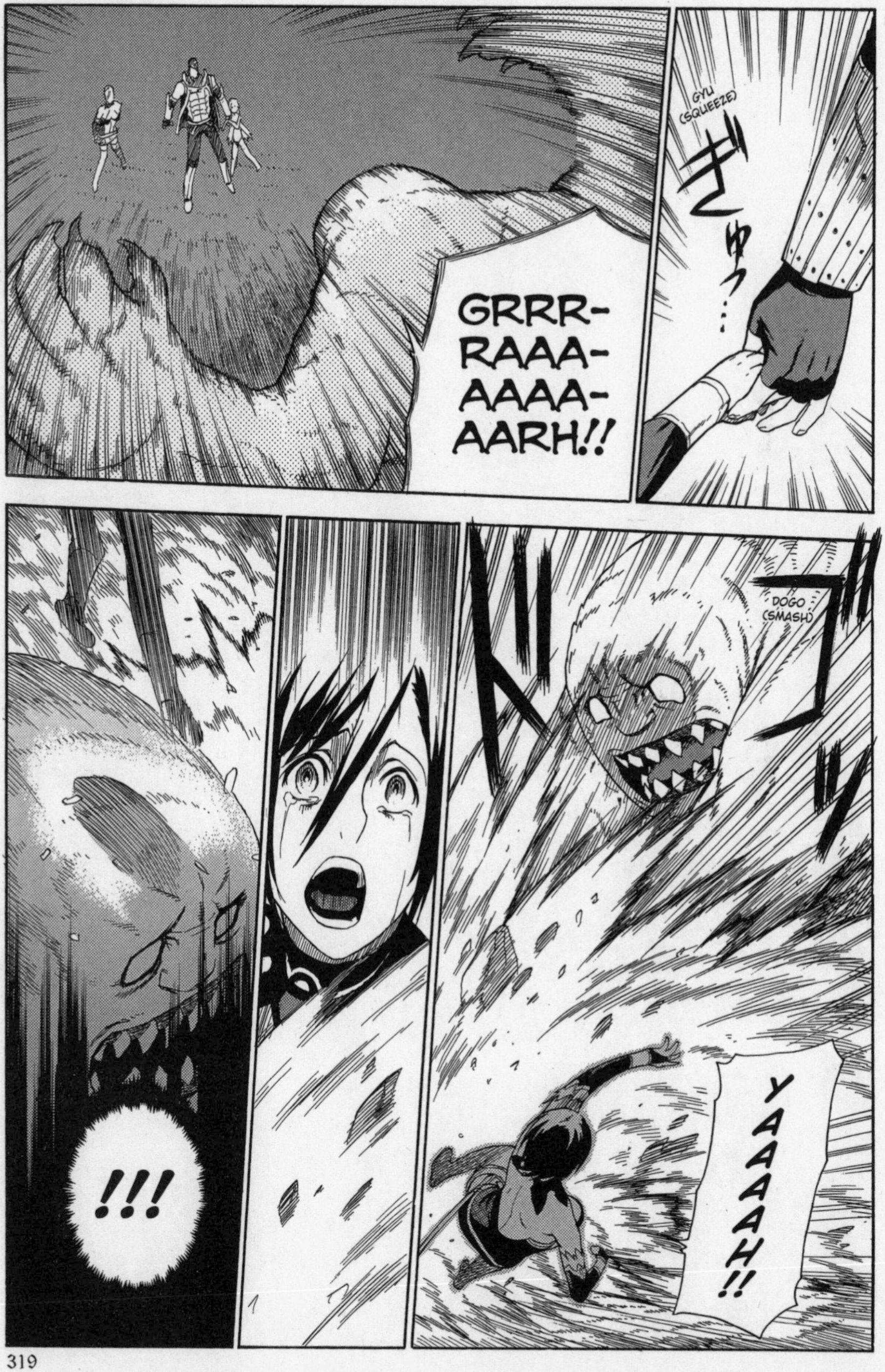
GYU (SQUEEZE)
ぎゅっ…
GRRR-RAAA-AAAA-AARH!!
DOGO (SMASH)
ドゴッ
YAAAAAH!!
!!!

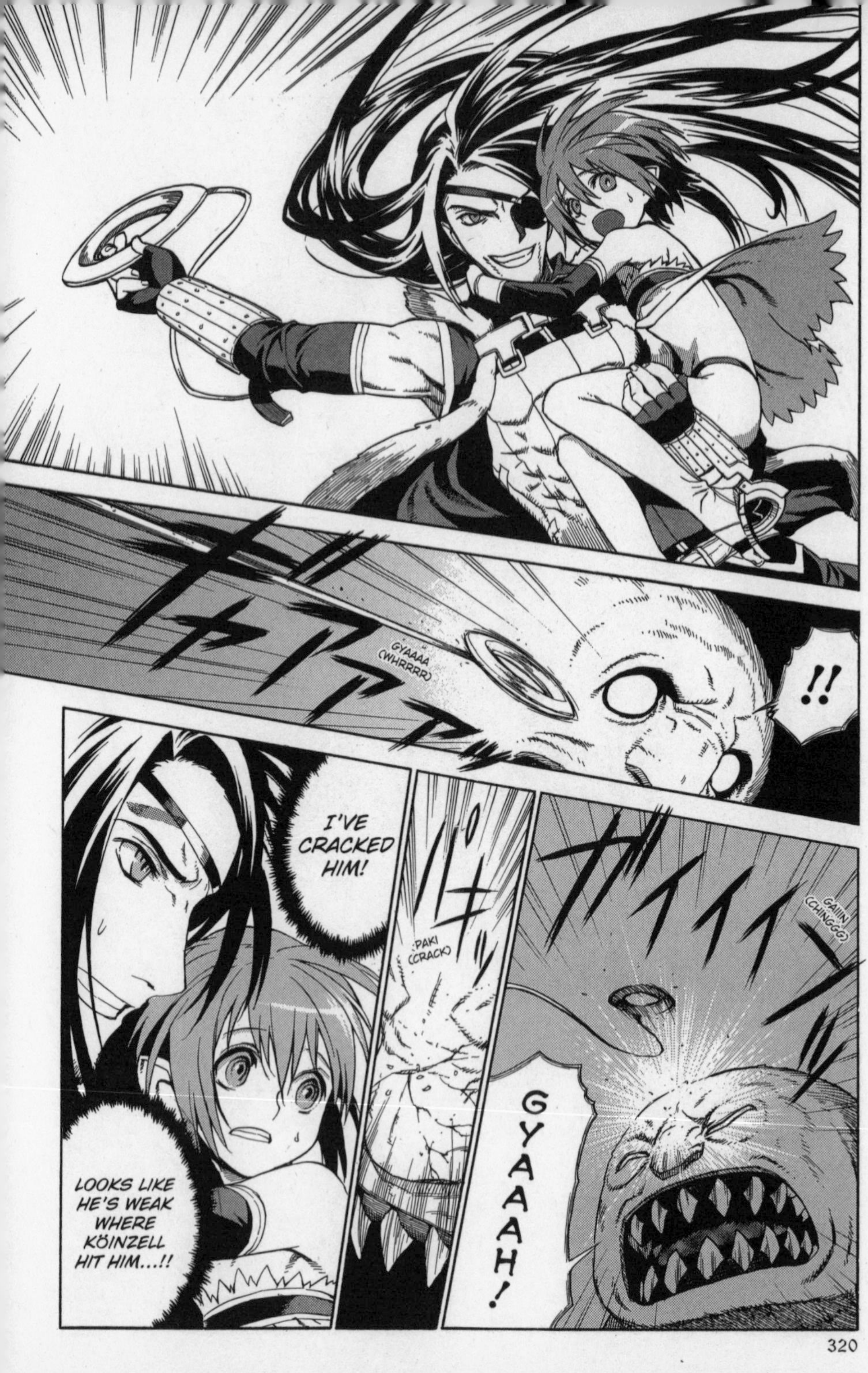
GYAAAA (WHRRRR)
!!
GAIIIN (CHINGGG)
GYAAAH!
PAKI (CRACK)
I'VE CRACKED HIM!
LOOKS LIKE HE'S WEAK WHERE KÖINZELL HIT HIM...!!

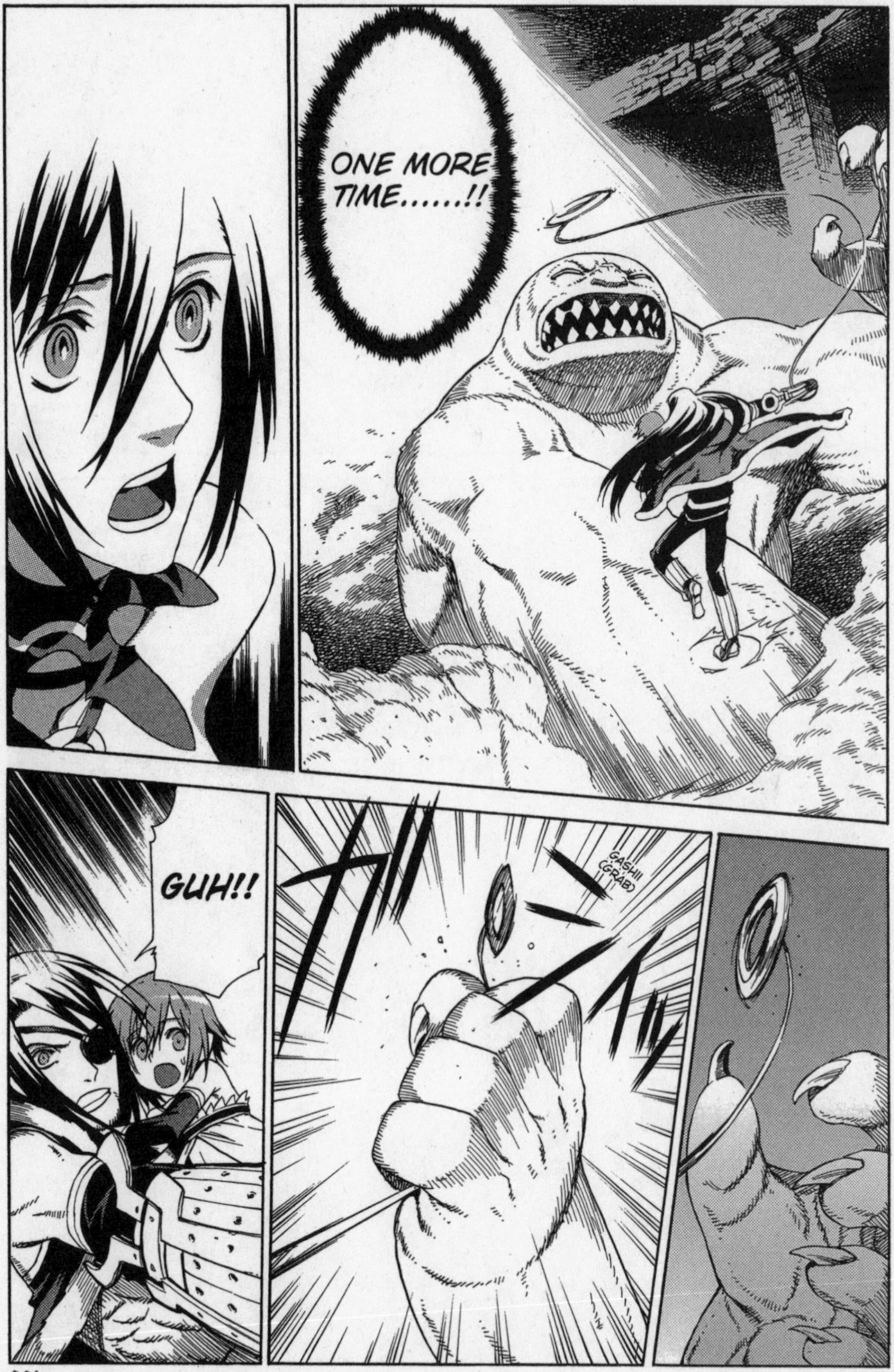
ONE MORE TIME......!!
GASHI! (GRAB)
GUH!!

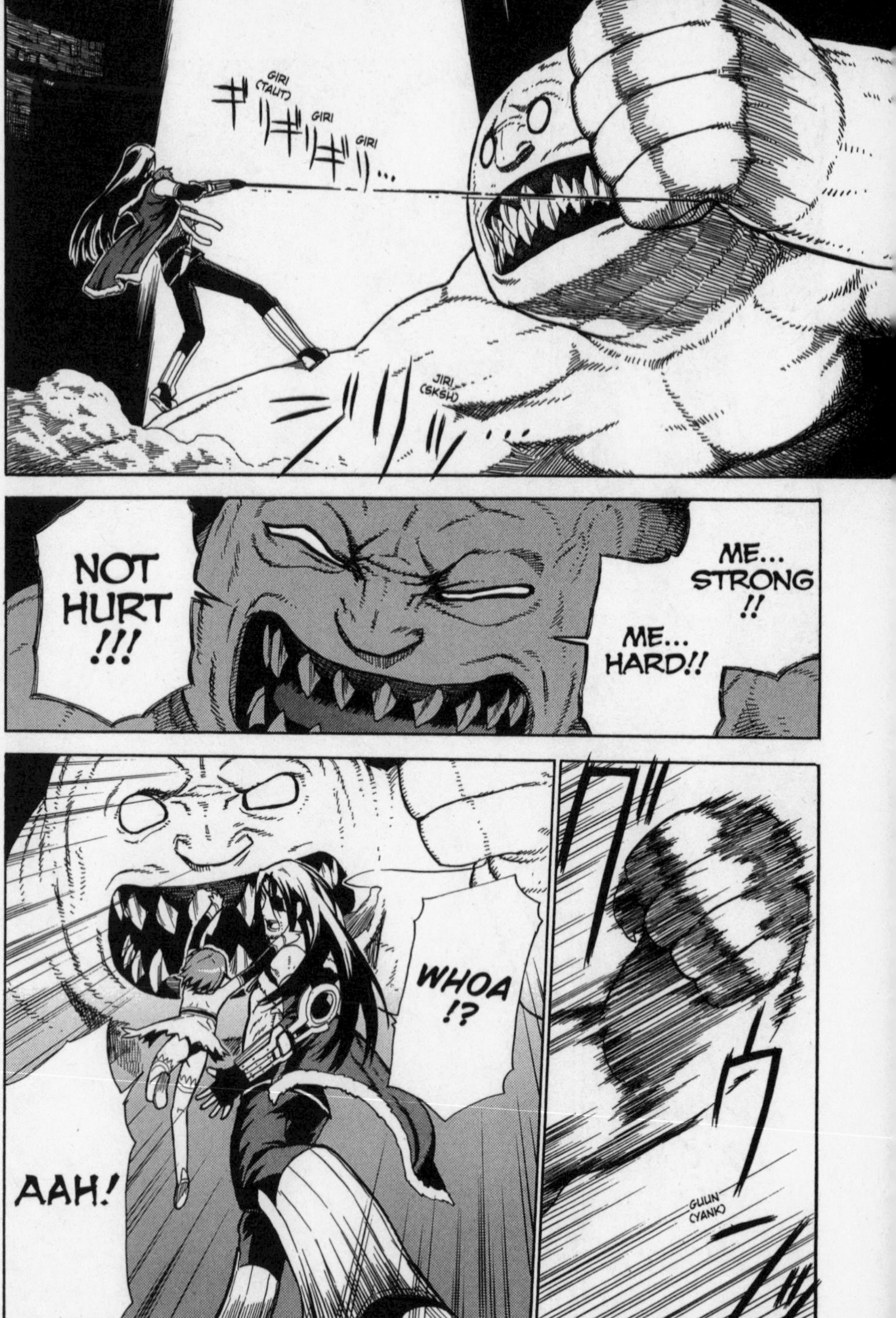
GIRI (TAUT)
ギリギリギリ…
GIRI
GIRI
JIRI (SKSH)
ME... STRONG!!
ME... HARD!!
NOT HURT!!!
GUUN (YANK)
WHOA!?
AAH!

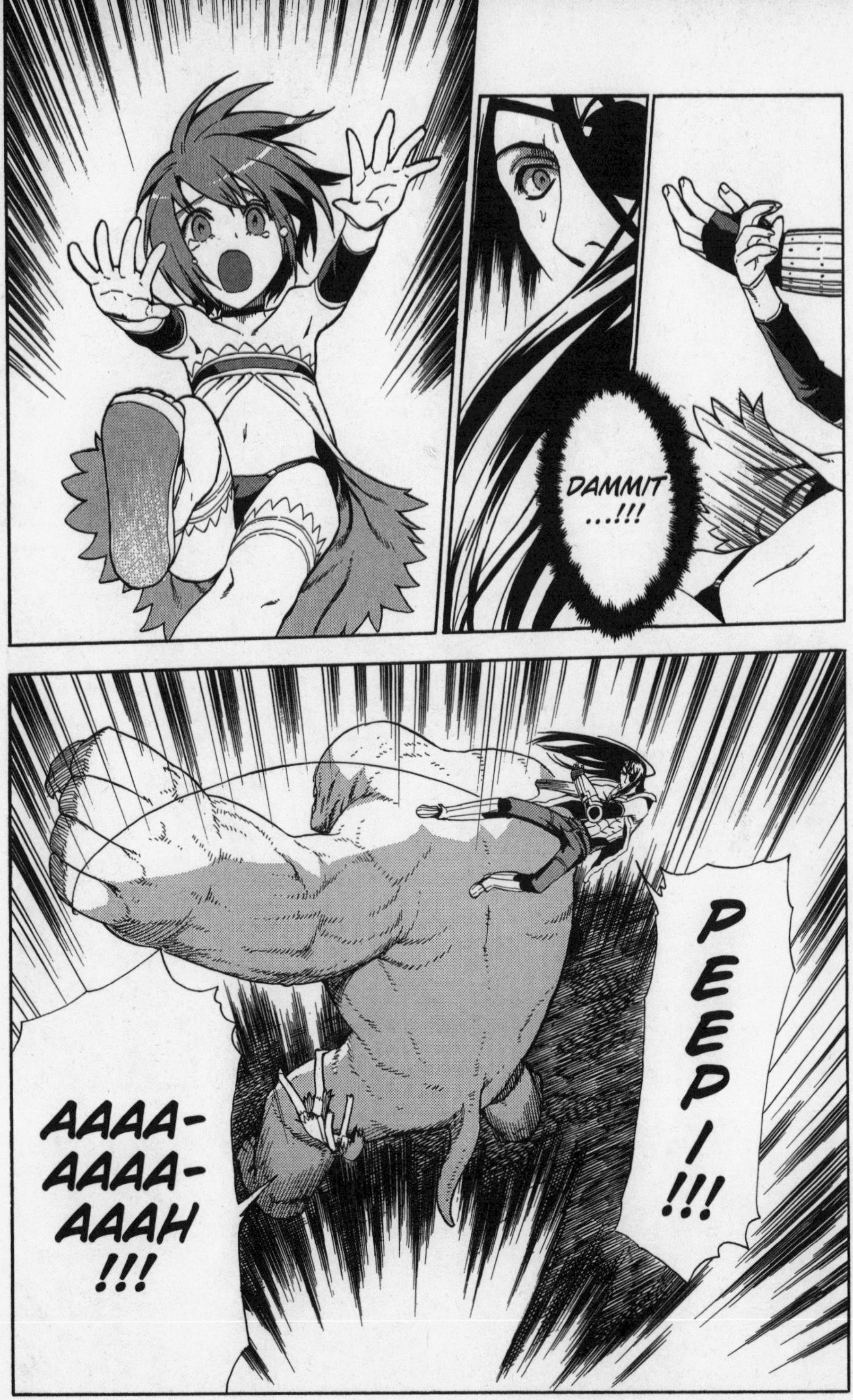
DAMMIT ...!!!
PEEP !!!!
AAAA-AAAA-AAAH !!!

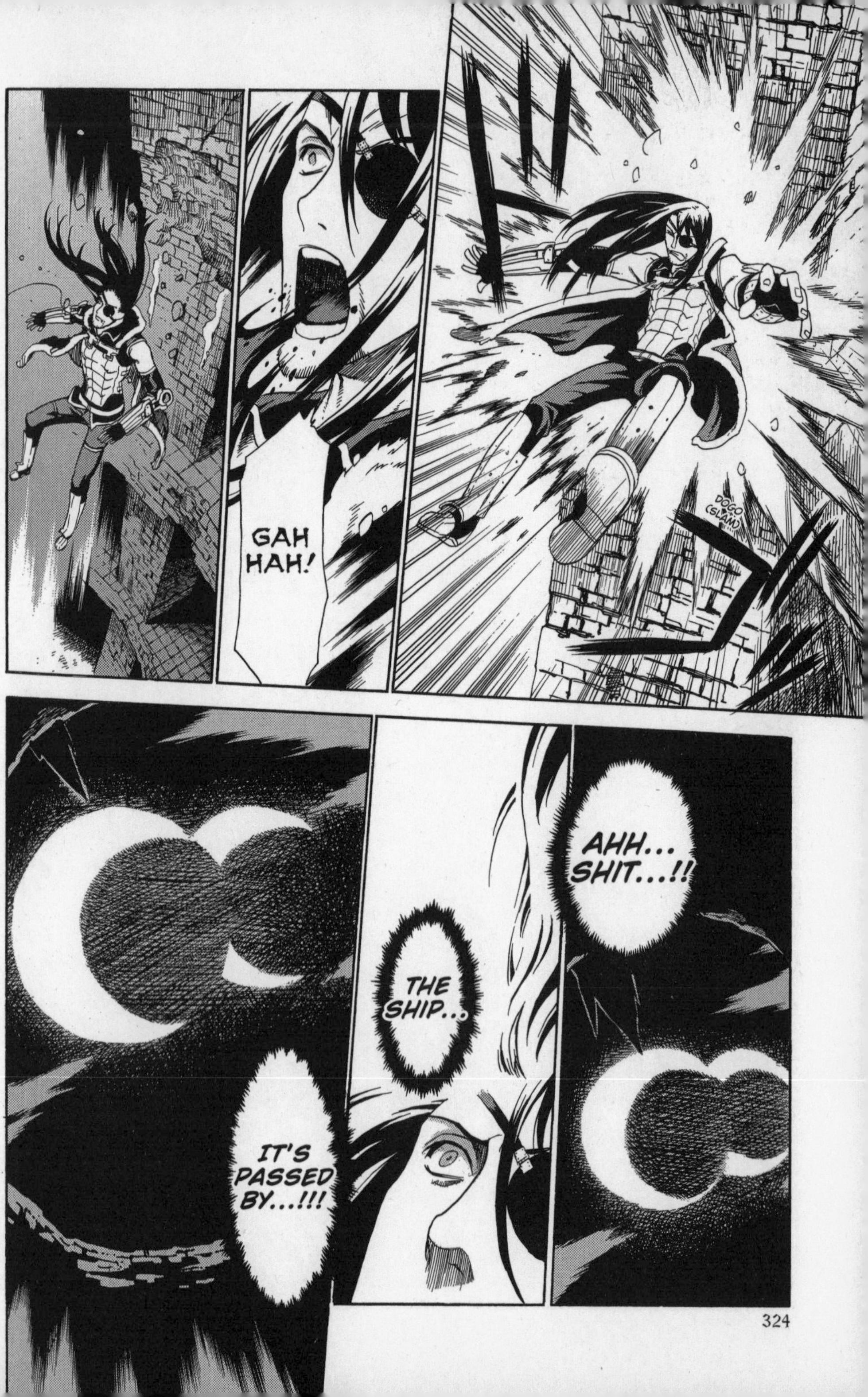
DOGO (SLAM)
GAH HAH!
AHH... SHIT...!!
THE SHIP...
IT'S PASSED BY...!!!

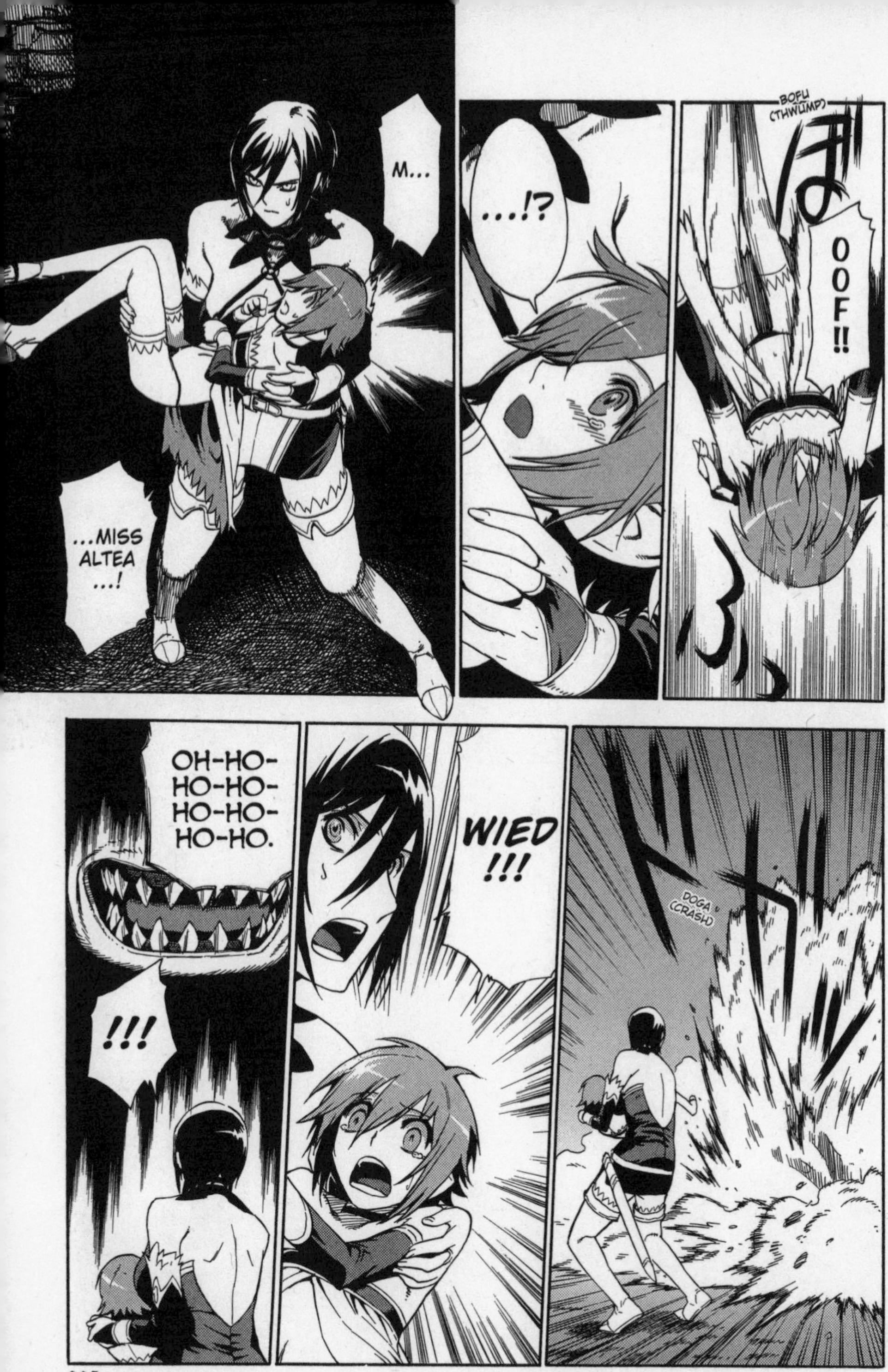
BOFU (THWUMP)
OOF!!
...!?
M...
...MISS ALTEA ...!
DOGA (CRASH)
WIED !!!
OH-HO-HO-HO-HO-HO-HO-HO.
!!!

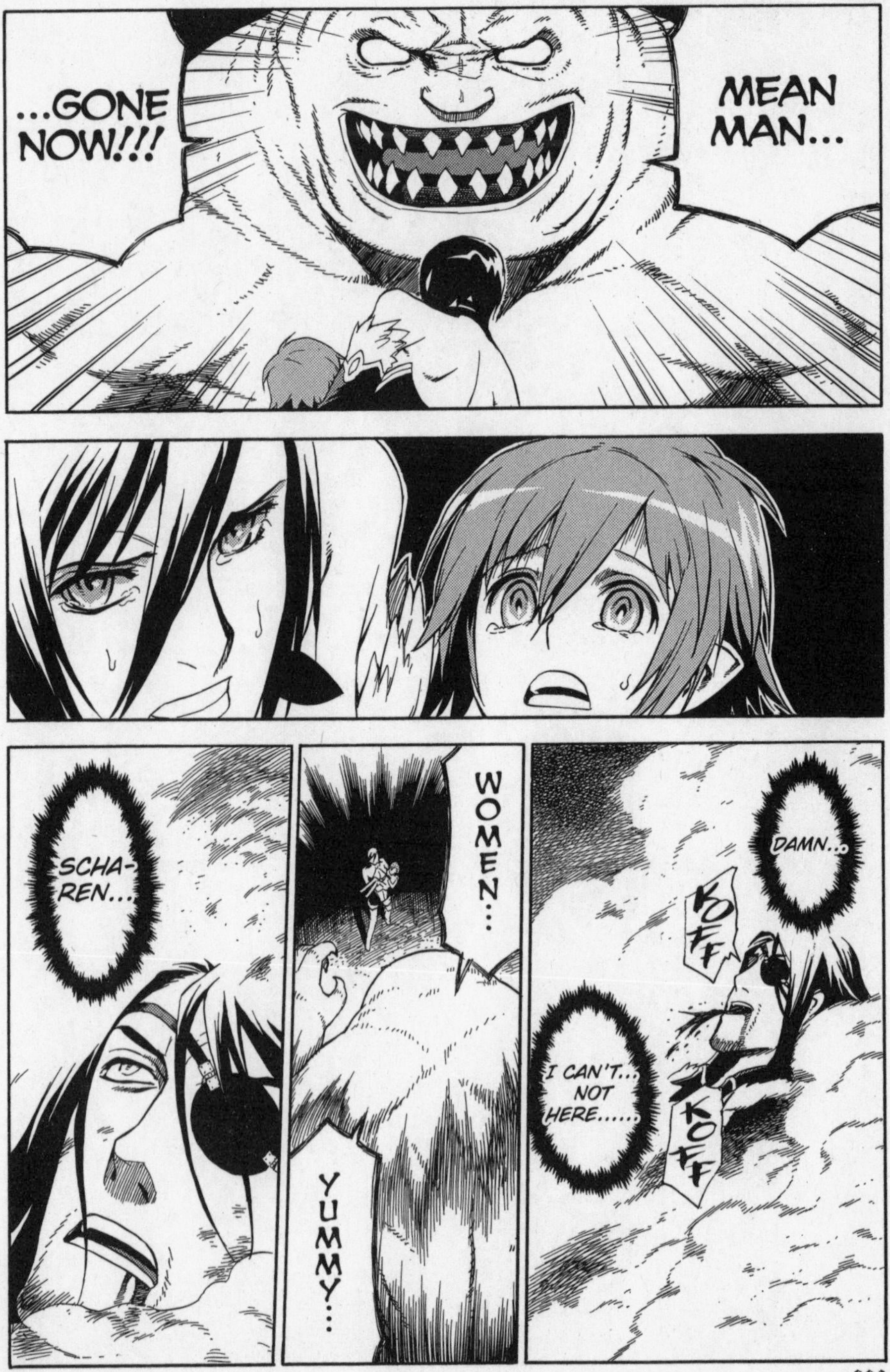
MEAN MAN...
...GONE NOW!!!
DAMN...
KOFF
I CAN'T... NOT HERE......
KOFF
WOMEN...
YUMMY...
SCHA-REN...

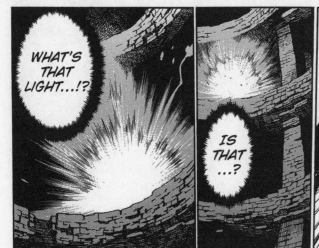

WHAT'S THAT LIGHT...!?

IS THAT...?

!?

RRRAAAAAAH!!

!!!!

WHO EAT FIRST?

WHO FIRST?

NOOOO!!!

N... NO......

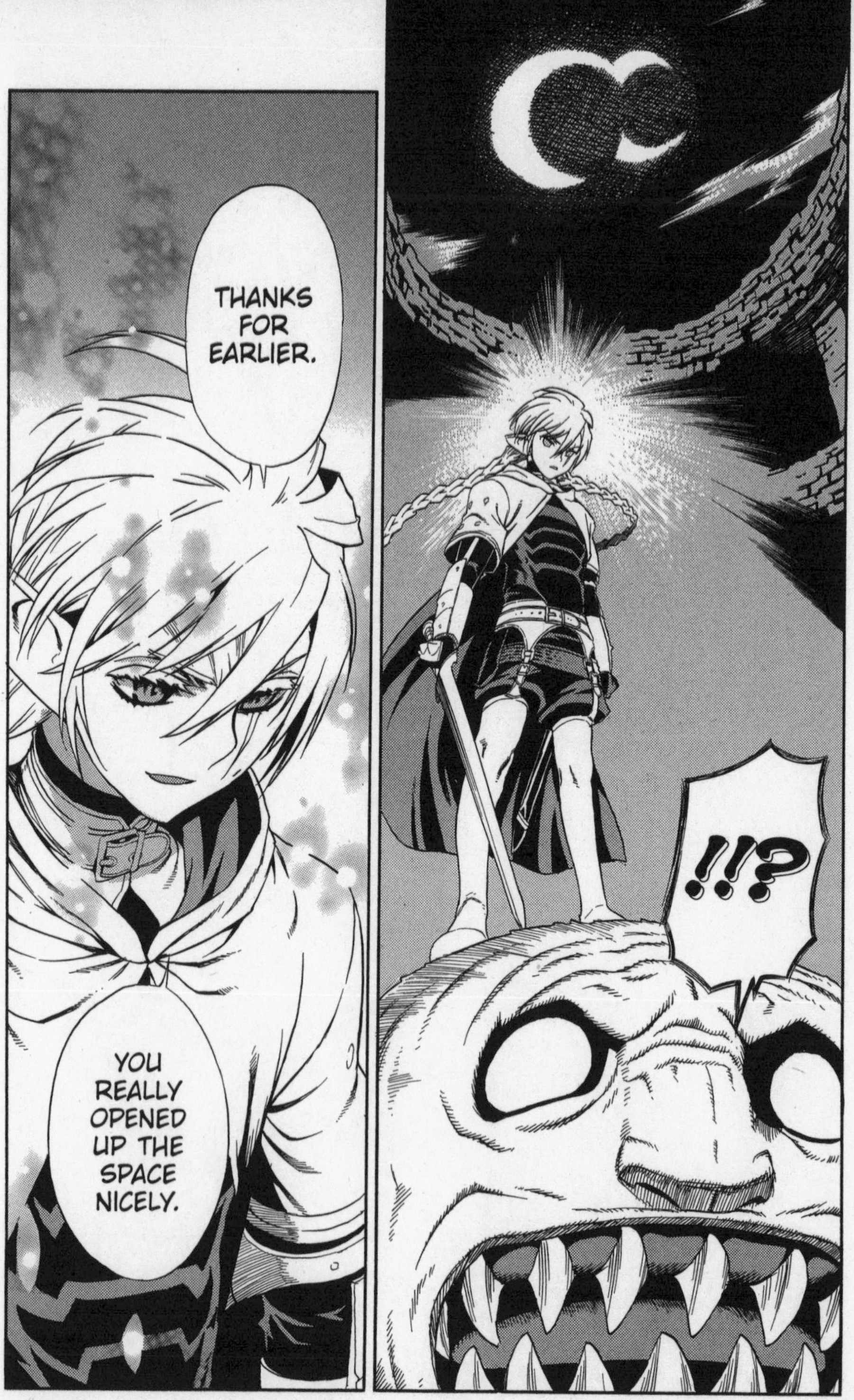
!!?
THANKS FOR EARLIER.
YOU REALLY OPENED UP THE SPACE NICELY.

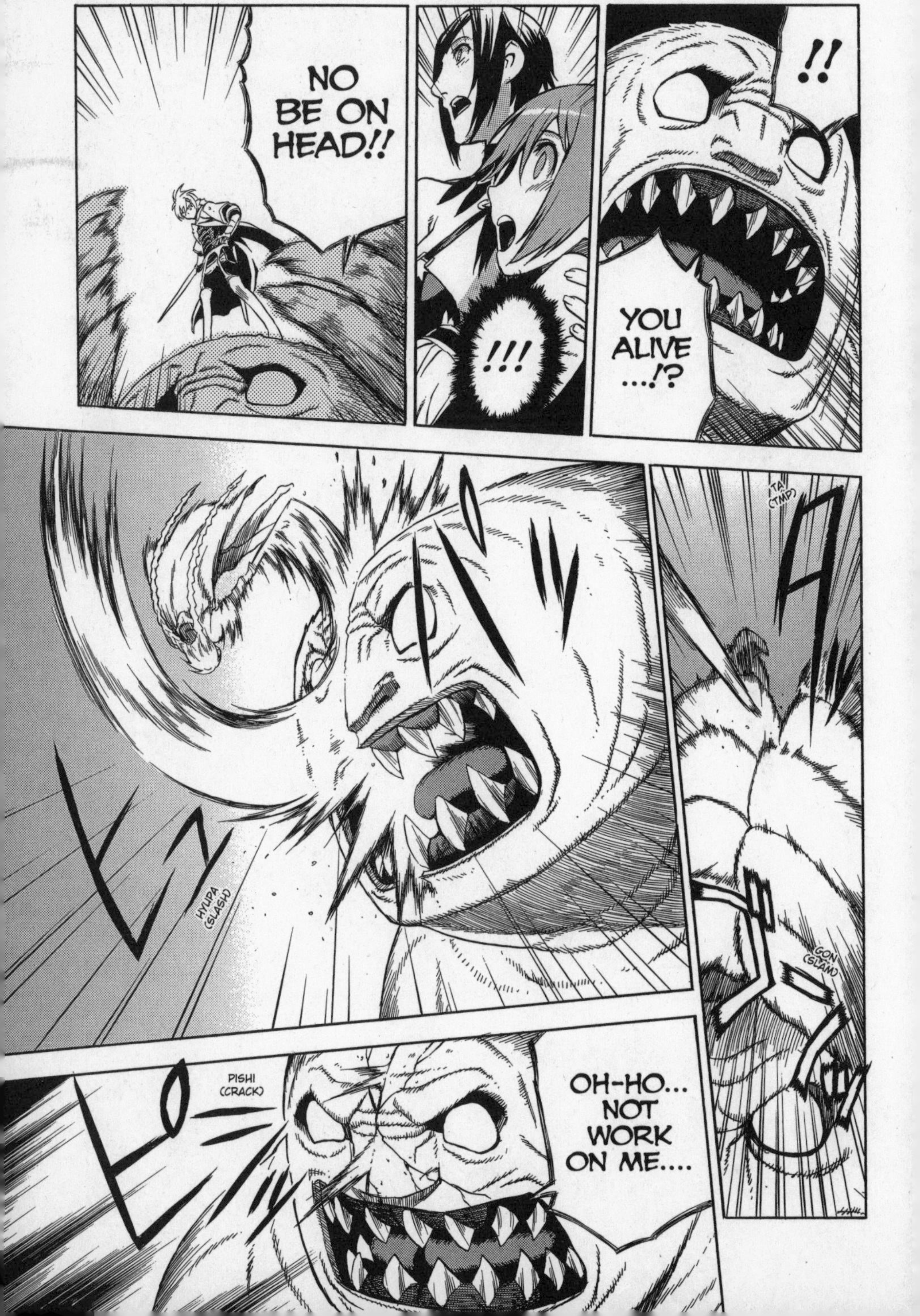
!!
YOU ALIVE ...!?
!!!
NO BE ON HEAD!!
TA (TMP)
GON (SLAM)
HYUPA (SLASH)
OH-HO... NOT WORK ON ME....
PISHI (CRACK)

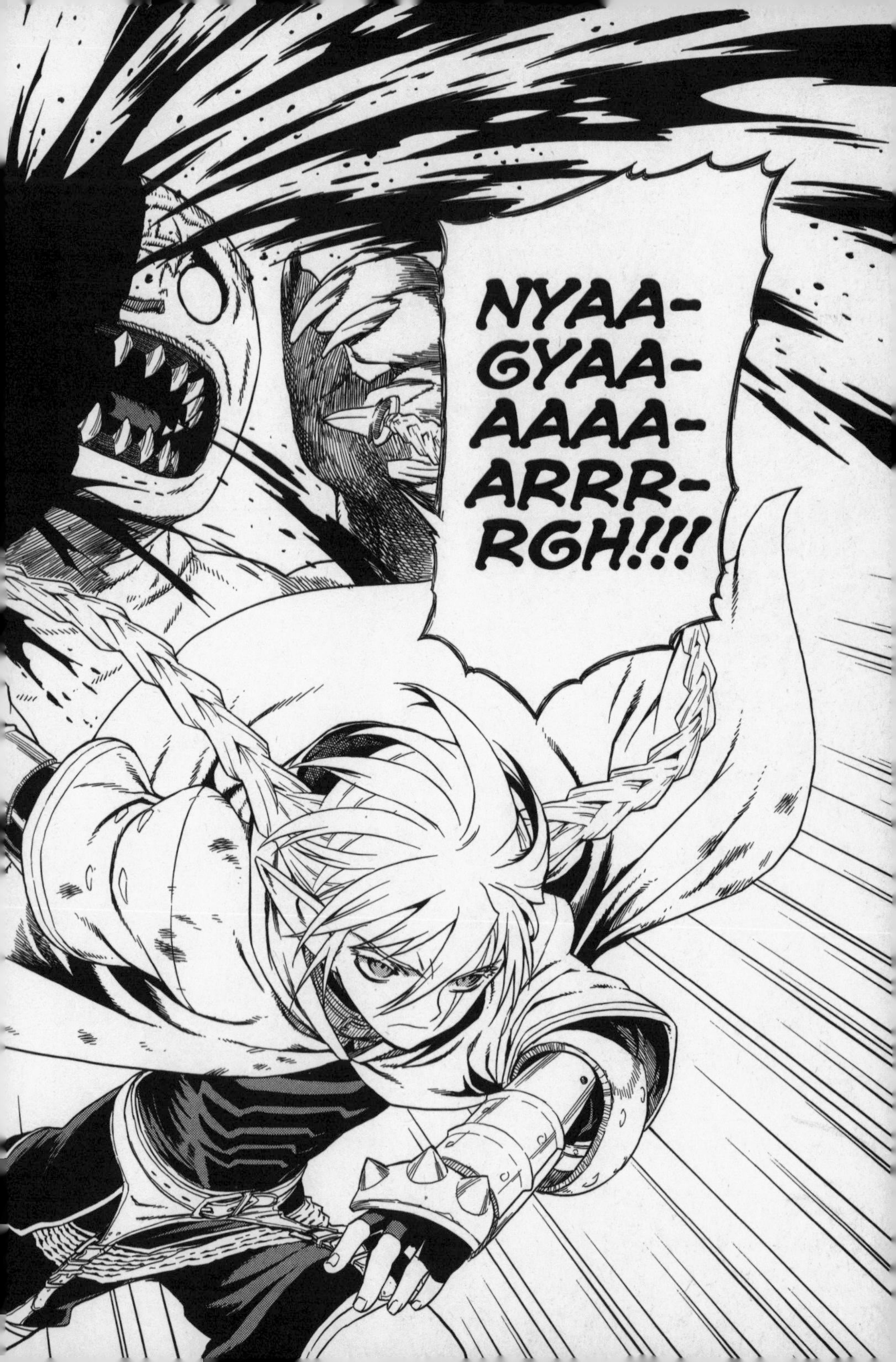
NYAA-GYAA-AAAA-ARRR-RGH!!!!

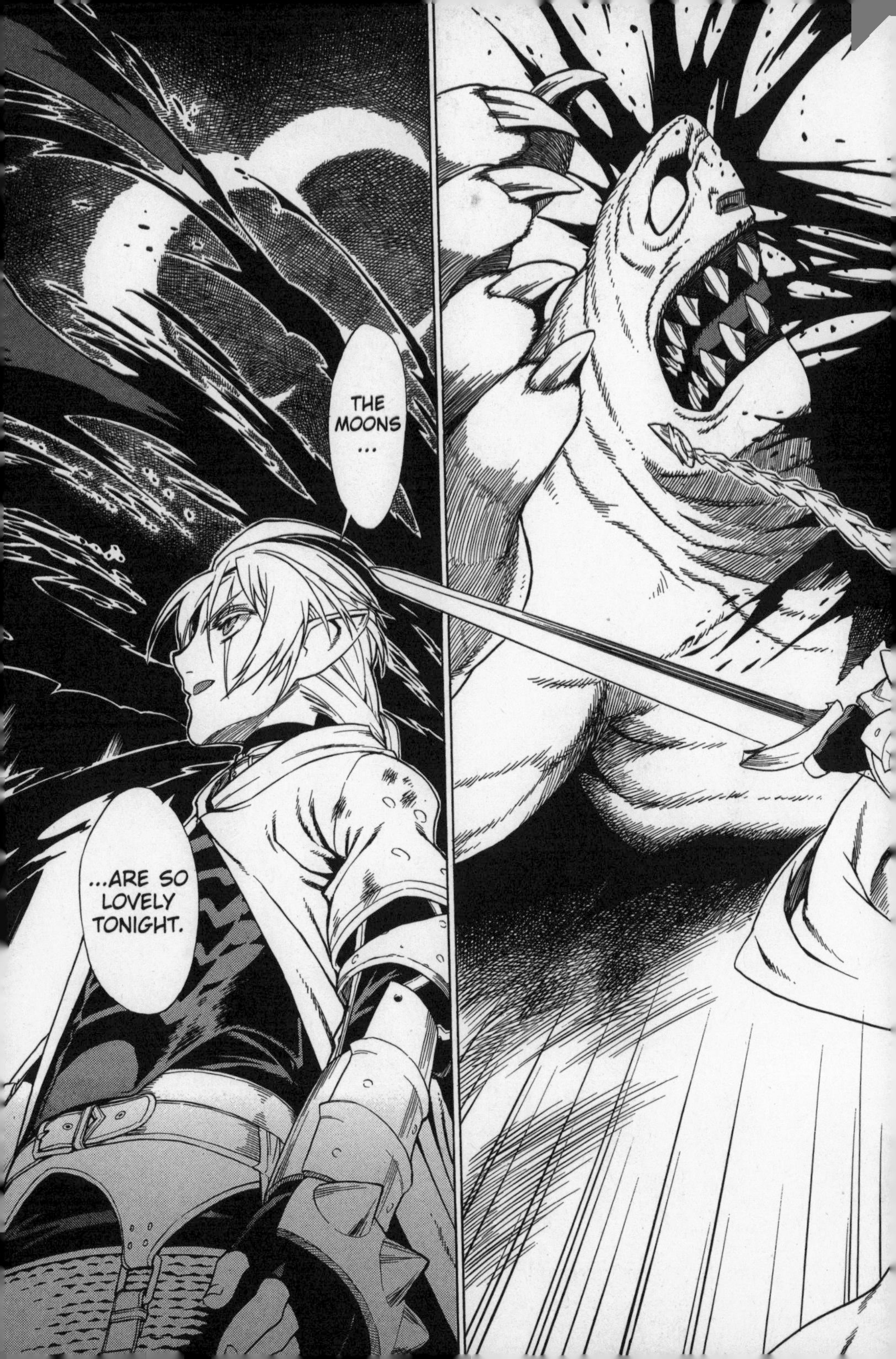
THE MOONS ...
...ARE SO LOVELY TONIGHT.

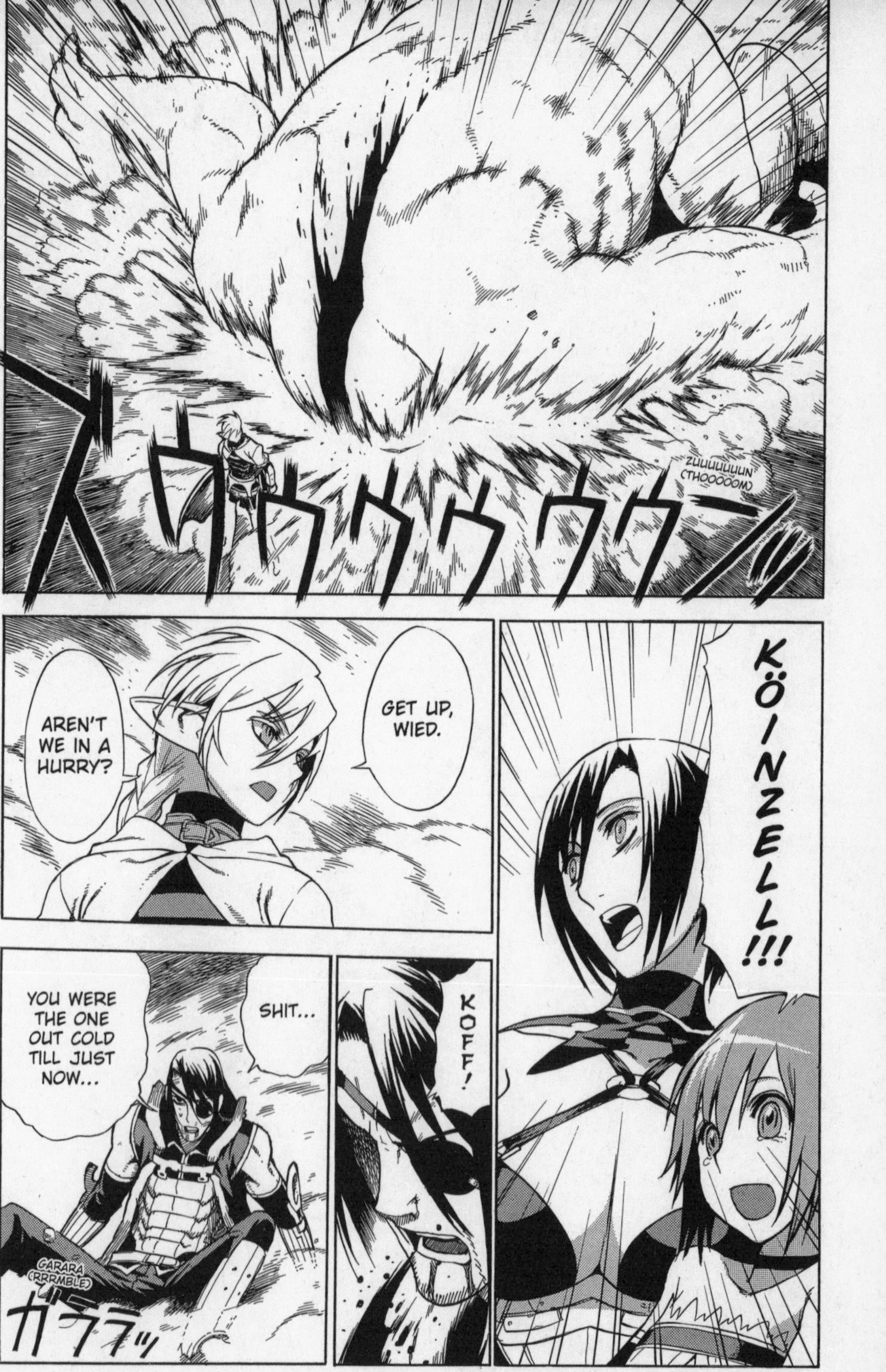
ZUUUUUUUN (THOOOOOM)
KÖINZELL!!!
GET UP, WIED.
AREN'T WE IN A HURRY?
KOFF!
SHIT...
YOU WERE THE ONE OUT COLD TILL JUST NOW...
GARARA (RRRMBLE)

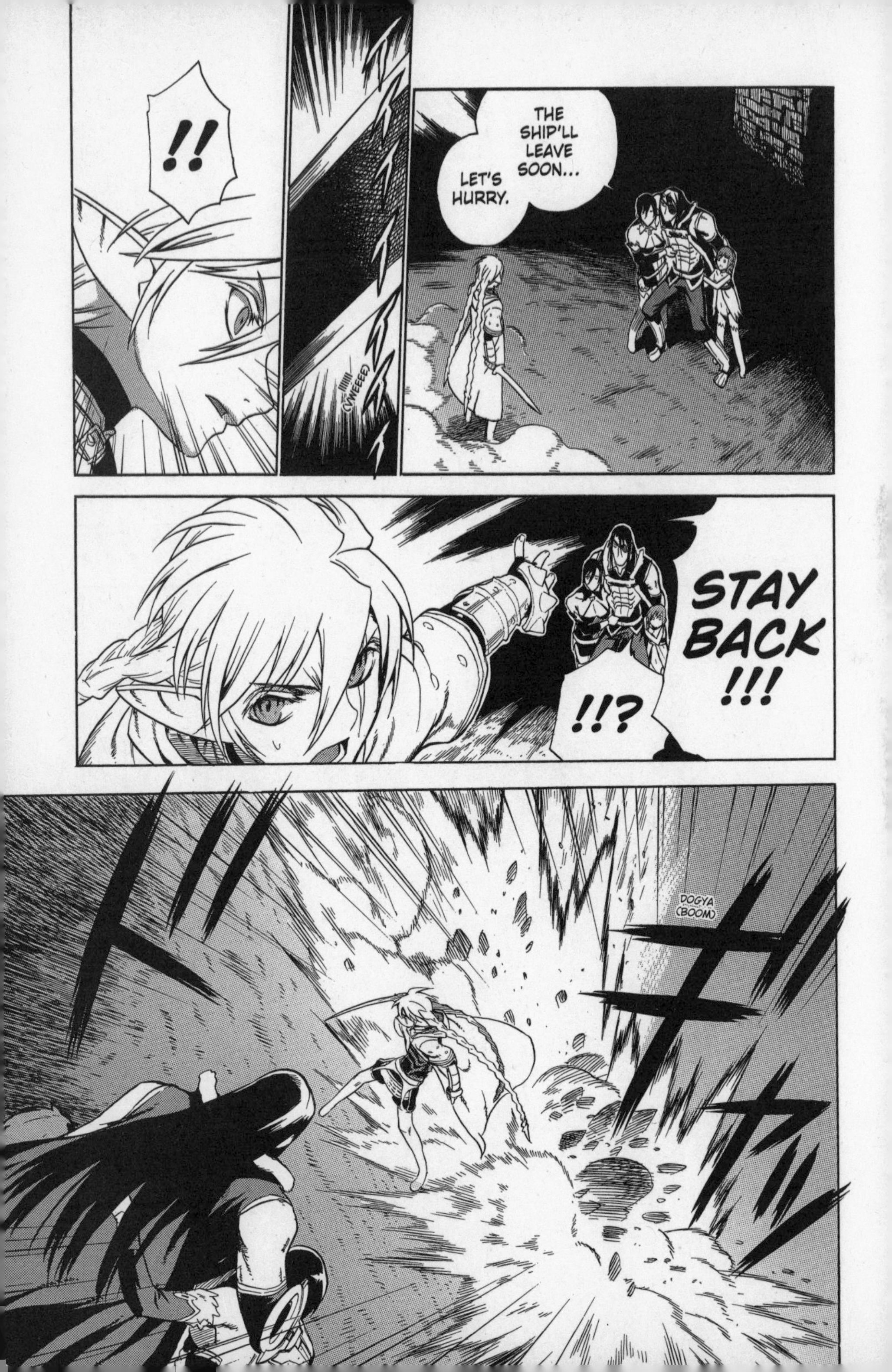
THE SHIP'LL LEAVE SOON...
LET'S HURRY.
(VWEEEE)
!!
STAY BACK!!!
!!?
DOGYA (BOOM)

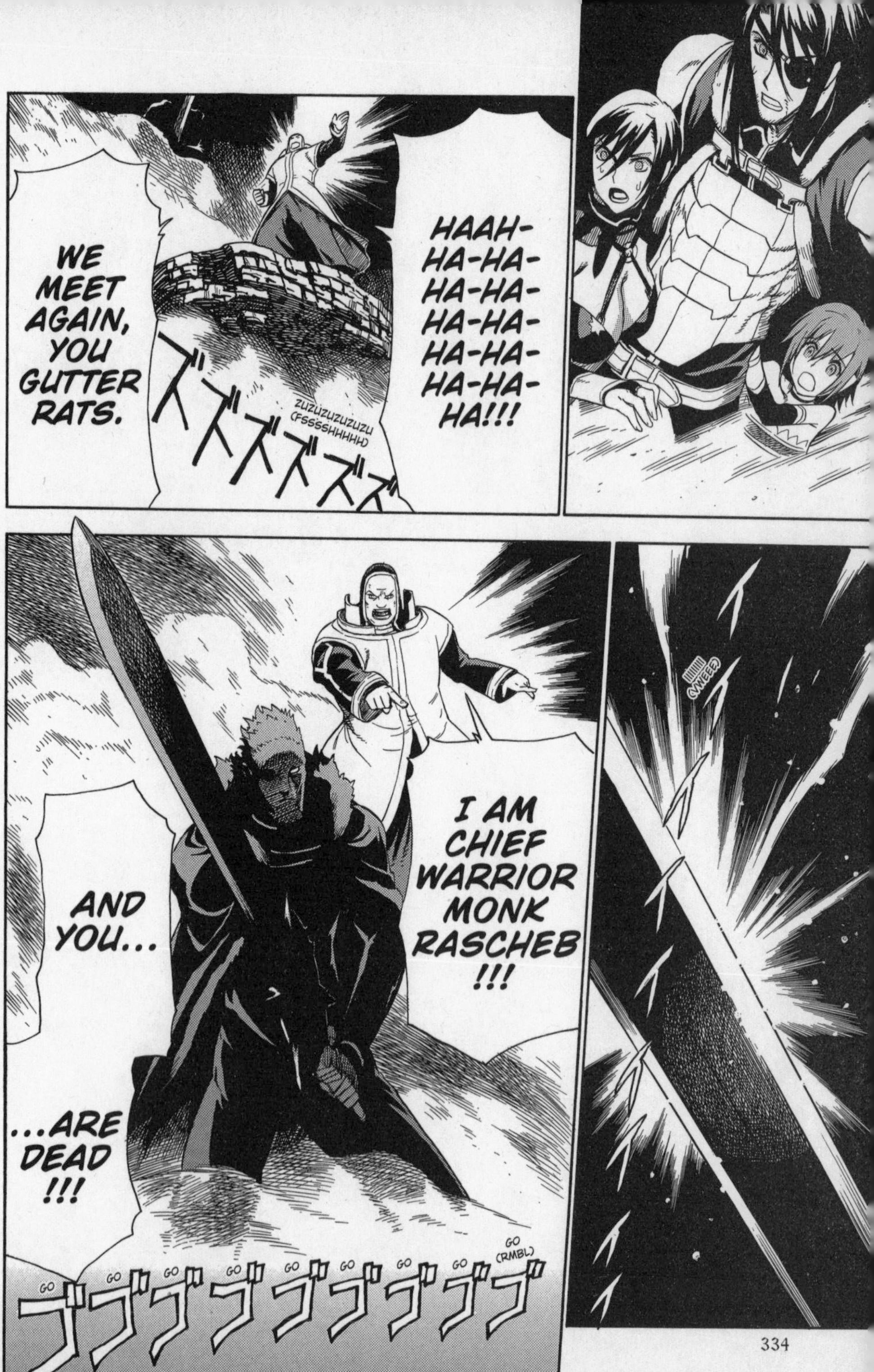
HAAH-HA-HA-HA-HA-HA-HA-HA-HA-HA-HA-HA!!!
WE MEET AGAIN, YOU GUTTER RATS.
ZUZUZUZUZUZU (FSSSSHHHHH)
(VWEE)
I AM CHIEF WARRIOR MONK RASCHEB!!!
AND YOU...
...ARE DEAD!!!
GO GO GO GO GO GO GO GO GO (RMBL)

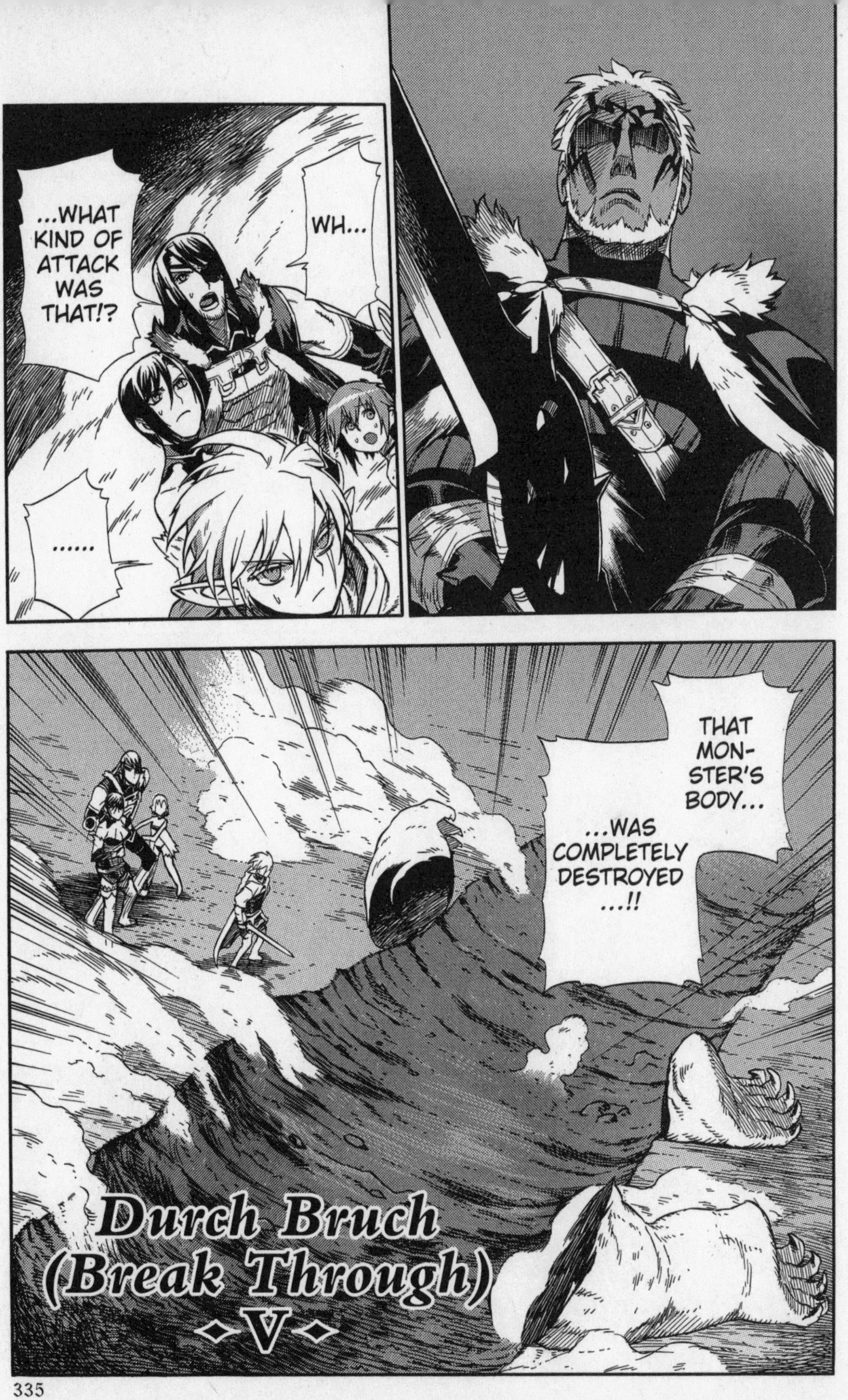
WH...
...WHAT KIND OF ATTACK WAS THAT!?
......
THAT MON-STER'S BODY...
...WAS COMPLETELY DESTROYED ...!!
Durch Bruch (Break Through) V

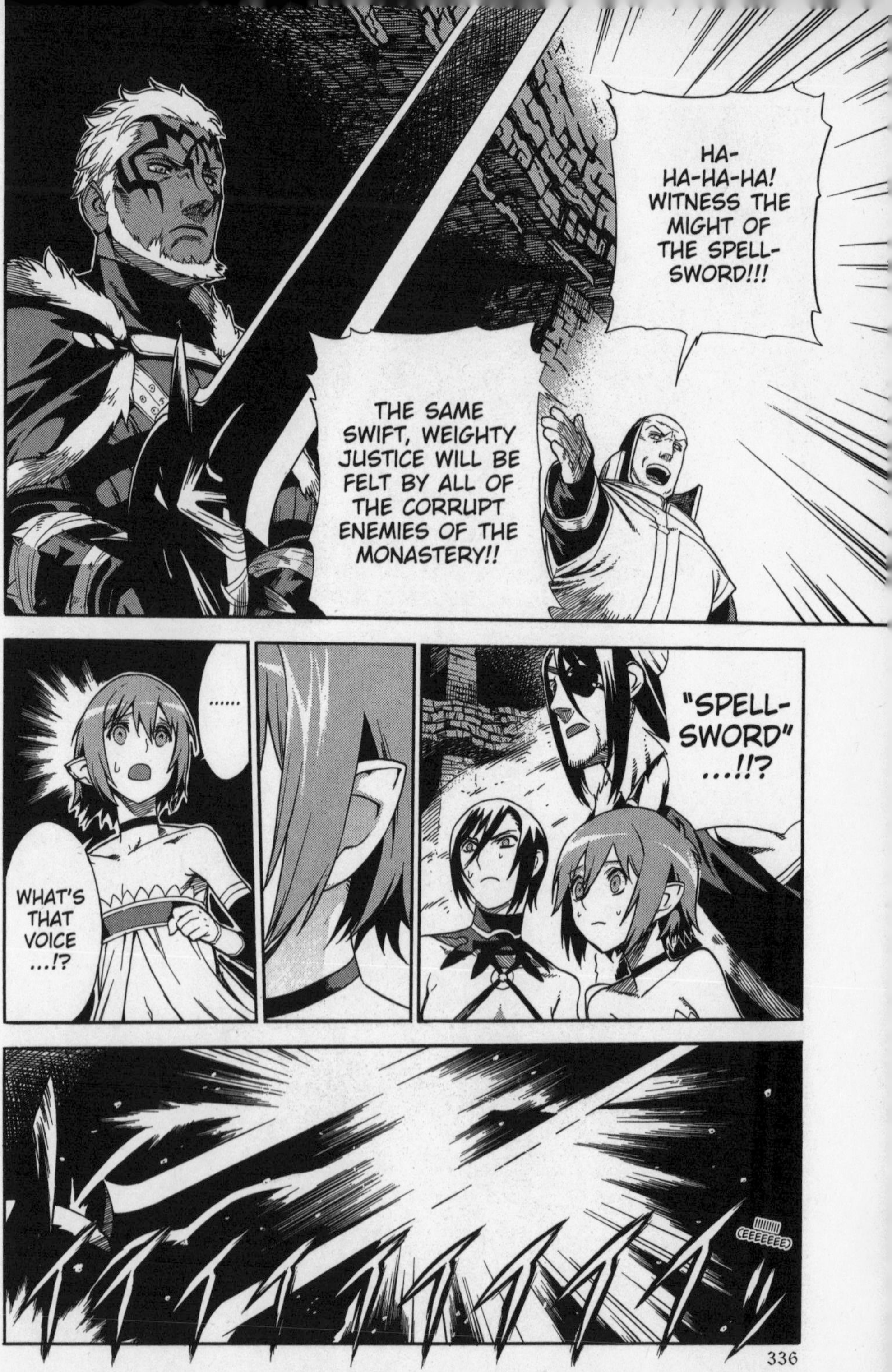
HA-HA-HA-HA! WITNESS THE MIGHT OF THE SPELL-SWORD!!!
THE SAME SWIFT, WEIGHTY JUSTICE WILL BE FELT BY ALL OF THE CORRUPT ENEMIES OF THE MONASTERY!!
"SPELL-SWORD" ...!!?
......
WHAT'S THAT VOICE ...!?
(EEEEEEE)

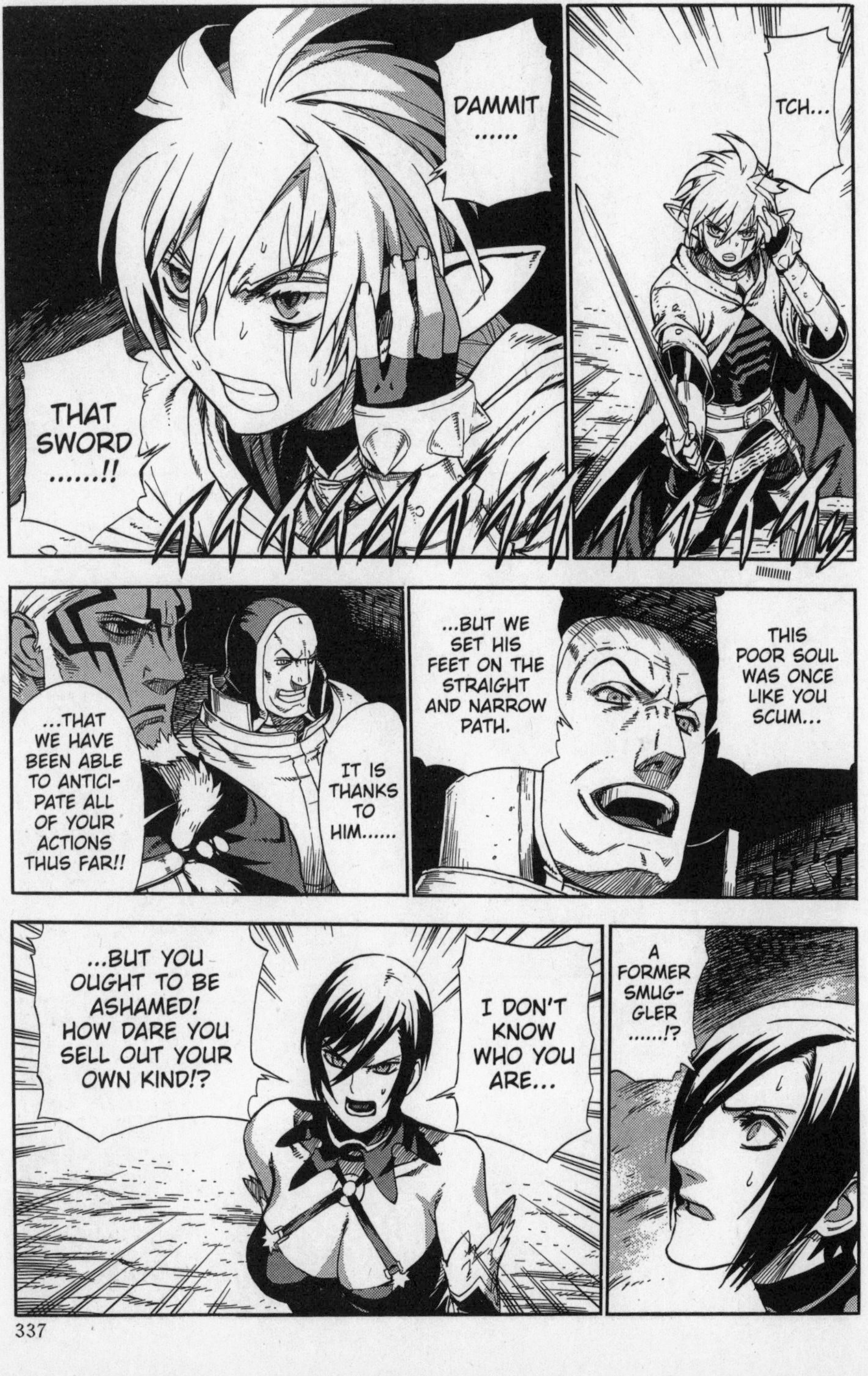
TCH...
DAMMIT ......
THAT SWORD ......!!
THIS POOR SOUL WAS ONCE LIKE YOU SCUM...
...BUT WE SET HIS FEET ON THE STRAIGHT AND NARROW PATH.
IT IS THANKS TO HIM......
...THAT WE HAVE BEEN ABLE TO ANTICI-PATE ALL OF YOUR ACTIONS THUS FAR!!
A FORMER SMUG-GLER ......!?
I DON'T KNOW WHO YOU ARE...
...BUT YOU OUGHT TO BE ASHAMED! HOW DARE YOU SELL OUT YOUR OWN KIND!?

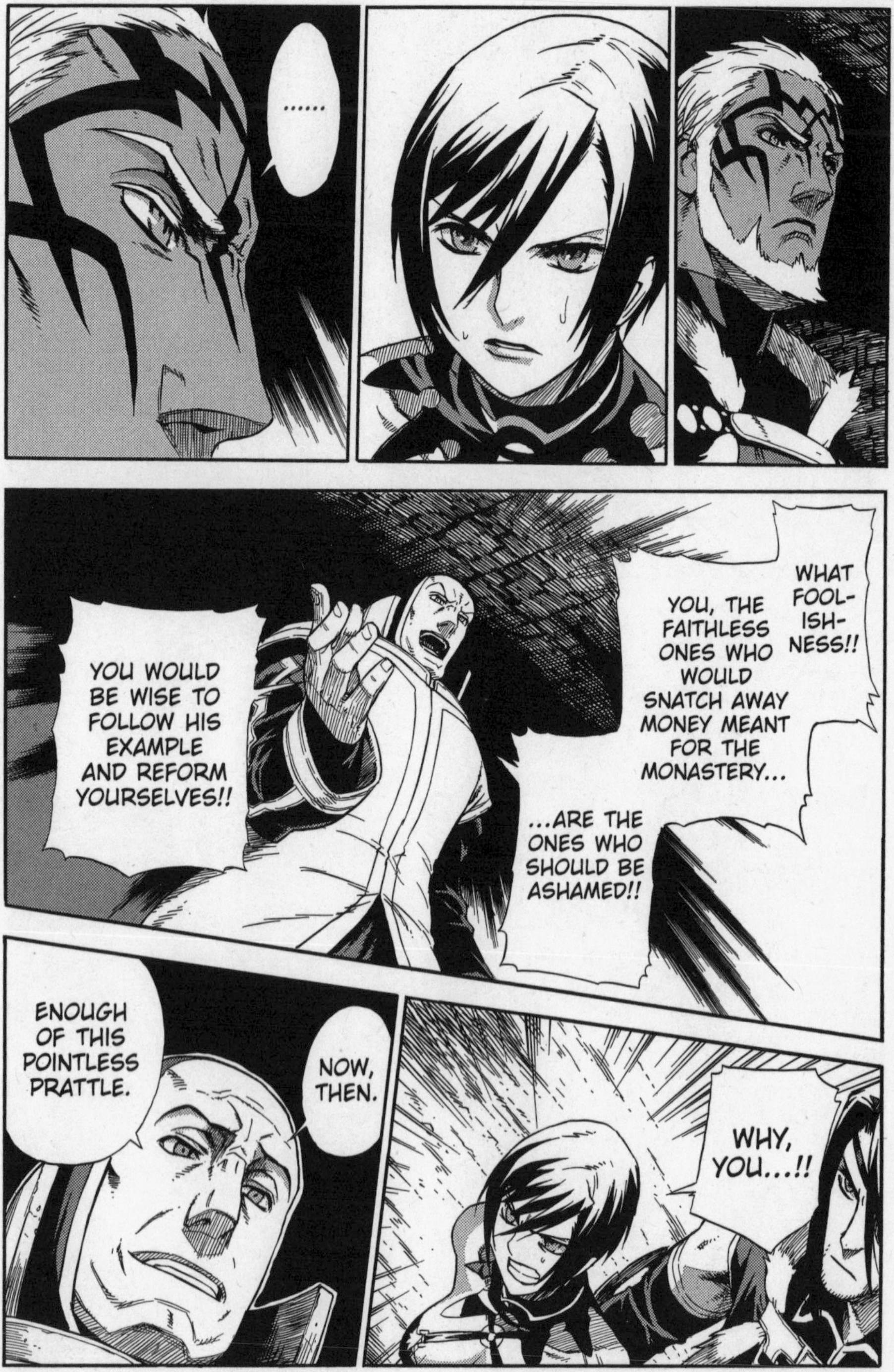
......
WHAT FOOLISHNESS!!
YOU, THE FAITHLESS ONES WHO WOULD SNATCH AWAY MONEY MEANT FOR THE MONASTERY...
...ARE THE ONES WHO SHOULD BE ASHAMED!!
YOU WOULD BE WISE TO FOLLOW HIS EXAMPLE AND REFORM YOURSELVES!!
WHY, YOU...!!
NOW, THEN.
ENOUGH OF THIS POINTLESS PRATTLE.

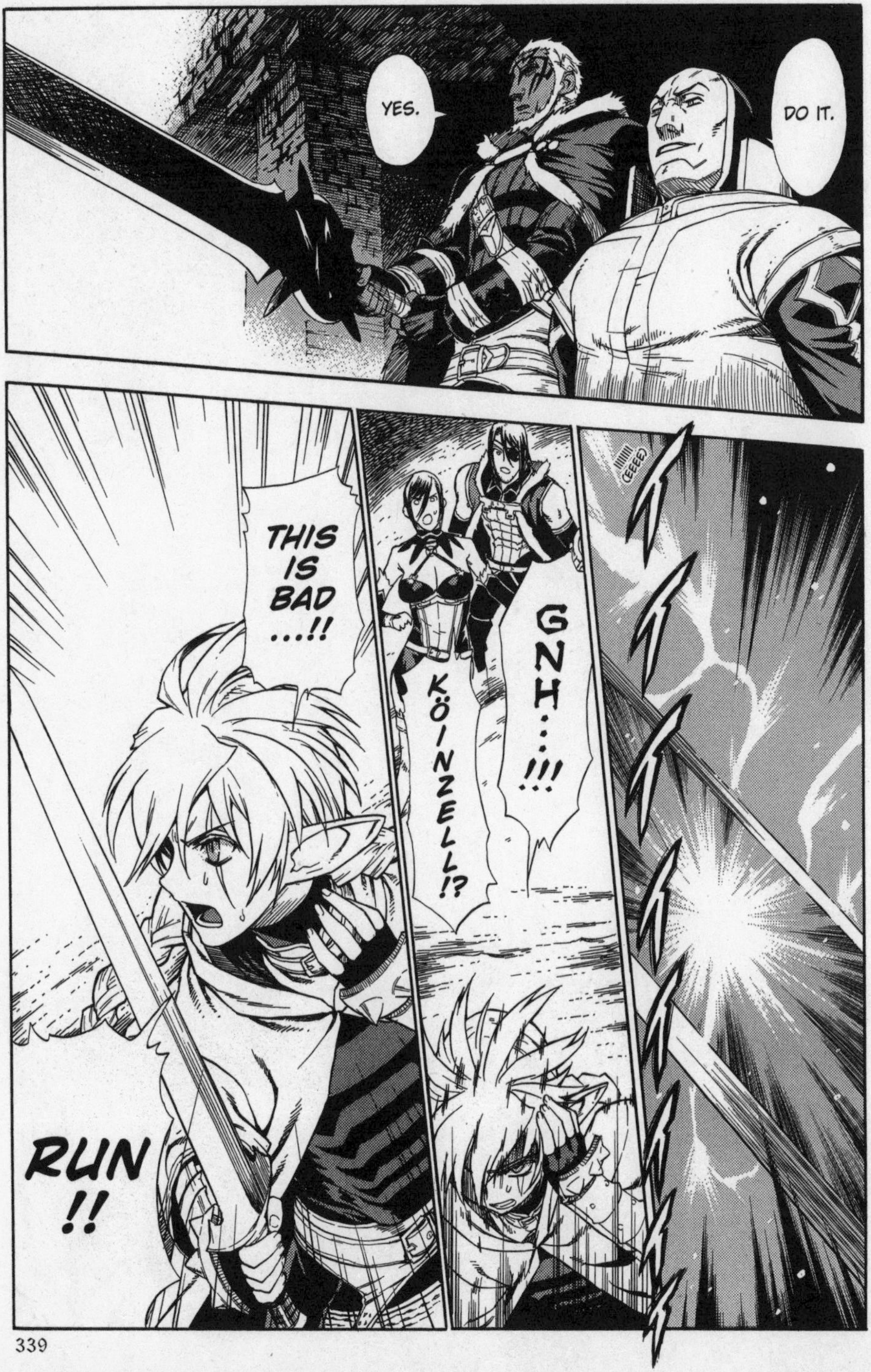
DO IT.
YES.
(EEEE)!!!!!!!
GNH...!!!
KÖINZELL!?
THIS IS BAD...!!
RUN!!

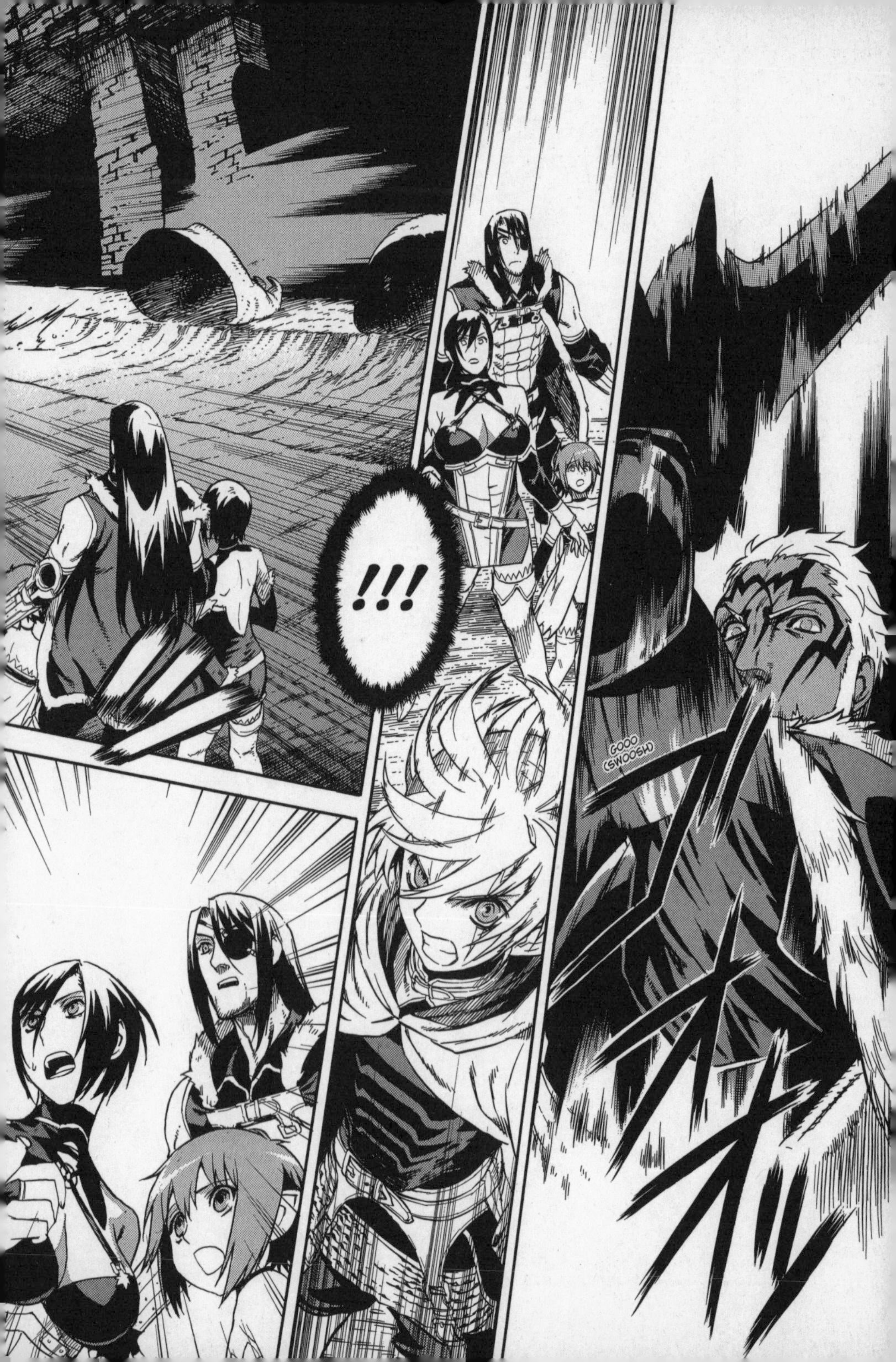
GOOO (SWOOSH)
!!!

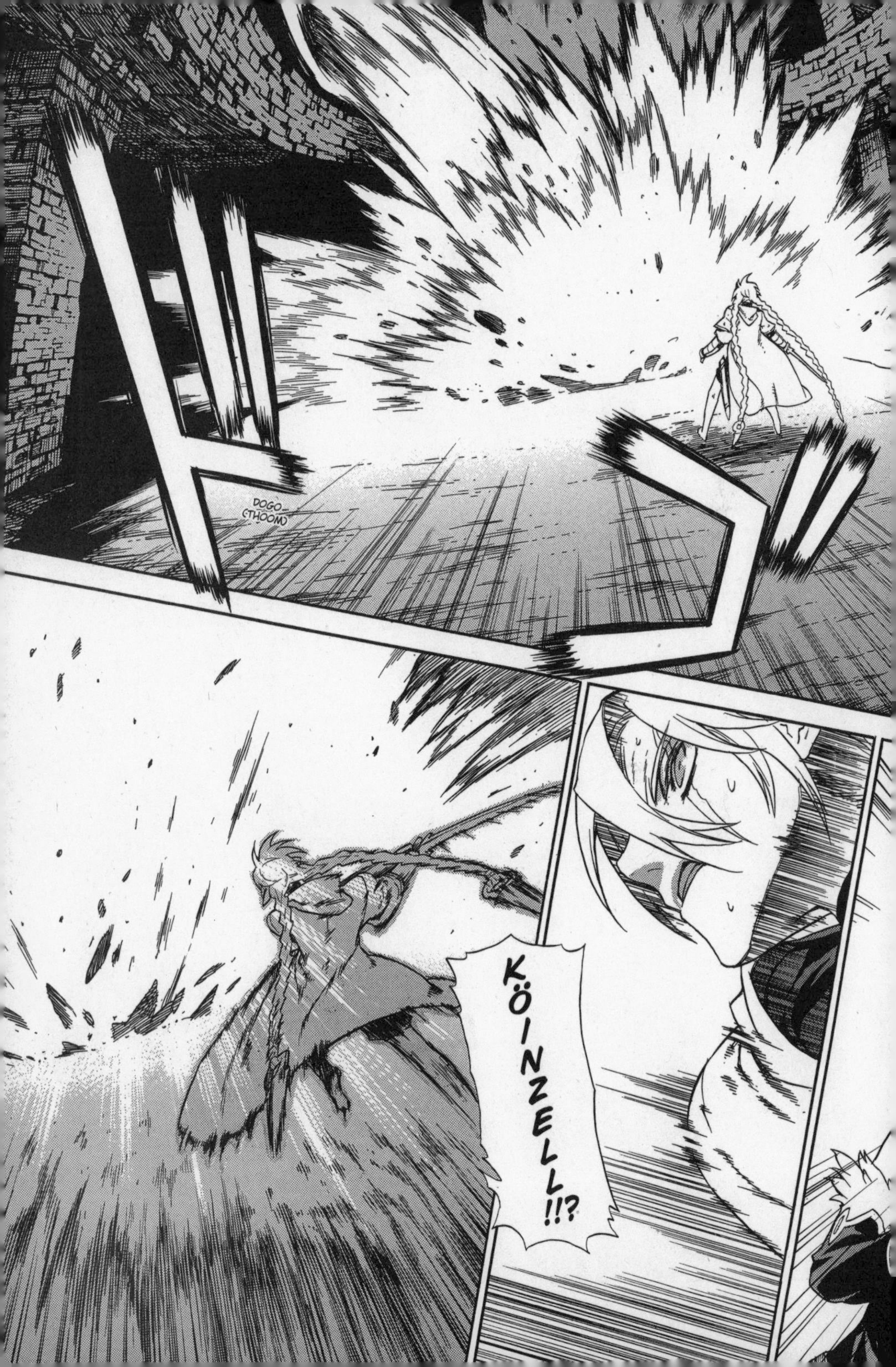
DOGO-
(THOOM)
KÖINZELL!!?

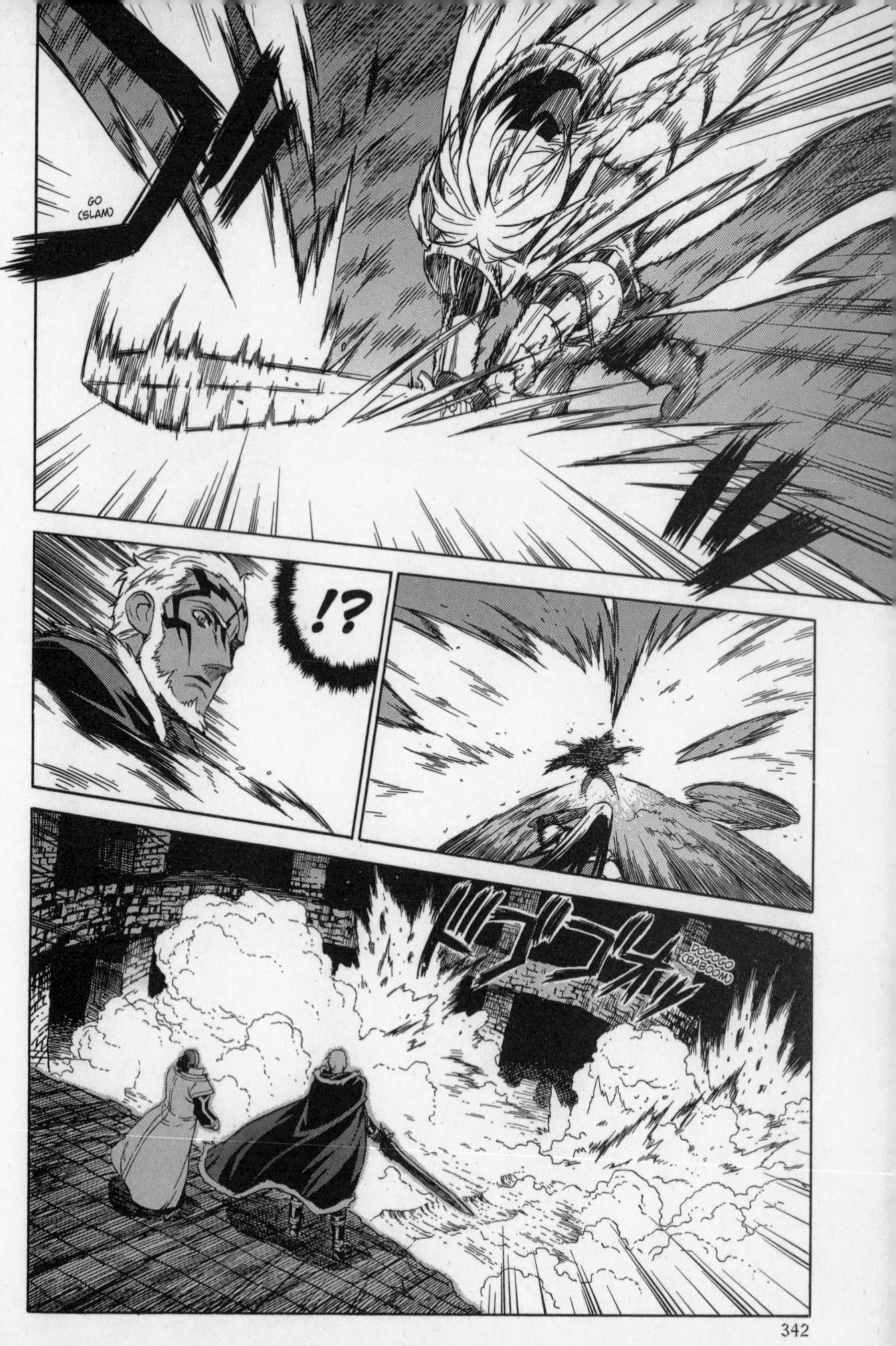
GO
(SLAM)
!?
DOGOGO
(BABOOM)

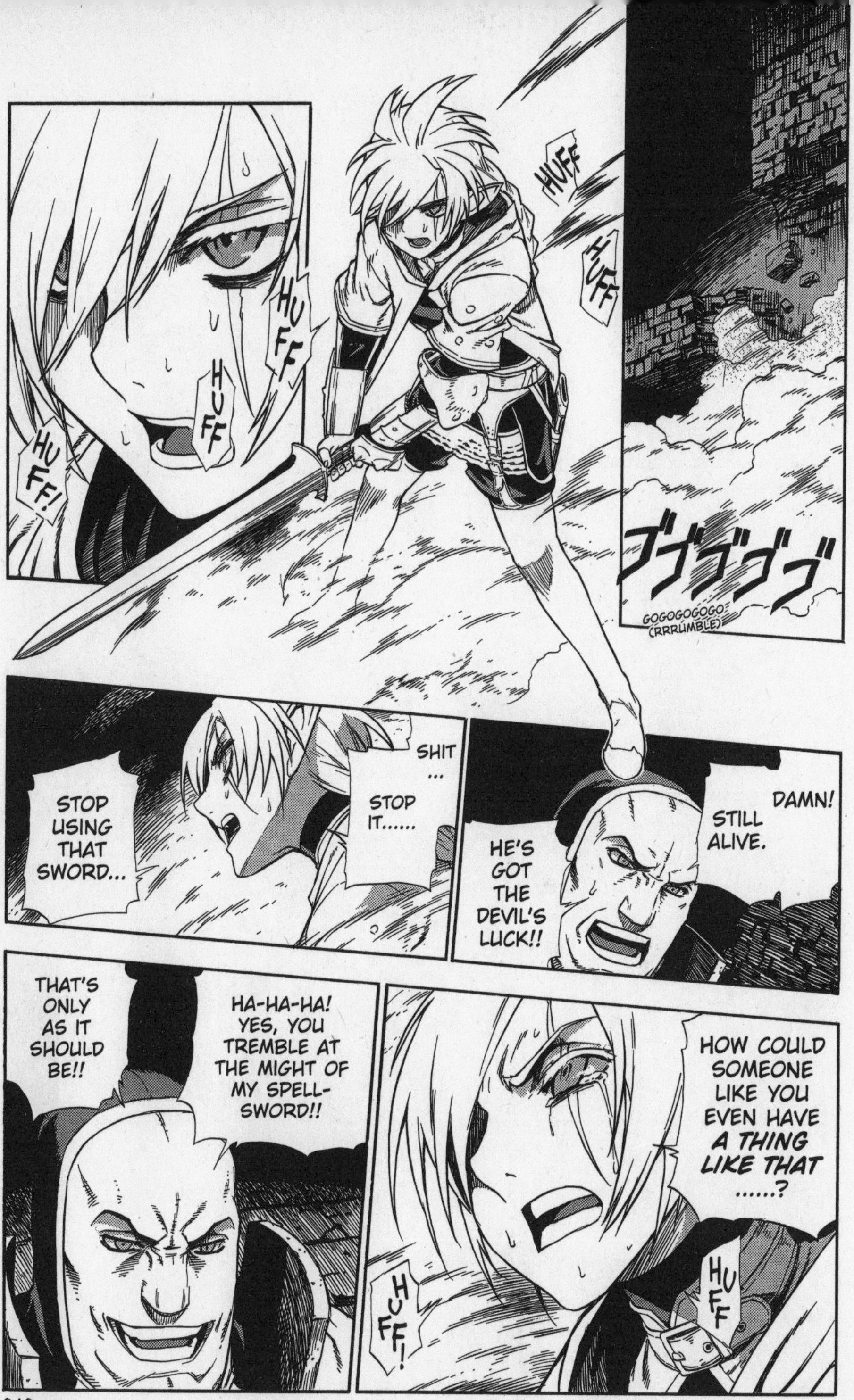
HUFF
HUFF
ゴゴゴゴゴ
GOGOGOGOGO (RRRUMBLE)
HUFF
HUFF
HUFF!
DAMN! STILL ALIVE.
HE'S GOT THE DEVIL'S LUCK!!
SHIT ...
STOP IT......
STOP USING THAT SWORD...
HOW COULD SOMEONE LIKE YOU EVEN HAVE *A THING LIKE THAT* ......?
HUFF
HUFF!
HA-HA-HA! YES, YOU TREMBLE AT THE MIGHT OF MY SPELL-SWORD!!
THAT'S ONLY AS IT SHOULD BE!!

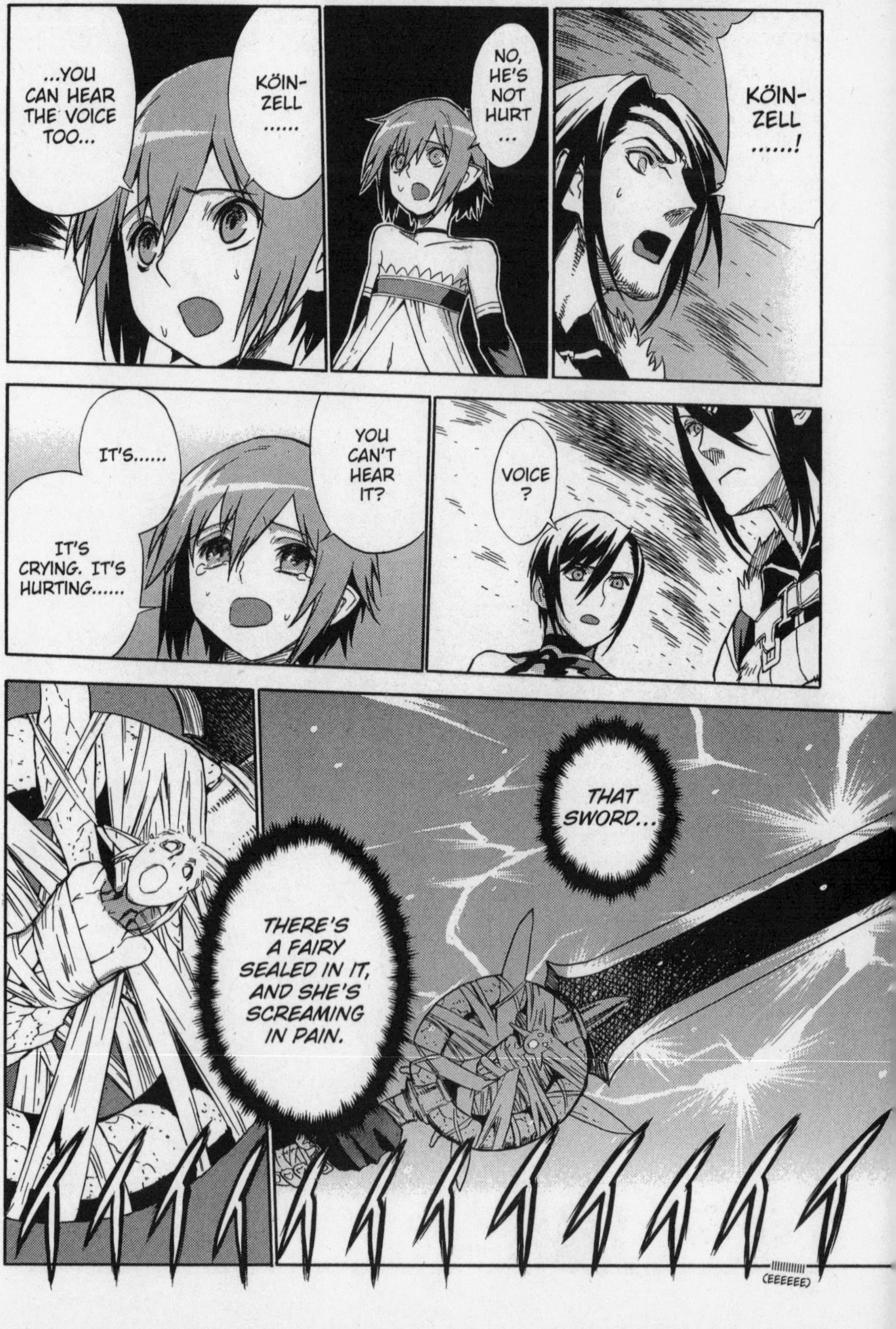
KÖIN-ZELL ......!
NO, HE'S NOT HURT ...
KÖIN-ZELL ......
...YOU CAN HEAR THE VOICE TOO...
VOICE?
YOU CAN'T HEAR IT?
IT'S......
IT'S CRYING. IT'S HURTING......
THAT SWORD...
THERE'S A FAIRY SEALED IN IT, AND SHE'S SCREAMING IN PAIN.
(EEEEEE)

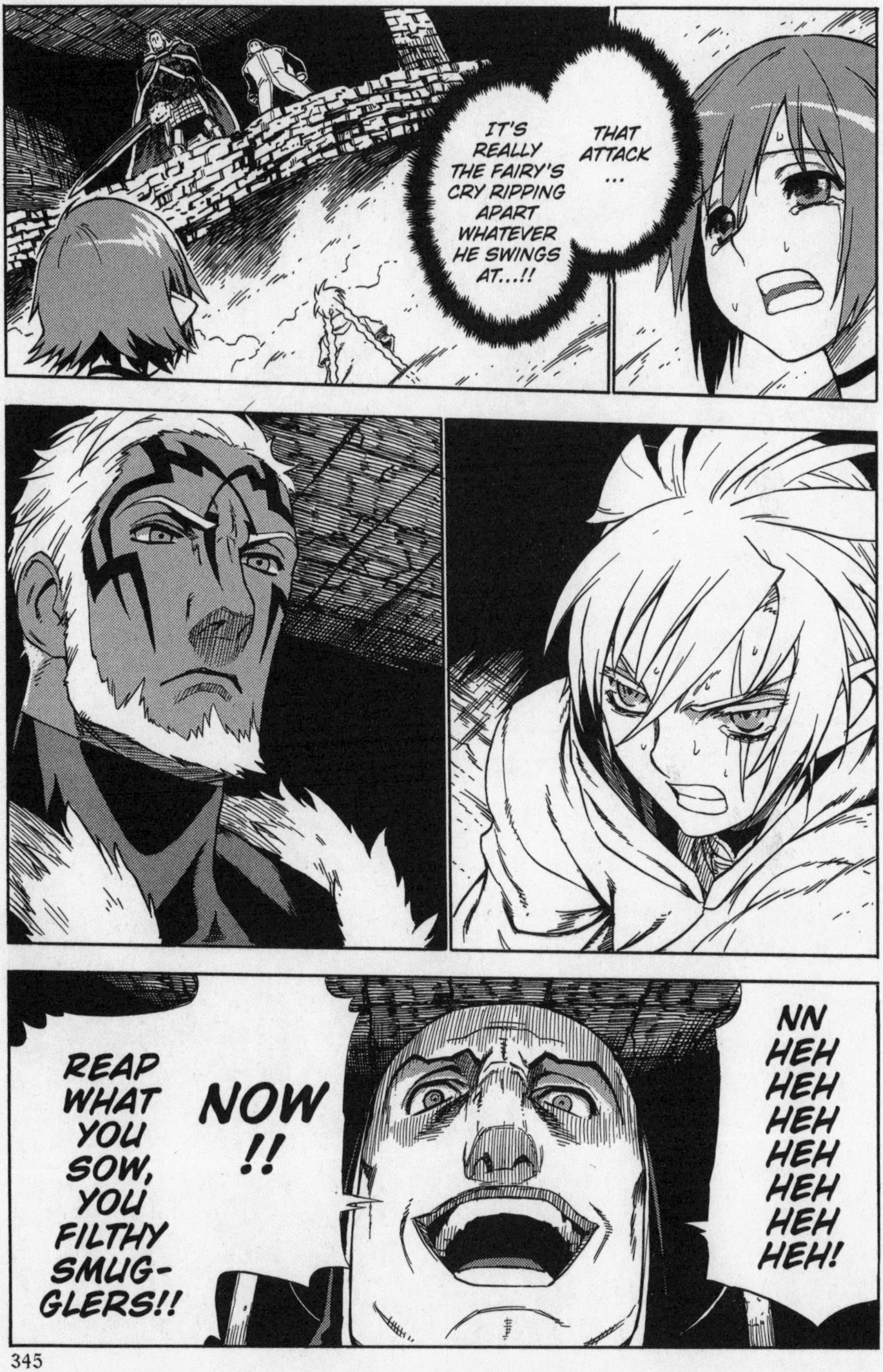
THAT ATTACK ...
IT'S REALLY THE FAIRY'S CRY RIPPING APART WHATEVER HE SWINGS AT...!!
NN HEH HEH HEH HEH HEH HEH HEH!
NOW !!
REAP WHAT YOU SOW, YOU FILTHY SMUG-GLERS!!

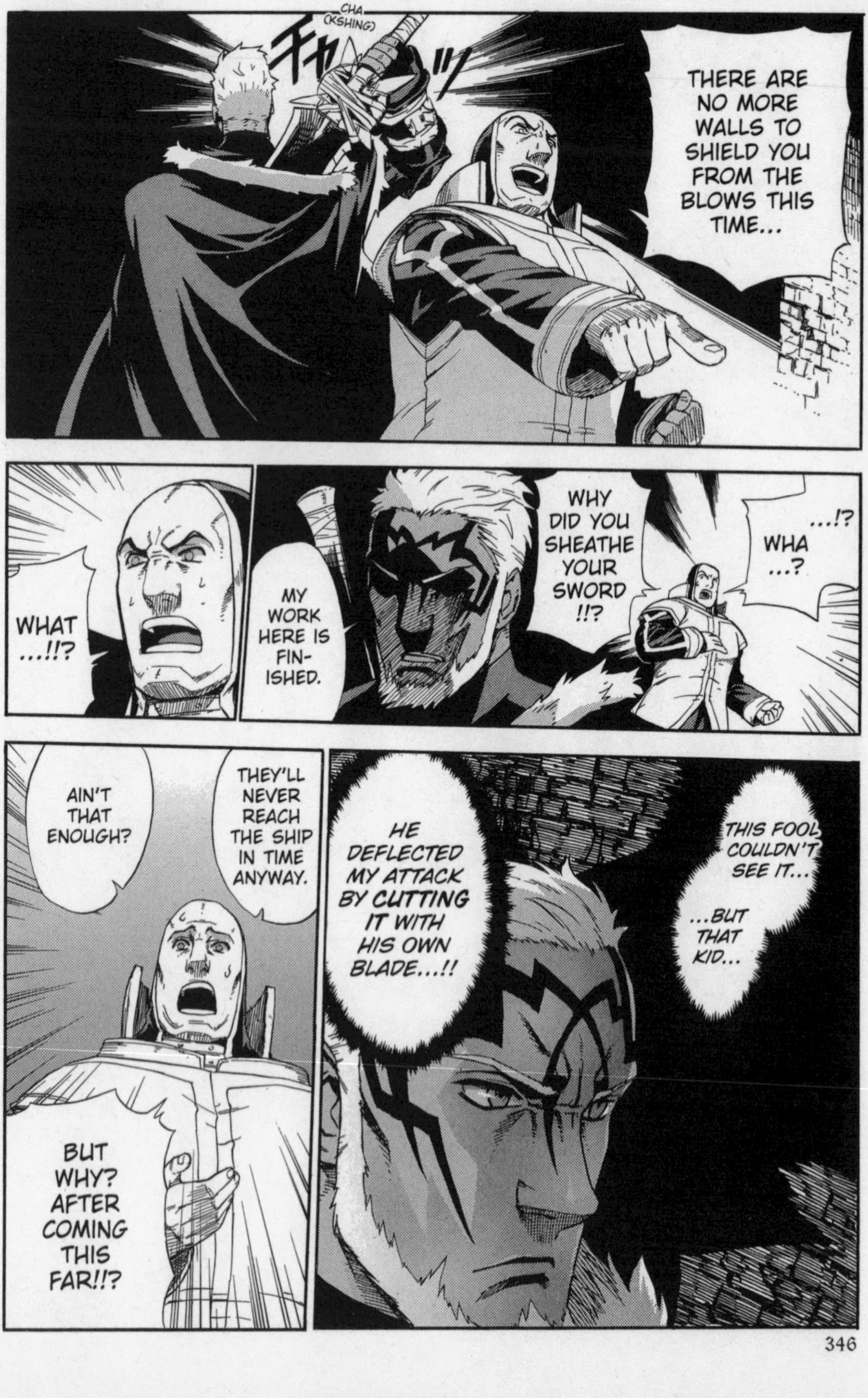
THERE ARE NO MORE WALLS TO SHIELD YOU FROM THE BLOWS THIS TIME...
CHA (KSHING)
...!? WHA...?
WHY DID YOU SHEATHE YOUR SWORD!!?
MY WORK HERE IS FIN-ISHED.
WHAT...!!?
THIS FOOL COULDN'T SEE IT...
...BUT THAT KID...
HE DEFLECTED MY ATTACK BY CUTTING IT WITH HIS OWN BLADE...!!
THEY'LL NEVER REACH THE SHIP IN TIME ANYWAY.
AIN'T THAT ENOUGH?
BUT WHY? AFTER COMING THIS FAR!!?

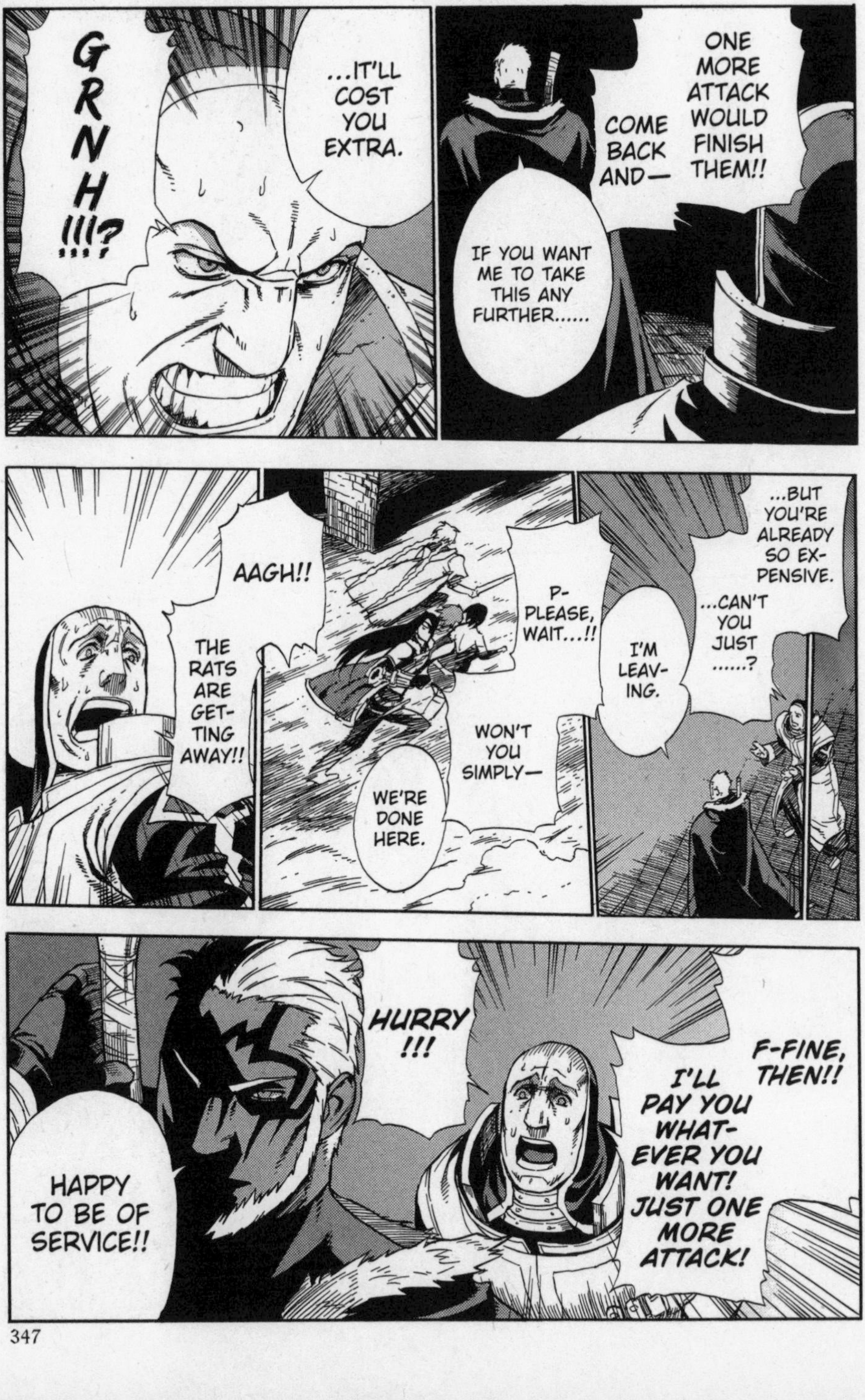
ONE MORE ATTACK WOULD FINISH THEM!!
COME BACK AND—
IF YOU WANT ME TO TAKE THIS ANY FURTHER......
...IT'LL COST YOU EXTRA.
GRNH!!!?
...BUT YOU'RE ALREADY SO EX-PENSIVE.
...CAN'T YOU JUST ......?
I'M LEAV-ING.
P-PLEASE, WAIT...!!
WON'T YOU SIMPLY—
WE'RE DONE HERE.
AAGH!!
THE RATS ARE GET-TING AWAY!!
F-FINE, THEN!!
I'LL PAY YOU WHAT-EVER YOU WANT! JUST ONE MORE ATTACK!
HURRY!!!
HAPPY TO BE OF SERVICE!!

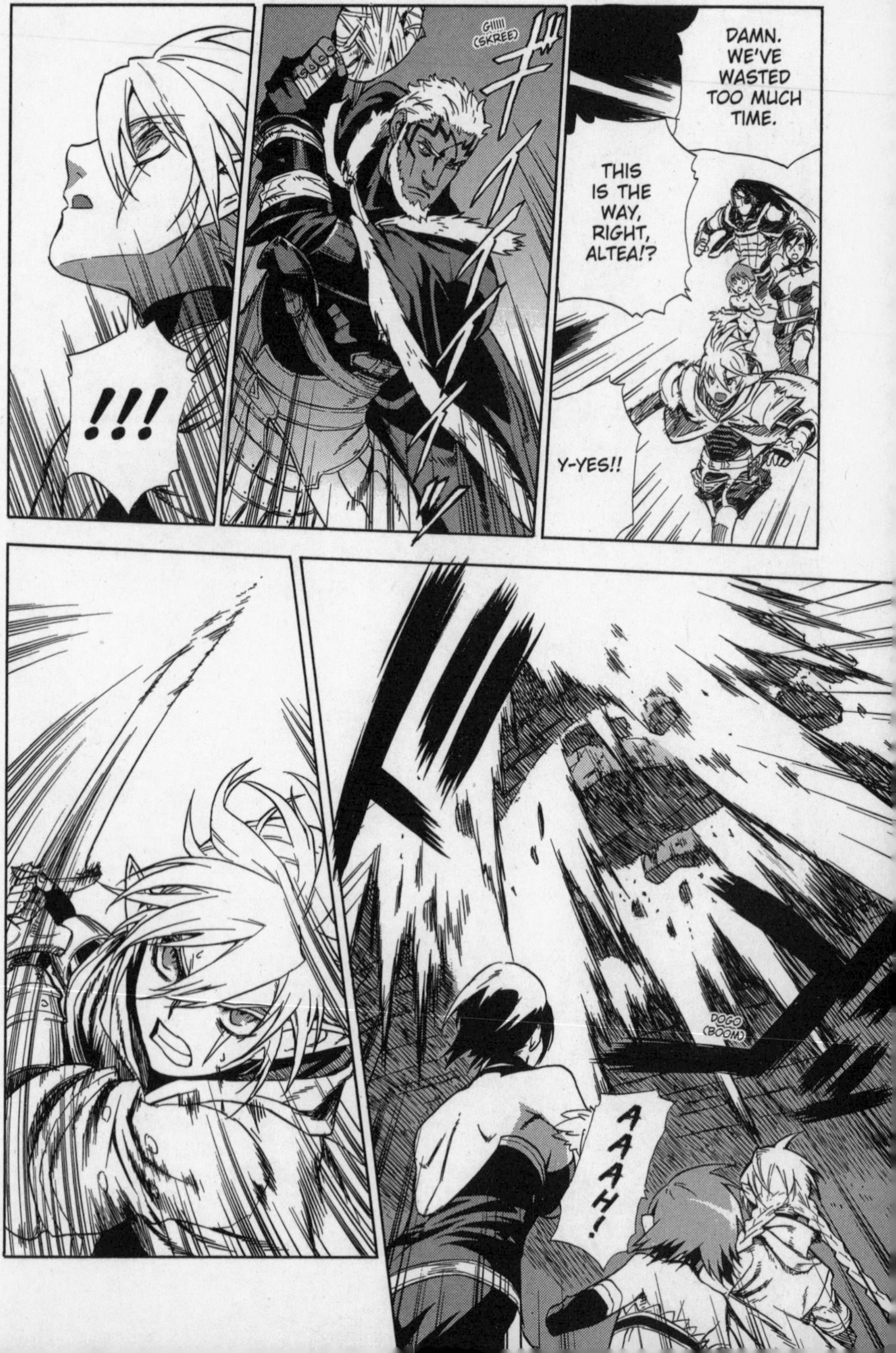
DAMN. WE'VE WASTED TOO MUCH TIME.
THIS IS THE WAY, RIGHT, ALTEA!?
Y-YES!!
GIIII (SKREE)
!!!
DOGO (BOOM)
AAAAH!

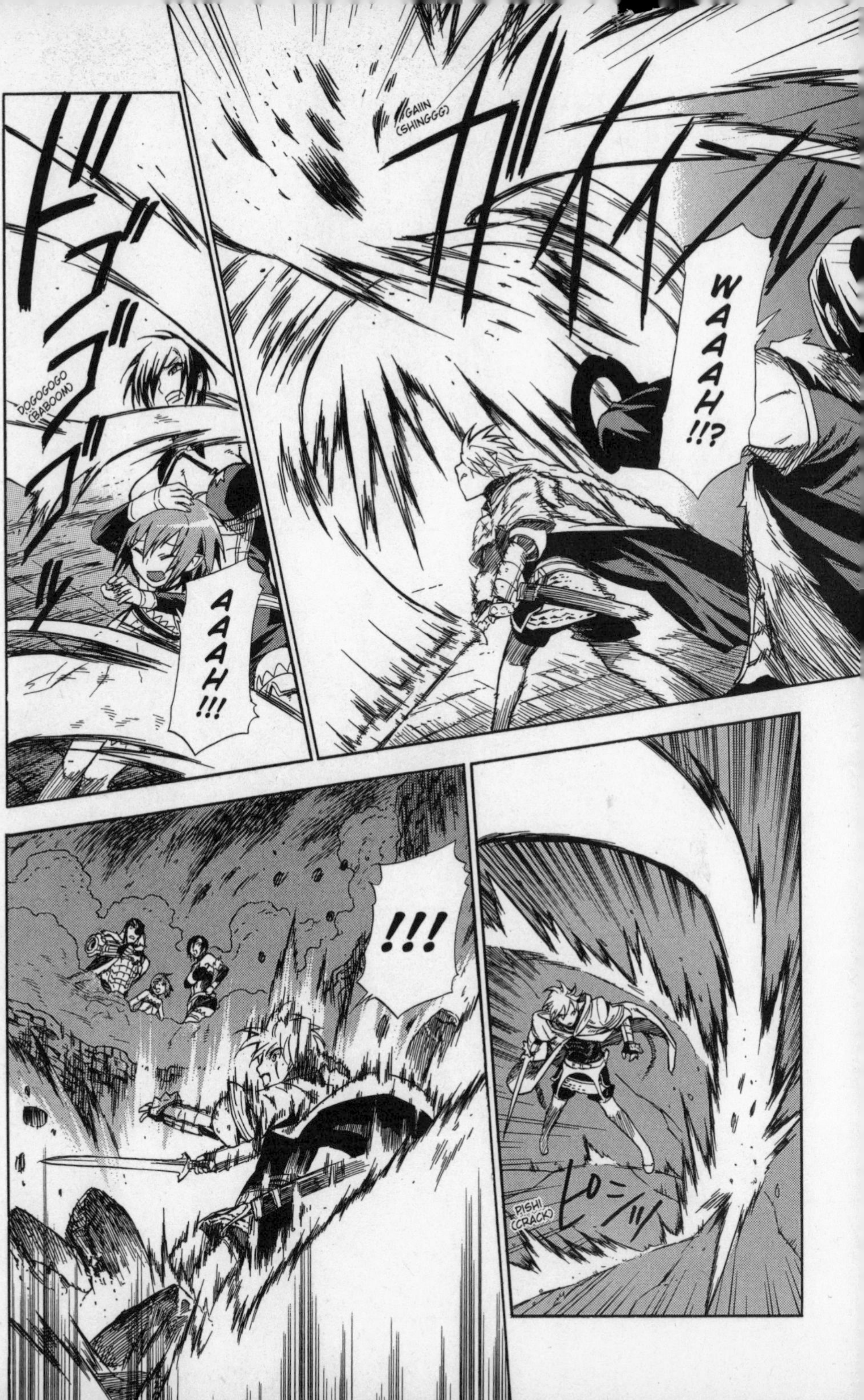
GAIIN (SHINGGG)
WAAAAH!!?
DOGOGOGO (BABOOM)
AAAAH!!!
PISHI (CRACK)
!!!

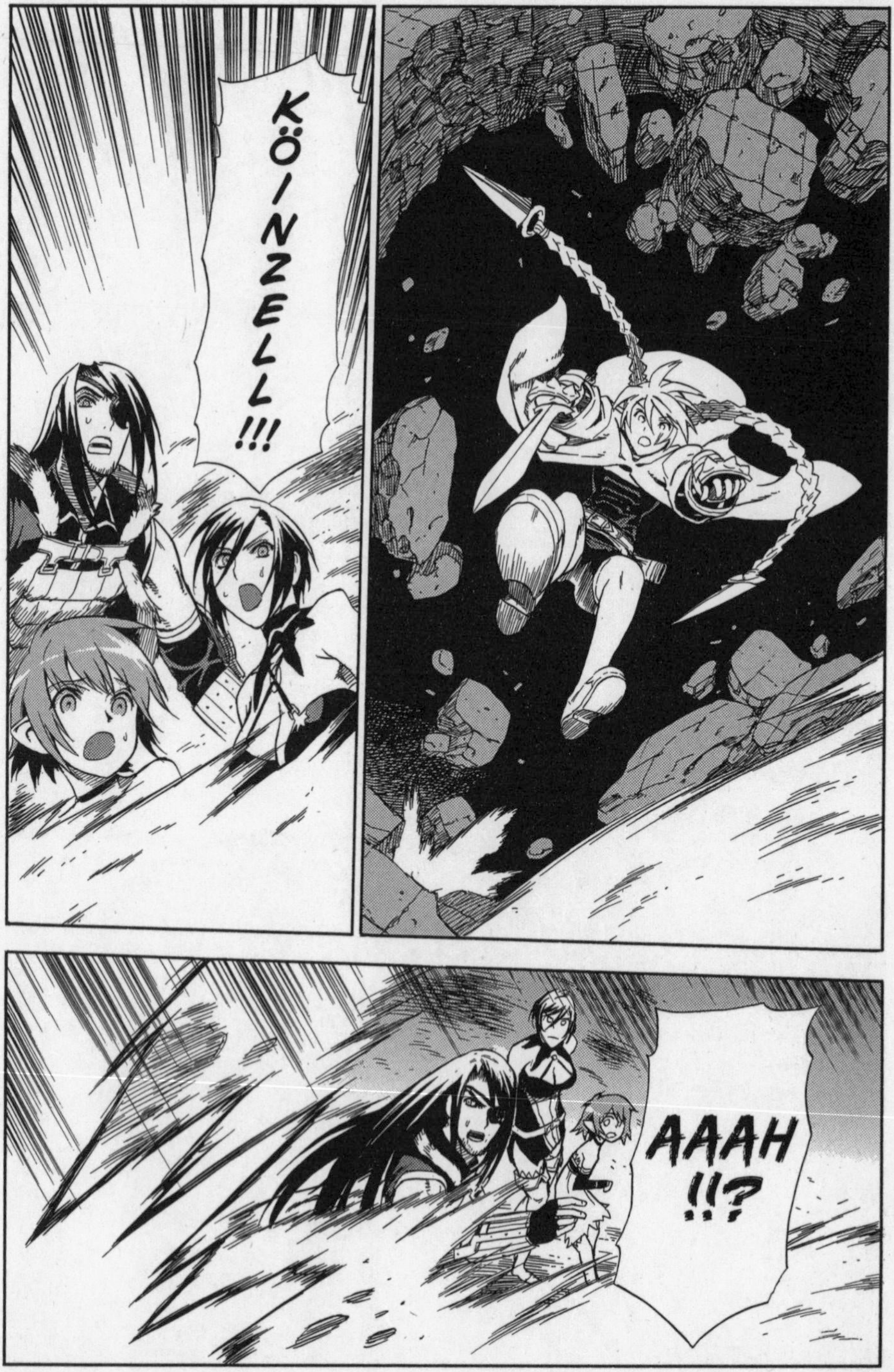
KÖINZELL!!!
AAAH!!?

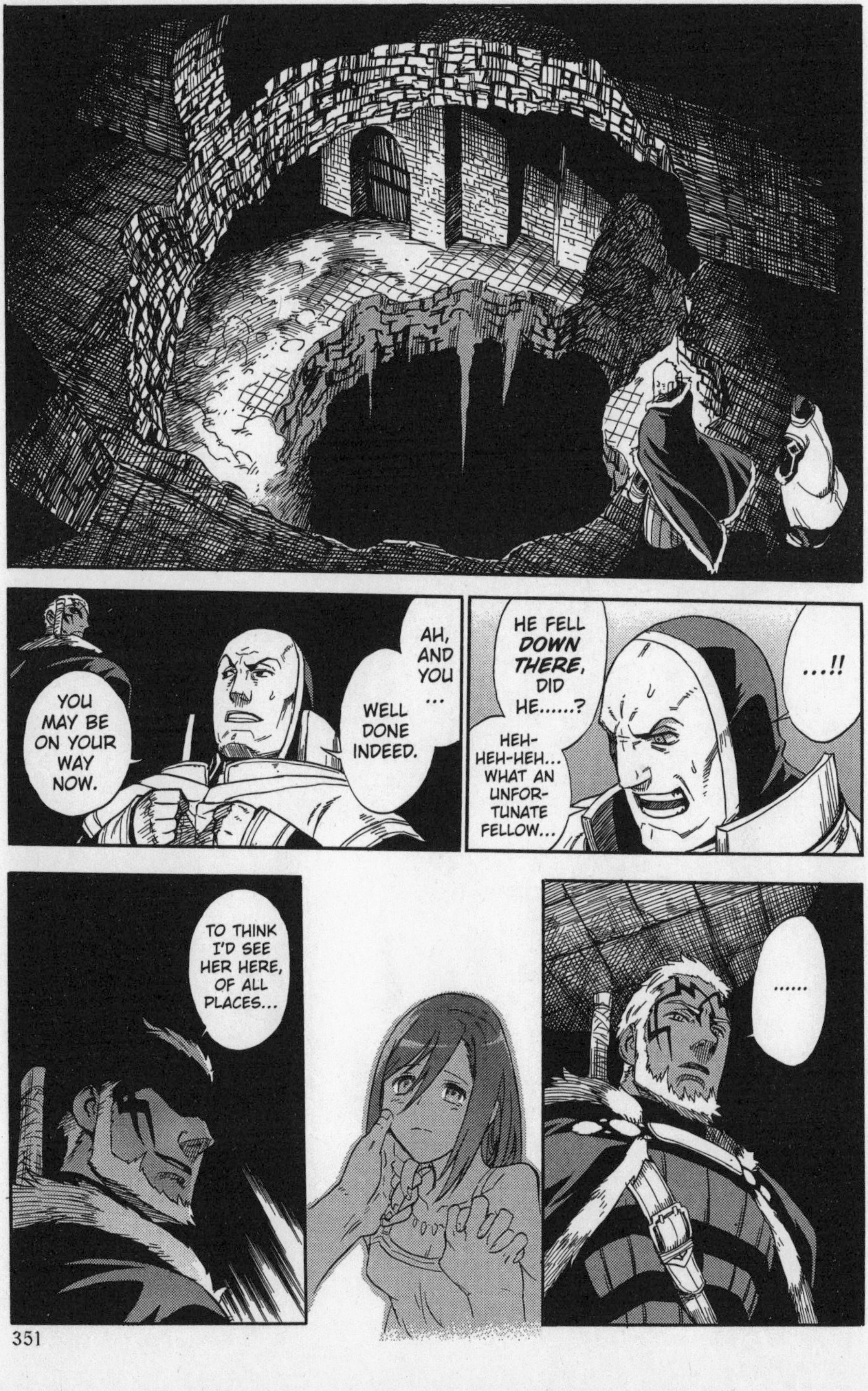
...!!
HE FELL *DOWN THERE,* DID HE......?
HEH-HEH-HEH... WHAT AN UNFORTUNATE FELLOW...
AH, AND YOU ...
WELL DONE INDEED.
YOU MAY BE ON YOUR WAY NOW.
......
TO THINK I'D SEE HER HERE, OF ALL PLACES...

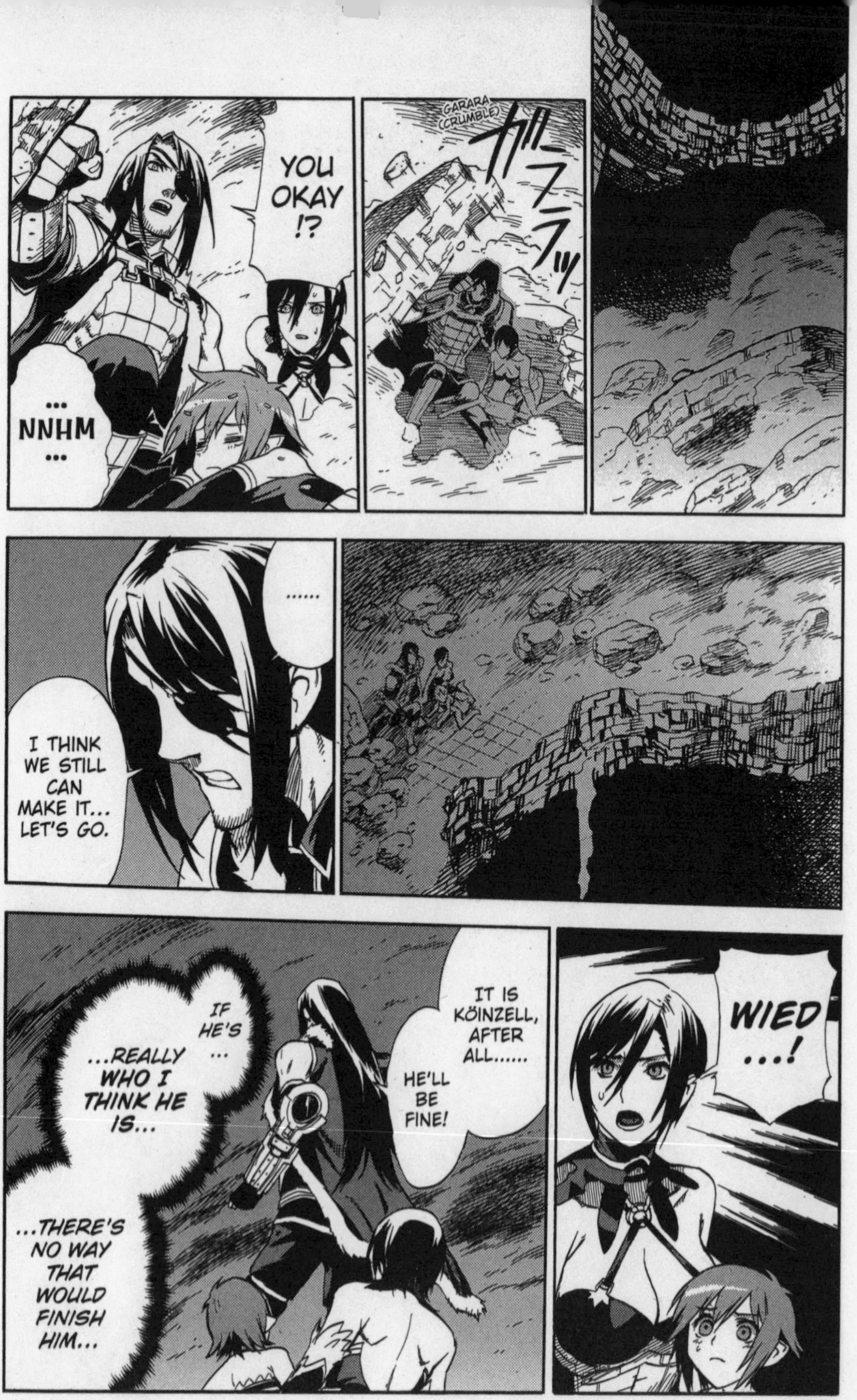
GARARA (CRUMBLE)
ガラララッ
YOU OKAY !?
... NNHM ...
......
I THINK WE STILL CAN MAKE IT... LET'S GO.
WIED ...!
IT IS KÖINZELL, AFTER ALL......
HE'LL BE FINE!
IF HE'S ...
...REALLY WHO I THINK HE IS...
...THERE'S NO WAY THAT WOULD FINISH HIM...

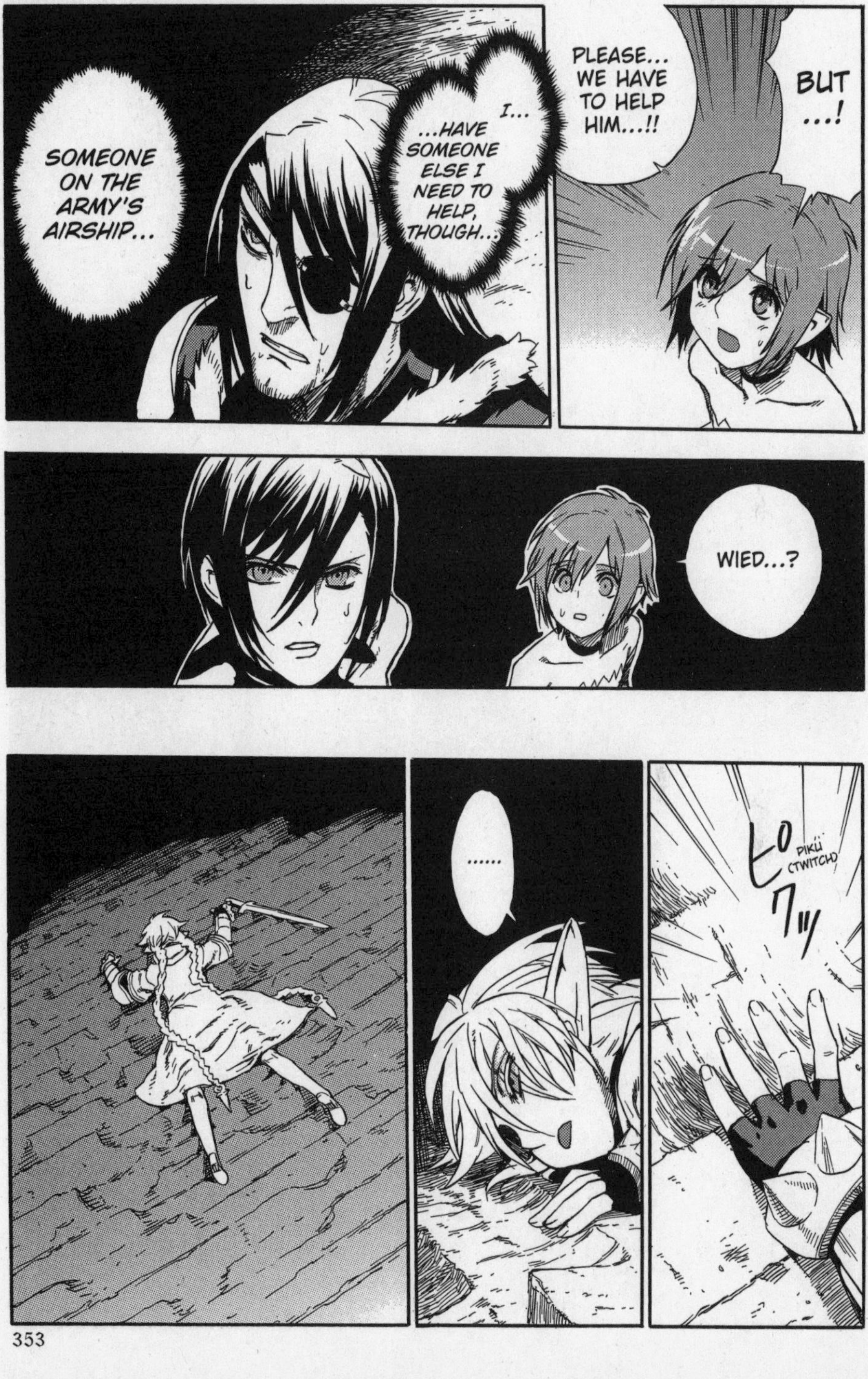
BUT ...!
PLEASE... WE HAVE TO HELP HIM...!!
I...
...HAVE SOMEONE ELSE I NEED TO HELP, THOUGH...
SOMEONE ON THE ARMY'S AIRSHIP...
WIED...?
ピクッ
PIKU (TWITCH)
......

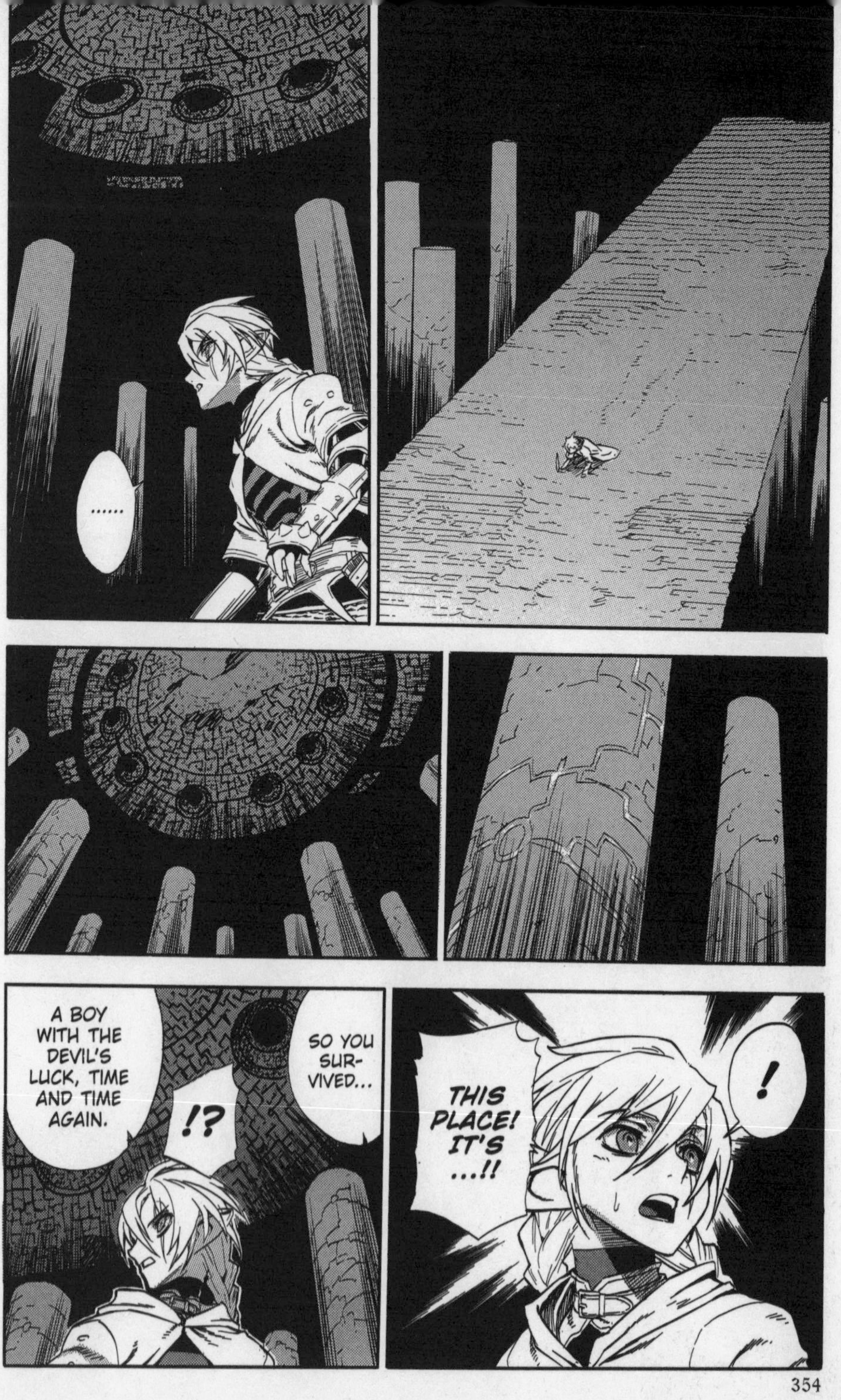
......
!
THIS PLACE! IT'S ...!!
SO YOU SURVIVED...
A BOY WITH THE DEVIL'S LUCK, TIME AND TIME AGAIN.
!?

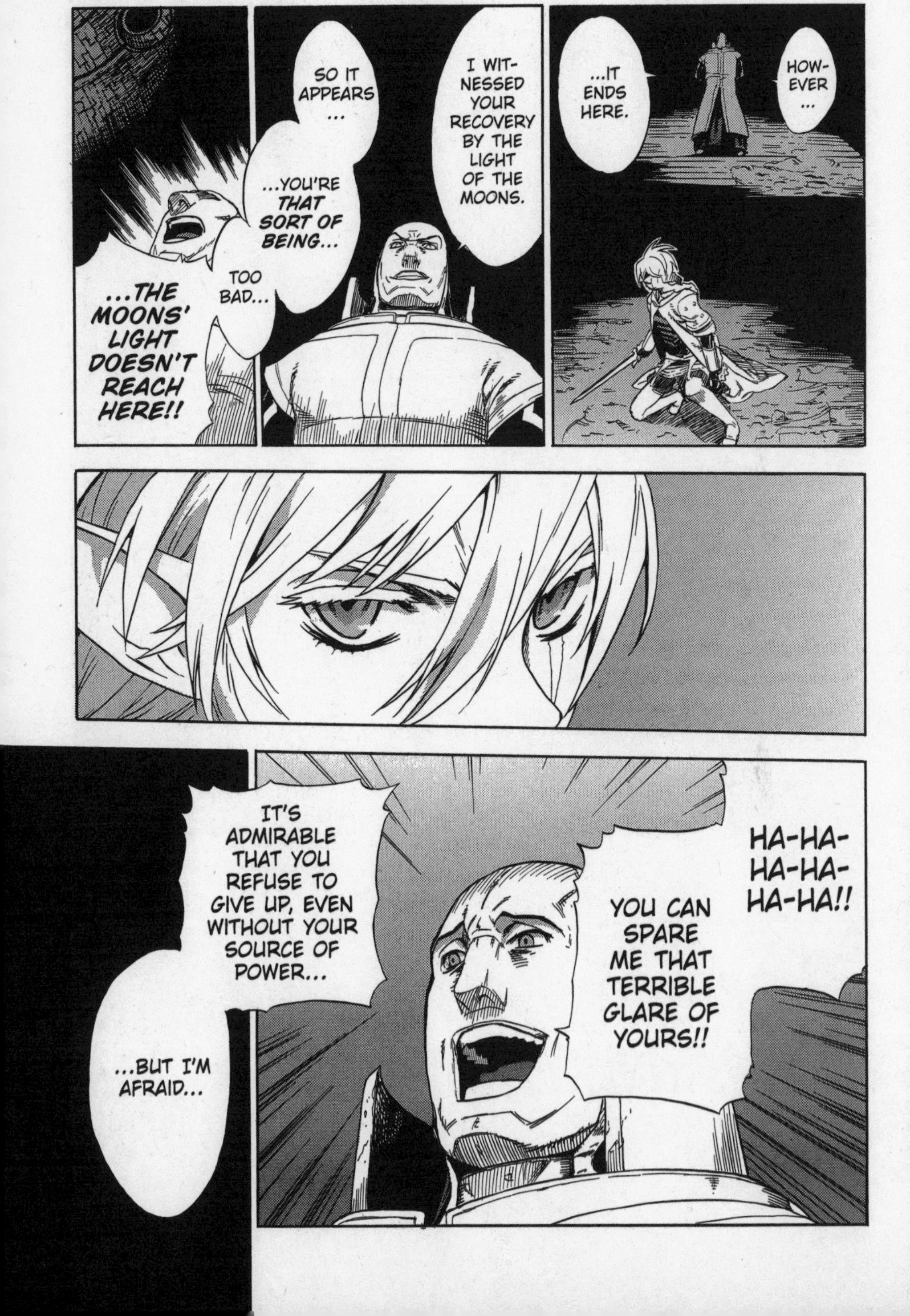
HOW-EVER...
...IT ENDS HERE.
I WIT-NESSED YOUR RECOVERY BY THE LIGHT OF THE MOONS.
SO IT APPEARS...
...YOU'RE THAT SORT OF BEING...
TOO BAD...
...THE MOONS' LIGHT DOESN'T REACH HERE!!
HA-HA-HA-HA-HA-HA!!
YOU CAN SPARE ME THAT TERRIBLE GLARE OF YOURS!!
IT'S ADMIRABLE THAT YOU REFUSE TO GIVE UP, EVEN WITHOUT YOUR SOURCE OF POWER...
...BUT I'M AFRAID...

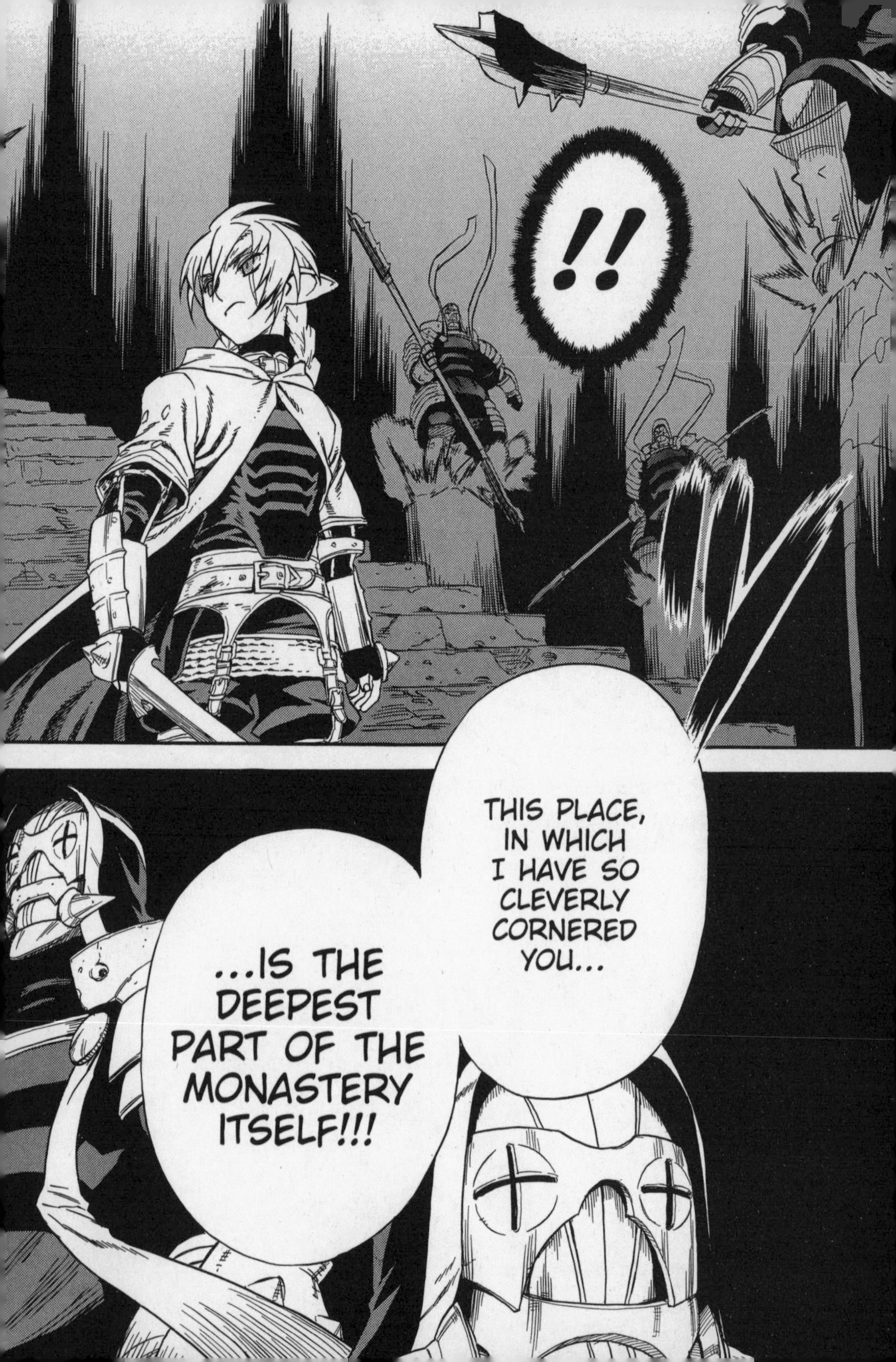
!!
THIS PLACE, IN WHICH I HAVE SO CLEVERLY CORNERED YOU...
...IS THE DEEPEST PART OF THE MONASTERY ITSELF!!!

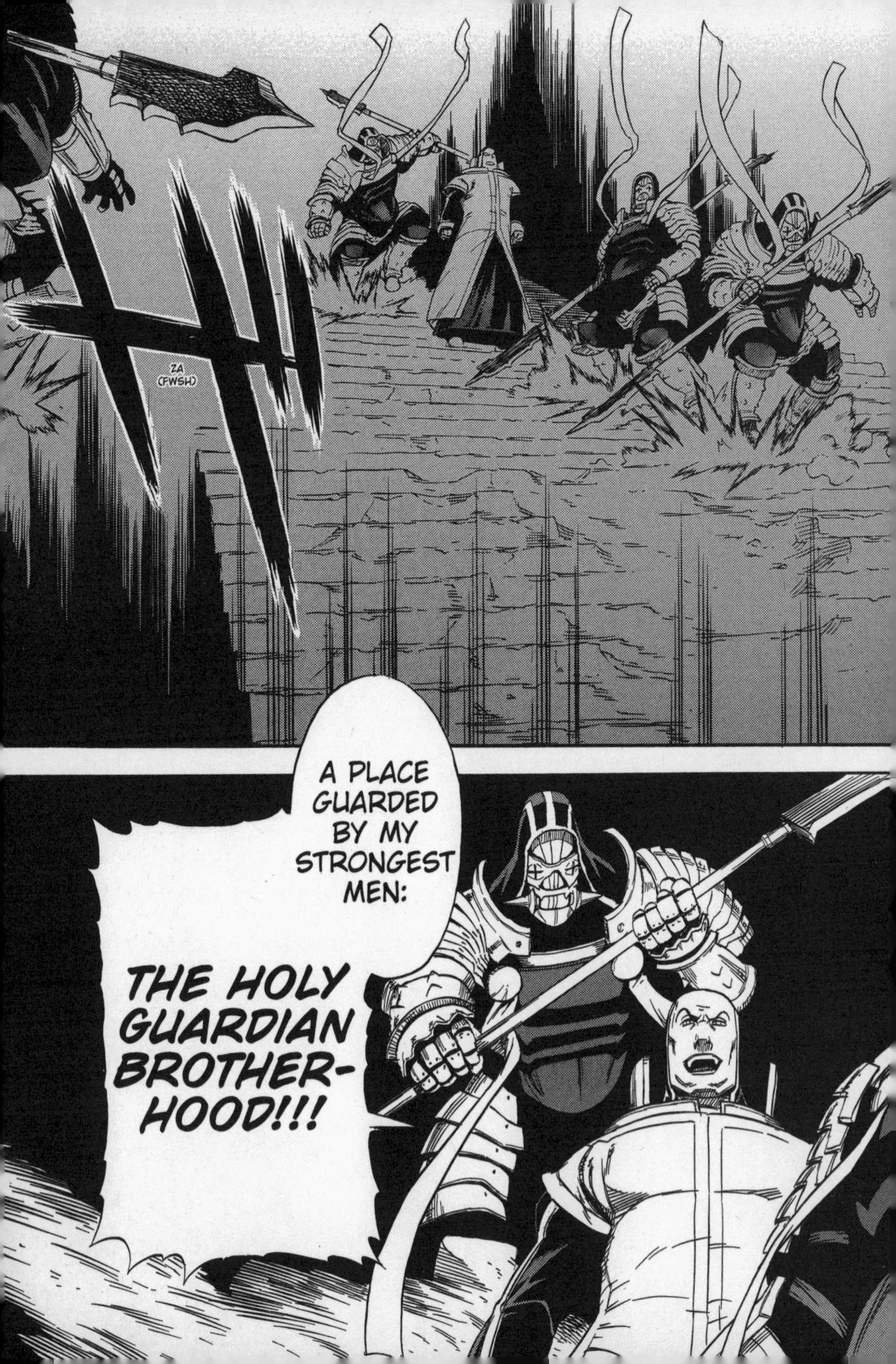
ZA
(FWSH)
A PLACE GUARDED BY MY STRONGEST MEN:
THE HOLY GUARDIAN BROTHER-HOOD!!!

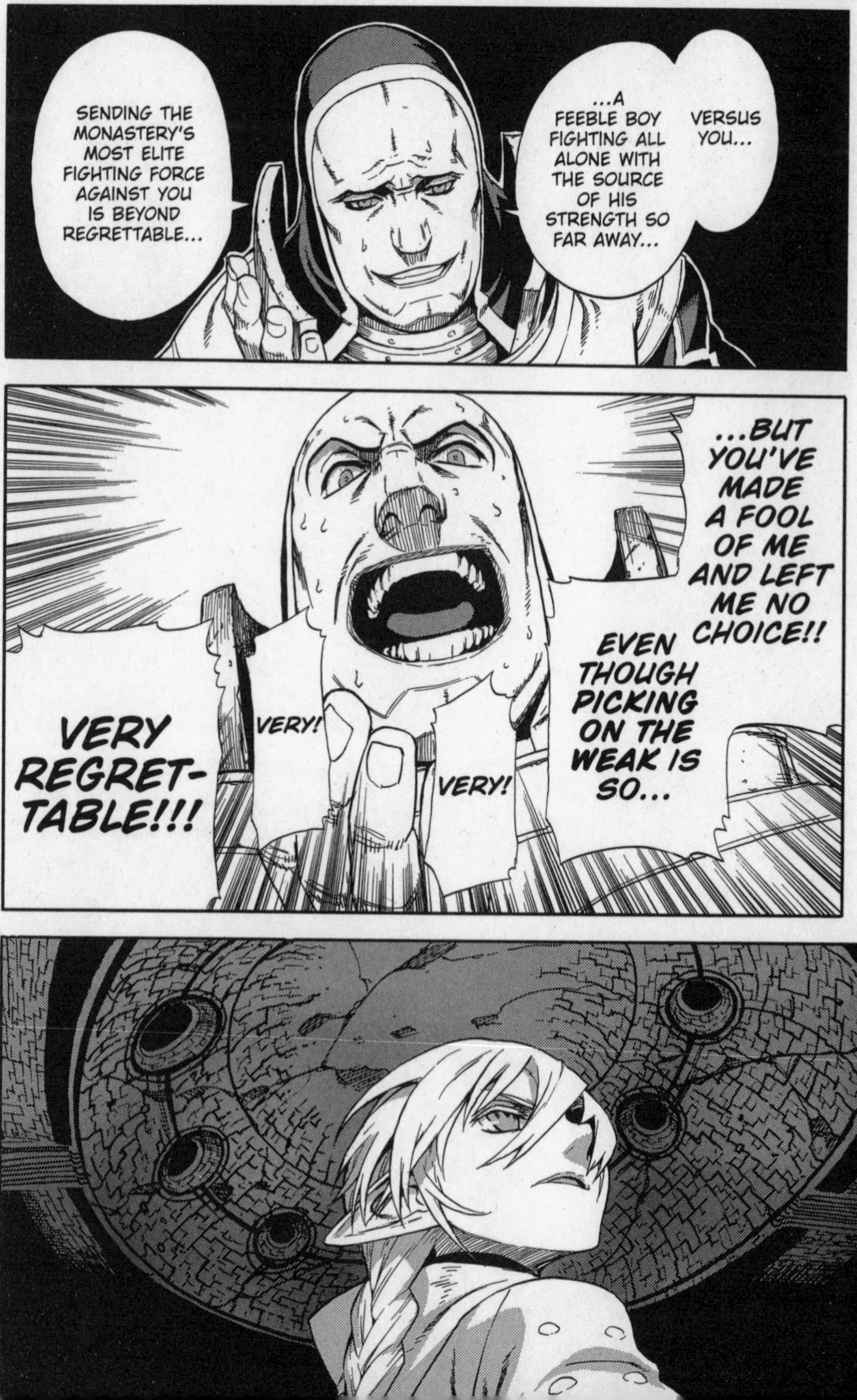

VERSUS YOU...
...A FEEBLE BOY FIGHTING ALL ALONE WITH THE SOURCE OF HIS STRENGTH SO FAR AWAY...
SENDING THE MONASTERY'S MOST ELITE FIGHTING FORCE AGAINST YOU IS BEYOND REGRETTABLE...
...BUT YOU'VE MADE A FOOL OF ME AND LEFT ME NO CHOICE!!
EVEN THOUGH PICKING ON THE WEAK IS SO...
VERY!
VERY!
VERY REGRET-TABLE!!!

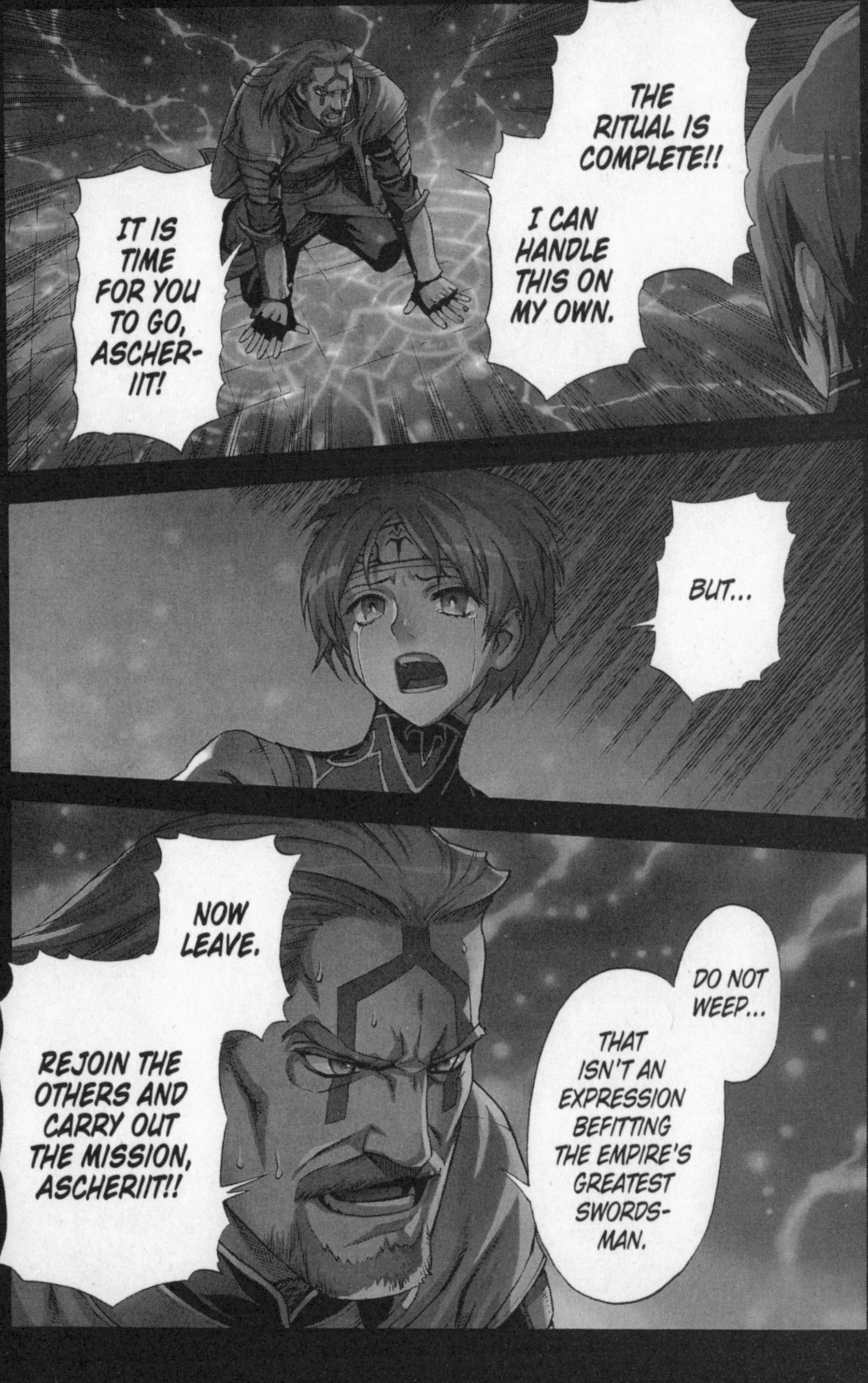
THE RITUAL IS COMPLETE!!
I CAN HANDLE THIS ON MY OWN.
IT IS TIME FOR YOU TO GO, ASCHER-IIT!
BUT...
DO NOT WEEP...
THAT ISN'T AN EXPRESSION BEFITTING THE EMPIRE'S GREATEST SWORDS-MAN.
NOW LEAVE.
REJOIN THE OTHERS AND CARRY OUT THE MISSION, ASCHERIIT!!

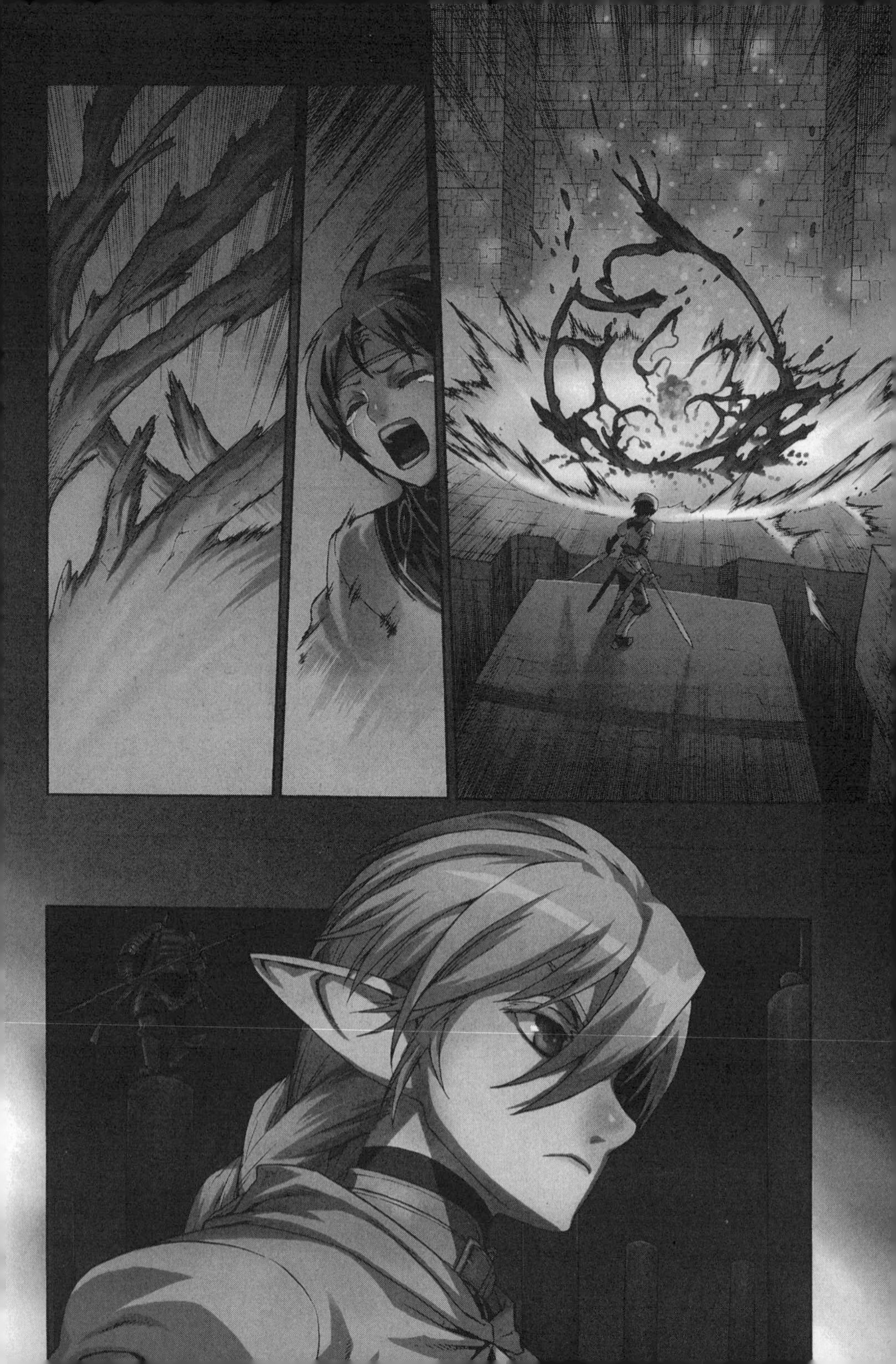

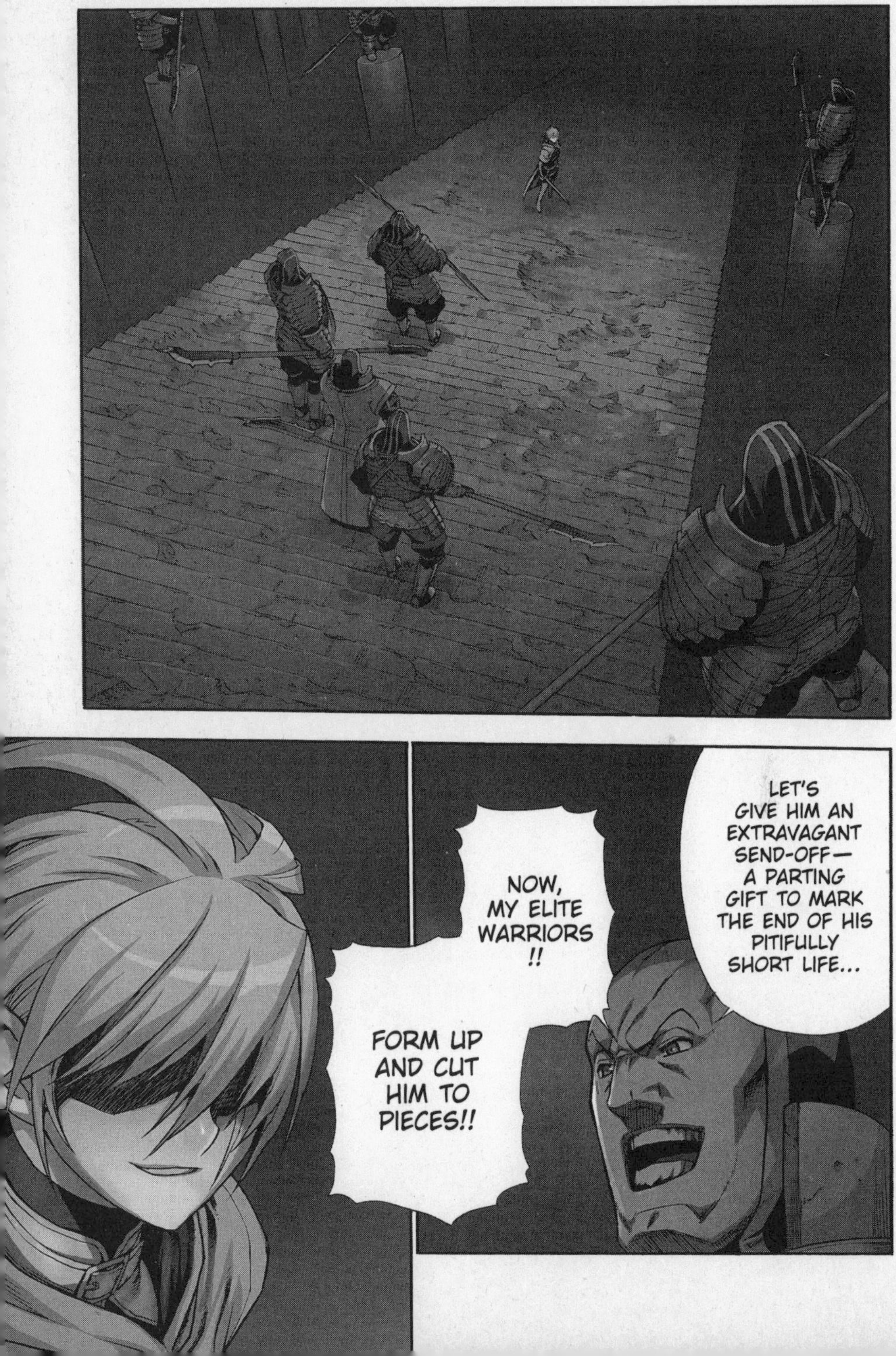
LET'S GIVE HIM AN EXTRAVAGANT SEND-OFF— A PARTING GIFT TO MARK THE END OF HIS PITIFULLY SHORT LIFE...
NOW, MY ELITE WARRIORS!!
FORM UP AND CUT HIM TO PIECES!!

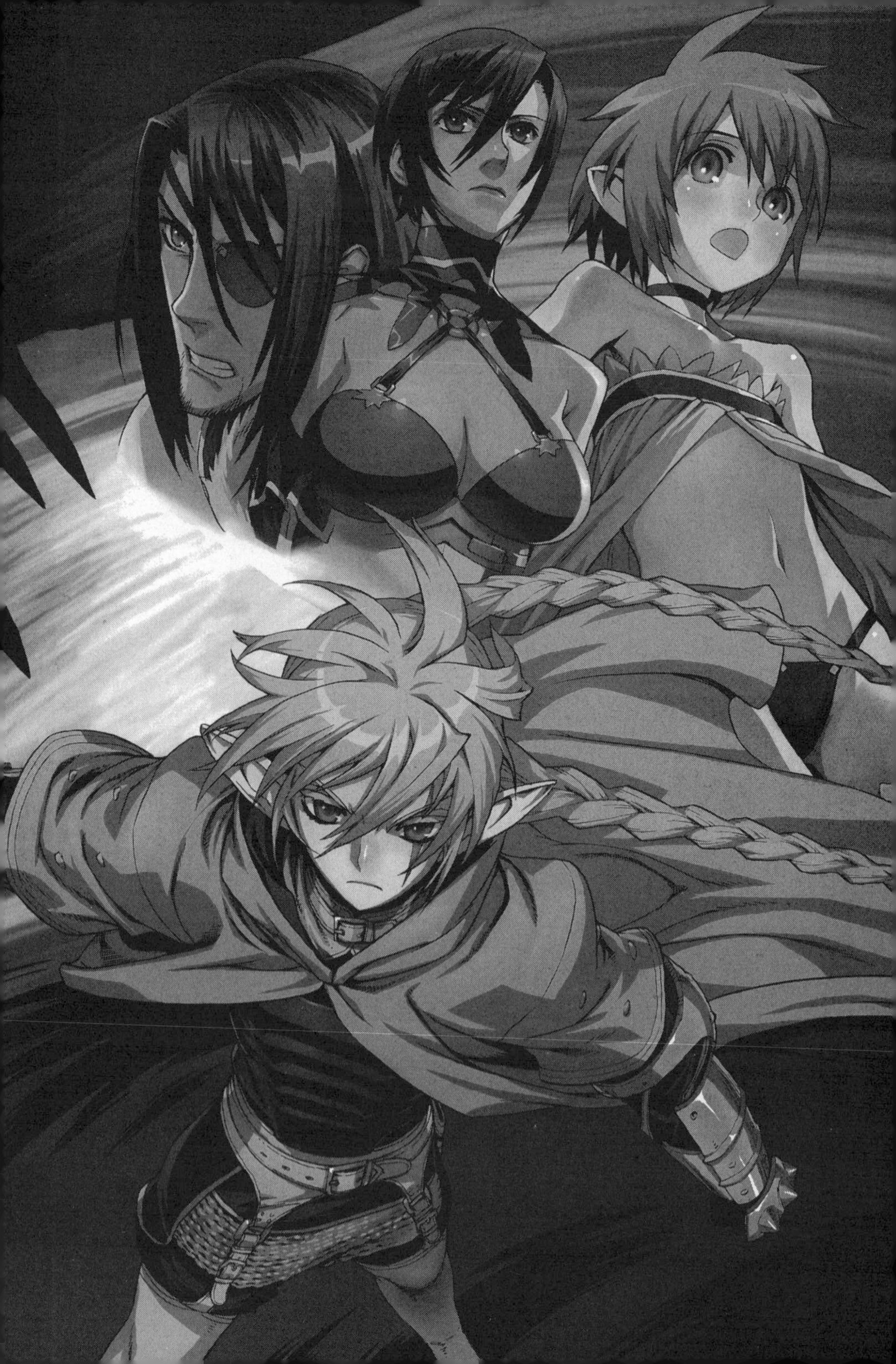

Durch Bruch (Break Through) ◆VI◆

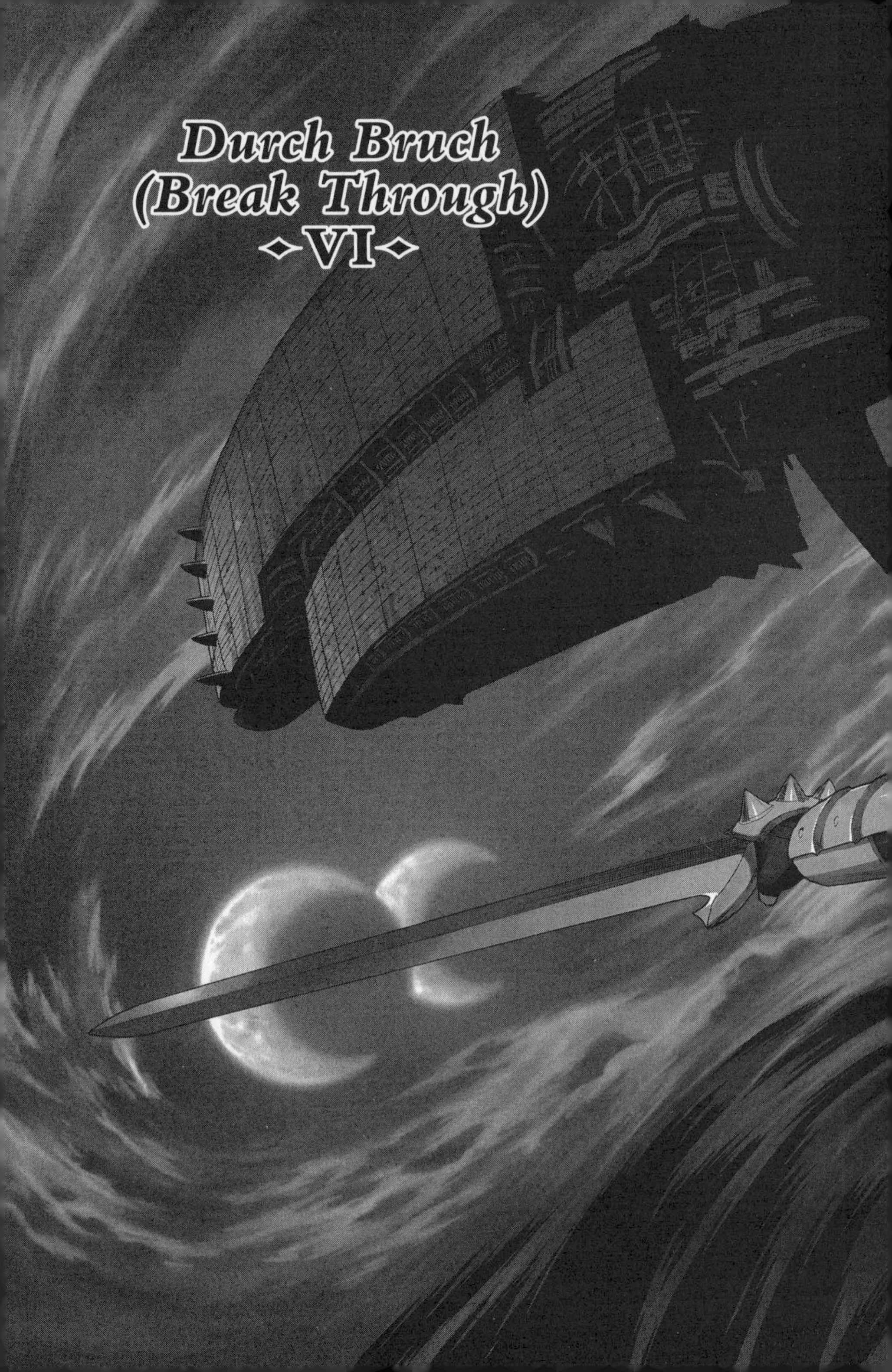

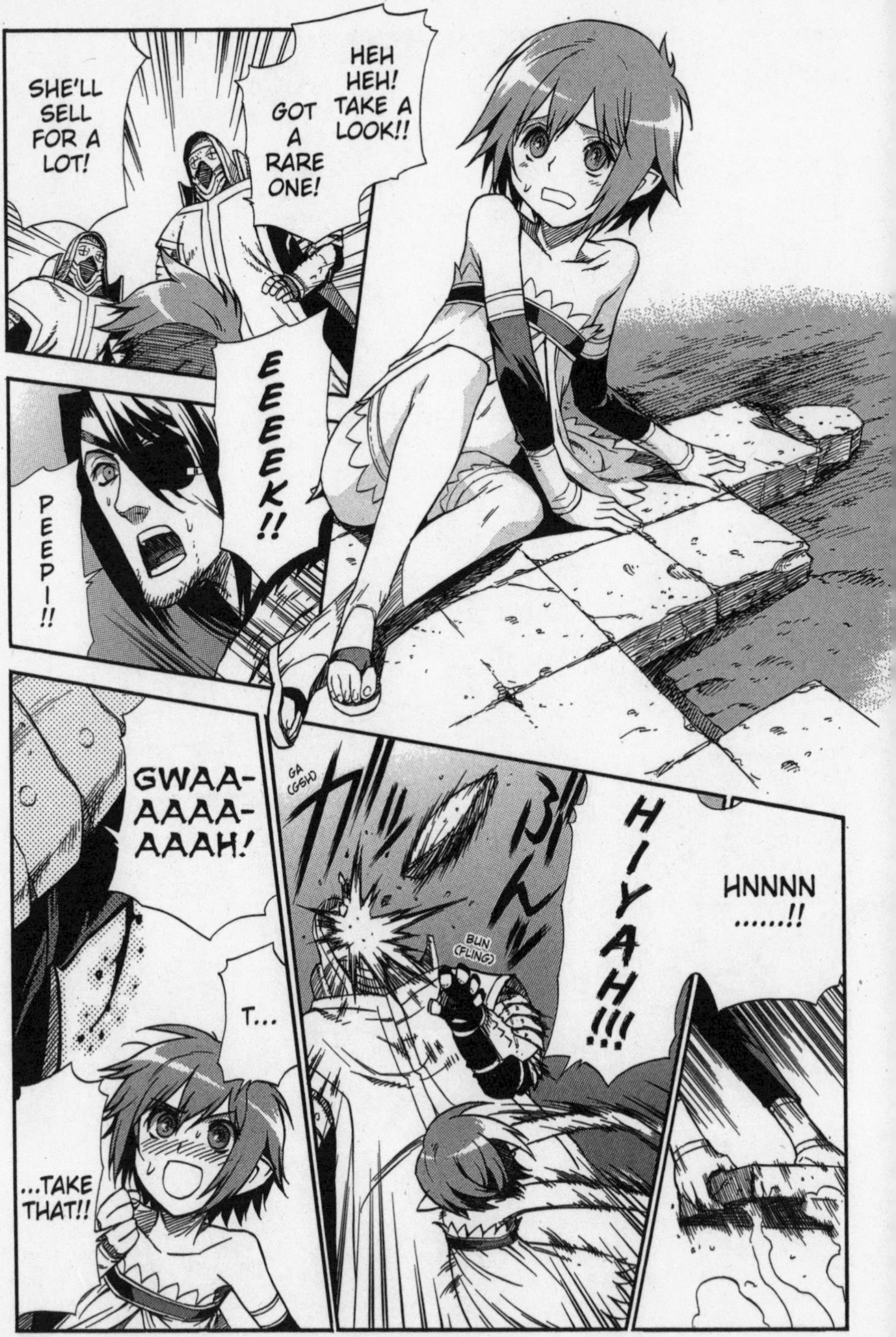
HEH HEH! TAKE A LOOK!!
GOT A RARE ONE!
SHE'LL SELL FOR A LOT!
EEEEEK!!
PEEPI-!!
HNNNN ......!!
HIYAH!!!
BUN (FLING)
GA (GSH)
GWAA-AAAA-AAAH!
T...
...TAKE THAT!!

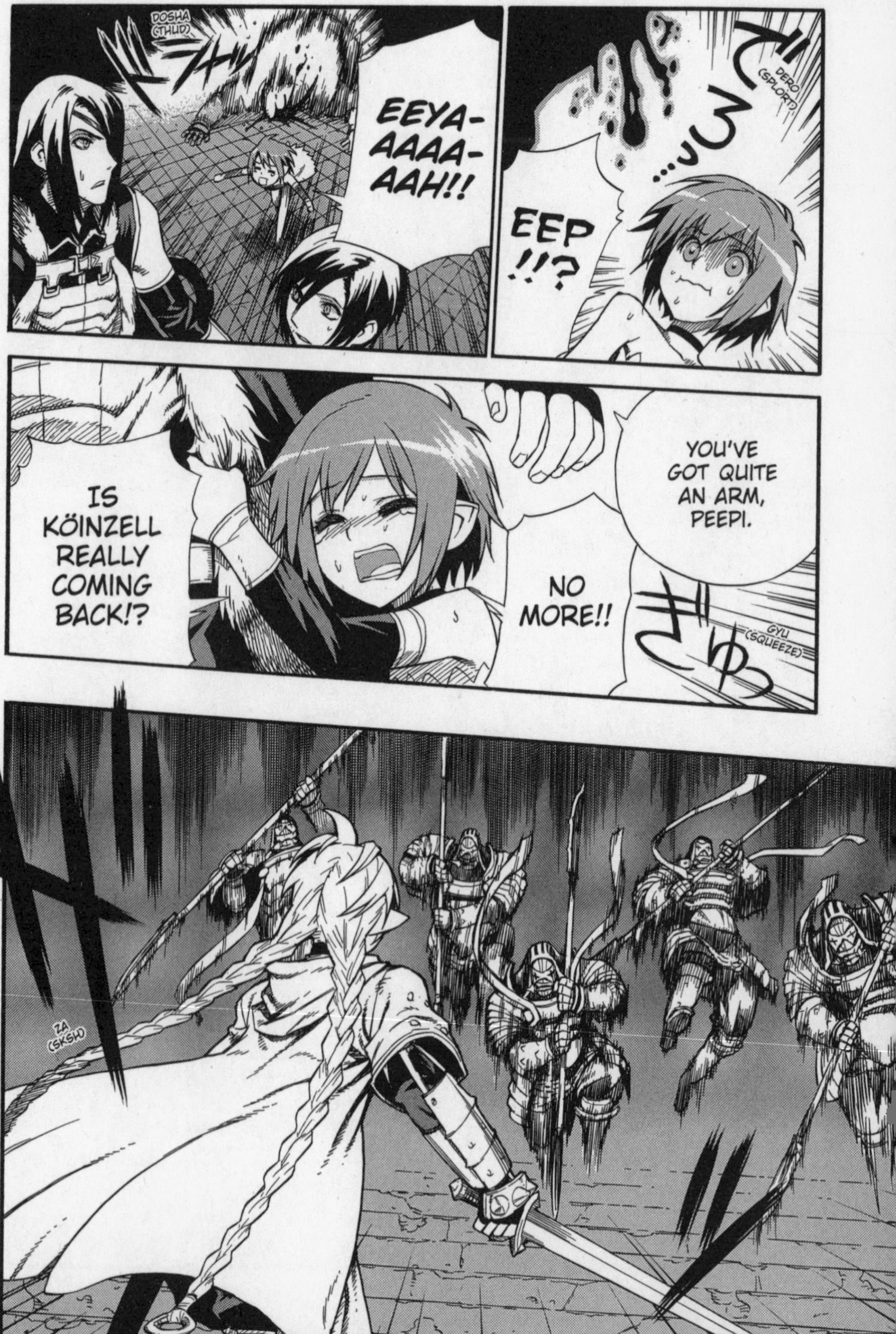
DERO (SPLORT)
EEP!!?
EEYA-AAAA-AAH!!
DOSHA (THUD)
YOU'VE GOT QUITE AN ARM, PEEPI.
GYU (SQUEEZE)
NO MORE!!
IS KÖINZELL REALLY COMING BACK!?
ZA (SKSH)

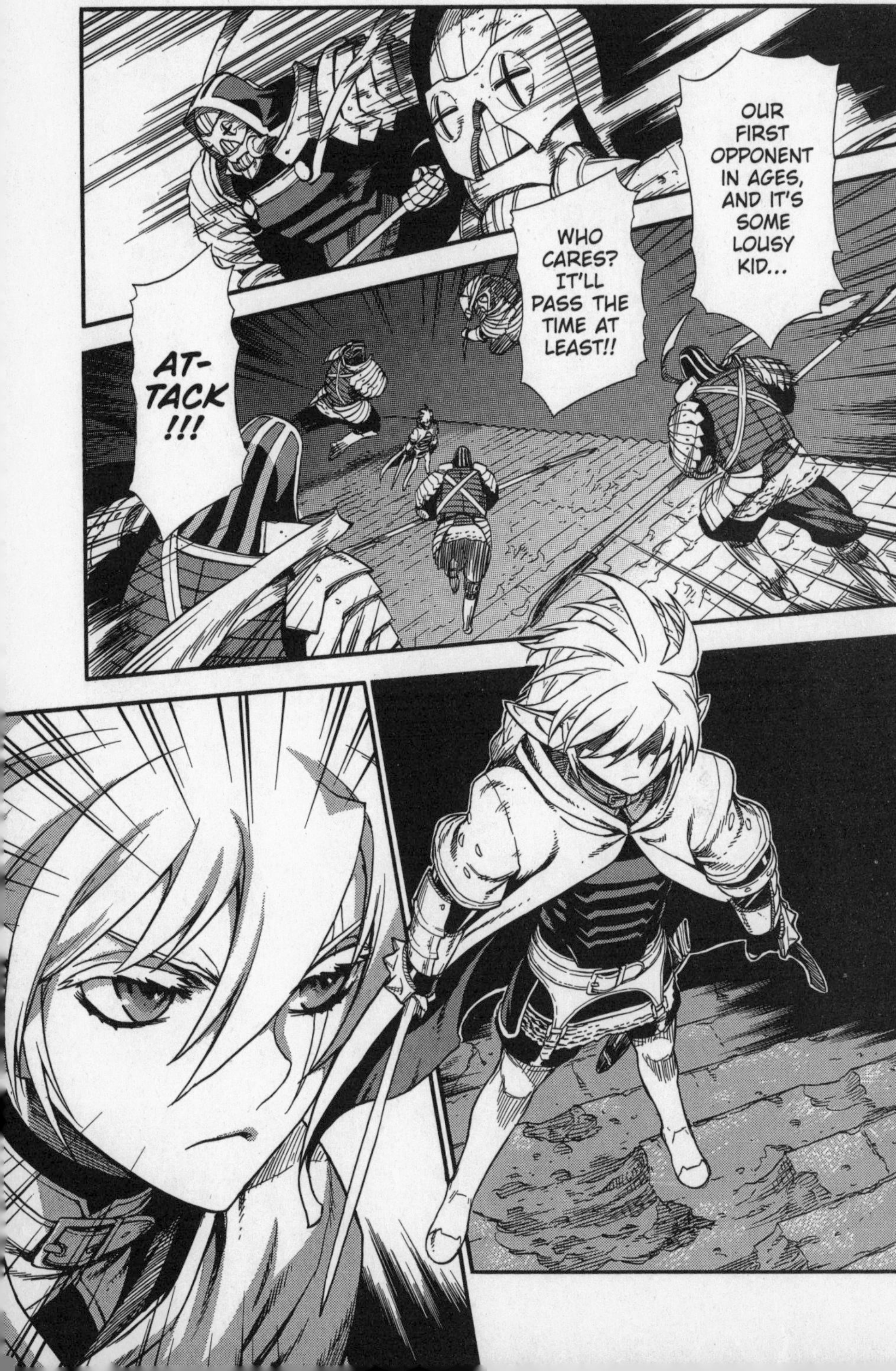
OUR FIRST OPPONENT IN AGES, AND IT'S SOME LOUSY KID...
WHO CARES? IT'LL PASS THE TIME AT LEAST!!
AT-TACK!!!

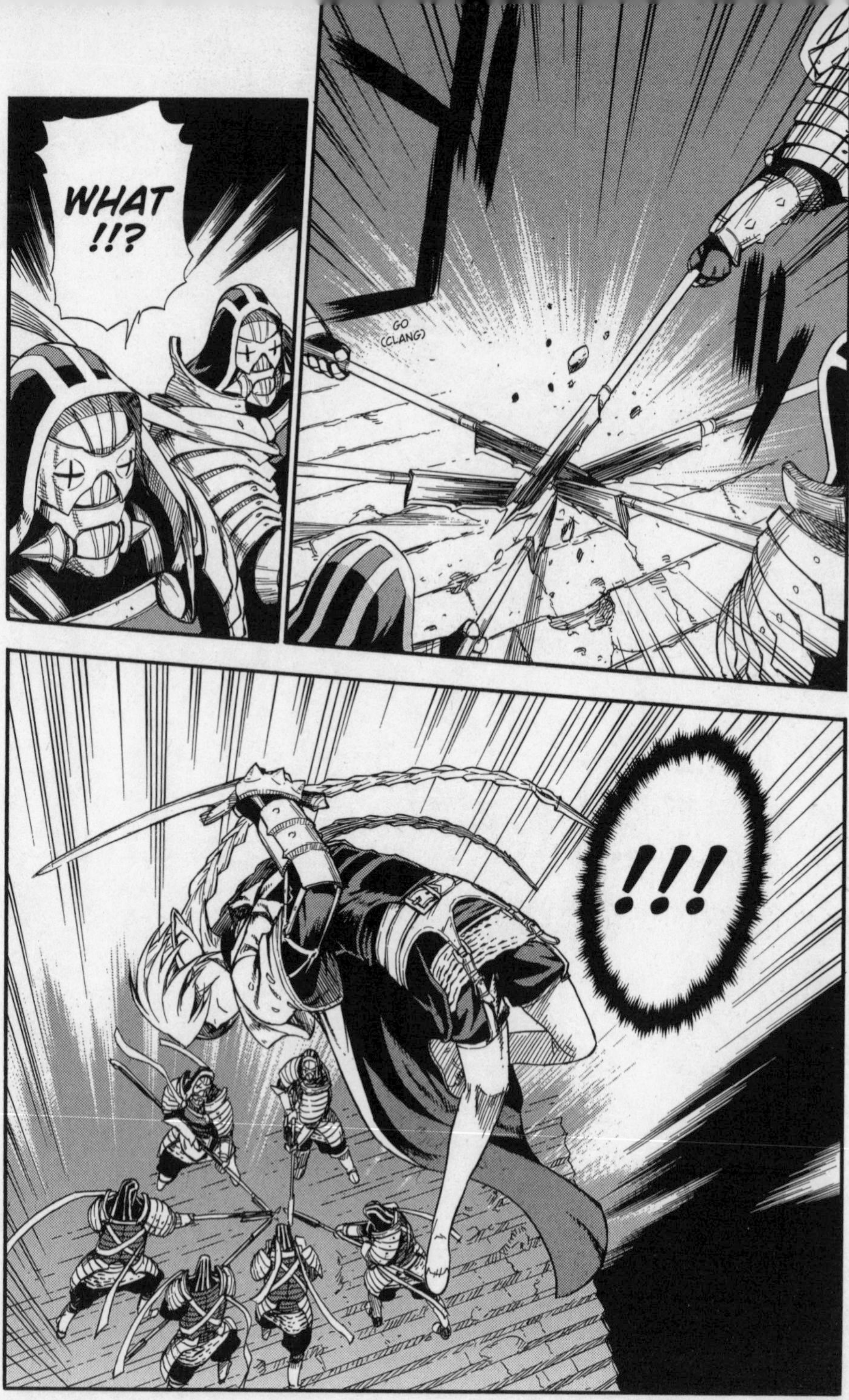
GO (CLANG)
WHAT !!?
!!!

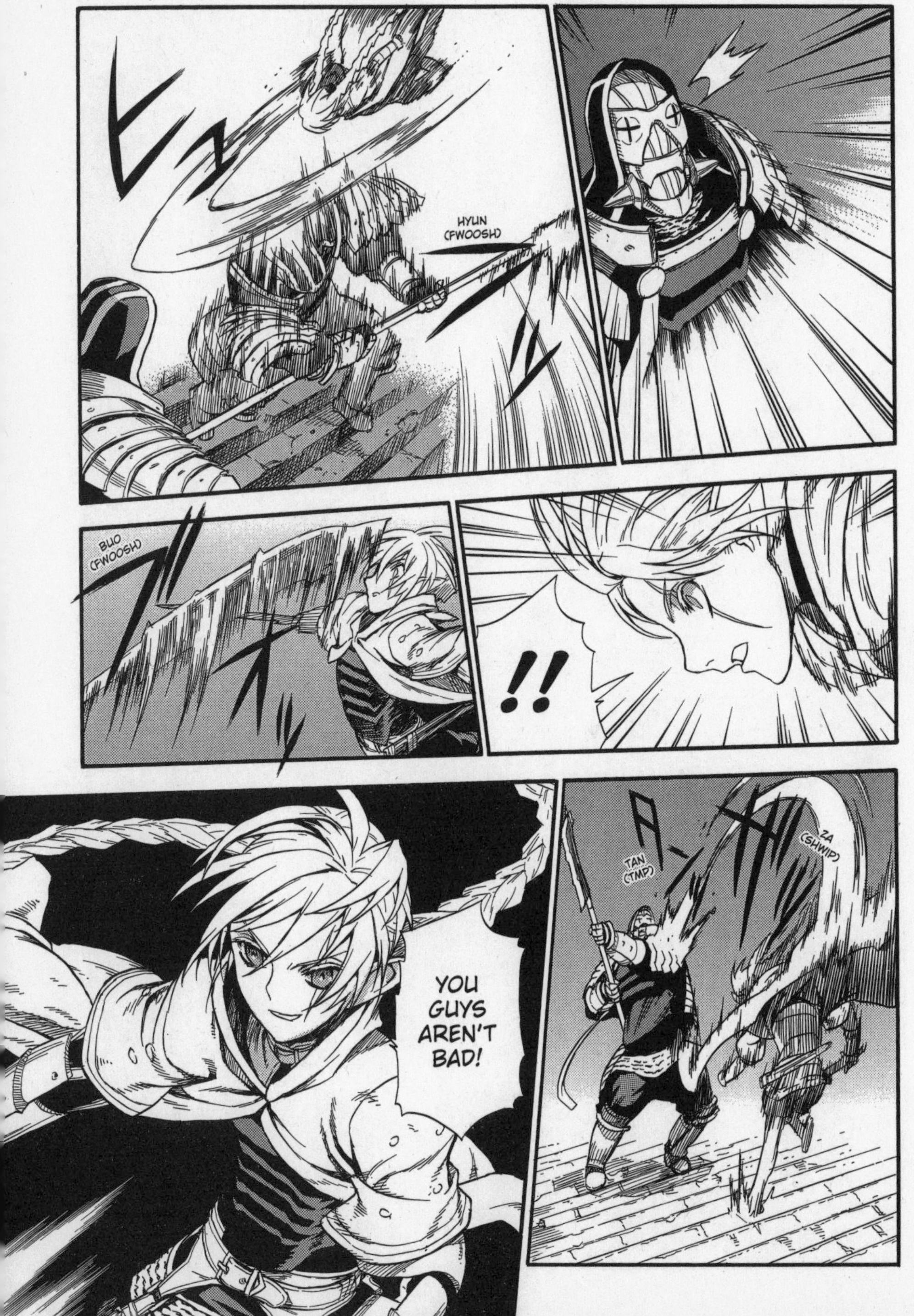
HYUN
(FWOOSH)
!!
BUO
(FWOOSH)
ZA
(SHWIP)
TAN
(TMP)
YOU GUYS AREN'T BAD!

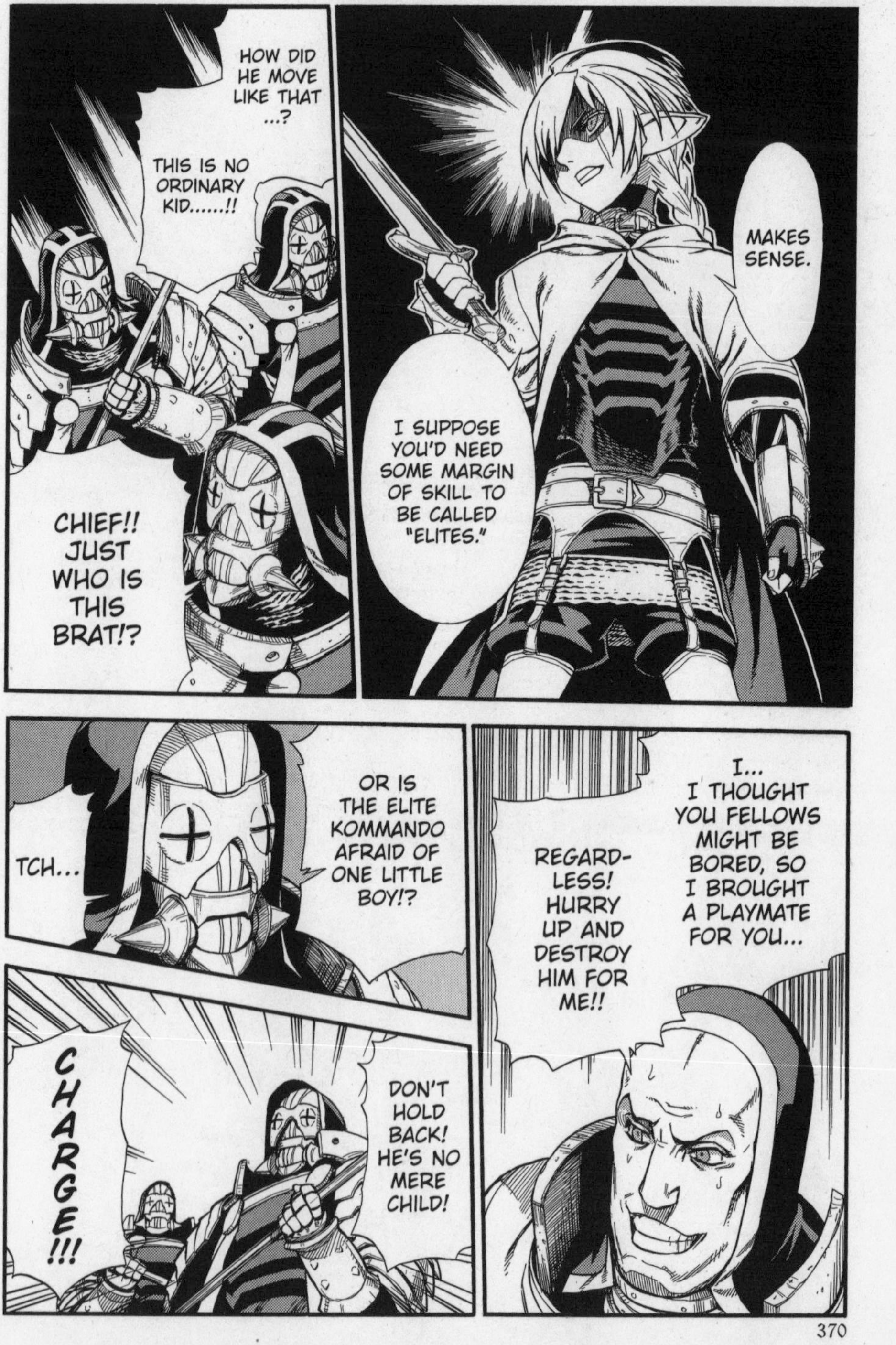
MAKES SENSE.
I SUPPOSE YOU'D NEED SOME MARGIN OF SKILL TO BE CALLED "ELITES."
HOW DID HE MOVE LIKE THAT ...?
THIS IS NO ORDINARY KID......!!
CHIEF!! JUST WHO IS THIS BRAT!?
I... I THOUGHT YOU FELLOWS MIGHT BE BORED, SO I BROUGHT A PLAYMATE FOR YOU...
REGARD-LESS! HURRY UP AND DESTROY HIM FOR ME!!
OR IS THE ELITE KOMMANDO AFRAID OF ONE LITTLE BOY!?
TCH...
DON'T HOLD BACK! HE'S NO MERE CHILD!
CHARGE!!!

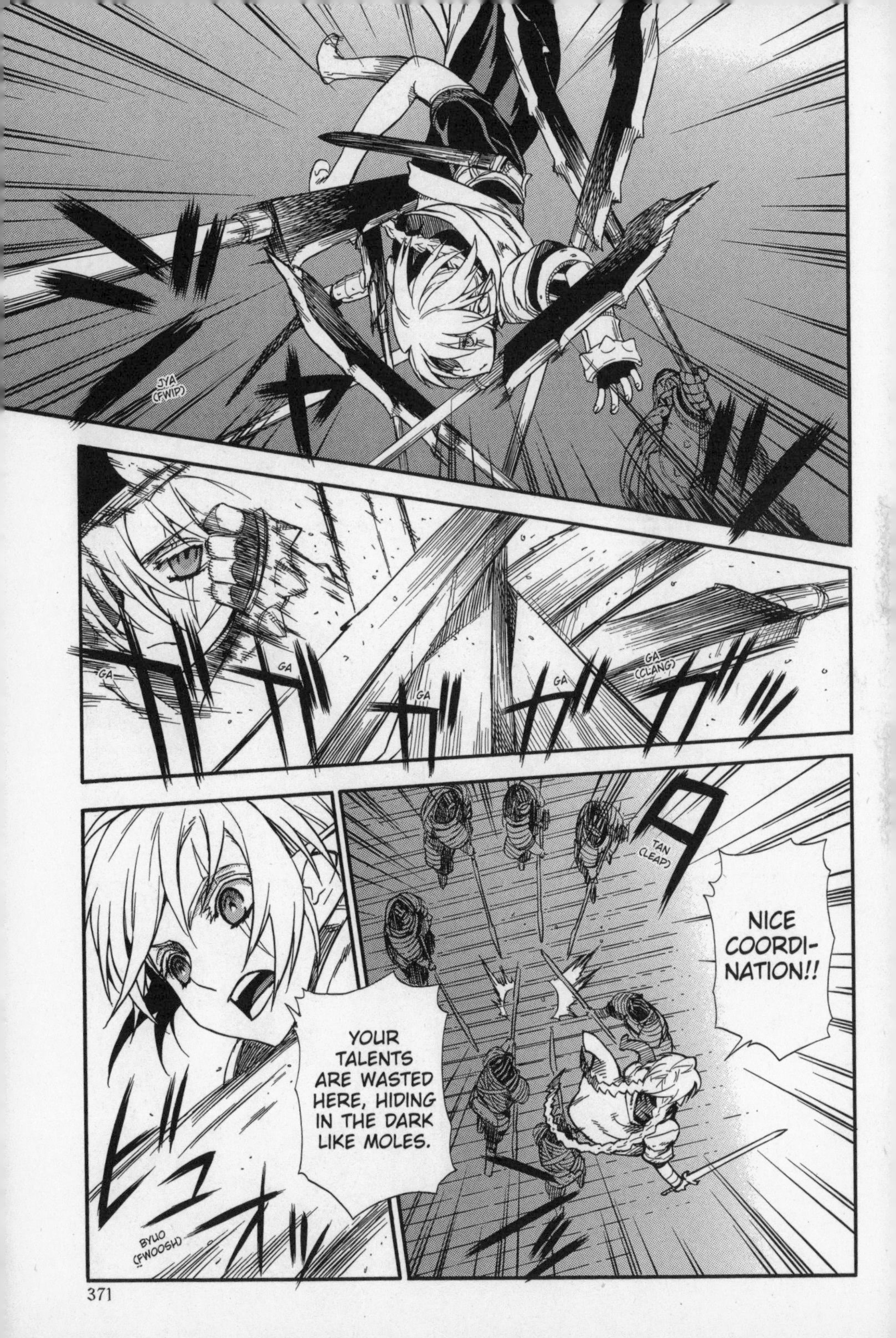

JYA (FWIP)
GA (CLANG)
GA
GA
GA
GA
TAN (LEAP)
NICE COORDI-NATION!!
YOUR TALENTS ARE WASTED HERE, HIDING IN THE DARK LIKE MOLES.
BYUO (FWOOSH)

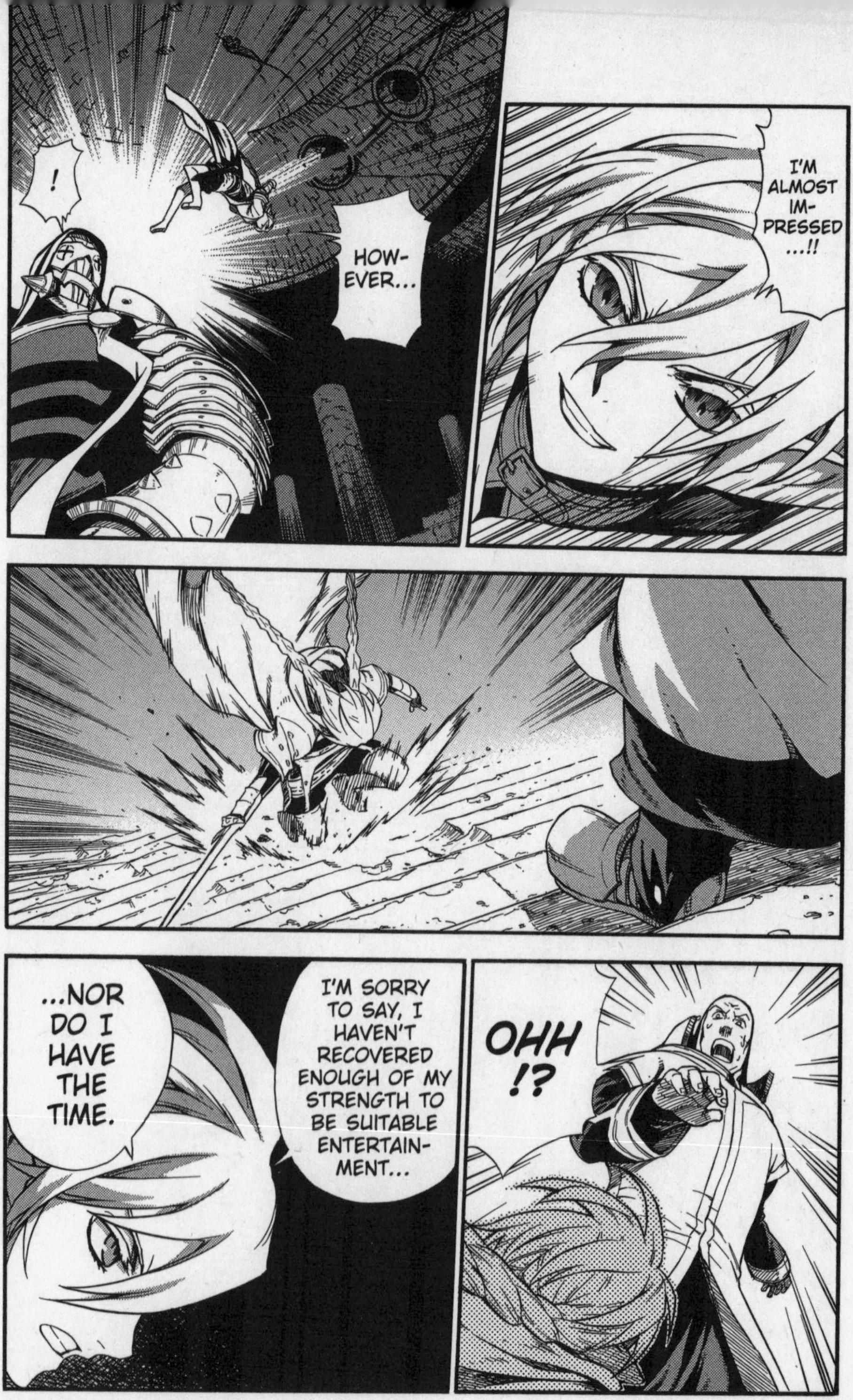
I'M ALMOST IM-PRESSED ...!!
HOW-EVER...
!
OHH !?
I'M SORRY TO SAY, I HAVEN'T RECOVERED ENOUGH OF MY STRENGTH TO BE SUITABLE ENTERTAIN-MENT...
...NOR DO I HAVE THE TIME.

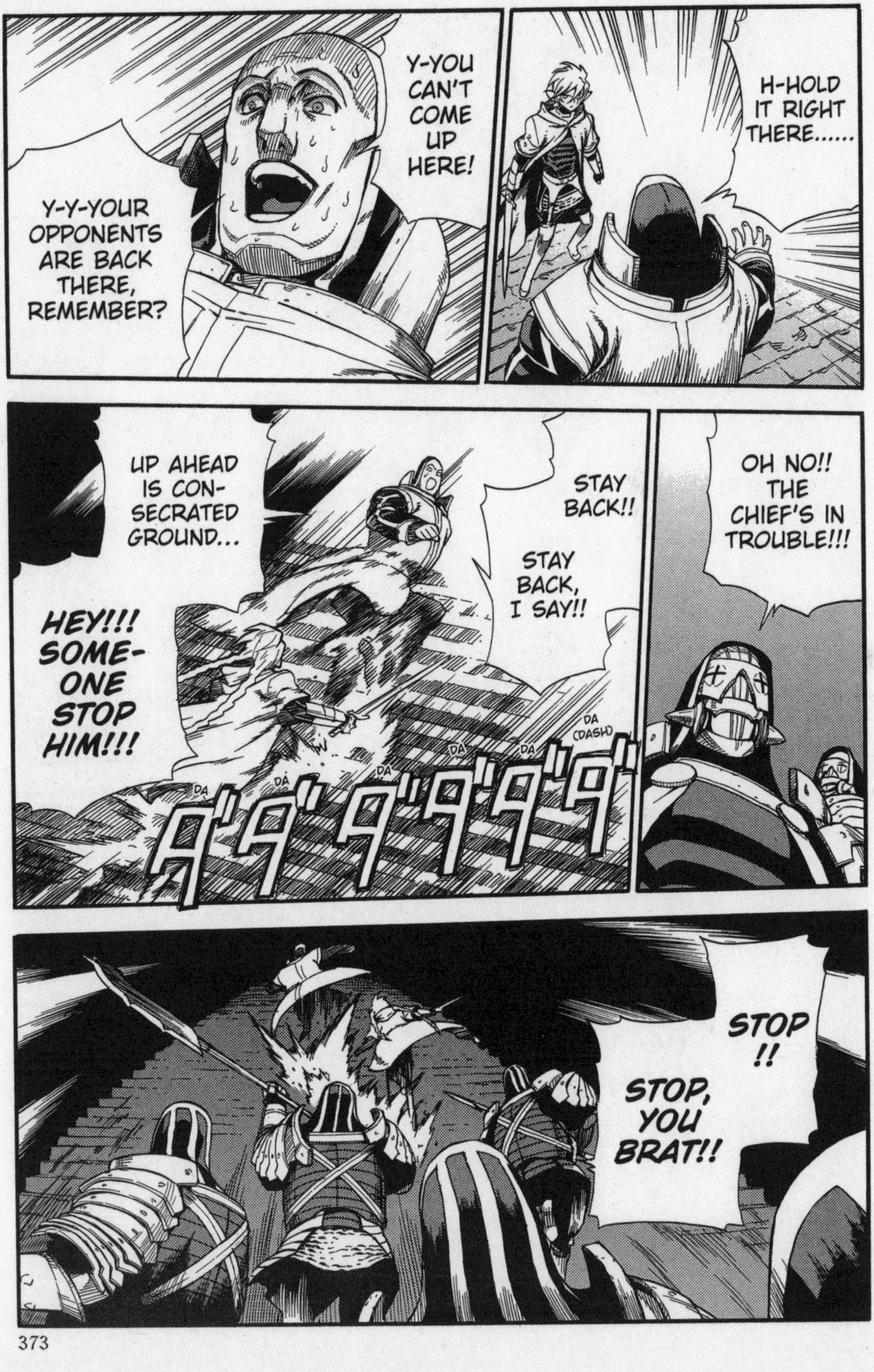
H-HOLD IT RIGHT THERE......
Y-YOU CAN'T COME UP HERE!
Y-Y-YOUR OPPONENTS ARE BACK THERE, REMEMBER?
OH NO!! THE CHIEF'S IN TROUBLE!!!
STAY BACK!!
STAY BACK, I SAY!!
UP AHEAD IS CON-SECRATED GROUND...
HEY!!! SOME-ONE STOP HIM!!!
DA (DASH)
DA
DA
DA
DA
DA
ダダダダダダダ
STOP!!
STOP, YOU BRAT!!

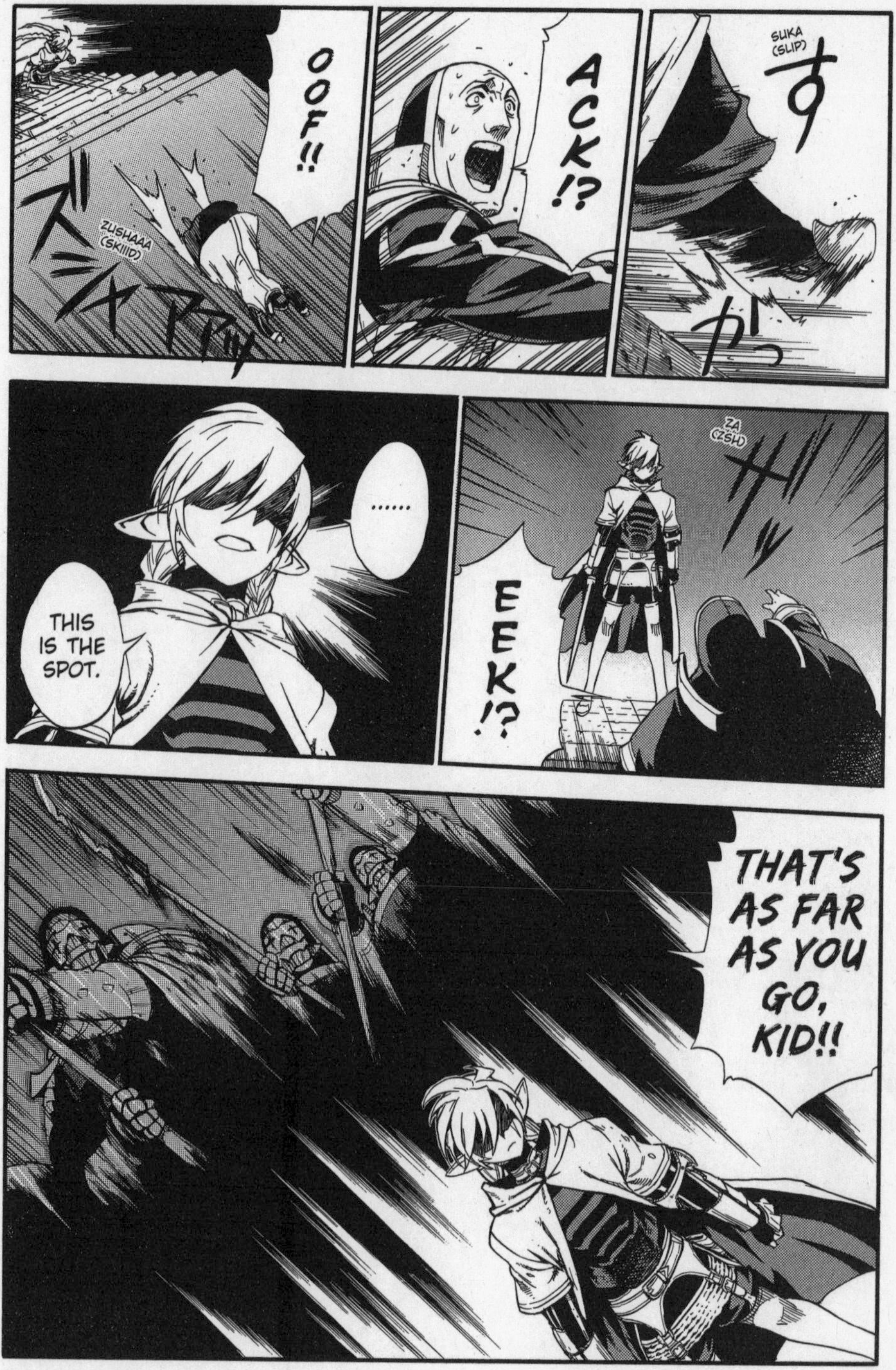
SUKA (SLIP)
す
ACK!?
OOF!!
ZUSHAAA (SKIID)
ZA (ZSH)
EEK!?
......
THIS IS THE SPOT.
THAT'S AS FAR AS YOU GO, KID!!

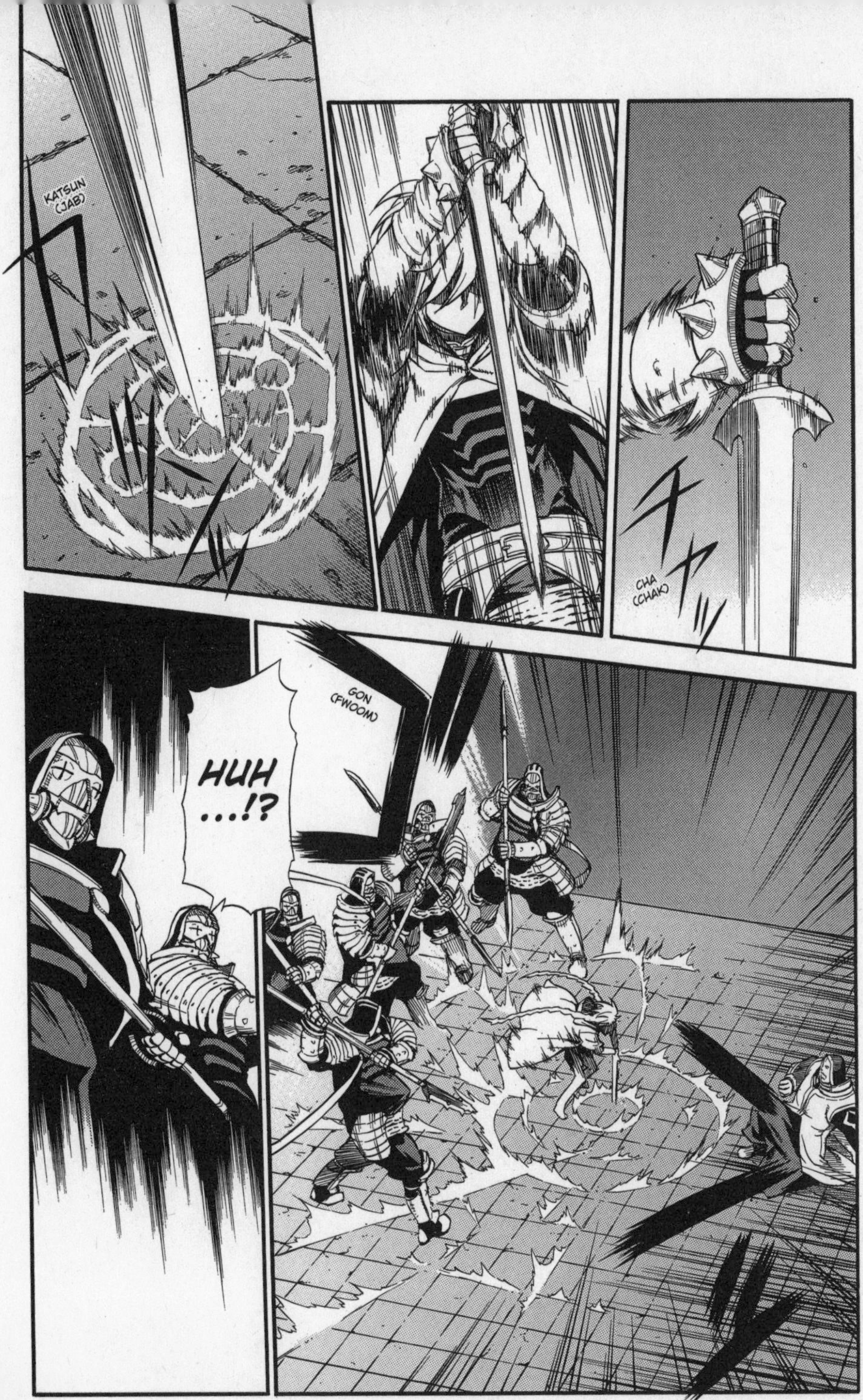
CHA (CHAK)
KATSUN (JAB)
GON (FWOOM)
HUH ...!?

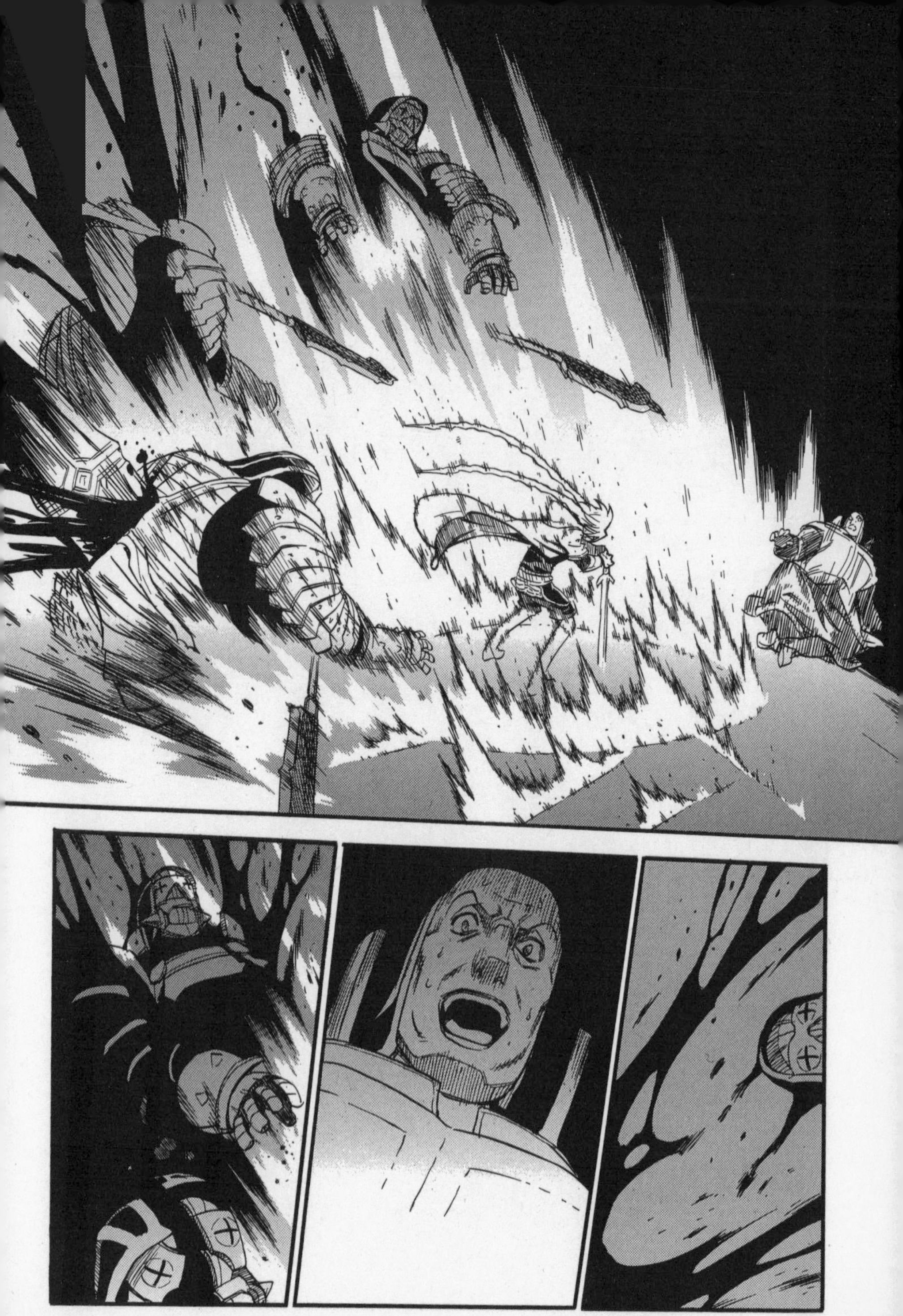

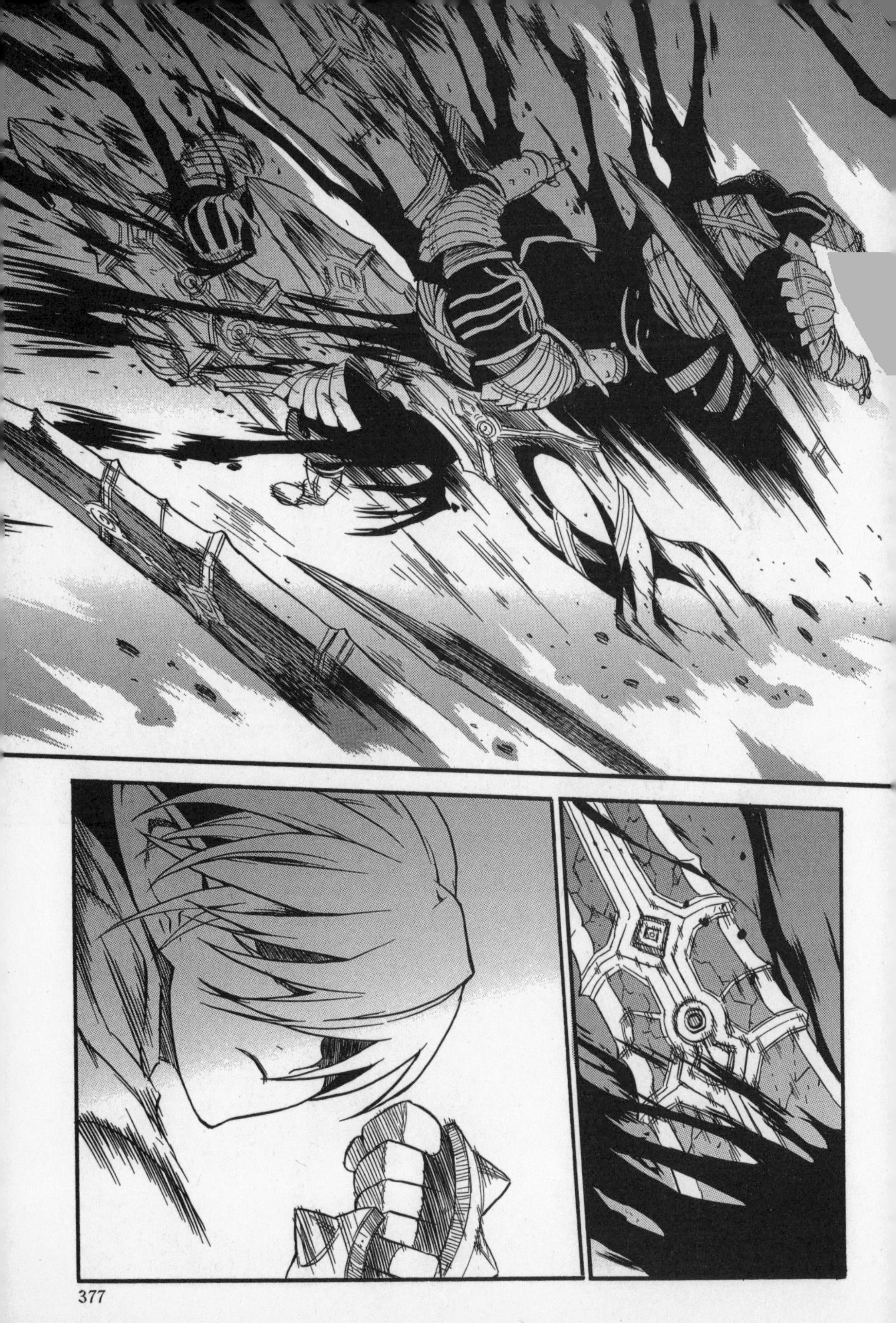

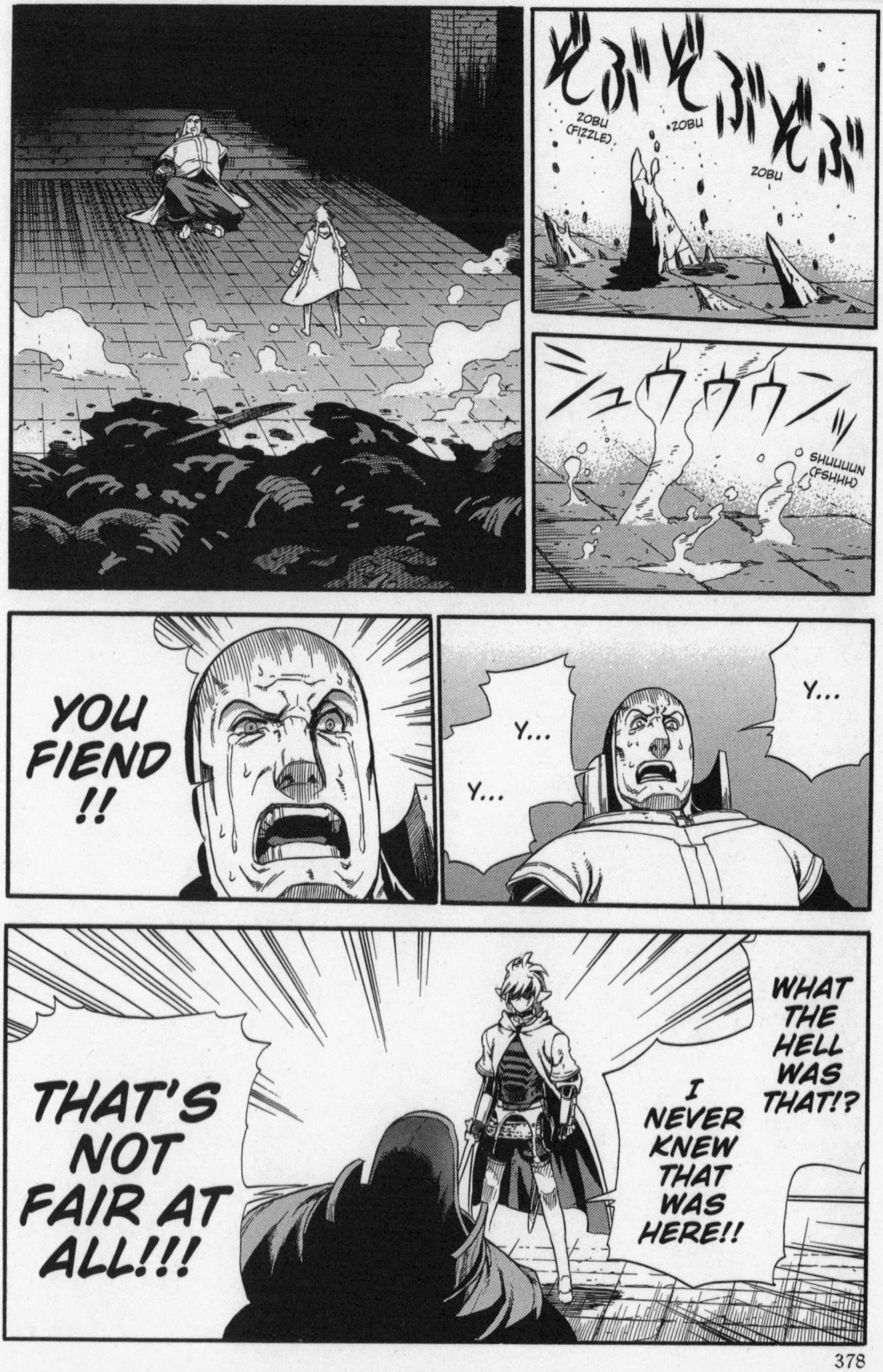
ぞぶぞぶぞぶ
ZOBU (FIZZLE)
ZOBU
ZOBU
シュウウウンッ
SHUUUUN (FSHHH)
Y...
Y...
Y...
YOU FIEND!!
WHAT THE HELL WAS THAT!?
I NEVER KNEW THAT WAS HERE!!
THAT'S NOT FAIR AT ALL!!!

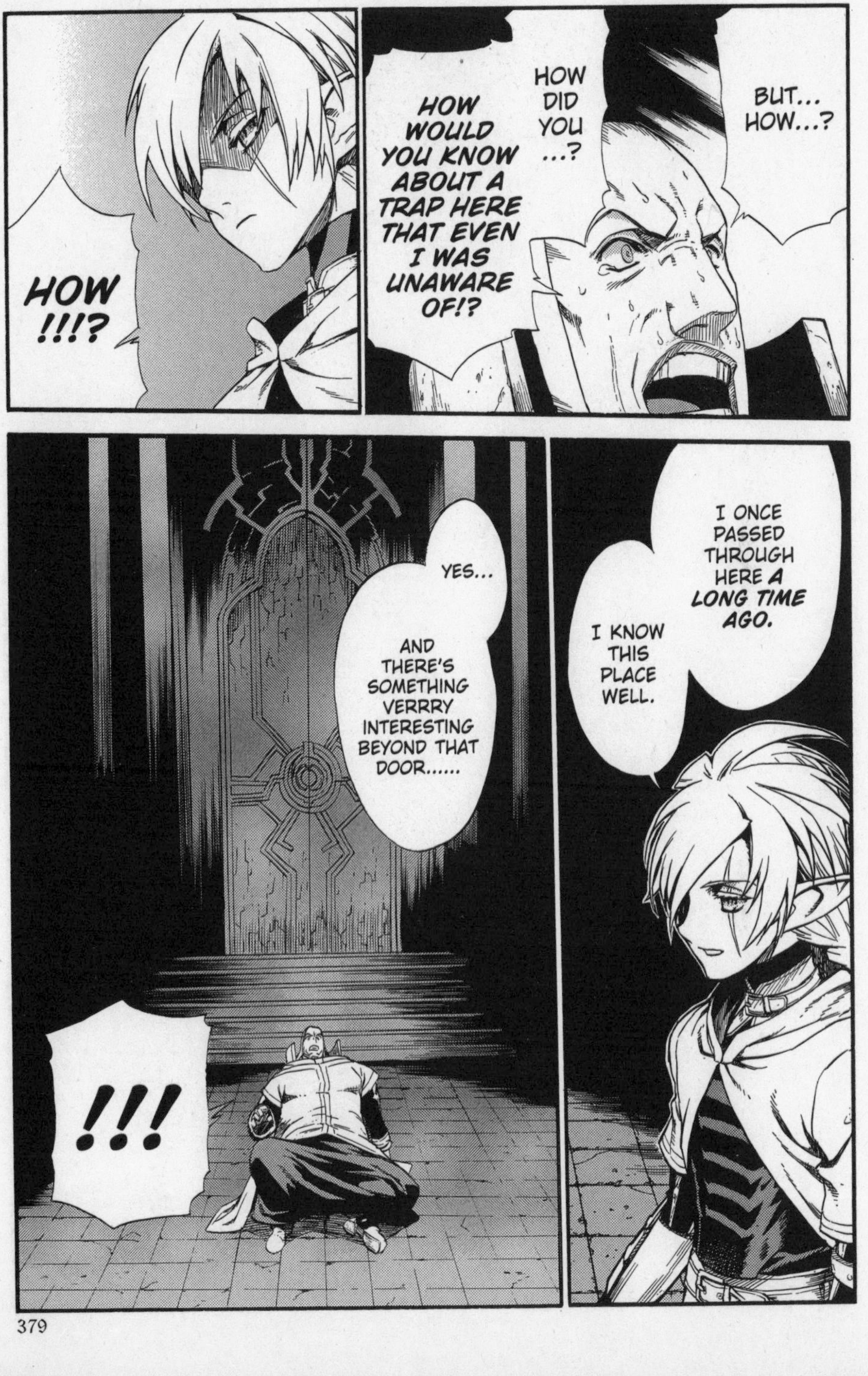
BUT... HOW...?
HOW DID YOU ...?
HOW WOULD YOU KNOW ABOUT A TRAP HERE THAT EVEN I WAS UNAWARE OF!?
HOW !!!?
I ONCE PASSED THROUGH HERE A LONG TIME AGO.
I KNOW THIS PLACE WELL.
YES...
AND THERE'S SOMETHING VERRRY INTERESTING BEYOND THAT DOOR......
!!!

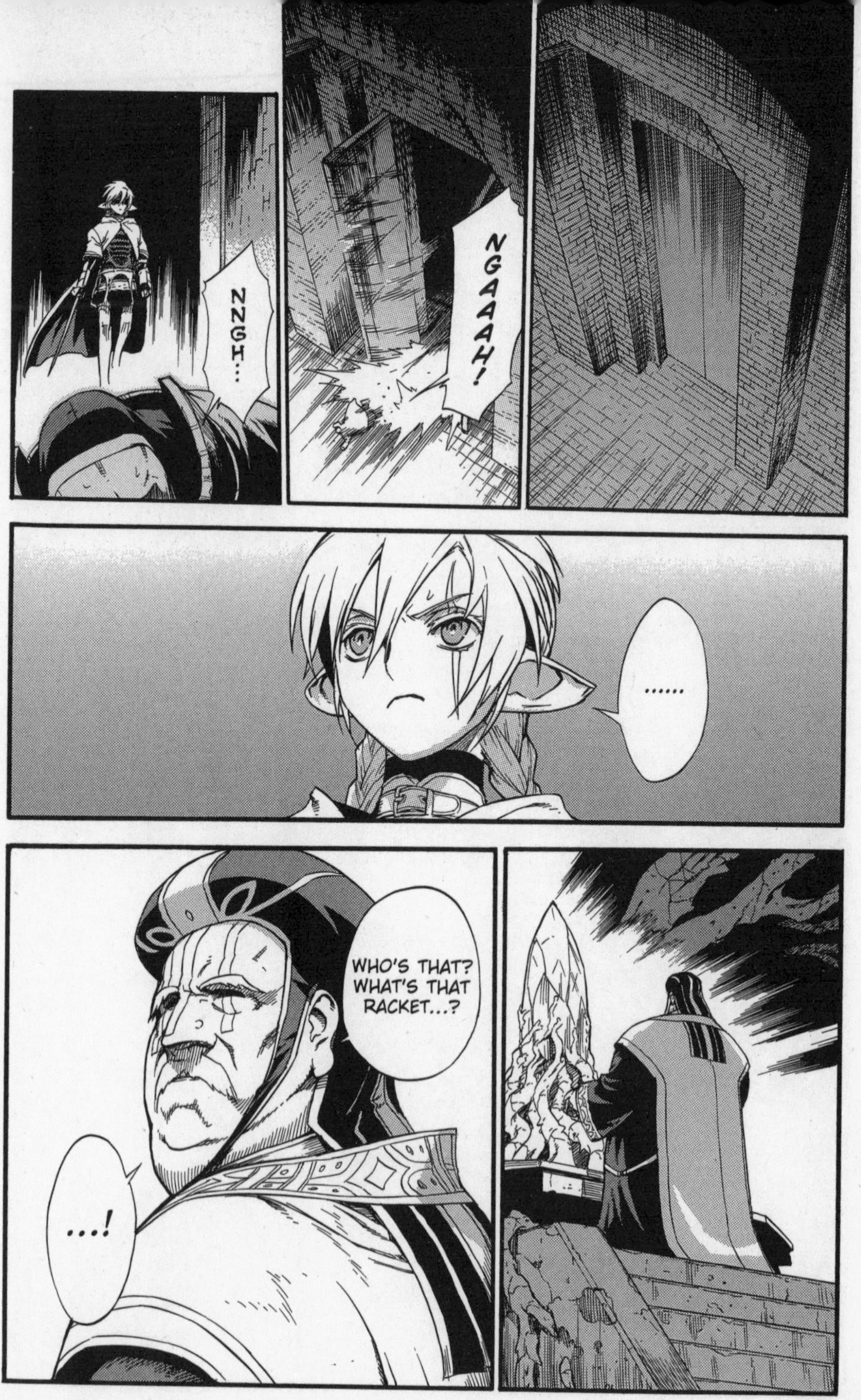
NGAAAH!
NNGH...
......
WHO'S THAT? WHAT'S THAT RACKET...?
...!

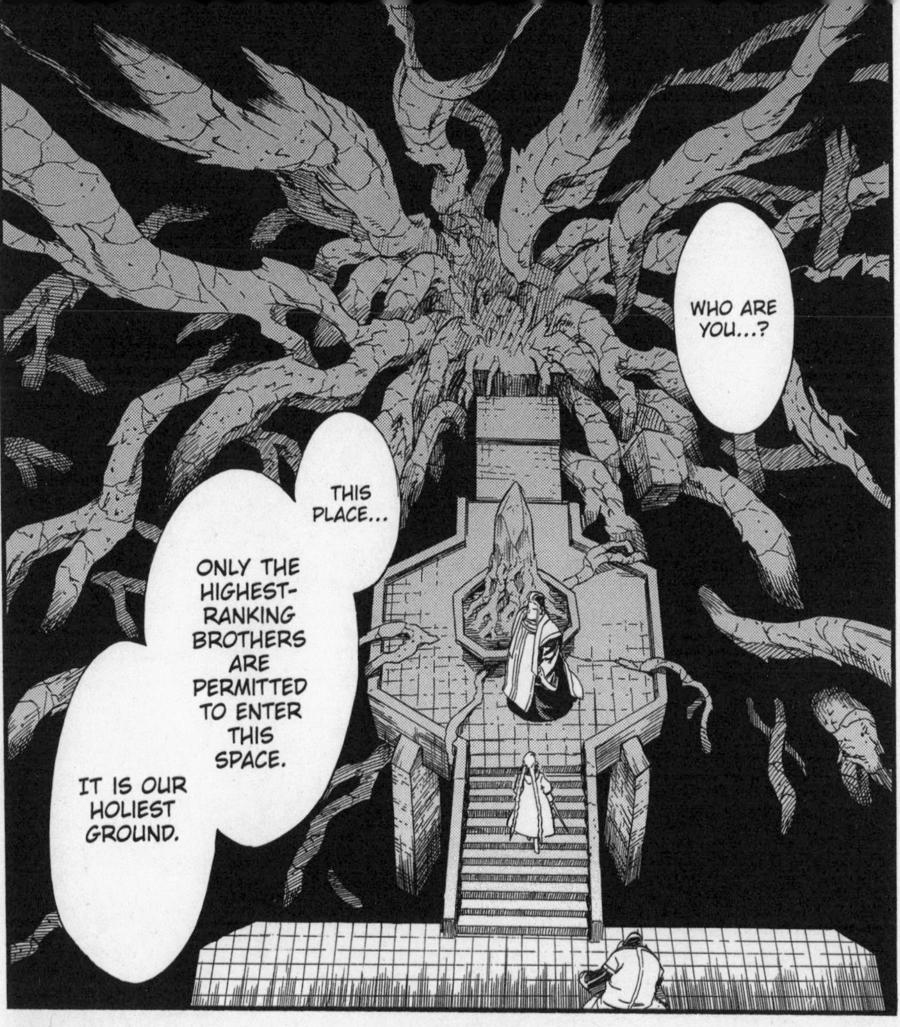
WHO ARE YOU...?
THIS PLACE...
ONLY THE HIGHEST-RANKING BROTHERS ARE PERMITTED TO ENTER THIS SPACE.
IT IS OUR HOLIEST GROUND.
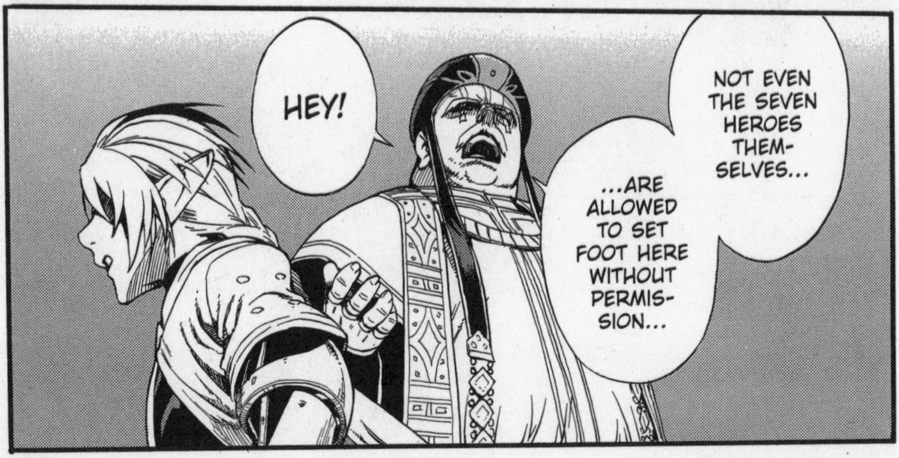
NOT EVEN THE SEVEN HEROES THEM-SELVES...
...ARE ALLOWED TO SET FOOT HERE WITHOUT PERMIS-SION...
HEY!

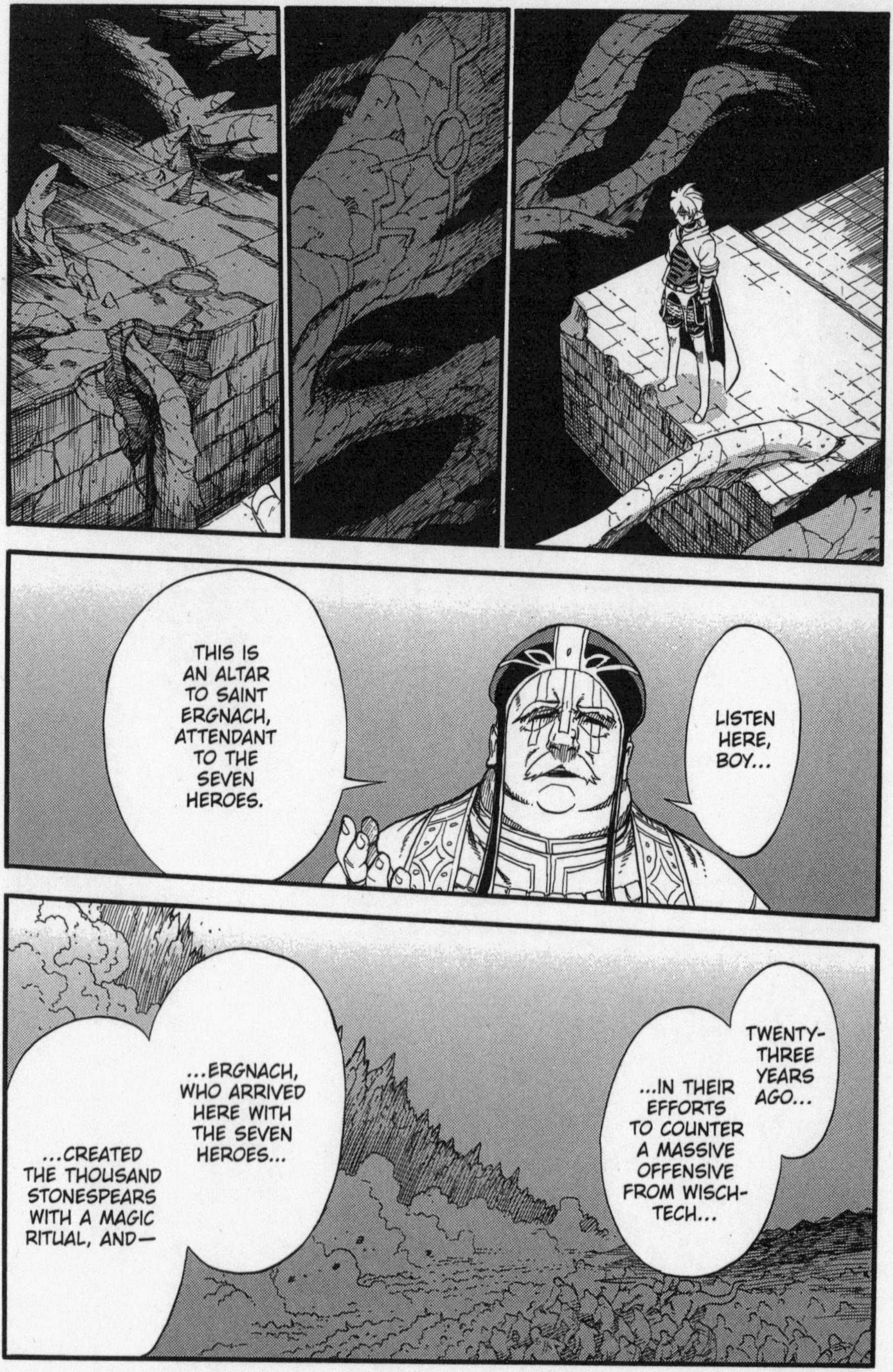
LISTEN HERE, BOY...
THIS IS AN ALTAR TO SAINT ERGNACH, ATTENDANT TO THE SEVEN HEROES.
TWENTY-THREE YEARS AGO...
...IN THEIR EFFORTS TO COUNTER A MASSIVE OFFENSIVE FROM WISCH-TECH...
...ERGNACH, WHO ARRIVED HERE WITH THE SEVEN HEROES...
...CREATED THE THOUSAND STONESPEARS WITH A MAGIC RITUAL, AND—

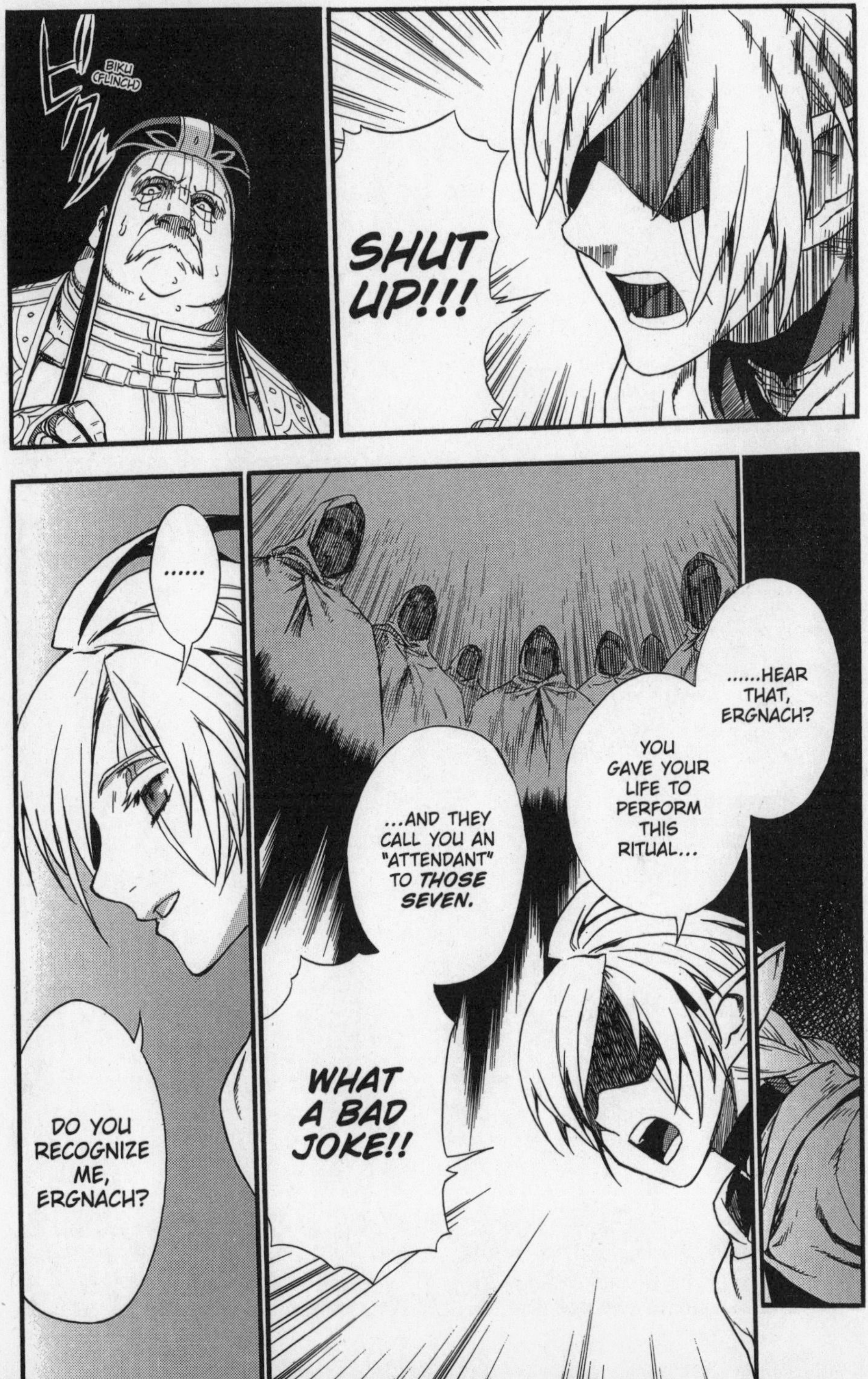
SHUT UP!!!
BIKU (FLINCH)
......HEAR THAT, ERGNACH?
YOU GAVE YOUR LIFE TO PERFORM THIS RITUAL...
...AND THEY CALL YOU AN "ATTENDANT" TO *THOSE SEVEN.*
WHAT A BAD JOKE!!
......
DO YOU RECOGNIZE ME, ERGNACH?

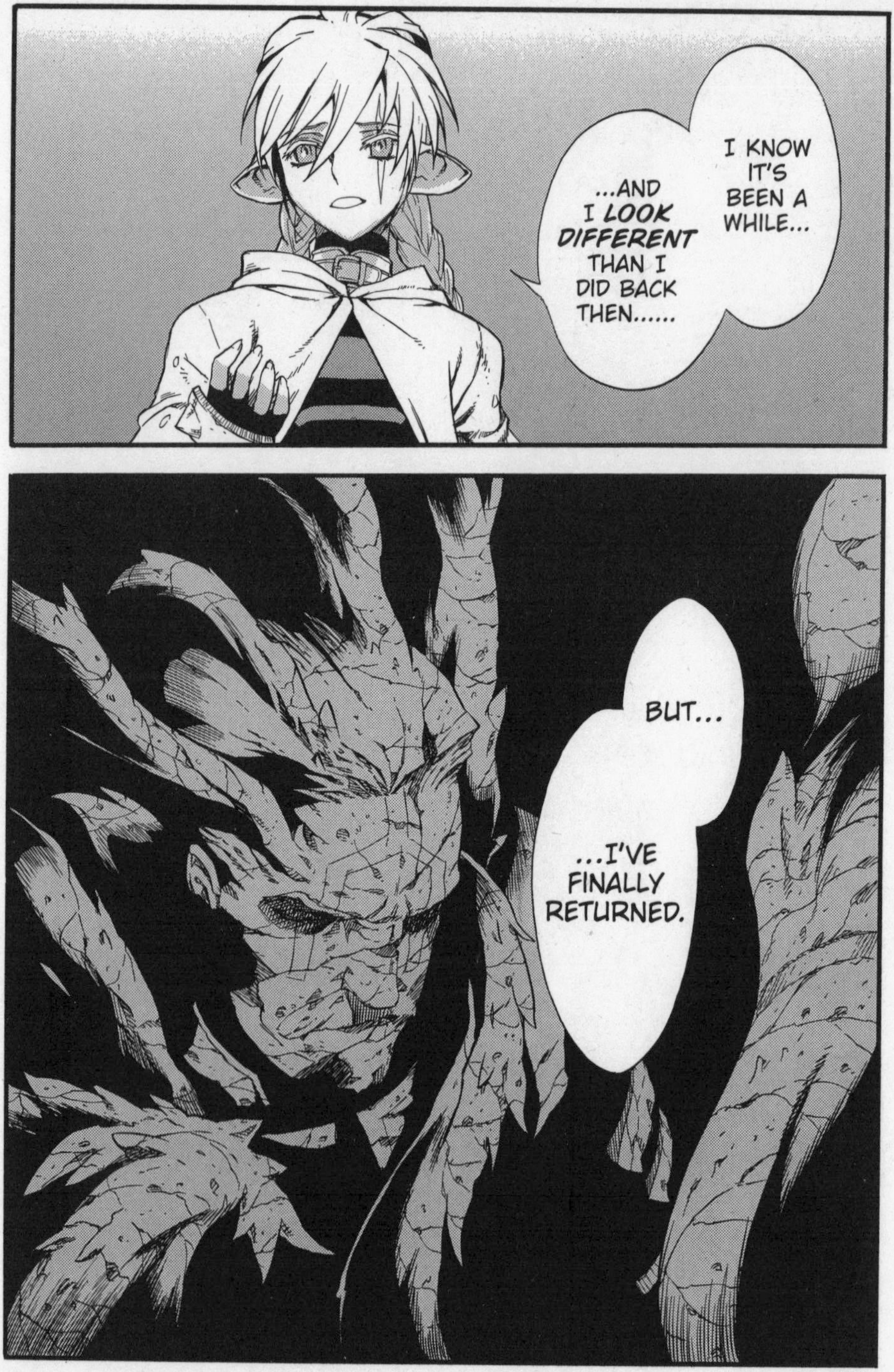
I KNOW IT'S BEEN A WHILE...
...AND I LOOK DIFFERENT THAN I DID BACK THEN......
BUT...
...I'VE FINALLY RETURNED.

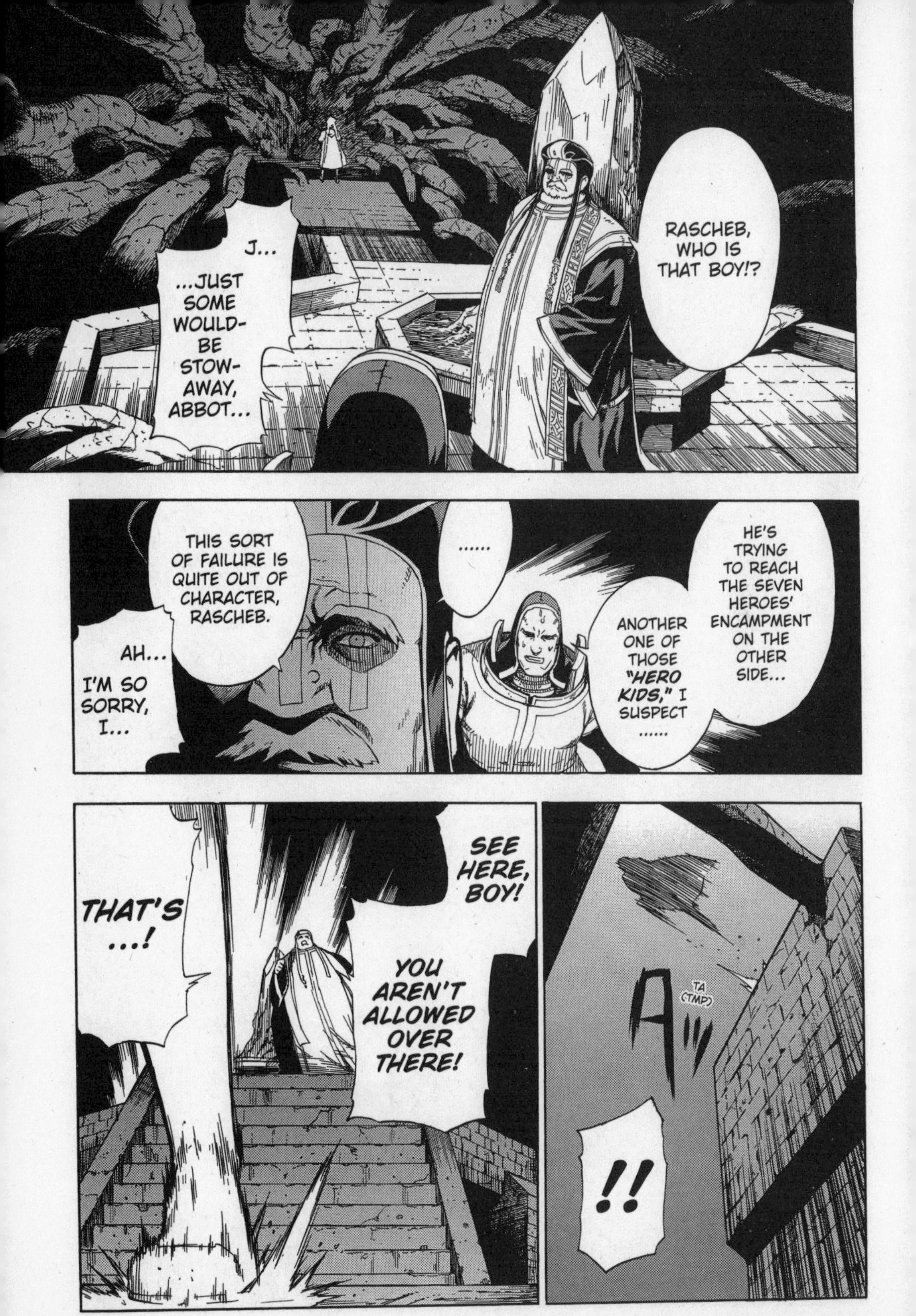
RASCHEB, WHO IS THAT BOY!?
J...
...JUST SOME WOULD-BE STOW-AWAY, ABBOT...
HE'S TRYING TO REACH THE SEVEN HEROES' ENCAMPMENT ON THE OTHER SIDE...
ANOTHER ONE OF THOSE "HERO KIDS," I SUSPECT ......
......
THIS SORT OF FAILURE IS QUITE OUT OF CHARACTER, RASCHEB.
AH... I'M SO SORRY, I...
TA (TMP)
!!
SEE HERE, BOY!
YOU AREN'T ALLOWED OVER THERE!
THAT'S ...!

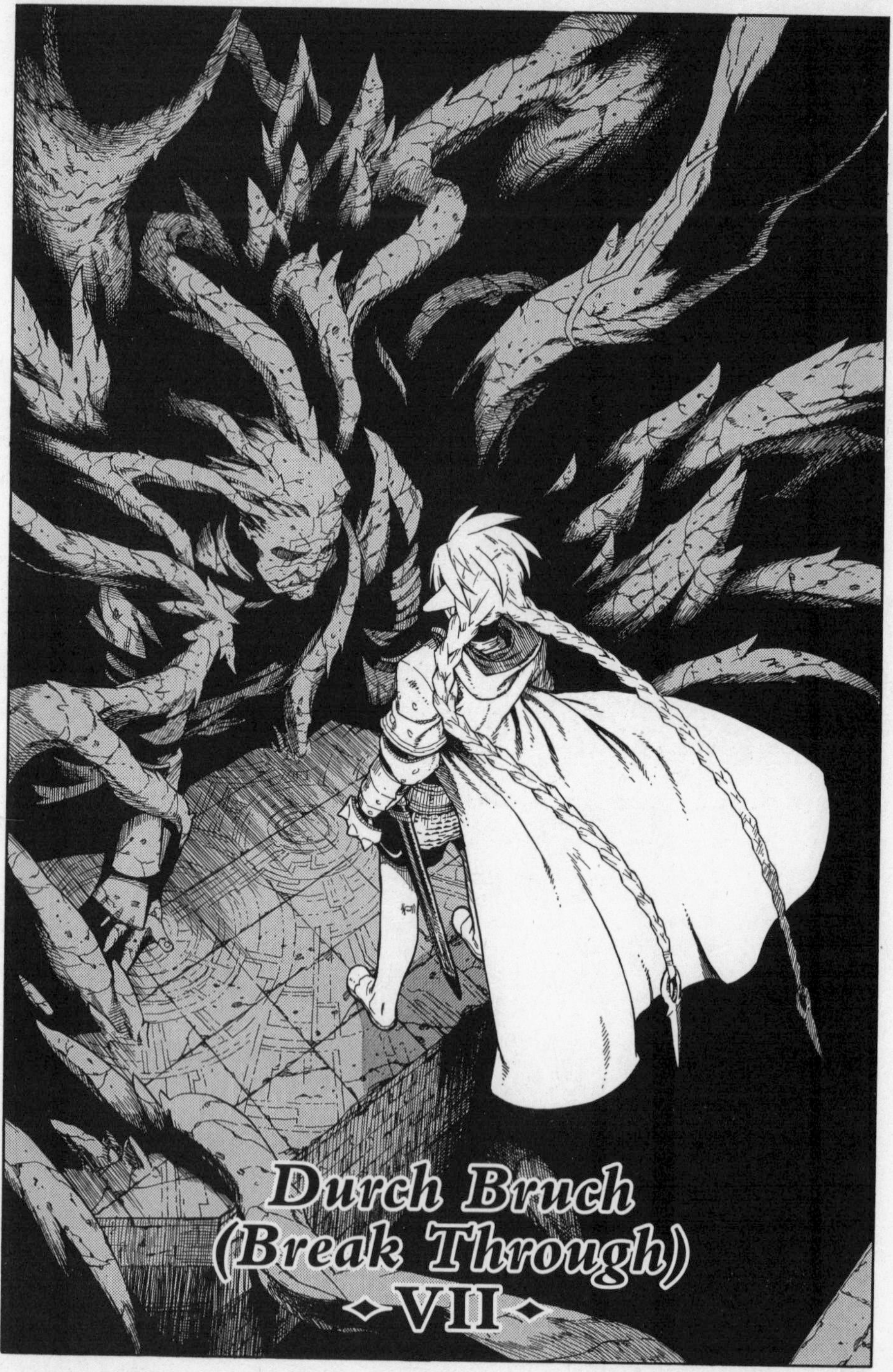
Durch Bruch
(Break Through)
VII

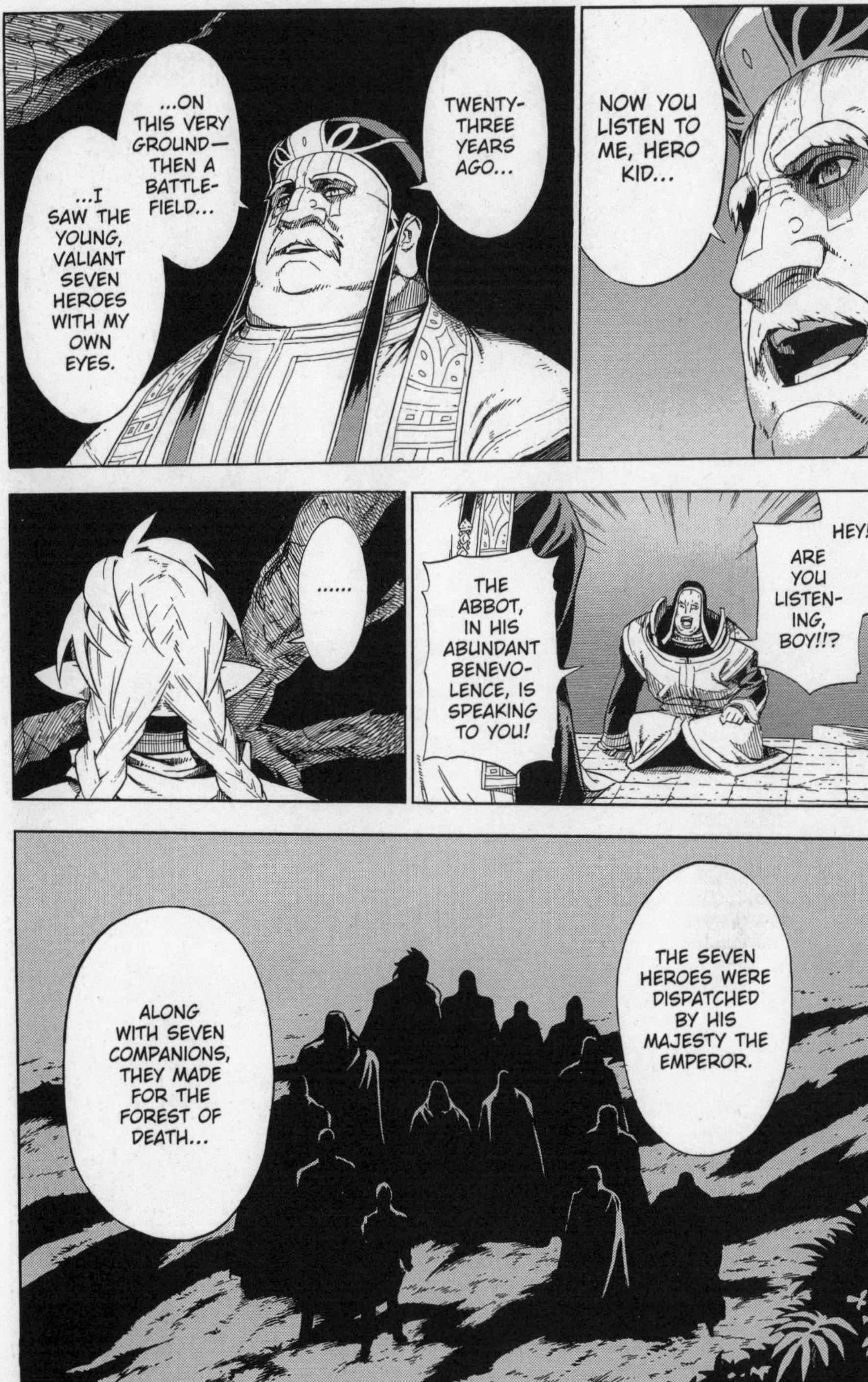
NOW YOU LISTEN TO ME, HERO KID...
TWENTY-THREE YEARS AGO...
...ON THIS VERY GROUND—THEN A BATTLEFIELD...
...I SAW THE YOUNG, VALIANT SEVEN HEROES WITH MY OWN EYES.
HEY! ARE YOU LISTENING, BOY!!?
THE ABBOT, IN HIS ABUNDANT BENEVOLENCE, IS SPEAKING TO YOU!
......
THE SEVEN HEROES WERE DISPATCHED BY HIS MAJESTY THE EMPEROR.
ALONG WITH SEVEN COMPANIONS, THEY MADE FOR THE FOREST OF DEATH...

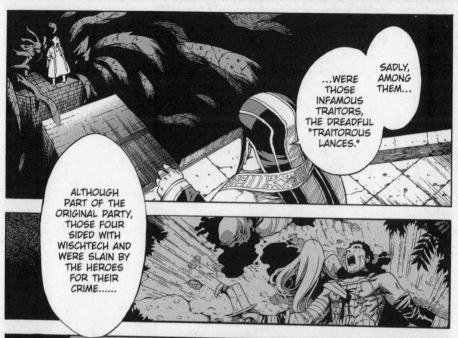

SADLY, AMONG THEM...

...WERE THOSE INFAMOUS TRAITORS, THE DREADFUL "TRAITOROUS LANCES."

ALTHOUGH PART OF THE ORIGINAL PARTY, THOSE FOUR SIDED WITH WISCHTECH AND WERE SLAIN BY THE HEROES FOR THEIR CRIME......

BUT I DIGRESS!!

THE SEVEN HEROES, SENSING THAT WISCHTECH WOULD LAUNCH AN INVASION HERE, COULD NOT LEAVE THIS PLACE TO THE MERCY OF INVADING FORCES!!

THEY PUT THEIR LIVES ON THE LINE TO PERFORM A RITUAL THAT WOULD ERECT A MASSIVE WALL!!

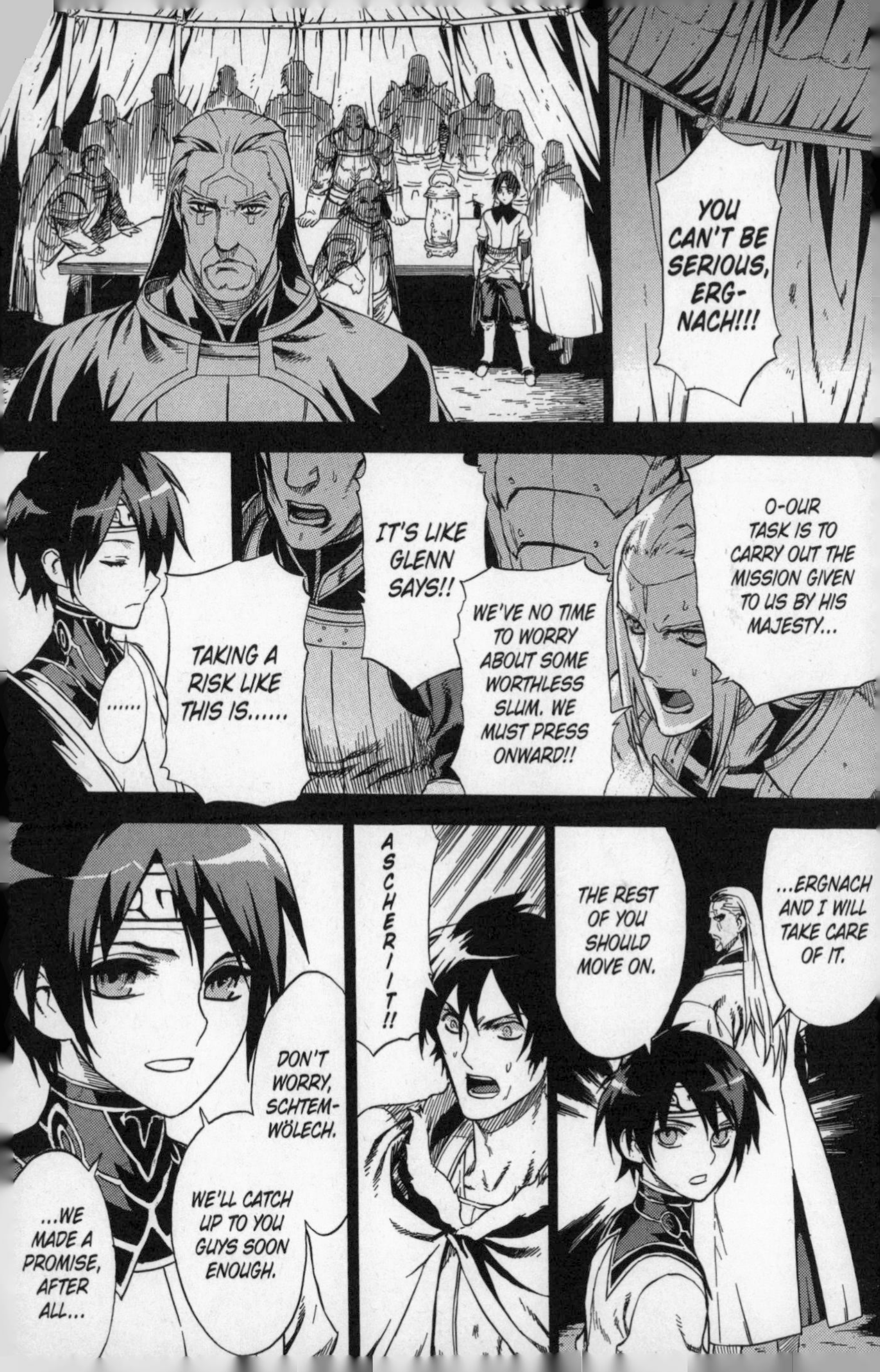

YOU CAN'T BE SERIOUS, ERG-NACH!!!
O-OUR TASK IS TO CARRY OUT THE MISSION GIVEN TO US BY HIS MAJESTY...
WE'VE NO TIME TO WORRY ABOUT SOME WORTHLESS SLUM. WE MUST PRESS ONWARD!!
IT'S LIKE GLENN SAYS!!
TAKING A RISK LIKE THIS IS......
......
...ERGNACH AND I WILL TAKE CARE OF IT.
THE REST OF YOU SHOULD MOVE ON.
ASCHERIIIT!!
DON'T WORRY, SCHTEM-WÖLECH.
WE'LL CATCH UP TO YOU GUYS SOON ENOUGH.
...WE MADE A PROMISE, AFTER ALL...

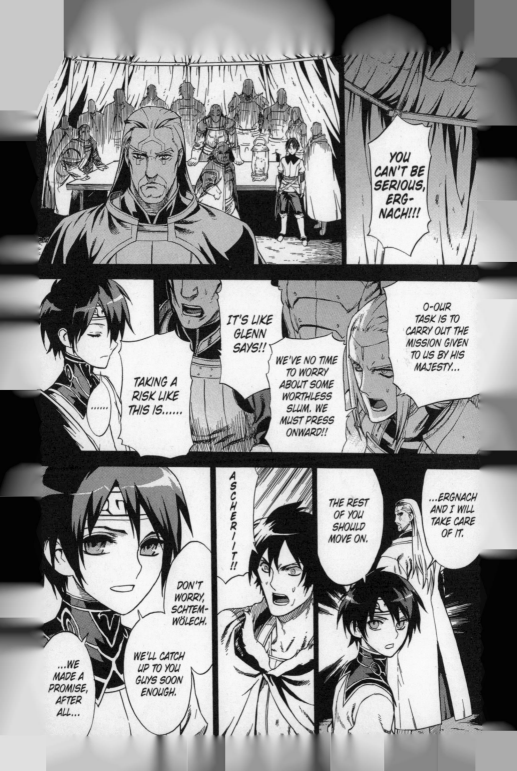

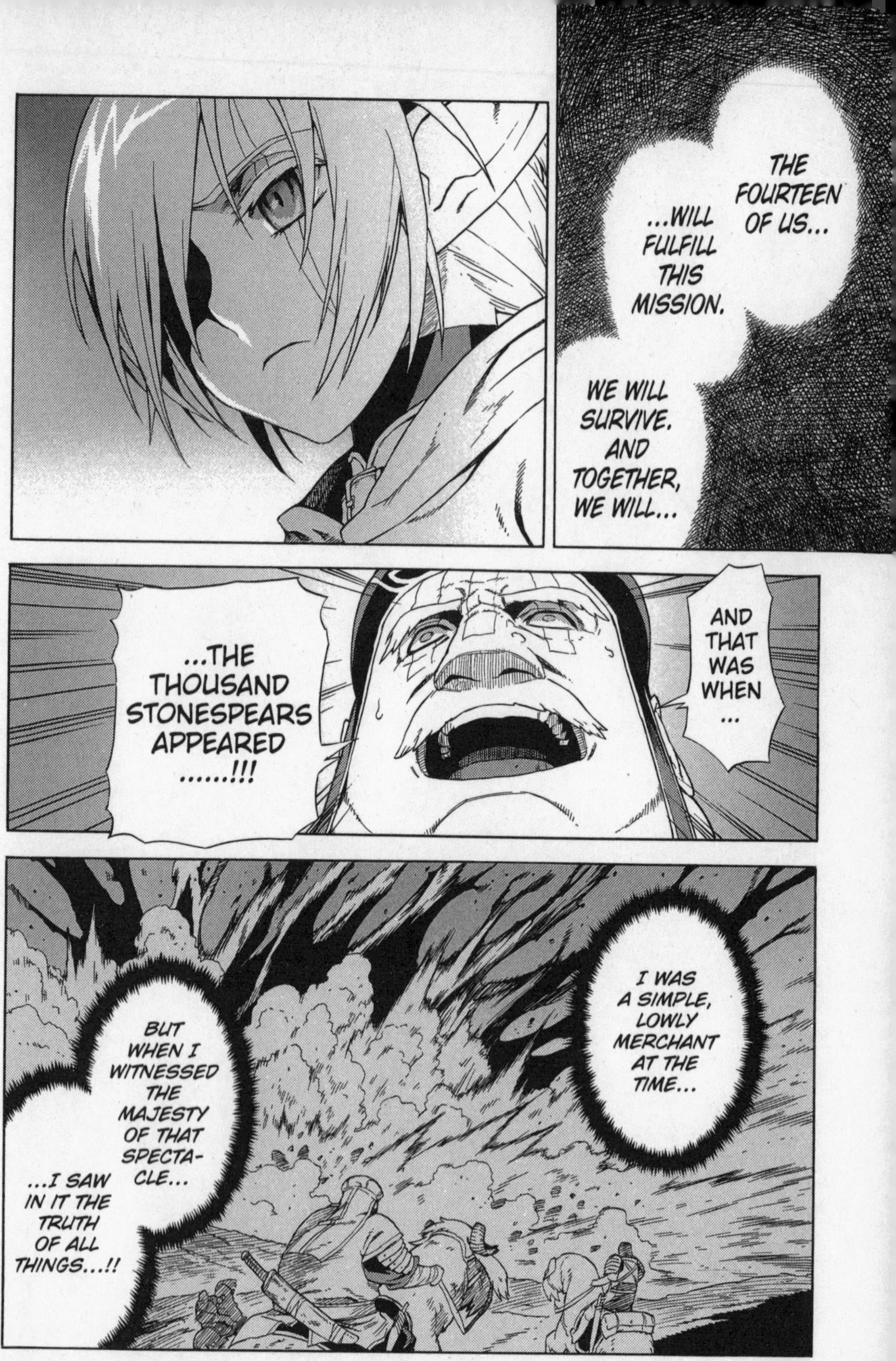
THE FOURTEEN OF US...
...WILL FULFILL THIS MISSION.
WE WILL SURVIVE. AND TOGETHER, WE WILL...
AND THAT WAS WHEN ...
...THE THOUSAND STONESPEARS APPEARED ......!!!
I WAS A SIMPLE, LOWLY MERCHANT AT THE TIME...
BUT WHEN I WITNESSED THE MAJESTY OF THAT SPECTACLE...
...I SAW IN IT THE TRUTH OF ALL THINGS...!!

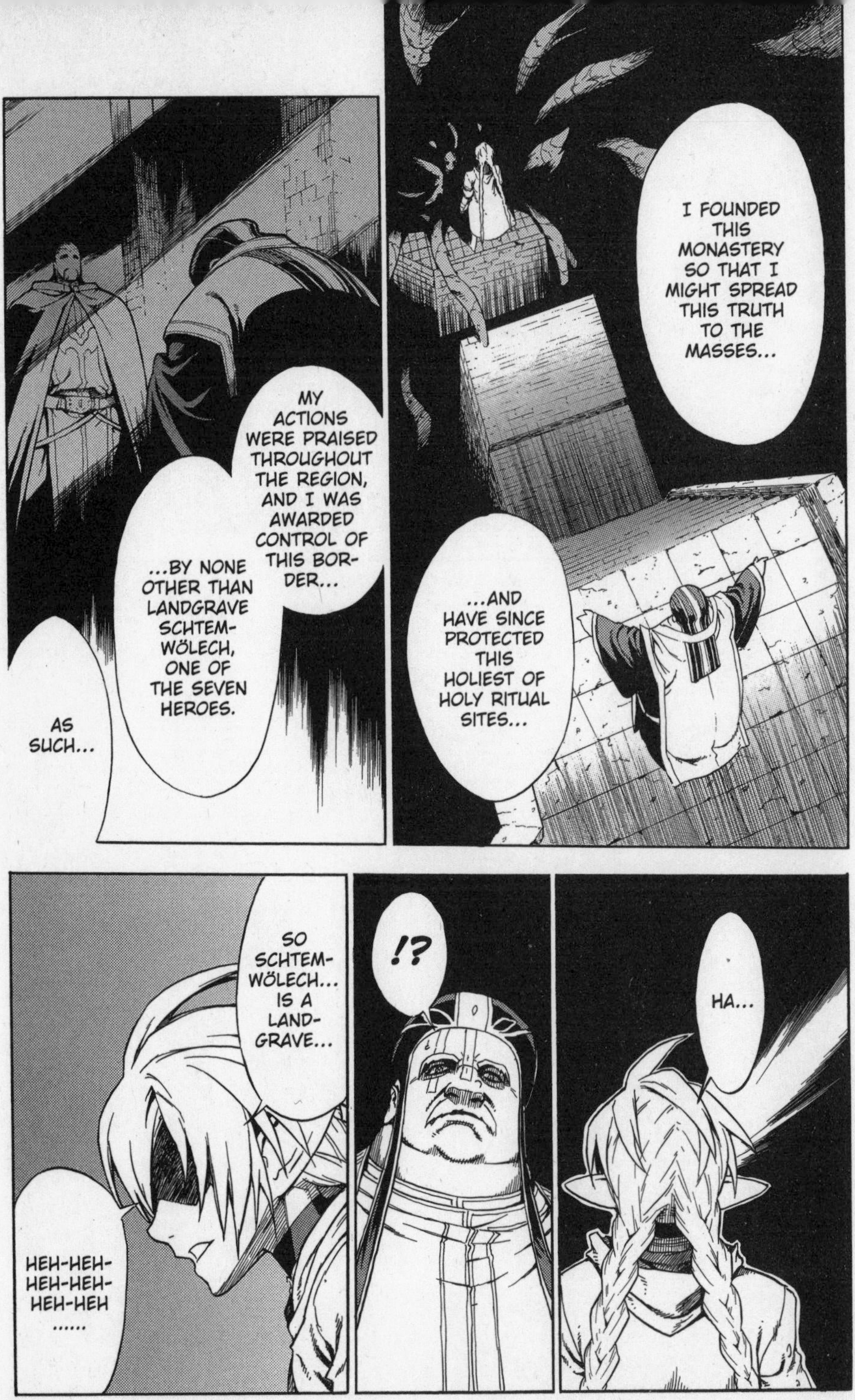
I FOUNDED THIS MONASTERY SO THAT I MIGHT SPREAD THIS TRUTH TO THE MASSES...
...AND HAVE SINCE PROTECTED THIS HOLIEST OF HOLY RITUAL SITES...
MY ACTIONS WERE PRAISED THROUGHOUT THE REGION, AND I WAS AWARDED CONTROL OF THIS BORDER...
...BY NONE OTHER THAN LANDGRAVE SCHTEMWÖLECH, ONE OF THE SEVEN HEROES.
AS SUCH...
HA...
!?
SO SCHTEMWÖLECH... IS A LANDGRAVE...
HEH-HEH-HEH-HEH-HEH-HEH......

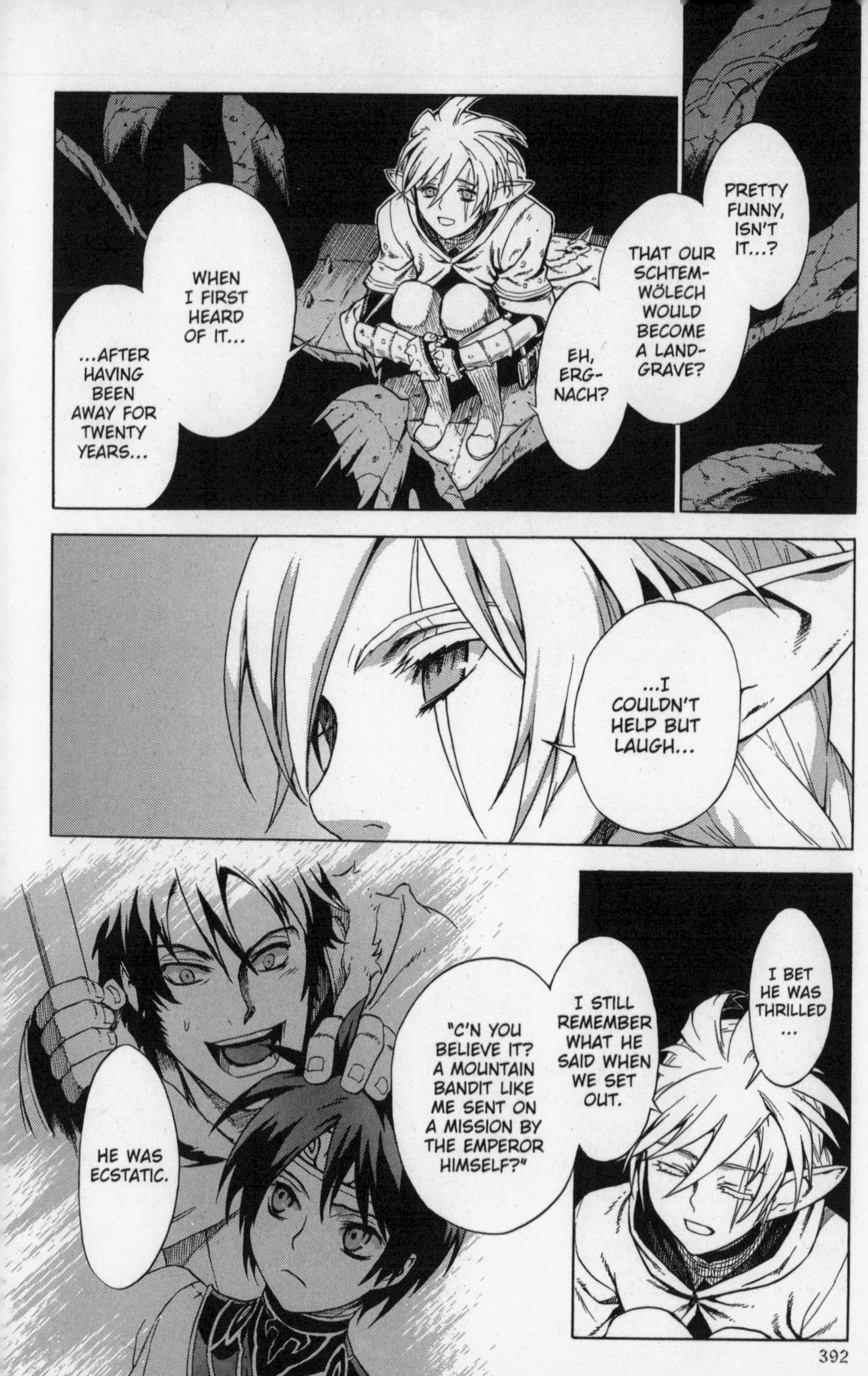
PRETTY FUNNY, ISN'T IT...?
THAT OUR SCHTEMWÖLECH WOULD BECOME A LANDGRAVE?
EH, ERGNACH?
WHEN I FIRST HEARD OF IT...
...AFTER HAVING BEEN AWAY FOR TWENTY YEARS...
...I COULDN'T HELP BUT LAUGH...
I BET HE WAS THRILLED...
I STILL REMEMBER WHAT HE SAID WHEN WE SET OUT.
"C'N YOU BELIEVE IT? A MOUNTAIN BANDIT LIKE ME SENT ON A MISSION BY THE EMPEROR HIMSELF?"
HE WAS ECSTATIC.

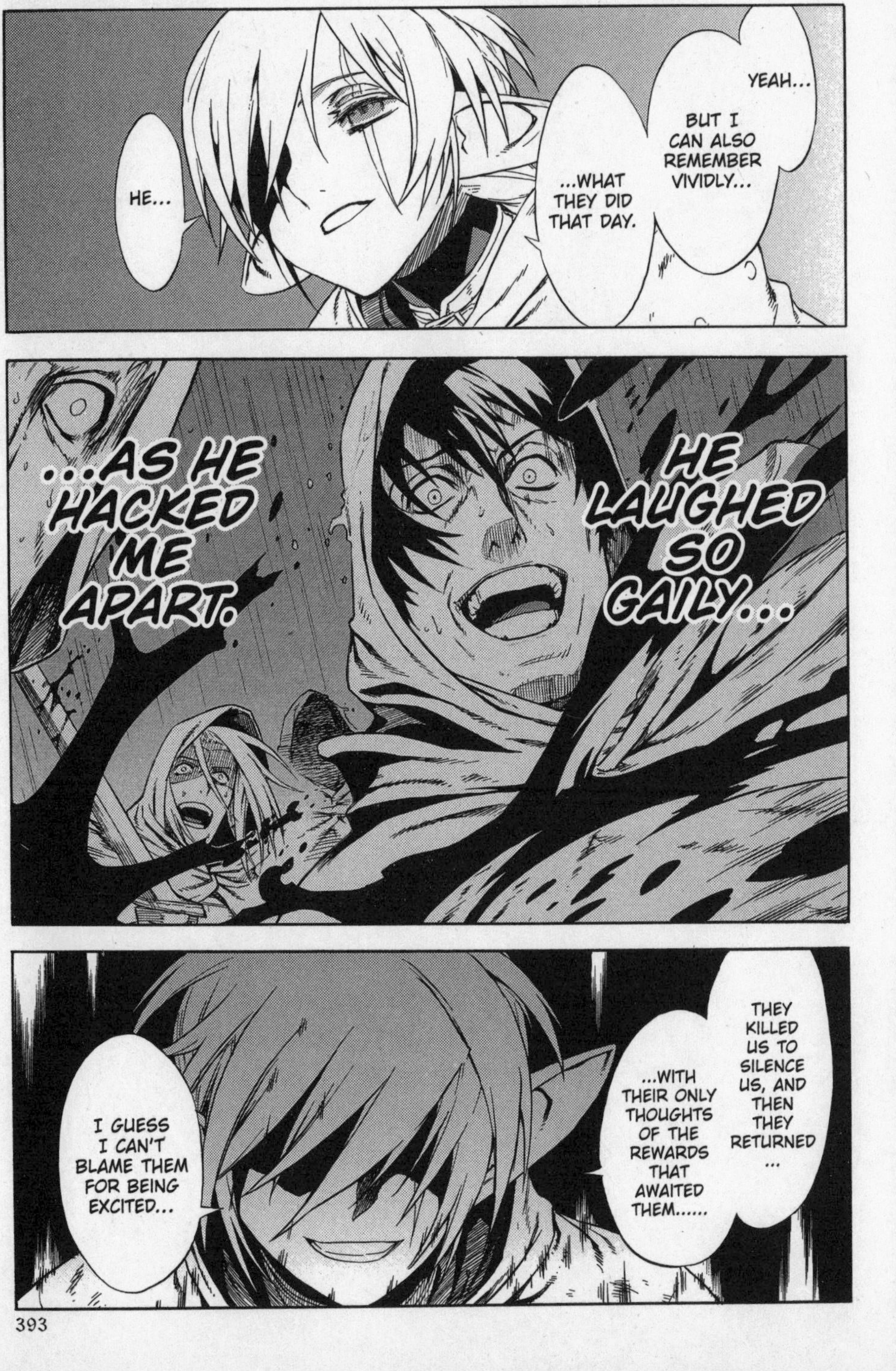
YEAH...
BUT I CAN ALSO REMEMBER VIVIDLY...
...WHAT THEY DID THAT DAY.
HE...
HE LAUGHED SO GAILY...
...AS HE HACKED ME APART.
THEY KILLED US TO SILENCE US, AND THEN THEY RETURNED ...
...WITH THEIR ONLY THOUGHTS OF THE REWARDS THAT AWAITED THEM......
I GUESS I CAN'T BLAME THEM FOR BEING EXCITED...

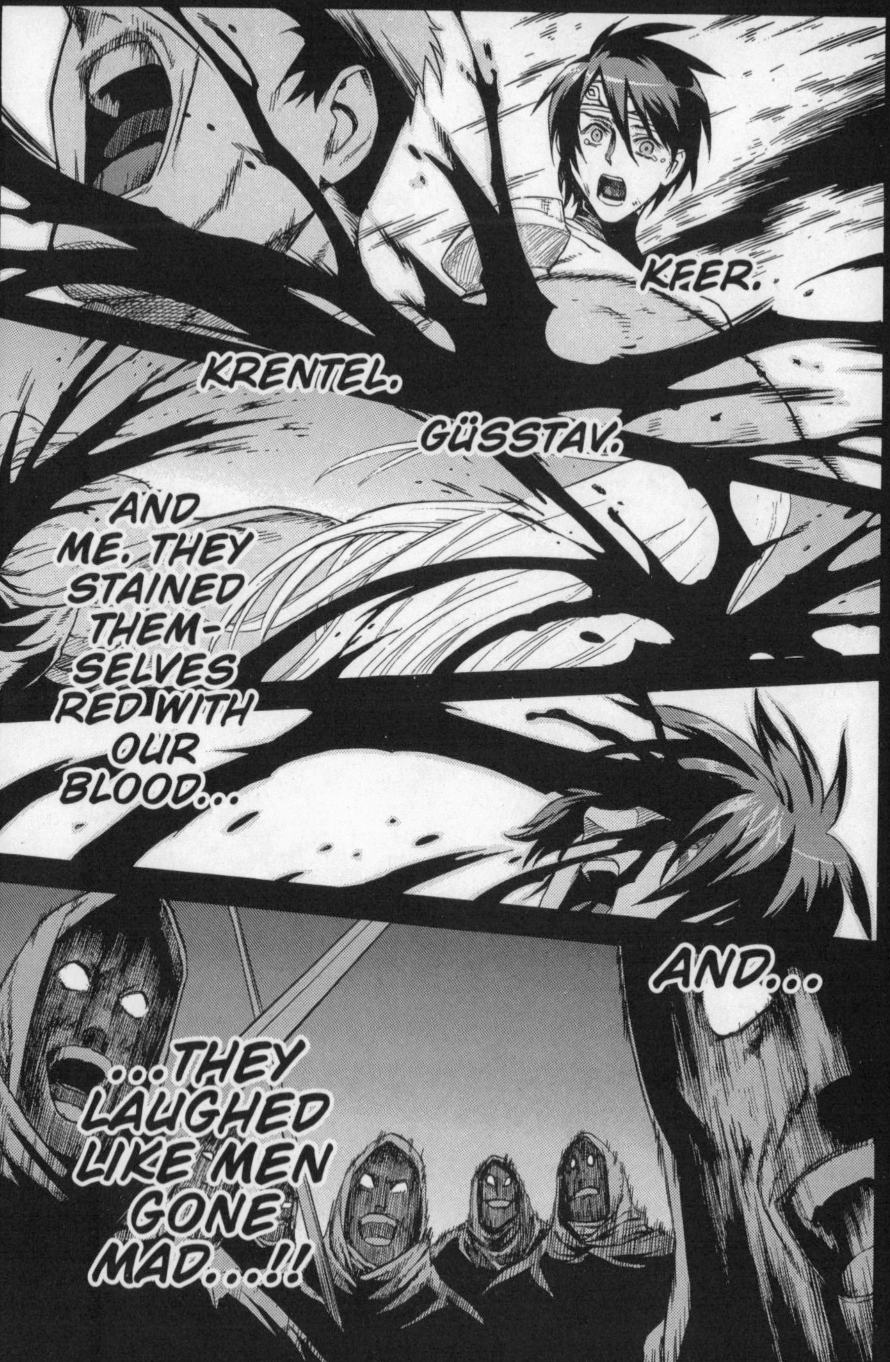
K.F.ER.
KRENTEL.
GÜSSTAV.
AND ME. THEY STAINED THEM-SELVES RED WITH OUR BLOOD...
AND...
...THEY LAUGHED LIKE MEN GONE MAD...!!

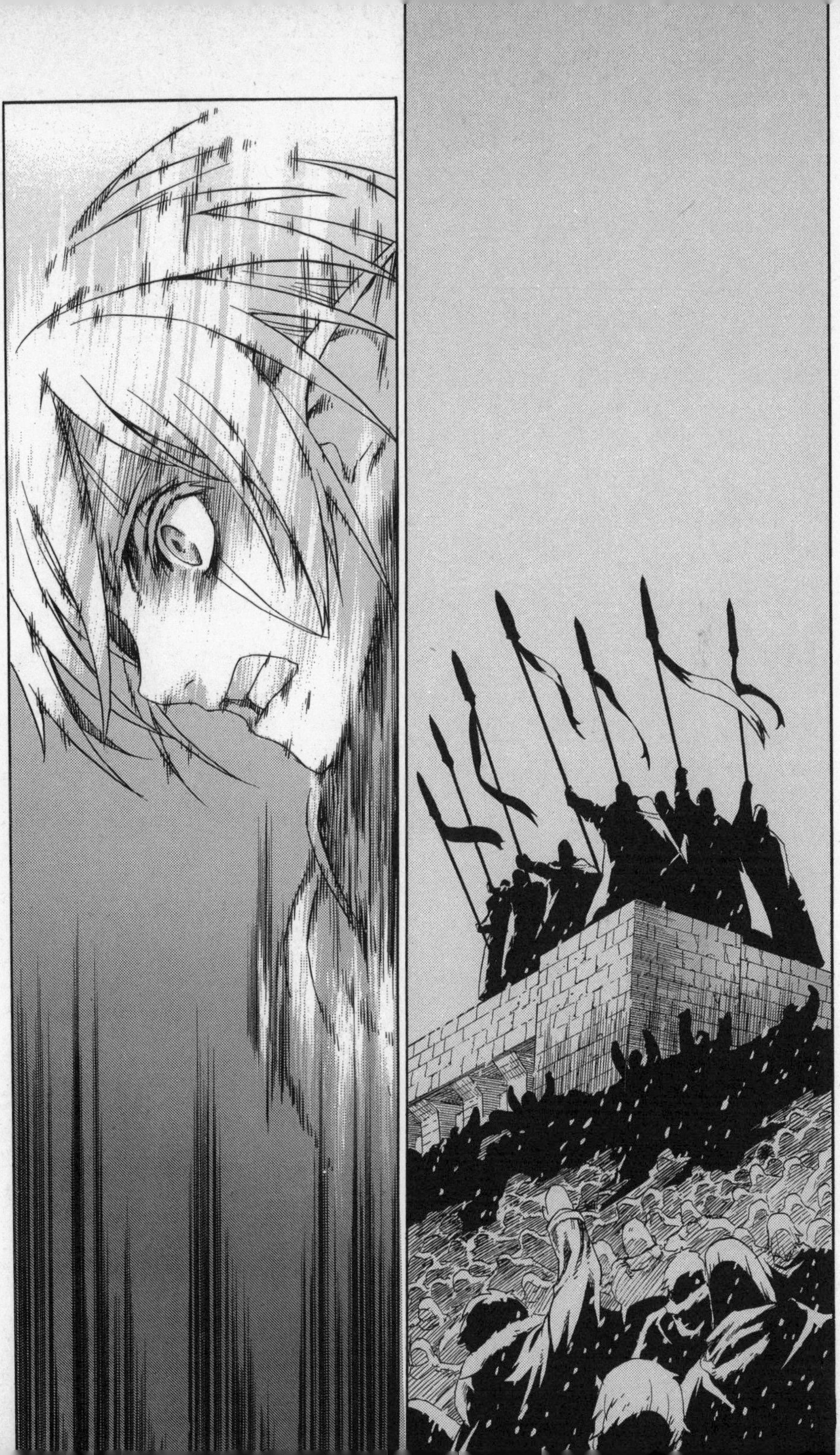

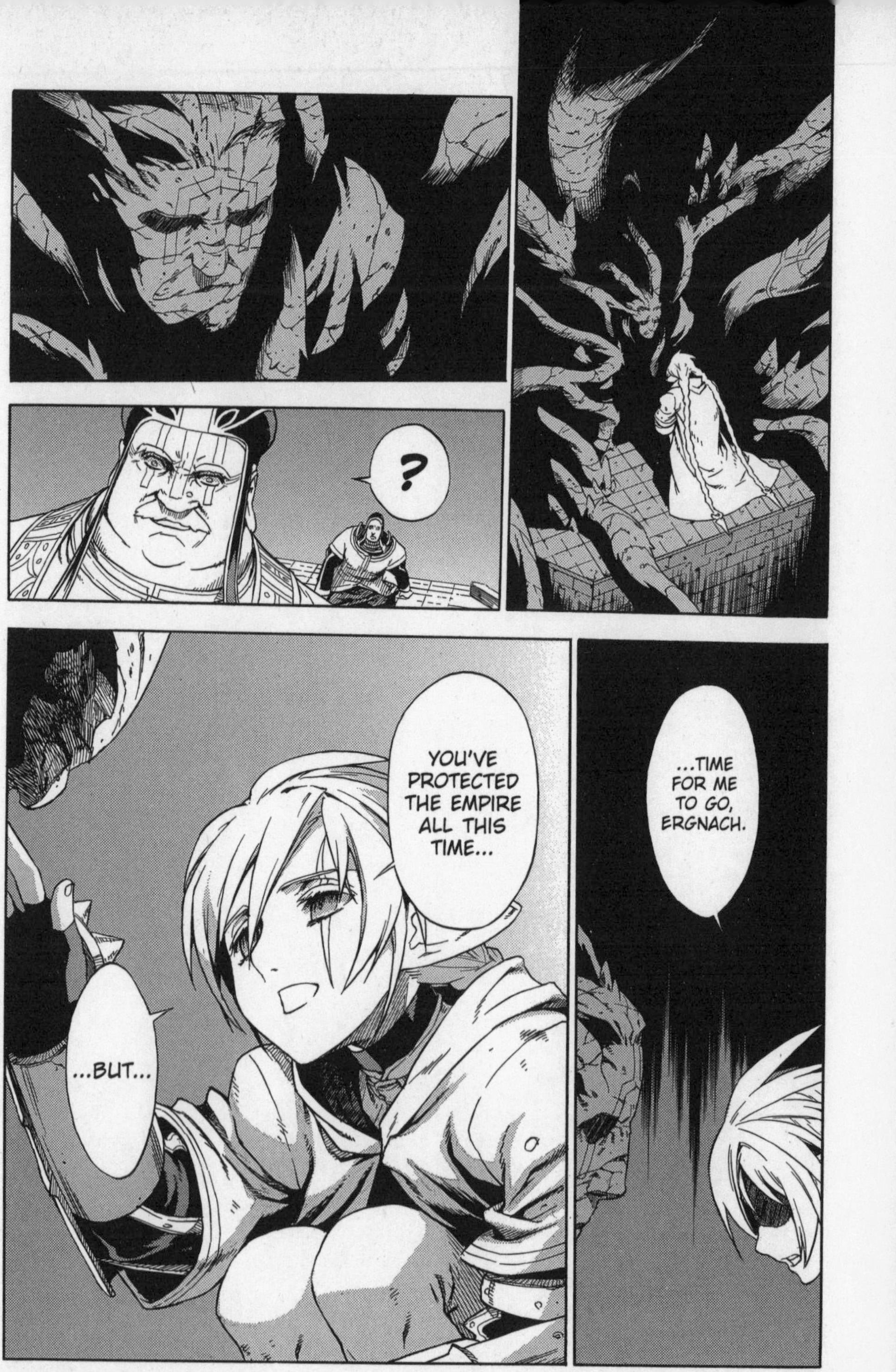
?
...TIME FOR ME TO GO, ERGNACH.
YOU'VE PROTECTED THE EMPIRE ALL THIS TIME...
...BUT...

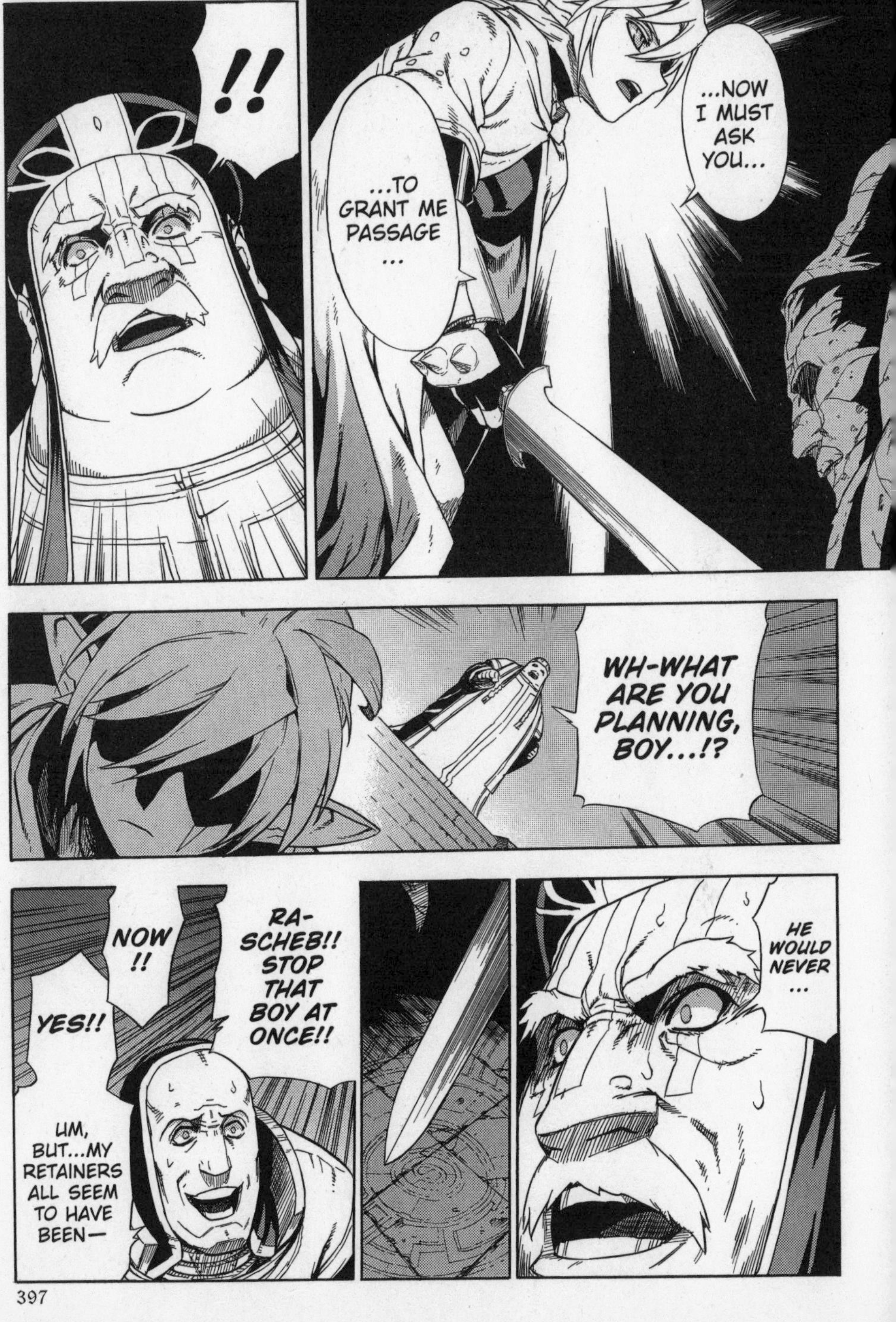

...NOW I MUST ASK YOU...
...TO GRANT ME PASSAGE ...
!!
WH-WHAT ARE YOU PLANNING, BOY...!?
HE WOULD NEVER ...
RA-SCHEB!! STOP THAT BOY AT ONCE!!
NOW !!
YES!!
UM, BUT...MY RETAINERS ALL SEEM TO HAVE BEEN—

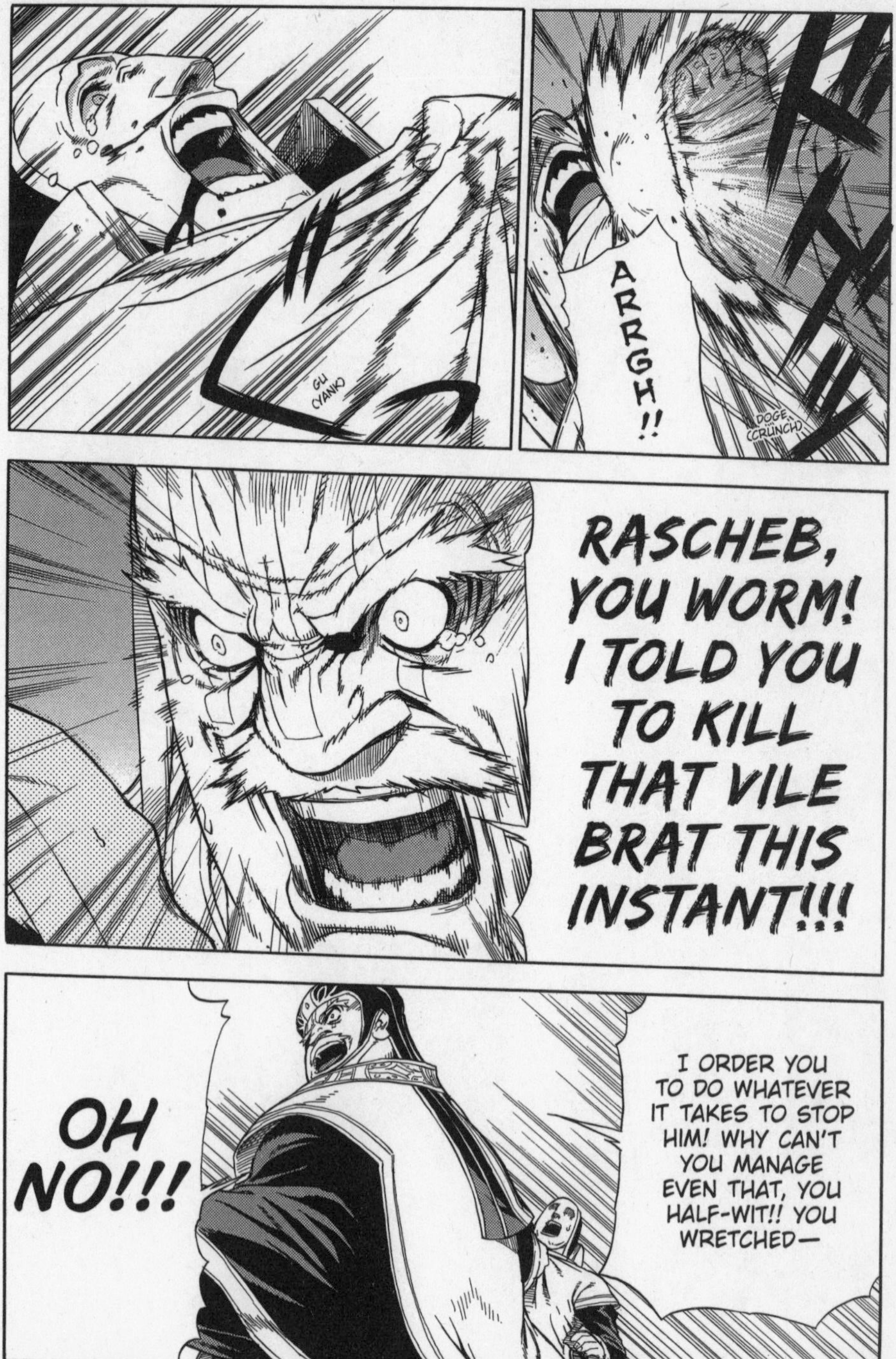
ARRGH!!
DOGE (CRUNCH)
GU (YANK)
RASCHEB, YOU WORM! I TOLD YOU TO KILL THAT VILE BRAT THIS INSTANT!!!
I ORDER YOU TO DO WHATEVER IT TAKES TO STOP HIM! WHY CAN'T YOU MANAGE EVEN THAT, YOU HALF-WIT!! YOU WRETCHED—
OH NO!!!

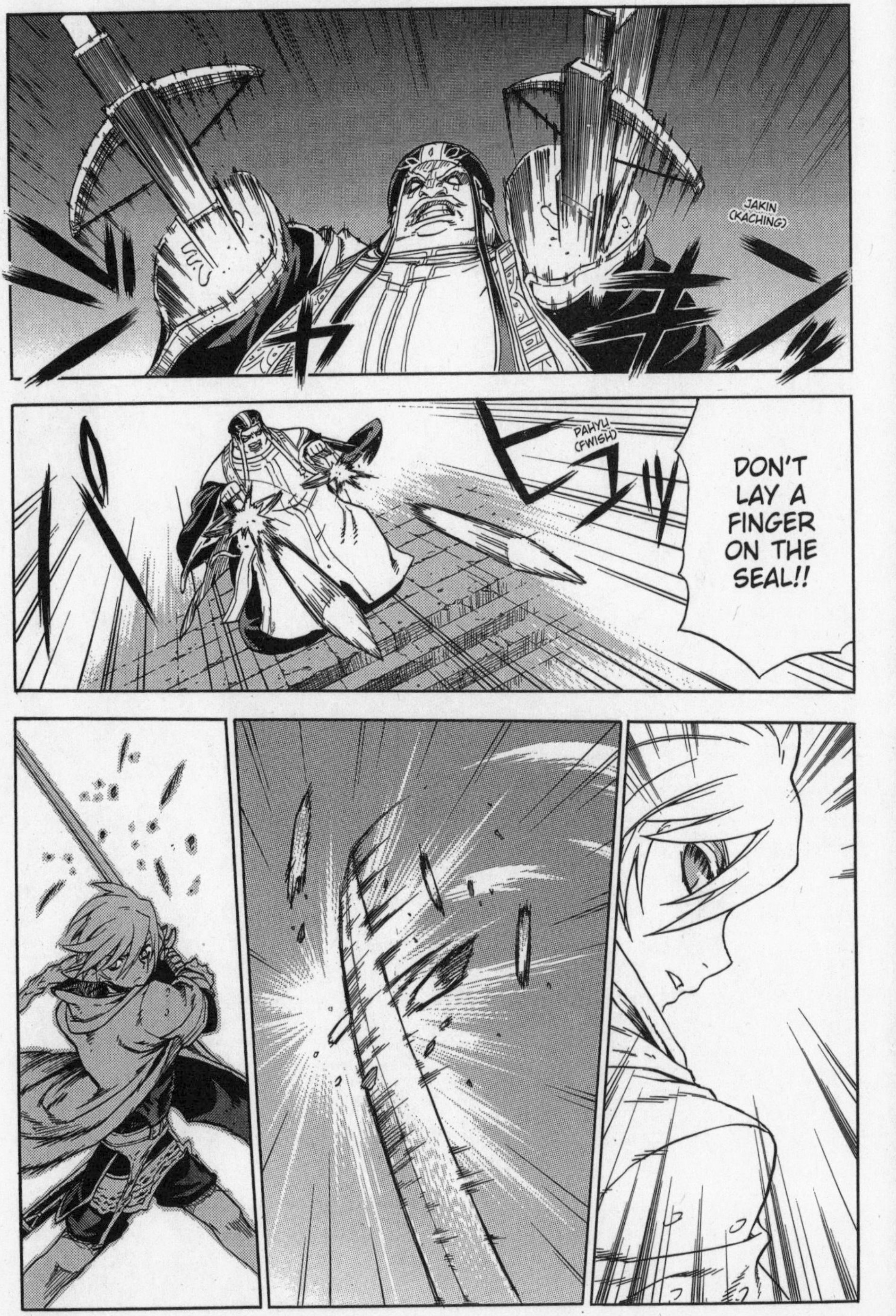
JAKIN
(KACHING)
PAHYU
(FWISH)
DON'T LAY A FINGER ON THE SEAL!!

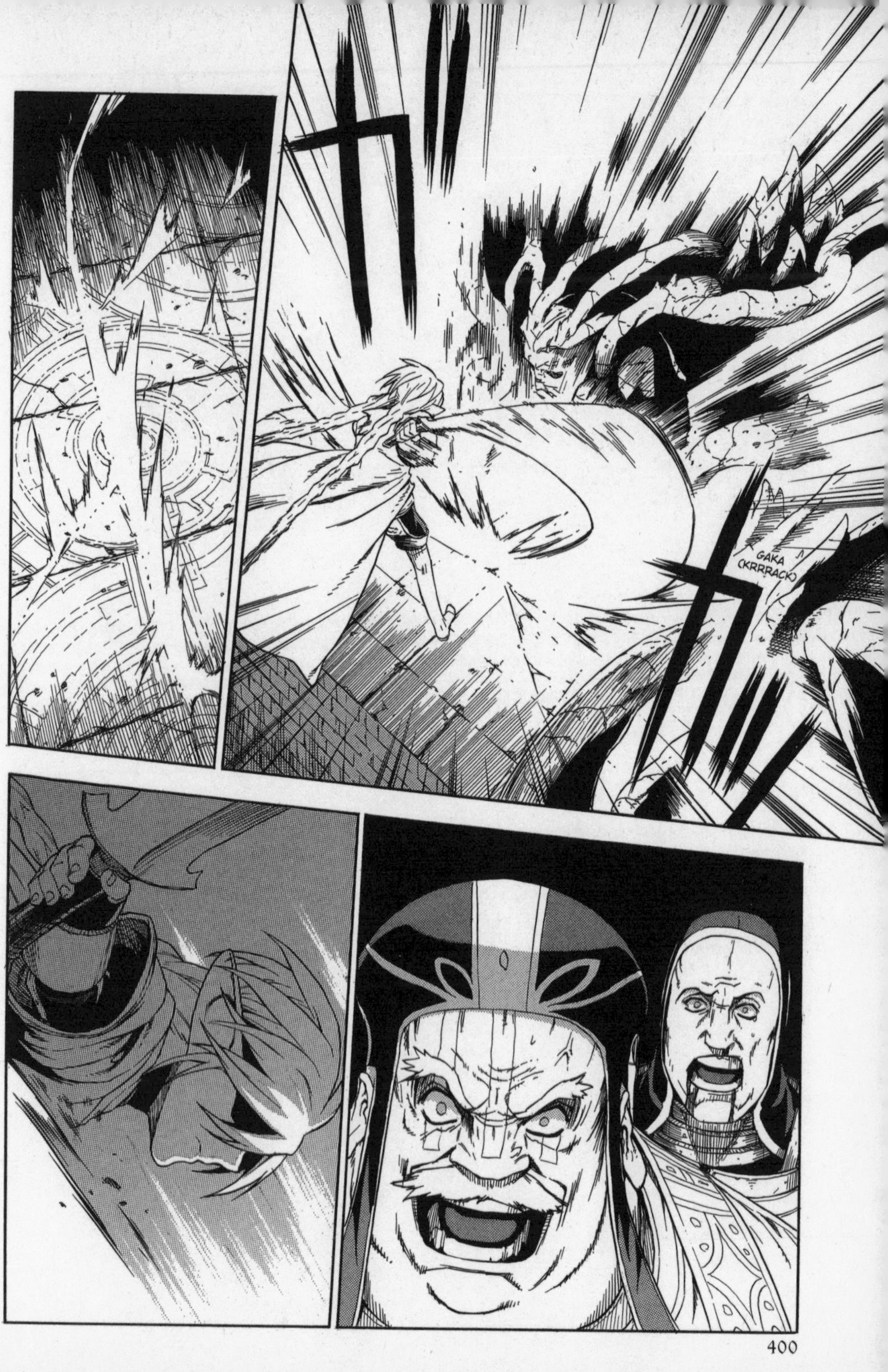
GAKA
(KRRRACK)

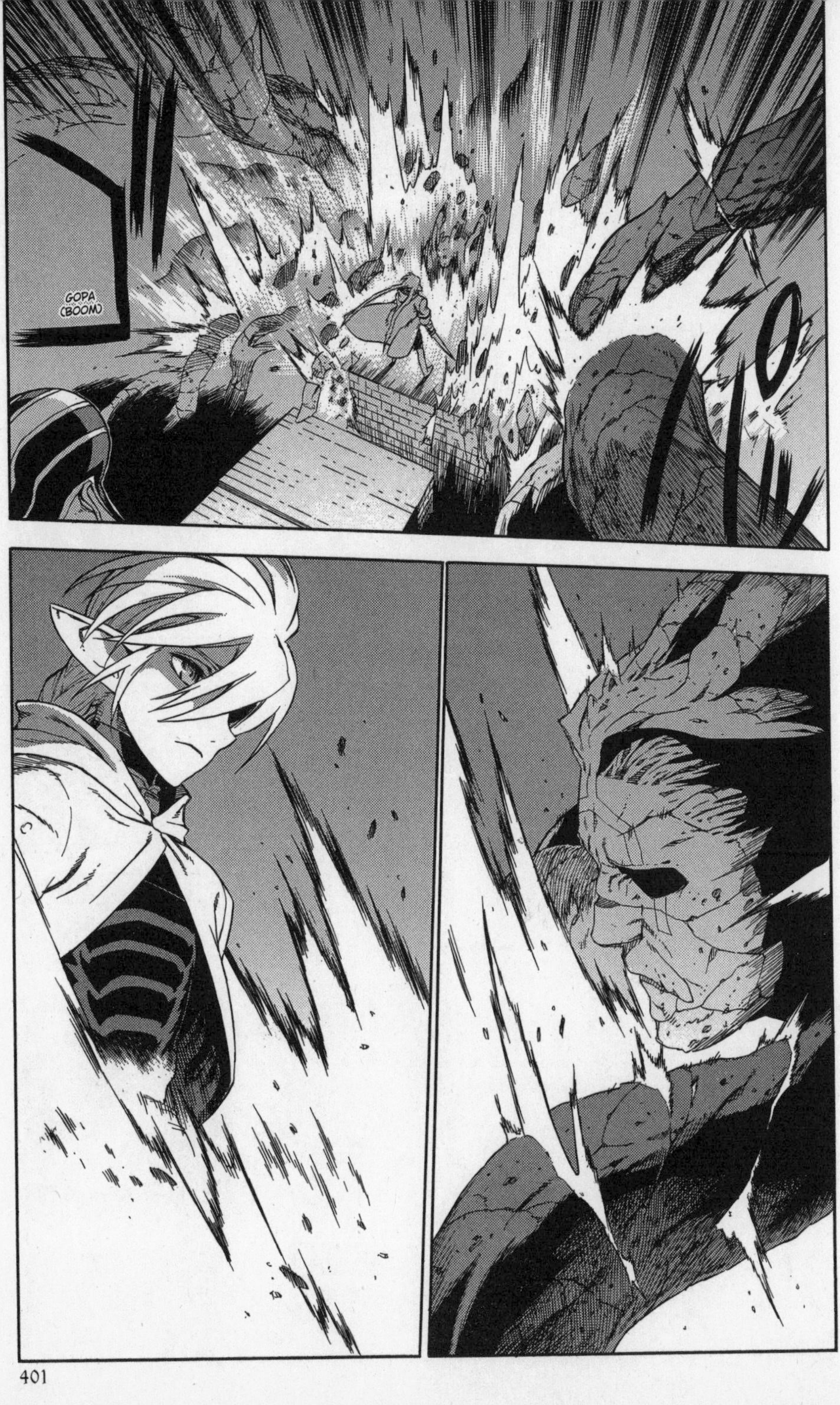
GOPA
(BOOM)

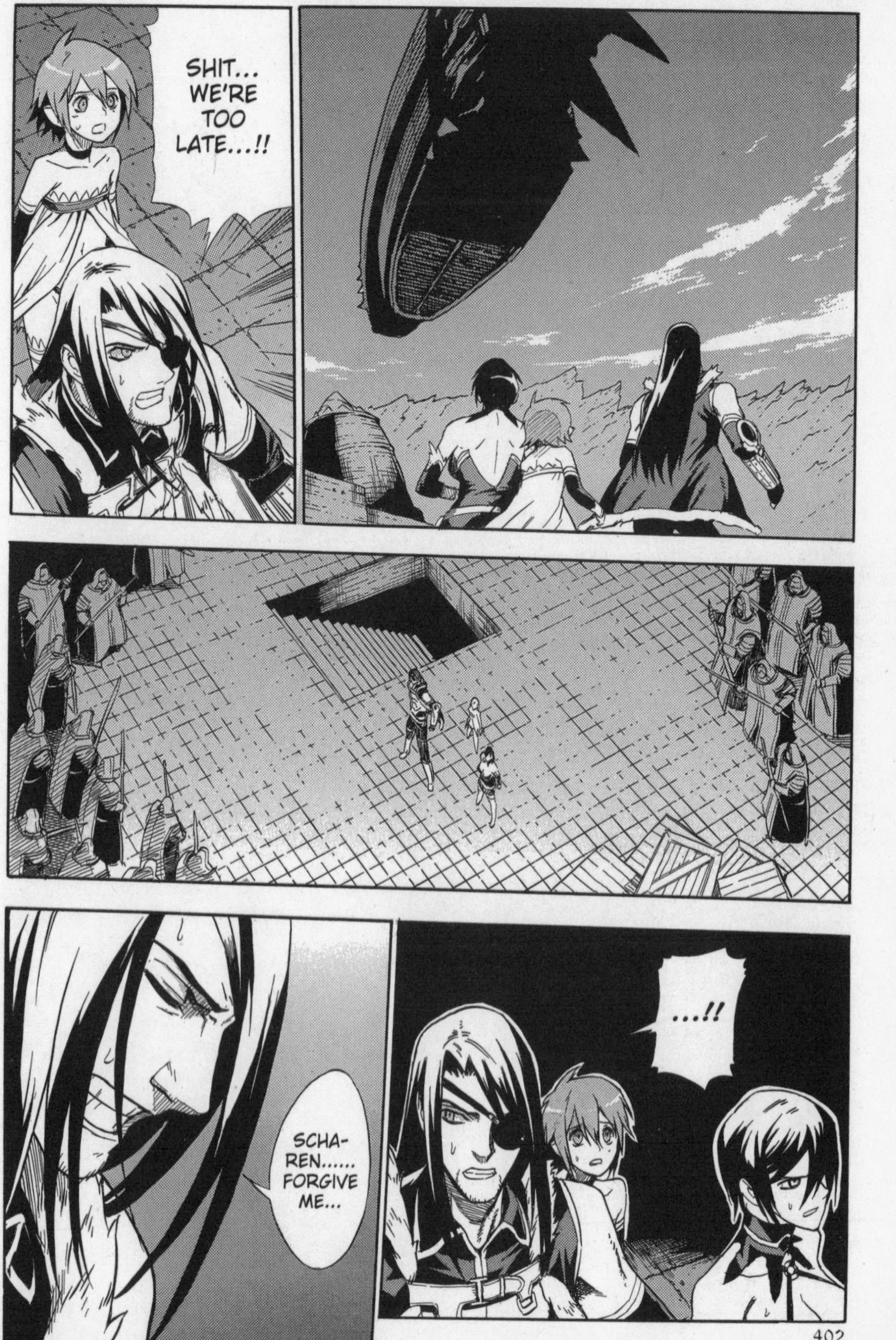
SHIT... WE'RE TOO LATE...!!
...!!
SCHA-REN...... FORGIVE ME...

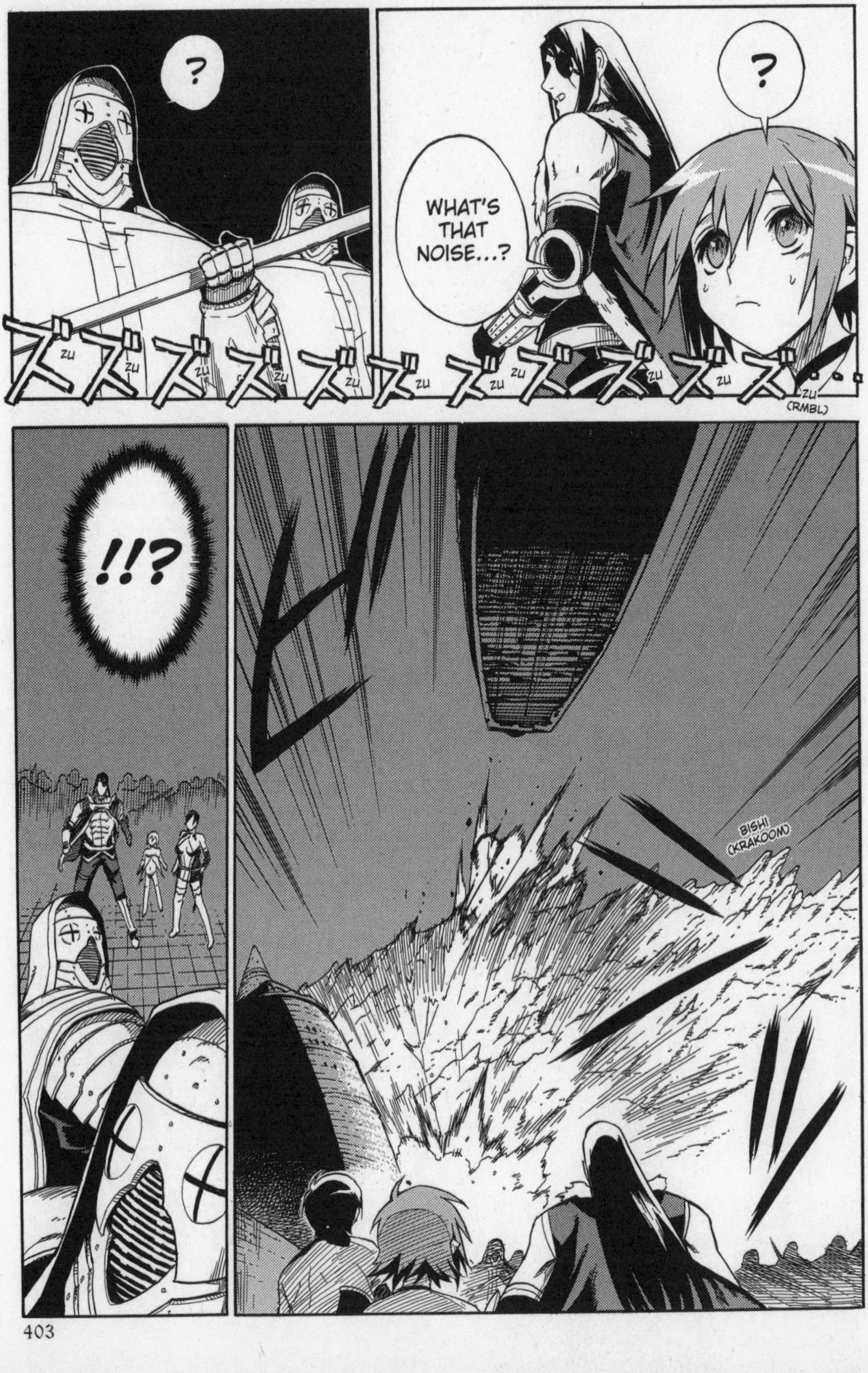
?
WHAT'S THAT NOISE...?
?
ズズズズズズズズズズズズ...
ZU ZU ZU ZU ZU ZU ZU ZU ZU ZU ZU ZU
(RMBL)
BISHI (KRAKOOM)
!!?

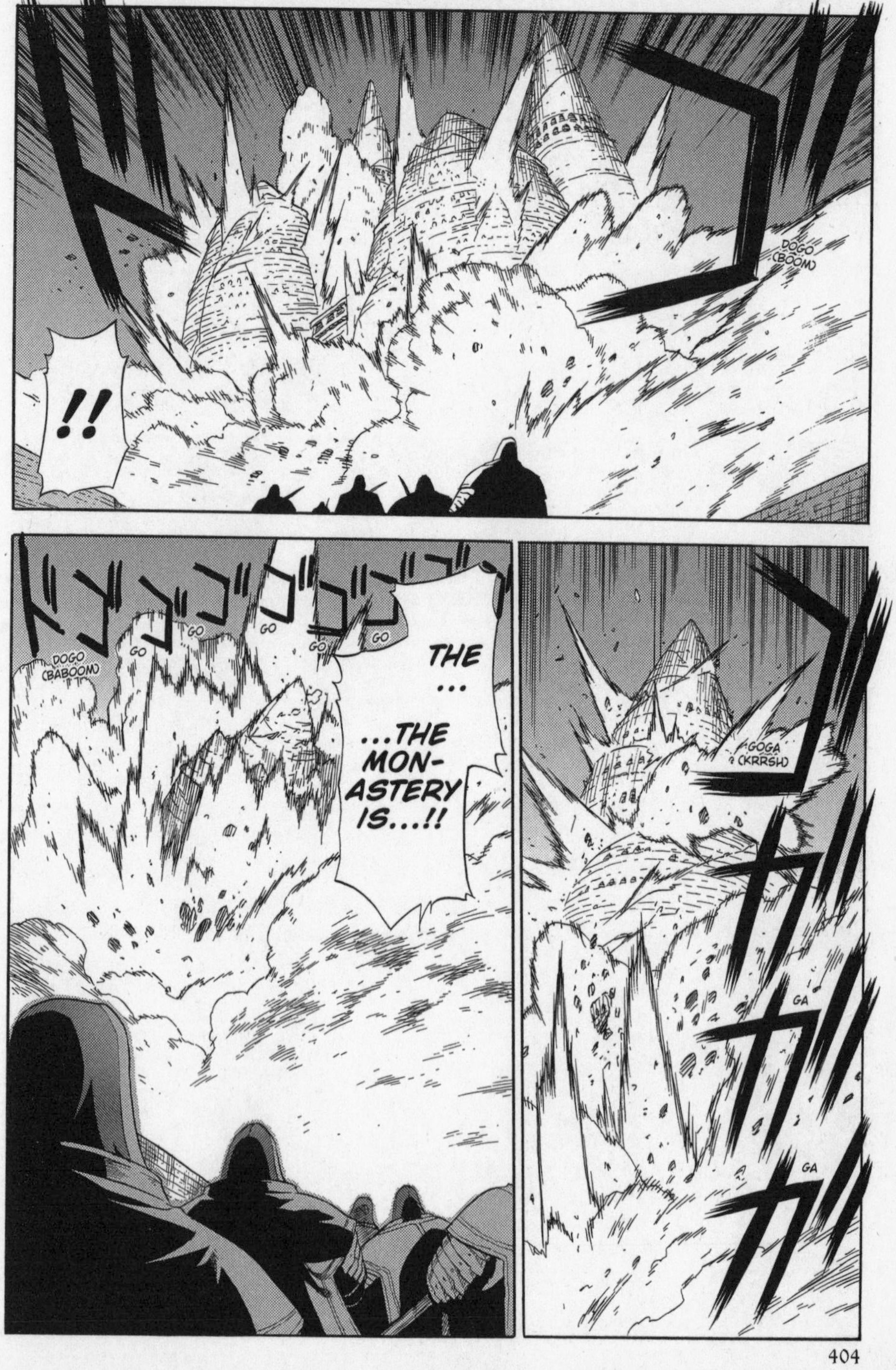
DOGO (BOOM)
!!
GOGA (KRRSH)
GA
GA
GO
GO
GO
GO
GO
DOGO (BABOOM)
THE ...
...THE MON-ASTERY IS...!!

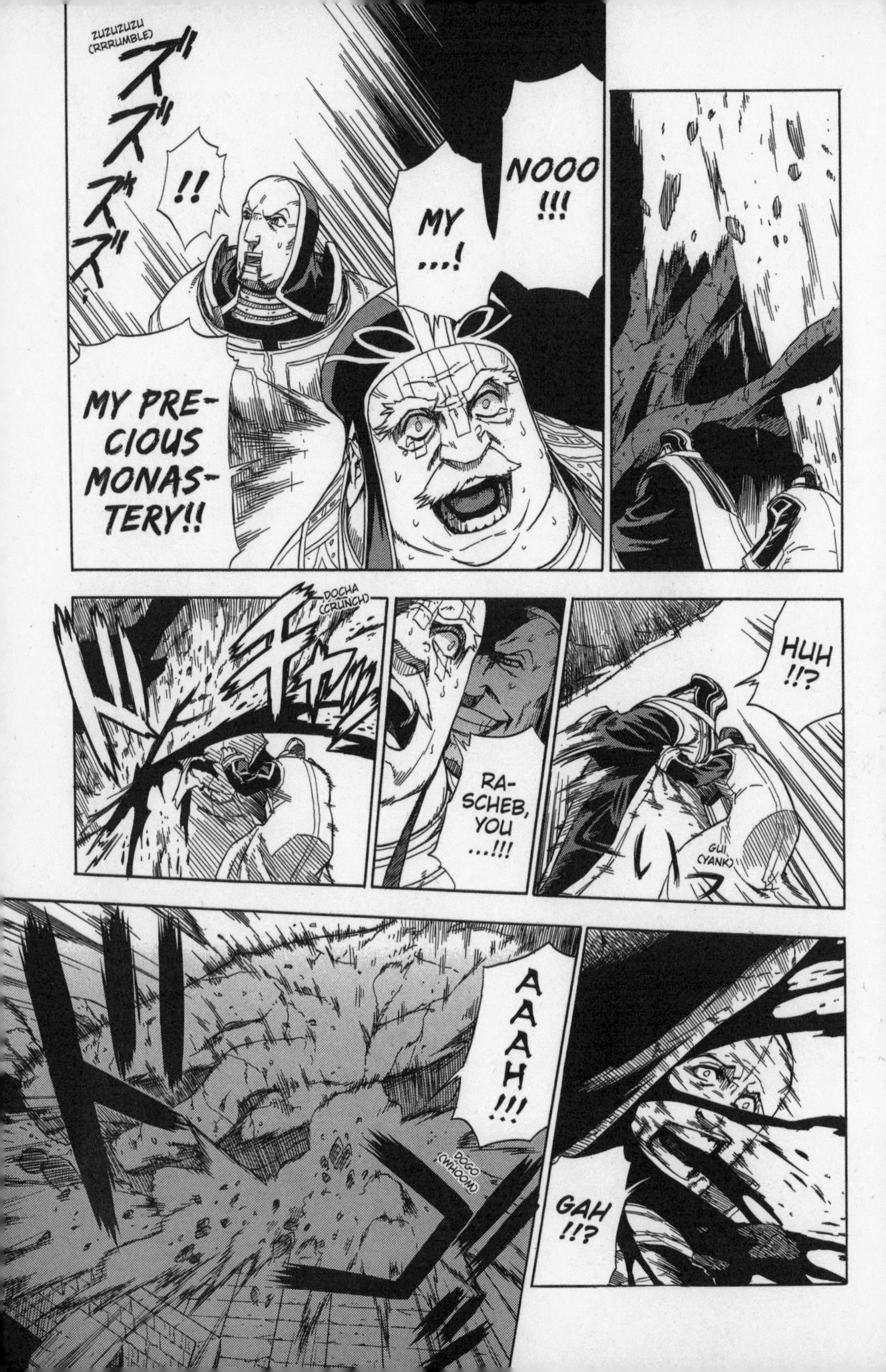
NOOO!!!
MY ...!
!!
ZUZUZUZU (RRRUMBLE)
MY PRE-CIOUS MONAS-TERY!!
HUH!!?
GUI (YANK)
RA-SCHEB, YOU ...!!!
DOCHA (CRUNCH)
GAH!!?
AAAH!!!
DOGO (WHOOM)

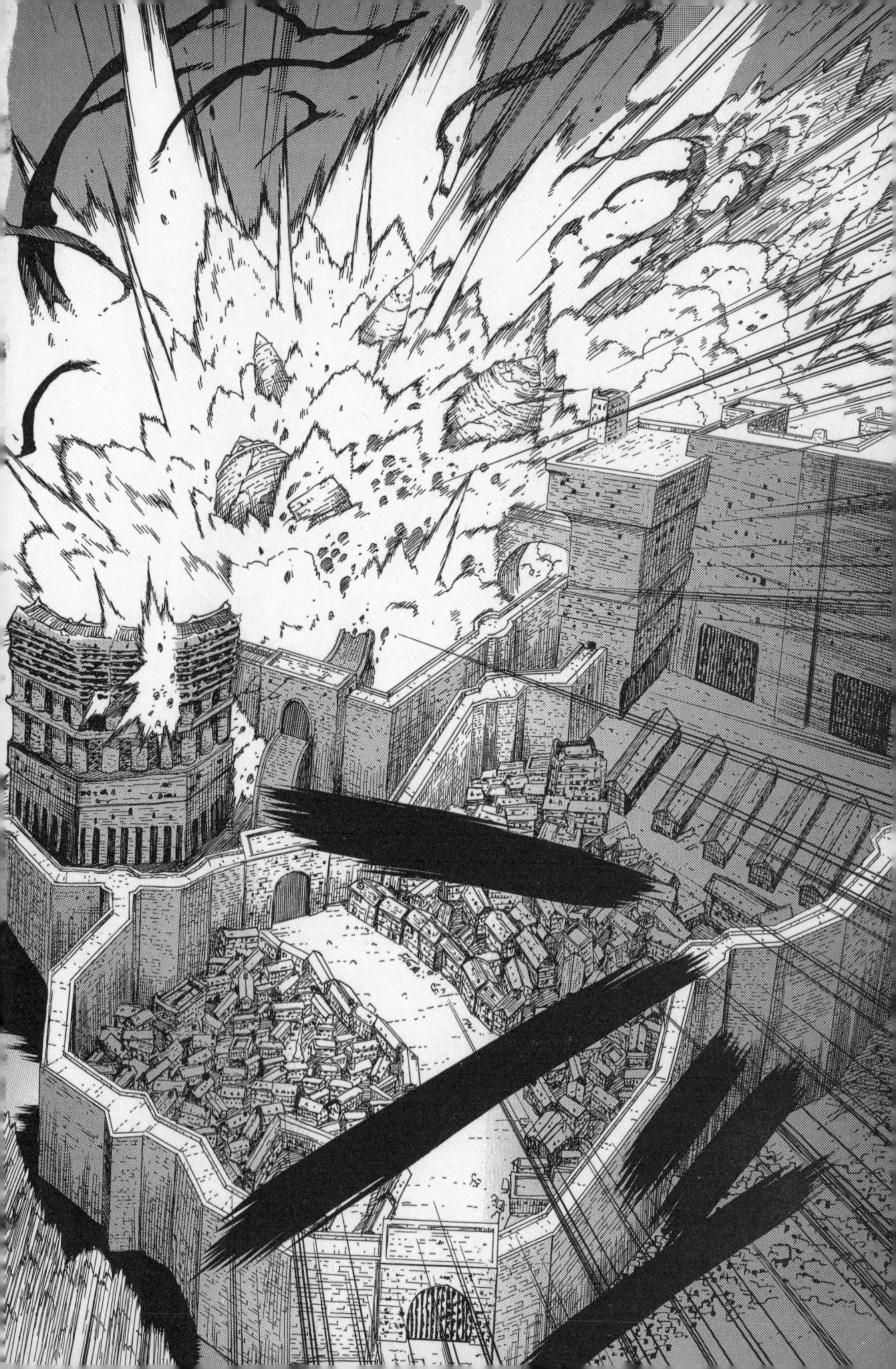

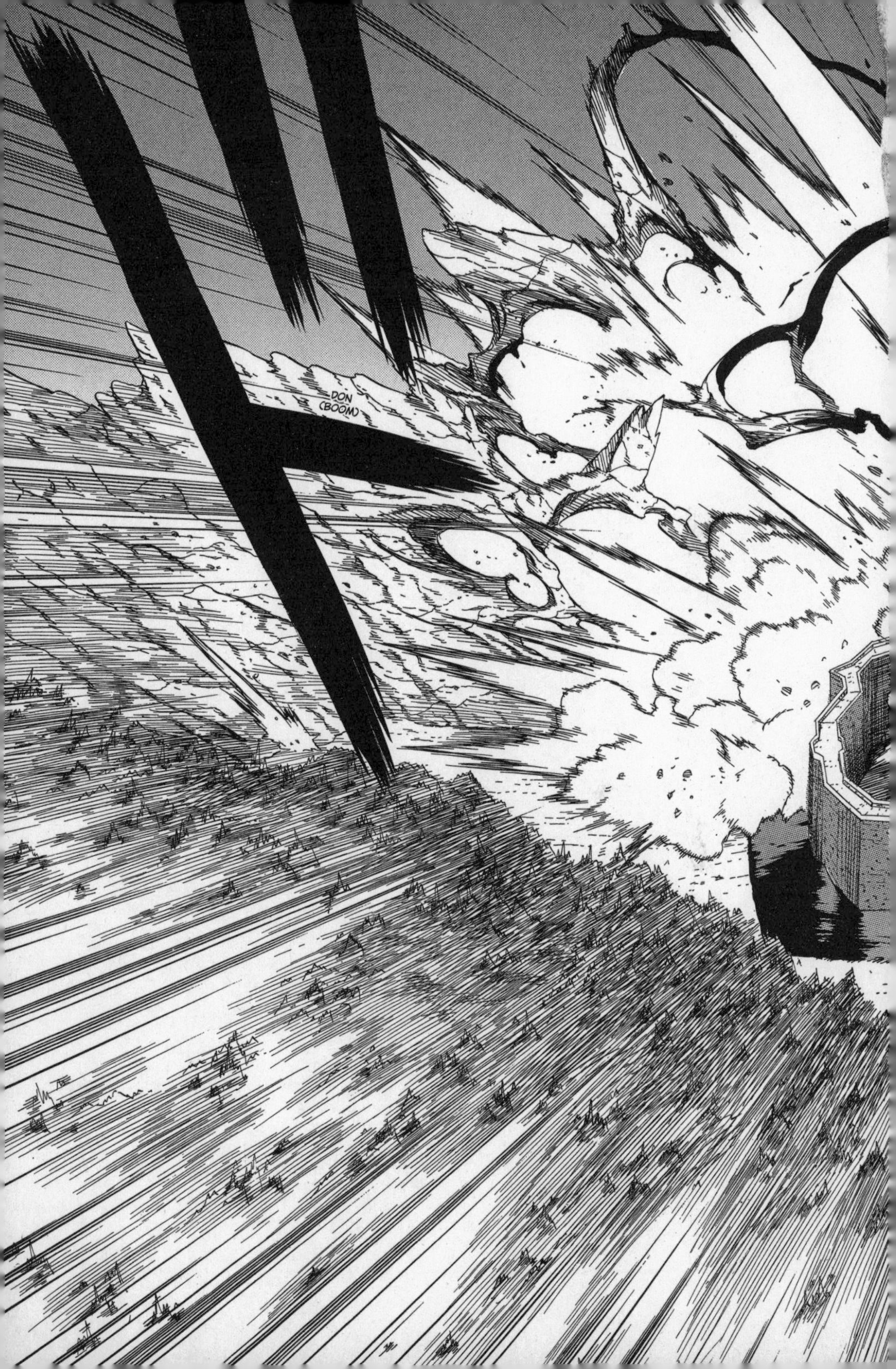
DON
(BOOM)

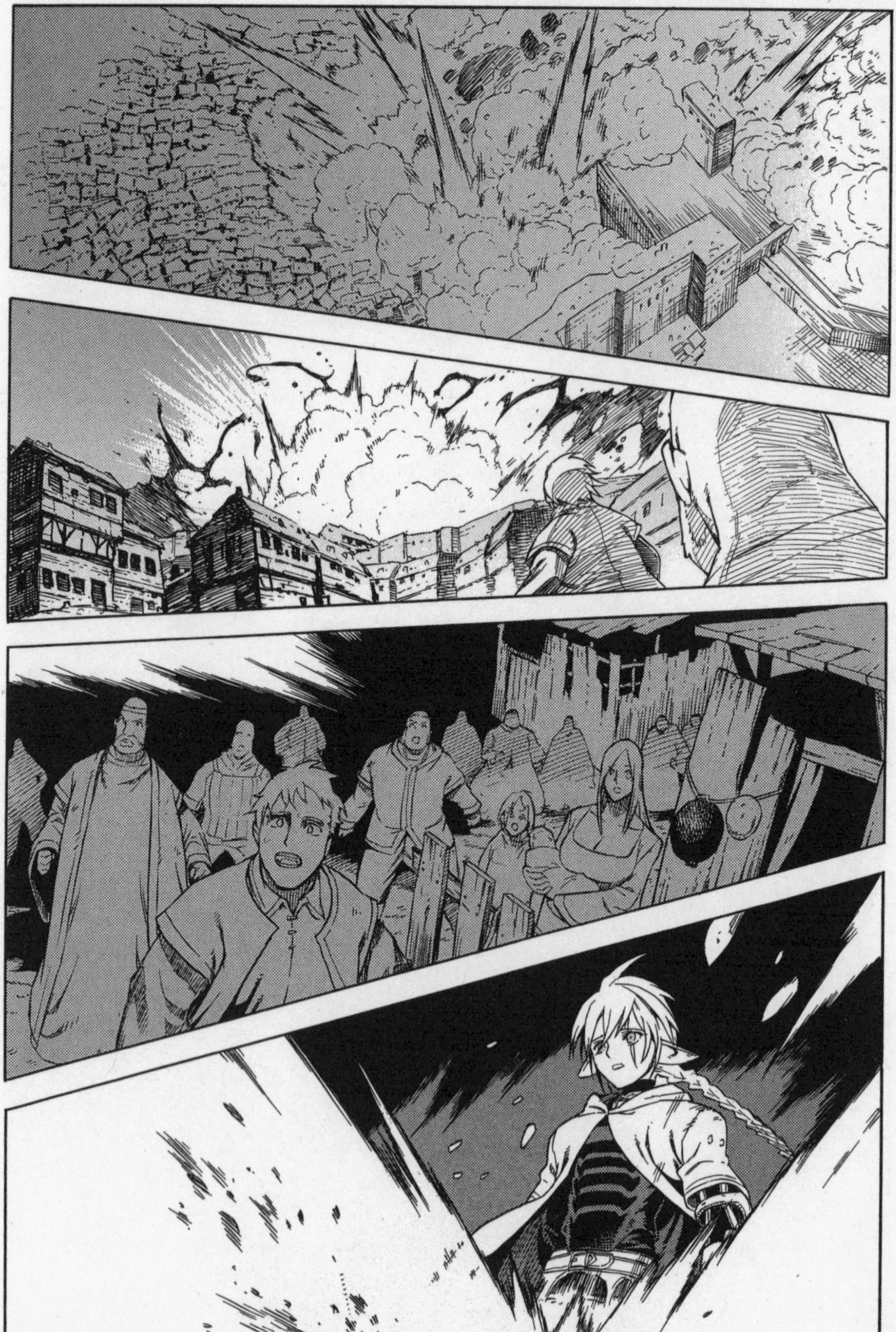

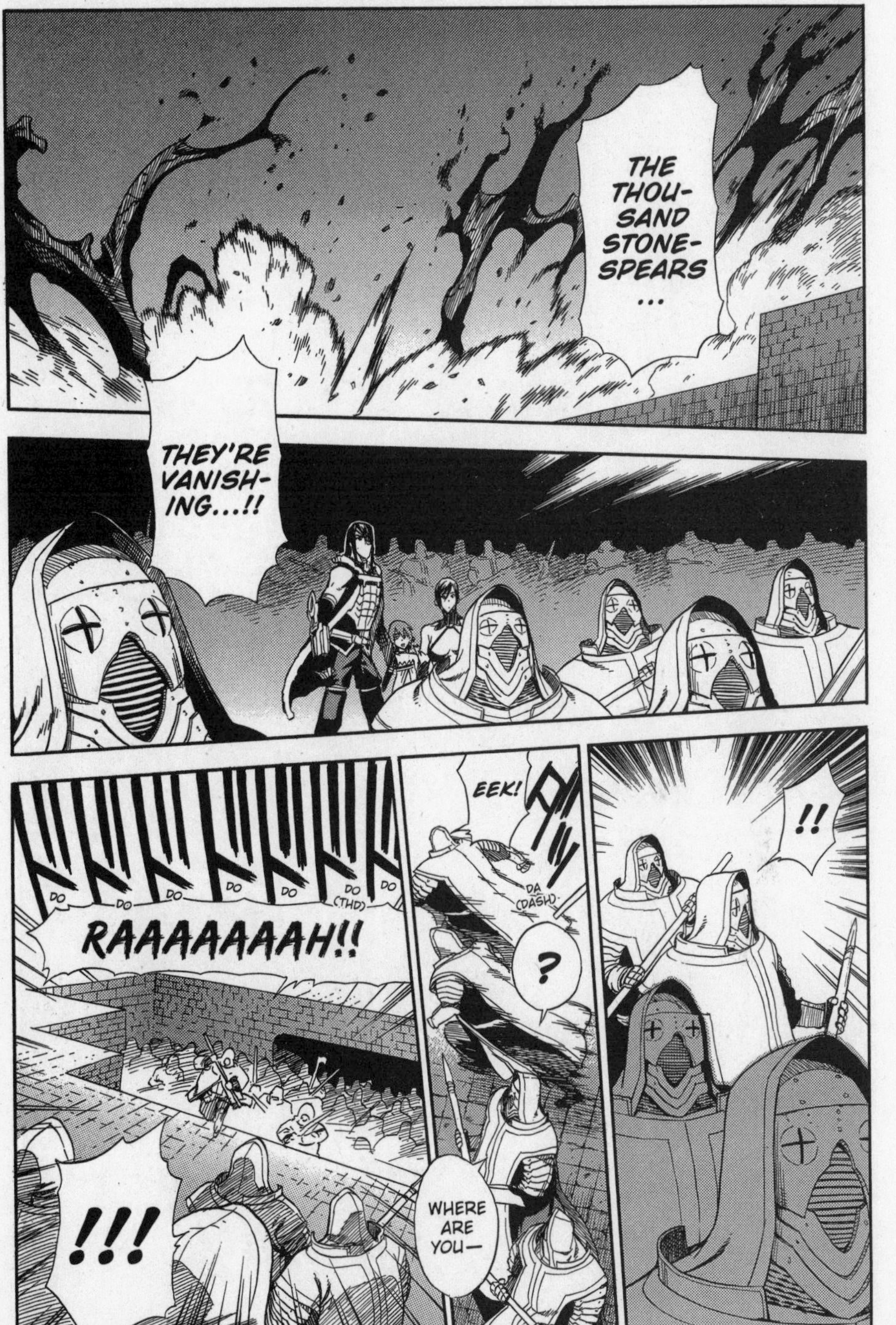
THE THOU-SAND STONE-SPEARS...
THEY'RE VANISH-ING...!!
!!
EEK!
DA (DASH)
?
WHERE ARE YOU—
DO DO DO DO DO DO DO (THD)
RAAAAAAAH!!
!!!

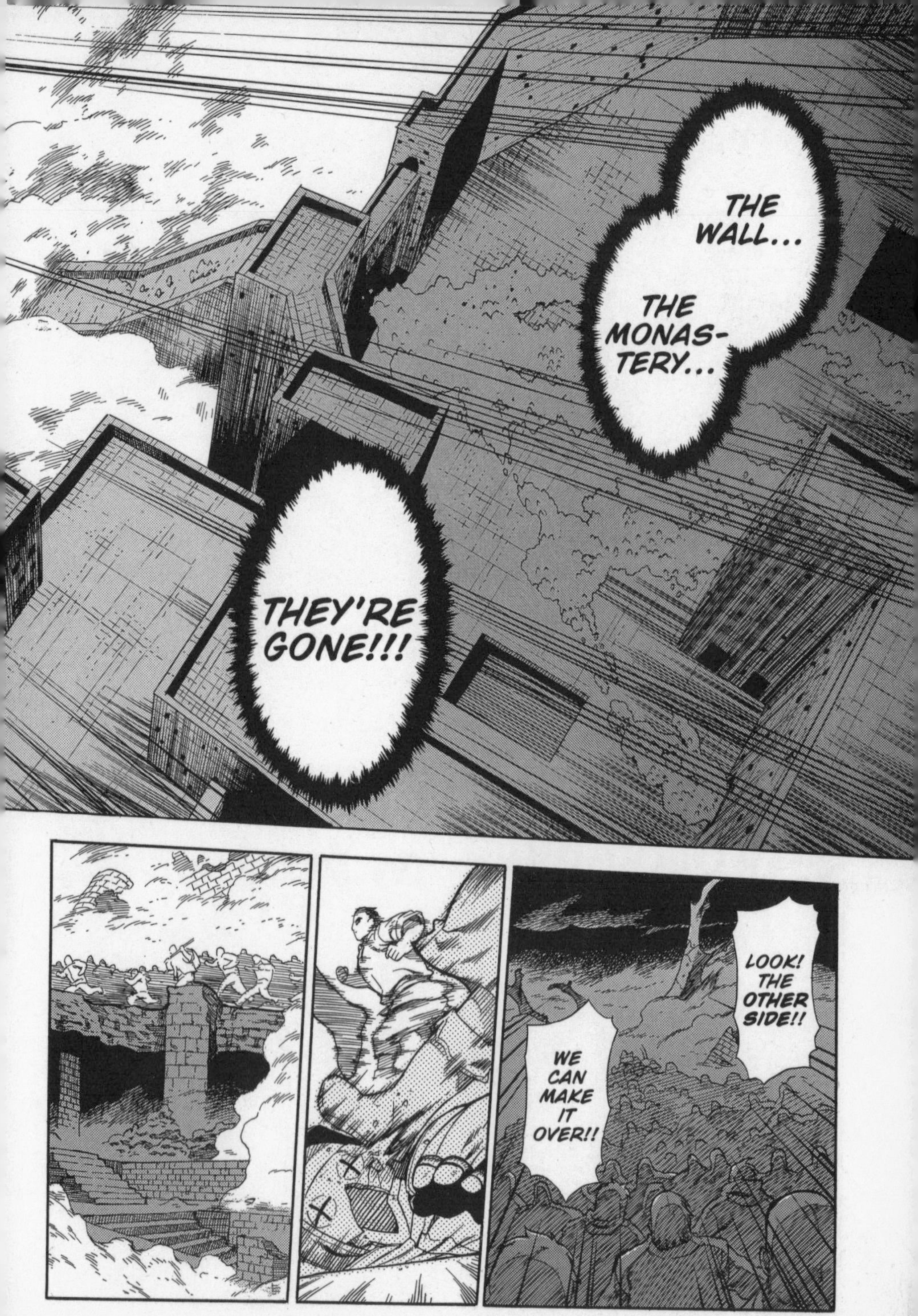
THE WALL...
THE MONAS-TERY...
THEY'RE GONE!!!
LOOK! THE OTHER SIDE!!
WE CAN MAKE IT OVER!!

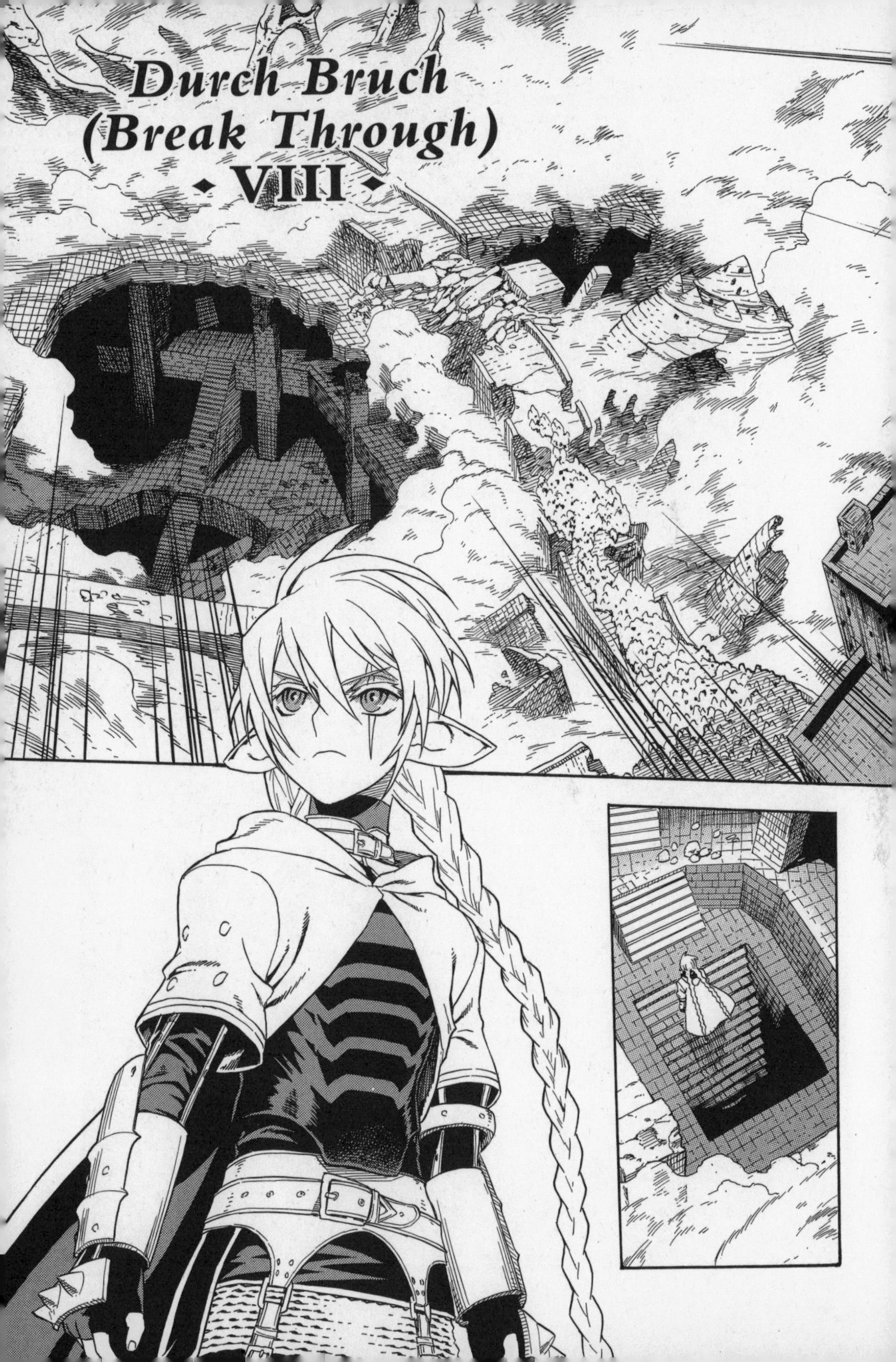
Durch Bruch
(Break Through)
• VIII •

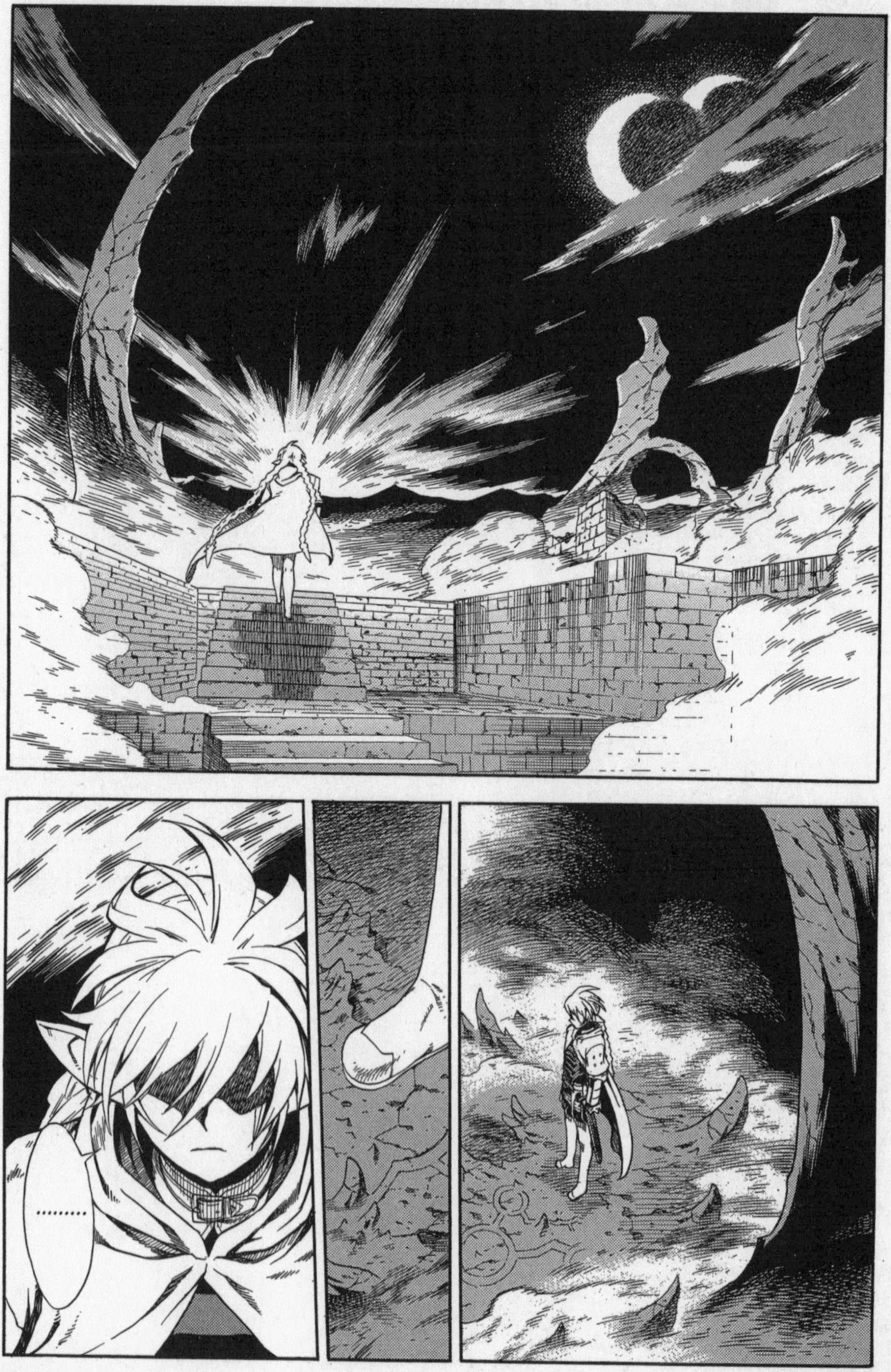
....

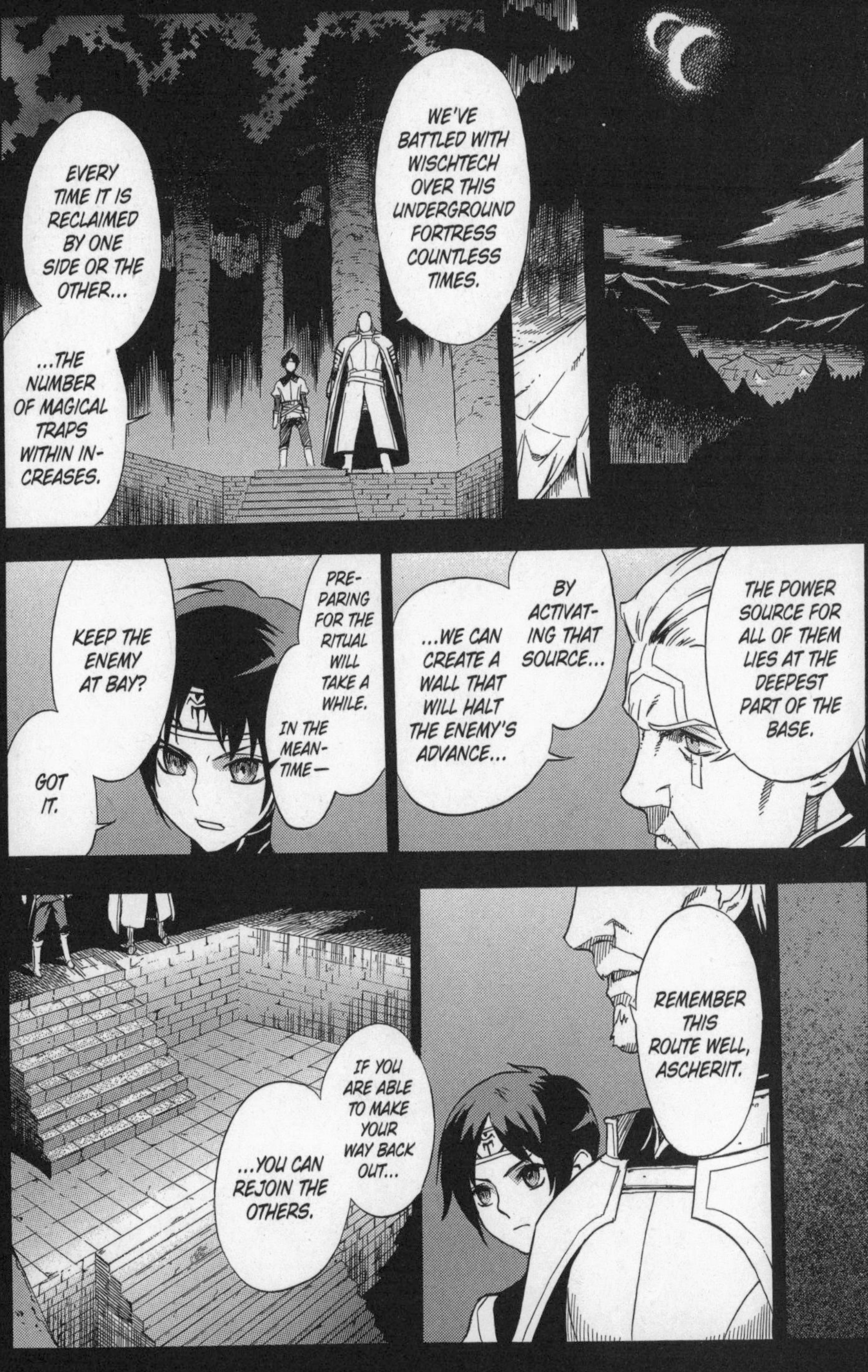
WE'VE BATTLED WITH WISCHTECH OVER THIS UNDERGROUND FORTRESS COUNTLESS TIMES.
EVERY TIME IT IS RECLAIMED BY ONE SIDE OR THE OTHER...
...THE NUMBER OF MAGICAL TRAPS WITHIN IN-CREASES.
THE POWER SOURCE FOR ALL OF THEM LIES AT THE DEEPEST PART OF THE BASE.
BY ACTIVAT-ING THAT SOURCE...
...WE CAN CREATE A WALL THAT WILL HALT THE ENEMY'S ADVANCE...
PRE-PARING FOR THE RITUAL WILL TAKE A WHILE.
IN THE MEAN-TIME—
KEEP THE ENEMY AT BAY?
GOT IT.
REMEMBER THIS ROUTE WELL, ASCHERIIT.
IF YOU ARE ABLE TO MAKE YOUR WAY BACK OUT...
...YOU CAN REJOIN THE OTHERS.

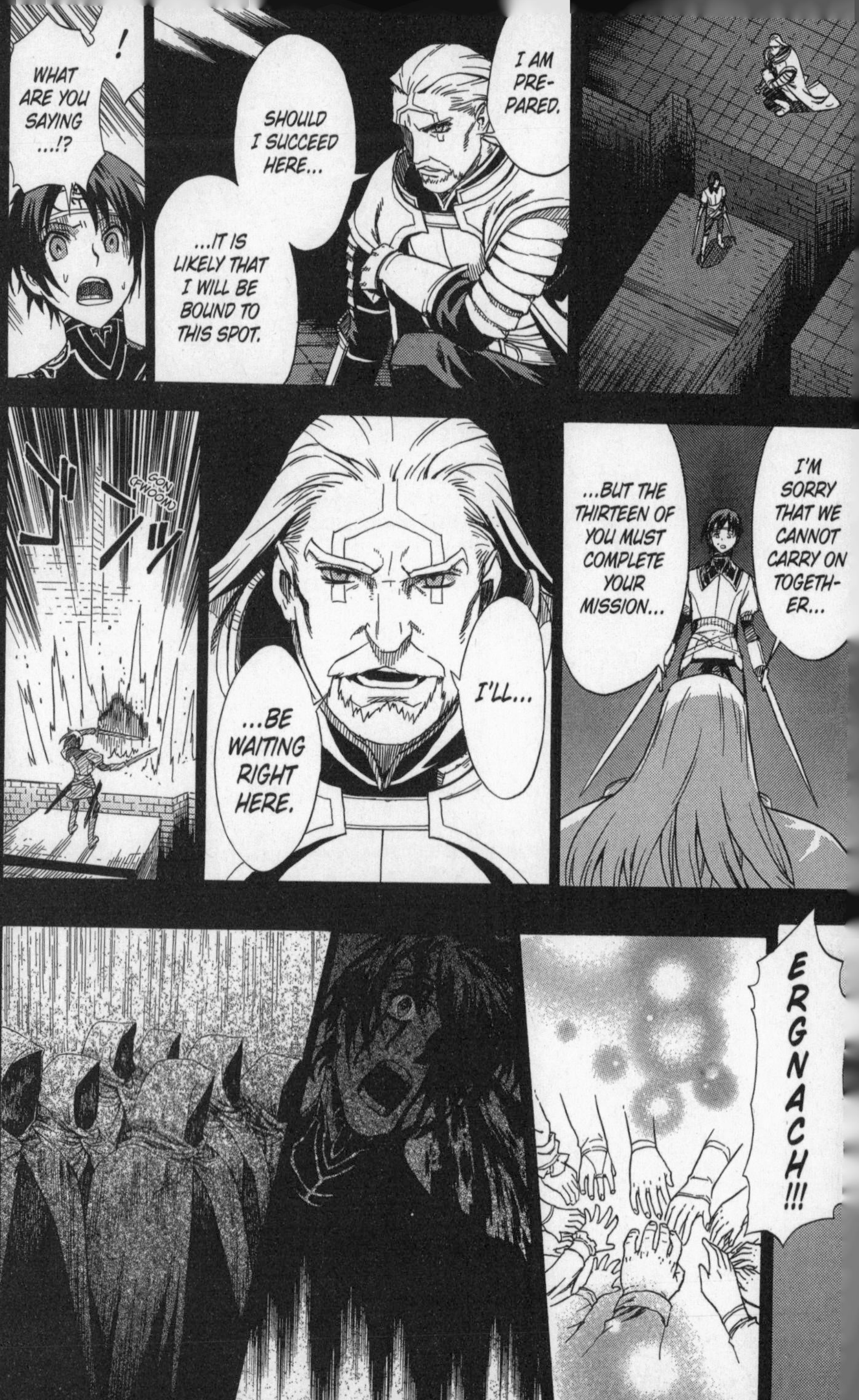
I AM PRE-PARED.
SHOULD I SUCCEED HERE...
...IT IS LIKELY THAT I WILL BE BOUND TO THIS SPOT.
!
WHAT ARE YOU SAYING ...!?
I'M SORRY THAT WE CANNOT CARRY ON TOGETH-ER...
...BUT THE THIRTEEN OF YOU MUST COMPLETE YOUR MISSION...
I'LL...
...BE WAITING RIGHT HERE.
GON (FWOOM)
ERGNACH!!!

......I'M SORRY... ERGNACH...

BUT NOW...

...I MUST GO AND KILL...

...GLENN AND THE OTHERS...

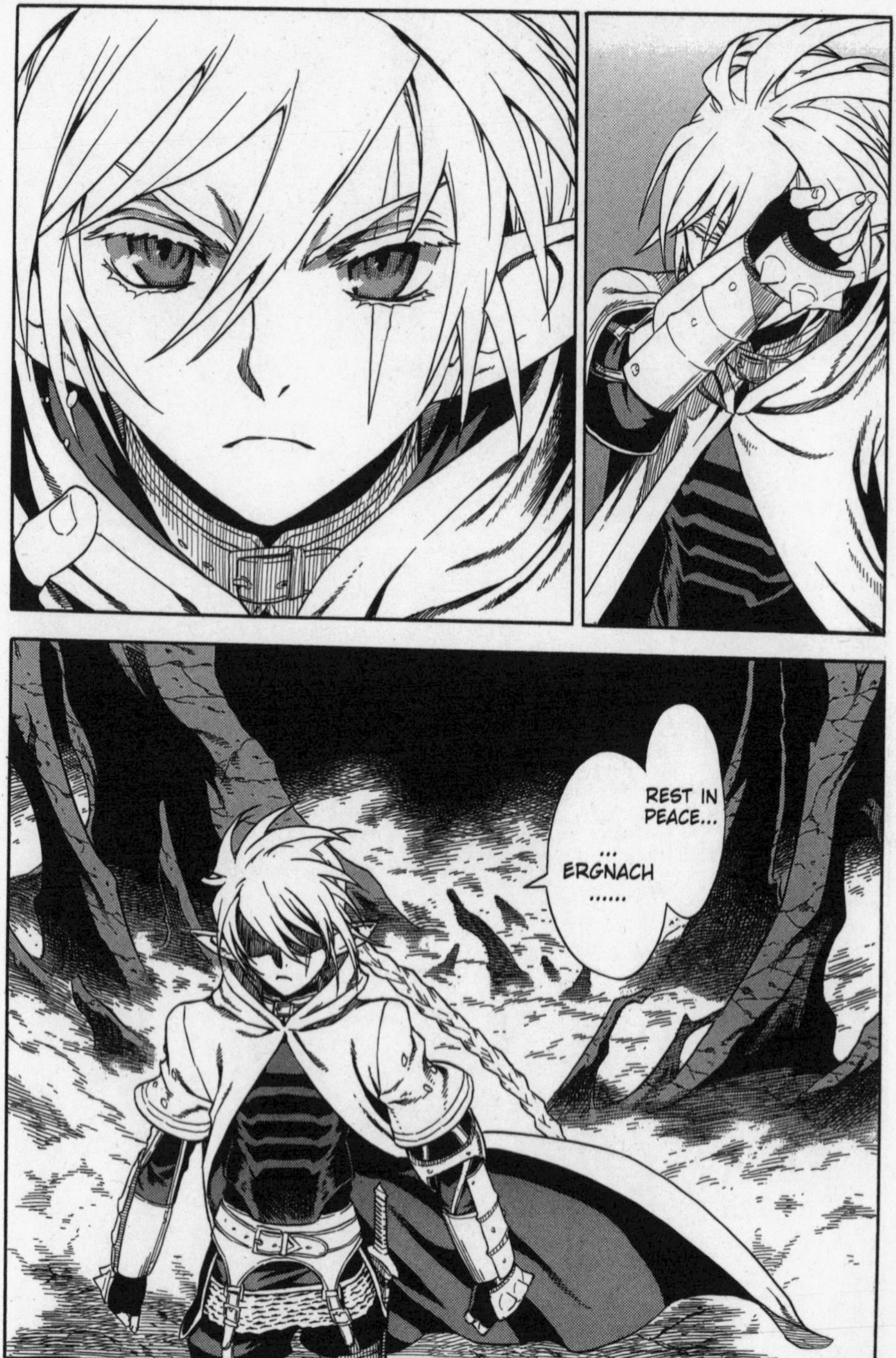
REST IN PEACE... ...ERGNACH ......

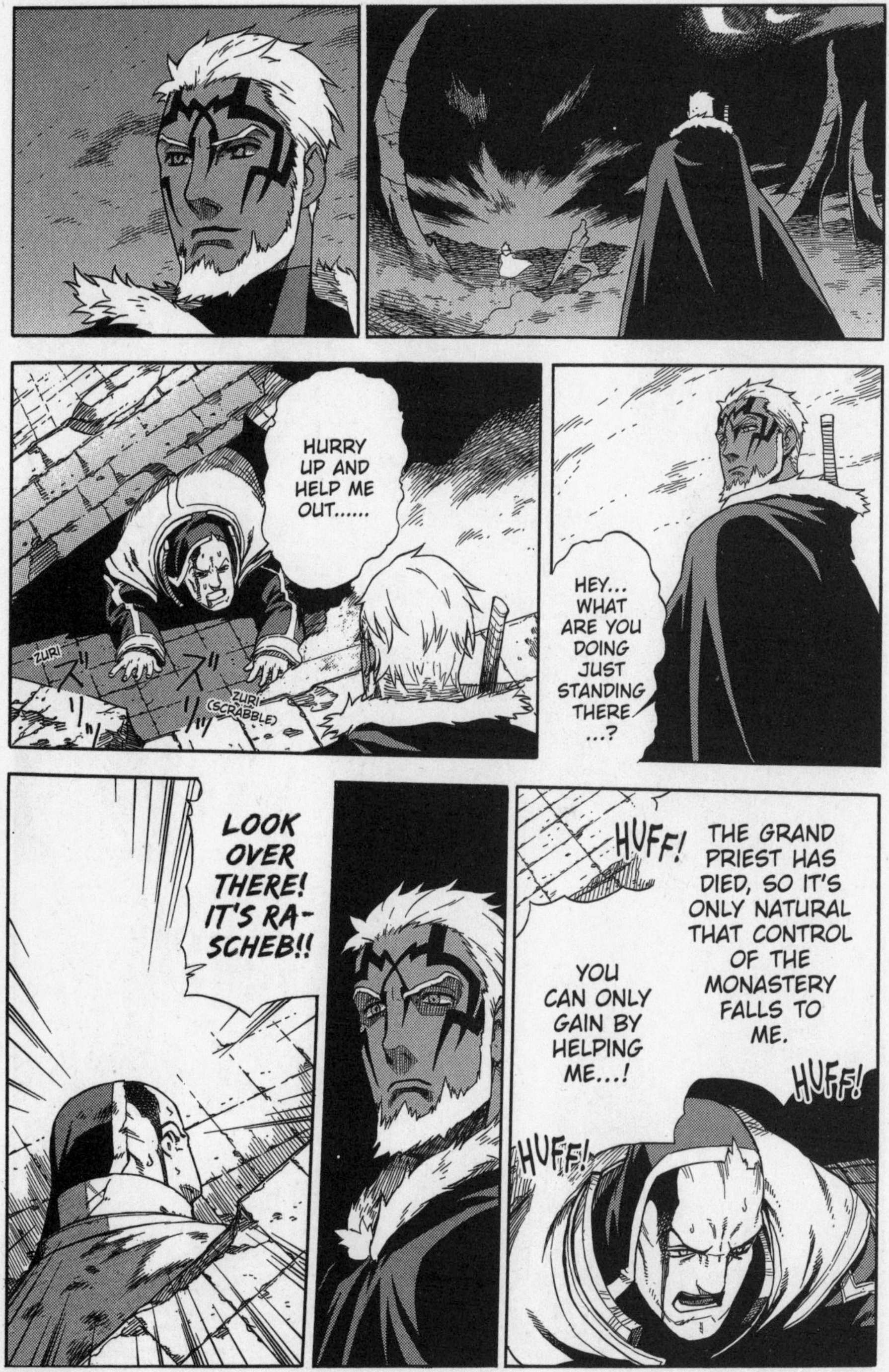
HEY... WHAT ARE YOU DOING JUST STANDING THERE ...?
HURRY UP AND HELP ME OUT......
ZURI
ZURI (SCRABBLE)
HUFF!
THE GRAND PRIEST HAS DIED, SO IT'S ONLY NATURAL THAT CONTROL OF THE MONASTERY FALLS TO ME.
YOU CAN ONLY GAIN BY HELPING ME...!
HUFF!
HUFF!
LOOK OVER THERE! IT'S RA-SCHEB!!

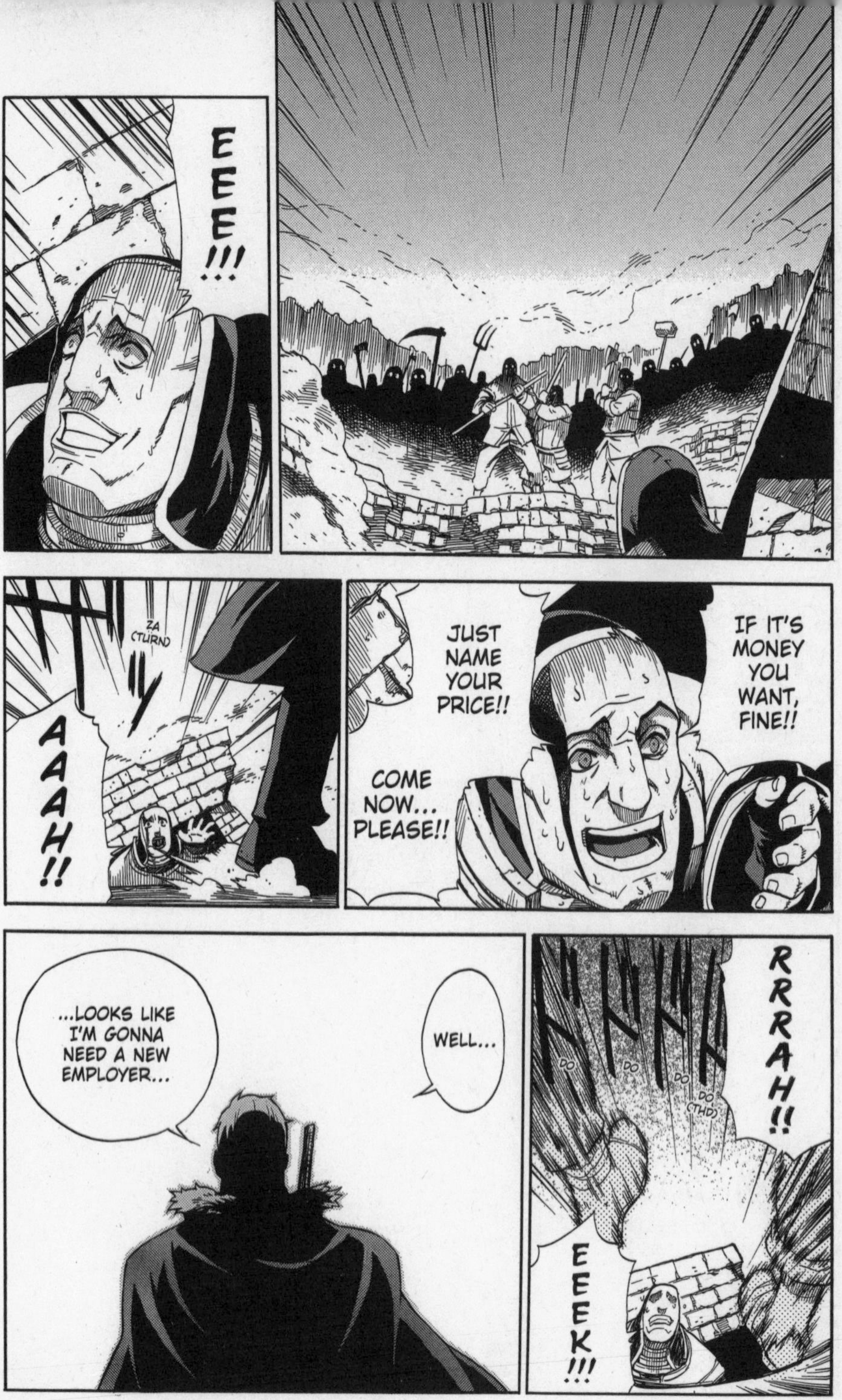
EEE!!!
IF IT'S MONEY YOU WANT, FINE!!
JUST NAME YOUR PRICE!!
COME NOW... PLEASE!!
ZA (TURN)
AAAH!!
RRRAH!!
DO DO DO DO (THD)
EEEK!!!
WELL...
...LOOKS LIKE I'M GONNA NEED A NEW EMPLOYER...

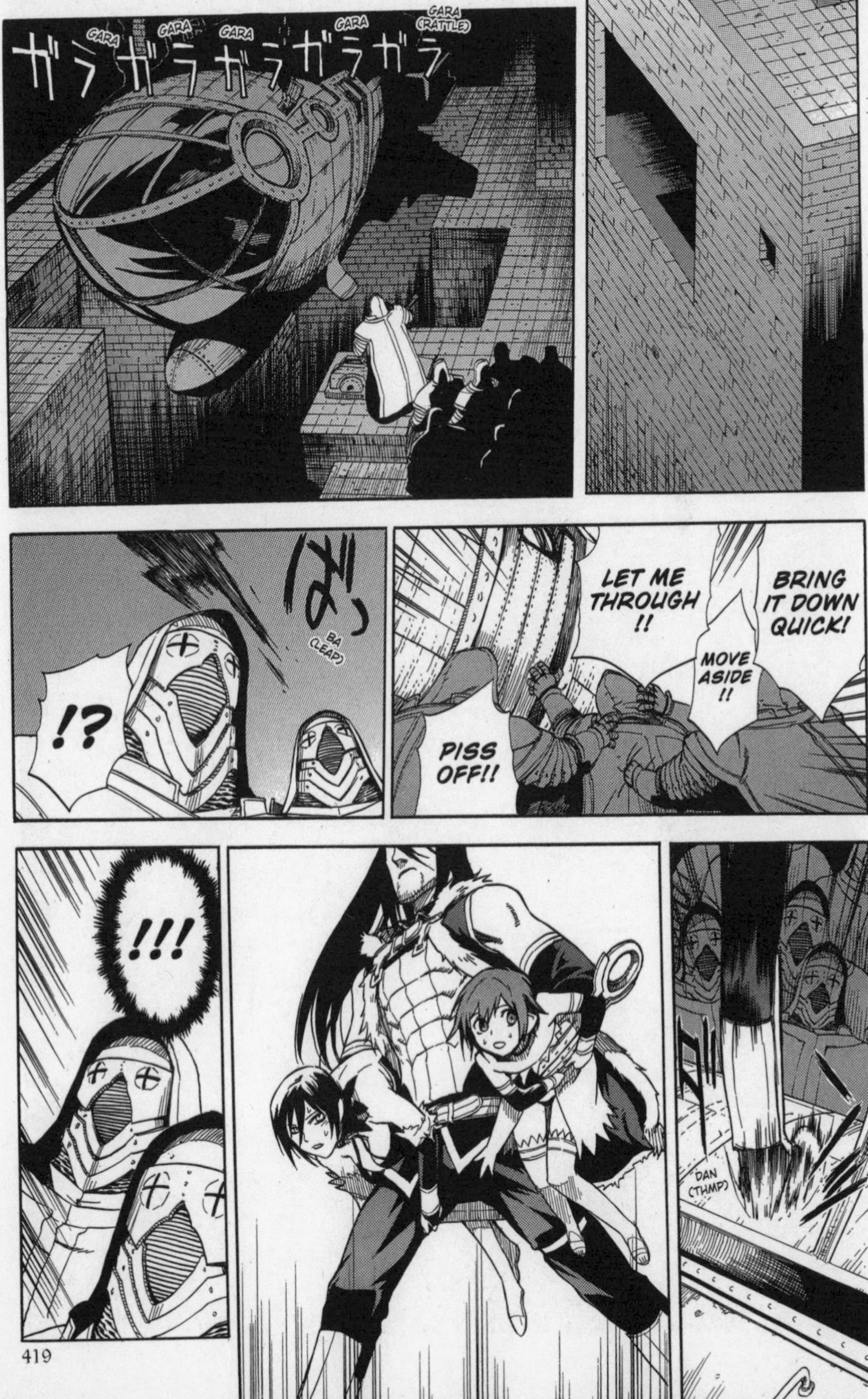

ガラガラガラガラ
GARA GARA GARA GARA (RATTLE)
BRING IT DOWN QUICK!
LET ME THROUGH!!
MOVE ASIDE!!
PISS OFF!!
ばっ
BA (LEAP)
!?
DAN (THMP)
!!!

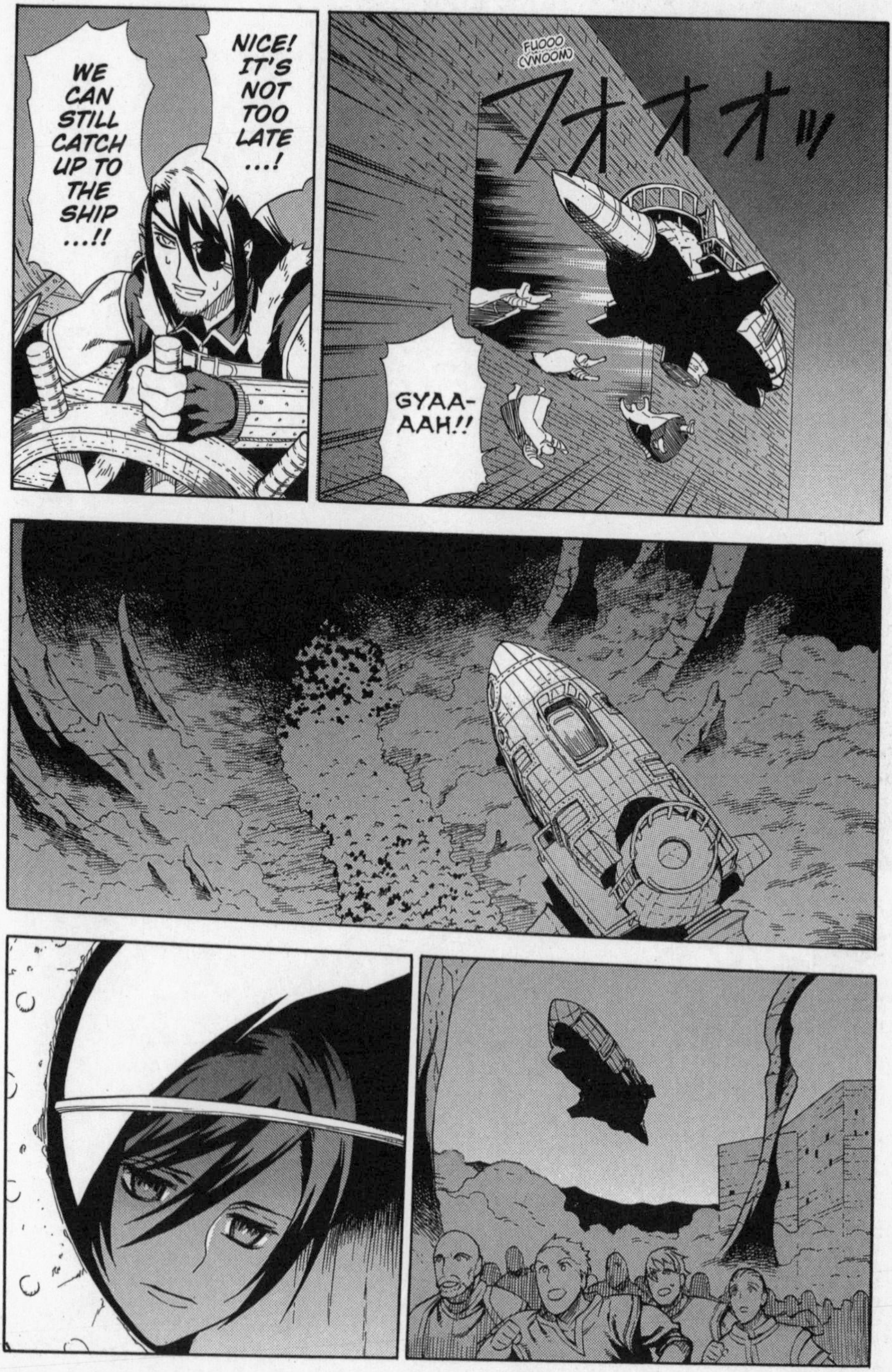
FUOOO (VWOOM)
フオオオッ
GYAA-AAH!!
NICE! IT'S NOT TOO LATE...!
WE CAN STILL CATCH UP TO THE SHIP...!!

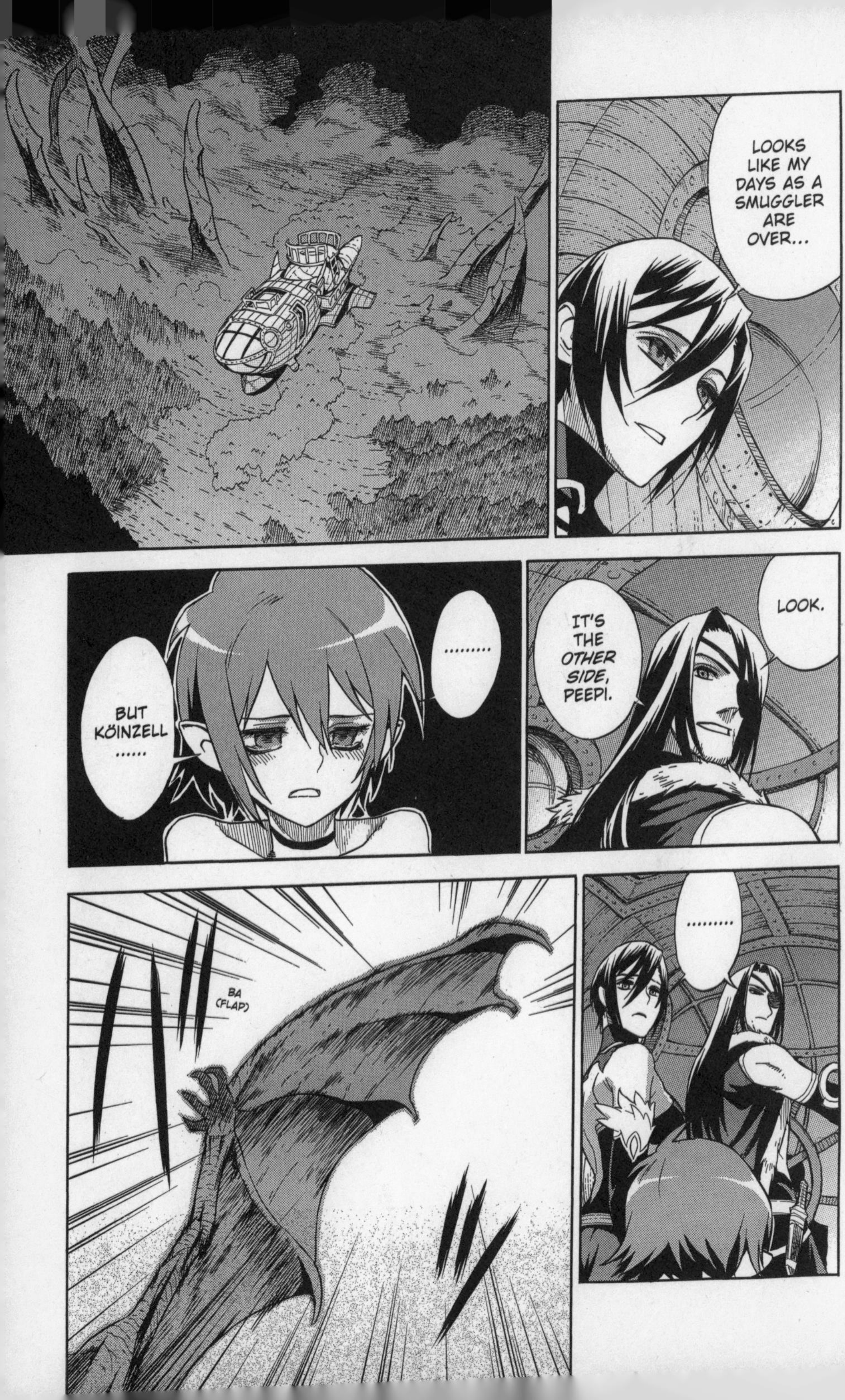
LOOKS LIKE MY DAYS AS A SMUGGLER ARE OVER...
LOOK.
IT'S THE *OTHER SIDE,* PEEPI.
....
BUT KÖINZELL ......
....
BA (FLAP)

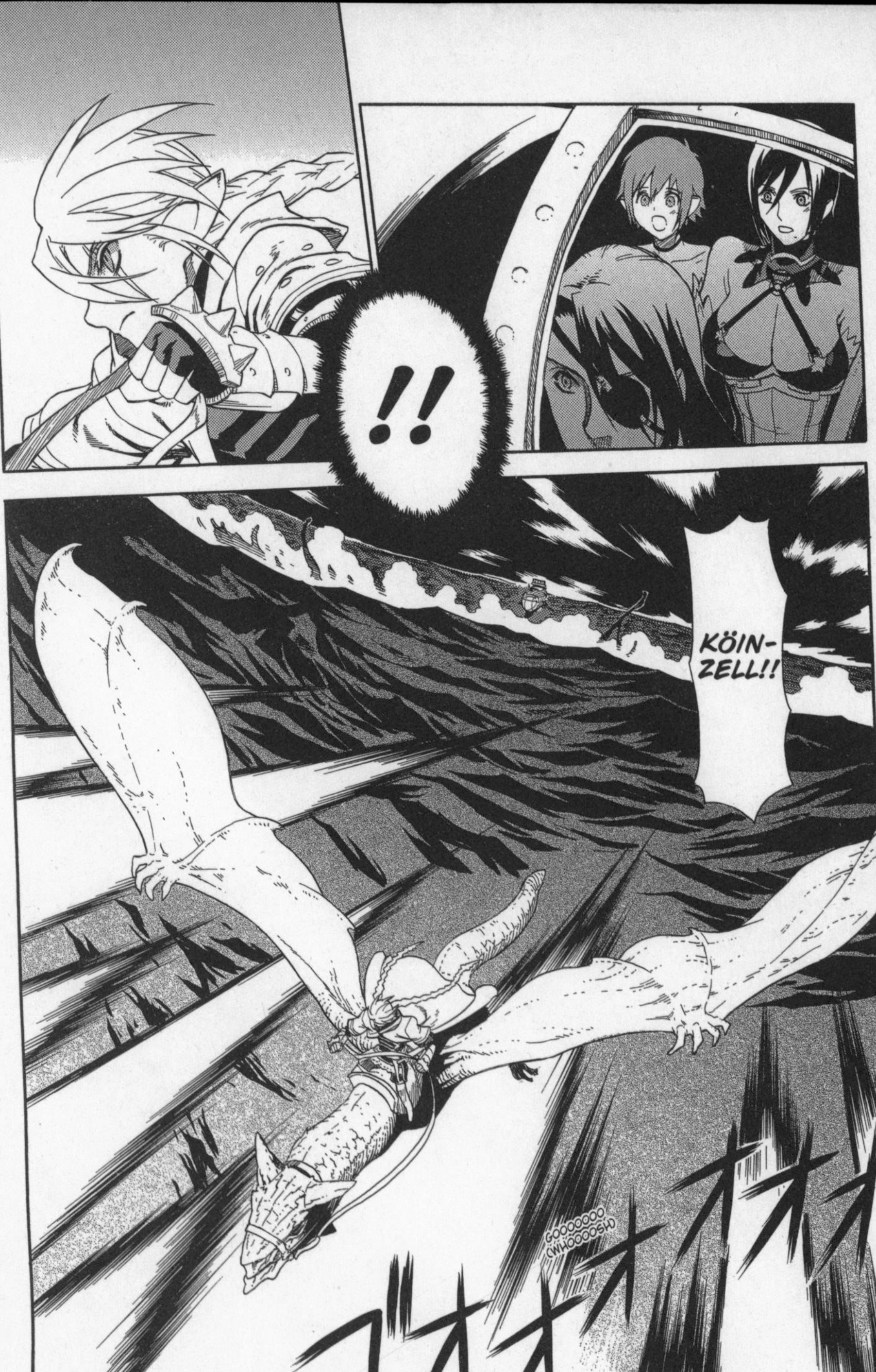
!!
KÖIN-ZELL!!
ゴオオオオオオ
GOOOOOOO (WHOOOOOSH)

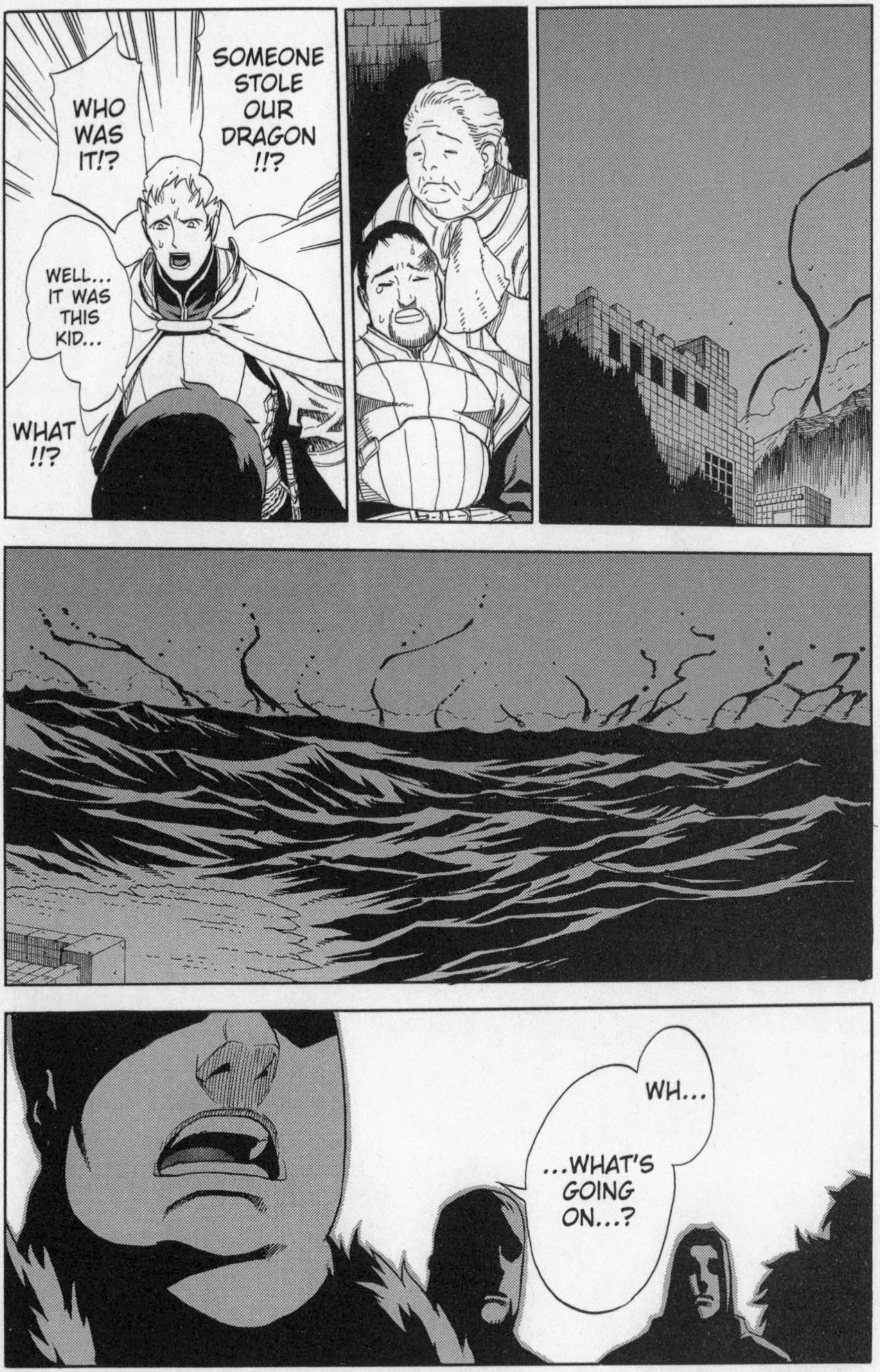
SOMEONE STOLE OUR DRAGON !!?
WHO WAS IT!?
WELL... IT WAS THIS KID...
WHAT !!?
WH...
...WHAT'S GOING ON...?

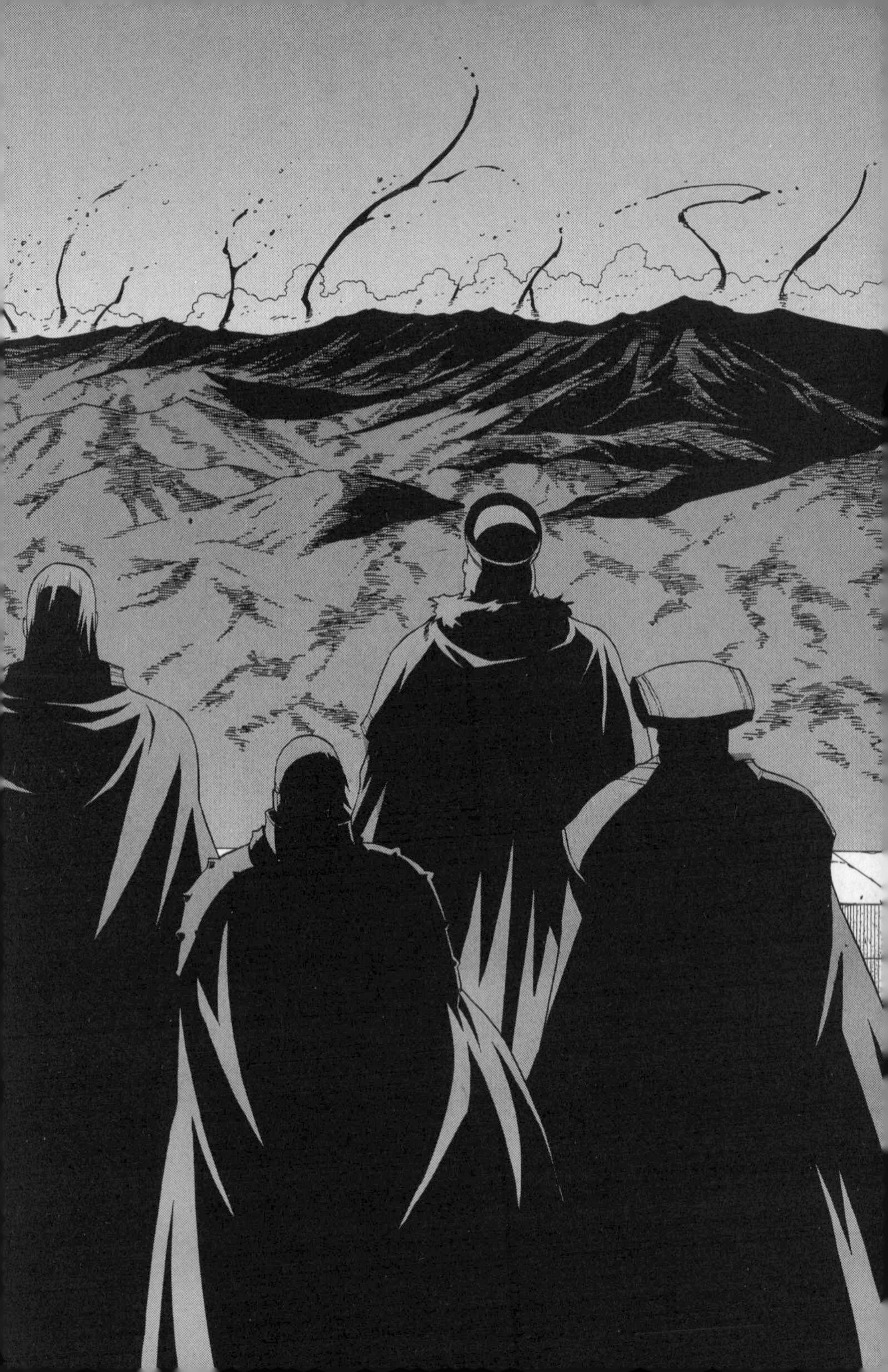

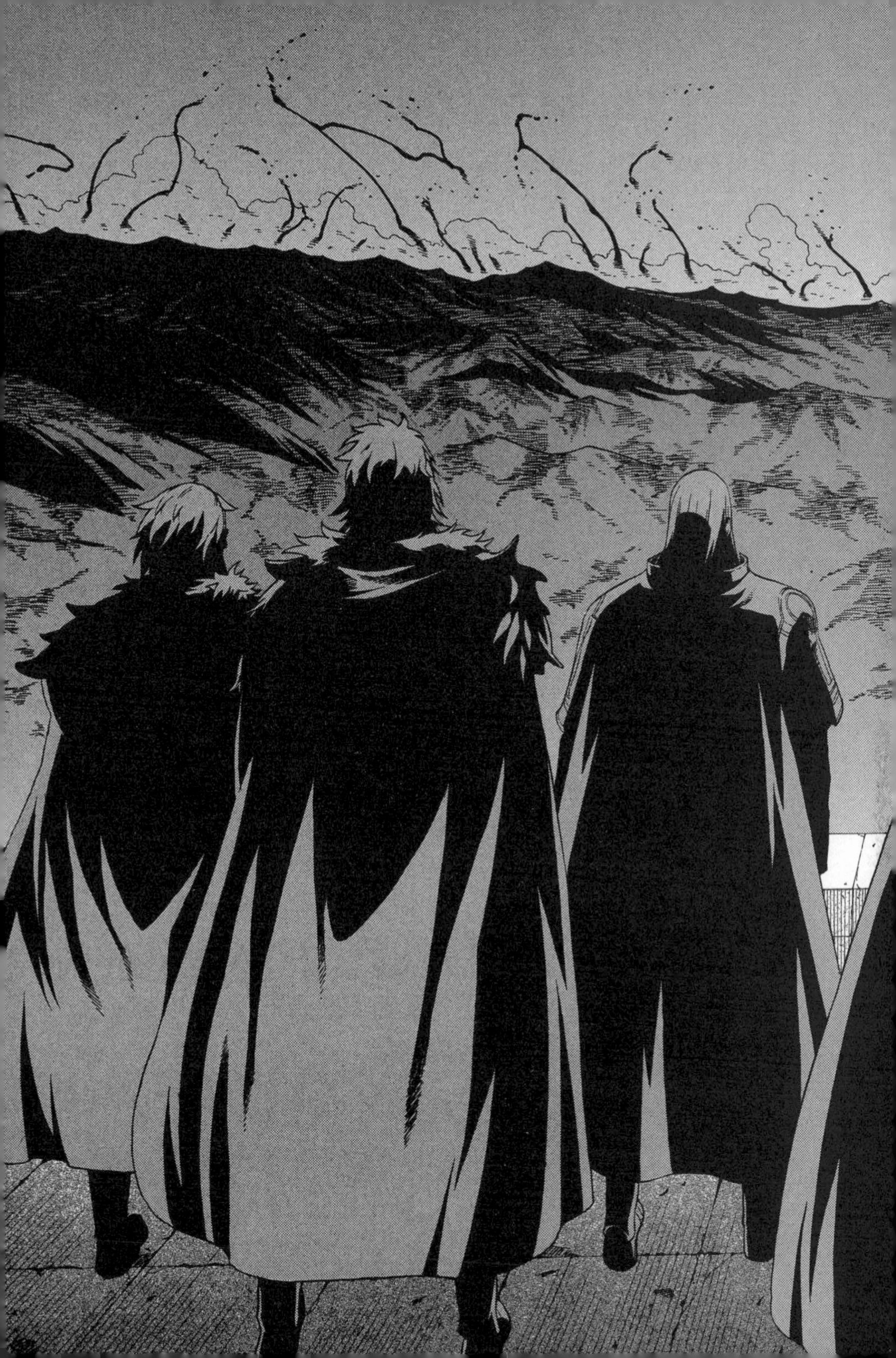

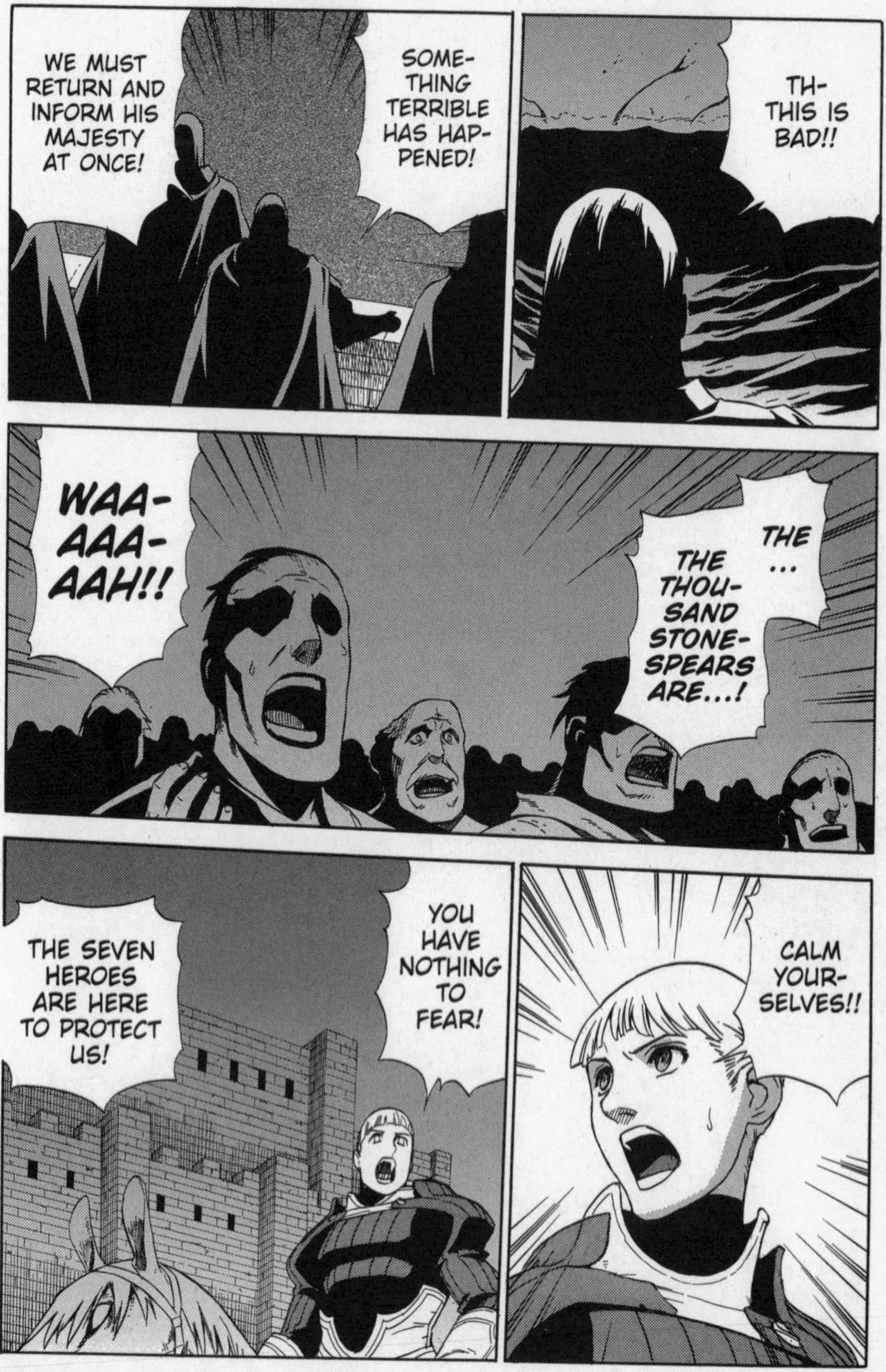
TH- THIS IS BAD!!
SOME-THING TERRIBLE HAS HAP-PENED!
WE MUST RETURN AND INFORM HIS MAJESTY AT ONCE!
THE...
THE THOU-SAND STONE-SPEARS ARE...!
WAA-AAA-AAH!!
CALM YOUR-SELVES!!
YOU HAVE NOTHING TO FEAR!
THE SEVEN HEROES ARE HERE TO PROTECT US!

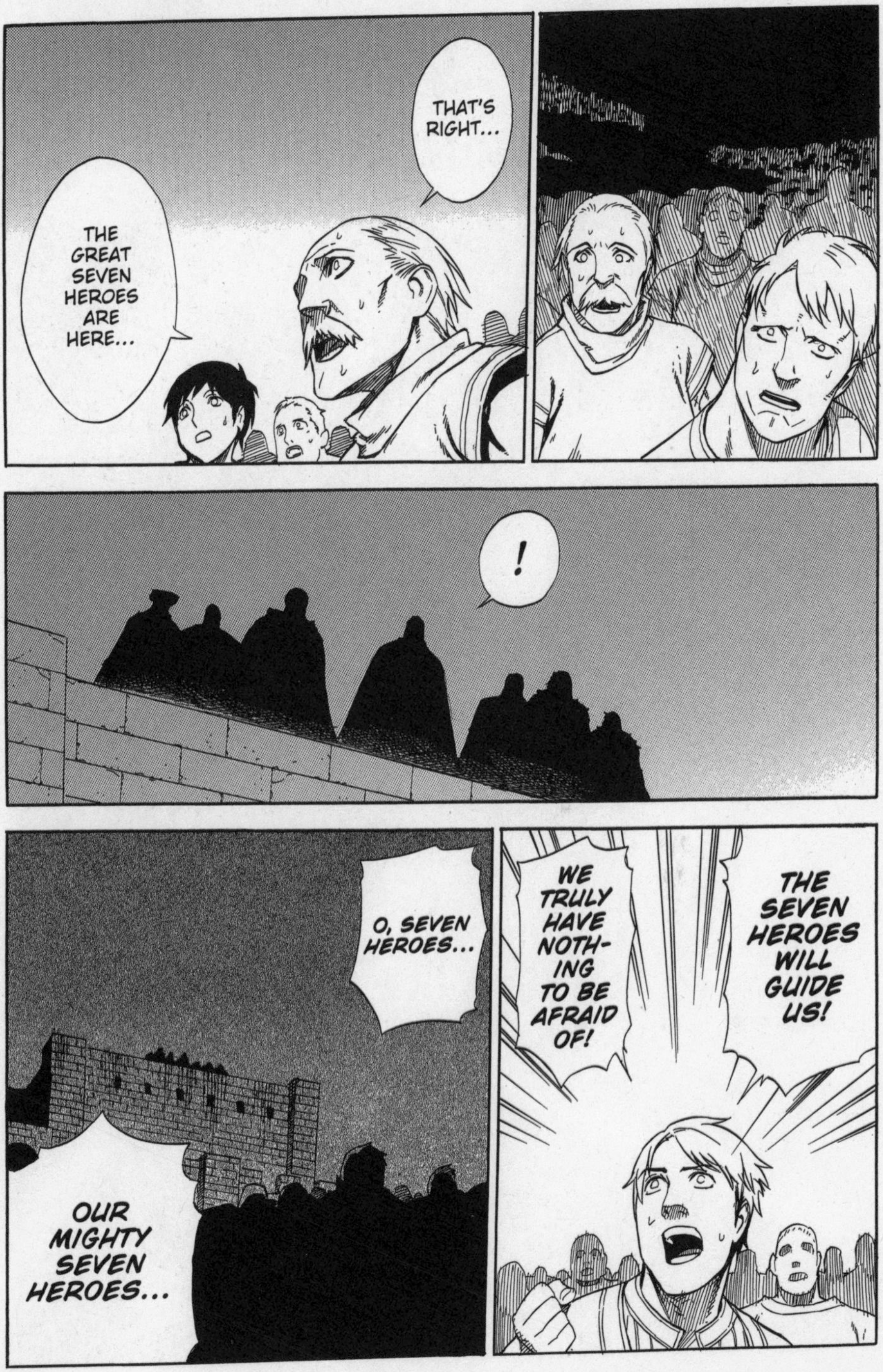
THAT'S RIGHT...
THE GREAT SEVEN HEROES ARE HERE...
!
THE SEVEN HEROES WILL GUIDE US!
WE TRULY HAVE NOTH-ING TO BE AFRAID OF!
O, SEVEN HEROES...
OUR MIGHTY SEVEN HEROES...

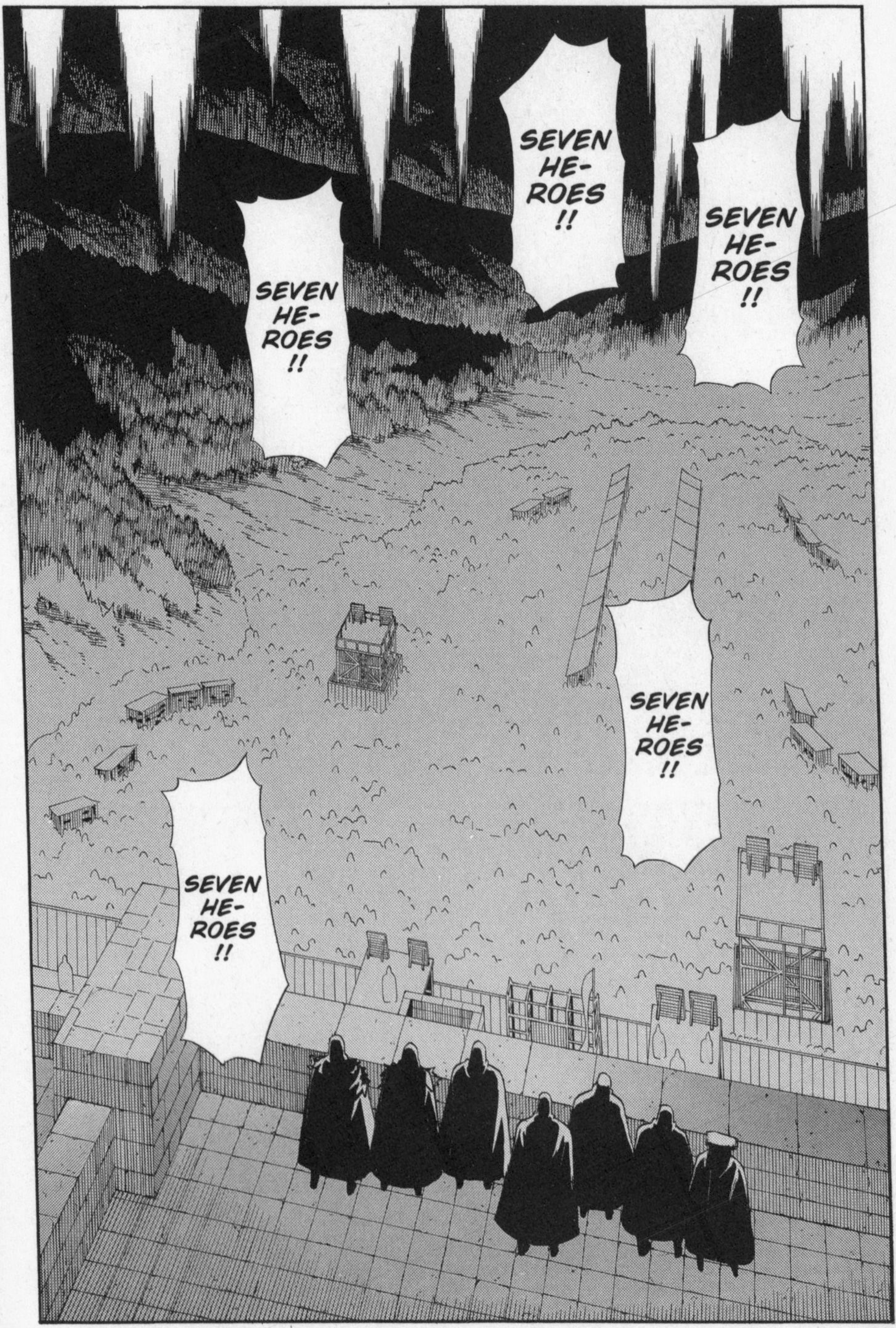
SEVEN HE-ROES !!
SEVEN HE-ROES !!
SEVEN HE-ROES !!
SEVEN HE-ROES !!
SEVEN HE-ROES !!

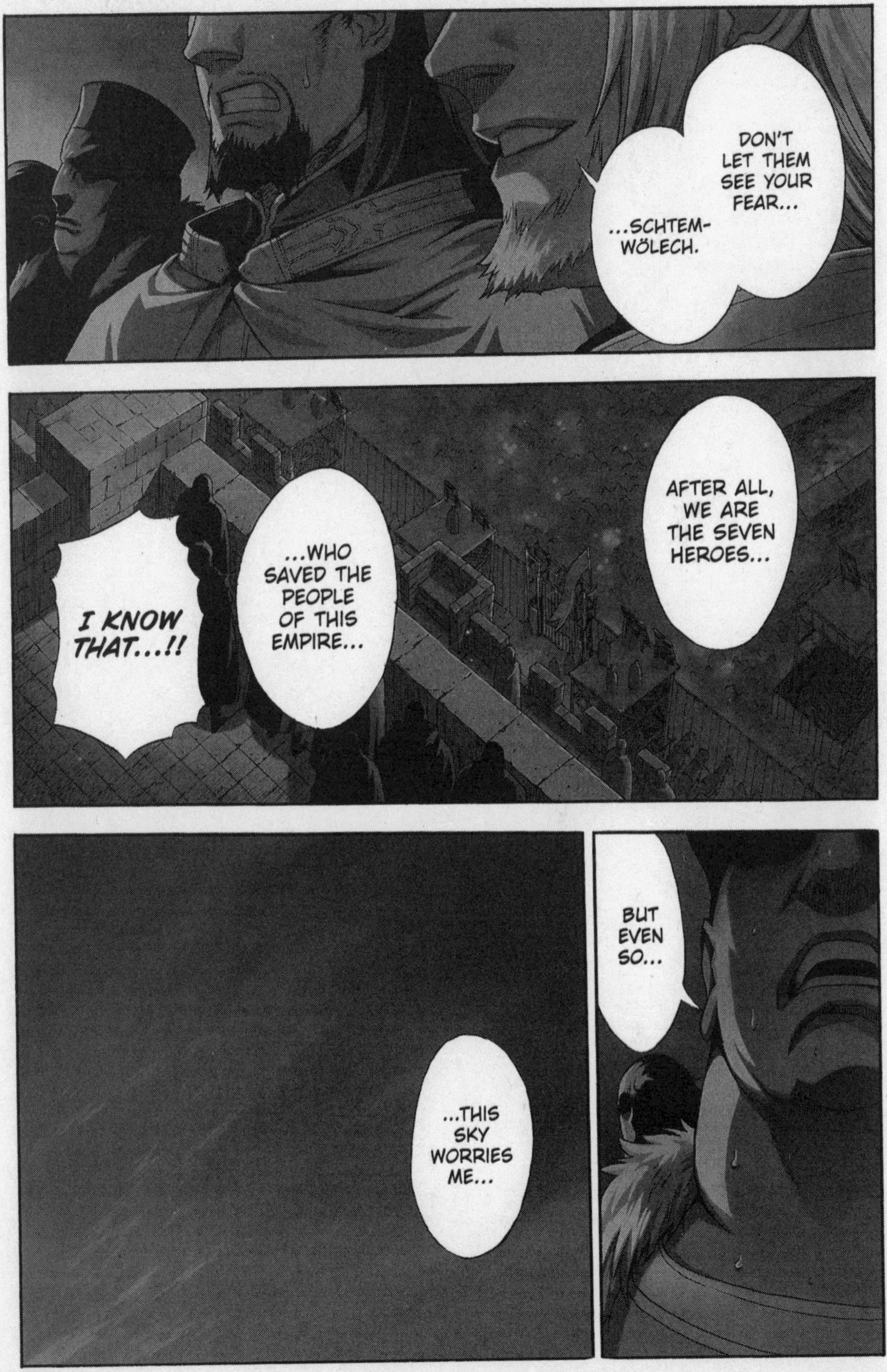
DON'T LET THEM SEE YOUR FEAR...
...SCHTEM-WÖLECH.
AFTER ALL, WE ARE THE SEVEN HEROES...
...WHO SAVED THE PEOPLE OF THIS EMPIRE...
I KNOW THAT...!!
BUT EVEN SO...
...THIS SKY WORRIES ME...

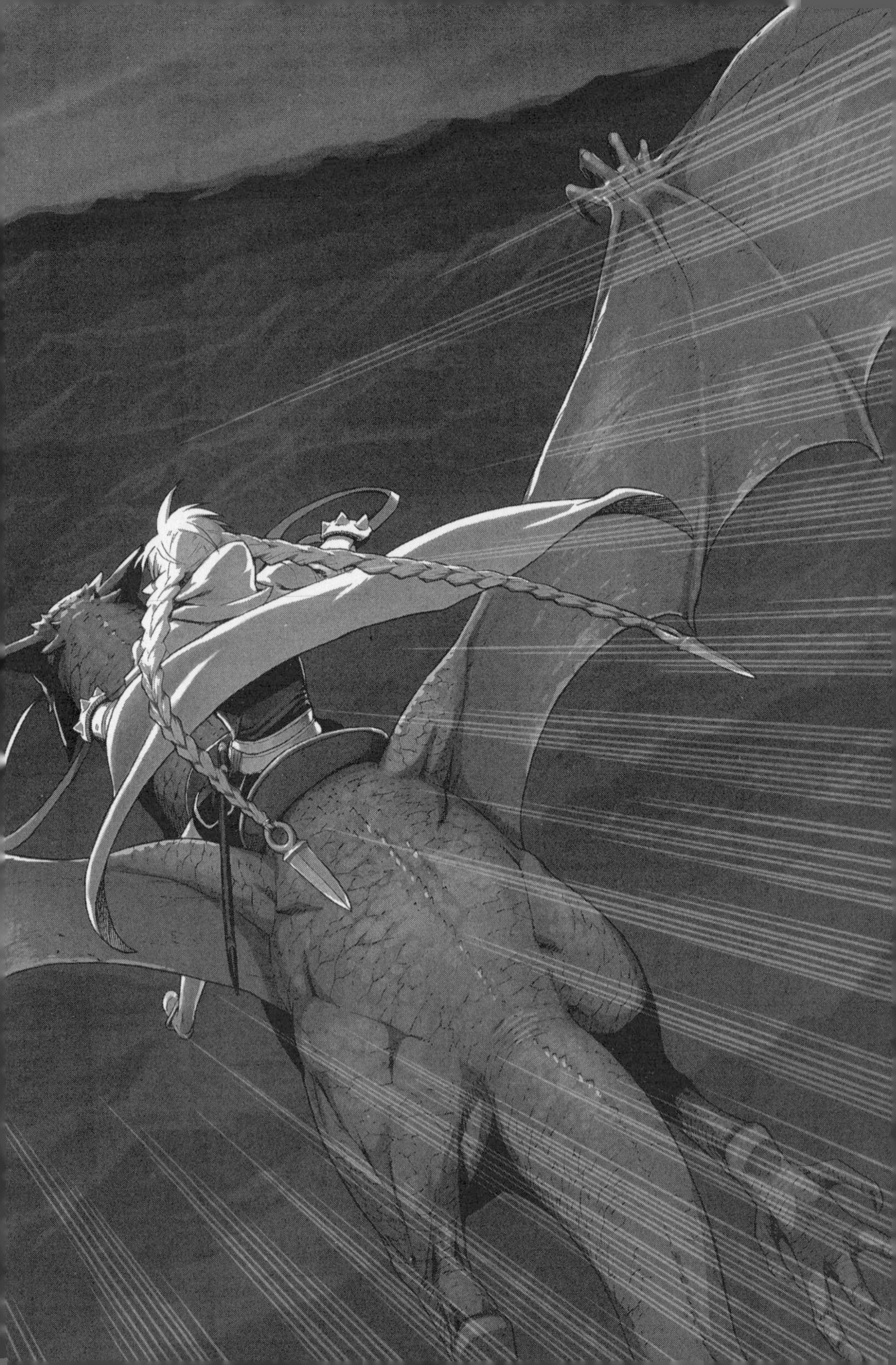

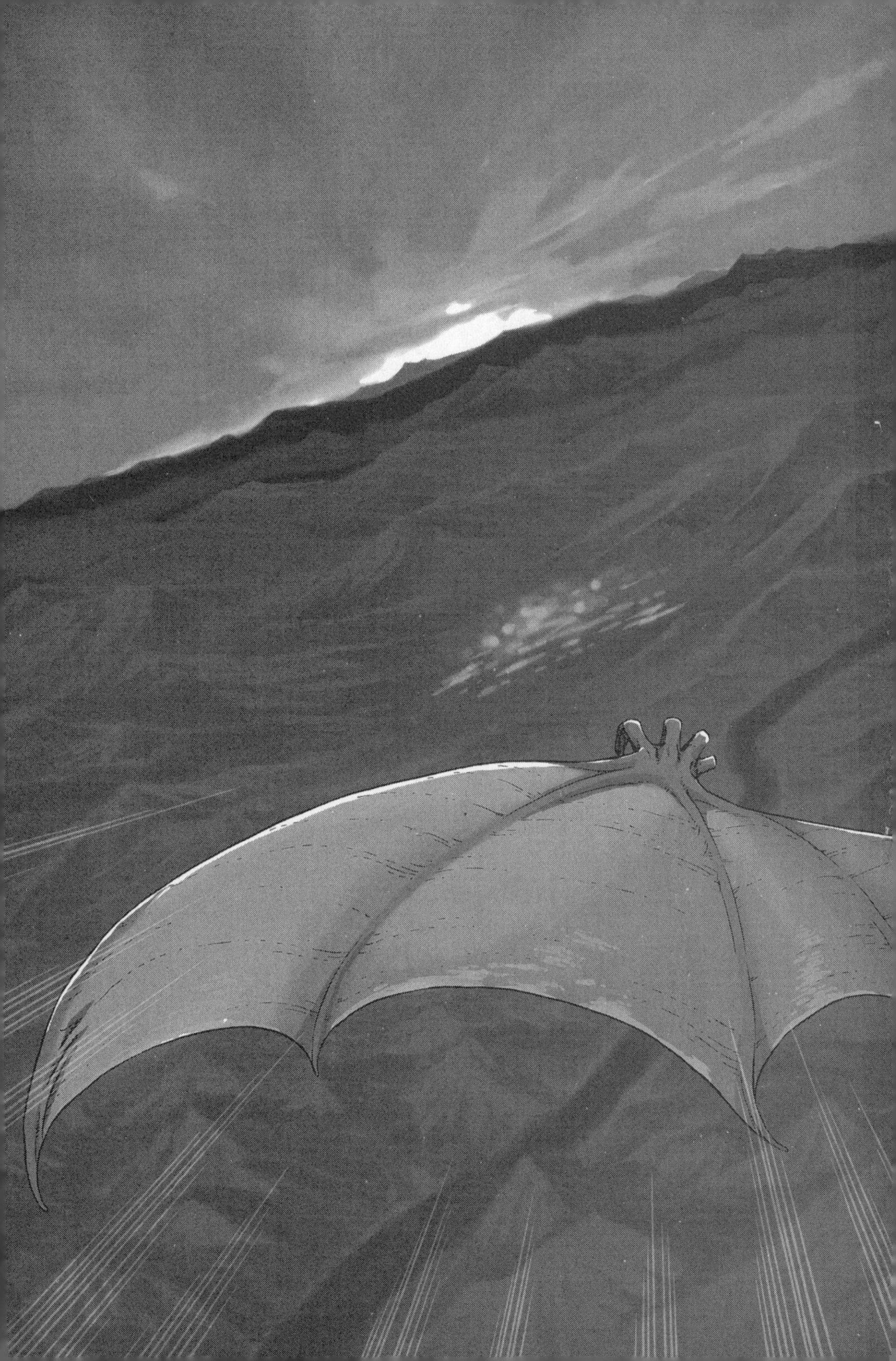

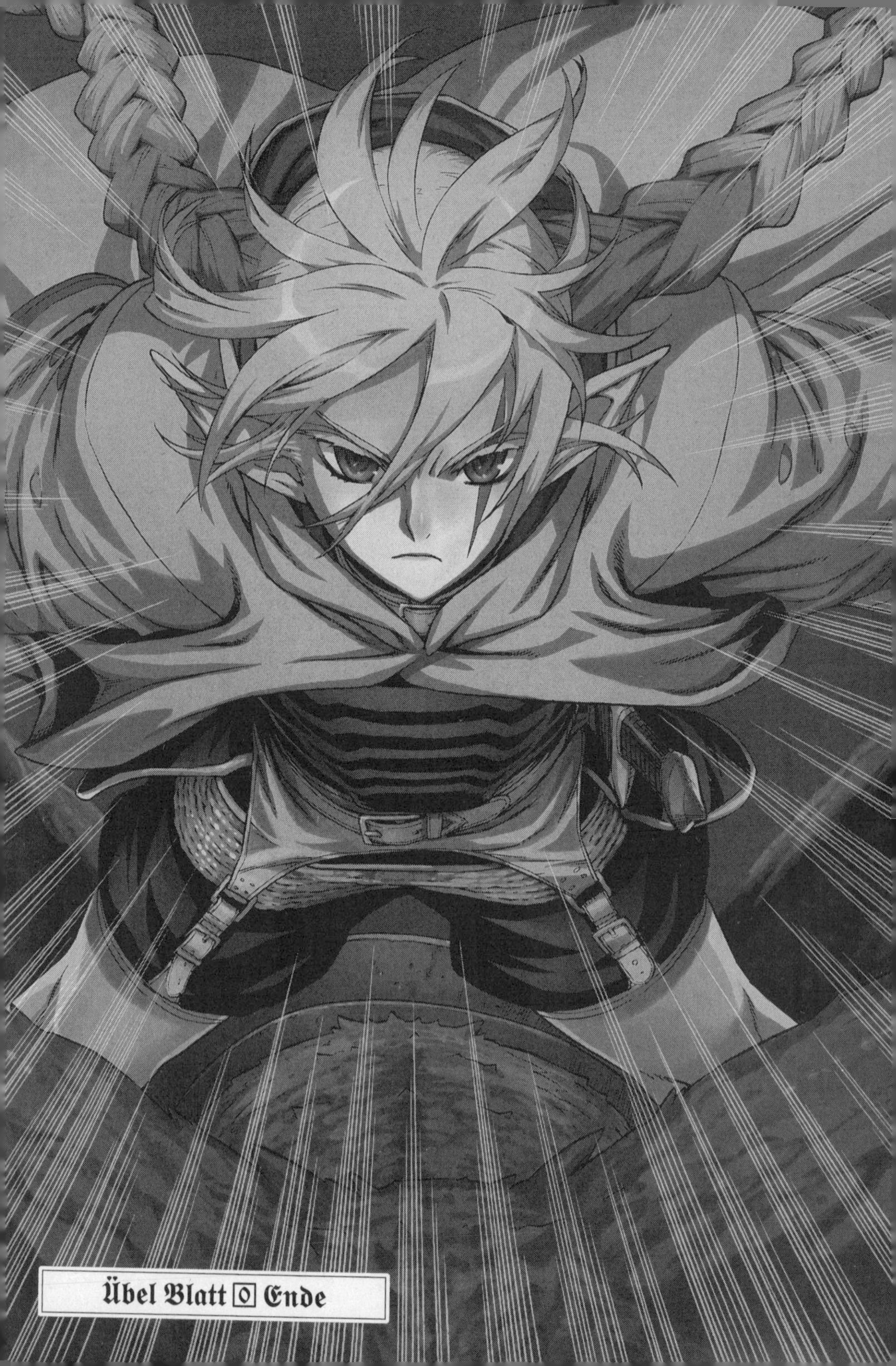
Übel Blatt 0 Ende

BORDER CITY RIELDE-VELEM

A city that lies directly on the border between Mollan—the easternmost landgravate of the Seven Heroes' domains (collectively known as Heldenstrasse)—and the margravate of Gormbark.

The underground fortress was originally constructed by Wischtech during the war, but it was captured and retaken from the forces of the empire several times throughout the fighting.

Each subsequent capture and withdrawal brought on the construction of additional rooms, passages, and traps, turning it into a complex and deadly piece of architecture.

In 3969 A.D., Ergnach—military strategist and disciple of Blatt Meister Ludift—created the Thousand Stonespears, halting the impending invasion from Wischtech.

After the great war, Rielde-Velem developed into a full-fledged border city, partly in thanks to the monastery.

The underground was initially sealed off once the fighting ended, but people from the borderlands began moving in on their own and eventually established an independent society in the space beneath the city proper.

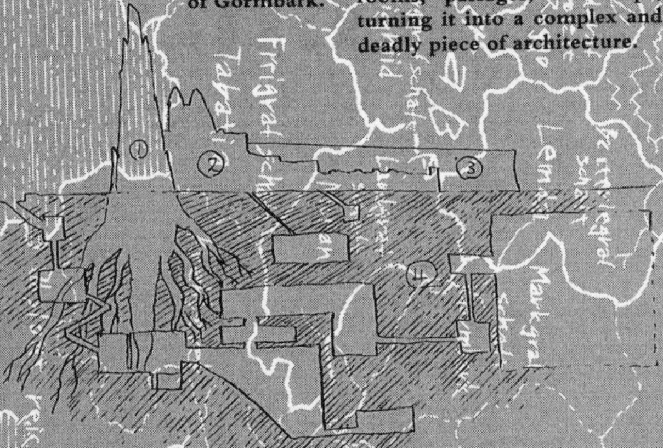

① Thousand Stonespears
② Monastery
③ Maschinendrache Port
④ Underground City (formerly the underground fortress)

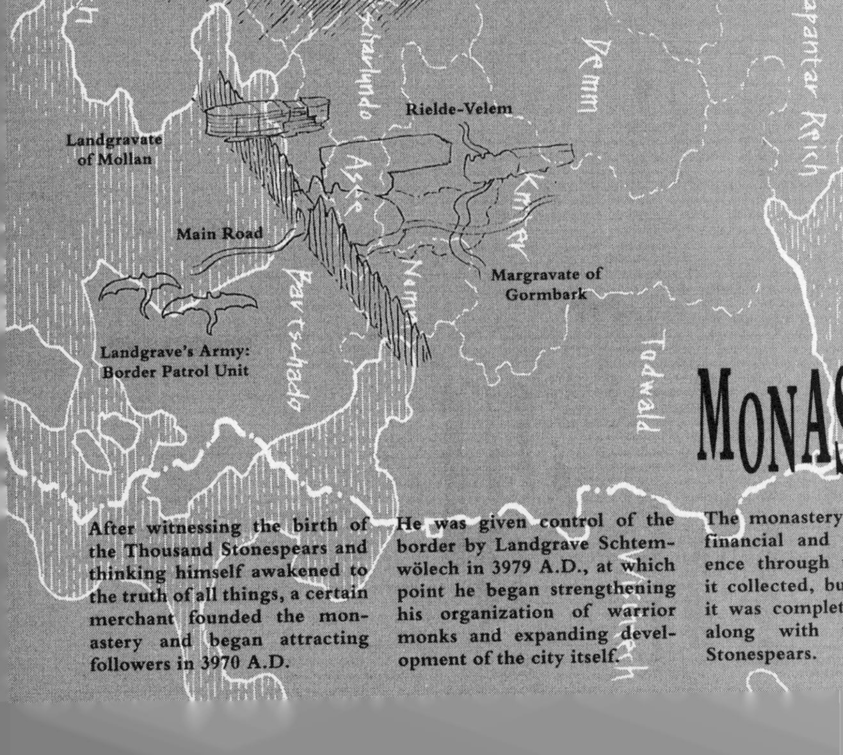
Rielde-Velem
Landgravate of Mollan
Main Road
Margravate of Gormbark
Landgrave's Army: Border Patrol Unit

MONASTERY

After witnessing the birth of the Thousand Stonespears and thinking himself awakened to the truth of all things, a certain merchant founded the monastery and began attracting followers in 3970 A.D.

He was given control of the border by Landgrave Schtemwölech in 3979 A.D., at which point he began strengthening his organization of warrior monks and expanding development of the city itself.

The monastery gained untold financial and political influence through the border tax it collected, but in 3992 A.D. it was completely annihilated along with the Thousand Stonespears.

Translation Notes

Title:
Übel Blatt translates to "evil/sinister blade" in German.

Page 20:
The original Japanese designates this world's calendar literally as "the year of the sacred gift," referring to the point in time when the gods granted Szaalenden to the people in year zero. Our own A.D. stands for *anno domini* ("the year of our Lord"), but in *Übel Blatt* the "D" stands for *donatio*, or "gift" in Latin, to reflect the gods' giving of Szaalenden.

Page 80:
The Japanese characters used for *Mondenbürgen* ("moon castles" in German) translate literally as "Moon Reading Palace." This fits with the astral prognosticating that is apparently performed there.

Page 100:
The German term that Güsstav uses, *Hoch Elfe*, as well as the characters used to spell it out in the Japanese edition, means "High Elf." The distinction between "fairy" and "elf" is not made—the broad term used in Japanese (*yousei*) covers both.

Page 109:
Blatt Meister translates to Blade Master in German.

übelBlatt

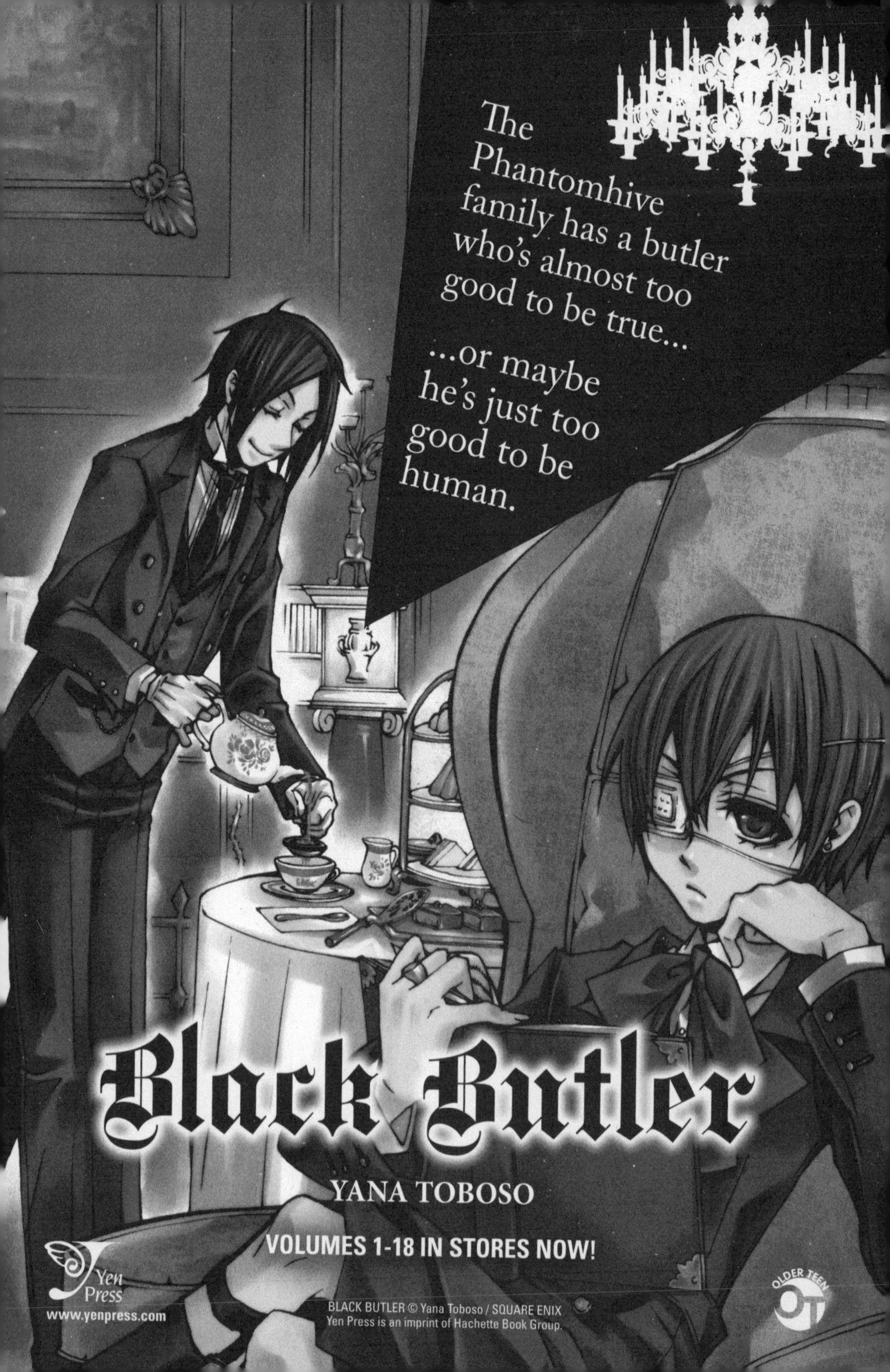
The Phantomhive family has a butler who's almost too good to be true...
...or maybe he's just too good to be human.
Black Butler
YANA TOBOSO
VOLUMES 1-18 IN STORES NOW!
Yen Press
www.yenpress.com
BLACK BUTLER © Yana Toboso / SQUARE ENIX
Yen Press is an imprint of Hachette Book Group.
OLDER TEEN
OT

To become the ultimate weapon, one must devour the souls of 99 humans...

and one witch.

Maka is a scythe meister, working to perfect her demon scythe until it is good enough to become Death's Weapon—the weapon used by Shinigami-sama, the spirit of Death himself. And if that isn't strange enough, her scythe also has the power to change form—into a human-looking boy!

VOLUMES 1-22 IN STORES NOW!

ÜBEL BLATT 0

ETOROUJI SHIONO

Translation: Caleb D. Cook • Lettering: Abigail Blackman

ÜBEL BLATT Vol. 0, 1 © 2005 Etorouji Shiono / SQUARE ENIX CO., LTD. First published in Japan in 2005 by SQUARE ENIX CO., LTD. English translation rights arranged with SQUARE ENIX CO., LTD. and Hachette Book Group through Tuttle-Mori Agency, Inc., Tokyo.

Translation © 2014 by SQUARE ENIX CO., LTD.

Yen Press
Hachette Book Group
1290 Avenue of the Americas
New York, NY 10104

www.HachetteBookGroup.com
www.YenPress.com

Yen Press is an imprint of Hachette Book Group, Inc.
The Yen Press name and logo are trademarks of Hachette Book Group, Inc.

First Yen Press Edition: October 2014

ISBN: 978-0-316-33616-1

10 9 8 7 6 5 4 3 2 1

BVG

Printed in the United States of America